Greening philosophy

A Fresh Introduction to the Field

AMBER L. KATHERINE

Kendall Hunt
publishing company

This book has been printed on recycled paper.

Cover credits:
Earthrise as seen from Apollo 8 orbiting the moon: Image provided by NASA.
Auguste Rodin's *The Thinker:* © Shutterstock, Inc. Used under license.

Kendall Hunt
publishing company
www.kendallhunt.com
Send all inquiries to:
4050 Westmark Drive
Dubuque, IA 52004-1840

Copyright © 2011 by Amber L. Katherine

ISBN 978-0-7575-8768-9

Printed in the United States of America
10 9 8 7 6 5 4 3 2 1

Table of Contents

Unit One ■■■ The Examined Life   25

Unit Two ■■■ Reality   115

Unit Three ■ ■ ■ Knowledge 253

Unit Four ▪ ▪ ▪ Values 385

*For Lindley and all the other Earthlings
that make life worth living.*

Acknowledgements

I am fortunate to teach for Santa Monica College, an educational institution genuinely committed to sustainability and global citizenship. Without the support of the College this project could not have been completed. The students in my classes during the past few years who have simultaneously studied philosophy and experimented with the development of this reader have gifted me with confidence in its viability and real world relevance. I am eternally grateful to have had Marilyn Frye as my graduate advisor and mentor and appreciate the many useful suggestions she offered in her generous reading of the introduction.

Thanks to my good friend and ecofeminist philosopher Chris Cuomo the introduction to this reader is smarter, sleeker, and greener than it would have been without her keen contributions. The editorial support of Katherine McCracken, a connoisseur of the English language, improved the text immensely. I am deeply grateful to my supportive colleagues, including Richard Tahvildaran, Eric Oifer, Christine Schultz, William Selby, David Phillips, Brian Lawson, and Sage Bennett who read the introduction and regularly indulged me in fruitful discussions about sustainability and greening the curriculum. Katie Phillips, my mother and dearest friend, offered more unconditional support and lavish praise all along the way than any academic projects deserves. Finally, heart-felt thanks to my amazing wife, Lindley Karstens, for her valuable insights, pragmatic sensibility, humor, and on-going inspiration.

Preface

This book is part of an emergent project in higher education called "greening the curriculum," the goal of which is to incorporate environmental awareness, or ecological literacy, into existing courses without changing the primary objectives of those courses. Given this understanding, "greening philosophy" need not be limited to specialty courses entitled "Environmental Philosophy" or "Environmental Ethics." This is not a book designed for an applied ethics course or an upper division course. This book is designed to do what any introductory reader is suppose to do, *introduce* the field of philosophy by way of classic and contemporary readings.

In the late twentieth century several readers emerged which introduced philosophy by way of multiculturalism. These readers played a vital role, ushering philosophy out of the dusty halls of ivory towers and into the streets where people from different walks of life were struggling to live together in a post-colonial world, offering students the chance to learn philosophy at the same time as they developed a pluralist consciousness. This reader carries on in this engaging tradition, offering students the opportunity to learn philosophy and at the same time to cultivate an environmental consciousness for global citizenship. If students today are going to meet the challenges of the twenty-first century they will need a rich understanding of the knowledge, reality, and ethics behind sustainability as well as the opportunity to debate the merits of becoming a global citizen.

For this project to succeed it must be a collective effort. Students and faculty that use this book are invited to offer their critiques and suggestions for future editions.

- Are there selections included here that you don't find necessary? Or, selections not included here that you believe ought to be included?
- What questions ought to be added or deleted from the questions that accompany each selection?
- What changes or additions should future editions include?

All feedback welcome: KATHERINE_AMBER@SMC.EDU

A Green Introduction to Philosophy

Amber L. Katherine

©NASA

Earthrise: The Dawning of the Age of Ecology

Before this famous photo was taken by an Apollo astronaut in 1968, no one had ever seen the planet from space. People had seen vast expanses of earth from mountaintops and then, after humans began to fly planes, from the sky. Not until the late 1960s did anyone have a glimpse of the whole. Before that experience was possible, some visionaries had imagined what Earth might look like "from above." Notably, in the fourth century B.C.E., Plato conjectured that the "true Earth" would appear as "a patchwork of colors . . . more numerous and beautiful than any we have ever seen." Later, during the Enlightenment, a few philosophers wondered whether seeing it whole could bring about a collective shift in consciousness. Would the realization that humanity shares a destiny on this lonely orb moving through space with no apparent destination provoke a reflective humility about our earthly existence?

It is ironic that the astronaut who first saw the whole earth on Christmas Eve in 1968 did it somewhat unintentionally. During this Apollo 8 mission to circumnavigate the moon, all eyes, monitoring machines, and

1

cameras were focused on the moon. On Apollo's fourth orbit Frank Borman glanced out a window and was awe-struck by the Earth rising over the lunar horizon. He grabbed his camera to snap an unscheduled shot and later described it as "the most beautiful, heart-catching sight of my life." In 1969, Friends of the Earth—the first global federation of grassroots environmental organizations—was founded, followed the next year by the creation of Earth Day, and two more years later by the first United Nations Conference on the Human Environment, called Earth Summit. In 1987, the United Nations World Commission on Environment and Development declared a "new reality" had been born with our ability to see our planet from space. In *Our Common Future,* the commission proclaimed that we could finally "see and study the Earth as an organism whose health depends on the health of all of its parts." Some say the greatest contribution of Apollo was not landing on the Moon, but bringing that photo home, the picture that woke the world up and marked the dawn of the Age of Ecology.

For a sense of the significance of our present moment, consider it in comparison to the dawning of what is known as the Modern Age. Imagine what it must have been like for Copernicus to figure out, as he did in 1543, that the Earth was not the center of the universe. Or think of Galileo's excitement in 1610 when he announced his evidence for the Copernican system in *The Starry Messenger.* The discovery of the planetary bodies circling Jupiter challenged the prevailing view that everything in the universe was revolving around the presumed centerpiece, Earth (geocentrism). The prevailing view was based on religious authority and ordinary sensory observations of the sun, the moon, and the stars moving daily through the sky from our stationary position on Earth. To declare that the sun was the center around which the earth moved (heliocentricism) was considered lunacy and heresy. Despite the danger of making such an unorthodox claim, the "new philosophers" courageously chipped away at the longstanding earth-centered paradigm which ruled in the schools of Europe. They willingly suffered infamy and persecution in the long struggle to bring the sun-centered paradigm to light.

Entrenched as we are in the modern world, it may seem equally absurd to imagine that we are on the brink of a new paradigm shift, a change just as important, that may unfold during our lifetimes. While no one can predict the future, there are many signs indicating this shift is already under way, including climate destabilization, global economic crises, and worldwide ecosystems degradation. Just as there were those who ignored or denied the evidence for heliocentricism in the sixteenth century; today there are those who, entranced by the existing paradigm, refuse to consider what these global signs of change portend for the future.

The similarities in these two historic moments—the Copernican revolution and the dawning of the ecological age—include not only facing the nay-saying forces invested in the existing order or facing one's own fear of the consequences of accepting new paradigms, but also owning up to the challenge of imagining what the future might hold and the hopeful exhilaration of building a new world.

Of course, during the Renaissance humanity's future existence did not turn on the shift away from geocentrism. We are living in even more exceptional times. The balance between humans and (nonhuman) nature is changing. Nature has always played an overriding role in determining the future of humans. Now humans have begun to determine the fate of the natural world, and all that is inextricably rooted in it.

Reality Check

For the first time in history, a future is conceivable in which human existence on Earth is diminished beyond recognition. Based on a scientific appraisal of the planet's condition called the *Millennium Ecosystem Assessment,* over a thousand experts have concluded, "Human actions are depleting Earth's natural capital, putting such strain on the environment that the ability of the planet's ecosystems to sustain future generations can no longer be taken for granted." In support of their findings, scientists offer evidence of ocean acidification, ozone depletion, deforestation, desertification, pollution, and exponential biodiversity loss. But on a more hopeful note, the assessment also shows that with timely and appropriate actions it is possible to reverse the degradation of many ecosystem services over the next forty or fifty years. However, the changes in policy and practice called for in the Assessment are substantial and not currently under way.

Perhaps those changes are not under way because our global environmental problems are not easily resolved through technological fixes or economic incentives. Such complex problems cannot be resolved through an easy choice to do what's right instead of wrong. The wicked network of problems that make up the "ecological crisis" has been forged over centuries by groups of people with conflicting perspectives and priorities, all striving for the good life. When one community's solution becomes another's problem, who can say what ought to be done? The changes in policy and practice required demand recognition that the roots of our problems lay not in the earth, but in humanity's deeply entrenched value systems and ways of life.

On one hand, the popular modern Western value system prize individualism, human ingenuity, free enterprise, and perpetual growth as the best means for realizing health, wealth, and happiness. There is no denying the important advances, especially in medicine and communications, made possible by using these values to guide us. On the other hand, several twentieth century developments have raised serious doubts about the "progress" bought by advanced techno-industrial societies. Doubters ask, if we are so happy why are depression, anxiety, alienation, and addiction so ubiquitous today? Are not unbridled economic production and unrestrained consumption directly responsible for overshooting the planet's carrying capacity? Can the growing disparities in material wealth among the world's people be explained apart from the exploits of corporate globalization? We may all be in the same boat, but we are not all in the same situation. We see things differently, in large part, because of our different relations to power, that is, to markets, banks, bombs, oil, and water. If the modern Western value paradigm is truly the basis for the global good life, skeptics wonder, why must it be backed by the military industrial complex? Can health, wealth, and happiness be secured for all—the growing multitudes of endangered species, climate refugees, exploited workers, malnourished children, people with AIDS, sectarians, and anti-Western discontents—through competition for dwindling resources, power struggles for international dominance or another bloody war?

"Sustainability" is the name of a twenty-first century conception of the good life which offers an alternative to the dominant paradigm. One articulation of a sustainable value system, called *The Earth Charter,* emphasizes respect and care for the community of life, ecological integrity, democracy, social and economic justice, and peace. The goal of "sustainable development", as defined in 1987 by the World Commission on Environment and Development, is "to ensure that humanity meets the needs of the present without compromising the ability of future generations to meet their own needs." Bringing about this magnitude of change at the global level will require acknowledging limits to growth, international cooperation and compromise, sharing resources more equitably, and the preservation of diverse cultures and lifeforms. Quality of life, in this view, is measured not so much by consumer experiences and material goods, as by access to fresh air and water; healthy active lifestyles which include more walking, biking, and gardening; and especially by meaningful community-based experiences. Conceptualized this way, health, wealth, and happiness means *being* more rather than *having* more.

Ours is a critical moment for humanity. The future for ourselves and our progeny will be made by the values we choose to live by today. The changes are coming so quickly, refusing to choose is a choice in itself. Should we stay the course of modern Western values that have enlightened our world to this point or should we change our values for the sake of a brighter future? How shall we decide which paradigm to affirm? Obviously, we ought to base our decision on reality. But what reality might justify one value over another? For assurance, shall we turn to God, a moral compass inherent in human nature, or an order of earthly existence? What's worse is the prospect that no moral order is given by reality, that values are relative. Would that mean any search for "the" good life is fundamentally misguided? If so, is there any hope that humanity could take a leap toward a particular future and build a consensus around it strong enough to weather the perfect storm of the twenty-first century?

These are not questions scientists alone can or should answer for us. As citizens committed to self-government we shoulder the responsibility for making decisions in the midst of uncertainty, controversy, and impending crisis. People who see the earth-shattering threats on humanity's horizon as somebody else's problem do not stand in a neutral zone beyond danger or reproach. For the good of ourselves and others the environmental situation calls on us to put our heads together, even if we don't see eye to eye. United by projects which demand ingenuity and collaboration humans have overcome our differences and achieved what no individual could do alone. Think, for example, of how thousands of people working together for millions of hours realized the dream of Project Apollo, or the Human Genome Project.

The changes in policy and practice needed to reverse the ongoing degradation of ecosystems and related human suffering calls for mobilizing educational institutions for sustainable development, also known as "greening the curriculum." This project entails infusing "ecological literacy" into new and existing courses, disciplines, and programs. Ecological literacy means, first, understanding the biosphere; i.e., the natural systems and cycles which together provide the basis for life on Earth; second, understanding the impacts of social, cultural, and political-economic systems on the biosphere; and third, developing the wisdom to balance the needs of humans with the health and integrity of the biosphere, to insure the planet's long-term livability and sustainability. While efforts to integrate ecological literacy into the curriculum have been underway for nearly forty years, ecological *illiteracy* is still pervasive among college graduates today. Just as medieval scholasticism did not easily give way to modern science, the necessary shift to a sustainable educational paradigm will require forward-thinking students and educators willing to think outside the box. The exciting thing about this newly emerging academic project is the chance it offers to make an original connection or an insightful contribution. Unlike traditional introductory courses that relegate beginners to what is already known, the academic project of greening invites you to participate in a knowledge-making process that calls for the kind of critical and creative thinking needed to analyze and help solve global environmental problems. The big question before us is this: Shall we work for a green paradigm shift or stay the course we're on? And on what basis can this choice of values be justified?

Having considered the "greening" project in historical context and in light of our contemporary situation, let's talk about philosophy generally, and then how greening philosophy will be approached in this introductory text.

Engaged Philosophy

I have been haunted by something a student asked me after he successfully completed the first introductory philosophy class I ever taught. After delivering a polite compliment on my teaching, he challenged me with a question: "But what does philosophy have to do with *real life?*" Over the years, I have attempted to meet his challenge by showing how philosophy has everything to do with the real world. But the case that it has nothing to do with real life is worthy of consideration.

Perhaps the first to have suggested that philosophy has *nothing* to do with real life was an ancient poet named Aristophanes. His infamous play on the subject, entitled *The Clouds,* depicts philosophy's founder, Socrates, as a fool bumbling along with his head in the clouds, unaware of the ground beneath his feet or where on earth he is heading. Because philosophy deals in abstract ideas, hypothetical speculation, and logical argument, some people say it amounts, at best, to an exercise of intellectual masturbation, and at worst, to an irrelevant waste of time. Accordingly, philosophers are stereotyped as armchair academics more concerned with arcane questions than with practical matters important to real people.

On the other hand, there are those who agree that philosophy has *everything* to do with real life. They argue that philosophy itself emerged as a real-world solution to a pressing political problem. The real world problem facing the aristocratic Greeks in 400 B.C.E. was how to critique the existing democratic regime. In the interest of overthrowing democracy, philosophy (defined as wisdom-loving) emerged as a dissident discourse, proclaiming that rule by the *wise* was superior to rule by the democratic *masses* (defined as irrational mobs). Hence, the Socratic search for the "essence" or "ideal" of justice was motivated by a real-world need for an eternal standard to measure and criticize existing injustices. In contrast with the armchair philosopher, Socrates provides an example of a public philosopher and citizen activist, advocating care for the self and soul of the city above a preoccupation with material wealth and reputation.

The complexity of our global problems urgently calls for a firm grasp of the tradition of Western philosophy as well as the conceptual tools and skills it has to offer. While this may not be immediately evident, studying philosophy matters. Hence, this introduction to philosophy offers a practical starting point for a sustainable future.

What is Philosophy?

Philosophy can be taken up as a professional pursuit or as a lifestyle by anyone who wishes to live life to its fullest. Professionals define the field by three subjects of inquiry: the nature of reality (metaphysics), the justification of belief (epistemology), and the conduct of life (ethics). Philosophy comes up for non-professionals when something happens that interrupts ordinary daily life that demands a reflective pause. These kinds of happenings naturally lead to a reconsideration of beliefs and actions in light of the "big" questions: Does God exist? What is the point of human existence? What can we know of reality? What values will guide us to happiness?

Defining "philosophy" is tough. We can consider the examples set by particular philosophers. Socrates made a daily practice of questioning and dialoging with others in pursuit of wisdom for right action. Aquinas lived to serve God, using reason and reflection to keep his actions in line with God's will. Nietzsche, a notorious critic of God-given reality, sought to live creatively, as if life were a work of art. The challenge of defining "philosophy" is to make it general enough to encompass the rich diversity of meanings forged by particular philosophers in different historical eras, but narrow enough to provide a useful starting point for a beginner. Since philosophy for the ancient Greeks and Romans was not what it was for the medieval Scholastics, which was not what it was for the Renaissance thinkers, or the Enlightenment thinkers, or the Existentialists, one does well to approach "philosophy" as a *contested* concept and a *living* practice. By the time you have completed this course—*after* you study who has lived and died to practice it and what ideas have won and lost in its arenas—*then* you will be well situated to define philosophy for yourself.

One useful starting point is to consider two competing schools on the subject of "philosophy." The *traditional* school holds that philosophy is a search, or a quest, or an exploration to *discover* the Truth (the capital "T" signifies a search for a universal, timeless, or absolute truth). According to this view, Truth is given like an image in the mirror. The task of the philosopher—motivated by a love of wisdom or curiosity or, perhaps, by human nature—is to distinguish true from false, reality from appearance, right from wrong, and to establish and defend the superiority of the former—i.e., the true, the real, and the right.

The *critical* school, on the other hand, holds that philosophy is a contest of wills, or a joust aimed not at discovery but at *invention*. In this view, truth is not given like an image in a mirror, but must be determined, or carved out of the chaos and ambiguity of experience through creative efforts like those of an artist sculpting a statue or a writer composing a poem. The task of the philosopher—motivated by will or desire or, perhaps, interest—is to *interpret* reality, to invent concepts, to make "maps" with strategic value, and to establish and defend his or her position in debates with those who see things differently, especially when something vital is at stake. According to this view, the determination of what counts as true, real, and right is the outcome of a struggle.

The field of philosophy has room enough for both these schools and others. In fact, some argue that progress depends on this pluralist starting point. Diversity of philosophical perspective is rich soil for new ideas to sprout and grow. Could Galileo have made his breakthroughs had he gone along with the prevailing views of his time? Wasn't modern science itself born out of the clash of opposing ideas? Differences of opinion invite analysis and evaluation of contrasting positions. Arguments are built up out of these analyses. These arguments, viewed as a series of historical developments in humanity's quest to answer life's big questions, provide a unique standpoint for reflection on one's life. The philosophical canon is not just a random collection of disparate answers. It's a tradition of thoughtful reading and writing handed down from one generation to the next for guidance and enrichment. Aristotle disagreed with Plato and wrote in response. Descartes criticized Aristotle and wrote in response. Some have called it "the great conversation" because philosophers "talk" with each other even across vast historical distances, agreeing and disagreeing, about the nature of the soul, or happiness, or how much free will humans have. Think of studying philosophy as listening in on this conversation. At first you listen to get acquainted, then to figure out where you stand in relation to the others, and after a while, as with any good conversation, you get sucked in. Surveying the tradition, you begin to discriminate between those philosophies that resonate with you and those you find quite alien. In the process you find your place and expand your sense of self. Just as you are the descendent of a family tradition, you are the descendent of the Western philosophical tradition. Study philosophy, in the words of the ancient Greek aphorism, to "know thyself."

Let's say something happens in your life that starts you wondering what brings happiness. Reading in the Western philosophical tradition is like taking in the view from a mountaintop. Just as sitting on a rock high above, overlooking a coastline or a city, invites reflection and provides perspective, reading Plato's view in the *Republic* encourages you to consider whether gaining rational control of your appetites might insure your happiness. Reading Aristotle's *Ethics* may provoke you to wonder whether happiness is even possible without loyal friends, a supportive family, and a good education. Reading Aquinas motivates a search for happiness through connection with God. Reading Rousseau can lead you to ask about how much your happiness depends on your closeness to nature. Have the ancient Greeks got it right? Or are the views of the medieval Christians, the early Moderns, or the twentieth century Existentialists more promising? There is more than one answer to the question of what insures happiness. From the philosophical mountaintop comes the clarity that happiness is a contested terrain the negotiation of which entails self-reflection and values clarification.

Consider the philosophers selected for this book. The list is like any to be found in an introductory philosophy textbook. What unites them? Of course, they are considered "great" philosophers in the Western canon. But what made them great? Millions of people have written philosophy, but only a few have made the list. What unites and distinguishes these few? Each of them became great through writing with a sense of purpose. Each wrote to challenge their predecessors and the reigning philosophical paradigm of their time. Each resisted the traditions out of which they emerged in creative and ingenious ways. They wrote philosophy to get humanity on a course to a better future. While each in his time was a change-maker, collectively they form the tradition of Western philosophy that is today a pillar of the existing paradigm.

There are some notable absences from the Western philosophical canon. We might ask, as many have asked in the past half century, where are the Native American and South American philosophers, the philosophers of color, and the women philosophers? In the same vein, we might wonder what the adjective "Western" does and does not refer to. These questions remind us not to assume that traditions, ours or others, represent answers to the big questions that are neutral or universal. In fact, traditions themselves are forged in political struggles, which is to say they embody the values championed by the winners more than those defended by the losers. One strategy for keeping this fact at the forefront, developed and practiced by feminist philosophers, is to "re-read the canon" with the following question in mind: How far and in what ways have socially inherited stereotypes and prejudices about women affected each philosopher's assumptions, concepts, and arguments? The same sort of question must be asked about how far particular philosophies reflect ruling class, racist, or ethnocentric assumptions. The point of this critical questioning is not to condemn the canon, but to recognize its weaknesses as well as its strengths and what it holds dear as well as what it ignores or disdains.

On "Greening" Philosophy

Just as we question the presence of sexist or ethnocentric prejudices embedded in the philosophies that constitute the Western canon, we can ask: How is "nature" conceptualized by each philosopher in the tradition? What assumptions have been made about relations between what is "human" and what is not? How and to what extent have socially inherited stereotypes about the natural world, embedded in the works of "great" philosophers, contributed to the impending ecological breakdown we face today? These "green" questions are genuinely open, although the debate has begun. Those inclined to make Western philosophy the villain argue there is an anthropocentric bias in its ideas about God, humans, nature, truth, and justice which is the foundation of our ecological demise. Others hope that Western philosophy's rich conceptual resources and powerful analytic tools can help solve the problems we face. The future is uncertain. The jury is still out. Learning to ask and being able to answer these big green questions will help cultivate the wisdom necessary to help solve twenty-first century environmental problems.

"Greening" is more about focus than content. It does not change the existing objectives of a course introducing philosophy, nor does it replace the selections most commonly found in introductory readers. "Greening" involves identifying and critically examining the arguments and values embedded in classic and contemporary philosophical writings, which is the primary task of every philosophical introduction. Greening philosophy does not mean following a prescribed path or party line. Rather, it means using the opportunity to study philosophy to cultivate the ecological literacy which will enable you to determine for yourself how best to insure a good life and sustainable future.

Focusing with an ecological lens offers a fresh perspective on traditional philosophical questions and problems. The tripartite division of the introductory philosophy course into reality, knowledge, and values lends itself brilliantly to the task of greening. As we identify and examine the views of reality handed down by philosophers through the ages, including the perennial questions about the relations between "spirit" and "body," between "God" and "humans," or between "mind" and "matter" it makes sense to reflect on the present relations between humanity and nature at the root of the environmental crisis. As we survey the philosophical terrain of knowledge, including the distinctions between logic and empirical observation, objectivity and subjectivity, and the forces that impede our efforts to get at the truth, it makes sense to reflect on *how* and *why* we have sought to understand the natural world. As we take up the ethical questions regarding how we *ought* to live, including questions about who counts as part of the moral community and which values promise passage to the good life, it makes sense to reflect on sustainability and ecological citizenship. In other words, to steer modern civilization toward a sustainable future we must inventory, evaluate, and possibly alter the dominant views on the real, the true, and the right.

If, as the consensus of the world's scientists suggests, human *behaviors* (e.g., consuming, producing, reproducing, polluting) are the *cause* of our worst environmental problems today, then it makes good sense to ask about what values or "ways of thinking" are informing, guiding, or fueling that behavior. As we make our way through the philosophical field, we will look for the causes of our ecological problems. At each point along the way—from the emergence of Western philosophy to the emergence of monotheism, to the birth of modern science, to the outset of industrial and technological civilization—we can pause and reflect on our philosophical evolution for the light it sheds on our present situation. We will also search for resources to solve our problems among the philosophical positions we study. Hence, the work of "greening" philosophy requires that we keep one eye on what the philosophers have said in their own terms and the other eye on how their ideas relate to the environmental situation we face today.

Resources

Robert Poole. *Earthrise: How Man First Saw the Earth.* (Yale University Press, 2008).

Millennium Ecosystem Assessment, called for by the United Nations Secretary-General Kofi Annan in 2000. Their findings provide a state-of-the-art scientific appraisal of the condition and trends in the world's ecosystems and the services they provide and the options to restore, conserve, or enhance the sustainable use of ecosystems. http://www.millenniumassessment.org/en/About.aspx#1

The World Commission on Environment and Development. *Our Common Future.* (Oxford University Press, 1987).

Spark Notes map of Western Philosophy http://sparkcharts.sparknotes.com/philosophy/philosophy/section6.php

Stanford Encyclopedia of Philosophy, edited by Edward N. Zalta, SEP is a dynamic, scholarly open-access digital library with entries written and updated by experts in the field. http://plato.stanford.edu/

Green Questions for Studying Philosophy:

- Can the causes of ecological collapse be found in Western assumptions about reality? Is there a metaphysical foundation to justify the shift to a sustainable order of values?

- What difference do our various ways of knowing reality make with respect to the natural world? What justification can be offered for truth claims made in the interests of sustainability?

- Have our ways of envisioning "moral community" left too many or too much outside our ethical consideration? How should we conceptualize "the good life" today?

- Are there conceptual resources buried in the philosophies of the past that, once excavated, could open up fruitful directions for a more sustainable future?

Reading & Writing Philosophy for a Change

Amber L. Katherine

start reading
or we're all screwed
— We

Instead of reading, we've been watching. We're like the people on the star liners in Wall•E perpetually fixed in our lounge chairs staring endlessly into the screens in front of our faces. Watching, especially television, enables the influx of market values which reinforce the existing paradigm of consumption-based prosperity. Instead of "start reading," TV sings the resounding imperative, "start buying." In the process of exclusively asserting this dogmatic message it short circuits the viewer's capacity for critical engagement and considering alternatives. While reading permits pause for thoughtful reflection, television impatiently prods one along. Viewers are socialized to watch passively for fear they will "miss something" if they begin to question or analyze. They don't call it "programming" for nothing. Even if you don't stop watching, start reading philosophy to become a wiser watcher.

It is not easy to hear the philosophers' voices from the past speaking in their unfamiliar tones and using their archaic terms, especially in the midst of the omnipresent chatter of the TV age. Becoming watchers means we mostly have not learned how to read in a deep, substantive way. Watchers flip through magazines at the same pace that images flash on the screen, or they nibble on books but abandon them as soon as their cell phones ring. It is rare to be alone with a book, without interruption, for hours on end, reading like a long-distance runner on a high. Taking on the readings in this collection will require mental agility, stamina, focus, and commitment. If you can get into the zone with each selection, you may find meeting the challenge of the book as satisfying as completing a marathon.

There is no denying that reading philosophy can be boring at times, especially if you don't understand a long string of obscure words, you don't know where the philosopher is trying to take you, and none of it seems relevant to your life here and now. Making contact with a philosophy written hundreds of years ago is not easy for a beginner looking for recognizable signposts. The temptation to give up on the original text and go rummaging around the Internet for a summary will be great. Succumbing to the urge is a mistake for the same reason it is misguided to avoid all the hills during marathon training. No pain, no gain. Becoming a strong reader requires the will to take on a masterwork, to swallow it whole, to make it your own. You do this by summoning the nerve to approach a difficult text actively. You set your intention to stay with it, beginning to end. You fight the boredom and doubt by taking an interest in what you might say to this writer and in what you might make of his or her work.

Reading is more than running your eyes over words. To get below the surface, read with a pen in hand. Put checks by, or highlight, points you understand, especially if you suspect they are main points. If you get lost, don't read the same paragraph over and over. Try taking another running start by using your markers to retrace the writer's trajectory to strengthen your sense of what they are aiming at. Keep moving. Reading philosophy inevitably involves coming upon passages that anyone might find confusing or unintelligible. When this happens, don't just assume the problem is you, and don't stop reading. The problem may well be you—perhaps you have stumbled on an idea you've never considered before. Or, the problem may not be you—perhaps the philosopher is being intentionally obscure in order to disturb a complacent reader who assumes she understands more than she does. Either way, keep reading, because getting to the end does not require command of every word or sentence or passage. Mark what escapes you with a question mark or note in the margin to keep it from thwarting your resolve to finish.

On your first read, listen with hungry ears for what the philosopher says. Who is he or she talking to, and why? What's at issue and what concepts are being used to discuss it? Give the philosopher the floor without interruption to insure you get the gist. If possible, read from beginning to end in one sitting. Your task, at this point, is to grasp the philosopher's position and perspective, as best you can, on its own terms. On your second pass, you may pause to look up unfamiliar words, dig between the lines, or linger over passages that arouse your interest.

After two readings, stand back and contemplate the work as a whole. Does it speak to you? How might you reply? Steer the conversation on to your terms. Try to discern what's in this philosophy for you. Could you use it to expand your artistic vision or to sharpen your wit? Each philosophy, whether you affirm it or reject it, offers a chance to cultivate you own philosophy. The process of considering each in turn and in their relations with each other will ultimately lead you to be able to assert with confidence, "I am a dualist," or "My philosophy is more Nietzschean than Darwinian," or "What the world needs now is more cosmopolitans." In other words, reading philosophy helps you find your place in the world.

Reading the Map: Interpretations

A philosopher is like a cartographer. Just as making a map involves value-laden decisions about what will and will not have a place on the map, the size and scale of whatever has a place, and where it stands in relation to everything else on the map. Developing a philosophy involves value-laden decisions about how to carve up the undifferentiated mass that is the universe of ideas into concepts, and how those concepts will stand in relation to each other and everything else the philosopher wishes to theorize. It is sometimes said that the map is not the territory to remind map users that the representation does not capture all aspects of the geographical mass it seeks to reflect. The same is true with philosophies. The philosophy is not the reality. It is a particular attempt to represent reality through concepts and arguments. The test of a good map and a good philosophy is how well it works to help the user locate her present position, desired goal, potential obstacles, and best options for traversing the distance between them.

Reading philosophy is like reading a map. As with any map, philosophical writing offers much more information and insight than a traveler needs at any given moment. When looking at a street map, you may only need to see the distance between two intersections; but the map offers scads of additional information. If you don't know where you're going, a map is practically useless. Philosophy is like that. If you are reading without direction, you can read and read and read and at the end of it you can find yourself asking, what was the point?

When reading philosophy keep in mind that, like a map, it can guide two people with different purposes in very different directions. For example, if one is reading Plato's *Republic* for a critique of democracy, she will be led to different conclusions about the nature and value of the text than one who is reading in order to make a case for the arts. Or if readers are reading to get to know Socrates, some will find a great moral exemplar while others will find an annoying, troublesome decadent. The same words on the page can suggest very different meanings, or *interpretations.*

Interpretations are representations or "constructions" of textual realities. Those that are thought to best mirror the author's meaning are most often considered the "authoritative" or "correct" interpretations. Philosophers debate about whether any interpretation *can* provide a perfect mirror of a text. Skeptics argue that because values are inherent in the work of interpretation, readings are always relative. In other words, since reading is not just vacuuming up all the ideas in your path, the criteria any particular reader uses to select what is essential or meaningful will vary. There are, to be sure, some interpretations that are important to know about either because many people have accepted them or because they offer unique, original insight. Not all interpretations are created equal. Some are historically more sensitive than others or achieve more coherence with a larger body of writings. Others might be political, personal, or just off the wall.

Interpretive Strategies for Critical Reading

When a bunch of interpretations cluster around a particular group of values, they constitute theoretical frameworks anyone can take up and use to examine any philosophy text. Taking up a particular framework to analyze a philosophical text is a strategy for reading the text with a sense of purpose or a particular destination in mind. Consider the following strategic possibilities for critical reading.

- **"Logical Critique"** ferrets out contradictions through a close examination of a text's main argument. An argument is a line of reasoning composed to demonstrate that something is, or is not, the case. Philosophical literature is most often evaluated by the strength of its arguments, specifically by the validity of its logic. Knowing the rules of logic provides a reader with a powerful set of tools for analyzing a text. And, conversely, reading philosophy is a good way to become acquainted with the most common logical moves. The first and most fundamental principle of logic, according to Aristotle, states that it cannot be the case that both A and not-A are true at the same time.
  - Are there contradictions in the philosophers reasoning process?
  - Does the conclusion follow logically from the reasons given to support it?
  - What counter-examples challenge the argument's main claims or conclusion?
- **"Class Critique"** is socio-political framework inspired by Karl Marx. It works to reveal the economic investments or class interests motivating the development of particular concepts and arguments. For example, focusing this interpretive framework on metaphysical belief led

Marx to suggest, "Religion is the opium of the masses," meaning it functions to numb the pain of capitalist exploitation or tranquilize the revolutionary impulse. Class critique has expanded to include classes other than economic ones, including; e.g., gender, race, ethnic, and national. Feminist Critique, for example, explores how patriarchal interests are embedded in language, concepts, dominant values, social structures, and ways of knowing.

- What class interests are served by this philosopher's standpoint?
- How does this philosophy support or challenge the economic (or patriarchal, etc.) status quo?

■ **"Genealogical Critique"** seeks to understand present realities as products of particular historical legacies. Just as a family genealogy traced through marriage and kinship lines reveals a dimension of your individual identity, this approach reveals how particular values and practices have intersected and evolved over time to create our collective beliefs, identities, and situations today. In this view, history is understood in terms of "a hazardous play of dominations" rather than a necessary unfolding in a progressive direction. Inspired by Nietzsche and Foucault, genealogical critique situates philosophical positions in their historical contexts to debunk assumptions about immutable origins. For example, instead of asking about the essence of truth, genealogists ask, when and how did our present understanding of truth emerge?

- What enabled the emergence of this philosopher's position?
- How did this value, reality, or method of inquiry become what it is for us?

■ **"Phenomenological Critique"** seeks to understand the world as it is experienced in its first-person felt immediacy, before attempts to reflect on it or theorize it. Since we can never capture the world as it is "in itself," we can at least apprehend what it is "for us." This approach reveals how various conceptual constructions obscure or distort our attempts to grasp particular realities on the basis of our "lived experience" alone.

- Does this philosophy correspond with my direct, sensorial experience?
- If I "bracket" my socially constructed assumptions, what might I discover?

Bringing these strategies to the work of reading the "great" texts of Western philosophy is a way to honor them, a way to energize the study of them, to breathe fresh life into them. These strategies can guide your reading by giving you direction about what to look for, but they do not determine what conclusions you will reach because your reading is always informed by your values.

Writing Philosophy: Beyond WFTT

Writing is rarely an end in itself. In the correctional facilities called colleges and universities, writing is normally writing-for-the-teacher (WFTT) in pursuit of the grade. In this mode, "What does she want?" is the question motivating a student's every key stroke. The student seeking an "A" delivers words on a page organized like so many soldiers in a brigade, marching to the orders of the commander-in-chief. Given the order for summary regurgitation, the end product will be a nice dry, unobjectionable report for the teacher, conveying no sign of intelligent life. The grade assigned will usually be determined by the number of mistakes highlighted by the teacher. Unfortunately, when the grade relation eclipses the teaching-learning relation, writing that is urgent, unusual, intriguing, insightful, joyful, or genuinely philosophical is rare. Prioritizing the teaching-learning relation calls for teachers who embrace their roles as change-makers rather than correctional officers. It calls for students who aspire to become more than just good direction-followers. To transcend the politic of resentment that keeps teachers and students working at cross-purposes, we must work together to get beyond WFTT.

We can begin by conceiving of writing as struggle and resistance. Not conflict as an end in itself, but in the pursuit of innovative transformation. As I have already pointed out, pushing for the ecological paradigm shift promises a struggle at least as immense as the shift from geocentricism to heliocentricism. Writing motivated by a struggle for change conducts heat. Think, for example, of how Rousseau's writing fired up the French revolution. If you want your writing to mean something, stop shoveling crap, and use it to do something that matters. Malign a repugnant idea. Praise some nonconformist wisdom. Prove resistance is not futile. Debunk assimilation to creativity-killing norms. Stand up for something.

No doubt, writing to resist is dangerous. What if you are flunked for writing a brilliant and biting critique of Socratic humility because the assignment called for analysis of his declaration that "the unexamined life is not worth living"? First, keep in mind, what doesn't kill you can make you stronger. So what if you miss the grade? It might be worth it if you learn (or teach) something valuable in the process. But second, while resistance entails risk, college writing isn't a zero-sum game. Play by the rules, but strive to interpret them in a way that maximizes your response potential. "Resistance" does not mean ignoring or refusing to follow instructions. That would be self-sabotage or defeat. Resistance to stifling academic norms—creative, dynamic, prolific resistance—means figuring out how to use an assignment to write something soul-satisfyingly great. Resistance in the game of greening philosophy is a win-win proposition.

And third, everything is dangerous. The danger of writing reports that conform to existing academic norms is that you will become a dutiful, docile report writer. If you think that the papers you write for the teacher are inconsequential products, you miss the big picture. Think of the educational system as a gigantic production machine processing human resources to meet various economic and political ends. Before you even registered, someone considered what use could be made of you after you graduate. Your paper isn't the product—you are. Education is a formative enterprise, but that doesn't mean you are powerless. What you choose to write puts the question of what you will become in your hands. Great writing will make you powerful. WFTT in every class, throughout your college career, will make you acquiescent. Writing to green philosophy for the project of solving our pressing environmental problems will make you a valued citizen and a leader. In a profound sense, you are what you write.

Free-writing

"Free-writing" is writing in your own words, without fear of judgment, to secure your understanding and connection with the philosopher. Free-writing frees you from the terrible obligation to think *before* you write. It encourages you to poke around freely with your pen. Your free-writes will prepare you for class discussions and provide fertile starting points for writing assignments.

Each of the selections in this book is preceded by a box with questions to stimulate an active reading and encourage you to dig deep. Right after your second reading choose a question and start "free-writing." You write not to record your answers, but to figure them out. Writing is the way to generate ideas, to explore them, milk them, challenge or defend them, abandon them, or revisit them. Nobody ever became great waiting for an idea to strike. After reading, always write. Write daily. Write hard. Write up the hills. Write through the walls. Write for the paradigm shift of the century. Start reading philosophy to get writing. Start writing to get going . . . or we're all screwed.

Free-write on Earthrise
Look at the image called Earthrise and imagine you are the person who first glimpsed the earth whole. Before reading on, pause for a few moments to focus and reflect on this image of Earth on your own terms. After your pause freely write in response to one or more of the following questions.

- What is it?
- Do you see something large or small? One or many? Made of what? Doing what?
- Is it living or dead? Does it work like a machine or like an organism? Does it have a soul or a mind?
- Does the image show all there is, or is there a reality behind what appears to your eyes?
- Does it make you feel separate and alone? Or part of an interconnected whole?
- Does it make you want to laugh? Or pray? Or cry? Or does it make you feel dizzy and nauseous?
- Do you wonder more *how* it came to be or *why* it came to be? Or, what it *means* that it has come to be?
- Of course it's a planet, but forget that for a moment and think *metaphorically:* What is it?
- Do you see *yourself* in the earth's image? Or something quite other than you?
- What is humanity's *relation* to the Earth?
- What does this image represent for humanity?

Debating

Although we don't see much of it in higher education today, debate is one of the best strategies for overcoming WFTT. There is nothing like being pressed to take a stand in a debate to start you thinking about what you *really* care about. Which side is more consistent with your values? Which position are you better equipped to defend? Depending on how thoroughly baked you've been in the teacher-pleasing mode, the pressure to take a stand may start you deciphering the teacher to determine which side she favors. Beware the tricky business of basing your position on what you *think* the teacher favors. If you decide to go against your gut, and for what you assume is the teacher's view, putting yourself in the position of being both for *and* against a particular position, your paper may reveal your ambiguity in unintended ways. Or you may decide to go with what you *think* is the teacher's position, but having misread his view, you inadvertently end up arguing against it. Or if the teacher cares more about how well you make your case than which side you take, you could waste a lot of time speculating on an irrelevant matter rather than thinking for yourself. If a teacher *really* wanted everyone to argue the side she favored, she could just make that the assignment and scrap the debate altogether. It is safe to assume that if a teacher is calling for a genuine debate, you are free to write for the position of your choice. Abnegate your freedom at your own risk.

Initially some are worried that a vigorous debate could turn a mild-mannered classroom into a bloody battlefield. This is not likely so long as everyone understands that *a debate is not a war.* A debate is a context in which healthy conflict, but not violence, is encouraged. The point of a war is to *kill* your opposition. In contrast, the point of a debate is to *persuade* your opposition. According to the Socratic Method, pitting one idea against another in a rational search for the strongest argument is the noble way to determine the truth in the absence of a neutral judge. A similar principle is at work in democracy, where the best policy is said to arise out of the competition of ideas in a free, transparent public arena. In a debate, stubbornly refusing to affirm the best argument is a sign of mental weakness. While it is rare for a combatant to change sides in a war, changing sides in a debate is the sign of an open mind. Seldom does the closed-minded interlocutor emerge the victor. A genuine philosophical debate is a values-clarification ordeal unlike all other academic exercises.

In a philosophical debate the best argument is built logically with well-supported claims, resistant to counter-examples, capable of meeting challenges raised by the opposition, and widely affirmed by the community of inquirers. Philosophers use a variety of tools to persuade, including allegories, analogies, conceptual distinctions, thought experiments, examples and counterexamples, logic, and rhetoric. Skillful interlocutors avoid strong-arming opponents with dirty looks, half-truths, or fallacies. In fact, it is a sign of strength in philosophical debate to extend "the principle of charity" to an opponent, which means looking at their argument in the best possible light. Most beginners are inclined to do just the opposite, an error called "the straw man fallacy." Instead of addressing your opposition's best argument, you ignore it in favor of an easy-to-knock-down caricature. The mistake here is to believe that your side can win the debate without re-futing or disposing of the other side's strongest argument. Hearing a for-midable challenge to your argument can be a humbling experience. But what's worse is not hearing it at all, because that leaves you vulnerable and unprepared to match the challenge. Competent debaters make their case on the basis of a two-pronged strategy: giving reasons *for* their own posi-tion and giving reasons *against* their opposition's best argument. One measure of victory is the persuasion of your opposition that their arguments cannot withstand your critical challenges.

In the heat of a debate there is an opportunity for a moment of truth. All the arguments are on the table, each having been subjected to several rounds of disputation. Everyone is focused intently on what the dispute is coming down to in its bare essence. Suddenly you are struck with an epiphany. In a concise burst of articulate matter, you convey your quantum leap in understanding. You say what's at stake without regard for consequences. You silence the room with your blunt honesty. One person claps. Then everyone at once, on both sides, is recognizing your point with robust applause. In this moment a leader emerges. Through debating you make yourself. By taking a stand you make yourself something other than the next report writer churned out by the educational factory.

Debate: Was the Apollo mission to the moon great?

If there were a Technology Olympics, the Apollo mission would have been a gold-medal winner. In the political arena, too, Apollo was a world champion. But what would Socrates say? Reflecting on the accomplishment, a philosopher might ask, what does it *mean* for humankind to have gone to the moon? What have humans *become* as a result of this accomplishment? Has it changed our standing in the universe? Are we happier, healthier, wiser, more powerful, or spiritually enlightened in virtue of this achievement? How does it affect human existence or advance our knowledge of reality? Does it mark a turning point in human relations with the natural world? What light can Apollo 11 shed on Being in all of its dimensions? In the Philosophy Olympics, where would Apollo 11 stand?

For an idea of what philosophers *do,* consider the following two perspectives on the matter. After reflecting on both, you decide which best answers the question of Apollo 11's greatness on the basis of your own philosophical assessment.

Suppose the Apollo advocate begins, "From a philosophical viewpoint, the greatness of Apollo 11 is evident in its demonstration of the power of the human mind. It exemplifies the best in humans, the vision, and will to overcome, to reach beyond, to strive for noble ideals, and demand of ourselves the excellence necessary for their realization. Nothing we call 'great' compares to the immensity of this ingenious production, or to the drive and determination that made it possible. The human spirit grew from this event by extending the reach of human reason."

The skeptic might reply: "The only reason everyone thinks Apollo was so great is that technology has such an exaggerated standing in modern life. In fact, prowess and cleverness in science and engineering is *the only* measure of greatness in today's gadget-obsessed world. Is not *creativity* a better criterion for judging greatness? Kicking a tin can to the moon is hardly noble when compared to circumnavigating the soul with a pen or a paintbrush. As Nietzsche once pointed out, 'The greatest events—they are not our loudest but our stillest hours.' "

Having established a point of difference worthy of more deliberation, each side presents an argument to support its conclusion. As you consider the arguments in turn, extend the *principle of charity* to both by considering each fully on its own terms, before you begin to evaluate their strengths and weaknesses.

The advocate proceeds: "Like astronauts, humans are naturally endowed with a will to boldly go where no one has gone before. Having thoroughly explored and studied the earth, the time has come to seek out what lies beyond. The Apollo mission is an affirmation of human progress and enlightenment. If progress in the human condition is measured by increasing freedom, then the spaceship's escape from the earthly chains of gravity symbolizes a great liberation from earthly limits. Apollo represents the opening of a fresh horizon for growth and new possibilities for meeting human needs. The more we expand our knowledge beyond the earth, the more powerful and impressive we become. If we can send a man to the moon, we can do anything. By lifting ourselves up from the dirt, where we have scrambled about with other animals for eons, we distinguish and honor humanity. Standing on the moon, the astronaut symbolizes the crowning achievement in the human quest for ascendance to an Archimedean point, an exquisitely objective view suitable for those who would be masters of their destiny."

The skeptic rejoins: "Are we now the masters of destiny we dreamed of becoming? Or are we merely batteries for the machine, more dependent on technology, more addicted than ever to fireworks and speed at the push of a button? Just because we *can* do something, does not mean we *ought* to do it. Apollo symbolizes, not progress, but the ego's thirst for conquest and a lack of respect for limits. In the nihilistic wasteland of modern life, the Apollo achievement is a measure of our longing for a passionate, meaningful, heroic existence. Turning our backs on our only home for the vast lonely expanse of nothingness reveals, not our glory, but our desperation and alienation. Having left earth, the astronauts discover not new horizons, but no horizons. Free of the earth's gravity there is no up or down, no east or west, no backward or forward. The moon is not a glorious destination, but an ignoble desolation. The astronaut, separated from life on earth and plugged into an artificial life-support system, represents the precarious situation of humanity today in advanced technological society. In our quest for ascendance we have forgotten the earth and what it is to be human. We are earthlings, not spacemen, connected to the planet by a sacred bond. The Apollo mission symbolizes the severing of that relation and a great fall from the grace of life-affirming existence."

Continued.

Which perspective points toward the true interpretation of the Apollo mission? Mull it over long enough and you may begin to wonder if there is a fact of the matter upon which to base a definitive judgment. What is a human— transcendent being or rooted earthling? What is good for humans—pursuit of limitless growth or respect for limits? What was the mission—progress or travesty? How do you decide among these conflicting values? Is there a *given* order of values to appeal to for answers? Even if some philosophers believe there is, the skeptics won't stop asking, given by who, or by what? This is what it means to say that philosophy is a *speculative* discipline. The fun of it is exploring values, framing the issues conceptually, making good arguments, refuting bad arguments, and sometimes, if you are really skillful and lucky, reaching agreements with your opposition without need of a judge!

■ Think for yourself to determine where you stand on the question of Apollo 11's greatness and compose an argument to defend your position.

The primary objective of this book is *not* simply to introduce you to the great thinkers in the Western tradition of philosophy. Rather, it is to *make* you a great thinker. A least it is to provide you the means to make yourself great. Hitherto, introductory readers have only presented various philosophies; the point is to *grow* them. The genius of this endeavor is that it puts all the fun back in studying philosophy. Instead of saying, "Bow down to the great minds of Western thought and assume the position for an examination of your comprehension," this book says, "Climb up on the shoulders of giants so that you may see farther, search boldly, and dare to think for yourself!" Here is a chance not just to study the insights of others, but to have your own insights, and not just for the fun of it—although becoming great has its exhilarations—but also because the big trouble humans are in today is calling for human ingenuity.

Resources

Julian Baggini & Peter S. Fosl, *The Philosopher's Toolkit: A Compendium of Philosophical Concepts and Methods,* (Blackwell, 2003). Provides eighty-seven entries, each of which explains how to use a concept or technique to accomplish philosophical work.

David Bartholomae and Anthony Petrosky, *Ways of Reading: An Anthology for Writers,* "**Introduction: Ways of Reading,**" (Bedford/St.Martin's, 2008). This introduction provides excellent guidance for the development of a strong, aggressive, labor-intensive reading and writing practice.

UNIT ONE:
The Examined Life

Introduction: An Education for a Life Worth Living

"Money Top Goal of College Freshman," was the headline of a recent *Los Angeles Times* article on what students hope to gain from a college education. According to a national survey of student attitudes conducted annually by UCLA, the percentage of students who reported their reason for going to college was to "be very well off financially" hit a record high (74%), while the percentage reporting they were attending in order to "develop a meaningful philosophy of life" was at an all time low (39%). This has not always been the case. In 1967 the numbers were reversed with the majority (86%) saying that a college education was for philosophical self-development and the minority (42%) saying it was a stepping stone to financial success.

Where you stand on the question of what education is *for* is probably related to what you think makes life 'worth living.' If wealth is what makes life worth living, you will probably think education ought to provide preparation for lucrative careers. If, on the other hand, you define a life worth living in nonmonetary terms, you will probably want something more meaningful from your education than a paycheck. What makes life worth living and what would an education for a life worth living include?

This unit challenges you to think broadly about what the goals of a 'good education' ought to be, and what you hope to become as a result of reaching those goals. It involves reflecting on means and ends. For those who enrolled in this course as a means of avoiding a fate worse than school, the challenge begins with a recognition that remaining enrolled and succeeding academically is a choice. Instead of being here right now, you might have chosen to be sleeping in your bed, watching television, making money at a job, or partying at the beach. You made a series of choices that landed you here, *now,* reading this book. Did you arrive here as a result of soul searching? Before you arrived, did you examine your options in terms of the values they embody? Did you give away your decision-making power, choosing impulsively? Even if you don't know why you chose this course, or what ends you think it ought to serve, you can take up the readings in this unit as a starting point for working out

25

your educational philosophy and begin using it to inform your decision-making for the rest of your life.

This unit begins with an allegory presented by the ancient Greek philosopher Plato in his most famous work, which is considered the first masterpiece in the Western philosophical tradition. In the *Republic,* a lengthy dialogue on justice, Plato lays out a plan for educating leaders who will be willing and able to govern a just society. "The Allegory of the Cave" illustrates the degrees to which humans may be enlightened or un-enlightened in regard to the Truth (including the essence of justice). Plato's hope is that students provided with an enlightening education might become leaders capable of governing in a manner that insures the good life. We will explore the use of this allegory as an interpretive tool throughout the book, asking for example, "Who is in the cave on Friedrich Nietzsche's view?" Or, "What does the pathway out of the cave symbolize for David Orr?" After completing the unit you will be able to put the allegory to use in an essay on your personal educational philosophy.

The nineteenth century German philosopher Nietzsche and contemporary American environmental theorist Orr give us two (mostly) contrasting answers to the question, *What is education for?* Both examine the purposes education *is* serving in their respective societies, in contrast with purposes each believes it *ought* to be serving. Both are motivated to change the dominant educational assumptions at work in their respective societies.

In several notable respects, their views diverge. Is education an end in itself or a means to some higher end? Should its aim be the realization of each individual's full human potential? Or should it aim to produce citizens capable of solving society's problems for the common good? Should education's goal be 'moral people,' 'responsible citizens,' or 'creators of great cultural productions'? To what extent can these competing ends be reconciled? Should we measure educational success by the upward mobility and economic standing of its graduates? Or should it be measured by its commitment to justice, standards of decency, and human survival? Or by artistic and intellectual productions representing the pinnacle of cultural advancement?

As you read look for two contrasting views which might be called the "classical" and the "pragmatic" perspectives on education, and think about where you stand in relation to each.

As is so often the case in philosophy, one question leads to another. Since the purpose of education depends on the sort of lives those seeking an education hope to live, it makes sense to ask, what is 'a life worth living'? In Plato's *Apology,* after Socrates is found guilty by the democratic citizens of Athens, he refuses lighter penalties that would hold back his philosophical mission on the grounds that "the unexamined life is not worth living."

What does this mean?

What, *exactly,* is examined in an 'examined life,' that is not examined in an unexamined one? How does this make the 'examined' one *more* worth living? As you search for clues to shed light on Socrates' view, reflect on what you think makes a human life worth living.

Of course it could be argued that every human life is worth living, including the life of a psychopath. That would be to miss the point of reflecting on what *makes* a life *genuinely worth living* ... that is, what makes a life so *good* that it would be worth dying for? Whatever that life might be, it is certainly what a 'good education' is supposed to be preparing you for.

Resources

An Inconvenient Truth: A Global Warning. Dir. Davis Guggenheim. Perf. Al Gore. (Paramount, 2006).

Brown, Eric, "Plato's Ethics and Politics in *The Republic,*" *The Stanford Encyclopedia of Philosophy,* edited by Edward N. Zalta. (Winter 2010 Edition, forthcoming). http://plato.stanford.edu/archives/win2010/entries/plato-ethics-politics/

Cockburn, Alexander, and St. Clair, Jeffrey, *Al Gore: A User's Manuel.* (Verso, 2000).

Leiter, Brian, "Nietzsche's Moral and Political Philosophy," *The Stanford Encyclopedia of Philosophy,* edited by Edward N. Zalta. (Summer 2010 Edition). http://plato.stanford.edu/archives/sum2010/entries/nietzsche-moral-political/

Metz, Thaddeus, "The Meaning of Life," *The Stanford Encyclopedia of Philosophy,* edited by Edward N. Zalta. (Fall 2008 Edition) http://plato.stanford.edu/archives/fall2008/entries/life-meaning/

Nails, Debra, "Socrates," *The Stanford Encyclopedia of Philosophy,* edited by Edward N. Zalta. (Spring 2010 Edition). http://plato.stanford.edu/archives/spr2010/entries/socrates/

Phillips, D. C., "Philosophy of Education," *The Stanford Encyclopedia of Philosophy,* edited by Edward N. Zalta. (Spring 2009 Edition). http://plato.stanford.edu/archives/spr2009/entries/education-philosophy/

Allegory of the Cave

from Republic

Plato
Translated by Benjamin Jowett

Book VII

And now, I said, let me show in a figure how far our nature is enlightened or unenlightened:—Behold! human beings living in a underground den, which has a mouth open towards the light and reaching all along the den; here they have been from their childhood, and have their legs and necks chained so that they cannot move, and can only see before them, being prevented by the chains from turning round their heads. Above and behind them a fire is blazing at a distance, and between the fire and the prisoners there is a raised way; and you will see, if you look, a low wall built along the way, like the screen which marionette players have in front of them, over which they show the puppets.

I see.

And do you see, I said, men passing along the wall carrying all sorts of vessels, and statues and figures of animals made of wood and stone and various materials, which appear over the wall? Some of them are talking, others silent.

You have shown me a strange image, and they are strange prisoners.

Like ourselves, I replied; and they see only their own shadows, or the shadows of one another, which the fire throws on the opposite wall of the cave?

True, he said; how could they see anything but the shadows if they were never allowed to move their heads?

And of the objects which are being carried in like manner they would only see the shadows?

Yes, he said.

And if they were able to converse with one another, would they not suppose that they were naming what was actually before them?

Very true.

And suppose further that the prison had an echo which came from the other side, would they not be sure to fancy when one of the passers-by spoke that the voice which they heard came from the passing shadow?

No question, he replied.

To them, I said, the truth would be literally nothing but the shadows of the images.

That is certain.

And now look again, and see what will naturally follow if the prisoners are released and disabused of their error. At first, when any of them is liberated and compelled suddenly to stand up and turn his neck round and walk and look towards the light, he will suffer sharp pains; the glare will distress him, and he will be unable to see the realities of which in his former state he had seen the shadows; and then conceive some one saying to him, that what he saw before was an illusion, but that now, when he is approaching nearer to being and his eye is turned towards more real existence, he has a clearer vision,—what will be his reply? And you may further imagine that his instructor is pointing to the objects as they pass and requiring him to name them,—will he not be perplexed? Will he not fancy that the shadows which he formerly saw are truer than the objects which are now shown to him?

Far truer.

And if he is compelled to look straight at the light, will he not have a pain in his eyes which will make him turn away to take refuge in the objects of vision which he can see, and which he will conceive to be in reality clearer than the things which are now being shown to him?

True, he said.

And suppose once more, that he is reluctantly dragged up a steep and rugged ascent, and held fast until he is forced into the presence of the sun himself, is he not likely to be pained and irritated? When he approaches the light his eyes will be dazzled, and he will not be able to see anything at all of what are now called realities.

Not all in a moment, he said.

He will require to grow accustomed to the sight of the upper world. And first he will see the shadows best, next the reflections of men and other objects in the water, and then the objects themselves; then he will gaze upon the light of the moon and the stars and the spangled heaven; and he will see the sky and the stars by night better than the sun or the light of the sun by day?

Certainly.

Last of all he will be able to see the sun, and not mere reflections of him in the water, but he will see him in his own proper place, and not in another; and he will contemplate him as he is.

Certainly.

He will then proceed to argue that this is he who gives the season and the years, and is the guardian of all that is in the visible world, and in a certain way the cause of all things which he and his fellows have been accustomed to behold?

Clearly, he said, he would first see the sun and then reason about him.

And when he remembered his old habitation, and the wisdom of the den and his fellow-prisoners, do you not suppose that he would felicitate himself on the change, and pity them?

Certainly, he would.

And if they were in the habit of conferring honours among themselves on those who were quickest to observe the passing shadows and to remark which of them went before, and which followed after, and which were together; and who were therefore best able to draw conclusions as to the future, do you think that he would care for such honours and glories, or envy the possessors of them? Would he not say with Homer, 'Better to be the poor servant of a poor master,' and to endure anything, rather than think as they do and live after their manner?

Yes, he said, I think that he would rather suffer anything than entertain these false notions and live in this miserable manner.

Imagine once more, I said, such an one coming suddenly out of the sun to be replaced in his old situation; would he not be certain to have his eyes full of darkness?

To be sure, he said.

And if there were a contest, and he had to compete in measuring the shadows with the prisoners who had never moved out of the den, while his sight was still weak, and before his eyes had become steady (and the time which would be needed to acquire this new habit of sight might be very considerable), would he not be ridiculous? Men would say of him that up he went and down he came without his eyes; and that it was better not even to think of ascending; and if any one tried to loose another and lead him up to the light, let them only catch the offender, and they would put him to death.

No question, he said.

■ ■ ■

Questions for Further Exploration:

- What does each of the symbols in Plato's allegory represent? Fill in the table.

SYMBOL	INTERPRETATION
Sun:	
Outside the cave:	
Escapee:	
Pathway out:	Knowledge
Inside the cave:	Self
Prisoners:	Societal Expectations
Shadow-casters:	Society
Shadows on the wall:	morals, values

- What point(s) did Plato hope to convey with his allegory?

- How might this allegory be used to interpret a contemporary event?

- Consider which symbols are associated with good/bad or positive/ negative meanings. What message(s) do these symbolic values imply about the earth?

On the Future of Our Educational Institutions

Friedrich Nietzsche
Translated by J. M. Kennedy

■ ■ ■

Listen, therefore, ladies and gentlemen, while I recount my harmless experience and the less harmless conversation between the two gentlemen whom, so far, I have not named.

Let us now imagine ourselves in the position of a young student—that is to say, in a position which, in our present age of bewildering movement and feverish excitability, has become an almost impossible one. It is necessary to have lived through it in order to believe that such careless self-lulling and comfortable indifference to the moment, or to time in general, are possible. In this condition I, and a friend about my own age, spent a year at the University of Bonn on the Rhine,—it was a year which, in its complete lack of plans and projects for the future, seems almost like a dream to me now—a dream framed, as it were, by two periods of growth. We two remained quiet and peaceful, although we were surrounded by fellows who in the main were very differently disposed, and from time to time we experienced considerable difficulty in meeting and resisting the somewhat too pressing advances of the young men of our own age. Now, however, that I can look upon the stand we had to take against these opposing forces, I cannot help associating them in my mind with those checks we are wont to receive in our dreams, as, for instance, when we imagine we are able to fly and yet feel ourselves held back by some incomprehensible power.

I and my friend had many reminiscences in common, and these dated from the period of our boyhood upwards. One of these I must relate to you, since it forms a sort of prelude to the harmless experience already mentioned. On the occasion of a certain journey up the Rhine, which we had made together one summer, it happened that he and I independently conceived the very same plan at the same hour and on the same spot, and we were so struck by this unwonted coincidence that we determined to carry the plan out forthwith. We resolved to found a kind of small club which would consist of ourselves and a few friends, and the object of which would be to provide us with a stable and binding organisation directing and adding interest to our creative impulses in art and literature; or, to put it more plainly: each of us would be pledged to present an original piece of work to the club once a month,—either a poem, a treatise, an architectural design, or a musical composition, upon which each of the others, in a friendly spirit, would have to pass free and unrestrained criticism.

We thus hoped, by means of mutual correction, to be able both to stimulate and to chasten our creative impulses and, as a matter of fact, the success of the scheme was such that we have both always felt a sort of respectful attachment for the hour and the place at which it first took shape in our minds.

This attachment was very soon transformed into a rite; for we all agreed to go, whenever it was possible to do so, once a year to that lonely spot near Rolandseck, where on that summer's day, while sitting together, lost in meditation, we were suddenly inspired by the same thought. Frankly speaking, the rules which were drawn up on the formation of the club were never very strictly observed; but owing to the very fact that we had many sins of omission on our conscience during our student-year in Bonn, when we were once more on the banks of the Rhine, we firmly resolved not only to observe our rule, but also to gratify our feelings and our sense of gratitude by reverently visiting that spot near Rolandseck on the day appointed.

It was, however, with some difficulty that we were able to carry our plans into execution; for, on the very day we had selected for our excursion, the large and lively students' association, which always hindered us in our flights, did their utmost to put obstacles in our way and to hold us back. Our association had organised a general holiday excursion to Rolandseck on the very day my friend and I had fixed upon, the object of the outing being to assemble all its members for the last time at the close of the half-year and to send them home with pleasant recollections of their last hours together.

The day was a glorious one; the weather was of the kind which, in our climate at least, only falls to our lot in late summer: heaven and earth merged harmoniously with one another, and, glowing wondrously in the sunshine, autumn freshness blended with the blue expanse above. Arrayed in the bright fantastic garb in which, amid the gloomy fashions now reigning, students alone may indulge, we boarded a steamer which was gaily decorated in our honour, and hoisted our flag on its mast. From both banks of the river there came at intervals the sound of signal-guns, fired according to our orders, with the view of acquainting both our host in Rolandseck and the inhabitants in the neighbourhood with our approach. I shall not speak of the noisy journey from the landing-stage, through the excited and expectant little place, nor shall I refer to the esoteric jokes exchanged between ourselves; I also make no mention of a feast which became both wild and noisy, or of an extraordinary musical production in the execution of which, whether as soloists or as chorus, we all ultimately had to share, and which I, as musical adviser of our club, had not only had to rehearse, but was then forced to conduct. Towards the end of this piece, which grew ever wilder and which was sung to ever quicker time, I made a sign to my friend, and just as the last chord rang like a yell through the building, he and I vanished, leaving behind us a raging pandemonium.

In a moment we were in the refreshing and breathless stillness of nature. The shadows were already lengthening, the sun still shone steadily, though it had sunk a good deal in the heavens, and from the green and glittering waves of the Rhine a cool breeze was wafted over our hot faces. Our solemn rite bound us only in so far as the latest hours of the day were concerned, and we therefore determined to employ the last moments of clear daylight by giving ourselves up to one of our many hobbies.

At that time we were passionately fond of pistol-shooting, and both of us in later years found the skill we had acquired as amateurs of great use in our military career. Our club servant happened to know the somewhat distant and elevated spot which we used as a range, and had carried our pistols there in advance. The spot lay near the upper border of the wood which covered the lesser heights behind Rolandseck: it was a small uneven plateau, close to the place we had consecrated in memory of its associations. On a wooded slope alongside of our shooting-range there was a small piece of ground which had been cleared of wood, and which made an ideal halting-place; from it one could get a view of the Rhine over the tops of the trees and the brushwood, so that the beautiful, undulating lines of the Seven Mountains and above all of the Drachenfels bounded the horizon against the group of trees, while in the centre of the bow formed by the glistening Rhine itself the island of Nonnenwörth stood out as if suspended in the river's arms. This was the place which had become sacred to us through the dreams and plans we had had in common, and to which we intended to withdraw, later in the evening,—nay, to which we should be obliged to withdraw, if we wished to close the day in accordance with the law we had imposed on ourselves.

At one end of the little uneven plateau, and not very far away, there stood the mighty trunk of an oak-tree, prominently visible against a background quite bare of trees and consisting merely of low undulating hills in the distance. Working together, we had once carved a pentagram in the side of this tree-trunk. Years of exposure to rain and storm had slightly deepened the channels we had cut, and the figure seemed a welcome target for our pistol-practice. It was already late in the afternoon when we

reached our improvised range, and our oak-stump cast a long and attenu-
ated shadow across the barren heath. All was still: thanks to the lofty trees
at our feet, we were unable to catch a glimpse of the valley of the Rhine
below. The peacefulness of the spot seemed only to intensify the loudness
of our pistol-shots—and I had scarcely fired my second barrel at the pentagram when I felt some one lay hold of my arm and noticed that my
friend had also some one beside him who had interrupted his loading.

Turning sharply on my heels I found myself face to face with an astonished old gentleman, and felt what must have been a very powerful dog
make a lunge at my back. My friend had been approached by a somewhat
younger man than I had; but before we could give expression to our surprise the older of the two interlopers burst forth in the following threatening and heated strain: "No! no!" he called to us, "no duels must be fought
here, but least of all must you young students fight one. Away with these
pistols and compose yourselves. Be reconciled, shake hands! What?—and
are you the salt of the earth, the intelligence of the future, the seed of our
hopes—and are you not even able to emancipate yourselves from the insane code of honour and its violent regulations? I will not cast any asper-
sions on your hearts, but your heads certainly do you no credit. You, whose
youth is watched over by the wisdom of Greece and Rome, and whose
youthful spirits, at the cost of enormous pains, have been flooded with the
light of the sages and heroes of antiquity,—can you not refrain from making the code of knightly honour—that is to say, the code of folly and
brutality—the guiding principle of your conduct?—Examine it rationally
once and for all, and reduce it to plain terms; lay its pitiable narrowness
bare, and let it be the touchstone, not of your hearts but of your minds. If
you do not regret it then, it will merely show that your head is not fitted for
work in a sphere where great gifts of discrimination are needful in order to
burst the bonds of prejudice, and where a well-balanced understanding is
necessary for the purpose of distinguishing right from wrong, even when
the difference between them lies deeply hidden and is not, as in this case,
so ridiculously obvious. In that case, therefore, my lads, try to go through
life in some other honourable manner; join the army or learn a handicraft
that pays its way."

To this rough, though admittedly just, flood of eloquence, we replied
with some irritation, interrupting each other continually in so doing: "In
the first place, you are mistaken concerning the main point; for we are not
here to fight a duel at all; but rather to practise pistol-shooting. Secondly,
you do not appear to know how a real duel is conducted;—do you suppose
that we should have faced each other in this lonely spot, like two highway-
men, without seconds or doctors, etc. etc.? Thirdly, with regard to the
question of duelling, we each have our own opinions, and do not require to

be waylaid and surprised by the sort of instruction you may feel disposed to give us."

This reply, which was certainly not polite, made a bad impression upon the old man. At first, when he heard that we were not about to fight a duel, he surveyed us more kindly: but when we reached the last passage of our speech, he seemed so vexed that he growled. When, however, we began to speak of our point of view, he quickly caught hold of his companion, turned sharply round, and cried to us in bitter tones: "People should not have points of view, but thoughts!" And then his companion added: "Be respectful when a man such as this even makes mistakes!"

Meanwhile, my friend, who had reloaded, fired a shot at the pentagram, after having cried: "Look out!" This sudden report behind his back made the old man savage; once more he turned round and looked sourly at my friend, after which he said to his companion in a feeble voice: "What shall we do? These young men will be the death of me with their firing."— "You should know," said the younger man, turning to us, "that your noisy pastimes amount, as it happens on this occasion, to an attempt upon the life of philosophy. You observe this venerable man,—he is in a position to beg you to desist from firing here. And when such a man begs——" "Well, his request is generally granted," the old man interjected, surveying us sternly.

As a matter of fact, we did not know what to make of the whole matter; we could not understand what our noisy pastimes could have in common with philosophy; nor could we see why, out of regard for polite scruples, we should abandon our shooting-range, and at this moment we may have appeared somewhat undecided and perturbed. The companion noticing our momentary discomfiture, proceeded to explain the matter to us.

"We are compelled," he said, "to linger in this immediate neighbourhood for an hour or so; we have a rendezvous here. An eminent friend of this eminent man is to meet us here this evening; and we had actually selected this peaceful spot, with its few benches in the midst of the wood, for the meeting. It would really be most unpleasant if, owing to your continual pistol-practice, we were to be subjected to an unending series of shocks; surely your own feelings will tell you that it is impossible for you to continue your firing when you hear that he who has selected this quiet and isolated place for a meeting with a friend is one of our most eminent philosophers."

This explanation only succeeded in perturbing us the more; for we saw a danger threatening us which was even greater than the loss of our shooting-range, and we asked eagerly, "Where is this quiet spot? Surely not to the left here, in the wood?"

"That is the very place."

"But this evening that place belongs to us," my friend interposed. "We must have it," we cried together.

Our long-projected celebration seemed at that moment more important than all the philosophies of the world, and we gave such vehement and animated utterance to our sentiments that in view of the incomprehensible nature of our claims we must have cut a somewhat ridiculous figure. At any rate, our philosophical interlopers regarded us with expressions of amused inquiry, as if they expected us to proffer some sort of apology. But we were silent, for we wished above all to keep our secret.

Thus we stood facing one another in silence, while the sunset dyed the tree-tops a ruddy gold. The philosopher contemplated the sun, his companion contemplated him, and we turned our eyes towards our nook in the woods which to-day we seemed in such great danger of losing. A feeling of sullen anger took possession of us. What is philosophy, we asked ourselves, if it prevents a man from being by himself or from enjoying the select company of a friend,—in sooth, if it prevents him from becoming a philosopher? For we regarded the celebration of our rite as a thoroughly philosophical performance. In celebrating it we wished to form plans and resolutions for the future, by means of quiet reflections we hoped to light upon an idea which would once again help us to form and gratify our spirit in the future, just as that former idea had done during our boyhood. The solemn act derived its very significance from this resolution, that nothing definite was to be done, we were only to be alone, and to sit still and meditate, as we had done five years before when we had each been inspired with the same thought. It was to be a silent solemnisation, all reminiscence and all future; the present was to be as a hyphen between the two. And fate, now unfriendly, had just stepped into our magic circle—and we knew not how to dismiss her;—the very unusual character of the circumstances filled us with mysterious excitement.

Whilst we stood thus in silence for some time, divided into two hostile groups, the clouds above waxed ever redder and the evening seemed to grow more peaceful and mild; we could almost fancy we heard the regular breathing of nature as she put the final touches to her work of art—the glorious day we had just enjoyed; when, suddenly, the calm evening air was rent by a confused and boisterous cry of joy which seemed to come from the Rhine. A number of voices could be heard in the distance—they were those of our fellow-students who by that time must have taken to the Rhine in small boats. It occurred to us that we should be missed and that we should also miss something: almost simultaneously my friend and I raised our pistols: our shots were echoed back to us, and with their echo there came from the valley the sound of a well-known cry intended as a signal of identification. For our passion for shooting had brought us both repute and ill-repute in our club. At the same time we were conscious that our behaviour towards the silent philosophical couple had been exceptionally ungentlemanly; they had been quietly contemplating us for some time, and when we fired the shock made them draw close up to each other. We hurried up to them, and each in our turn cried out: "Forgive us. That was our last shot, and it was intended for our friends on the Rhine. They have understood us, do you hear? If you insist upon having that place among the trees, grant us at least the permission to recline there also. You will find a number of benches on the spot: we shall not disturb you; we shall sit quite still and shall not utter a word: but it is now past seven o'clock and we *must* go there at once.

"That sounds more mysterious than it is," I added after a pause; "we have made a solemn vow to spend this coming hour on that ground, and there were reasons for the vow. The spot is sacred to us, owing to some pleasant associations, it must also inaugurate a good future for us. We shall therefore endeavour to leave you with no disagreeable recollections of our meeting—even though we have done much to perturb and frighten you."

The philosopher was silent; his companion, however, said: "Our promises and plans unfortunately compel us not only to remain, but also to spend the same hour on the spot you have selected. It is left for us to decide whether fate or perhaps a spirit has been responsible for this extraordinary coincidence."

"Besides, my friend," said the philosopher, "I am not half so displeased with these warlike youngsters as I was. Did you observe how quiet they were a moment ago, when we were contemplating the sun? They neither spoke nor smoked, they stood stone still, I even believe they meditated."

Turning suddenly in our direction, he said: "*Were* you meditating? Just tell me about it as we proceed in the direction of our common trysting-place." We took a few steps together and went down the slope into the warm balmy air of the woods where it was already much darker. On the way my friend openly revealed his thoughts to the philosopher, he confessed how much he had feared that perhaps to-day for the first time a philosopher was about to stand in the way of his philosophising.

The sage laughed. "What? You were afraid a philosopher would prevent your philosophising? This might easily happen: and you have not yet experienced such a thing? Has your university life been free from experience? You surely attend lectures on philosophy?"

This question discomfited us; for, as a matter of fact, there had been no element of philosophy in our education up to that time. In those days, moreover, we fondly imagined that everybody who held the post and possessed the dignity of a philosopher must perforce be one: we were inexperienced and badly informed. We frankly admitted that we had not yet belonged to any philosophical college, but that we would certainly make up for lost time.

"Then what," he asked, "did you mean when you spoke of philosophising?" Said I, "We are at a loss for a definition. But to all intents and purposes we meant this, that we wished to make earnest endeavours to consider the best possible means of becoming men of culture." "That is a good deal and at the same time very little," growled the philosopher; "just you think the matter over. Here are our benches, let us discuss the question exhaustively: I shall not disturb your meditations with regard to how you are to become men of culture. I wish you success and—points of view, as in your duelling questions; brand-new, original, and enlightened points of view. The philosopher does not wish to prevent your philosophising: but refrain at least from disconcerting him with your pistol-shots. Try to imitate the Pythagoreans to-day: they, as servants of a true philosophy, had to remain silent for five years—possibly you may also be able to remain silent for five times fifteen minutes, as servants of your own future culture, about which you seem so concerned."

We had reached our destination: the solemnisation of our rite began. As on the previous occasion, five years ago, the Rhine was once more flowing beneath a light mist, the sky seemed bright and the woods exhaled the same fragrance. We took our places on the farthest corner of the most distant bench; sitting there we were almost concealed, and neither the philosopher nor his companion could see our faces. We were alone: when the sound of the philosopher's voice reached us, it had become so blended with the rustling leaves and with the buzzing murmur of the myriads of living things inhabiting the wooded height, that it almost seemed like the music of nature; as a sound it resembled nothing more than a distant monotonous plaint. We were indeed undisturbed.

Some time elapsed in this way, and while the glow of sunset grew steadily paler the recollection of our youthful undertaking in the cause of culture waxed ever more vivid. It seemed to us as if we owed the greatest debt of gratitude to that little society we had founded; for it had done more than merely supplement our public school training; it had actually been the only fruitful society we had had, and within its frame we even placed our public school life, as a purely isolated factor helping us in our general efforts to attain to culture.

We knew this, that, thanks to our little society, no thought of embracing any particular career had ever entered our minds in those days. The all too frequent exploitation of youth by the State, for its own purposes—that is to say, so that it may rear useful officials as quickly as possible and guarantee their unconditional obedience to it by means of excessively severe examinations—had remained quite foreign to our education. And to show

how little we had been actuated by thoughts of utility or by the prospect of speedy advancement and rapid success, on that day we were struck by the comforting consideration that, even then, we had not yet decided what we should be—we had not even troubled ourselves at all on this head. Our little society had sown the seeds of this happy indifference in our souls and for it alone we were prepared to celebrate the anniversary of its foundation with hearty gratitude. I have already pointed out, I think, that in the eyes of the present age, which is so intolerant of anything that is not useful, such purposeless enjoyment of the moment, such a lulling of one's self in the cradle of the present, must seem almost incredible and at all events blameworthy. How useless we were! And how proud we were of being useless! We used even to quarrel with each other as to which of us should have the glory of being the more useless. We wished to attach no importance to anything, to have strong views about nothing, to aim at nothing; we wanted to take no thought for the morrow, and desired no more than to recline comfortably like good-for-nothings on the threshold of the present; and we did—bless us!

—That, ladies and gentlemen, was our standpoint then!—

Absorbed in these reflections, I was just about to give an answer to the question of the future of *our* Educational Institutions in the same self-sufficient way, when it gradually dawned upon me that the "natural music," coming from the philosopher's bench had lost its original character and travelled to us in much more piercing and distinct tones than before. Suddenly I became aware that I was listening, that I was eavesdropping, and was passionately interested, with both ears keenly alive to every sound. I nudged my friend who was evidently somewhat tired, and I whispered: "Don't fall asleep! There is something for us to learn over there. It applies to us, even though it be not meant for us."

For instance, I heard the younger of the two men defending himself with great animation while the philosopher rebuked him with ever increasing vehemence. "You are unchanged," he cried to him, "unfortunately unchanged. It is quite incomprehensible to me how you can still be the same as you were seven years ago, when I saw you for the last time and left you with so much misgiving. I fear I must once again divest you, however reluctantly, of the skin of modern culture which you have donned meanwhile;—and what do I find beneath it? The same immutable 'intelligible' character forsooth, according to Kant; but unfortunately the same unchanged 'intellectual' character, too—which may also be a necessity, though not a comforting one. I ask myself to what purpose have I lived as a philosopher, if, possessed as you are of no mean intelligence and a genuine thirst for knowledge, all the years you have spent in my company have left no deeper impression upon you. At present you are behaving as if you had not even heard the cardinal principle of all culture, which I went to such pains to inculcate upon you during our former intimacy. Tell me,—what was that principle?"

"I remember," replied the scolded pupil, "you used to say no one would strive to attain to culture if he knew how incredibly small the number of really cultured people actually is, and can ever be. And even this number of really cultured people would not be possible if a prodigious multitude, from reasons opposed to their nature and only led on by an alluring delusion, did not devote themselves to education. It were therefore a mistake publicly to reveal the ridiculous disproportion between the number of really cultured people and the enormous magnitude of the educational apparatus. Here lies the whole secret of culture—namely, that an innumerable host of men struggle to achieve it and work hard to that end, ostensibly in their own interests, whereas at bottom it is only in order that it may be possible for the few to attain to it."

"That is the principle," said the philosopher,—"and yet you could so far forget yourself as to believe that you are one of the few? This thought has occurred to you—I can see. That, however, is the result of the worthless character of modern education. The rights of genius are being democratised in order that people may be relieved of the labour of acquiring culture, and their need of it. Every one wants if possible to recline in the shade of the tree planted by genius, and to escape the dreadful necessity of working for him, so that his procreation may be made possible. What? Are you too proud to be a teacher? Do you despise the thronging multitude of learners? Do you speak contemptuously of the teacher's calling? And, aping my mode of life, would you fain live in solitary seclusion, hostilely isolated from that multitude? Do you suppose that you can reach at one bound what I ultimately had to win for myself only after long and determined struggles, in order even to be able to live like a philosopher? And do you not fear that solitude will wreak its vengeance upon you? Just try living the life of a hermit of culture. One must be blessed with overflowing wealth in order to live for the good of all on one's own resources! Extraordinary youngsters! They felt it incumbent upon them to imitate what is precisely most difficult and most high,—what is possible only to the master, when they, above all, should know how difficult and dangerous this is, and how many excellent gifts may be ruined by attempting it!"

"I will conceal nothing from you, sir," the companion replied. "I have heard too much from your lips at odd times and have been too long in your company to be able to surrender myself entirely to our present system of education and instruction. I am too painfully conscious of the disastrous errors and abuses to which you used to call my attention—though I very well know that I am not strong enough to hope for any success were I to struggle ever so valiantly against them. I was overcome by a feeling of general discouragement; my recourse to solitude was the result neither of pride nor arrogance. I would fain describe to you what I take to be the nature of the educational questions now attracting such enormous and pressing attention. It seemed to me that I must recognise two main directions in the forces at work—two seemingly antagonistic tendencies, equally deleterious in their action, and ultimately combining to produce their results: a striving to achieve the greatest possible *expansion* of education on the one hand, and a tendency to *minimise and weaken* it on the other. The first-named would, for various reasons, spread learning among the greatest number of people; the second would compel education to renounce its highest, noblest and sublimest claims in order to subordinate itself to some other department of life—such as the service of the State.

"I believe I have already hinted at the quarter in which the cry for the greatest possible expansion of education is most loudly raised. This expansion belongs to the most beloved of the dogmas of modern political economy. As much knowledge and education as possible; therefore the greatest possible supply and demand—hence as much happiness as possible:—that is the formula. In this case utility is made the object and goal of education,—utility in the sense of gain—the greatest possible pecuniary gain. In the quarter now under consideration culture would be defined as that point of vantage which enables one to 'keep in the van of one's age,' from which one can see all the easiest and best roads to wealth, and with which one controls all the means of communication between men and nations. The purpose of education, according to this scheme, would be to rear the most 'current' men possible,—'current' being used here in the sense in which it is applied to the coins of the realm. The greater the number of such men, the happier a nation will be; and this precisely is the purpose of our modern educational institutions: to help every one, as far as his nature will allow, to become 'current'; to develop him so that his particular degree of knowledge and science may yield him the greatest possible amount of happiness and pecuniary gain. Every one must be able to form some sort of estimate of himself; he must know how much he may reasonably expect from life. The 'bond between intelligence and property' which this point of view postulates has almost the force of a moral principle. In this quarter all culture is loathed which isolates, which sets goals beyond gold and gain, and which requires time: it is customary to dispose of such eccentric tendencies in education as systems of 'Higher Egotism,' or of 'Immoral Culture—Epicureanism.' According to the morality reigning here, the demands are quite different; what is required above all is 'rapid education,' so that a money-earning creature may be produced with all speed; there is even a desire to make this education so thorough that a creature may be reared that will be able to earn a *great deal* of money. Men are allowed only the precise amount of culture which is compatible with the interests of gain; but that amount, at least, is expected from them. In short: mankind has a necessary right to happiness on earth—that is why culture is necessary—but on that account alone!"

"I must just say something here," said the philosopher. "In the case of the view you have described so clearly, there arises the great and awful danger that at some time or other the great masses may overleap the middle classes and spring headlong into this earthly bliss. That is what is now called 'the social question.' It might seem to these masses that education for the greatest number of men was only a means to the earthly bliss of the few: the 'greatest possible expansion of education' so enfeebles education that it can no longer confer privileges or inspire respect. The most general form of culture is simply barbarism. But I do not wish to interrupt your discussion."

The companion continued: "There are yet other reasons, besides this beloved economical dogma, for the expansion of education that is being striven after so valiantly everywhere. In some countries the fear of religious oppression is so general, and the dread of its results so marked, that people in all classes of society long for culture and eagerly absorb those elements of it which are supposed to scatter the religious instincts. Elsewhere the State, in its turn, strives here and there for its own preservation, after the greatest possible expansion of education, because it always feels strong enough to bring the most determined emancipation, resulting from culture, under its yoke, and readily approves of everything which tends to extend culture, provided that it be of service to its officials or soldiers, but in the main to itself, in its competition with other nations. In this case, the foundations of a State must be sufficiently broad and firm to constitute a fitting counterpart to the complicated arches of culture which it supports, just as in the first case the traces of some former religious tyranny must still be felt for a people to be driven to such desperate remedies. Thus, wherever I hear the masses raise the cry for an expansion of education, I am wont to ask myself whether it is stimulated by a greedy lust of gain and property, by the memory of a former religious persecution, or by the prudent egotism of the State itself.

"On the other hand, it seemed to me that there was yet another tendency, not so clamorous, perhaps, but quite as forcible, which, hailing from various quarters, was animated by a different desire,—the desire to minimise and weaken education.

"In all cultivated circles people are in the habit of whispering to one another words something after this style: that it is a general fact that, owing to the present frantic exploitation of the scholar in the service of his science, his *education* becomes every day more accidental and more uncertain. For the study of science has been extended to such interminable lengths that he who, though not exceptionally gifted, yet possesses fair abilities, will need to devote himself exclusively to one branch and ignore all others if he ever wish to achieve anything in his work. Should he then elevate himself above the herd by means of his speciality, he still remains one of them in regard to all else,—that is to say, in regard to all the most important things in life. Thus, a specialist in science gets to resemble nothing so much as a factory workman who spends his whole life in turning one particular screw or handle on a certain instrument or machine, at which occupation he acquires the most consummate skill. In Germany, where we know how to drape such painful facts with the glorious garments of fancy, this narrow specialisation on the part of our learned men is even admired, and their ever greater deviation from the path of true culture is regarded as a moral phenomenon. 'Fidelity in small things,' 'dogged faithfulness,' become expressions of highest eulogy, and the lack of culture outside the speciality is flaunted abroad as a sign of noble sufficiency.

"For centuries it has been an understood thing that one alluded to scholars alone when one spoke of cultured men; but experience tells us that it would be difficult to find any necessary relation between the two classes to-day. For at present the exploitation of a man for the purpose of science is accepted everywhere without the slightest scruple. Who still ventures to ask, What may be the value of a science which consumes its minions in this vampire fashion? The division of labour in science is practically struggling towards the same goal which religions in certain parts of the world are consciously striving after,—that is to say, towards the decrease and even the destruction of learning. That, however, which, in the case of certain religions, is a perfectly justifiable aim, both in regard to their origin and their history, can only amount to self-immolation when transferred to the realm of science. In all matters of a general and serious nature, and above all, in regard to the highest philosophical problems, we have now already reached a point at which the scientific man, as such, is no longer allowed to speak. On the other hand, that adhesive and tenacious stratum which has now filled up the interstices between the sciences—Journalism—believes it has a mission to fulfil here, and this it does, according to its own particular lights—that is to say, as its name implies, after the fashion of a day-labourer.

"It is precisely in journalism that the two tendencies combine and become one. The expansion and the diminution of education here join hands. The newspaper actually steps into the place of culture, and he who, even as a scholar, wishes to voice any claim for education, must avail himself of this viscous stratum of communication which cements the seams between all forms of life, all classes, all arts, and all sciences, and which is as firm and reliable as news paper is, as a rule. In the news-paper the peculiar educational aims of the present culminate, just as the journalist, the servant of the moment, has stepped into the place of the genius, of the leader for all time, of the deliverer from the tyranny of the moment. Now, tell me, distinguished master, what hopes could I still have in a struggle against the general topsy-turvification of all genuine aims for education; with what courage can I, a single teacher, step forward, when I know that the moment any seeds of real culture are sown, they will be mercilessly crushed by the roller of this pseudo-culture? Imagine how useless the most energetic work on the part of the individual teacher must be, who would fain lead a pupil back into the distant and evasive Hellenic world and to the real home of culture, when in less than an hour, that same pupil will have recourse to a newspaper, the latest novel, or one of those learned books, the very style of which already bears the revolting impress of modern barbaric culture——"

"Now, silence a minute!" interjected the philosopher in a strong and sympathetic voice. "I understand you now, and ought never to have spoken so crossly to you. You are altogether right, save in your despair. I shall now proceed to say a few words of consolation."

Questions for Further Exploration:

- What does this lecture reveal about Nietzsche's philosophy of education?

- What is Nietzsche's critique of "modern times" in his world?

- What is the philosophical significance of the natural setting of Nietzsche's story?

- Consider Nietzsche's story in terms of Plato's allegory. What might each of the symbols (the cave, prisoners, shadows, escapee, outside, the sun, etc.) represent in Nietzsche's view?

- Select a quote to begin a free-write on your educational experience.

What Is Education For?

Six myths about the foundations of modern education, and six new principles to replace them

David Orr

If today is a typical day on planet Earth, we will lose 116 square miles of rainforest, or about an acre a second. We will lose another 72 square miles to encroaching deserts, as a result of human mismanagement and over-population. We will lose 40 to 100 species, and no one knows whether the number is 40 or 100. Today the human population will increase by 250,000. And today we will add 2,700 tons of chlorofluorocarbons to the atmosphere and 15 million tons of carbon. Tonight the Earth will be a little hotter, its waters more acidic, and the fabric of life more threadbare.

The truth is that many things on which your future health and prosperity depend are in dire jeopardy: climate stability, the resilience and productivity of natural systems, the beauty of the natural world, and biological diversity.

It is worth noting that this is not the work of ignorant people. It is, rather, largely the result of work by people with BAs, BSs, LLBs, MBAs, and PhDs. Elie Wiesel made a similar point to the Global Forum in Moscow last winter when he said that the designers and perpetrators of the Holocaust were the heirs of Kant and Goethe. In most respects the Germans were the best educated people on Earth, but their education did not serve as an adequate barrier to barbarity. What was wrong with their education? In Wiesel's words: "It emphasized theories instead of values, concepts rather than human beings, abstraction rather than consciousness, answers instead of questions, ideology and efficiency rather than conscience."

What is Education For?, by David Orr, reprinted by permission from In Context, No. 27, Winter 1991, copyright © 1990, 1996 by Context Institute, www.context.org

The same could be said of the way our education has prepared us to think about the natural world. It is a matter of no small consequence that the only people who have lived sustainably on the planet for any length of time could not read, or, like the Amish, do not make a fetish of reading. My point is simply that education is no guarantee of decency, prudence, or wisdom. More of the same kind of education will only compound our problems. This is not an argument for ignorance, but rather a statement that the worth of education must now be measured against the standards of decency and human survival—the issues now looming so large before us in the decade of the 1990s and beyond. It is not education that will save us, but education of a certain kind.

Sane Means, Mad Ends

What went wrong with contemporary culture and with education? There is some insight in literature: Christopher Marlowe's Faust, who trades his soul for knowledge and power; Mary Shelley's Dr. Frankenstein, who refuses to take responsibility for his creation; Herman Melville's Captain Ahab, who says "All my means are sane, my motive and object mad." In these characters we encounter the essence of the modern drive to dominate nature.

Historically, Francis Bacon's proposed union between knowledge and power foreshadows the contemporary alliance between government, business, and knowledge that has wrought so much mischief. Galileo's separation of the intellect foreshadows the dominance of the analytical mind over that part given to creativity, humor, and wholeness. And in Descartes' epistemology, one finds the roots of the radical separation of self and object. Together these three laid the foundations for modern education, foundations now enshrined in myths we have come to accept without question. Let me suggest six.

First, there is the myth that *ignorance is a solvable problem.* Ignorance is *not* a solvable problem, but rather an inescapable part of the human condition. The advance of knowledge always carries with it the advance of some form of ignorance. In 1930, after Thomas Midgely Jr. discovered CFCs, what had previously been a piece of trivial ignorance became a critical, life-threatening gap in the human understanding of the biosphere. No one thought to ask "what does this substance do to what?" until the early 1970s, and by 1990 CFCs had created a general thinning of the ozone layer worldwide. With the discovery of CFCs knowledge increased; but like the circumference of an expanding circle, ignorance grew as well.

A second myth is that *with enough knowledge and technology we can manage planet Earth.* "Managing the planet" has a nice a ring to it. It appeals to our fascination with digital readouts, computers, buttons and dials. But the complexity of Earth and its life systems can never be safely managed. The ecology of the top inch of topsoil is still largely unknown, as is its relationship to the larger systems of the biosphere.

What might be managed is *us:* human desires, economies, politics, and communities. But our attention is caught by those things that avoid the hard choices implied by politics, morality, ethics, and common sense. It makes far better sense to reshape ourselves to fit a finite planet than to attempt to reshape the planet to fit our infinite wants.

A third myth is that *knowledge is increasing and by implication human goodness.* There is an information explosion going on, by which I mean a rapid increase of data, words, and paper. But this explosion should not be taken for an increase in knowledge and wisdom, which cannot so easily by measured. What can be said truthfully is that some knowledge is increasing while other kinds of knowledge are being lost. David Ehrenfeld has pointed out that biology departments no longer hire faculty in such areas as systematics, taxonomy, or ornithology. In other words, important knowledge is being lost because of the recent overemphasis on molecular biology and genetic engineering, which are more lucrative, but not more important, areas of inquiry. We still lack the science of land health that Aldo Leopold called for half a century ago.

It is not just knowledge in certain areas that we're losing, but vernacular knowledge as well, by which I mean the knowledge that people have of their places. In the words of Barry Lopez:

"[I am] forced to the realization that something strange, if not dangerous, is afoot. Year by year the number of people with firsthand experience in the land dwindles. Rural populations continue to shift to the cities. . . . In the wake of this loss of personal and local knowledge, the knowledge from which a real geography is derived, the knowledge on which a country must ultimately stand, has come something hard to define but I think sinister and unsettling."

In the confusion of data with knowledge is a deeper mistake that learning will make us better people. But learning, as Loren Eiseley once said, is endless and "In itself it will never make us ethical [people]." Ultimately, it may be the knowledge of the good that is most threatened by all of our other advances. All things considered, it is possible that we are becoming more ignorant of the things we must know to live well and sustainably on the Earth.

A fourth myth of higher education is that *we can adequately restore that which we have dismantled.* In the modern curriculum we have fragmented the world into bits and pieces called disciplines and subdisciplines. As a result, after 12 or 16 or 20 years of education, most students graduate without any broad integrated sense of the unity of things. The consequences for their personhood and for the planet are large. For example, we routinely produce economists who lack the most rudimentary knowledge of ecology. This explains why our national accounting systems do not subtract the costs of biotic impoverishment, soil erosion, poisons in the air or water, and resource depletion from gross national product. We add the price of the sale of a bushel of wheat to GNP while forgetting to subtract the three bushels of topsoil lost in its production. As a result of incomplete education, we've fooled ourselves into thinking that we are much richer than we are.

Fifth, there is a myth that *the purpose of education is that of giving you the means for upward mobility and success.* Thomas Merton once identified this as the "mass production of people literally unfit for anything except to take part in an elaborate and completely artificial charade." When asked to write about his own success, Merton responded by saying that "if it so happened that I had once written a best seller, this was a pure accident, due to inattention and naiveté, and I would take very good care never to do the same again." His advice to students was to "be anything you like, be madmen, drunks, and bastards of every shape and form, but at all costs avoid one thing: success."

The plain fact is that the planet does not need more "successful" people. But it does desperately need more peacemakers, healers, restorers, storytellers, and lovers of every shape and form. It needs people who live well in their places. It needs people of moral courage willing to join the fight to make the world habitable and humane. And these needs have little to do with success as our culture has defined it.

Finally, there is a myth that *our culture represents the pinnacle of human achievement:* we alone are modern, technological, and developed. This, of course, represents cultural arrogance of the worst sort, and a gross misreading of history and anthropology. Recently this view has taken the form that we won the cold war and that the triumph of capitalism over communism is complete. Communism failed because it produced too little at too high a cost. But capitalism has also failed because it produces too much, shares too little, also at too high a cost to our children and grandchildren. Communism failed as an ascetic morality. Capitalism failed because it destroys morality altogether. This is not the happy world that any number of feckless advertisers and politicians describe. We have built a world of sybaritic wealth for a few and Calcuttan poverty for a growing underclass. At its worst it is a world of crack on the streets, insensate violence, anomie, and the most desperate kind of poverty. The fact is that we live in a disintegrating culture. In the words of Ron Miller, editor of *Holistic Review:*

"Our culture does not nourish that which is best or noblest in the human spirit. It does not cultivate vision, imagination, or aesthetic or spiritual sensitivity. It does not encourage gentleness, generosity, caring, or compassion. Increasingly in the late 20th Century, the economic-technocratic-statist worldview has become a monstrous destroyer of what is loving and life-affirming in the human soul."

What Education Must be For

Measured against the agenda of human survival, how might we rethink education? Let me suggest six principles.

First, *all education is environmental education.* By what is included or excluded we teach students that they are part of or apart from the natural world. To teach economics, for example, without reference to the laws of thermodynamics or those of ecology is to teach a fundamentally important ecological lesson: that physics and ecology have nothing to do with the economy. That just happens to be dead wrong. The same is true throughout all of the curriculum.

A second principle comes from the Greek concept of *paideia. The goal of education is not mastery of subject matter, but of one's person.* Subject matter is simply the tool. Much as one would use a hammer and chisel to carve a block of marble, one uses ideas and knowledge to forge one's own personhood. For the most part we labor under a confusion of ends and means, thinking that the goal of education is to stuff all kinds of facts, techniques, methods, and information into the student's mind, regardless of how and with what effect it will be used. The Greeks knew better.

Third, I would like to propose that *knowledge carries with it the responsibility to see that it is well used in the world.* The results of a great deal of contemporary research bear resemblance to those foreshadowed by Mary Shelley: monsters of technology and its byproducts for which no one takes responsibility or is even expected to take responsibility. Whose responsibility is Love Canal? Chernobyl? Ozone depletion? The Valdez oil spill? Each of these tragedies were possible because of knowledge created for which no one was ultimately responsible. This may finally come to be seen for what I think it is: a problem of scale. Knowledge of how to do vast and risky things has far outrun our ability to use it responsibly. Some of it cannot be used responsibly, which is to say safely and to consistently good purposes.

Fourth, *we cannot say that we know something until we understand the effects of this knowledge on real people and their communities.* I grew up near Youngstown, Ohio, which was largely destroyed by corporate decisions to "disinvest" in the economy of the region. In this case MBAs, educated in the tools of leveraged buyouts, tax breaks, and capital mobility have done what no invading army could do: they destroyed an American city with total impunity on behalf of something called the "bottom line." But the bottom line for society includes other costs, those of unemployment, crime, higher divorce rates, alcoholism, child abuse, lost savings, and wrecked lives. In this instance what was taught in the business schools and economics departments did not include the value of good communities or the human costs of a narrow destructive economic rationality that valued efficiency and economic abstractions above people and community.

My fifth principle follows and is drawn from William Blake. It has to do with *the importance of "minute particulars" and the power of examples over words.* Students hear about global responsibility while being educated in institutions that often invest their financial weight in the most irresponsible things. The lessons being taught are those of hypocrisy and ultimately despair. Students learn, without anyone ever saying it, that they are helpless to overcome the frightening gap between ideals and reality. What is desperately needed are faculty and administrators who provide role models of integrity, care, thoughtfulness, *and* institutions that are capable of embodying ideals wholly and completely in all of their operations.

Finally, I would like to propose that *the way learning occurs is as important as the content of particular courses.* Process is important for learning. Courses taught as lecture courses tend to induce passivity. Indoor classes create the illusion that learning only occurs inside four walls isolated from what students call without apparent irony the "real world." Dissecting frogs in biology classes teaches lessons about nature that no one would verbally profess. Campus architecture is crystallized pedagogy that often reinforces passivity, monologue, domination, and artificiality. My point is simply that students are being taught in various and subtle ways beyond the content of courses.

An Assignment for the Campus

If education is to be measured against the standard of sustainability, what can be done? I would like to make four propsals. First, I would like to propose that you engage in a campus-wide dialogue about the way you conduct your business as educators. Does four years here make your graduates better planetary citizens or does it make them, in Wendell Berry's words, "itinerant professional vandals"? Does this college contribute to the development of a sustainable regional economy or, in the name of efficiency, to the processes of destruction?

My second suggestion is to examine resource flows on this campus: food, energy, water, materials, and waste. Faculty and students should together study the wells, mines, farms, feedlots, and forests that supply the campus as well as the dumps where you send your waste. Collectively, begin a process of finding ways to shift the buying power of this institution to support better alternatives that do less environmental damage, lower carbon dioxide emissions, reduce use of toxic substances, promote energy efficiency and the use of solar energy, help to build a sustainable regional economy, cut long-term costs, and provide an example to other institutions. The results of these studies should be woven into the curriculum as interdisplinary courses, seminars, lectures, and research. No student should graduate without understanding how to analyze resource flows and without the opportunity to participate in the creation of real solutions to real problems.

Third, reexamaine how your endowment works. Is it invested according to the Valdez principles? Is it invested in companies doing responsible things that the world needs? Can some part of it be invested locally to help leverage energy efficiency and the evolution of a sustainable economy throughout the region?

Finally, I propose that you set a goal of ecological literacy for all of your students. No student should graduate from this or any other educational institution without a basic comprehension of:

- the laws of thermodynamics
- the basic principles of ecology
- carrying capacity
- energetics
- least-cost, end-use analysis
- how to live well in a place
- limits of technology
- appropriate scale
- sustainable agriculture and forestry
- steady-state economics
- environmental ethics

Do graduates of this college, in Aldo Leopold's words, know that "they are only cogs in an ecological mechanism such that, if they will work with that mechanism, their mental wealth and material wealth can expand indefinitely (and) if they refuse to work with it, it will ultimately grind them to dust." Leopold asked: "If education does not teach us these things, then what is education for?"

Questions for Further Exploration:

- What does this lecture reveal about Orr's philosophy of education?

- Consider Orr's speech in terms of Plato's allegory: What might each of the symbols (the cave, shadows, escapee, outside, the sun, etc.) represent in Orr's view?

- On what points in their critiques and educational philosophies do Nietzsche and Orr agree and disagree? Who makes the better argument?

- Free-write on your response to Orr's critique of modern education.

Apology

Plato
Translated by Benjamin Jowett

How you, O Athenians, have been affected by my accusers, I cannot tell; but I know that they almost made me forget who I was—so persuasively did they speak; and yet they have hardly uttered a word of truth. But of the many falsehoods told by them, there was one which quite amazed me;—I mean when they said that you should be upon your guard and not allow yourselves to be deceived by the force of my eloquence. To say this, when they were certain to be detected as soon as I opened my lips and proved myself to be anything but a great speaker, did indeed appear to me most shameless—unless by the force of eloquence they mean the force of truth; for is such is their meaning, I admit that I am eloquent. But in how different a way from theirs! Well, as I was saying, they have scarcely spoken the truth at all; but from me you shall hear the whole truth: not, however, delivered after their manner in a set oration duly ornamented with words and phrases. No, by heaven! but I shall use the words and arguments which occur to me at the moment; for I am confident in the justice of my cause (Or, I am certain that I am right in taking this course.): at my time of life I ought not to be appearing before you, O men of Athens, in the character of a juvenile orator—let no one expect it of me. And I must beg of you to grant me a favour:—If I defend myself in my accustomed manner, and you hear me using the words which I have been in the habit of using in the agora, at the tables of the money-changers, or anywhere else, I would ask you not to be surprised, and not to interrupt me on this account. For I am more than seventy years of age, and appearing now for the first time in a court of law, I am quite a stranger to the language of the place; and therefore I would have you regard me as if I were really a stranger, whom you would excuse if he spoke in his native tongue, and after the fashion of his country:—Am I making an unfair request of you? Never mind the manner, which may or may not be good; but think only of the truth of my words, and give heed to that: let the speaker speak truly and the judge decide justly.

And first, I have to reply to the older charges and to my first accusers, and then I will go on to the later ones. For of old I have had many accusers, who have accused me falsely to you during many years; and I am more afraid of them than of Anytus and his associates, who are dangerous, too, in their own way. But far more dangerous are the others, who began when you were children, and took possession of your minds with their falsehoods, telling of one Socrates, a wise man, who speculated about the heaven above, and searched into the earth beneath, and made the worse appear the better cause. The disseminators of this tale are the accusers whom I dread; for their hearers are apt to fancy that such enquirers do not believe in the existence of the gods. And they are many, and their charges against me are of ancient date, and they were made by them in the days when you were more impressible than you are now—in childhood, or it may have been in youth—and the cause when heard went by default, for there was none to answer. And hardest of all, I do not know and cannot tell the names of my accusers; unless in the chance case of a Comic poet. All who from envy and malice have persuaded you—some of them having first convinced themselves—all this class of men are most difficult to deal with; for I cannot have them up here, and cross-examine them, and therefore I must simply fight with shadows in my own defence, and argue when there is no one who answers. I will ask you then to assume with me, as I was saying, that my opponents are of two kinds; one recent, the other ancient: and I hope that you will see the propriety of my answering the latter first, for these accusations you heard long before the others, and much oftener.

Well, then, I must make my defence, and endeavour to clear away in a short time, a slander which has lasted a long time. May I succeed, if to succeed be for my good and yours, or likely to avail me in my cause! The task is not an easy one; I quite understand the nature of it. And so leaving the event with God, in obedience to the law I will now make my defence.

I will begin at the beginning, and ask what is the accusation which has given rise to the slander of me, and in fact has encouraged Meletus to proof this charge against me. Well, what do the slanderers say? They shall be my prosecutors, and I will sum up their words in an affidavit: 'Socrates is an evil-doer, and a curious person, who searches into things under the earth and in heaven, and he makes the worse appear the better cause; and he teaches the aforesaid doctrines to others.' Such is the nature of the accusation: it is just what you have yourselves seen in the comedy of Aristophanes (Aristoph., Clouds.), who has introduced a man whom he calls Socrates, going about and saying that he walks in air, and talking a deal of nonsense concerning matters of which I do not pretend to know either much or little—not that I mean to speak disparagingly of any one who is a student of natural philosophy. I should be very sorry if Meletus could bring so grave a charge against me. But the simple truth is, O Athenians, that I have nothing to do with physical speculations. Very many of those here present are witnesses to the truth of this, and to them I appeal. Speak then, you who have heard me, and tell your neighbours whether any of you have ever known me hold forth in few words or in many upon such matters . . . You hear their answer. And from what they say of this part of the charge you will be able to judge of the truth of the rest.

As little foundation is there for the report that I am a teacher, and take money; this accusation has no more truth in it than the other. Although, if a man were really able to instruct mankind, to receive money for giving instruction would, in my opinion, be an honour to him. There is Gorgias of Leontium, and Prodicus of Ceos, and Hippias of Elis, who go the round of the cities, and are able to persuade the young men to leave their own citizens by whom they might be taught for nothing, and come to them whom they not only pay, but are thankful if they may be allowed to pay them. There is at this time a Parian philosopher residing in Athens, of whom I have heard; and I came to hear of him in this way:—I came across a man who has spent a world of money on the Sophists, Callias, the son of Hipponicus, and knowing that he had sons, I asked him: 'Callias,' I said, 'if your two sons were foals or calves, there would be no difficulty in finding some one to put over them; we should hire a trainer of horses, or a farmer probably, who would improve and perfect them in their own proper virtue and excellence; but as they are human beings, whom are you thinking of placing over them? Is there any one who understands human and political virtue? You must have thought about the matter, for you have sons; is there any one?' 'There is,' he said. 'Who is he?' said I; 'and of what country? and what does he charge?' 'Evenus the Parian,' he replied; 'he is the man, and his charge is five minae.' Happy is Evenus, I said to myself, if he really has this wisdom, and teaches at such a moderate charge. Had I the same, I should have been very proud and conceited; but the truth is that I have no knowledge of the kind.

I dare say, Athenians, that some one among you will reply, 'Yes, Socrates, but what is the origin of these accusations which are brought against you; there must have been something strange which you have been doing? All these rumours and this talk about you would never have arisen if you had been like other men: tell us, then, what is the cause of them, for we should be sorry to judge hastily of you.' Now I regard this as a fair challenge, and I will endeavour to explain to you the reason why I am called wise and have such an evil fame. Please to attend then. And although some of you may think that I am joking, I declare that I will tell you the entire truth. Men of Athens, this reputation of mine has come of a certain sort of wisdom which I possess. If you ask me what kind of wisdom, I reply, wisdom such as may perhaps be attained by man, for to that extent I am inclined to believe that I am wise; whereas the persons of whom I was speaking have a superhuman wisdom which I may fail to describe, because I have it not myself; and he who says that I have, speaks falsely, and is taking away my character. And here, O men of Athens, I must beg you not to interrupt me, even if I seem to say something extravagant. For the word which I will speak is not mine. I will refer you to a witness who is worthy of credit; that witness shall be the God of Delphi—he will tell you about my wisdom, if I have any, and of what sort it is. You must have known Chaerephon; he was early a friend of mine, and also a friend of yours, for he shared in the recent exile of the people, and returned with you. Well, Chaerephon, as you know, was very impetuous in all his doings, and he went to Delphi and boldly asked the oracle to tell him whether—as I was saying, I must beg you not to interrupt—he asked the oracle to tell him whether anyone was wiser than I was, and the Pythian prophetess answered, that there was no man wiser. Chaerephon is dead himself; but his brother, who is in court, will confirm the truth of what I am saying.

Why do I mention this? Because I am going to explain to you why I have such an evil name. When I heard the answer, I said to myself. What can the god mean? and what is the interpretation of his riddle? for I know that I have no wisdom, small or great. What then can he mean when he says that I am the wisest of men? And yet he is a god, and cannot lie; that would be against his nature. After long consideration, I thought of a method of trying the question. I reflected that if I could only find a man wiser than myself, then I might go to the god with a refutation in my hand. I should say to him, 'Here is a man who is wiser than I am; but you said that I was the wisest.' Accordingly I went to one who had the reputation of wisdom, and observed him—his name I need not mention; he was a politician whom I selected for examination—and the result was as follows: When I began to talk with him, I could not help thinking that he was not really wise, although he was thought wise by many, and still wiser by himself; and thereupon I tried to explain to him that he thought himself wise, but was not really wise; and the consequence was that he hated me, and his enmity was shared by several who were present and heard me. So I left him, saying to myself, as I went away: Well, although I do not suppose that either of us knows anything really beautiful and good, I am better off than he is,—for he knows nothing, and thinks that he knows; I neither know nor think that I know. In this latter particular, then, I seem to have slightly the advantage of him. Then I went to another who had still higher pretensions to wisdom, and my conclusion was exactly the same. Whereupon I made another enemy of him, and of many others besides him.

Then I went to one man after another, being not unconscious of the enmity which I provoked, and I lamented and feared this: but necessity was laid upon me,—the word of God, I thought, ought to be considered first. And I said to myself, Go I must to all who appear to know, and find out the meaning of the oracle. And I swear to you, Athenians, by the dog I swear!—for I must tell you the truth—the result of my mission was just this: I found that the men most in repute were all but the most foolish; and that others less esteemed were really wiser and better. I will tell you the tale of my wanderings and of the 'Herculean' labours, as I may call them, which I endured only to find at last the oracle irrefutable. After the politicians, I went to the poets; tragic, dithyrambic, and all sorts. And there, I said to myself, you will be instantly detected; now you will find out that you are more ignorant than they are. Accordingly, I took them some of the most elaborate passages in their own writings, and asked what was the meaning of them—thinking that they would teach me something. Will you believe me? I am almost ashamed to confess the truth, but I must say that there is hardly a person present who would not have talked better about their poetry than they did themselves. Then I knew that not by wisdom do poets write poetry, but by a sort of genius and inspiration; they are like diviners or soothsayers who also say many fine things, but do not understand the meaning of them. The poets appeared to me to be much in the same case; and I further observed that upon the strength of their poetry they believed themselves to be the wisest of men in other things in which they were not wise. So I departed, conceiving myself to be superior to them for the same reason that I was superior to the politicians.

At last I went to the artisans. I was conscious that I knew nothing at all, as I may say, and I was sure that they knew many fine things; and here I was not mistaken, for they did know many things of which I was ignorant, and in this they certainly were wiser than I was. But I observed that even the good artisans fell into the same error as the poets;—because they were good workmen they thought that they also knew all sorts of high matters, and this defect in them overshadowed their wisdom; and therefore I asked myself on behalf of the oracle, whether I would like to be as I was, neither having their knowledge nor their ignorance, or like them in both; and I made answer to myself and to the oracle that I was better off as I was.

This inquisition has led to my having many enemies of the worst and most dangerous kind, and has given occasion also to many calumnies. And I am called wise, for my hearers always imagine that I myself possess the wisdom which I find wanting in others: but the truth is, O men of Athens, that God only is wise; and by his answer he intends to show that the wisdom of men is worth little or nothing; he is not speaking of Socrates, he is only using my name by way of illustration, as if he said, He, O men, is the wisest, who, like Socrates, knows that his wisdom is in truth worth nothing. And so I go about the world, obedient to the god, and search and make enquiry into the wisdom of any one, whether citizen or stranger, who appears to be wise; and if he is not wise, then in vindication of the oracle I show him that he is not wise; and my occupation quite absorbs me, and I have no time to give either to any public matter of interest or to any concern of my own, but I am in utter poverty by reason of my devotion to the god.

There is another thing:—young men of the richer classes, who have not much to do, come about me of their own accord; they like to hear the pretenders examined, and they often imitate me, and proceed to examine others; there are plenty of persons, as they quickly discover, who think that they know something, but really know little or nothing; and then those who are examined by them instead of being angry with themselves are angry with me: This confounded Socrates, they say: this villainous misleader of youth!—and then if somebody asks them, Why, what evil does he practise or teach? they do not know, and cannot tell; but in order that they may not appear to be at a loss, they repeat the ready-made charges which are used against all philosophers about teaching things up in the clouds and under the earth, and having no gods, and making the worse appear the better cause; for they do not like to confess that their pretence of knowledge has been detected—which is the truth; and as they are numerous and ambitious and energetic, and are drawn up in battle array and have persuasive tongues, they have filled your ears with their loud and inveterate calumnies. And this is the reason why my three accusers, Meletus and Anytus and Lycon, have set upon me; Meletus, who has a quarrel with me on behalf of the poets; Anytus, on behalf of the craftsmen and politicians; Lycon, on behalf of the rhetoricians: and as I said at the beginning, I cannot expect to get rid of such a mass of calumny all in a moment. And this, O men of Athens, is the truth and the whole truth; I have concealed nothing, I have dissembled nothing. And yet, I know that my plainness of speech makes them hate me, and what is their hatred but a proof that I am speaking the truth?—Hence has arisen the prejudice against me; and this is the reason of it, as you will find out either in this or in any future enquiry.

I have said enough in my defence against the first class of my accusers; I turn to the second class. They are headed by Meletus, that good man and true lover of his country, as he calls himself. Against these, too, I must try to make a defence:—Let their affidavit be read: it contains something of this kind: It says that Socrates is a doer of evil, who corrupts the youth; and who does not believe in the gods of the state, but has other new divinities of his own. Such is the charge; and now let us examine the particular counts. He says that I am a doer of evil, and corrupt the youth; but I say, O men of Athens, that Meletus is a doer of evil, in that he pretends to be in earnest when he is only in jest, and is so eager to bring men to trial from a pretended zeal and interest about matters in which he really never had the smallest interest. And the truth of this I will endeavour to prove to you.

Come hither, Meletus, and let me ask a question of you. You think a great deal about the improvement of youth?

Yes, I do.

Tell the judges, then, who is their improver; for you must know, as you have taken the pains to discover their corrupter, and are citing and accusing me before them. Speak, then, and tell the judges who their improver is.—Observe, Meletus, that you are silent, and have nothing to say. But is not this rather disgraceful, and a very considerable proof of what I was saying, that you have no interest in the matter? Speak up, friend, and tell us who their improver is.

The laws.

But that, my good sir, is not my meaning. I want to know who the person is, who, in the first place, knows the laws.

The judges, Socrates, who are present in court.

What, do you mean to say, Meletus, that they are able to instruct and improve youth?

Certainly they are.

What, all of them, or some only and not others?

All of them.

By the goddess Here, that is good news! There are plenty of improvers, then. And what do you say of the audience,—do they improve them?

Yes, they do.

And the senators?

Yes, the senators improve them.

But perhaps the members of the assembly corrupt them?—or do they too improve them?

They improve them.

Then every Athenian improves and elevates them; all with the exception of myself; and I alone am their corrupter? Is that what you affirm?

That is what I stoutly affirm.

I am very unfortunate if you are right. But suppose I ask you a question: How about horses? Does one man do them harm and all the world good? Is not the exact opposite the truth? One man is able to do them good, or at least not many;—the trainer of horses, that is to say, does them good, and others who have to do with them rather injure them? Is not that true, Meletus, of horses, or of any other animals? Most assuredly it is; whether you and Anytus say yes or no. Happy indeed would be the condition of youth if they had one corrupter only, and all the rest of the world were their improvers. But you, Meletus, have sufficiently shown that you never had a thought about the young: your carelessness is seen in your not caring about the very things which you bring against me.

And now, Meletus, I will ask you another question—by Zeus I will: Which is better, to live among bad citizens, or among good ones? Answer, friend, I say; the question is one which may be easily answered. Do not the good do their neighbours good, and the bad do them evil?

Certainly.

And is there anyone who would rather be injured than benefited by those who live with him? Answer, my good friend, the law requires you to answer—does any one like to be injured?

Certainly not.

And when you accuse me of corrupting and deteriorating the youth, do you allege that I corrupt them intentionally or unintentionally?

Intentionally, I say.

But you have just admitted that the good do their neighbours good, and the evil do them evil. Now, is that a truth which your superior wisdom has recognized thus early in life, and am I, at my age, in such darkness and ignorance as not to know that if a man with whom I have to live is corrupted by me, I am very likely to be harmed by him; and yet I corrupt him, and intentionally, too—so you say, although neither I nor any other human being is ever likely to be convinced by you. But either I do not corrupt them, or I corrupt them unintentionally; and on either view of the case you lie. If my offence is unintentional, the law has no cognizance of unintentional offences: you ought to have taken me privately, and warned and admonished me; for if I had been better advised, I should have left off doing what I only did unintentionally—no doubt I should; but you would have nothing to say to me and refused to teach me. And now you bring me up in this court, which is a place not of instruction, but of punishment.

It will be very clear to you, Athenians, as I was saying, that Meletus has no care at all, great or small, about the matter. But still I should like to know, Meletus, in what I am affirmed to corrupt the young. I suppose you mean, as I infer from your indictment, that I teach them not to acknowledge the gods which the state acknowledges, but some other new divinities or spiritual agencies in their stead. These are the lessons by which I corrupt the youth, as you say.

Yes, that I say emphatically.

Then, by the gods, Meletus, of whom we are speaking, tell me and the court, in somewhat plainer terms, what you mean! for I do not as yet understand whether you affirm that I teach other men to acknowledge some gods, and therefore that I do believe in gods, and am not an entire atheist—this you do not lay to my charge,—but only you say that they are not the same gods which the city recognizes—the charge is that they are different gods. Or do you mean that I am an atheist simply, and a teacher of atheism?

I mean the latter—that you are a complete atheist.

What an extraordinary statement! Why do you think so, Meletus? Do you mean that I do not believe in the godhead of the sun or moon, like other men?

I assure you, judges, that he does not: for he says that the sun is stone, and the moon earth.

Friend Meletus, you think that you are accusing Anaxagoras: and you have but a bad opinion of the judges, if you fancy them illiterate to such a degree as not to know that these doctrines are found in the books of Anaxagoras the Clazomenian, which are full of them. And so, forsooth, the youth are said to be taught them by Socrates, when there are not unfrequently exhibitions of them at the theatre (Probably in allusion to Aristophanes who caricatured, and to Euripides who borrowed the notions of Anaxagoras, as well as to other dramatic poets.) (price of admission one drachma at the most); and they might pay their money, and laugh at Socrates if he pretends to father these extraordinary views. And so, Meletus, you really think that I do not believe in any god?

I swear by Zeus that you believe absolutely in none at all.

Nobody will believe you, Meletus, and I am pretty sure that you do not believe yourself. I cannot help thinking, men of Athens, that Meletus is reckless and impudent, and that he has written this indictment in a spirit of mere wantonness and youthful bravado. Has he not compounded a riddle, thinking to try me? He said to himself:—I shall see whether the wise Socrates will discover my facetious contradiction, or whether I shall be able to deceive him and the rest of them. For he certainly does appear to me to contradict himself in the indictment as much as if he said that Socrates is guilty of not believing in the gods, and yet of believing in them—but this is not like a person who is in earnest.

I should like you, O men of Athens, to join me in examining what I conceive to be his inconsistency; and do you, Meletus, answer. And I must remind the audience of my request that they would not make a disturbance if I speak in my accustomed manner.

Did ever man, Meletus, believe in the existence of human things, and not of human beings? . . . I wish, men of Athens, that he would answer, and not be always trying to get up an interruption. Did ever any man believe in horsemanship, and not in horses? or in flute-playing, and not in flute-players? No, my friend; I will answer to you and to the court, as you refuse to answer for yourself. There is no man who ever did. But now please to answer the next question: Can a man believe in spiritual and divine agencies, and not in spirits or demigods?

He cannot.

How lucky I am to have extracted that answer, by the assistance of the court! But then you swear in the indictment that I teach and believe in divine or spiritual agencies (new or old, no matter for that); at any rate, I believe in spiritual agencies,—so you say and swear in the affidavit; and yet if I believe in divine beings, how can I help believing in spirits or demigods;—must I not? To be sure I must; and therefore I may assume that your silence gives consent. Now what are spirits or demigods? Are they not either gods or the sons of gods?

Certainly they are.

But this is what I call the facetious riddle invented by you: the demigods or spirits are gods, and you say first that I do not believe in gods, and then again that I do believe in gods; that is, if I believe in demigods. For if the demigods are the illegitimate sons of gods, whether by the nymphs or by any other mothers, of whom they are said to be the sons— what human being will ever believe that there are no gods if they are the sons of gods? You might as well affirm the existence of mules, and deny that of horses and asses. Such nonsense, Meletus, could only have been intended by you to make trial of me. You have put this into the indictment because you had nothing real of which to accuse me. But no one who has a particle of understanding will ever be convinced by you that the same men can believe in divine and superhuman things, and yet not believe that there are gods and demigods and heroes.

I have said enough in answer to the charge of Meletus: any elaborate defence is unnecessary, but I know only too well how many are the enmities which I have incurred, and this is what will be my destruction if I am destroyed;—not Meletus, nor yet Anytus, but the envy and detraction of the world, which has been the death of many good men, and will probably be the death of many more; there is no danger of my being the last of them.

Some one will say: And are you not ashamed, Socrates, of a course of life which is likely to bring you to an untimely end? To him I may fairly answer: There you are mistaken: a man who is good for anything ought not to calculate the chance of living or dying; he ought only to consider whether in doing anything he is doing right or wrong—acting the part of a good man or of a bad. Whereas, upon your view, the heroes who fell at Troy were not good for much, and the son of Thetis above all, who altogether despised danger in comparison with disgrace; and when he was so eager to slay Hector, his goddess mother said to him, that if he avenged his companion Patroclus, and slew Hector, he would die himself—'Fate,' she said, in these or the like words, 'waits for you next after Hector;' he, receiving this warning, utterly despised danger and death, and instead of fearing them, feared rather to live in dishonour, and not to avenge his friend. 'Let me die forthwith,' he replies, 'and be avenged of my enemy, rather than abide here by the beaked ships, a laughing-stock and a burden of the earth.' Had Achilles any thought of death and danger? For wherever a man's place is, whether the place which he has chosen or that in which he has been placed by a commander, there he ought to remain in the hour of danger; he should not think of death or of anything but of disgrace. And this, O men of Athens, is a true saying.

Strange, indeed, would be my conduct, O men of Athens, if I who, when I was ordered by the generals whom you chose to command me at Potidaea and Amphipolis and Delium, remained where they placed me, like any other man, facing death—if now, when, as I conceive and imagine, God orders me to fulfil the philosopher's mission of searching into myself and other men, I were to desert my post through fear of death, or any other fear; that would indeed be strange, and I might justly be arraigned in court for denying the existence of the gods, if I disobeyed the oracle because I was afraid of death, fancying that I was wise when I was not wise. For the fear of death is indeed the pretence of wisdom, and not real wisdom, being a pretence of knowing the unknown; and no one knows whether death, which men in their fear apprehend to be the greatest evil, may not be the greatest good. Is not this ignorance of a disgraceful sort, the ignorance which is the conceit that a man knows what he does not know? And in this respect only I believe myself to differ from men in general, and may perhaps claim to be wiser than they are:—that whereas I know but little of the world below, I do not suppose that I know: but I do know that injustice and disobedience to a better, whether God or man, is evil and dishonourable, and I will never fear or avoid a possible good rather than a certain evil. And therefore if you let me go now, and are not convinced by Anytus, who said that since I had been prosecuted I must be put to death; (or if not that I ought never to have been prosecuted at all); and that if I escape now, your sons will all be utterly ruined by listening to my words—if you say to me, Socrates, this time we will not mind Anytus, and you shall be let off, but upon one condition, that you are not to enquire and speculate in this way any more, and that if you are caught doing so again you shall die;—if this was the condition on which you let me go, I should reply: Men of Athens, I honour and love you; but I shall obey God rather than you, and while I have life and strength I shall never cease from the practice and teaching of philosophy, exhorting any one whom I meet and saying to him after my manner: You, my friend,—a citizen of the great and mighty and wise city of Athens,—are you not ashamed of heaping up the greatest amount of money and honour and reputation, and caring so little about wisdom and truth and the greatest improvement of the soul, which you never regard or heed at all? And if the person with whom I am arguing, says: Yes, but I do care; then I do not leave him or let him go at once; but I proceed to interrogate and examine and cross-examine him, and if I think that he has no virtue in him, but only says that he has, I reproach him with undervaluing the greater, and overvaluing the less. And I shall repeat the same words to every one whom I meet, young and old, citizen and alien, but especially to the citizens, inasmuch as they are my brethren. For know that this is the command of God; and I believe that no greater good has ever happened in the state than my service to the God. For I do nothing but go about persuading you all, old and young alike, not to take thought for your persons or your properties, but first and chiefly to care about the greatest improvement of the soul. I tell you that virtue is not given by money, but that from virtue comes money and every other good of man, public as well as private. This is my teaching, and if this is the doctrine which corrupts the youth, I am a mischievous person. But if any one says that this is not my teaching, he is speaking an untruth. Wherefore, O men of Athens, I say to you, do as Anytus bids or not as Anytus bids, and either acquit me or not; but whichever you do, understand that I shall never alter my ways, not even if I have to die many times.

Men of Athens, do not interrupt, but hear me; there was an understanding between us that you should hear me to the end: I have something more to say, at which you may be inclined to cry out; but I believe that to hear me will be good for you, and therefore I beg that you will not cry out. I would have you know, that if you kill such an one as I am, you will injure yourselves more than you will injure me. Nothing will injure me, not Meletus nor yet Anytus—they cannot, for a bad man is not permitted to injure a better than himself. I do not deny that Anytus may, perhaps, kill him, or drive him into exile, or deprive him of civil rights; and he may imagine, and others may imagine, that he is inflicting a great injury upon him: but there I do not agree. For the evil of doing as he is doing—the evil of unjustly taking away the life of another—is greater far.

And now, Athenians, I am not going to argue for my own sake, as you may think, but for yours, that you may not sin against the God by condemning me, who am his gift to you. For if you kill me you will not easily find a successor to me, who, if I may use such a ludicrous figure of speech, am a sort of gadfly, given to the state by God; and the state is a great and noble steed who is tardy in his motions owing to his very size, and requires to be stirred into life. I am that gadfly which God has attached to the state, and all day long and in all places am always fastening upon you, arousing and persuading and reproaching you. You will not easily find another like me, and therefore I would advise you to spare me. I dare say that you may feel out of temper (like a person who is suddenly awakened from sleep), and you think that you might easily strike me dead as Anytus advises, and then you would sleep on for the remainder of your lives, unless God in his care of you sent you another gadfly. When I say that I am given to you by God, the proof of my mission is this:—if I had been like other men, I should not have neglected all my own concerns or patiently seen the neglect of them during all these years, and have been doing yours, coming to you individually like a father or elder brother, exhorting you to regard virtue; such conduct, I say, would be unlike human nature. If I had gained anything, or if my exhortations had been paid, there would have been some sense in my doing so; but now, as you will perceive, not even the impudence of my accusers dares to say that I have ever exacted or sought pay of any one; of that they have no witness. And I have a sufficient witness to the truth of what I say—my poverty.

Some one may wonder why I go about in private giving advice and busying myself with the concerns of others, but do not venture to come forward in public and advise the state. I will tell you why. You have heard me speak at sundry times and in divers places of an oracle or sign which comes to me, and is the divinity which Meletus ridicules in the indictment. This sign, which is a kind of voice, first began to come to me when I was a child; it always forbids but never commands me to do anything which I am going to do. This is what deters me from being a politician. And rightly, as I think. For I am certain, O men of Athens, that if I had engaged in politics, I should have perished long ago, and done no good either to you or to myself. And do not be offended at my telling you the truth: for the truth is, that no man who goes to war with you or any other multitude, honestly striving against the many lawless and unrighteous deeds which are done in a state, will save his life; he who will fight for the right, if he would live even for a brief space, must have a private station and not a public one.

I can give you convincing evidence of what I say, not words only, but what you value far more—actions. Let me relate to you a passage of my own life which will prove to you that I should never have yielded to injustice from any fear of death, and that 'as I should have refused to yield' I must have died at once. I will tell you a tale of the courts, not very interesting perhaps, but nevertheless true. The only office of state which I ever held, O men of Athens, was that of senator: the tribe Antiochis, which is my tribe, had the presidency at the trial of the generals who had not taken up the bodies of the slain after the battle of Arginusae; and you proposed to try them in a body, contrary to law, as you all thought afterwards; but at the time I was the only one of the Prytanes who was opposed to the illegality, and I gave my vote against you; and when the orators threatened to impeach and arrest me, and you called and shouted, I made up my mind that I would run the risk, having law and justice with me, rather than take part in your injustice because I feared imprisonment and death. This happened in the days of the democracy. But when the oligarchy of the Thirty was in power, they sent for me and four others into the rotunda, and bade us bring Leon the Salaminian from Salamis, as they wanted to put him to death. This was a specimen of the sort of commands which they were always giving with the view of implicating as many as possible in their crimes; and then I showed, not in word only but in deed, that, if I may be allowed to use such an expression, I cared not a straw for death, and that my great and only care was lest I should do an unrighteous or unholy thing. For the strong arm of that oppressive power did not frighten me into doing wrong; and when we came out of the rotunda the other four went to Salamis and fetched Leon, but I went quietly home. For which I might have lost my life, had not the power of the Thirty shortly afterwards come to an end. And many will witness to my words.

Now do you really imagine that I could have survived all these years, if I had led a public life, supposing that like a good man I had always maintained the right and had made justice, as I ought, the first thing? No indeed, men of Athens, neither I nor any other man. But I have been always the same in all my actions, public as well as private, and never have I yielded any base compliance to those who are slanderously termed my disciples, or to any other. Not that I have any regular disciples. But if any one likes to come and hear me while I am pursuing my mission, whether he be young or old, he is not excluded. Nor do I converse only with those who pay; but any one, whether he be rich or poor, may ask and answer me and listen to my words; and whether he turns out to be a bad man or a good one, neither result can be justly imputed to me; for I never taught or professed to teach him anything. And if any one says that he has ever learned or heard anything from me in private which all the world has not heard, let me tell you that he is lying.

But I shall be asked, Why do people delight in continually conversing with you? I have told you already, Athenians, the whole truth about this matter: they like to hear the cross-examination of the pretenders to wisdom; there is amusement in it. Now this duty of cross-examining other men has been imposed upon me by God; and has been signified to me by oracles, visions, and in every way in which the will of divine power was ever intimated to any one. This is true, O Athenians, or, if not true, would be soon refuted. If I am or have been corrupting the youth, those of them who are now grown up and have become sensible that I gave them bad advice in the days of their youth should come forward as accusers, and take their revenge; or if they do not like to come themselves, some of their relatives, fathers, brothers, or other kinsmen, should say what evil their families have suffered at my hands. Now is their time. Many of them I see in the court. There is Crito, who is of the same age and of the same deme with myself, and there is Critobulus his son, whom I also see. Then again there is Lysanias of Sphettus, who is the father of Aeschines—he is present; and also there is Antiphon of Cephisus, who is the father of Epigenes; and there are the brothers of several who have associated with me. There is Nicostratus the son of Theosdotides, and the brother of Theodotus (now Theodotus himself is dead, and therefore he, at any rate, will not seek to stop him); and there is Paralus the son of Demodocus, who had a brother Theages; and Adeimantus the son of Ariston, whose brother Plato is present; and Aeantodorus, who is the brother of Apollodorus, whom I also see. I might mention a great many others, some of whom Meletus should have produced as witnesses in the course of his speech; and let him still produce them, if he has forgotten—I will make way for him. And let him say, if he has any testimony of the sort which he can produce. Nay, Athenians, the very opposite is the truth. For all these are ready to witness on behalf of the corrupter, of the injurer of their kindred, as Meletus and Anytus call me; not the corrupted youth only—there might have been a motive for that—but their uncorrupted elder relatives. Why should they too support me with their testimony? Why, indeed, except for the sake of truth and justice, and because they know that I am speaking the truth, and that Meletus is a liar.

Well, Athenians, this and the like of this is all the defence which I have to offer. Yet a word more. Perhaps there may be some one who is offended at me, when he calls to mind how he himself on a similar, or even a less serious occasion, prayed and entreated the judges with many tears, and how he produced his children in court, which was a moving spectacle, together with a host of relations and friends; whereas I, who am probably in danger of my life, will do none of these things. The contrast may occur to his mind, and he may be set against me, and vote in anger because he is displeased at me on this account. Now if there be such a person among you,—mind, I do not say that there is,—to him I may fairly reply: My friend, I am a man, and like other men, a creature of flesh and blood, and not 'of wood or stone,' as Homer says; and I have a family, yes, and sons, O Athenians, three in number, one almost a man, and two others who are still young; and yet I will not bring any of them hither in order to petition you for an acquittal. And why not? Not from any self-assertion or want of respect for you. Whether I am or am not afraid of death is another question, of which I will not now speak. But, having regard to public opinion, I feel that such conduct would be discreditable to myself, and to you, and to the whole state. One who has reached my years, and who has a name for wisdom, ought not to demean himself. Whether this opinion of me be deserved or not, at any rate the world has decided that Socrates is in some way superior to other men. And if those among you who are said to be superior in wisdom and courage, and any other virtue, demean themselves in this way, how shameful is their conduct! I have seen men of reputation, when they have been condemned, behaving in the strangest manner: they seemed to fancy that they were going to suffer something dreadful if they died, and that they could be immortal if you only allowed them to live; and I think that such are a dishonour to the state, and that any stranger coming in would have said of them that the most eminent men of Athens, to whom the Athenians themselves give honour and command, are no better than women. And I say that these things ought not to be done by those of us who have a reputation; and if they are done, you ought not to permit them; you ought rather to show that you are far more disposed to condemn the man who gets up a doleful scene and makes the city ridiculous, than him who holds his peace.

But, setting aside the question of public opinion, there seems to be something wrong in asking a favour of a judge, and thus procuring an acquittal, instead of informing and convincing him. For his duty is, not to make a present of justice, but to give judgment; and he has sworn that he will judge according to the laws, and not according to his own good pleasure; and we ought not to encourage you, nor should you allow yourselves to be encouraged, in this habit of perjury—there can be no piety in that. Do not then require me to do what I consider dishonourable and impious and wrong, especially now, when I am being tried for impiety on the indictment of Meletus. For if, O men of Athens, by force of persuasion and entreaty I could overpower your oaths, then I should be teaching you to believe that there are no gods, and in defending should simply convict myself of the charge of not believing in them. But that is not so—far otherwise. For I do believe that there are gods, and in a sense higher than that in which any of my accusers believe in them. And to you and to God I commit my cause, to be determined by you as is best for you and me.

There are many reasons why I am not grieved, O men of Athens, at the vote of condemnation. I expected it, and am only surprised that the votes are so nearly equal; for I had thought that the majority against me would have been far larger; but now, had thirty votes gone over to the other side, I should have been acquitted. And I may say, I think, that I have escaped Meletus. I may say more; for without the assistance of Anytus and Lycon, any one may see that he would not have had a fifth part of the votes, as the law requires, in which case he would have incurred a fine of a thousand drachmae.

And so he proposes death as the penalty. And what shall I propose on my part, O men of Athens? Clearly that which is my due. And what is my due? What return shall be made to the man who has never had the wit to be idle during his whole life; but has been careless of what the many care for—wealth, and family interests, and military offices, and speaking in the assembly, and magistracies, and plots, and parties. Reflecting that I was really too honest a man to be a politician and live, I did not go where I could do no good to you or to myself; but where I could do the greatest good privately to every one of you, thither I went, and sought to persuade every man among you that he must look to himself, and seek virtue and wisdom before he looks to his private interests, and look to the state before he looks to the interests of the state; and that this should be the order which he observes in all his actions. What shall be done to such an one? Doubtless some good thing, O men of Athens, if he has his reward; and the good should be of a kind suitable to him. What would be a reward suitable to a poor man who is your benefactor, and who desires leisure that he may instruct you? There can be no reward so fitting as maintenance in the Prytaneum, O men of Athens, a reward which he deserves far more than the citizen who has won the prize at Olympia in the horse or chariot race, whether the chariots were drawn by two horses or by many. For I am in want, and he has enough; and he only gives you the appearance of happiness, and I give you the reality. And if I am to estimate the penalty fairly, I should say that maintenance in the Prytaneum is the just return.

Perhaps you think that I am braving you in what I am saying now, as in what I said before about the tears and prayers. But this is not so. I speak rather because I am convinced that I never intentionally wronged any one, although I cannot convince you—the time has been too short; if there were a law at Athens, as there is in other cities, that a capital cause should not be decided in one day, then I believe that I should have convinced you. But I cannot in a moment refute great slanders; and, as I am convinced that I never wronged another, I will assuredly not wrong myself. I will not say of myself that I deserve any evil, or propose any penalty. Why should I? because I am afraid of the penalty of death which Meletus proposes? When I do not know whether death is a good or an evil, why should I propose a penalty which would certainly be an evil? Shall I say imprisonment? And why should I live in prison, and be the slave of the magistrates of the year—of the Eleven? Or shall the penalty be a fine, and imprisonment until the fine is paid? There is the same objection. I should have to lie in prison, for money I have none, and cannot pay. And if I say exile (and this may possibly be the penalty which you will affix), I must indeed be blinded by the love of life, if I am so irrational as to expect that when you, who are my own citizens, cannot endure my discourses and words, and have found them so grievous and odious that you will have no more of them, others are likely to endure me. No indeed, men of Athens, that is not very likely. And what a life should I lead, at my age, wandering from city to city, ever changing my place of exile, and always being driven out! For I am quite sure that wherever I go, there, as here, the young men will flock to me; and if I drive them away, their elders will drive me out at their request; and if I let them come, their fathers and friends will drive me out for their sakes.

Some one will say: Yes, Socrates, but cannot you hold your tongue, and then you may go into a foreign city, and no one will interfere with you? Now I have great difficulty in making you understand my answer to this. For if I tell you that to do as you say would be a disobedience to the God, and therefore that I cannot hold my tongue, you will not believe that I am serious; and if I say again that daily to discourse about virtue, and of those other things about which you hear me examining myself and others, is the greatest good of man, and that the unexamined life is not worth living, you are still less likely to believe me. Yet I say what is true, although a thing of which it is hard for me to persuade you. Also, I have never been accustomed to think that I deserve to suffer any harm. Had I money I might have estimated the offence at what I was able to pay, and not have been much the worse. But I have none, and therefore I must ask you to proportion the fine to my means. Well, perhaps I could afford a mina, and therefore I propose that penalty: Plato, Crito, Critobulus, and Apollodorus, my friends here, bid me say thirty minae, and they will be the sureties. Let thirty minae be the penalty; for which sum they will be ample security to you.

Not much time will be gained, O Athenians, in return for the evil name which you will get from the detractors of the city, who will say that you killed Socrates, a wise man; for they will call me wise, even although I am not wise, when they want to reproach you. If you had waited a little while, your desire would have been fulfilled in the course of nature. For I am far advanced in years, as you may perceive, and not far from death. I am speaking now not to all of you, but only to those who have condemned me to death. And I have another thing to say to them: you think that I was convicted because I had no words of the sort which would have procured my acquittal—I mean, if I had thought fit to leave nothing undone or unsaid. Not so; the deficiency which led to my conviction was not of words— certainly not. But I had not the boldness or impudence or inclination to address you as you would have liked me to do, weeping and wailing and lamenting, and saying and doing many things which you have been accustomed to hear from others, and which, as I maintain, are unworthy of me. I thought at the time that I ought not to do anything common or mean when in danger: nor do I now repent of the style of my defence; I would rather die having spoken after my manner, than speak in your manner and live. For neither in war nor yet at law ought I or any man to use every way of escaping death. Often in battle there can be no doubt that if a man will throw away his arms, and fall on his knees before his pursuers, he may escape death; and in other dangers there are other ways of escaping death, if a man is willing to say and do anything. The difficulty, my friends, is not to avoid death, but to avoid unrighteousness; for that runs faster than death. I am old and move slowly, and the slower runner has overtaken me, and my accusers are keen and quick, and the faster runner, who is unrighteousness, has overtaken them. And now I depart hence condemned by you to suffer the penalty of death,—they too go their ways condemned by the truth to suffer the penalty of villainy and wrong; and I must abide by my award—let them abide by theirs. I suppose that these things may be regarded as fated,—and I think that they are well.

And now, O men who have condemned me, I would fain prophesy to you; for I am about to die, and in the hour of death men are gifted with prophetic power. And I prophesy to you who are my murderers, that immediately after my departure punishment far heavier than you have inflicted on me will surely await you. Me you have killed because you wanted to escape the accuser, and not to give an account of your lives. But that will not be as you suppose: far otherwise. For I say that there will be more accusers of you than there are now; accusers whom hitherto I have restrained: and as they are younger they will be more inconsiderate with you, and you will be more offended at them. If you think that by killing men you can prevent some one from censuring your evil lives, you are mistaken; that is not a way of escape which is either possible or honourable; the easiest and the noblest way is not to be disabling others, but to be improving yourselves. This is the prophecy which I utter before my departure to the judges who have condemned me.

Friends, who would have acquitted me, I would like also to talk with you about the thing which has come to pass, while the magistrates are busy, and before I go to the place at which I must die. Stay then a little, for we may as well talk with one another while there is time. You are my friends, and I should like to show you the meaning of this event which has happened to me. O my judges—for you I may truly call judges—I should like to tell you of a wonderful circumstance. Hitherto the divine faculty of which the internal oracle is the source has constantly been in the habit of opposing me even about trifles, if I was going to make a slip or error in any matter; and now as you see there has come upon me that which may be thought, and is generally believed to be, the last and worst evil. But the oracle made no sign of opposition, either when I was leaving my house in the morning, or when I was on my way to the court, or while I was speaking, at anything which I was going to say; and yet I have often been stopped in the middle of a speech, but now in nothing I either said or did touching the matter in hand has the oracle opposed me. What do I take to be the explanation of this silence? I will tell you. It is an intimation that what has happened to me is a good, and that those of us who think that death is an evil are in error. For the customary sign would surely have opposed me had I been going to evil and not to good.

Let us reflect in another way, and we shall see that there is great reason to hope that death is a good; for one of two things—either death is a state of nothingness and utter unconsciousness, or, as men say, there is a change and migration of the soul from this world to another. Now if you suppose that there is no consciousness, but a sleep like the sleep of him who is undisturbed even by dreams, death will be an unspeakable gain. For if a person were to select the night in which his sleep was undisturbed even by dreams, and were to compare with this the other days and nights of his life, and then were to tell us how many days and nights he had passed in the course of his life better and more pleasantly than this one, I think that any man, I will not say a private man, but even the great king will not find many such days or nights, when compared with the others. Now if death be of such a nature, I say that to die is gain; for eternity is then only a single night. But if death is the journey to another place, and there, as men say, all the dead abide, what good, O my friends and judges, can be greater than this? If indeed when the pilgrim arrives in the world below, he is delivered from the professors of justice in this world, and finds the true judges who are said to give judgment there, Minos and Rhadamanthus and Aeacus and Triptolemus, and other sons of God who were righteous in their own life, that pilgrimage will be worth making. What would not a man give if he might converse with Orpheus and Musaeus and Hesiod and Homer? Nay, if this be true, let me die again and again. I myself, too, shall have a wonderful interest in there meeting and conversing with Palamedes, and Ajax the son of Telamon, and any other ancient hero who has suffered death through an unjust judgment; and there will be no small pleasure, as I think, in comparing my own sufferings with theirs. Above all, I shall then be able to continue my search into true and false knowledge; as in this world, so also in the next; and I shall find out who is wise, and who pretends to be wise, and is not. What would not a man give, O judges, to be able to examine the leader of the great Trojan expedition; or Odysseus or Sisyphus, or numberless others, men and women too! What infinite delight would there be in conversing with them and asking them questions! In another world they do not put a man to death for asking questions: assuredly not. For besides being happier than we are, they will be immortal, if what is said is true.

Wherefore, O judges, be of good cheer about death, and know of a certainty, that no evil can happen to a good man, either in life or after death. He and his are not neglected by the gods; nor has my own approaching end happened by mere chance. But I see clearly that the time had arrived when it was better for me to die and be released from trouble; wherefore the oracle gave no sign. For which reason, also, I am not angry with my condemners, or with my accusers; they have done me no harm, although they did not mean to do me any good; and for this I may gently blame them.

Still I have a favour to ask of them. When my sons are grown up, I would ask you, O my friends, to punish them; and I would have you trouble them, as I have troubled you, if they seem to care about riches, or anything, more than about virtue; or if they pretend to be something when they are really nothing,—then reprove them, as I have reproved you, for not caring about that for which they ought to care, and thinking that they are something when they are really nothing. And if you do this, both I and my sons will have received justice at your hands.

The hour of departure has arrived, and we go our ways—I to die, and you to live. Which is better God only knows.

He speaks of the "Internal Oracle" - instinct?

Questions for Further Exploration:

- What is your take on Socrates? Consider what he says in his defense and the strategy he employs in defending himself. Was he wise or foolish? What are his strengths and weaknesses? Would you describe him as a gadfly, player, hero, victim, villain, or something else? (Is he the Dali Lama, Michael Moore, etc. . . ?)

- What is Socrates' critique of popular Athenian values? What alternative values does he advocate and/or exemplify?

- Gathering what you can from Plato's account, what does Socrates mean by living the "examined life"? How would Nietzsche or Orr define that concept? What might each say one ought to examine before acting to live the best life?

- If he were here, what would Socrates say about the causes of the contemporary environmental crises? Do his teachings offer any insight that might be useful in the movement towards a sustainable civilization?

Republic

Plato
Translated by Benjamin Jowett

Book I

■ ■ ■

Well said, Cephalus, I replied; but as concerning justice, what is it?—to speak the truth and to pay your debts—no more than this? And even to this are there not exceptions? Suppose that a friend when in his right mind has deposited arms with me and he asks for them when he is not in his right mind, ought I to give them back to him? No one would say that I ought or that I should be right in doing so, any more than they would say that I ought always to speak the truth to one who is in his condition.

You are quite right, he replied.

But then, I said, speaking the truth and paying your debts is not a correct definition of justice.

Quite correct, Socrates, if Simonides is to be believed, said Polemarchus interposing.

I fear, said Cephalus, that I must go now, for I have to look after the sacrifices, and I hand over the argument to Polemarchus and the company.

Is not Polemarchus your heir? I said.

To be sure, he answered, and went away laughing to the sacrifices.

Tell me then, O thou heir of the argument, what did Simonides say, and according to you truly say, about justice?

He said that the repayment of a debt is just, and in saying so he appears to me to be right.

I should be sorry to doubt the word of such a wise and inspired man, but his meaning, though probably clear to you, is the reverse of clear to me. For he certainly does not mean, as we were now saying that I ought to return a return a deposit of arms or of anything else to one who asks for it when he is not in his right senses; and yet a deposit cannot be denied to be a debt.

True.

Then when the person who asks me is not in his right mind I am by no means to make the return?

Certainly not.

When Simonides said that the repayment of a debt was justice, he did not mean to include that case?

Certainly not; for he thinks that a friend ought always to do good to a friend and never evil.

You mean that the return of a deposit of gold which is to the injury of the receiver, if the two parties are friends, is not the repayment of a debt,—that is what you would imagine him to say?

Yes.

And are enemies also to receive what we owe to them?

To be sure, he said, they are to receive what we owe them, and an enemy, as I take it, owes to an enemy that which is due or proper to him—that is to say, evil.

Simonides, then, after the manner of poets, would seem to have spoken darkly of the nature of justice; for he really meant to say that justice is the giving to each man what is proper to him, and this he termed a debt.

That must have been his meaning, he said.

By heaven! I replied; and if we asked him what due or proper thing is given by medicine, and to whom, what answer do you think that he would make to us?

He would surely reply that medicine gives drugs and meat and drink to human bodies.

And what due or proper thing is given by cookery, and to what?

Seasoning to food.

And what is that which justice gives, and to whom?

If, Socrates, we are to be guided at all by the analogy of the preceding instances, then justice is the art which gives good to friends and evil to enemies.

That is his meaning then?

I think so.

And who is best able to do good to his friends and evil to his enemies in time of sickness?

The physician.

Or when they are on a voyage, amid the perils of the sea?

The pilot.

And in what sort of actions or with a view to what result is the just man most able to do harm to his enemy and good to his friends?

In going to war against the one and in making alliances with the other.

But when a man is well, my dear Polemarchus, there is no need of a physician?

No.

And he who is not on a voyage has no need of a pilot?

No.

Then in time of peace justice will be of no use?

I am very far from thinking so.

You think that justice may be of use in peace as well as in war?

Yes.

Like husbandry for the acquisition of corn?

Yes.

Or like shoemaking for the acquisition of shoes,—that is what you mean?

Yes.

And what similar use or power of acquisition has justice in time of peace?

In contracts, Socrates, justice is of use.

And by contacts you mean partnerships?

Exactly.

But is the just man or the skilful player a more useful and better partner at a game of draughts?

The skilful player.

And in the laying of bricks and stones is the just man a more useful or better partner than the builder?

Quite the reverse.

Then in what sort of partnership is the just man a better partner than the harp-player, as in playing the harp the harp-player is certainly a better partner than the just man?

In a money partnership.

Yes, Polemarchus, but surely not in the use of money; for you do not want a just man to be your counsellor the purchase or sale of a horse; a man who is knowing about horses would be better for that, would he not?

Certainly.

And when you want to buy a ship, the shipwright or the pilot would be better?

True.

Then what is that joint use of silver or gold in which the just man is to be preferred?

When you want a deposit to be kept safely.

You mean when money is not wanted, but allowed to lie?

Precisely.

That is to say, justice is useful when money is useless?

That is the inference.

And when you want to keep a pruning-hook safe, then justice is useful to the individual and to the state; but when you want to use it, then the art of the vine-dresser?

Clearly.

And when you want to keep a shield or a lyre, and not to use them, you would say that justice is useful; but when you want to use them, then the art of the soldier or of the musician?

Certainly.

And so of all the other things;—justice is useful when they are useless, and useless when they are useful?

That is the inference.

Then justice is not good for much. But let us consider this further point: Is not he who can best strike a blow in a boxing match or in any kind of fighting best able to ward off a blow?

Certainly.

And he who is most skilful in preventing or escaping from a disease is best able to create one?

True.

And he is the best guard of a camp who is best able to steal a march upon the enemy?

Certainly.

Then he who is a good keeper of anything is also a good thief?

That, I suppose, is to be inferred.

Then if the just man is good at keeping money, he is good at stealing it.

That is implied in the argument.

Then after all the just man has turned out to be a thief. And this is a lesson which I suspect you must have learnt out of Homer; for he, speaking of Autolycus, the maternal grandfather of Odysseus, who is a favourite of his, affirms that

'He was excellent above all men in theft and perjury.'

And so, you and Homer and Simonides are agreed that justice is an art of theft; to be practised however 'for the good of friends and for the harm of enemies,'—that was what you were saying?

No, certainly not that, though I do not now know what I did say; but I still stand by the latter words.

Well, there is another question: By friends and enemies do we mean those who are so really, or only in seeming?

Surely, he said, a man may be expected to love those whom he thinks good, and to hate those whom he thinks evil.

Yes, but do not persons often err about good and evil: many who are not good seem to be so, and conversely?

That is true.

Then to them the good will be enemies and the evil will be their friends? True.

And in that case they will be right in doing good to the evil and evil to the good?

Clearly.

But the good are just and would not do an injustice?

True.

Then according to your argument it is just to injure those who do no wrong?

Nay, Socrates; the doctrine is immoral.

Then I suppose that we ought to do good to the just and harm to the unjust?

I like that better.

But see the consequence:—Many a man who is ignorant of human nature has friends who are bad friends, and in that case he ought to do harm to them; and he has good enemies whom he ought to benefit; but, if so, we shall be saying the very opposite of that which we affirmed to be the meaning of Simonides.

Very true, he said: and I think that we had better correct an error into which we seem to have fallen in the use of the words 'friend' and 'enemy.'

What was the error, Polemarchus? I asked.

We assumed that he is a friend who seems to be or who is thought good.

And how is the error to be corrected?

We should rather say that he is a friend who is, as well as seems, good; and that he who seems only, and is not good, only seems to be and is not a friend; and of an enemy the same may be said.

You would argue that the good are our friends and the bad our enemies?

Yes.

And instead of saying simply as we did at first, that it is just to do good to our friends and harm to our enemies, we should further say: It is just to do good to our friends when they are good and harm to our enemies when they are evil?

Yes, that appears to me to be the truth.

But ought the just to injure any one at all?

Undoubtedly he ought to injure those who are both wicked and his enemies.

When horses are injured, are they improved or deteriorated?

The latter.

Deteriorated, that is to say, in the good qualities of horses, not of dogs?

Yes, of horses.

And dogs are deteriorated in the good qualities of dogs, and not of horses?

Of course.

And will not men who are injured be deteriorated in that which is the proper virtue of man?

Certainly.

And that human virtue is justice?

To be sure.

Then men who are injured are of necessity made unjust?

That is the result.

But can the musician by his art make men unmusical?

Certainly not.

Or the horseman by his art make them bad horsemen?

Impossible.

And can the just by justice make men unjust, or speaking generally, can the good by virtue make them bad?

Assuredly not.

Any more than heat can produce cold?

It cannot.

Or drought moisture?

Clearly not.

Nor can the good harm any one?

Impossible.

And the just is the good?

Certainly.

Then to injure a friend or any one else is not the act of a just man, but of the opposite, who is the unjust?

I think that what you say is quite true, Socrates.

Then if a man says that justice consists in the repayment of debts, and that good is the debt which a man owes to his friends, and evil the debt which he owes to his enemies,—to say this is not wise; for it is not true, if, as has been clearly shown, the injuring of another can be in no case just.

I agree with you, said Polemarchus.

Then you and I are prepared to take up arms against any one who attributes such a saying to Simonides or Bias or Pittacus, or any other wise man or seer?

I am quite ready to do battle at your side, he said.

Shall I tell you whose I believe the saying to be?

Whose?

I believe that Periander or Perdiccas or Xerxes or Ismenias the Theban, or some other rich and mighty man, who had a great opinion of his own power, was the first to say that justice is 'doing good to your friends and harm to your enemies.'

Most true, he said.

Yes, I said; but if this definition of justice also breaks down, what other can be offered?

Several times in the course of the discussion Thrasymachus had made an attempt to get the argument into his own hands, and had been put down by the rest of the company, who wanted to hear the end. But when Polemarchus and I had done speaking and there was a pause, he could no longer hold his peace; and, gathering himself up, he came at us like a wild beast, seeking to devour us. We were quite panic-stricken at the sight of him.

He roared out to the whole company: What folly, Socrates, has taken possession of you all? And why, sillybillies, do you knock under to one another? I say that if you want really to know what justice is, you should not only ask but answer, and you should not seek honour to yourself from the refutation of an opponent, but have your own answer; for there is many a one who can ask and cannot answer. And now I will not have you say that justice is duty or advantage or profit or gain or interest, for this sort of nonsense will not do for me; I must have clearness and accuracy.

I was panic-stricken at his words, and could not look at him without trembling. Indeed I believe that if I had not fixed my eye upon him, I should have been struck dumb: but when I saw his fury rising, I looked at him first, and was therefore able to reply to him.

Thrasymachus, I said, with a quiver, don't be hard upon us. Polemarchus and I may have been guilty of a little mistake in the argument, but I can assure you that the error was not intentional. If we were seeking for a piece of gold, you would not imagine that we were 'knocking under to one another,' and so losing our chance of finding it. And why, when we are seeking for justice, a thing more precious than many pieces of gold, do you say that we are weakly yielding to one another and not doing our utmost to get at the truth? Nay, my good friend, we are most willing and anxious to do so, but the fact is that we cannot. And if so, you people who know all things should pity us and not be angry with us.

How characteristic of Socrates! he replied, with a bitter laugh;—that's your ironical style! Did I not foresee—have I not already told you, that whatever he was asked he would refuse to answer, and try irony or any other shuffle, in order that he might avoid answering?

You are a philosopher, Thrasymachus, I replied, and well know that if you ask a person what numbers make up twelve, taking care to prohibit him whom you ask from answering twice six, or three times four, or six times two, or four times three, 'for this sort of nonsense will not do for me,'—then obviously, if that is your way of putting the question, no one can answer you. But suppose that he were to retort, 'Thrasymachus, what do you mean? If one of these numbers which you interdict be the true answer to the question, am I falsely to say some other number which is not the right one?—is that your meaning?'—How would you answer him?

Just as if the two cases were at all alike! he said.

Why should they not be? I replied; and even if they are not, but only appear to be so to the person who is asked, ought he not to say what he thinks, whether you and I forbid him or not?

I presume then that you are going to make one of the interdicted answers?

I dare say that I may, notwithstanding the danger, if upon reflection I approve of any of them.

But what if I give you an answer about justice other and better, he said, than any of these? What do you deserve to have done to you?

Done to me!—as becomes the ignorant, I must learn from the wise— that is what I deserve to have done to me.

What, and no payment! a pleasant notion!

I will pay when I have the money, I replied.

But you have, Socrates, said Glaucon: and you, Thrasymachus, need be under no anxiety about money, for we will all make a contribution for Socrates.

Yes, he replied, and then Socrates will do as he always does—refuse to answer himself, but take and pull to pieces the answer of some one else.

Why, my good friend, I said, how can any one answer who knows, and says that he knows, just nothing; and who, even if he has some faint notions of his own, is told by a man of authority not to utter them? The natural thing is, that the speaker should be some one like yourself who professes to know and can tell what he knows. Will you then kindly answer, for the edification of the company and of myself?

Glaucon and the rest of the company joined in my request and Thrasymachus, as any one might see, was in reality eager to speak; for he thought that he had an excellent answer, and would distinguish himself. But at first he to insist on my answering; at length he consented to begin. Behold, he said, the wisdom of Socrates; he refuses to teach himself, and goes about learning of others, to whom he never even says Thank you.

That I learn of others, I replied, is quite true; but that I am ungrateful I wholly deny. Money I have none, and therefore I pay in praise, which is all I have: and how ready I am to praise any one who appears to me to speak well you will very soon find out when you answer; for I expect that you will answer well.

Listen, then, he said; I proclaim that justice is nothing else than the interest of the stronger. And now why do you not me? But of course you won't.

Let me first understand you, I replied. Justice, as you say, is the interest of the stronger. What, Thrasymachus, is the meaning of this? You cannot mean to say that because Polydamas, the pancratiast, is stronger than we are, and finds the eating of beef conducive to his bodily strength, that to eat beef is therefore equally for our good who are weaker than he is, and right and just for us?

That's abominable of you, Socrates; you take the words in the sense which is most damaging to the argument.

Not at all, my good sir, I said; I am trying to understand them; and I wish that you would be a little clearer.

Well, he said, have you never heard that forms of government differ; there are tyrannies, and there are democracies, and there are aristocracies?

Yes, I know.

And the government is the ruling power in each state?

Certainly.

And the different forms of government make laws democratical, aristocratical, tyrannical, with a view to their several interests; and these laws, which are made by them for their own interests, are the justice which they deliver to their subjects, and him who transgresses them they punish as a breaker of the law, and unjust. And that is what I mean when I say that in all states there is the same principle of justice, which is the interest of the government; and as the government must be supposed to have power, the only reasonable conclusion is, that everywhere there is one principle of justice, which is the interest of the stronger.

Now I understand you, I said; and whether you are right or not I will try to discover. But let me remark, that in defining justice you have yourself used the word 'interest' which you forbade me to use. It is true, however, that in your definition the words 'of the stronger' are added.

A small addition, you must allow, he said.

Great or small, never mind about that: we must first enquire whether what you are saying is the truth. Now we are both agreed that justice is interest of some sort, but you go on to say 'of the stronger'; about this addition I am not so sure, and must therefore consider further.

Proceed.

I will; and first tell me, Do you admit that it is just or subjects to obey their rulers?

I do.

But are the rulers of states absolutely infallible, or are they sometimes liable to err?

To be sure, he replied, they are liable to err.

Then in making their laws they may sometimes make them rightly, and sometimes not?

True.

When they make them rightly, they make them agreeably to their interest; when they are mistaken, contrary to their interest; you admit that?

Yes.

And the laws which they make must be obeyed by their subjects,—and that is what you call justice?

Doubtless.

Then justice, according to your argument, is not only obedience to the interest of the stronger but the reverse?

What is that you are saying? he asked.

I am only repeating that you are saying, I believe. But let us consider: Have we not admitted that the rulers may be mistaken about their own interest in what they command, and also that to obey them is justice? Has not that been admitted?

Yes.

Then you must also have acknowledged justice not to be for the interest of the stronger, when the rulers unintentionally command things to be done which are to their own injury. For if, as you say, justice is the obedience which the subject renders to their commands, in that case, O wisest of men, is there any escape from the conclusion that the weaker are commanded to do, not what is for the interest, but what is for the injury of the stronger?

Nothing can be clearer, Socrates, said Polemarchus.

Yes, said Cleitophon, interposing, if you are allowed to be his witness.

But there is no need of any witness, said Polemarchus, for Thrasymachus himself acknowledges that rulers may sometimes command what is not for their own interest, and that for subjects to obey them is justice.

Yes, Polemarchus,—Thrasymachus said that for subjects to do what was commanded by their rulers is just.

Yes, Cleitophon, but he also said that justice is the interest of the stronger, and, while admitting both these propositions, he further acknowledged that the stronger may command the weaker who are his subjects to do what is not for his own interest; whence follows that justice is the injury quite as much as the interest of the stronger.

But, said Cleitophon, he meant by the interest of the stronger what the stronger thought to be his interest,—this was what the weaker had to do; and this was affirmed by him to be justice.

Those were not his words, rejoined Polemarchus.

Never mind, I replied, if he now says that they are, let us accept his statement. Tell me, Thrasymachus, I said, did you mean by justice what the stronger thought to be his interest, whether really so or not?

Certainly not, he said. Do you suppose that I call him who is mistaken the stronger at the time when he is mistaken?

Yes, I said, my impression was that you did so, when you admitted that the ruler was not infallible but might be sometimes mistaken.

You argue like an informer, Socrates. Do you mean, for example, that he who is mistaken about the sick is a physician in that he is mistaken? or that he who errs in arithmetic or grammar is an arithmetician or grammarian at the me when he is making the mistake, in respect of the mistake? True, we say that the physician or arithmetician or grammarian has made a mistake, but this is only a way of speaking; for the fact is that neither the grammarian nor any other person of skill ever makes a mistake in so far as he is what his name implies; they none of them err unless their skill fails them, and then they cease to be skilled artists. No artist or sage or ruler errs at the time when he is what his name implies; though he is commonly said to err, and I adopted the common mode of speaking. But to be perfectly accurate, since you are such a lover of accuracy, we should say that the ruler, in so far as he is the ruler, is unerring, and, being unerring, always commands that which is for his own interest; and the subject is required to execute his commands; and therefore, as I said at first and now repeat, justice is the interest of the stronger.

Indeed, Thrasymachus, and do I really appear to you to argue like an informer?

Certainly, he replied.

And you suppose that I ask these questions with any design of injuring you in the argument?

Nay, he replied, 'suppose' is not the word—I know it; but you will be found out, and by sheer force of argument you will never prevail.

I shall not make the attempt, my dear man; but to avoid any misunderstanding occurring between us in future, let me ask, in what sense do you speak of a ruler or stronger whose interest, as you were saying, he being the superior, it is just that the inferior should execute—is he a ruler in the popular or in the strict sense of the term?

In the strictest of all senses, he said. And now cheat and play the informer if you can; I ask no quarter at your hands. But you never will be able, never.

And do you imagine, I said, that I am such a madman as to try and cheat, Thrasymachus? I might as well shave a lion.

Why, he said, you made the attempt a minute ago, and you failed.

Enough, I said, of these civilities. It will be better that I should ask you a question: Is the physician, taken in that strict sense of which you are speaking, a healer of the sick or a maker of money? And remember that I am now speaking of the true physician.

A healer of the sick, he replied.

And the pilot—that is to say, the true pilot—is he a captain of sailors or a mere sailor?

A captain of sailors.

The circumstance that he sails in the ship is not to be taken into account; neither is he to be called a sailor; the name pilot by which he is distinguished has nothing to do with sailing, but is significant of his skill and of his authority over the sailors.

Very true, he said.

Now, I said, every art has an interest?

Certainly.

For which the art has to consider and provide?

Yes, that is the aim of art.

And the interest of any art is the perfection of it—this and nothing else?

What do you mean?

I mean what I may illustrate negatively by the example of the body. Suppose you were to ask me whether the body is self-sufficing or has wants, I should reply: Certainly the body has wants; for the body may be ill and require to be cured, and has therefore interests to which the art of medicine ministers; and this is the origin and intention of medicine, as you will acknowledge. Am I not right?

Quite right, he replied.

But is the art of medicine or any other art faulty or deficient in any quality in the same way that the eye may be deficient in sight or the ear fail of hearing, and therefore requires another art to provide for the interests of seeing and hearing—has art in itself, I say, any similar liability to fault or defect, and does every art require another supplementary art to provide for its interests, and that another and another without end? Or have the arts to look only after their own interests? Or have they no need either of themselves or of another?—having no faults or defects, they have no need to correct them, either by the exercise of their own art or of any other; they have only to consider the interest of their subject-matter. For every art remains pure and faultless while remaining true—that is to say, while perfect and unimpaired. Take the words in your precise sense, and tell me whether I am not right.

Yes, clearly.

Then medicine does not consider the interest of medicine, but the interest of the body?

True, he said.

Nor does the art of horsemanship consider the interests of the art of horsemanship, but the interests of the horse; neither do any other arts care for themselves, for they have no needs; they care only for that which is the subject of their art?

True, he said.

But surely, Thrasymachus, the arts are the superiors and rulers of their own subjects?

To this he assented with a good deal of reluctance.

Then, I said, no science or art considers or enjoins the interest of the stronger or superior, but only the interest of the subject and weaker?

He made an attempt to contest this proposition also, but finally acquiesced.

Then, I continued, no physician, in so far as he is a physician, considers his own good in what he prescribes, but the good of his patient; for the true physician is also a ruler having the human body as a subject, and is not a mere money-maker; that has been admitted?

Yes.

And the pilot likewise, in the strict sense of the term, is a ruler of sailors and not a mere sailor?

That has been admitted.

And such a pilot and ruler will provide and prescribe for the interest of the sailor who is under him, and not for his own or the ruler's interest?

He gave a reluctant 'Yes.'

Then, I said, Thrasymachus, there is no one in any rule who, in so far as he is a ruler, considers or enjoins what is for his own interest, but always what is for the interest of his subject or suitable to his art; to that he looks, and that alone he considers in everything which he says and does.

When we had got to this point in the argument, and every one saw that the definition of justice had been completely upset, Thrasymachus, instead of replying to me, said: Tell me, Socrates, have you got a nurse?

Why do you ask such a question, I said, when you ought rather to be answering?

Because she leaves you to snivel, and never wipes your nose: she has not even taught you to know the shepherd from the sheep.

What makes you say that? I replied.

Because you fancy that the shepherd or neatherd fattens or tends the sheep or oxen with a view to their own good and not to the good of himself or his master; and you further imagine that the rulers of states, if they are

They are arguing whether Rulers are after their own interest or the interest of everyone which in turn is their own.

true rulers, never think of their subjects as sheep, and that they are not studying their own advantage day and night. Oh, no; and so entirely astray are you in your ideas about the just and unjust as not even to know that justice and the just are in reality another's good; that is to say, the interest of the ruler and stronger, and the loss of the subject and servant; and injustice the opposite; for the unjust is lord over the truly simple and just: he is the stronger, and his subjects do what is for his interest, and minister to his happiness, which was very far from being their own. Consider further, most foolish Socrates, that the just is always a loser in comparison with the unjust. First of all, in private contracts: wherever the unjust is the partner of the just you will find that, when the partnership is dissolved, the unjust man has always more and the just less. Secondly, in their dealings with the State: when there is an income-tax, the just man will pay more and the unjust less on the same amount of income; and when there is anything to be received the one gains nothing and the other much. Observe also what happens when they take an office; there is the just man neglecting his affairs and perhaps suffering other losses, and getting nothing out of the public, because he is just; moreover he is hated by his friends and acquaintance for refusing to serve them in unlawful ways. But all this is reversed in the case of the unjust man. I am speaking, as before, of injustice on a large scale in which the advantage of the unjust is more apparent; and my meaning will be most clearly seen if we turn to that highest form of injustice in which the criminal is the happiest of men, and the sufferers or those who refuse to do injustice are the most miserable—that is to say tyranny, which by fraud and force takes away the property of others, not little by little but wholesale; comprehending in one, things sacred as well as profane, private and public; for which acts of wrong, if he were detected perpetrating any one of them singly, he would be punished and incur great disgrace—they who do such wrong in particular cases are called robbers of temples, and man-stealers and burglars and swindlers and thieves. But when a man besides taking away the money of the citizens has made slaves of them, then, instead of these names of reproach, he is termed happy and blessed, not only by the citizens but by all who hear of his having achieved the consummation of injustice. For mankind censure injustice, fearing that they may be the victims of it and not because they shrink from committing it. And thus, as I have shown, Socrates, injustice, when on a sufficient scale, has more strength and freedom and mastery than justice; and, as I said at first, justice is the interest of the stronger, whereas injustice is a man's own profit and interest.

Thrasymachus, when he had thus spoken, having, like a bath-man, deluged our ears with his words, had a mind to go away. But the company would not let him; they insisted that he should remain and defend his position; and I myself added my own humble request that he would not leave us. Thrasymachus, I said to him, excellent man, how suggestive are your remarks! And are you going to run away before you have fairly taught or learned whether they are true or not? Is the attempt to determine the way of man's life so small a matter in your eyes—to determine how life may be passed by each one of us to the greatest advantage?

And do I differ from you, he said, as to the importance of the enquiry?

You appear rather, I replied, to have no care or thought about us, Thrasymachus—whether we live better or worse from not knowing what you say you know, is to you a matter of indifference. Prithee, friend, do not keep your knowledge to yourself; we are a large party; and any benefit which you confer upon us will be amply rewarded. For my own part I openly declare that I am not convinced, and that I do not believe injustice to be more gainful than justice, even if uncontrolled and allowed to have free play. For, granting that there may be an unjust man who is able to commit injustice either by fraud or force, still this does not convince me of the superior advantage of injustice, and there may be others who are in the same predicament with myself. Perhaps we may be wrong; if so, you in your wisdom should convince us that we are mistaken in preferring justice to injustice.

And how am I to convince you, he said, if you are not already convinced by what I have just said; what more can I do for you? Would you have me put the proof bodily into your souls?

Heaven forbid! I said; I would only ask you to be consistent; or, if you change, change openly and let there be no deception. For I must remark, Thrasymachus, if you will recall what was previously said, that although you began by defining the true physician in an exact sense, you did not observe a like exactness when speaking of the shepherd; you thought that the shepherd as a shepherd tends the sheep not with a view to their own good, but like a mere diner or banquetter with a view to the pleasures of the table; or, again, as a trader for sale in the market, and not as a shepherd. Yet surely the art of the shepherd is concerned only with the good of his subjects; he has only to provide the best for them, since the perfection of the art is already ensured whenever all the requirements of it are satisfied. And that was what I was saying just now about the ruler. I conceived that the art of the ruler, considered as ruler, whether in a state or in private life, could only regard the good of his flock or subjects; whereas you seem to think that the rulers in states, that is to say, the true rulers, like being in authority.

Think! Nay, I am sure of it.

Then why in the case of lesser offices do men never take them willingly without payment, unless under the idea that they govern for the advantage not of themselves but of others? Let me ask you a question: Are not the several arts different, by reason of their each having a separate function? And, my dear illustrious friend, do say what you think, that we may make a little progress.

Yes, that is the difference, he replied.

And each art gives us a particular good and not merely a general one—medicine, for example, gives us health; navigation, safety at sea, and so on?

Yes, he said.

And the art of payment has the special function of giving pay: but we do not confuse this with other arts, any more than the art of the pilot is to be confused with the art of medicine, because the health of the pilot may be improved by a sea voyage. You would not be inclined to say, would you, that navigation is the art of medicine, at least if we are to adopt your exact use of language?

Certainly not.

Or because a man is in good health when he receives pay you would not say that the art of payment is medicine?

I should not.

Nor would you say that medicine is the art of receiving pay because a man takes fees when he is engaged in healing?

Certainly not.

And we have admitted, I said, that the good of each art is specially confined to the art?

Yes.

Then, if there be any good which all artists have in common, that is to be attributed to something of which they all have the common use?

True, he replied.

And when the artist is benefited by receiving pay the advantage is gained by an additional use of the art of pay, which is not the art professed by him?

He gave a reluctant assent to this.

Then the pay is not derived by the several artists from their respective arts. But the truth is, that while the art of medicine gives health, and the art of the builder builds a house, another art attends them which is the art of pay. The various arts may be doing their own business and benefiting that over which they preside, but would the artist receive any benefit from his art unless he were paid as well?

I suppose not.

But does he therefore confer no benefit when he works for nothing?

Certainly, he confers a benefit.

Then now, Thrasymachus, there is no longer any doubt that neither arts nor governments provide for their own interests; but, as we were before saying, they rule and provide for the interests of their subjects who are the weaker and not the stronger—to their good they attend and not to the good of the superior. And this is the reason, my dear Thrasymachus, why, as I was just now saying, no one is willing to govern; because no one likes to take in hand the reformation of evils which are not his concern without remuneration. For, in the execution of his work, and in giving his orders to another, the true artist does not regard his own interest, but always that of his subjects; and therefore in order that rulers may be willing to rule, they must be paid in one of three modes of payment: money, or honour, or a penalty for refusing.

What do you mean, Socrates? said Glaucon. The first two modes of payment are intelligible enough, but what the penalty is I do not understand, or how a penalty can be a payment.

You mean that you do not understand the nature of this payment which to the best men is the great inducement to rule? Of course you know that ambition and avarice are held to be, as indeed they are, a disgrace?

Very true.

And for this reason, I said, money and honour have no attraction for them; good men do not wish to be openly demanding payment for governing and so to get the name of hirelings, nor by secretly helping themselves out of the public revenues to get the name of thieves. And not being ambitious they do not care about honour. Wherefore necessity must be laid upon them, and they must be induced to serve from the fear of punishment. And this, as I imagine, is the reason why the forwardness to take office, instead of waiting to be compelled, has been deemed dishonourable. Now the worst part of the punishment is that he who refuses to rule is liable to be ruled by one who is worse than himself. And the fear of this, as I conceive, induces the good to take office, not because they would, but because they cannot help—not under the idea that they are going to have any benefit or enjoyment themselves, but as a necessity, and because they are not able to commit the task of ruling to any one who is better than themselves, or indeed as good. For there is reason to think that if a city were composed entirely of good men, then to avoid office would be as much an object of contention as to obtain office is at present; then we should have plain proof that the true ruler is not meant by nature to regard his own interest, but that of his subjects; and every one who knew this would choose rather to receive a benefit from another than to have the trouble of conferring one. So far am I from agreeing with Thrasymachus that justice is the interest of the stronger. This latter question need not be further discussed at present; but when Thrasymachus says that the life of the unjust is more advantageous than that of the just, his new statement appears to me to be of a far more serious character. Which of us has spoken truly? And which sort of life, Glaucon, do you prefer?

I for my part deem the life of the just to be the more advantageous, he answered.

Did you hear all the advantages of the unjust which Thrasymachus was rehearsing?

Yes, I heard him, he replied, but he has not convinced me.

Then shall we try to find some way of convincing him, if we can, that he is saying what is not true?

Most certainly, he replied.

If, I said, he makes a set speech and we make another recounting all the advantages of being just, and he answers and we rejoin, there must be a numbering and measuring of the goods which are claimed on either side, and in the end we shall want judges to decide; but if we proceed in our enquiry as we lately did, by making admissions to one another, we shall unite the offices of judge and advocate in our own persons.

Very good, he said.

And which method do I understand you to prefer? I said.

That which you propose.

Well, then, Thrasymachus, I said, suppose you begin at the beginning and answer me. You say that perfect injustice is more gainful than perfect justice?

Yes, that is what I say, and I have given you my reasons.

And what is your view about them? Would you call one of them virtue and the other vice?

Certainly.

I suppose that you would call justice virtue and injustice vice?

What a charming notion! So likely too, seeing that I affirm injustice to be profitable and justice not.

What else then would you say?

The opposite, he replied.

And would you call justice vice?

No, I would rather say sublime simplicity.

Then would you call injustice malignity?

No; I would rather say discretion.

And do the unjust appear to you to be wise and good?

Yes, he said; at any rate those of them who are able to be perfectly unjust, and who have the power of subduing states and nations; but perhaps you imagine me to be talking of cutpurses. Even this profession if undetected has advantages, though they are not to be compared with those of which I was just now speaking.

I do not think that I misapprehend your meaning, Thrasymachus, I replied; but still I cannot hear without amazement that you class injustice with wisdom and virtue, and justice with the opposite.

Certainly I do so class them.

Now, I said, you are on more substantial and almost unanswerable ground; for if the injustice which you were maintaining to be profitable had been admitted by you as by others to be vice and deformity, an answer might have been given to you on received principles; but now I perceive that you will call injustice honourable and strong, and to the unjust you will attribute all the qualities which were attributed by us before to the just, seeing that you do not hesitate to rank injustice with wisdom and virtue.

You have guessed most infallibly, he replied.

Then I certainly ought not to shrink from going through with the argument so long as I have reason to think that you, Thrasymachus, are speaking your real mind; for I do believe that you are now in earnest and are not amusing yourself at our expense.

I may be in earnest or not, but what is that to you?—to refute the argument is your business.

Very true, I said; that is what I have to do: But will you be so good as answer yet one more question? Does the just man try to gain any advantage over the just?

Far otherwise; if he did would not be the simple amusing creature which he is.

And would he try to go beyond just action?

He would not.

And how would he regard the attempt to gain an advantage over the unjust; would that be considered by him as just or unjust?

He would think it just, and would try to gain the advantage; but he would not be able.

Whether he would or would not be able, I said, is not to the point. My question is only whether the just man, while refusing to have more than another just man, would wish and claim to have more than the unjust?

Yes, he would.

And what of the unjust—does he claim to have more than the just man and to do more than is just?

Of course, he said, for he claims to have more than all men.

And the unjust man will strive and struggle to obtain more than the unjust man or action, in order that he may have more than all?

True.

We may put the matter thus, I said—the just does not desire more than his like but more than his unlike, whereas the unjust desires more than both his like and his unlike?

Nothing, he said, can be better than that statement.

And the unjust is good and wise, and the just is neither?

Good again, he said.

And is not the unjust like the wise and good and the just unlike them?

Of course, he said, he who is of a certain nature, is like those who are of a certain nature; he who is not, not.

Each of them, I said, is such as his like is?

Certainly, he replied.

Very good, Thrasymachus, I said; and now to take the case of the arts: you would admit that one man is a musician and another not a musician?

Yes.

And which is wise and which is foolish?

Clearly the musician is wise, and he who is not a musician is foolish.

And he is good in as far as he is wise, and bad in as far as he is foolish?

Yes.

And you would say the same sort of thing of the physician?

Yes.

And do you think, my excellent friend, that a musician when he adjusts the lyre would desire or claim to exceed or go beyond a musician in the tightening and loosening the strings?

I do not think that he would.

But he would claim to exceed the non-musician?

Of course.

And what would you say of the physician? In prescribing meats and drinks would he wish to go beyond another physician or beyond the practice of medicine?

He would not.

But he would wish to go beyond the non-physician?

Yes.

And about knowledge and ignorance in general; see whether you think that any man who has knowledge ever would wish to have the choice of saying or doing more than another man who has knowledge. Would he not rather say or do the same as his like in the same case?

That, I suppose, can hardly be denied.

And what of the ignorant? would he not desire to have more than either the knowing or the ignorant?

I dare say.

And the knowing is wise?

Yes.

And the wise is good?

True.

Then the wise and good will not desire to gain more than his like, but more than his unlike and opposite?

I suppose so.

Whereas the bad and ignorant will desire to gain more than both?

Yes.

But did we not say, Thrasymachus, that the unjust goes beyond both his like and unlike? Were not these your words?

They were.

And you also said that the just will not go beyond his like but his unlike?

Yes.

Then the just is like the wise and good, and the unjust like the evil and ignorant?

That is the inference.

And each of them is such as his like is?

That was admitted.

Then the just has turned out to be wise and good and the unjust evil and ignorant.

Thrasymachus made all these admissions, not fluently, as I repeat them, but with extreme reluctance; it was a hot summer's day, and the perspiration poured from him in torrents; and then I saw what I had never seen before, Thrasymachus blushing. As we were now agreed that justice was virtue and wisdom, and injustice vice and ignorance, I proceeded to another point:

Well, I said, Thrasymachus, that matter is now settled; but were we not also saying that injustice had strength; do you remember?

Yes, I remember, he said, but do not suppose that I approve of what you are saying or have no answer; if however I were to answer, you would be quite certain to accuse me of haranguing; therefore either permit me to have my say out, or if you would rather ask, do so, and I will answer 'Very good,' as they say to story-telling old women, and will nod 'Yes' and 'No.'

Certainly not, I said, if contrary to your real opinion.

Yes, he said, I will, to please you, since you will not let me speak. What else would you have?

Nothing in the world, I said; and if you are so disposed I will ask and you shall answer.

Proceed.

Then I will repeat the question which I asked before, in order that our examination of the relative nature of justice and injustice may be carried on regularly. A statement was made that injustice is stronger and more powerful than justice, but now justice, having been identified with wisdom and virtue, is easily shown to be stronger than injustice, if injustice is ignorance; this can no longer be questioned by any one. But I want to view the matter, Thrasymachus, in a different way: You would not deny that a state may be unjust and may be unjustly attempting to enslave other states, or may have already enslaved them, and may be holding many of them in subjection?

True, he replied; and I will add that the best and most perfectly unjust state will be most likely to do so.

I know, I said, that such was your position; but what I would further consider is, whether this power which is possessed by the superior state can exist or be exercised without justice or only with justice.

If you are right in you view, and justice is wisdom, then only with justice; but if I am right, then without justice.

I am delighted, Thrasymachus, to see you not only nodding assent and dissent, but making answers which are quite excellent.

That is out of civility to you, he replied.

You are very kind, I said; and would you have the goodness also to inform me, whether you think that a state, or an army, or a band of robbers and thieves, or any other gang of evil-doers could act at all if they injured one another?

No indeed, he said, the could not.

But if they abstained from injuring one another, then they might act together better?

Yes.

And this is because injustice creates divisions and hatreds and fighting, and justice imparts harmony and friendship; is not that true, Thrasymachus?

I agree, he said, because I do not wish to quarrel with you.

How good of you, I said; but I should like to know also whether injustice, having this tendency to arouse hatred, wherever existing, among slaves or among freemen, will not make them hate one another and set them at variance and render them incapable of common action?

Certainly.

And even if injustice be found in two only, will they not quarrel and fight, and become enemies to one another and to the just

They will.

And suppose injustice abiding in a single person, would your wisdom say that she loses or that she retains her natural power?

Let us assume that she retains her power.

Yet is not the power which injustice exercises of such a nature that wherever she takes up her abode, whether in a city, in an army, in a family, or in any other body, that body is, to begin with, rendered incapable of united action by reason of sedition and distraction; and does it not become its own enemy and at variance with all that opposes it, and with the just? Is not this the case?

Yes, certainly.

And is not injustice equally fatal when existing in a single person; in the first place rendering him incapable of action because he is not at unity with himself, and in the second place making him an enemy to himself and the just? Is not that true, Thrasymachus?

Yes.

And O my friend, I said, surely the gods are just?

Granted that they are.

But if so, the unjust will be the enemy of the gods, and the just will be their friend?

Feast away in triumph, and take your fill of the argument; I will not oppose you, lest I should displease the company.

Well then, proceed with your answers, and let me have the remainder of my repast. For we have already shown that the just are clearly wiser and better and abler than the unjust, and that the unjust are incapable of common action; nay more, that to speak as we did of men who are evil acting at any time vigorously together, is not strictly true, for if they had been perfectly evil, they would have laid hands upon one another; but it is evident that there must have been some remnant of justice in them, which enabled them to combine; if there had not been they would have injured one another as well as their victims; they were but half-villains in their enterprises; for had they been whole villains, and utterly unjust, they would have been utterly incapable of action. That, as I believe, is the truth of the matter, and not what you said at first. But whether the just have a better and happier life than the unjust is a further question which we also proposed to consider. I think that they have, and for the reasons which to have given; but still I should like to examine further, for no light matter is at stake, nothing less than the rule of human life.

Proceed.

I will proceed by asking a question: Would you not say that a horse has some end?

I should.

And the end or use of a horse or of anything would be that which could not be accomplished, or not so well accomplished, by any other thing?

I do not understand, he said.

Let me explain: Can you see, except with the eye?

Certainly not.

Or hear, except with the ear?

No.

These then may be truly said to be the ends of these organs?

They may.

But you can cut off a vine-branch with a dagger or with a chisel, and in many other ways?

Of course.

And yet not so well as with a pruning-hook made for the purpose?
True.
May we not say that this is the end of a pruning-hook?
We may.
Then now I think you will have no difficulty in understanding my meaning when I asked the question whether the end of anything would be that which could not be accomplished, or not so well accomplished, by any other thing?
I understand your meaning, he said, and assent.
And that to which an end is appointed has also an excellence? Need I ask again whether the eye has an end?
It has.
And has not the eye an excellence?
Yes.
And the ear has an end and an excellence also?
True.
And the same is true of all other things; they have each of them an end and a special excellence?
That is so.
Well, and can the eyes fulfil their end if they are wanting in their own proper excellence and have a defect instead?
How can they, he said, if they are blind and cannot see?
You mean to say, if they have lost their proper excellence, which is sight; but I have not arrived at that point yet. I would rather ask the question more generally, and only enquire whether the things which fulfil their ends fulfil them by their own proper excellence, and fail of fulfilling them by their own defect?
Certainly, he replied.
I might say the same of the ears; when deprived of their own proper excellence they cannot fulfil their end?
True.
And the same observation will apply to all other things?
I agree.
Well; and has not the soul an end which nothing else can fulfil? for example, to superintend and command and deliberate and the like. Are not these functions proper to the soul, and can they rightly be assigned to any other?
To no other.
And is not life to be reckoned among the ends of the soul?
Assuredly, he said.
And has not the soul an excellence also?
Yes.

And can she or can she not fulfil her own ends when deprived of that excellence?

She cannot.

Then an evil soul must necessarily be an evil ruler and superintendent, and the good soul a good ruler?

Yes, necessarily.

And we have admitted that justice is the excellence of the soul, and injustice the defect of the soul?

That has been admitted.

Then the just soul and the just man will live well, and the unjust man will live ill?

That is what your argument proves.

And he who lives well is blessed and happy, and he who lives ill the reverse of happy?

Certainly.

Then the just is happy, and the unjust miserable?

So be it.

But happiness and not misery is profitable.

Of course.

Then, my blessed Thrasymachus, injustice can never be more profitable than justice.

Let this, Socrates, he said, be your entertainment at the Bendidea.

For which I am indebted to you, I said, now that you have grown gentle towards me and have left off scolding. Nevertheless, I have not been well entertained; but that was my own fault and not yours. As an epicure snatches a taste of every dish which is successively brought to table, he not having allowed himself time to enjoy the one before, so have I gone from one subject to another without having discovered what I sought at first, the nature of justice. I left that enquiry and turned away to consider whether justice is virtue and wisdom or evil and folly; and when there arose a further question about the comparative advantages of justice and injustice, I could not refrain from passing on to that. And the result of the whole discussion has been that I know nothing at all. For I know not what justice is, and therefore I am not likely to know whether it is or is not a virtue, nor can I say whether the just man is happy or unhappy.

Book II

With these words I was thinking that I had made an end of the discussion; but the end, in truth, proved to be only a beginning. For Glaucon, who is always the most pugnacious of men, was dissatisfied at Thrasymachus' retirement; he wanted to have the battle out. So he said to me: Socrates, do you wish really to persuade us, or only to seem to have persuaded us, that to be just is always better than to be unjust?

I should wish really to persuade you, I replied, if I could.

Then you certainly have not succeeded. Let me ask you now:—How would you arrange goods—are there not some which we welcome for their own sakes, and independently of their consequences, as, for example, harmless pleasures and enjoyments, which delight us at the time, although nothing follows from them?

I agree in thinking that there is such a class, I replied.

Is there not also a second class of goods, such as knowledge, sight, health, which are desirable not only in themselves, but also for their results?

Certainly, I said.

And would you not recognize a third class, such as gymnastic, and the care of the sick, and the physician's art; also the various ways of money-making—these do us good but we regard them as disagreeable; and no one would choose them for their own sakes, but only for the sake of some reward or result which flows from them?

There is, I said, this third class also. But why do you ask?

Because I want to know in which of the three classes you would place justice?

In the highest class, I replied,—among those goods which he who would be happy desires both for their own sake and for the sake of their results.

Then the many are of another mind; they think that justice is to be reckoned in the troublesome class, among goods which are to be pursued for the sake of rewards and of reputation, but in themselves are disagreeable and rather to be avoided.

I know, I said, that this is their manner of thinking, and that this was the thesis which Thrasymachus was maintaining just now, when he censured justice and praised injustice. But I am too stupid to be convinced by him.

I wish, he said, that you would hear me as well as him, and then I shall see whether you and I agree. For Thrasymachus seems to me, like a snake, to have been charmed by your voice sooner than he ought to have been; but to my mind the nature of justice and injustice have not yet been made clear. Setting aside their rewards and results, I want to know what they are in themselves, and how they inwardly work in the soul. If you, please, then, I will revive the argument of Thrasymachus. And first I will speak of the nature and origin of justice according to the common view of them. Secondly, I will show that all men who practise justice do so against their will, of necessity, but not as a good. And thirdly, I will argue that there is reason in this view, for the life of the unjust is after all better far than the life of the just—if what they say is true, Socrates, since I myself am not of their opinion. But still I acknowledge that I am perplexed when I hear the voices of Thrasymachus and myriads of others dinning in my ears; and, on the other hand, I have never yet heard the superiority of justice to injustice maintained by any one in a satisfactory way. I want to hear justice praised in respect of itself; then I shall be satisfied, and you are the person from whom I think that I am most likely to hear this; and therefore I will praise the unjust life to the utmost of my power, and my manner of speaking will indicate the manner in which I desire to hear you too praising justice and censuring injustice. Will you say whether you approve of my proposal?

Indeed I do; nor can I imagine any theme about which a man of sense would oftener wish to converse.

I am delighted, he replied, to hear you say so, and shall begin by speaking, as I proposed, of the nature and origin of justice.

They say that to do injustice is, by nature, good; to suffer injustice, evil; but that the evil is greater than the good. And so when men have both done and suffered injustice and have had experience of both, not being able to avoid the one and obtain the other, they think that they had better agree among themselves to have neither; hence there arise laws and mutual covenants; and that which is ordained by law is termed by them lawful and just. This they affirm to be the origin and nature of justice;—it is a mean or compromise, between the best of all, which is to do injustice and not be punished, and the worst of all, which is to suffer injustice without the power of retaliation; and justice, being at a middle point between the two, is tolerated not as a good, but as the lesser evil, and honoured by reason of the inability of men to do injustice. For no man who is worthy to be called a man would ever submit to such an agreement if he were able to resist; he would be mad if he did. Such is the received account, Socrates, of the nature and origin of justice.

Now that those who practice justice do so involuntarily and because they have not the power to be unjust will best appear if we imagine something of this kind: having given both to the just and the unjust power to do what they will, let us watch and see whither desire will lead them; then we shall discover in the very act the just and unjust man to be proceeding along the same road, following their interest, which all natures deem to be their good, and are only diverted into the path of justice by the force of law. The liberty which we are supposing may be most completely given to them in the form of such a power as is said to have been possessed by Gyges, the ancestor of Croesus the Lydian. According to the tradition, Gyges was a shepherd in the service of the king of Lydia; there was a great storm, and an earthquake made an opening in the earth at the place where he was feeding his flock. Amazed at the sight, he descended into the opening, where, among other marvels, he beheld a hollow brazen horse, having doors, at which he stooping and looking in saw a dead body of stature, as appeared to him, more than human, and having nothing on but a gold ring; this he took from the finger of the dead and reascended. Now the shepherds met together, according to custom, that they might send their monthly report about the flocks to the king; into their assembly he came having the ring on his finger, and as he was sitting among them he chanced to turn the collet of the ring inside his hand, when instantly he became invisible to the rest of the company and they began to speak of him as if he were no longer present. He was astonished at this, and again touching the ring he turned the collet outwards and reappeared; he made several trials of the ring, and always with the same result—when he turned the collet inwards he became invisible, when outwards he reappeared. Whereupon he contrived to be chosen one of the messengers who were sent to the court; where as soon as he arrived he seduced the queen, and with her help conspired against the king and slew him, and took the kingdom. Suppose now that there were two such magic rings, and the just put on one of them and the unjust the other; no man can be imagined to be of such an iron nature that he would stand fast in justice. No man would keep his hands off what was not his own when he could safely take what he liked out of the market, or go into houses and lie with any one at his pleasure, or kill or release from prison whom he would, and in all respects be like a God among men. Then the actions of the just would be as the actions of the unjust; they would both come at last to the same point. And this we may truly affirm to be a great proof that a man is just, not willingly or because he thinks that justice is any good to him individually, but of necessity, for wherever any one thinks that he can safely be unjust, there he is unjust. For all men believe in their hearts that injustice is far more profitable to the individual than justice, and he who argues as I have been supposing, will say that they are right. If you could imagine any one obtaining this power of becoming invisible, and never doing any wrong or touching what was another's, he would be thought by the lookers-on to be a most wretched idiot, although they would praise him to one another's faces, and keep up appearances with one another from a fear that they too might suffer injustice. Enough of this.

Now, if we are to form a real judgment of the life of the just and unjust, we must isolate them; there is no other way; and how is the isolation to be effected? I answer: Let the unjust man be entirely unjust, and the just man entirely just; nothing is to be taken away from either of them, and both are to be perfectly furnished for the work of their respective lives.

Causes me to ponder my Question of whether we can have a moral society without Religion is fear

First, let the unjust be like other distinguished masters of craft; like the skilful pilot or physician, who knows intuitively his own powers and keeps within their limits, and who, if he fails at any point, is able to recover himself. So let the unjust make his unjust attempts in the right way, and lie hidden if he means to be great in his injustice: (he who is found out is nobody:) for the highest reach of injustice is, to be deemed just when you are not. Therefore I say that in the perfectly unjust man we must assume the most perfect injustice; there is to be no deduction, but we must allow him, while doing the most unjust acts, to have acquired the greatest reputation for justice. If he have taken a false step he must be able to recover himself; he must be one who can speak with effect, if any of his deeds come to light, and who can force his way where force is required his courage and strength, and command of money and friends. And at his side let us place the just man in his nobleness and simplicity, wishing, as Aeschylus says, to be and not to seem good. There must be no seeming, for if he seem to be just he will be honoured and rewarded, and then we shall not know whether he is just for the sake of justice or for the sake of honours and rewards; therefore, let him be clothed in justice only, and have no other covering; and he must be imagined in a state of life the opposite of the former. Let him be the best of men, and let him be thought the worst; then he will have been put to the proof; and we shall see whether he will be affected by the fear of infamy and its consequences. And let him continue thus to the hour of death; being just and seeming to be unjust. When both have reached the uttermost extreme, the one of justice and the other of injustice, let judgment be given which of them is the happier of the two.

■ ■ ■

Questions for Further Exploration:

- Notice how Socrates leads in the pursuit of the definition of "justice" through a series of arguments by analogy. As you read, highlight or check each analogy. Which are his strongest and weakest analogies? Upon what analogy does his most important claim about justice rest?

- Does Plato extend 'the principle of charity' in his engagement with his opposition? What rhetorical devices does Plato employ in his presentation of Thrasymachus?

- Compare and contrast the positions taken by Thrasymachus and Socrates. With regard to the nature of justice, whose interests does it serve? Between "the just" and "the unjust," which life provides the greatest advantage? Where do you stand in this debate?

- Consider the idea of "climate justice" or "environmental justice" in light of the definitions offered by Socrates and Thrasymachus. Which one offers the most promise for ensuring a "good life" in the twenty-first century?

- If you came upon a ring with the power to make you invisible, as Gyges did, what would you use it to do? What conclusions follow from this thought experiment?

Our Purpose

The Nobel Peace Prize Lecture
Oslo, 2007

Al Gore

Your Majesties, Your Royal Highnesses, Honorable members of the Norwegian Nobel Committee, Excellencies, ladies and gentlemen.

I have a purpose here today. It is a purpose I have tried to serve for many years. I have prayed that God would show me a way to accomplish it.

Sometimes, without warning, the future knocks on our door with a precious and painful vision of what might be. One hundred and nineteen years ago, a wealthy inventor read his own obituary, mistakenly published years before his death. Wrongly believing the inventor had just died, a newspaper printed a harsh judgment of his life's work, unfairly labeling him "The Merchant of Death" because of his invention—dynamite. Shaken by this condemnation, the inventor made a fateful choice to serve the cause of peace.

Seven years later, Alfred Nobel created this prize and the others that bear his name.

Seven years ago tomorrow, I read my own political obituary in a judgment that seemed to me harsh and mistaken—if not premature. But that unwelcome verdict also brought a precious if painful gift: an opportunity to search for fresh new ways to serve my purpose.

Unexpectedly, that quest has brought me here. Even though I fear my words cannot match this moment, I pray what I am feeling in my heart will be communicated clearly enough that those who hear me will say, "We must act."

The distinguished scientists with whom it is the greatest honor of my life to share this award have laid before us a choice between two different futures—a choice that to my ears echoes the words of an ancient prophet: "Life or death, blessings or curses. Therefore, choose life, that both thou and thy seed may live."

We, the human species, are confronting a planetary emergency—a threat to the survival of our civilization that is gathering ominous and destructive potential even as we gather here. But there is hopeful news as well: We have the ability to solve this crisis and avoid the worst—though not all—of its consequences, if we act boldly, decisively and quickly.

However, despite a growing number of honorable exceptions, to many of the world's leaders are still best described in the words Winston Churchill applied to those who ignored Adolf Hitler's threat: "They go on in strange paradox, decided only to be undecided, resolved to be irresolute, adamant for drift, solid for fluidity, all powerful to be impotent."

So today, we dumped another 70 million tons of global-warming pollution into the thin shell of atmosphere surrounding our planet, as if it were an open sewer. And tomorrow, we will dump a slightly larger amount, with the cumulative concentrations now trapping more and more heat from the sun.

As a result, the Earth has a fever. And the fever is rising. The experts have told us it is not a passing affliction that will heal by itself. We asked for a second opinion. And a third. And a fourth. And the consistent conclusion, restated with unprecedented alarm, is that something basic is wrong.

We are what is wrong, and we must make it right.

Last September 21, as the Northern Hemisphere tilted away from the sun, scientists reported with increasing distress that the North Polar ice cap is "falling off a cliff." One study estimated that it could be completely gone during summer in less than 22 years. Another new study, to be presented by U.S. Navy researchers later this week, warns it could happen in as little as 7 years.

Seven years from now.

In the last few months, it has been harder and harder to misinterpret the signs that our world is spinning out of kilter. Major cities in North and South America, Asia, and Australia are nearly out of water due to massive droughts and melting glaciers. Desperate farmers are losing their livelihoods. Peoples in the frozen Arctic and on low-lying Pacific Islands are planning evacuations of places they have long called home. Unprecedented wildfires have forced a half million people from their homes in one country and caused a national emergency that almost brought down the government in another. Climate refugees have migrated into areas already inhabited by people with different cultures, religions, and traditions, increasing the potential for conflict. Stronger storms in the Pacific and Atlantic have threatened whole cities. Millions have been displaced by massive flooding in South Asia, Mexico, and 18 countries in Africa. As temperature extremes have increased, tens of thousands have lost their lives. We are recklessly burning and clearing our forests and driving more and more species into extinction. The very web of life on which we depend is being ripped and frayed.

We never intended to cause all this destruction, just as Alfred Nobel never intended that dynamite be used for waging war. He had hoped his invention would promote human progress. We shared that same worthy goal when we began burning massive quantities of coal, then oil and methane.

Even in Nobel's time, there were a few warnings of the likely consequences. One of the very first winners of the prize in chemistry worried that, "We are evaporating our coal mines into the air." After performing 10,000 equations by hand, Svante Arrhenius calculated that the Earth's average temperature would increase by many degrees if we doubled the amount of CO_2 in the atmosphere.

Seventy years later, my teacher, Roger Revelle, and his colleague, Dave Keeling, began to precisely document the increasing CO_2 levels day by day.

But unlike most other forms of pollution, CO_2 is invisible, tasteless, and odorless—which has helped keep the truth about what it is doing to our climate out of sight and out of mind. Moreover, the catastrophe now threatening us is unprecedented—and we often confuse the unprecedented with the improbable.

We also find it hard to imagine making the massive changes that are now necessary to solve the crisis. And when large truths are genuinely inconvenient, whole societies can, at least for a time, ignore them. Yet as George Orwell reminds us: "Sooner or later a false belief bump up against solid reality, usually on a battlefield."

In the years since this prize was first awarded, the entire relationship between humankind and the Earth has been radically transformed. And still, we have remained largely oblivious to the impact of our cumulative actions.

Indeed, without realizing it, we have begun to wage war on the Earth itself. Now, we and the Earth's climate are locked in a relationship familiar to war planners: "Mutually assured destruction."

More than 2 decades ago, scientists calculated that nuclear war could throw so much debris and smoke into the air that it would block life-giving sunlight from our atmosphere, causing a "nuclear winter." Their eloquent warnings here in Oslo helped galvanize the world's resolve to halt the nuclear arms race.

Now science is warning us that if we do not quickly reduce the global warming pollution that is trapping so much of the heat our planet normally radiates back out of the atmosphere, we are in danger of creating a permanent "carbon summer."

As the American poet Robert Frost wrote, "Some say the world will end in fire; some say in ice." Either, he notes, "would suffice."

But neither need be our fate. It is time to make peace with the planet.

We must quickly mobilize our civilization with the urgency and resolve that has previously been seen only when nations mobilized for war. These prior struggles for survival were won when leaders found words at the 11th hour that released a mighty surge of courage, hope, and readiness to sacrifice for a protracted and mortal challenge.

These were not comforting and misleading assurances that the threat was not real or imminent; that it would affect others but not ourselves; that ordinary life might be lived even in the presence of extraordinary threat; that Providence could be trusted to do for us what we would not do for ourselves.

No, these were calls to come to the defense of the common future. They were calls upon the courage, generosity, and strength of entire peoples, citizens of every class and condition who were ready to stand against the threat once asked to do so. Our enemies in those times calculated that free people would not rise to the challenge; they were, of course, catastrophically wrong.

Now comes the threat of climate crisis—a threat that is real, rising, imminent, and universal. Once again, it is the 11th hour. The penalties for ignoring this challenge are immense and growing and, at some near point would be unsustainable and unrecoverable. For now we still have the power to choose our fate, and the remaining question is only this: Have we the will to act vigorously and in time, or will we remain imprisoned by a dangerous illusion?

Mahatma Gandhi awakened the largest democracy on Earth and forged a shared resolve with what he called *satyagraha,* or "truth force."

In every land, the truth—once known—has the power to set us free.

Truth also has the power to unite us and bridge the distance between "me" and "we," creating the basis for common effort and shared responsibility.

There is an African proverb that says, "If you want to go quickly, go alone. If you want to go far, go together." We need to go far, quickly.

We must abandon the conceit that individual, isolated, private actions are the answer. They can and do help. But they will not take us far enough without collective action. At the same time, we must ensure that in mobilizing globally, we do not invite the establishment of ideological conformity and a new lock-step "ism."

That means adopting principles, values, laws, and treaties that release creativity and initiative at every level of society in multifold responses originating concurrently and spontaneously.

This new consciousness requires expanding the possibilities inherent in all humanity. The innovators who will devise a new way to harness the sun's energy for pennies or invent an engine that's carbon negative may live in Lagos or Mumbai or Montevideo. We must ensure that entrepreneurs and inventors everywhere on the globe have the chance to change the world.

When we unite for a moral purpose that is manifestly good and true, the spiritual energy unleashed can transform us. The generation that defeated fascism throughout the world in the 1940s found, in rising to meet their awesome challenge, that they had gained the moral authority and long-term vision to launch the Marshall Plan, the United Nations, and a new level of global cooperation and foresight that unified Europe and facilitated the emergence of democracy and prosperity in Germany, Japan, Italy, and much of the world. One of their visionary leaders said, "It is time we steered by the stars and not by the lights of every passing ship."

In the last year of that war, you gave the Peace Prize to a man from my hometown of 2,000 people, Carthage, Tennessee. Cordell Hull was described by Franklin Roosevelt as the "Father of the United Nations." He was an inspiration and hero to my own father, who followed Hull in the Congress and the U.S. Senate and in his commitment to world peace and global cooperation.

My parents spoke often of Hull, always in tones of reverence and admiration. Eight weeks ago, when you announced this prize, the deepest emotion I felt was when I saw the headline in my hometown paper that simply noted I had won the same prize that Cordell Hull had won. In that moment, I knew what my father and mother would have felt were they alive.

Just as Hull's generation found moral authority in rising to solve the world crisis caused by fascism, so too can we find our greatest opportunity in rising to solve the climate crisis. In the kanji characters used in both Chinese and Japanese, "crisis" is written with two symbols—the first meaning "danger," the second, "opportunity."

By facing and removing the danger of the climate crisis, we have the opportunity to gain the moral authority and vision to vastly increase our own capacity to solve other crises that have been too long ignored.

We must understand the connections between the climate crisis and the afflictions of poverty, hunger, HIV/AIDS and other pandemics. As these problems are linked, so too must be their solutions. We must begin by making the common rescue of the global environment the central organizing principle of the world community.

Fifteen years ago, I made that case at the Earth Summit in Rio de Janeiro. Ten years ago, I presented it in Kyoto. This week, I will urge the delegates in Bali to adopt a bold mandate for a treaty that establishes a universal global cap on emissions and uses the market in emissions trading to efficiently allocate resources to the most effective opportunities for speedy reductions.

This treaty should be ratified and brought into effect everywhere in the world by the beginning of 2010—two years sooner than presently contemplated. The pace of our response must be accelerated to match the accelerating pace of the crisis itself.

Heads of state should meet early next year to review what was accomplished in Bali and take personal responsibility for addressing this crisis. It is not unreasonable to ask, given the gravity of our circumstances, that these heads of state meet every three months until the treaty is completed.

We also need a moratorium on the construction of any new generating facility that burns coal without the capacity to safely trap and store carbon dioxide.

And most important of all, we need to put a price on carbon—with a CO_2 tax that is then rebated back to the people, progressively, according to the laws of each nation, in ways that shift the burden of taxation from employment to pollution. This is by far the most effective and simplest way to accelerate solutions to this crisis.

The world needs an alliance—especially of those nations that weigh heaviest in the scales where Earth is in the balance. I salute Europe and Japan for the steps they've taken in recent years to meet the challenge, and the new government in Australia, which has made solving the climate crisis its first priority.

But the outcome will be decisively influenced by two nations that are now failing to do enough: the United States and China. While India is also growing fast in importance, it should be absolutely clear that it is the two largest CO_2 emitters—most of all, my own country—that will need to make the boldest moves or stand accountable before history for their failure to act.

Both countries should stop using the other's behavior as an excuse for stalemate and instead develop an agenda for mutual survival in a shared global environment.

These are the last few years of decision, but they can be the first years of a bright and hopeful future if we do what we must. No one should believe a solution will be found without effort, without cost, without change. Let us acknowledge that if we wish to redeem squandered time and speak again with moral authority, then these are the hard truths:

The way ahead is difficult. The outer boundary of what we currently believe is feasible is still far short of what we actually must do. Moreover, between here and there, across the unknown, falls the shadow.

That is just another way of saying that we have to expand the boundaries of what is possible. In the words of the Spanish poet, Antonio Machado, "Pathwalker, there is no path. You must make the path as you walk."

We are standing at the most fateful fork in the path. So I want to end as I began, with a vision of two futures—each a palpable possibility—and with a prayer that we will see with vivid clarity the necessity of choosing between those two futures, and the urgency of making the right choice now.

The great Norwegian playwright, Henrik Ibsen, wrote, "One of these days, the younger generation will come knocking at my door."

The future is knocking at our door right now. Make no mistake, the next generation will ask us one of two questions. Either they will ask: "What were you thinking; why didn't you act?"

Or they will ask instead: "How did you find the moral courage to rise and successfully resolve a crisis that so many said was impossible to solve?"

We have everything we need to get started, save perhaps political will, but political will is a renewable resource.

So let us renew it and say together: "We have a purpose. We are many. For this purpose, we will rise and we will act."

Questions for Further Exploration:

- Why does Gore believe that we must make it our common moral purpose to respond to the climate crisis? How does he think we ought to respond? Are you with or against him in this global environmental project?

- "Truth," Gore claims, "has the power to unite us and bridge the distance between 'me' and 'we,' creating the basis for common effort and shared responsibility." Is this true in your experience? Free-write about a specific occurrence that supports or challenges his claim.

- What's your take on Gore? What are his strengths and weaknesses? Would you describe him as a gadfly, player, hero, victim, villain, or something else? In what respects is Gore like or unlike Socrates?

UNIT TWO:
Reality

Introduction to Greening Metaphysics

Why bother sorting through philosophies of reality when we are faced with "real" problems that urgently demand our best attention and action? This seemingly straight-forward question ironically holds its own answer.

The question assumes that our "real" problems are readily apparent, indisputable, and agreed upon by everyone. In fact, they are not, as is revealed in the debate over climate change. The emphasis on "real" problems and what's "really" going on assumes a particular conception of reality which justifies a call to action while ignoring both the contest over what counts as "reality" and those who deny the validity of the call to action. There is an ongoing debate as to whether or not there *really* is an environmental crisis. Those who argue there *is* a crisis depend on a particular conception of reality to make their case. Similarly, those who *deny* there is a crisis depend on a particular conception of reality to make their case. Hence, the need to bother with sorting through philosophies of reality is called for by the role these philosophies play in adjudicating claims on our attention and behavior.

In addition to determining the conception of reality needed to justify the best environmental solutions, the work of sorting through philosophies of reality is worth the effort for the hope of change it inspires. If it is true that ideas about reality have informed and influenced the human choices that have created environmental problems, it makes sense that reconsidering and revising our ideas will move us toward solutions. In case there is a metaphysical foundation for an ecological world view that calls people to more sustainable ways of life, it is surely worth the effort to *discover* it. If it turns out there is no such reality, the work of *searching* may bring us closer to the sobering realization that we still must *act,* and may inform sustainable decision-making in the future. While it may be naïve to believe that changing *ideas* alone can solve problems, there is no wisdom in decision-making without first thinking long and hard about reality.

There are several common ways to explore Western philosophies of reality. We might ask, "How many essentially different kinds of realities are there?" *Monists* claim all of reality is one. *Dualists* argue there are two basic realities. *Pluralists* maintain there are many realities. *Nihilists* say there is no (given order of) reality at all. We might also ask, what is the relation between various kinds of reality; e.g. what is the relation between "the mind" and "the body"? Philosophers explore metaphysical theories using a few important distinctions, including: appearance/reality, actuality/potentiality, transcendence/immanence, organic/mechanistic, necessary/contingent, and substance/process. These distinctions are used to explore questions about the nature of particular realities; e.g., "Is God a substance or a process?" "Is the physical world an organism or a mechanism?" This unit is organized historically to reveal the manner in which various metaphysical questions and concepts have emerged through time.

Sorting through philosophies of reality helps us to understand our place in the order of things. What are the most basic substances or processes upon which everything else depends? What is the reality of a human being? Are humans essentially the same or different than other 'beings,' and in what respects? What is God's relation to the natural world? What is the reality of the natural world? Do natural beings, like trees or bees, have a soul, spirit, or mind? Is there a given order of relations among all existing beings? To answer these questions, it may be useful to use Plato's Allegory of the Cave as a common reference point as you work your way through this survey of Western conceptions of reality. The shadows on the wall of the cave represent the lowest form of reality, while the sun represents the highest form of reality. Among philosophers who share the view that reality is given in this value-laden way, the higher forms of reality are understood as *really* real, or *genuinely* real in contrast with the lower forms, which are understood as mere *appearances.* As you take up each metaphysical philosophy, ask yourself how Plato's Allegory might be used to reveal the values embedded in its concepts and distinctions.

Resources

Avatar. Dir. James Cameron, (Twentieth Century Fox, 2009).

Bertram, Christopher, "Jean Jacques Rousseau," *The Stanford Encyclopedia of Philosophy* edited by Edward N. Zalta, (Winter 2010 Edition, forthcoming). http://plato.stanford.edu/archives/win2010/entries/rousseau/

Creation: The True Story of Charles Darwin. Dir. Jon Amiel, (Recorded Picture Company with BBC Films and Ocean Pictures, 2010).

Crowell, Steven, "Existentialism," *The Stanford Encyclopedia of Philosophy* edited by Edward N. Zalta, (Winter 2010 Edition, forthcoming). http://plato.stanford.edu/archives/win2010/entries/existentialism/

God in America, a 2010 documentary series, co-produced by American Experience and Frontline, features the relationship between metaphysics and politics in the 400 year history of America from the first settlements to the present. All four episodes are available free online.

Hatfield, Gary, "René Descartes," *The Stanford Encyclopedia of Philosophy,* edited by Edward N. Zalta, (Spring 2009 Edition). http://plato.stanford.edu/archives/spr2009/entries/descartes/

Human, All Too Human, a 1999 BBC documentary television series features the lives of three existentialist philosophers: Friedrich Nietzsche, Martin Heidegger, and Jean-Paul Sartre. All three episodes are available free online.

Ismael, Jenann, "Quantum Mechanics," *The Stanford Encyclopedia of Philosophy* edited by Edward N. Zalta, (Fall 2009 Edition). http://plato.stanford.edu/archives/fall2009/entries/qm/

Lennox, James, "Darwinism," *The Stanford Encyclopedia of Philosophy* edited by Edward N. Zalta, (Fall 2010 Edition). http://plato.stanford.edu/archives/fall2010/entries/darwinism/

Lorenz, Hendrik, "Ancient Theories of Soul," *The Stanford Encyclopedia of Philosophy,* edited by Edward N. Zalta, (Summer 2009 Edition). http://plato.stanford.edu/archives/sum2009/entries/ancient-soul/

Mindwalk. Dir. Bernt Capra. The Atlas Production Company presents a Lintschinger/Cohen Production, 1990. Based on *The Turning Point* by Fritjof Capra.

McInerny, Ralph and O'Callaghan, John, "Saint Thomas Aquinas," *The Stanford Encyclopedia of Philosophy* edited by Edward N. Zalta, (Winter 2009 Edition). http://plato.stanford.edu/archives/win2009/entries/aquinas/

Ramsey, William, "Eliminative Materialism," *The Stanford Encyclopedia of Philosophy* edited by Edward N. Zalta, (Fall 2008 Edition). http://plato.stanford.edu/archives/fall2008/entries/materialism-eliminative/

Richard Dawkins interviews Dan Dennett for "The Genius of Charles Darwin," the Channel 4 UK TV program which won British Broadcasting Awards' "Best Documentary Series" of 2008, (49 min). http://www.youtube.com/watch?v=5lfTPTFN94o

Wieland, Carl. "*Avatar* and the 'new' evolutionary religion," *Creation Ministries International* (January 5, 2010). http://creation.com/avatar-movie-review

Wierenga, Edward, "Omnipresence," *The Stanford Encyclopedia of Philosophy* edited by Edward N. Zalta, (Fall 2009 Edition). http://plato.stanford.edu/archives/fall2009/entries/omnipresence/

Questions for Further Exploration:

- What values are embedded in various theories of reality?

- What does each metaphysical theory reveal about the nature of humans, the nature of nature, and the nature of relations between humans and the natural world?

- What can metaphysics reveal about the cause(s) of ecological problems?

- Can the causes of ecological destruction be found in particular Western assumptions about reality?

- What conceptualization of reality encourages the best ecological practices and policies?

- Is there a metaphysical justification for the shift to a sustainable order of values?

- Are there conceptual resources buried in Western metaphysical theories that could open up fruitful directions for a more sustainable future?

Phaedo

Plato

■ ■ ■

Now consider, my good friend, if you and I are agreed on another point which I think will help us to understand the question better. Do you think that a philosopher will care very much about what are called pleasures, such as the pleasures of eating and drinking?

Certainly not, Socrates, said Simmias.

Or about the pleasures of sexual passion?

Indeed, no.

And, do you think that he holds the remaining cares of the body in high esteem? Will he think much of getting fine clothes, and sandals, and other bodily adornments, or will he despise them, except so far as he is absolutely forced to meddle with them?

The real philosopher, I think, will despise them, he replied.

In short, said he, you think that his studies are not concerned with the body? He stands aloof from it, as far as he can, and turns toward the soul?

I do.

Well then, in these matters, first, it is clear that the philosopher releases his soul from communion with the body, so far as he can, beyond all other men?

It is.

And does not the world think, Simmias, that if a man has no pleasure in such things, and does not take his share in them, his life is not worth living? Do not they hold that he who thinks nothing of bodily pleasures is almost as good as dead?

Indeed you are right.

But what about the actual acquisition of wisdom? If the body is taken as a companion in the search for wisdom, is it a hindrance or not? For example, do sight and hearing convey any real truth to men? Are not the very poets forever telling us that we neither hear nor see anything accurately? But if these senses of the body are not accurate or clear, the others will hardly be so, for they are all less perfect than these, are they not?

Yes, I think so, certainly, he said.

Then when does the soul attain truth? he asked. We see that, as often as she seeks to investigate anything in company with the body, the body leads her astray.

True.

Is it not by reasoning, if at all, that any real truth becomes manifest to her?

Yes.

And she reasons best, I suppose, when none of the senses, whether hearing, or sight, or pain, or pleasure, harasses her; when she has dismissed the body, and released herself as far as she can from all intercourse or contact with it, and so, coming to be as much alone with herself as is possible, strives after real truth.

That is so.

And here too the soul of the philosopher very greatly despises the body, and flies from it, and seeks to be alone by herself, does she not?

Clearly.

And what do you say to the next point, Simmias? Do we say that there is such a thing as absolute justice, or not?

Indeed we do.

And absolute beauty, and absolute good?

Of course.

Have you ever seen any of them with your eyes?

Indeed I have not, he replied.

Did you ever grasp them with any bodily sense? I am speaking of all absolutes, whether size, or health, or strength; in a word, of the essence or real being of everything. Is the very truth of things contemplated by the body? Is it not rather the case that the man who prepares himself most carefully to apprehend by his intellect the essence of each thing which he examines will come nearest to the knowledge of it?

Certainly.

And will not a man attain to this pure thought most completely if he goes to each thing, as far as he can, and his mind alone, taking neither sight nor any other sense along with his reason in the process of thought, to be an encumbrance? In every case he will pursue pure and absolute being, with his pure intellect alone. He will be set free as far as possible from the eye and the ear and, in short, from the whole body, because intercourse with the body troubles the soul, and hinders her from gaining truth and wisdom. Is it not he who will attain the knowledge of real being, if any man will?

Your words are admirably true, Socrates, said Simmias.

And, he said, must not all this cause real philosophers to reflect, and make them say to each other, It seems that there is a narrow path which will bring us safely to our journey's end, with reason as our guide. As long as we have this body, and an evil of that sort is mingled with our souls, we shall never fully gain what we desire; and that is truth. For the body is forever taking up our time with the care which it needs; and, besides, whenever diseases attack it, they hinder us in our pursuit of real being. It fills us with passions, and desires, and fears, and all manner of phantoms, and much foolishness; and so, as the saying goes, in very truth we can never think at all for it. It alone and its desires cause wars and factions and battles; for the origin of all wars is the pursuit of wealth, and we are forced to pursue wealth because we live in slavery to the cares of the body. And therefore, for all these reasons, we have no leisure for philosophy. And last of all, if we ever are free from the body for a time, and then turn to examine some matter, it falls in our way at every step of the inquiry, and causes confusion and trouble and panic, so that we cannot see the truth for it. Verily we have learned that if we are to have any pure knowledge at all, we must be freed from the body; the soul by herself must behold things as they are. Then, it seems, after we are dead, we shall gain the wisdom which we desire, and for which we say we have a passion, but not while we are alive, as the argument shows. For if it be not possible to have pure knowledge while the body is with us, one of two things must be true: either we cannot gain knowledge at all, or we can gain it only after death. For then, and not till then, will the soul exist by herself, separate from the body. And while we live, we shall come nearest to knowledge, if we have no communion or intercourse with the body beyond what is absolutely necessary, and if we are not defiled with its nature. We must live pure from it until God himself releases us. And when we are thus pure and released from its follies, we shall dwell, I suppose, with others who are pure like ourselves, and we shall of ourselves know all that is pure; and that my be the truth. For I think that the impure is not allowed to attain to the pure. Such, Simmias, I fancy must needs be the language and the reflections of the true lovers of knowledge. Do you not agree with me?

Most assuredly I do, Socrates.

And, my friend, said Socrates, if this be true, I have good hope that, when I read the place whither I am going, I shall there, if anywhere, gain fully that which we have sought so earnestly in the past. And so I shall set forth cheerfully on the journey that is appointed me today, and so may every man who thinks that his mind is prepared and purified.

That is quite true, said Simmias.

And does not the purification consist, as we have said, in separating the soul from the body, as far as is possible, and in accustoming her to collect and rally herself together from the body on every side, and to dwell alone by herself as much as she can, both now and hereafter, released from the bondage of the body?

Yes, certainly, he said.

Is not what we call death a release and separation of the soul from the body?

Undoubtedly, he replied.

And the true philosopher, we hold, is alone in his constant desire to set his soul free? His study is simply the release and separation of the soul from the body, is it not?

Clearly.

Would it not be absurd then, as I began by saying, for a man to complain at death coming to him, when in his life he has been preparing himself to live as nearly in a state of death as he could? Would not that be absurd?

Yes, indeed.

In truth, then, Simmias, he said, the true philosopher studies to die, and to him of all men is death least terrible. Now look at the matter in this way. In everything he is at enmity with his body, and he longs to possess his soul alone. Would it not then be most unreasonable if he were to fear and complain when he has his desire, instead of rejoicing to go to the place where he hopes to gain the wisdom that he has passionately longed for all his life, and to be released from the company of his enemy? Many a man has willingly gone to the other world, when a human love or wife or son has died, in the hope of seeing there those whom he longed for, and of being with them: and will a man who has a real passion for wisdom, and a firm hope of really finding wisdom in the other world and nowhere else, grieve at death, and not depart rejoicing? Nay, my friend, you ought not to think that, if he be truly a philosopher. He will be firmly convinced that there and nowhere else will he meet with wisdom in its purity. And if this be so, would it not, I repeat, be very unreasonable for such a man to fear death?

Yes, indeed, he replied, it would.

Does not this show clearly, he said, that any man whom you see grieving at the approach of death is after all no lover of wisdom, but a lover of his body? He is also, most likely, a lover either of wealth, or of honor, or, it may be, of both.

Yes, he said, it is as you say.

Well then, Simmias, he went on, does not what is called courage belong especially to the philosopher?

Certainly I think so, he replied.

And does not temperance, the quality which even the world calls temperance, and which means to despise and control and govern the passions—does not temperance belong only to such men as most despise the body, and pass their lives in philosophy?

Of necessity, he replied.

For if you will consider the courage and the temperance of other men, said he, you will find that they are strange things.

How so, Socrates?

You know, he replied, that all other men regard death as one of the great evils to which mankind is subject?

Indeed they do, he said.

And when the brave men of them submit to death, do not they do so from a fear of still greater evils?

Yes.

Then all men but the philosopher are brave from fear and because they are afraid. Yet it is rather a strange thing for a man to be brave out of fear and cowardice.

Indeed it is.

And are not the orderly men of them in exactly the same case? Are not they temperate from a kind of intemperance? We should say that this cannot be; but in them this state of foolish temperance comes to that. They desire certain pleasures, and fear to lose them; and so they abstain from other pleasures because they are mastered by these. Intemperance is defined to mean being under the dominion of pleasure, yet they only master certain pleasures because they are mastered by others. But that is exactly what I said just now—that, in a way, they are made temperate from intemperance.

It seems to be so.

My dear Simmias, I fear that virtue is not really to be bought in this way, by bartering pleasure for pleasure, and pain for pain, and fear for fear, and the greater for the less, like coins. There is only one sterling coin for which all these things ought to be exchanged, and that is wisdom. All that is bought and sold for this and with this, whether courage, or temperance, or justice, is real; in one word, true virtue cannot be without wisdom, and it matters nothing whether pleasure, and fear, and all other such things are present or absent. But I think that the virtue which is composed of pleasures and fears bartered with one another, and severed from wisdom, is only a shadow of true virtue, and that it has no freedom, nor health, nor truth. True virtue in reality is a kind of purifying from all these things; and temperance, and justice, and courage, and wisdom itself are the purification. And I fancy that the men who established our mysteries had a very real meaning: in truth they have been telling us in parables all the time that whosoever comes to Hades uninitiated and profane will lie in the mire, while he that has been purified and initiated shall dwell with the gods. For "the thyrsus-bearers are many," as they say in the mysteries, "but the inspired few." And by these last, I believe, are meant only the true philosophers. And I in my life have striven as hard as I was able, and have left nothing undone, that I might become one of them. Whether I have striven in the right way, and whether I have succeeded or not, I suppose that I shall learn in a little while, when I reach the other world, if it be the will of god.

That is my defense, Simmias and Cebes, to show that I have reason for not being angry or grieved at leaving you and my masters here. I believe that in the next world, no less than in this, I shall meet with good masters and friends, though the multitude are incredulous of it. And if I have been more successful with you in my defense than I was with my Athenian judges, it is well.

When Socrates had finished, Cebes replied to him, and said, I think that for the most part you are right, Socrates. But men are very incredulous of what you have said of the soul. They fear that she will no longer exist anywhere when she has left the body, but that she will be destroyed and perish on the very day of death. They think that the moment that she is released and leaves the body, she will be dissolved and vanish away like breath or smoke, and thenceforward cease to exist at all. If she were to exist somewhere as a whole, released from the evils which you enumerated just now, we should have good reason to hope, Socrates, that what you way is true. But it will need no little persuasion and assurance to show that the soul exists after death, and continues to possess any power or wisdom.

True, Cebes, said Socrates; but what are we to do? Do you wish to converse about these matters and see if what I say is probable?

I for one, said Cebes, should gladly hear your opinion about them.

I think, said Socrates, that no one who heard me now, even if he were a comic poet, would say that I am an idle talker about things which do not concern me. So, if you wish it, let us examine this question.

Let us consider whether or not the souls of men exist in the next world after death, thus. There is an ancient belief, which we remember, that on leaving this world they exist there, and that they return hither and are born again from the dead. But if it be true that the living are born from the dead, our souls must exist in the other world; otherwise they could not be born again. It will be a sufficient proof that this is so if we can really prove that the living are born only from the dead. But if this is not so, we shall have to find some other argument.

Exactly, said Cebes.

Well, said he, the easiest way of answering the question will be to consider it not in relation to men only, but also in relation to all animals and plants, and in short to all things that are generated. Is it the case that everything which has an opposite is generated only from its opposite? By opposites I mean the honorable and the base, the just and the unjust, and so on in a thousand other instances. Let us consider then whether it is necessary for everything that has an opposite to be generated only from its own opposite. For instance, when anything becomes greater, I suppose it must first have been less and then become greater?

Yes.

And if a thing becomes less, it must have been greater, and afterward become less?

That is so, said he.

And further, the weaker is generated from the stronger, and the swifter from the slower?

Certainly.

And the worse is generated from the better, and the more just from the more unjust?

Of course.

Then it is sufficiently clear to us that all things are generated in this way, opposites from opposites?

Quite so.

And in every pair of opposites, are there not two generations between the two members of the pair, from the one to the other, and then back again from the other to the first? Between the greater and the less are growth and diminution, and we say that the one grows and the other diminishes, do we not?

Yes, he said.

And there is division and composition, and cold and hot, and so on. In fact, is it not a universal law, even though we do not always express it in so many words, that opposites are generated always from one another, and that there is a process of generation from one to the other?

It is, he replied.

Well, said he, is there an opposite to life, in the same way that sleep is the opposite of being awake?

Certainly, he answered.

What is it?

Death, he replied.

Then if life and death are opposites, they are generated the one from the other: they are two, and between them there are two generations. Is it not so?

Of course.

Now, said Socrates, I will explain to you one of the two pairs of opposites of which I spoke just now, and its generations, and you shall explain to me the other. Sleep is the opposite of waking. From sleep is produced the state of waking, and from the state of waking is produced sleep. Their generations are, first, to fall asleep; secondly, to awake. Is that clear? he asked.

Yes, quite.

Now then, said he, do you tell me about life and death. Death is the opposite of life, is it not?

It is.

And they are generated the one from the other?

Yes.

Then what is that which is generated from the living?

The dead, he replied.

And what is generated from the dead?

I must admit that it is the living.

Then living things and living men are generated from the dead, Cebes?

Clearly, said he.

Then our souls exist in the other world? he said.

Apparently.

Now of these two generations the one is certain? Death I suppose is certain enough, is it not?

Yes, quite, he replied.

What then shall we do? said he. Shall we not assign an opposite generation to correspond? Or is nature imperfect here? Must we not assign some opposite generation to dying?

I think so, certainly, he said.

And what must it be?

To come to life again.

And if there be such a thing as a return to life, he said, it will be a generation from the dead to the living, will it not?

It will, certainly.

Then we are agreed on this point: namely, that the living are generated from the dead no less than the dead from the living. But we agreed that, if this be so, it is a sufficient proof that the souls of the dead must exist somewhere, whence they come into being again.

I think, Socrates, that that is the necessary result of our premises.

And I think, Cebes, said he, that our conclusion has not been an unfair one. For if opposites did not always correspond with opposites as they are generated, moving as it were round in a circle, and there were generation in a straight line forward from one opposite only, with no turning or return to the other, then, you know, all things would come at length to have the same form and be in the same state, and would cease to be generated at all.

What do you mean? he asked.

It is not at all hard to understand my meaning, he replied. If, for example, the one opposite, to go to sleep, existed without the corresponding opposite, to wake up, which is generated from the first, then all nature would at last make the tale of Endymion meaningless, and he would no longer be conspicuous; for everything else would be in the same state of sleep that he was in. And if all things were compounded together and never separated, the Chaos of Anaxagoras would soon be realized. Just in the same way, my dear Cebes, if all things in which there is any life were to die, and when they were dead were to remain in that form and not come to life again, would not the necessary result be that everything at last would be dead, and nothing alive? For if living things were generated from other sources than death, and were to die, the result is inevitable that all things would be consumed by death. Is it not so?

It is indeed, I think, Socrates, said Cebes; I think that what you say is perfectly true.

Yes, Cebes, he said, I think it is certainly so. We are not misled into this conclusion. The dead do come to life again, and the living are generated from them, and the souls of the dead exist; and with the souls of the good it is well, and with the souls of the evil it is evil.

And besides, Socrates, rejoined Cebes, if the doctrine which you are fond of stating, that our learning is only a process of recollection, be true, then I suppose we must have learned at some former time what we recollect now. And that would be impossible unless our souls had existed somewhere before they came into this human form. So that is another reason for believing the soul immortal.

But, Cebes, interrupted Simmias, what are the proofs of that? Recall them to me; I am not very clear about them at present.

One argument, answered Cebes, and the strongest of all, is that if you question men about anything in the right way, they will answer you correctly of themselves. But they would not have been able to do that unless they had had within themselves knowledge and right reason. Again, show them such things as geometrical diagrams, and the proof of the doctrine is complete.*

And if that does not convince you, Simmias, said Socrates, look at the matter in another way and see if you agree then. You have doubts, I know, how what is called knowledge can be recollection.

Nay, replied Simmias, I do not doubt. But I want to recollect the argument about recollection. What Cebes undertook to explain has nearly brought your theory back to me and convinced me. But I am nonetheless ready to hear you undertake to explain it.

In this way, he returned. We are agreed, I suppose, that if a man remembers anything, he must have known it at some previous time.

---

*For an example of this see Meno 82a–86b.

Certainly, he said.

And are we agreed that when knowledge comes in the following way, it is recollection? When a man has seen or heard anything, or has perceived it by some other sense, and then knows not that thing only, but has also in his mind an impression of some other thing, of which the knowledge is quite different, are we not right in saying that he remembers the thing of which he has an impression in his mind?

What do you mean?

I mean this. The knowledge of a man is different from the knowledge of a lyre, is it not?

Certainly.

And you know that when lovers see a lyre, or a garment, or anything that their favorites are wont to use, they have this feeling. They know the lyre, and in their mind they receive the image of the youth whose the lyre was. That is recollection. For instance, someone seeing Simmias often is reminded of Cebes; and there are endless examples of the same thing.

Indeed there are, said Simmias.

Is not that a kind of recollection, he said; and more especially when a man has this feeling with reference to things which the lapse of time and inattention have made him forget?

Yes, certainly, he replied.

Well, he went on, is it possible to recollect a man on seeing the picture of a horse, or the picture of a lyre? Or to recall Simmias on seeing a picture of Cebes?

Certainly.

And it is possible to recollect Simmias himself on seeing a picture of Simmias?

No doubt, he said.

Then in all these cases there is recollection caused by similar objects, and also by dissimilar objects?

There is.

But when a man has a recollection caused by similar objects, will he not have a further feeling and consider whether the likeness to that which he recollects is defective in any way or not?

He will, he said.

Now see if this is true, he went on. Do we not believe in the existence of equality—not the equality of pieces of wood or of stones, but something beyond that—equality in the abstract? Shall we say that there is such a thing, or not?

Yes indeed, said Simmias, most empathically we will.

And do we know what this abstract equality is?

Certainly, he replied.

Where did we get the knowledge of it? Was it not from seeing the equal pieces of wood, and stones, and the like, which we were speaking of just now? Did we not form from them the idea of abstract equality, which is different from them? Or do you think that it is not different? Consider the question in this way. Do not equal pieces of wood and stones appear to us sometimes equal and sometimes unequal, though in fact they remain the same all the time?

Certainly they do.

But did absolute equals ever seem to you to be unequal, or abstract equality to be inequality?

No, never, Socrates.

Then equal things, he said, are not the same as abstract equality?

No, certainly not, Socrates.

Yet it was from these equal things, he said, which are different from abstract equality, that you have conceived and got your knowledge of abstract equality?

That is quite true, he replied.

And that whether it is like them or unlike them?

Certainly.

But that makes no difference, he said. As long as the sight of one thing brings another thing to your mind, there must be recollection, whether or no the two things are like.

That is so.

Well then, said he, do the equal pieces of wood, and other similar equal things, of which we have been speaking, affect us at all this way? Do they seem to us to be equal, in the way that abstract equality is equal? Do they come short of being like abstract equality, or not?

Indeed, they come very short of it, he replied.

Are we agreed about this? A man sees something and thinks to himself, "This thing that I see aims at being like some other thing, but it comes short and cannot be like that other thing: it is inferior"; must not the man who thinks that have known at some previous time that other thing, which he says that it resembles, and to which it is inferior?

He must.

Well, have we ourselves had the same sort of feeling with reference to equal things, and to abstract equality?

Yes, certainly.

Then we must have had knowledge of equality before we first saw equal things, and perceived that they all strive to be like equality, and all come short of it.

That is so.

And we are agreed also that we have not, nor could we have, obtained the idea of equality except from sight or touch or some other sense; the same is true of all the senses.

Yes, Socrates, for the purposes of the argument that is so.

At any rate, it is by the senses that we must perceive that all sensible objects strive to resemble absolute equality, and are inferior to it. Is not that so?

Yes.

Then before we began to see, and to hear, and to use the other senses, we must have received the knowledge of the nature of abstract and real equality; otherwise we could not have compared equal sensible objects with abstract equality, and seen that the former in all cases strive to be like the latter, though they are always inferior to it?

That is the necessary consequence of what we have been saying, Socrates.

Did we not see, and hear, and possess the other senses as soon as we were born?

Yes, certainly.

And we must have received the knowledge of abstract equality before we had these senses?

Yes.

Then, it seems, we must have received that knowledge before we were born?

It does.

Now if we received this knowledge before our birth, and were born with it, we knew, both before and at the moment of our birth, not only the equal, and the greater, and the less, but also everything of the same kind, did we not? Our present reasoning does not refer only to equality. It refers just as much to absolute good, and absolute beauty, and absolute justice, and absolute holiness; in short, I repeat, to everything which we mark with the name of the real, in the questions and answers of our dialectic. So we must have received our knowledge of all realities before we were born.

That is so.

And we must always be born with this knowledge, and must always retain it throughout life, if we have not each time forgotten it, after having received it. For to know means to receive and retain knowledge, and not to have lost it. Do not we mean by forgetting, the loss of knowledge, Simmias?

Yes, certainly, Socrates, he said.

But, I suppose, if it be the case that we lost at birth the knowledge which we received before we were born, and then afterward, by using our senses on the objects of sense, recovered the knowledge which we had previously possessed, then what we call learning is the recovering of knowledge which is already ours. And are we not right in calling that recollection?

Certainly.

For we have found it possible to perceive a thing by sight, or hearing, or any other sense, and thence to form a notion of some other thing, like or unlike, which had been forgotten, but with which this thing was associated. And therefore, I say, one of two things must be true. Either we are all born with this knowledge and retain it all our life; or, after birth, those whom we say are learning are only recollecting, and our knowledge is recollection.

Yes indeed, that is undoubtedly true, Socrates.

Then which do you choose, Simmias? Are we born with knowledge or do we recollect the things of which we have received knowledge before our birth?

I cannot say at present, Socrates.

Well, have you an opinion about this question? Can a man who knows give an account of what he knows, or not? What do you think about that?

Yes, of course he can, Socrates.

And do you think that everyone can give an account of the ideas of which we have been speaking?

I wish I did, indeed, said Simmias, but I am very much afraid that by this time tomorrow there will no longer be any man living able to do so as it should be done.

Then, Simmias, he said, you do not think that all men know these things?

Certainly not.

Then they recollect what they once learned?

Necessarily.

And when did our souls gain this knowledge? It cannot have been after we were born men.

No, certainly not.

Then it was before?

Yes.

Then, Simmias, our souls existed formerly, apart from our bodies, and possessed intelligence before they came into man's shape.

Unless we receive this knowledge at the moment of birth, Socrates. That time still remains.

Well, my friend, and at what other time do we lose it? We agreed just now that we are not born with it; do we lose it at the same moment that we gain it, or can you suggest any other time?

I cannot, Socrates. I did not see that I was talking nonsense.

Then, Simmias, he said, is not this the truth? If, as we are forever re-peating, beauty, and good, and the other ideas really exist, and if we refer all the objects of sensible perception to these ideas which were formerly ours, and which we find to be ours still, and compare sensible objects with them, then, just as they exist, our souls must have existed before ever we were born. But if they do not exist, then our reasoning will have been thrown away. Is it so? If these ideas exist, does it not at once follow that our souls must have existed before we were born, and if they do not exist, then neither did our souls?

Admirably put, Socrates, said Simmias. I think that the necessity is the same for the one as for the other. The reasoning has reached a place of safety in the common proof of the existence of our souls before we were born and of the existence of the ideas of which you spoke. Nothing is so evidence to me as that beauty, and good, and other ideas which you spoke of just now have a very real existence indeed. Your proof is quite sufficient for me.

But what of Cebes? said Socrates. I must convince Cebes too.

I think that he is satisfied, said Simmias, though he is the most skepti-cal of men in argument. But I think that he is perfectly convinced that our souls existed before we were born.

But I do not think myself, Socrates, he continued, that you have proved that the soul will continue to exist when we are dead. The common fear which Cebes spoke of, that she [the soul] may be scattered to the winds at death, and that death may be the end of her existence, still stands in the way. Assuming that the soul is generated and comes together from some other elements, and exists before she ever enters the human body, why should she not come to an end and be destroyed, after she has entered into the body, when she is released from it?

You are right, Simmias, said Cebes. I think that only half the required proof has been given. It has been shown that our souls existed before we were born; but it must also be shown that our souls will continue to exist after we are dead, no less than that they existed before we were born, if the proof is to be complete.

That has been shown already, Simmias and Cebes, said Socrates, if you will combine this reasoning with our previous conclusion, that all life is generated from death. For if the soul exists in a previous state and if, when she comes into life and is born, she can only be born from death, and from a state of death, must she not exist after death too, since she has to be born again? So the point which you speak of has been already proved.

Still I think that you and Simmias would be glad to discuss this ques-tion further. Like children, you are afraid that the wind will really blow the soul away and disperse her when she leaves the body, especially if a man happens to die in a storm and not in a calm.

Cebes laughed and said, Try and convince us as if we were afraid, Socrates; or rather, do not think that we are afraid ourselves. Perhaps there is a child within us who has these fears. Let us try and persuade him not to be afraid of death, as if it were a bugbear.

You must charm him every day, until you have charmed him away, said Socrates.

And where shall we find a good charmer, Socrates, he asked, now that you are leaving us?

Hellas is a large country, Cebes, he replied, and good men may doubtless be found in it; and the nations of the Barbarians are many. You must search them all through for such a charmer, sparing neither money nor labor; for there is nothing on which you could spend money more profitably. And you must search for him among yourselves too, for you will hardly find a better charmer than yourselves.

That shall be done, said Cebes. But let us return to the point where we left off, if you will.

Yes, I will: why not?

Very good, he replied.

Well, said Socrates, must we not ask ourselves this question? What kind of thing is liable to suffer dispersion, and for what kind of thing have we to fear dispersion? And then we must see whether the soul belongs to that kind or not, and be confident or afraid about our own souls accordingly.

That is true, he answered.

Now is it not the compound and composite which is naturally liable to be dissolved in the same way in which it was compounded? And is not what is uncompounded alone not liable to dissolution, if anything is not?

I think that that is so, said Cebes.

And what always remains in the same state and unchanging is most likely to be uncompounded, and what is always changing and never the same is most likely to be compounded, I suppose?

Yes, I think so.

Now let us return to what we were speaking of before in the discussion, he said. Does the being, which in our dialectic we define as meaning absolute existence, remain always in exactly the same state, or does it change? Do absolute equality, absolute beauty, and every other absolute existence, admit of any change at all? Or does absolute existence in each case, being essentially uniform, remain the same and unchanging, and never in any case admit of any sort or kind of change whatsoever?

It must remain the same and unchanging, Socrates, said Cebes.

And what of the many beautiful things, such as men, and horses, and garments, and the like, and of all which bears the names of the ideas, whether equal, or beautiful, or anything else? Do they remain the same or is it exactly the opposite with them? In short, do they never remain the same at all, either in themselves or in their relations?

These things, said Cebes, never remain the same.

You can touch them, and see them, and perceive them with the other sense, while you can grasp the unchanging only by the reasoning of the intellect. These latter are invisible and not seen. Is it not so?

That is perfectly true, he said.

Let us assume then, he said, if you will, that there are two kinds of existence, the one visible, the other invisible.

Yes, he said.

And the invisible is unchanging, while the visible is always changing.

Yes, he said again.

Are not we men made up of body and soul?

There is nothing else, he replied.

And which of these kinds of existence should we say that the body is most like, and most akin to?

The visible, he replied; that is quite obvious.

And the soul? Is that visible or invisible?

It is invisible to man, Socrates, he said.

But we mean by visible and invisible, visible and invisible to man; do we not?

Yes; that is what we mean.

Then what do we say of the soul? Is it visible or not visible?

It is not visible.

Then is it invisible?

Yes.

Then the soul is more like the invisible than the body; and the body is like the visible.

That is necessarily so, Socrates.

Have we not also said that, when the soul employs the body in any inquiry, and makes use of sight, or hearing, or any other sense—for inquiry with the body means inquiry with the senses—she is dragged away by it to the things which never remain the same, and wanders about blindly, and becomes confused and dizzy, like a drunken man, from dealing with things that are ever changing?

Certainly.

But when she investigates any question by herself, she goes away to the pure, and eternal, and immortal, and unchangeable, to which she is akin, and so she comes to be ever with it, as soon as she is by herself, and can be so; and then she rests from her wanderings and dwells with it unchangingly, for she is dealing with what is unchanging. And is not this state of the soul called wisdom?

Indeed, Socrates, you speak well and truly, he replied.

Which kind of existence do you think from our former and our present arguments that the soul is more like and more akin to?

I think, Socrates, he replied, that after this inquiry the very dullest man would agree that the soul is infinitely more like the unchangeable than the changeable.

And the body?

That is like the changeable.

Consider the matter in yet another way. When the soul and the body are united, nature ordains the one to be a slave and to be ruled, and the other to be master and to rule. Tell me once again, which do you think is like the divine, and which is like the mortal? Do you not think that the divine naturally rules and has authority, and that the mortal naturally is ruled and is a slave?

I do.

Then which is the soul like?

That is quite plain, Socrates. The soul is like the divine, and the body is like the mortal.

Now tell me, Cebes, is the result of all that we have said that the soul is most like the divine, and the immortal, and the intelligible, and the uniform, and the indissoluble, and the unchangeable; while the body is most like the human, and the mortal, and the unintelligible, and the multiform, and the dissoluble, and the changeable? Have we any other argument to show that this is not so, my dear Cebes?

We have not.

Then if this is so, is it not the nature of the body to be dissolved quickly, and of the soul to be wholly or very nearly indissoluble?

Certainly.

You observe, he said, that after a man is dead, the visible part of him, his body, which lies in the visible world and which we call the corpse, which is subject to dissolution and decomposition, is not dissolved and decomposed at once? It remains as it was for a considerable time, and even for a long time, if a man dies with his body in good condition and in the vigor of life. And when the body falls in and is embalmed, like the mummies of Egypt, it remains nearly entire for an immense time. And should it decay, yet some parts of it, such as the bones and muscles, may almost be said to be immortal. Is it not so?

Yes.

And shall we believe that the soul, which is invisible, and which goes hence to a place that is like herself, glorious, and pure, and invisible, to Hades, which is rightly called the unseen world, to dwell with the good and wise God, whither, if it be the will of God, my soul too must shortly go—shall we believe that the soul, whose nature is so glorious, and pure, and invisible, is blown away by the winds and perishes as soon as she leaves the body, as the world says? Nay, dear Cebes and Simmias, it is not so. I will tell you what happens to a soul which is pure at her departure, and which in her life has had no intercourse that she could avoid with the body, and so draws after her, when she dies, no taint of the body, but has shunned it, and gathered herself into herself, for such has been her constant study—and that only means that she has loved wisdom rightly, and has truly practiced how to die. Is not this the practice of death?

Yes, certainly.

Does not the soul, which is in that state, go away to the invisible that is like herself, and to the divine, and the immortal, and the wise, where she is released from error, and folly, and fear, and fierce passions, and all the other evils that fall to the lot of men, and is happy, and for the rest of time lives in very truth with the gods, as they say that the initiated do? Shall we affirm this, Cebes?

Yes, certainly, said Cebes.

But if she be defiled and impure when she leaves the body, from being ever with it, and serving it and loving it, and from being besotted by it and by its desires and pleasures, so that she thinks nothing true but what is bodily and can be touched, and seen, and eaten, and drunk, and used for men's lusts; if she has learned to hate, and tremble at, and fly from what is dark and invisible to the eye, and intelligible and apprehended by philosophy—do you think that a soul which is in that state will be pure and without alloy at her departure?

No, indeed, he replied.

She is penetrated, I suppose, by the corporeal, which the unceasing intercourse and company and care of the body has made a part of her nature.

Yes.

And, my dear friend, the corporeal must be burdensome, and heavy, and earthy, and visible; and it is by this that such a soul is weighed down and dragged back to the visible world, because she is afraid of the invisible world of Hades, and haunts, it is said, the graves and tombs, where shadowy forms of souls have been seen, which are the phantoms of souls which were impure at their release and still cling to the visible; which is the reason why they are seen.

That is likely enough, Socrates.

That is likely, certainly, Cebes; and these are not the souls of the good, but of the evil, which are compelled to wander in such places as a punishment for the wicked lives that they have lived; and their wanderings continue until, from the desire for the corporeal that clings to them, they are again imprisoned in a body.

And, he continued, they are imprisoned, probably, in the bodies of animals with habits similar to the habits which were theirs in their lifetime.

What do you mean by that, Socrates?

I mean that men who have practiced unbridled gluttony, and wantonness, and drunkenness probably enter the bodies of asses and suchlike animals. Do you not think so?

Certainly that is very likely.

And those who have chosen injustice, and tyranny, and robbery enter the bodies of wolves, and hawks, and kites. Where else should we say that such souls go?

No doubt, said Cebes, they go into such animals.

In short, it is quite plain, he said, whither each soul goes; each enters an animal with habits like its own.

Certainly, he replied, that is so.

And of these, he said, the happiest, who go to the best place, are those who have practiced the popular and social virtues which are called temperance and justice, and which come from habit and practice, without philosophy or reason.

And why are they the happiest?

Because it is probable that they return into a mild and social nature like their own, such as that of bees, or wasps, or ants; or, it may be, into the bodies of men, and that from them are made worthy citizens.

Very likely.

But none but the philosopher or the lover of knowledge, who is wholly pure when he goes hence, is permitted to go to the race of the gods; and therefore, my friends, Simmias and Cebes, the true philosopher is temperate and refrains from all the pleasures of the body, and does not give himself up to them. It is not squandering his substance and poverty that he fears, as the multitude and the lovers of wealth do; nor again does he dread the dishonor and disgrace of wickedness, like the lovers of power and honor. It is not for these reasons that he is temperate.

No, it would be unseemly in him if he were, Socrates, said Cebes.

Indeed it would, he replied, and therefore all those who have any care for their souls, and who do not spend their lives in forming and molding their bodies, bid farewell to such persons, and do not walk in their ways, thinking that they know not whither they are going. They themselves turn and follow whithersoever philosophy leads them, for they believe that they ought not to resist philosophy, or its deliverance and purification.

How, Socrates?

I will tell you, he replied. The lovers of knowledge know that when philosophy receives the soul, she is fast bound in the body, and fastened to it; she is unable to contemplate what is, by herself, or except through the bars of her prison house, the body; and she is wallowing in utter ignorance. And philosophy sees that the dreadful thing about the imprisonment is that it is caused by lust, and that the captive herself is an accomplice in her own captivity. The lovers of knowledge, I repeat, know that philosophy takes the soul when she is in this condition, and gently encourages her, and strives to release her from her captivity, showing her that the perceptions of the eye, and the ear, and the other senses are full of deceit, and persuading her to stand aloof from the senses and to use them only when she must, and exhorting her to rally and gather herself together, and to trust only to herself and to the real existence which she of her own self apprehends, and to believe that nothing which is subject to change, and which she perceives by other faculties, has any truth, for such things are visible and sensible, while what she herself sees is apprehended by reason and invisible. The soul of the true philosopher thinks that it would be wrong to resist this deliverance from captivity, and therefore she holds aloof, so far as she can, from pleasure, and desire, and pain, and fear; for she reckons that when a man has vehement pleasure, or fear, or pain, or desire, he suffers from them not merely the evils which might be expected, such as sickness or some loss arising from the indulgence of his desires; he suffers what is the greatest and last of evils, and does not take it into account.

What do you mean, Socrates? asked Cebes.

I mean that when the soul of any man feels vehement pleasure or pain, she is forced at the same time to think that the object, whatever it be, of these sensations is the most distinct and truest, when it is not. Such objects are chiefly visible ones, are they not?

They are.

And is it not in this state that the soul is most completely in bondage to the body?

■ ■ ■

Questions for Further Exploration:

■ What is a "real philosopher" in Plato's view? In the search for wisdom is the body (e.g., sight and hearing) a hindrance?

■ According to Plato, what sort of a reality is a "soul"? What sorts of beings have souls? What is the soul in relation to life and death? Is the soul immortal? If the soul is immortal, does it possess power and wisdom after the person dies?

■ What arguments are offered for the immortality of the soul?

■ In contrast with soul-lovers who seek wisdom and virtue, Plato suggests that body-lovers seek pleasure, wealth, or honor. What are the implications of Plato's veneration of the soul and denigration of the body for human relations with the earth?

■ Free-write your view on the soul. Compare and contrast your view and reasoning with Plato's.

De Anima

Aristotle

On the Soul
Book II

1. Let the foregoing suffice as our account of the views concerning the soul which have been handed on by our predecessors; let us now make as it were a completely fresh start, endeavouring to answer the question, What is soul? i.e. to formulate the most general possible account of it.

We say that substance is one kind of what is, and that in several senses: in the sense of matter or that which in itself is not a this, and in the sense of form or essence, which is that precisely in virtue of which a thing is called a this, and thirdly in the sense of that which is compounded of both. Now matter is potentiality, form actuality; and actuality is of two kinds, one as e.g. knowledge, the other as e.g. reflecting.

Among substances are by general consent reckoned bodies and especially natural bodies; for they are the principles of all other bodies. Of natural bodies some have life in them, others not; by life we mean self-nutrition and growth and decay. It follows that every natural body which has life in it is a substance in the sense of a composite.

Now given that there are bodies of such and such a kind, viz. having life, the soul cannot be a body; for the body is the subject or matter, not what is attributed to it. Hence the soul must be a substance in the sense of the form of a natural body having life potentially within it. But substance is actuality, and thus soul is the actuality of a body as above characterized. Now there are two kinds of actuality corresponding to knowledge and to reflecting. It is obvious that the soul is an actuality like knowledge; for both sleeping and waking presuppose the existence of soul, and of these waking corresponds to reflecting, sleeping to knowledge possessed but not employed, and knowledge of something is temporally prior.

That is why the soul is an actuality of the first kind of a natural body having life potentially in it. The body so described is a body which is organized. The parts of plants in spite of their extreme simplicity are organs; e.g. the leaf serves to shelter the pericarp, the pericarp to shelter the fruit, while the roots of plants are analogous to the mouth of animals, both serving for the absorption of food. If, then, we have to give a general formula applicable to all kinds of soul, we must describe it as an actuality of the first kind of a natural organized body. That is why we can dismiss as unnecessary the question whether the soul and the body are one: it is as though we were to ask whether the wax and its shape are one, or generally the matter of a thing and that of which it is the matter. Unity has many senses (as many as "is" has), but the proper one is that of actuality.

We have now given a general answer to the question, What is soul? It is substance in the sense which corresponds to the account of a thing. That means that it is what it is to be for a body of the character just assigned. Suppose that a tool, e.g. an axe, were a natural body, then being an axe would have been its essence, and so its soul; if this disappeared from it, it would have ceased to be an axe, except in name. As it is, it is an axe; for it is not of a body of that sort that what it is to be, i.e. its account, is a soul, but of a natural body of a particular kind, viz. one having in itself the power of setting itself in movement and arresting itself. Next, apply this doctrine in the case of the parts of the living body. Suppose that the eye were an animal—sight would have been its soul, for sight is the substance of the eye which corresponds to the account, the eye being merely the matter of seeing; when seeing is removed the eye is no longer an eye, except in name—no more than the eye of a statue or of a painted figure. We must now extend our consideration from the parts to the whole living body; for what the part is to the part, that the whole faculty of sense is to the whole sensitive body as such.

We must not understand by that which is potentially capable of living what has lost the soul it had, but only what still retains it; but seeds and fruits are bodies which are potentially of that sort. Consequently, while waking is actuality in a sense corresponding to the cutting and the seeing, the soul is actuality in the sense corresponding to sight and the power in the tool; the body corresponds to what is in potentiality; as the pupil *plus* the power of sight constitutes the eye, so the soul *plus* the body constitutes the animal.

From this it is clear that the soul is inseparable from its body, or at any rate that certain parts of it are (if it has parts)—for the actuality of some of them is the actuality of the parts themselves. Yet some may be separable because they are not the actualities of any body at all. Further, we have no light on the problem whether the soul may not be the actuality of its body in the sense in which the sailor is the actuality of the ship.

This must suffice as our sketch or outline of the nature of soul.

2. Since what is clear and more familiar in account emerges from what in itself is confused but more observable by us, we must reconsider our results from this point of view. For it is not enough for a definitional account to express as most now do the mere fact; it must include and exhibit the cause also. At present definitions are given in a form analogous to the conclusion of an argument; e.g. What is squaring? The construction of an equilateral rectangle equal to a given oblong rectangle. Such a definition is in form equivalent to a conclusion. One that tells us that squaring is the discovery of a mean proportional discloses the cause of what is defined.

We resume our inquiry from a fresh starting-point by calling attention to the fact that what has soul in it differs from what has not in that the former displays life. Now this word has more than one sense, and provided any one alone of these is found in a thing we say that thing is living—viz. thinking or perception or local movement and rest, or movement in the sense of nutrition, decay and growth. Hence we think of plants also as living, for they are observed to possess in themselves an originative power through which they increase or decrease in all spatial directions; they do not grow up but not down—they grow alike in both, indeed in all, directions; and that holds for everything which is constantly nourished and continues to live, so long as it can absorb nutriment.

This power of self-nutrition can be separated from the other powers mentioned, but not they from it—in mortal beings at least. The fact is obvious in plants; for it is the only psychic power they possess.

This is the originative power the possession of which leads us to speak of things as *living* at all, but it is the possession of sensation that leads us for the first time to speak of living things as *animals;* for even those beings which possess no power of local movement but do possess the power of sensation we call animals and not merely living things.

The primary form of sense is touch, which belongs to all animals. Just as the power of self-nutrition can be separated from touch and sensation generally, so touch can be separated from all other forms of sense. (By the power of self-nutrition we mean that part of the soul which is common to plants and animals: all animals whatsoever are observed to have the sense of touch.) What the explanation of these two facts is, we must discuss later. At present we must confine ourselves to saying that soul is the source of these phenomena and is characterized by them, viz. by the powers of self-nutrition, sensation, thinking, and movement.

Is each of these a soul or a part of a soul? And if a part, a part merely distinguishable by definition or a part distinct in local situation as well? In the case of certain of these powers, the answers to these questions are easy, in the case of others we are puzzled what to say. Just as in the case of plants which when divided are observed to continue to live though separated from one another (thus showing that in *their* case the soul of each individual plant was actually one, potentially many), so we notice a similar result in other varieties of soul, i.e. in insects which have been cut in two; each of the segments possesses both sensation and local movement; and if sensation, necessarily also imagination and appetition; for, where there is sensation, there is also pleasure and pain, and, where these, necessarily also desire.

We have no evidence as yet about thought or the power of reflexion; it seems to be a different kind of soul, differing as what is eternal from what is perishable; it alone is capable of being separated. All the other parts of soul, it is evident from what we have said, are, in spite of certain statements to the contrary, incapable of separate existence though, of course, distinguishable by definition. If opining is distinct from perceiving, to be capable of opining and to be capable of perceiving must be distinct, and so with all the other forms of living above enumerated. Further, some animals possess all these parts of soul, some certain of them only, others one only (this is what enables us to classify animals); the cause must be considered later. A similar arrangement is found also within the field of the senses; some classes of animals have all the senses, some only certain of them, others only one, the most indispensable, touch.

Since the expression "that whereby we live and perceive" has two meanings, just like the expression "that whereby we know"—that may mean either knowledge or the soul, for we can speak of knowing *by* either, and similarly that whereby we are in health may be either health or the body or some part of the body; and since of these knowledge or health is a form, essence, or account, or if we so express it an activity of a recipient matter—knowledge of what is capable of knowing, health of what is capable of being made healthy (for the activity of that which is capable of originating change seems to take place in what is changed or altered); further, since it is the soul by which primarily we live, perceive, and think:—it follows that the soul must be an account and essence, not matter or a subject. For, as we said, the word substance has three meanings—form, matter, and the complex of both—and of these matter is potentiality, form actuality. Since then the complex here is the living thing, the body cannot be the actuality of the soul; it is the soul which is the actuality of a certain kind of body. Hence the rightness of the view that the soul cannot *be* without a body, while it cannot be a body; it is not a body but something relative to a body. That is why it is *in* a body, and a body of a definite kind. It was a mistake, therefore, to do as former thinkers did, merely to fit it into a body without adding a definite specification of the kind or character of that body, although evidently one chance thing will not receive another. It comes about as reason requires: the actuality of any given thing can only be realized in what is already potentially that thing, i.e. in a matter of its own appropriate to it. From all this it is plain that soul is an actuality or account of something that possesses a potentiality of being such.

3. Of the psychic powers above enumerated some kinds of living things, as we have said, possess all, some less than all, others one only. Those we have mentioned are the nutritive, the appetitive, the sensory, the locomotive, and the power of thinking. Plants have none but the first, the nutritive, while another order of living things has this *plus* the sensory. If any order of living things has the sensory, it must also have the appetitive; for appetite is the genus of which desire, passion, and wish are the species; now all animals have one sense at least, viz. touch, and whatever has a sense has the capacity for pleasure and pain and therefore has pleasant and painful objects present to it, and wherever these are present, there is desire, for desire is appetition of what is pleasant. Further, all animals have the sense for food (for touch is the sense for food); the food of all living things consists of what is dry, moist, hot, cold, and these are the qualities apprehended by touch; all other sensible qualities are apprehended by touch only indirectly. Sounds, colours, and odours contribute nothing to nutriment; flavours fall within the field of tangible qualities. Hunger and thirst are forms of desire, hunger a desire for what is dry and hot, thirst a desire for what is cold and moist; flavour is a sort of seasoning added to both. We must later clear up these points, but at present it may be enough to say that all animals that possess the sense of touch have also appetition. The case of imagination is obscure; we must examine it later. Certain kinds of animals possess in addition the power of locomotion, and still others, i.e. man and possibly another order like man or superior to him, the power of thinking and thought. It is now evident that a single definition can be given of soul only in the same sense as one can be given of figure. For, as in that case there is no figure apart from triangle and those that follow in order, so here there is no soul apart from the forms of soul just enumerated. It is true that a common definition can be given for figure which will fit all figures without expressing the peculiar nature of any figure. So here in the case of soul and its specific forms. Hence it is absurd in this and similar cases to look for a common definition which will not express the peculiar nature of anything that is and will not apply to the approrate indivisible species, while at the same time omitting to look for an account which will. The cases of figure and soul are exactly parallel; for the particulars subsumed under the common name in both cases—figures and living

beings—constitute a series, each successive term of which potentially contains its predecessor, e.g. the square the triangle, the sensory power the self-nutritive. Hence we must ask in the case of each order of living things, What is its soul, i.e. What is the soul of plant, man, beast? Why the terms are related in this serial way must form the subject of examination. For the power of perception is never found apart from the power of self-nutrition, while—in plants—the latter is found isolated from the former. Again, no sense is found apart from that of touch, while touch *is* found by itself; many animals have neither sight, hearing, nor smell. Again, among living things that possess sense some have the power of locomotion, some not. Lastly, certain living beings—a small minority—possess calculation and thought, for (among mortal beings) those which possess calculation have all the other powers above mentioned, while the converse does not hold—indeed some live by imagination alone, while others have not even imagination. Reflective thought presents a different problem.

It is evident that the way to give the most adequate definition of soul is to seek in the case of *each* of its forms for the most appropriate definition.

■ ■ ■

Book III

■ ■ ■

4. Turning now to the part of the soul with which the soul knows and (whether this is separable from the others in definition only, or spatially as well) we have to inquire what differentiates this part, and how thinking can take place.

If thinking is like perceiving, it must be either a process in which the soul is acted upon by what is capable of being thought, or a process different from but analogous to that. The thinking part of the soul must therefore be, while impassible, capable of receiving the form of an object; that is, must be potentially identical in character with its object without being the object. Thought must be related to what is thinkable, as sense is to what is sensible.

Therefore, since everything is a possible object of thought, mind in order, as Anaxagoras says, to dominate, that is, to know, must be pure from all admixture; for the co-presence of what is alien to its nature is a hindrance and a block: it follows that it can have no nature of its own, other than that of having a certain capacity. Thus that in the soul which is called thought (by thought I mean that whereby the soul thinks and judges) is, before it thinks, not actually any real thing. For this reason it cannot reasonably be regarded as blended with the body: if so, it would acquire some quality, e.g. warmth or cold, or even have an organ like the sensitive faculty: as it is, it has none. It was a good idea to call the soul "the place of forms," though this description holds only of the thinking soul, and even this is the forms only potentially, not actually.

Observation of the sense-organs and their employment reveals a distinction between the impassibility of the sensitive faculty and that of the faculty of thought. After strong stimulation of a sense we are less able to exercise it than before, as e.g. in the case of a loud sound we cannot hear easily immediately after, or in the case of a bright colour or a powerful odour we cannot see or smell, but in the case of thought thinking about an object that is highly thinkable renders it more and not less able afterwards to think of objects that are less thinkable: the reason is that while the faculty of sensation is dependent upon the body, thought is separable from it.

When thought has become each thing in the way in which a man who actually knows is said to do so (this happens when he is now able to exercise the power on his own initiative), its condition is still one of potentiality, but in a different sense from the potentiality which preceded the acquisition of knowledge by learning or discovery; and thought is then able to think of itself.

Since we can distinguish between a magnitude and what it is to be a magnitude, and between water and what it is to be water, and so in many other cases (though not in all; for in certain cases the thing and its form are identical), flesh and what it is to be flesh are discriminated either by different faculties, or by the same faculty in two different states; for flesh necessarily involves matter and is like what is snub-nosed, a *this* in a *this*. Now it is by means of the sensitive faculty that we discriminate the hot and the cold, i.e. the factors which combined in a certain ratio constitute flesh: the essential character of flesh is apprehended by something different either wholly separate from the sensitive faculty or related to it as a bent line to the same line when it has been straightened out.

Again in the case of abstract objects what is straight is analogous to what is snub-nosed; for it necessarily implies a continuum: its constitutive essence is different, if we may distinguish between straightness and what is straight: let us take it to be twoness. It must be apprehended, therefore, by a different power or by the same power in a different state. To sum up, in so far as the realities it knows are capable of being separated from their matter, so it is also with the powers of thought.

The problem might be suggested: if thinking is a passive affection, then if thought is simple and impassible and has nothing in common with anything else, as Anaxagoras says, how can it come to think at all? For interaction between two factors is held to require a precedent community of nature between the factors. Again it might be asked, is thought a possible object of thought to itself? For if thought is thinkable *per se* and what is thinkable is in kind one and the same, then either thought will belong to everything, or it will contain some element common to it with all other realities which makes them all thinkable.

Have not we already disposed of the difficulty about interaction involving a common element, when we said that thought is in a sense potentially whatever is thinkable, though actually it is nothing until it has thought? What it thinks must be in it just as characters may be said to be on a writing-table on which as yet nothing actually stands written: this is exactly what happens with thought.

Thought is itself thinkable in exactly the same way as its objects are. For in the case of objects which involve no matter, what thinks and what is thought are identical; for speculative knowledge and its object are identical. (Why thought is not always thinking we must consider later.) In the case of those which contain matter each of the objects of thought is only potentially present. It follows that while they will not have thought in them (for thought is a potentiality of them only in so far as they are capable of being disengaged from matter) thought may yet be thinkable.

5. Since in every class of things, as in nature as a whole, we find two factors involved, a matter which is potentially all the particulars included in the class, a cause which is productive in the sense that it makes them all (the latter standing to the former, as e.g. an art to its material), these distinct elements must likewise be found within the soul.

And in fact thought, as we have described it, is what it is by virtue of becoming all things, while there is another which is what it is by virtue of making all things: this is a sort of positive state like light; for in a sense light makes potential colours into actual colours.

Thought in this sense of it is separable, impassible, unmixed, since it is in its essential nature activity (for always the active is superior to the passive factor, the originating force to the matter).

Actual knowledge is identical with its object: in the individual, potential knowledge is in time prior to actual knowledge, but absolutely it is not prior even in time. It does not sometimes think and sometimes not think. When separated it is alone just what it is, and this above is immortal and eternal (we do not remember because, while this is impossible, passive thought is perishable); and without this nothing thinks.

■ ■ ■

Questions for Further Exploration:

- How does Aristotle conceptualize the "soul"? What aspect of a "substance" is the soul? How do the concepts of "potentiality" and "actuality" help explain the soul? What role does the soul play in relation to life and death? Is the soul immortal?

- According to Aristotle's pluralist classification, what life forms have "souls" and what characterizes each one?

- Compare and contrast Plato's and Aristotle's views of the "soul." Which view is closest to your view, and why?

- What are the implications of Aristotle's unification of body and soul for human relations with the earth? Are people more likely to respect plants and animals if they are understood to have souls?

Summa Theologica

First Part

Thomas Aquinas

Third Article [I, Q. 2, Art. 3]

Whether God Exists? God does Not exist ?

Objection 1: It seems that God does not exist; because if one of two contraries be infinite, the other would be altogether destroyed. But the word "God" means that He is infinite goodness. If, therefore, God existed, there would be no evil discoverable; but there is evil in the world. Therefore God does not exist.

Obj. 2: Further, it is superfluous to suppose that what can be accounted for by a few principles has been produced by many. But it seems that everything we see in the world can be accounted for by other principles, supposing God did not exist. For all natural things can be reduced to one principle which is nature; and all voluntary things can be reduced to one principle which is human reason, or will. Therefore there is no need to suppose God's existence.

On the contrary, It is said in the person of God: "I am Who am." (Ex. 3:14) God Does Exist 5

I answer that, The existence of God can be proved in five ways.

The first and more manifest way is the argument from motion. It is certain, and evident to our senses, that in the world some things are in motion. Now whatever is in motion is put in motion by another, for nothing can be in motion except it is in potentiality to that towards which it is in motion; whereas a thing moves inasmuch as it is in act. For motion is nothing else than the reduction of something from potentiality to actuality. But nothing can be reduced from potentiality to actuality, except by something in a state of actuality. Thus that which is actually hot, as fire, makes wood, which is potentially hot, to be actually hot, and thereby moves and changes it. Now it is not possible that the same thing should be at once in actuality and potentiality in the same respect, but only in different respects. For what is actually

149

hot cannot simultaneously be potentially hot; but it is simultaneously potentially cold. It is therefore impossible that in the same respect and in the same way a thing should be both mover and moved, i.e. that it should move itself. Therefore, whatever is in motion must be put in motion by another. If that by which it is put in motion be itself put in motion, then this also must needs be put in motion by another, and that by another again. But this cannot go on to infinity, because then there would be no first mover, and, consequently, no other mover; seeing that subsequent movers move only inasmuch as they are put in motion by the first mover; as the staff moves only because it is put in motion by the hand. Therefore it is necessary to arrive at a first mover, put in motion by no other; and this everyone understand to be God.

The second way is from the nature of the efficient cause. In the world of sense we find there is an order of efficient causes. There is no case known (neither is it, indeed, possible) in which a thing is found to be the efficient cause of itself; for so it would be prior to itself, which is impossible. Now in efficient causes it is not possible to go on to infinity, because in all efficient causes following in order, the first is the cause of the intermediate cause, and the intermediate is the cause of the ultimate cause, whether the intermediate cause be several, or only one. Now to take away the cause is to take away the effect. Therefore, if there be no first cause among efficient causes, there will be no ultimate, nor any intermediate cause. But if in efficient causes it is possible to go on to infinity, there will be no first efficient cause, neither will there be an ultimate effect, nor any intermediate efficient causes; all of which is plainly false. Therefore it is necessary to admit a first efficient cause, to which everyone gives the name of God.

The third way is taken from possibility and necessity, and runs thus. We find in nature things that are possible to be and not to be, since they are found to be generated, and to corrupt, and consequently, they are possible to be and not to be. But it is impossible for these always to exist, for that which is possible not to be at some time is not. Therefore, if everything is possible not to be, then at one time there could have been nothing in existence. Now if this were true, even now there would be nothing in existence, because that which does not exist only begins to exist by something already existing. Therefore, if at one time nothing was in existence, it would have been impossible for anything to have begun to exist; and thus even now nothing would be in existence—which is absurd. Therefore, not all beings are merely possible, but there must exist something the existence of which is necessary. But every necessary thing either has its necessity caused by another, or not. Now it is impossible to go on to infinity in necessary things which have their necessity caused by another, as has been already proved in regard to efficient causes. Therefore we cannot but postulate the existence of some being having of itself its own necessity, and not receiving it from another, but rather causing in others their necessity. This all men speak of as God.

The fourth way is taken from the gradation to be found in things. Among beings there are some more and some less good, true, noble and the like. But _more_ and _less_ are predicated of different things, according as they resemble in their different ways something which is the maximum, as a thing is said to be hotter according as it more nearly resembles that which is hottest; so that there is something which is truest, something best, something noblest and, consequently, something which is uttermost being; for those things that are greatest in truth are greatest in being, as it is written in _Metaph._ ii. Now the maximum in any genus is the cause of all in that genus; as fire, which is the maximum heat, is the cause of all hot things. Therefore there must also be something which is to all beings the cause of their being, goodness, and every other perfection; and this we call God.

The fifth way is taken from the governance of the world. We see that things which lack intelligence, such as natural bodies, act for an end, and this is evident from their acting always, or nearly always, in the same way, so as to obtain the best result. Hence it is plain that not fortuitously, but designedly, do they achieve their end. Now whatever lacks intelligence cannot move towards an end, unless it be directed by some being endowed with knowledge and intelligence; as the arrow is shot to its mark by the archer. Therefore some intelligent being exists by whom all natural things are directed to their end; and this being we call God.

Reply Obj. 1: As Augustine says (Enchiridion xi): "Since God is the highest good, He would not allow any evil to exist in His works, unless His omnipotence and goodness were such as to bring good even out of evil." This is part of the infinite goodness of God, that He should allow evil to exist, and out of it produce good.

Reply Obj. 2: Since nature works for a determinate end under the direction of a higher agent, whatever is done by nature must needs be traced back to God, as to its first cause. So also whatever is done voluntarily must also be traced back to some higher cause other than human reason or will, since these can change or fail; for all things that are changeable and capable of defect must be traced back to an immovable and self-necessary first principle, as was shown in the body of the Article.

First Article [I, Q. 3, Art. 1]

Whether God Is a Body?

Objection 1: It seems that God is a body. For a body is that which has the three dimensions. But Holy Scripture attributes the three dimensions to God, for it is written: "He is higher than Heaven, and what wilt thou do? He is deeper than Hell, and how wilt thou know? The measure of Him is longer than the earth and broader than the sea" (Job 11:8, 9). Therefore God is a body.

Obj. 2: Further, everything that has figure is a body, since figure is a quality of quantity. But God seems to have figure, for it is written: "Let us make man to our image and likeness" (Gen. 1:26). Now a figure is called an image, according to the text: "Who being the brightness of His glory and the figure," i.e. the image, "of His substance" (Heb. 1:3). Therefore God is a body.

Not A Body ■ ■ ■ 3

On the contrary, It is written in the Gospel of St. John (John 4:24): "God is a spirit."

I answer that, It is absolutely true that God is not a body; and this can be shown in three ways. First, because no body is in motion unless it be put in motion, as is evident from induction. Now it has been already proved (Q. 2, A. 3), that God is the First Mover, and is Himself unmoved. Therefore it is clear that God is not a body. Secondly, because the first being must of necessity be in act, and in no way in potentiality. For although in any single thing that passes from potentiality to actuality, the potentiality is prior in time to the actuality; nevertheless, absolutely speaking, actuality is prior to potentiality; for whatever is in potentiality can be reduced into actuality only by some being in actuality. Now it has been already proved that God is the First Being. It is therefore impossible that in God there should be any potentiality. But every body is in potentiality because the continuous, as such, is divisible to infinity; it is therefore impossible that God should be a body. Thirdly, because God is the most noble of beings. Now it is impossible for a body to be the most noble of beings; for a body must be either animate or inanimate; and an animate body is manifestly nobler than any inanimate body. But an animate body is not animate precisely as body; otherwise all bodies would be animate. Therefore its animation depends upon some other thing, as our body depends for its animation on the soul. Hence that by which a body becomes animated must be nobler than the body. Therefore it is impossible that God should be a body.

■ ■ ■

Seventh Article [I, Q. 3, Art. 7]

Whether God Is Altogether Simple?   Not Simple?

Objection 1: It seems that God is not altogether simple. For whatever is from God must imitate Him. Thus from the first being are all beings;

and from the first good is all good. But in the things which God has made, nothing is altogether simple. Therefore neither is God altogether simple.

Obj. 2: Further, whatever is best must be attributed to God. But with us that which is composite is better than that which is simple; thus, chemical compounds are better than simple elements, and animals than the parts that compose them. Therefore it cannot be said that God is altogether simple.

On the contrary, Augustine says (De Trin. iv, 6,7): "God is truly and absolutely simple."

I answer that, The absolute simplicity of God may be shown in many ways. First, from the previous articles of this question. For there is neither composition of quantitative parts in God, since He is not a body; nor composition of matter and form; nor does His nature differ from His _suppositum_; nor His essence from His existence; neither is there in Him composition of genus and difference, nor of subject and accident. Therefore, it is clear that God is nowise composite, but is altogether simple. Secondly, because every composite is posterior to its component parts, and is dependent on them; but God is the first being, as shown above (Q. 2, A. 3). Thirdly, because every composite has a cause, for things in themselves different cannot unite unless something causes them to unite. But God is uncaused, as shown above (Q. 2, A. 3), since He is the first efficient cause. Fourthly, because in every composite there must be potentiality and actuality; but this does not apply to God; for either one of the parts actuates another, or at least all the parts are potential to the whole. Fifthly, because nothing composite can be predicated of any single one of its parts. And this is evident in a whole made up of dissimilar parts; for no part of a man is a man, nor any of the parts of the foot, a foot. But in wholes made up of similar parts, although something which is predicated of the whole may be predicated of a part (as a part of the air is air, and a part of water, water), nevertheless certain things are predicable of the whole which cannot be predicated of any of the parts; for instance, if the whole volume of water is two cubits, no part of it can be two cubits. Thus in every composite there is something which is not it itself. But, even if this could be said of whatever has a form, viz. that it has something which is not it itself, as in a white object there is something which does not belong to the essence of white; nevertheless in the form itself, there is nothing besides itself. And so, since God is absolute form, or rather absolute being, He can be in no way composite. Hilary implies this argument, when he says (De Trin. vii): "God, Who is strength, is not made up of things that are weak; nor is He Who is light, composed of things that are dim."

■ ■ ■

Questions for Further Exploration:

- How does Aquinas refute the objection that the existence of evil in the world contradicts the existence of an infinitely good God?

- How does he refute the objection that nature and human reason can account for everything we see in the world and hence the existence of God is superfluous?

- What five lines of argument are offered for the existence of God? Which is the best/worst argument in your view?

- How does Aquinas define God? What does this definition imply about humanity's relation to God and to the natural world?

- Consider Aquinas' philosophy in terms of Plato's allegory. From his view, what might each of the symbols (the cave, prisoners, shadows, escapee, outside, the sun, etc.) represent?

- Free-write: Do you believe in God? What kind of relations between humans and the natural world follow from this belief?

The Historical Roots
of Our Ecological Crisis

Lynn White, Jr.

■ ■ ■

Since both our technological and our scientific movements got their start, acquired their character, and achieved world dominance in the Middle Ages, it would seem that we cannot understand their nature or their present impact upon ecology without examining fundamental medieval assumptions and developments.

Medieval View of Man and Nature

Until recently, agriculture has been the chief occupation even in "advanced" societies; hence, any change in methods of tillage has much importance. Early plows, drawn by two oxen, did not normally turn the sod but merely scratched it. Thus, cross-plowing was needed and fields tended to be squarish. In the fairly light soils and semiarid climates of the Near East and Mediterranean, this worked well. But such a plow was inappropriate to the wet climate and often sticky soils of northern Europe. By the latter part of the 7th century after Christ, however, following obscure beginnings, certain northern peasants were using an entirely new kind of plow, equipped with a vertical knife to cut the line of the furrow, a horizontal share to slice under the sod, and a moldboard to turn it over. The friction of this plow with the soil was so great that it normally required not two but eight oxen. It attacked the land with such violence that cross-plowing was not needed, and fields tended to be shaped in long strips.

In the days of the scratch-plow, fields were distributed generally in units capable of supporting a single family. Subsistence farming was the presupposition. But no peasant owned eight oxen: to use the new and more efficient plow, peasants pooled their oxen to form large plow-teams, originally receiving (it would appear) plowed strips in proportion to their contribution. Thus, distribution of land was based no longer on the needs of a family but, rather, on the capacity of a power machine to till the earth. Man's relation to the soil was profoundly changed. Formerly man had been part of nature; now he was the exploiter of nature. Nowhere else in the world did farmers develop any analogous agricultural implement. Is it coincidence that modern technology, with its ruthlessness toward nature, has so largely been produced by descendants of these peasants of northern Europe?

This same exploitive attitude appears slightly before A.D. 830 in Western illustrated calendars. In older calendars the months were shown as passive personifications. The new Frankish calendars, which set the style for the Middle Ages, are very different: they show men coercing the world around them—plowing, harvesting, chopping trees, butchering pigs. Man and nature are two things, and man is master.

These novelties seem to be in harmony with larger intellectual patterns. What people do about their ecology depends on what they think about themselves in relation to things around them. Human ecology is deeply conditioned by beliefs about our nature and destiny—that is, by religion. To Western eyes this is very evident in, say, India or Ceylon. It is equally true of ourselves and of our medieval ancestors.

The victory of Christianity over paganism was the greatest psychic revolution in the history of our culture. It has become fashionable today to say that, for better or worse, we live in the "post-Christian age." Certainly the forms of our thinking and language have largely ceased to be Christian, but to my eye the substance often remains amazingly akin to that of the past. Our daily habits of action, for example, are dominated by an implicit faith in perpetual progress which was unknown either to Greco-Roman antiquity or to the Orient. It is rooted in, and is indefensible apart from, Judeo-Christian theology. The fact that Communists share it merely helps to show what can be demonstrated on many other grounds: that Marxism, like Islam, is a Judeo-Christian heresy. We continue today to live, as we have lived for about 1700 years, very largely in a context of Christian axioms.

What did Christianity tell people about their relations with the environment? While many of the world's mythologies provide stories of creation, Greco-Roman mythology was singularly incoherent in this respect. Like Aristotle, the intellectuals of the ancient West denied that the visible world had a beginning. Indeed, the idea of a beginning was impossible in the framework of their cyclical notion of time. In sharp contrast, Christianity inherited from Judaism not only a concept of time as nonrepetitive and linear but also a striking story of creation. By gradual stages a loving and all-powerful God had created light and darkness, the heavenly bodies, the earth and all its plants, animals, birds, and fishes. Finally, God had created Adam and, as an afterthought, Eve to keep man from being lonely. Man named all the animals, thus establishing his dominance over them. God planned all of this explicitly for man's benefit and rule: no item in the physical creation had any purpose save to serve man's purposes. And, although man's body is made of clay, he is not simply part of nature: he is made in God's image.

Especially in its Western form, Christianity is the most anthropocentric religion the world has seen. As early as the 2nd century both Tertullian and Saint Irenaeus of Lyons were insisting that when God shaped Adam he was foreshadowing the image of the incarnate Christ, the Second Adam. Man shares, in great measure, God's transcendence of nature. Christianity, in absolute contrast to ancient paganism and Asia's religions (except, perhaps, Zorastrianism), not only established a dualism of man and nature but also insisted that it is God's will that man exploit nature for his proper ends.

At the level of the common people this worked out in an interesting way. In Antiquity every tree, every spring, every stream, every hill had its own genius loci, its guardian spirit. These spirits were accessible to men, but were very unlike men; centaurs, fauns, and mermaids show their ambivalence. Before one cut a tree, mined a mountain, or dammed a brook, it was important to placate the spirit in charge of that particular situation, and to keep it placated. By destroying pagan animism, Christianity made it possible to exploit nature in a mood of indifference to the feelings of natural objects.

It is often said that for animism the Church substituted the cult of saints. True; but the cult of saints is functionally quite different from animism. The saint is not in natural objects; he may have special shrines, but his citizenship is in heaven. Moreover, a saint is entirely a man; he can be approached in human terms. In addition to saints, Christianity of course also had angels and demons inherited from Judaism and perhaps, at one remove, from Zorastrianism. But these were all as mobile as the saints themselves. The spirits in natural objects, which formerly had protected nature from man, evaporated. Man's effective monopoly on spirit in this world was confirmed, and the old inhibitions to the exploitation of nature crumbled.

When one speaks in such sweeping terms, a note of caution is in order. Christianity is a complex faith, and its consequences differ in differing contexts. What I have said may well apply to the medieval West, where in fact technology made spectacular advances. But the Greek East, a highly civilized realm of equal Christian devotion, seems to have produced no marked technological innovation after the late 7th century, when Greek fire was invented. The key to the contrast may perhaps be found in a difference in the tonality of piety and thought which students of comparative theology find between the Greek and the Latin Churches. The Greeks believed that sin was intellectual blindness, and that salvation was found in illumination, orthodoxy—that is, clear thinking. The Latins, on the other hand, felt that sin was moral evil, and that salvation was to be found in right conduct. Eastern theology has been intellectualist. Western theology has been voluntarist. The Greek saint contemplates; the Western saint acts. The implications of Christianity for the conquest of nature would emerge more easily in the Western atmosphere.

The Christian dogma of creation, which is found in the first clause of all the Creeds, has another meaning for our comprehension of today's ecologic crisis. By revelation, God had given man the Bible, the Book of Scripture. But since God had made nature, nature also must reveal the divine mentality. The religious study of nature for the better understanding of God was known as natural theology. In the early Church, and always in the Greek East, nature was conceived primarily as a symbolic system through which God speaks to men: the ant is a sermon to sluggards; rising flames are the symbol of the soul's aspiration. The view of nature was essentially artistic rather than scientific. While Byzantium preserved and copied great numbers of ancient Greek scientific texts, science as we conceive it could scarcely flourish in such an ambience.

However, in the Latin West by the early 13th century natural theology was following a very different bent. It was ceasing to be the decoding of the physical symbols of God's communication with man and was becoming the effort to understand God's mind by discovering how his creation operates. The rainbow was no longer simply a symbol of hope first sent to Noah after the Deluge: Robert Grosseteste, Friar Roger Bacon, and Theodoric of Freiberg produced startlingly sophisticated work on the optics of the rainbow, but they did it as a venture in religious understanding. From the 13th century onward, up to and including Leitnitz and Newton, every major scientist, in effect, explained his motivations in religious terms. Indeed, if Galileo had not been so expert an amateur theologian he would have got into far less trouble: the professionals resented his intrusion. And Newton seems to have regarded himself more as a theologian than as a scientist. It was not until the late 18th century that the hypothesis of God became unnecessary to many scientists.

It is often hard for the historian to judge, when men explain why they are doing what they want to do, whether they are offering real reasons or merely culturally acceptable reasons. The consistency with which scientists during the long formative centuries of Western science said that the task and the reward of the scientist was "to think God's thoughts after him" leads one to believe that this was their real motivation. If so, then modern Western science was cast in a matrix of Christian theology. The dynamism of religious devotion shaped by the Judeo-Christian dogma of creation, gave it impetus.

An Alternative Christian View

We would seem to be headed toward conclusions unpalatable to many Christians. Since both science and technology are blessed words in our contemporary vocabulary, some may be happy at the notions, first, that viewed historically, modern science is an extrapolation of natural theology and, second, that modern technology is at least partly to be explained as an Occidental, voluntarist realization of the Christian dogma of man's transcendence of, and rightful master over, nature. But, as we now recognize, somewhat over a century ago science and technology—hitherto quite separate activities—joined to give mankind powers which, to judge by many of the ecologic effects, are out of control. If so, Christianity bears a huge burden of guilt.

I personally doubt that disastrous ecologic backlash can be avoided simply by applying to our problems more science and more technology. Our science and technology have grown out of Christian attitudes toward man's relation to nature which are almost universally held not only by Christians and neo-Christians but also by those who fondly regard themselves as post-Christians. Despite Copernicus, all the cosmos rotates around our little globe. Despite Darwin, we are not, in our hearts, part of the natural process. We are superior to nature, contemptuous of it, willing to use it for our slightest whim. The newly elected Governor of California, like myself a churchman but less troubled than I, spoke for the Christian tradition when he said (as is alleged), "when you've seen one redwood tree, you've seen them all." To a Christian a tree can be no more than a physical fact. The whole concept of the sacred grove is alien to Christianity and to the ethos of the West. For nearly 2 millennia Christian missionaries have been chopping down sacred groves, which are idolatrous because they assume spirit in nature.

What we do about ecology depends on our ideas of the man-nature relationship. More science and more technology are not going to get us out of the present ecologic crisis until we find a new religion, or rethink our old one. The beatniks, who are the basic revolutionaries of our time, show a sound instinct in their affinity for Zen Buddhism, which conceives of the man-nature relationship as very nearly the mirror image of the Christian view. Zen, however, is as deeply conditioned by Asian history as Christianity is by the experience of the West, and I am dubious of its viability among us.

Possibly we should ponder the greatest radical in Christian history since Christ: Saint Francis of Assisi. The prime miracle of Saint Francis is the fact that he did not end at the stake, as many of his left-wing followers did. He was so clearly heretical that a General of the Franciscan Order, Saint Bonavlentura, a great and perceptive Christian, tried to suppress the early accounts of Franciscanism. The key to an understanding of Francis is his belief in the virtue of humility—not merely for the individual but for man as a species. Francis tried to depose man from his monarchy over creation and set up a democracy of all God's creatures. With him the ant is no longer simply a homily for the lazy, flames a sign of the thrust of the soul toward union with God; now they are Brother Ant and Sister Fire, praising the Creator in their own ways as Brother Man does in his.

Later commentators have said that Francis preached to the birds as a rebuke to men who would not listen. The records do not read so: he urged the little birds to praise God, and in spiritual ecstasy they flapped their wings and chirped rejoicing. Legends of saints, especially the Irish saints, had long told of their dealings with animals but always, I believe, to show their human dominance over creatures. With Francis it is different. The land around Gubbio in the Apennines was ravaged by a fierce wolf. Saint Francis, says the legend, talked to the wolf and persuaded him of the error of his ways. The wolf repented, died in the odor of sanctity, and was buried in consecrated ground.

What Sir Steven Ruciman calls "the Franciscan doctrine of the animal soul" was quickly stamped out. Quite possibly it was in part inspired, consciously or unconsciously, by the belief in reincarnation held by the Cathar heretics who at that time teemed in Italy and southern France, and who presumably had got it originally from India. It is significant that at just the same moment, about 1200, traces of metempsychosis are found also in western Judaism, in the Provencal Cabbala. But Francis held neither to transmigration of souls nor to pantheism. His view of nature and of man rested on a unique sort of pan-psychism of all things animate and inaminate, designed for the glorification of their transcendent Creator, who, in the ultimate gesture of cosmic humility, assumed flesh, lay helpless in a manger, and hung dying on a scaffold.

I am not suggesting that many contemporary Americans who are concerned about our ecologic crisis will be either able or willing to counsel with wolves or exhort birds. However, the present increasing disruption of the global environment is the product of a dynamic technology and science which were originating in the Western medieval world against which

Saint Francis was rebelling in so original a way. Their growth cannot be understood historically apart from distinctive attitudes toward nature which are deeply grounded in Christian dogma. The fact that most people do not think of these attitudes as Christian is irrelevant. No new set of basic values has been accepted in our society to displace those of Christianity. Hence we shall continue to have a worsening ecologic crisis until we reject the Christian axiom that nature has no reason for existence save to serve man.

The greatest spiritual revolutionary in Western history, Saint Francis, proposed what he thought was an alternative Christian view of nature and man's relation to it; he tried to substitute the idea of the equality of all creatures, including man, for the idea of man's limitless rule of creation. He failed. Both our present science and our present technology are so tinctured with orthodox Christian arrogance toward nature that no solution for our ecologic crisis can be expected from them alone. Since the roots of our trouble are so largely religious, the remedy must also be essentially religious, whether we call it that or not. We must rethink and refeel our nature and destiny. The profoundly religious, but heretical, sense of the primitive Franciscans for the spiritual autonomy of all parts of nature may point a direction. I propose Francis as a patron saint for ecologists.

Questions for Further Exploration:

- How does White explain the change he finds in man's relation to nature in the medieval West during the latter part of the seventh century A.D.?

- What is the metaphysical meaning of White's claim that "The victory of Christianity over paganism was the greatest psychic revolution in the history of our culture"?

- According to Judeo-Christian monotheism, man shares God's transcendence of nature and God created nature to serve man's purposes. What are the ecological implications of this anthropocentricism?

- According to White, how did pagan animism prevent the exploitation of nature?

- Compare and contrast Franciscan pan-psychism with Aristotelian animism and Aquinas' monotheism.

- Free-write: Is the root of the ecologic crisis the metaphysical assumption that man is the only natural being made in God's image? Does the reality of being human entail dominion over nature?

Meditations on First Philosophy

René Descartes

Meditation I
Of the Things of Which We May Doubt

love!

1. Several years have now elapsed since I first became aware that I had accepted, even from my youth, many false opinions for true, and that consequently what I afterward based on such principles was highly doubtful; and from that time I was convinced of the necessity of undertaking once in my life to rid myself of all the opinions I had adopted, and of commencing anew the work of building from the foundation, if I desired to establish a firm and abiding superstructure in the sciences. But as this enterprise appeared to me to be one of great magnitude, I waited until I had attained an age so mature as to leave me no hope that at any stage of life more advanced I should be better able to execute my design. On this account, I have delayed so long that I should henceforth consider I was doing wrong were I still to consume in deliberation any of the time that now remains for action. To-day, then, since I have opportunely freed my mind from all cares and am happily disturbed by no passions], and since I am in the secure possession of leisure in a peaceable retirement, I will at length apply myself earnestly and freely to the general overthrow of all my former opinions.

2. But, to this end, it will not be necessary for me to show that the whole of these are false—a point, perhaps, which I shall never reach; but as even now my reason convinces me that I ought not the less carefully to withhold belief from what is not entirely certain and indubitable, than from what is manifestly false, it will be sufficient to justify the rejection of the whole if I shall find in each some ground for doubt. Nor for this purpose will it be necessary even to deal with each belief individually, which would be truly an endless labor; but, as the removal from below of the foundation necessarily involves the downfall of the whole edifice, I will at once approach the criticism of the principles on which all my former beliefs rested.

3. All that I have, up to this moment, accepted as possessed of the highest truth and certainty, I received either from or through the senses. I observed, however, that these sometimes misled us; and it is the part of prudence not to place absolute confidence in that by which we have even once been deceived.

4. But it may be said, perhaps, that, although the senses occasionally mislead us respecting minute objects, and such as are so far removed from us as to be beyond the reach of close observation, there are yet many other of their informations (presentations), of the truth of which it is manifestly impossible to doubt; as for example, that I am in this place, seated by the fire, clothed in a winter dressing gown, that I hold in my hands this piece of paper, with other intimations of the same nature. But how could I deny that I possess these hands and this body, and withal escape being classed with persons in a state of insanity, whose brains are so disordered and clouded by dark bilious vapors as to cause them pertinaciously to assert that they are monarchs when they are in the greatest poverty; or clothed in gold] and purple when destitute of any covering; or that their head is made of clay, their body of glass, or that they are gourds? I should certainly be not less insane than they, were I to regulate my procedure according to examples so extravagant. *(realist) view*

5. Though this be true, I must nevertheless here consider that I am a man, and that, consequently, I am in the habit of sleeping, and representing to myself in dreams those same things, or even sometimes others less probable, which the insane think are presented to them in their waking moments. How often have I dreamt that I was in these familiar circumstances, that I was dressed, and occupied this place by the fire, when I was lying undressed in bed? At the present moment, however, I certainly look upon this paper with eyes wide awake; the head which I now move is not asleep; I extend this hand consciously and with express purpose, and I perceive it; the occurrences in sleep are not so distinct as all this. But I cannot forget that, at other times I have been deceived in sleep by similar illusions; and, attentively considering those cases, I perceive so clearly that there exist no certain marks by which the state of waking can ever be distinguished from sleep, that I feel greatly astonished; and in amazement I almost persuade myself that I am now dreaming.

6. Let us suppose, then, that we are dreaming, and that all these particulars—namely, the opening of the eyes, the motion of the head, the forth-putting of the hands—are merely illusions; and even that we really possess neither an entire body nor hands such as we see. Nevertheless it must be admitted that least that the objects which appear to us in sleep are, as it were, painted representations which could not have been formed unless in the likeness of realities; and, therefore, that those general objects, at

[margin: lack of better term]

[margin: imagine those not in reality are not in reality]

[margin: Argument for Realism]

all events, namely, eyes, a head, hands, and an entire body, are not simply imaginary, but really existent. For, in truth, painters themselves, even when they study to represent sirens and satyrs by forms the most fantastic and extraordinary, cannot bestow upon them natures absolutely new, but can only make a certain medley of the members of different animals; or if they chance to imagine something so novel that nothing at all similar has ever been seen before, and such as is, therefore, purely fictitious and absolutely false, it is at least certain that the colors of which this is composed are real. And on the same principle, although these general objects, viz. a body], eyes, a head, hands, and the like, be imaginary, we are nevertheless absolutely necessitated to admit the reality at least of some other objects still more simple and universal than these, of which, just as of certain real colors, all those images of things, whether true and real, or false and fantastic, that are found in our consciousness (cogitatio), are formed.

7. To this class of objects seem to belong corporeal nature in general and its extension; the figure of extended things, their quantity or magnitude, and their number, as also the place in, and the time during, which they exist, and other things of the same sort.

8. We will not, therefore, perhaps reason illegitimately if we conclude from this that Physics, Astronomy, Medicine, and all the other sciences that have for their end the consideration of composite objects, are indeed of a doubtful character; but that Arithmetic, Geometry, and the other sciences of the same class, which regard merely the simplest and most general objects, and scarcely inquire whether or not these are really existent, contain somewhat that is certain and indubitable: for whether I am awake or dreaming, it remains true that two and three make five, and that a square has but four sides; nor does it seem possible that truths so apparent can ever fall under a suspicion of falsity or incertitude].

9. Nevertheless, the belief that there is a God who is all powerful, and who created me, such as I am, has, for a long time, obtained steady possession of my mind. How, then, do I know that he has not arranged that there should be neither earth, nor sky, nor any extended thing, nor figure, nor magnitude, nor place, providing at the same time, however, for the rise in me of the perceptions of all these objects, and] the persuasion that these do not exist otherwise than as I perceive them? And further, as I sometimes think that others are in error respecting matters of which they believe themselves to possess a perfect knowledge, how do I know that I am not also deceived each time I add together two and three, or number the sides of a square, or form some judgment still more simple, if more simple indeed can be imagined? But perhaps Deity has not been willing that I should be thus deceived, for he is said to be supremely good. If, however, it were repugnant to the goodness of Deity to have created me subject to

constant deception, it would seem likewise to be contrary to his goodness to allow me to be occasionally deceived; and yet it is clear that this is permitted.

10. Some, indeed, might perhaps be found who would be disposed rather to deny the existence of a Being so powerful than to believe that there is nothing certain. But let us for the present refrain from opposing this opinion, and grant that all which is here said of a Deity is fabulous: nevertheless, in whatever way it be supposed that I reach the state in which I exist, whether by fate, or chance, or by an endless series of antecedents and consequents, or by any other means, it is clear (since to be deceived and to err is a certain defect) that the probability of my being so imperfect as to be the constant victim of deception, will be increased exactly in proportion as the power possessed by the cause, to which they assign my origin, is lessened. To these reasonings I have assuredly nothing to reply, but am constrained at last to avow that there is nothing of all that I formerly believed to be true of which it is impossible to doubt, and that not through thoughtlessness or levity, but from cogent and maturely considered reasons; so that henceforward, if I desire to discover anything certain, I ought not the less carefully to refrain from assenting to those same opinions than to what might be shown to be manifestly false.

11. But it is not sufficient to have made these observations; care must be taken likewise to keep them in remembrance. For those old and customary opinions perpetually recur—long and familiar usage giving them the right of occupying my mind, even almost against my will, and subduing my belief; nor will I lose the habit of deferring to them and confiding in them so long as I shall consider them to be what in truth they are, viz, opinions to some extent doubtful, as I have already shown, but still highly probable, and such as it is much more reasonable to believe than deny. It is for this reason I am persuaded that I shall not be doing wrong, if, taking an opposite judgment of deliberate design, I become my own deceiver, by supposing, for a time, that all those opinions are entirely false and imaginary, until at length, having thus balanced my old by my new prejudices, my judgment shall no longer be turned aside by perverted usage from the path that may conduct to the perception of truth. For I am assured that, meanwhile, there will arise neither peril nor error from this course, and that I cannot for the present yield too much to distrust, since the end I now seek is not action but knowledge.

12. I will suppose, then, not that Deity, who is sovereignly good and the fountain of truth, but that some malignant demon, who is at once exceedingly potent and deceitful, has employed all his artifice to deceive me; I will suppose that the sky, the air, the earth, colors, figures, sounds, and all external things, are nothing better than the illusions of dreams, by means

of which this being has laid snares for my credulity; I will consider myself as without hands, eyes, flesh, blood, or any of the senses, and as falsely believing that I am possessed of these; I will continue resolutely fixed in this belief, and if indeed by this means it be not in my power to arrive at the knowledge of truth, I shall at least do what is in my power, viz, suspend my judgment], and guard with settled purpose against giving my assent to what is false, and being imposed upon by this deceiver, whatever be his power and artifice. But this undertaking is arduous, and a certain indolence insensibly leads me back to my ordinary course of life; and just as the captive, who, perchance, was enjoying in his dreams an imaginary liberty, when he begins to suspect that it is but a vision, dreads awakening, and conspires with the agreeable illusions that the deception may be prolonged; so I, of my own accord, fall back into the train of my former beliefs, and fear to arouse myself from my slumber, lest the time of laborious wakefulness that would succeed this quiet rest, in place of bringing any light of day, should prove inadequate to dispel the darkness that will arise from the difficulties that have now been raised.

Meditation II
Of the Nature of the Human Mind; And that it is More Easily Known than the Body

1. The Meditation of yesterday has filled my mind with so many doubts, that it is no longer in my power to forget them. Nor do I see, meanwhile, any principle on which they can be resolved; and, just as if I had fallen all of a sudden into very deep water, I am so greatly disconcerted as to be unable either to plant my feet firmly on the bottom or sustain myself by swimming on the surface. I will, nevertheless, make an effort, and try anew the same path on which I had entered yesterday, that is, proceed by casting aside all that admits of the slightest doubt, not less than if I had discovered it to be absolutely false; and I will continue always in this track until I shall find something that is certain, or at least, if I can do nothing more, until I shall know with certainty that there is nothing certain. Archimedes, that he might transport the entire globe from the place it occupied to another, demanded only a point that was firm and immovable; so, also, I shall be entitled to entertain the highest expectations, if I am fortunate enough to discover only one thing that is certain and indubitable.

2. I suppose, accordingly, that all the things which I see are false (fictitious); I believe that none of those objects which my fallacious memory represents ever existed; I suppose that I possess no senses; I believe that body, figure, extension, motion, and place are merely fictions of my mind.

What is there, then, that can be esteemed true? Perhaps this only, that there is absolutely nothing certain.

3. But how do I know that there is not something different altogether from the objects I have now enumerated, of which it is impossible to entertain the slightest doubt? Is there not a God, or some being, by whatever name I may designate him, who causes these thoughts to arise in my mind? But why suppose such a being, for it may be I myself am capable of producing them? Am I, then, at least not something? But I before denied that I possessed senses or a body; I hesitate, however, for what follows from that? Am I so dependent on the body and the senses that without these I cannot exist? But I had the persuasion that there was absolutely nothing in the world, that there was no sky and no earth, neither minds nor bodies; was I not, therefore, at the same time, persuaded that I did not exist? Far from it; I assuredly existed, since I was persuaded. But there is I know not what being, who is possessed at once of the highest power and the deepest cunning, who is constantly employing all his ingenuity in deceiving me. Doubtless, then, I exist, since I am deceived; and, let him deceive me as he may, he can never bring it about that I am nothing, so long as I shall be conscious that I am something. So that it must, in fine, be maintained, all things being maturely and carefully considered, that this proposition (pronunciatum) I am, I exist, is necessarily true each time it is expressed by me, or conceived in my mind.

4. But I do not yet know with sufficient clearness what I am, though assured that I am; and hence, in the next place, I must take care, lest perchance I inconsiderately substitute some other object in room of what is properly myself, and thus wander from truth, even in that knowledge (cognition) which I hold to be of all others the most certain and evident. For this reason, I will now consider anew what I formerly believed myself to be, before I entered on the present train of thought; and of my previous opinion I will retrench all that can in the least be invalidated by the grounds of doubt I have adduced, in order that there may at length remain nothing but what is certain and indubitable.

5. What then did I formerly think I was? Undoubtedly I judged that I was a man. But what is a man? Shall I say a rational animal? Assuredly not; for it would be necessary forthwith to inquire into what is meant by animal, and what by rational, and thus, from a single question, I should insensibly glide into others, and these more difficult than the first; nor do I now possess enough of leisure to warrant me in wasting my time amid subtleties of this sort. I prefer here to attend to the thoughts that sprung up of themselves in my mind, and were inspired by my own nature alone, when I applied myself to the consideration of what I was. In the first place, then, I thought that I possessed a countenance, hands, arms, and all the

fabric of members that appears in a corpse, and which I called by the name of body. It further occurred to me that I was nourished, that I walked, perceived, and thought, and all those actions I referred to the soul; but what the soul itself was I either did not stay to consider, or, if I did, I imagined that it was something extremely rare and subtile, like wind, or flame, or ether, spread through my grosser parts. As regarded the body, I did not even doubt of its nature, but thought I distinctly knew it, and if I had wished to describe it according to the notions I then entertained, I should have explained myself in this manner: By body I understand all that can be terminated by a certain figure; that can be comprised in a certain place, and so fill a certain space as there from to exclude every other body; that can be perceived either by touch, sight, hearing, taste, or smell; that can be moved in different ways, not indeed of itself, but by something foreign to it by which it is touched and from which it receives the impression]; for the power of self-motion, as likewise that of perceiving and thinking, I held as by no means pertaining to the nature of body; on the contrary, I was somewhat astonished to find such faculties existing in some bodies.

6. But as to myself, what can I now say that I am], since I suppose there exists an extremely powerful, and, if I may so speak, malignant being, whose whole endeavors are directed toward deceiving me? Can I affirm that I possess any one of all those attributes of which I have lately spoken as belonging to the nature of body? After attentively considering them in my own mind, I find none of them that can properly be said to belong to myself. To recount them were idle and tedious. Let us pass, then, to the attributes of the soul. The first mentioned were the powers of nutrition and walking; but, if it be true that I have no body, it is true likewise that I am capable neither of walking nor of being nourished. Perception is another attribute of the soul; but perception to is impossible without the body; besides, I have frequently, during sleep, believed that I perceived objects which I afterward observed I did not in reality perceive. Thinking is another attribute of the soul; and here I discover what properly belongs to myself. This alone is inseparable from me. I am—I exist: this is certain; but how often? As often as I think; for perhaps it would even happen, if I should wholly cease to think, that I should at the same time altogether cease to be. I now admit nothing that is not necessarily true. I am therefore, precisely speaking, only a thinking thing, that is, a mind (mens sive animus), understanding, or reason, terms whose signification was before unknown to me. I am, however, a real thing, and really existent; but what thing? The answer was, a thinking thing.

7. The question now arises, am I aught besides? I will stimulate my imagination with a view to discover whether I am not still something more than a thinking being. Now it is plain I am not the assemblage of members

called the human body; I am not a thin and penetrating air diffused through all these members, or wind, or flame, or vapor, or breath, or any of all the things I can imagine; for I supposed that all these were not, and, without changing the supposition, I find that I still feel assured of my existence. But it is true, perhaps, that those very things which I suppose to be non-existent, because they are unknown to me, are not in truth different from myself whom I know. This is a point I cannot determine, and do not now enter into any dispute regarding it. I can only judge of things that are known to me: I am conscious that I exist, and I who know that I exist inquire into what I am. It is, however, perfectly certain that the knowledge of my existence, thus precisely taken, is not dependent on things, the existence of which is as yet unknown to me: and consequently it is not dependent on any of the things I can feign in imagination. Moreover, the phrase itself, I frame an image (efffingo), reminds me of my error; for I should in truth frame one if I were to imagine myself to be anything, since to imagine is nothing more than to contemplate the figure or image of a corporeal thing; but I already know that I exist, and that it is possible at the same time that all those images, and in general all that relates to the nature of body, are merely dreams or chimeras]. From this I discover that it is not more reasonable to say, I will excite my imagination that I may know more distinctly what I am, than to express myself as follows: I am now awake, and perceive something real; but because my perception is not sufficiently clear, I will of express purpose go to sleep that my dreams may represent to me the object of my perception with more truth and clearness. And, therefore, I know that nothing of all that I can embrace in imagination belongs to the knowledge which I have of myself, and that there is need to recall with the utmost care the mind from this mode of thinking, that it may be able to know its own nature with perfect distinctness.

8. But what, then, am I? A thinking thing, it has been said. But what is a thinking thing? It is a thing that doubts, understands, conceives], affirms, denies, wills, refuses; that imagines also, and perceives.

9. Assuredly it is not little, if all these properties belong to my nature. But why should they not belong to it? Am I not that very being who now doubts of almost everything; who, for all that, understands and conceives certain things; who affirms one alone as true, and denies the others; who desires to know more of them, and does not wish to be deceived; who imagines many things, sometimes even despite his will; and is likewise percipient of many, as if through the medium of the senses. Is there nothing of all this as true as that I am, even although I should be always dreaming, and although he who gave me being employed all his ingenuity to deceive me? Is there also any one of these attributes that can be properly distinguished from my thought, or that can be said to be separate from my-

self? For it is of itself so evident that it is I who doubt, I who understand, and I who desire, that it is here unnecessary to add anything by way of rendering it more clear. And I am as certainly the same being who imagines; for although it may be (as I before supposed) that nothing I imagine is true, still the power of imagination does not cease really to exist in me and to form part of my thought. In fine, I am the same being who perceives, that is, who apprehends certain objects as by the organs of sense, since, in truth, I see light, hear a noise, and feel heat. But it will be said that these presentations are false, and that I am dreaming. Let it be so. At all events it is certain that I seem to see light, hear a noise, and feel heat; this cannot be false, and this is what in me is properly called perceiving (sentire), which is nothing else than thinking.

■ ■ ■

Questions for Further Exploration:

■ In his search for a foundation for the sciences, Descartes resolves to overthrow any and all beliefs about reality that he found it possible to doubt. What is the first indubitable belief about reality he discovers?

The belief of the Senses.

■ According to Descartes, what is the essence of being human? What are the attributes of the "body" and "mind"?

■ What argument does Descartes offer to support his mind/body dualism?

■ Free-write your response to Descartes' question: "Am I so dependent on the body and the senses that without these I cannot exist?"

Tell her u will Cru long Cod

172

Discourse on the Method of Rightly Conducting the Reason, and Seeking Truth in the Sciences

René Descartes

Part V

■ ■ ■

Nor will this appear at all strange to those who are acquainted with the variety of movements performed by the different automata, or moving machines fabricated by human industry, and that with help of but few pieces compared with the great multitude of bones, muscles, nerves, arteries, veins, and other parts that are found in the body of each animal. Such persons will look upon this body as a machine made by the hands of God, which is incomparably better arranged, and adequate to movements more admirable than is any machine of human invention. And here I specially stayed to show that, were there such machines exactly resembling organs and outward form an ape or any other irrational animal, we could have no means of knowing that they were in any respect of a different nature from these animals; but if there were machines bearing the image of our bodies and capable of imitating our actions as far as it is morally possible, there would still remain two most certain tests whereby to know that they were not therefore really men. Of these the first is that they could never use words or other signs arranged in such a manner as is competent to us in order to declare our thoughts to others: for we may easily conceive a machine to be so constructed that it emits vocables, and even that it emits some correspondent to the action upon it of external objects which cause a change in its organs; for example, if touched in a particular place it may demand what we wish to say to it; if in another it may cry out that it is hurt, and such like; but not that it should arrange them variously so as appositely to reply to what is said in its presence, as men of the lowest grade of intellect can do. The second test is, that although such machines might execute many things with equal or perhaps greater perfection than any of us, they would, without doubt, fail in certain others from which it could be discovered that they did not act from knowledge, but solely from the disposition of their organs: for while reason is an universal instrument that is alike available on every occasion, these organs, on the contrary, need a particular arrangement for each particular action; whence it must be morally impossible that there should exist in any machine a diversity of organs sufficient to enable it to act in all the occurrences of life, in the way in which our reason enables us to act. Again, by means of these two tests we may likewise know the difference between men and brutes. For it is highly deserving of remark, that there are no men so dull and stupid, not even idiots, as to be incapable of joining together different words, and thereby constructing a declaration by which to make their thoughts understood; and that on the other hand, there is no other animal, however perfect or happily circumstanced, which can do the like. Nor does this inability arise from want of organs: for we observe that magpies and parrots can utter words like ourselves, and are yet unable to speak as we do, that is, so as to show that they understand what they say; in place of which men born deaf and dumb, and thus not less, but rather more than the brutes, destitute of the organs which others use in speaking, are in the habit of spontaneously inventing certain signs by which they discover their thoughts to those who, being usually in their company, have leisure to learn their language. And this proves not only that the brutes have less reason than man, but that they have none at all: for we see that very little is required to enable a person to speak; and since a certain inequality of capacity is observable among animals of the same species, as well as among men, and since some are more capable of being instructed than others, it is incredible that the most perfect ape or parrot of its species, should not in this be equal to the most stupid infant of its kind or at least to one that was crackbrained, unless the soul of brutes were of a nature wholly different from ours. And we ought not to confound speech with the natural movements which indicate the passions, and can be imitated by machines as well as manifested by animals; nor must it be thought with certain of the ancients, that the brutes speak, although we do not understand their language. For if such were the case, since they are endowed with many organs analogous to ours, they could as easily communicate their thoughts to us as to their fellows. It is also very worthy of remark, that, though there are many animals which manifest more industry than we in certain of their actions, the same animals are yet observed to show none at all in many others: so that the circumstance that they do better than we does not prove that they are endowed with mind, for it would thence follow that they possessed greater reason than any of us, and could surpass us in all things; on the contrary, it rather proves that they are destitute of reason, and that it is nature which acts in them according to the disposition of their organs: thus it is seen, that a clock composed only of wheels and weights can number the hours and measure time more exactly than we with all our skin.

I had after this described the reasonable soul, and shown that it could by no means be educed from the power of matter, as the other things of which I had spoken, but that it must be expressly created; and that it is not sufficient that it be lodged in the human body exactly like a pilot in a ship, unless perhaps to move its members, but that it is necessary for it to be joined and united more closely to the body, in order to have sensations and appetites similar to ours, and thus constitute a real man. I here entered, in conclusion, upon the subject of the soul at considerable length, because it is of the greatest moment: for after the error of those who deny the existence of God, an error which I think I have already sufficiently refuted, there is none that is more powerful in leading feeble minds astray from the straight path of virtue than the supposition that the soul of the brutes is of the same nature with our own; and consequently that after this life we have nothing to hope for or fear, more than flies and ants; in place of which, when we know how far they differ we much better comprehend the reasons which establish that the soul is of a nature wholly independent of the body, and that consequently it is not liable to die with the latter and, finally, because no other causes are observed capable of destroying it, we are naturally led hence to judge that it is immortal.

Questions for Further Exploration:

- Descartes claims that animal bodies are comparable to man-made machines. Compare and contrast them in order to support or challenge his claim.

- What two tests does Descartes claim will enable one to distinguish humans from animals? What counter-examples might undermine his conclusions?

- What metaphysical conclusions does Descartes reach on the basis of these two tests?

- What does Descartes' mind/body dualism mean for human/nature relations?

- Speculate: Why is it commonplace among environmentalists to argue that Cartesian dualism lies at the root of the environmental crisis?

- Free-write: Are you a Cartesian dualist?

The Ethics

Benedict de Spinoza
Translated by R. H. M. Elwes

Part I: Concerning God
Definitions

I. By that which is 'self-caused' I mean that of which the essence involves existence, or that of which the nature is only conceivable as existent.

II. A thing is called 'finite after its kind' when it can be limited by another thing of the same nature; for instance, a body is called finite because we always conceive another greater body. So, also, a thought is limited by another thought, but a body is not limited by thought, nor a thought by body.

III. By 'substance' I mean that which is in itself, and is conceived through itself: in other words, that of which a conception can be formed independently of any other conception.

IV. By 'attribute' I mean that which the intellect perceives as constituting the essence of substance.

V. By 'mode' I mean the modifications ("affectiones") of substance, or that which exists in, and is conceived through, something other than itself.

VI. By 'God' I mean a being absolutely infinite—that is, a substance consisting in infinite attributes, of which each expresses eternal and infinite essentiality.

Explanation—I say absolutely infinite, not infinite after its kind: for, of a thing infinite only after its kind, infinite attributes may be denied; but that which is absolutely infinite, contains in its essence whatever expresses reality, and involves no negation.

VII. That thing is called 'free,' which exists solely by the necessity of its own nature, and of which the action is determined by itself alone. On the other hand, that thing is necessary, or rather constrained, which is determined by something external to itself to a fixed and definite method of existence or action.

VIII. By 'eternity' I mean existence itself, in so far as it is conceived necessarily to follow solely from the definition of that which is eternal.

Explanation—Existence of this kind is conceived as an eternal truth, like the essence of a thing and, therefore, cannot be explained by means of continuance or time, though continuance may be conceived without a beginning or end.

AXIOMS. I. Everything which exists, exists either in itself or in something else.

II. That which cannot be conceived through anything else must be conceived through itself.

III. From a given definite cause an effect necessarily follows; and, on the other hand, if no definite cause be granted, it is impossible that an effect can follow.

IV. The knowledge of an effect depends on and involves the knowledge of a cause.

V. Things which have nothing in common cannot be understood, the one by means of the other; the conception of one does not involve the conception of the other.

VI. A true idea must correspond with its ideate or object.

VII. If a thing can be conceived as non-existing, its essence does not involve existence.

PROPOSITIONS. I. Substance is by nature prior to its modifications.

Proof—This is clear from Def. iii. and v.

II. Two substances, whose attributes are different, have nothing in common.

Proof—Also evident from Def. iii. For each must exist in itself, and be conceived through itself; in other words, the conception of one does not imply the conception of the other.

III. Things which have nothing in common cannot be one the cause of the other.

Proof—If they have nothing in common, it follows that one cannot be apprehended by means of the other (Ax. v.), and, therefore, one cannot be the cause of the other (Ax. iv.). Q.E.D.

IV. Two or more distinct things are distinguished one from the other, either by the difference of the attributes of the substances, or by the difference of their modifications.

Proof—Everything which exists, exists either in itself or in something else (Ax. i.),—that is (by Def. iii. and v.), nothing is granted in addition to the understanding, except substance and its modifications. Nothing is, therefore, given besides the understanding, by which several things may be distinguished one from the other, except the substances, or, in other words (see Ax. iv.), their attributes and modifications. Q.E.D.

V. There cannot exist in the universe two or more substances having the same nature or attribute.

Proof—If several distinct substances be granted, they must be distinguished one from the other, either by the difference of their attributes, or by the difference of their modifications (Prop. iv.). If only by the difference of their attributes, it will be granted that there cannot be more than one with an identical attribute. If by the difference of their modifications—as substance is naturally prior to its modifications (Prop. i.)—it follows that setting the modifications aside, and considering substance in itself, that is truly, (Def. iii. and vi.), there cannot be conceived one substance different from another—that is (by Prop. iv.), there cannot be granted several substances, but one substance only. Q.E.D.

■ ■ ■

XIV. Besides God no substance can be granted or conceived.

Proof—As God is a being absolutely infinite, of whom no attribute that expresses the essence of substance can be denied (by Def. vi.), and he necessarily exists (by Prop. xi.); if any substance besides God were granted, it would have to be explained by some attribute of God, and thus two substances with the same attribute would exist, which (by Prop. v.) is absurd; therefore, besides God no substance can be granted, or consequently be conceived. If it could be conceived, it would necessarily have to be conceived as existent; but this (by the first part of this proof) is absurd. Therefore, besides God no substance can be granted or conceived. Q.E.D.

Corollary I.—Clearly, therefore: 1. God is one, that is (by Def. vi.) only one substance can be granted in the universe, and that substance is absolutely infinite, as we have already indicated (in the note to Prop. x.).

Corollary II.—It follows: 2. That extension and thought are either attributes of God or (by Ax. i.) accidents ("affectiones") of the attributes of God.

■ ■ ■

XVIII. God is the indwelling and not the transient cause of all things.

Proof—All things which are, are in God, and must be conceived through God (by Prop. xv.), therefore (by Prop. xvi., Cor. i.) God is the cause of those things which are in him. This is our first point. Further, besides God there can be no substance (by Prop. xiv.), that is nothing in itself external to God. This is our second point. God, therefore, is the indwelling and not the transient cause of all things. Q.E.D.

■ ■ ■

XXIX. Nothing in the universe is contingent, but all things are conditioned to exist and operate in a particular manner by the necessity of the divine nature.

Proof—Whatsoever is, is in God (Prop. xv.). But God cannot be called a thing contingent. For (by Prop. xi.) he exists necessarily, and not contingently. Further, the modes of the divine nature follow therefrom necessarily, and not contingently (Prop. xvi.); and they thus follow, whether we consider the divine nature absolutely, or whether we consider it as in any way conditioned to act (Prop. xxvii.). Further, God is not only the cause of these modes, in so far as they simply exist (by Prop. xxiv., Cor.), but also in so far as they are considered as conditioned for operating in a particular manner (Prop. xxvi.). If they be not conditioned by God (Prop. xxvi.), it is impossible, and not contingent, that they should condition themselves; contrariwise, if they be conditioned by God, it is impossible, and not contingent, that they should render themselves unconditioned. Wherefore all things are conditioned by the necessity of the divine nature, not only to exist, but also to exist and operate in a particular manner, and there is nothing that is contingent. Q.E.D.

*****Note—Before going any further, I wish here to explain, what we should understand by nature viewed as active (natura naturans), and nature viewed as passive (natura naturata). I say to explain, or rather call attention to it, for I think that, from what has been said, it is sufficiently clear, that by nature viewed as active we should understand that which is in itself, and is conceived through itself, or those attributes of substance, which express eternal and infinite essence, in other words (Prop. xiv., Cor. i., and Prop. xvii., Cor. ii.) God, in so far as he is considered as a free cause.

By nature viewed as passive I understand all that which follows from the necessity of the nature of God, or of any of the attributes of God, that is, all the modes of the attributes of God, in so far as they are considered as things which are in God, and which without God cannot exist or be conceived.

■ ■ ■

Part IV: Of Human Bondage, or the Strength of the Emotions
Preface

■ ■ ■

Now we showed in the Appendix to Part I., that Nature does not work with an end in view. For the eternal and infinite Being, which we call God or Nature, acts by the same necessity as that whereby it exists. For we have shown, that by the same necessity of its nature, whereby it exists, it likewise works (I:xvi.). The reason or cause why God or Nature exists, and the reason why he acts, are one and the same. Therefore, as he does not exist for the sake of an end, so neither does he act for the sake of an end; of his existence and of his action there is neither origin nor end. Wherefore, a cause which is called final is nothing else but human desire, in so far as it is considered as the origin or cause of anything. For example, when we say that to be inhabited is the final cause of this or that house, we mean nothing more than that a man, conceiving the conveniences of household life, had a desire to build a house. Wherefore, the being inhabited, in so far as it is regarded as a final cause, is nothing else but this particular desire, which is really the efficient cause; it is regarded as the primary cause, because men are generally ignorant of the causes of their desires. They are, as I have often said already, conscious of their own actions and appetites, but ignorant of the causes whereby they are determined to any particular desire. Therefore, the common saying that Nature sometimes falls short, or blunders, and produces things which are imperfect, I set down among the glosses treated of in the Appendix to Part 1. Perfection and imperfection, then, are in reality merely modes of thinking, or notions which we form from a comparison among one another of individuals of the same species; hence I said above (II:Def.vi.), that by reality and perfection I mean the same thing. For we are wont to refer all the individual things in nature to one genus, which is called the highest genus, namely, to the category of Being, whereto absolutely all individuals in nature belong. Thus, in so far as we refer the individuals in nature to this category, and comparing them one with another, find that some possess more of being or reality than others, we, to this extent, say that some are more perfect than others. Again, in so far as we attribute to them anything implying negation—as term, end, infirmity, etc., we, to this extent, call them imperfect, because they do not affect our mind so much as the things which we call perfect, not because they have any intrinsic deficiency, or because Nature has blundered. For nothing lies within the scope of a thing's nature, save that which follows from the necessity of the nature of its efficient cause, and whatsoever follows from the necessity of the nature of its efficient cause necessarily comes to pass.

■ ■ ■

Questions for Further Exploration:

- On what grounds does Spinoza refute Cartesian dualism?

- How does Spinoza define God? What does this definition imply about God's relation to humanity and to the natural world?

- What metaphysical claims does Spinoza articulate using the contingent/necessary distinction? What is his position on the existence of individual "free will"?

- What is the significance of the distinction Spinoza makes between "nature viewed as active" (natura naturans) and "nature viewed as passive" (natura naturata)?

- Free-write: What follows from Spinoza's argument that all reality is one (monism)?

Discourse on the Origin of Inequality

Jean-Jacques Rousseau
Translated by Donald A. Cress

Preface

Of all the branches of human knowledge, the most useful and the least advanced seems to me to be that of man;[2] and I dare say that the inscription on the temple at Delphi alone contained a precept more important and more difficult than all the huge tomes of the moralists. Thus I regard the subject of this discourse as one of the most interesting questions that philosophy is capable of proposing, and unhappily for us, one of the thorniest that philosophers can attempt to resolve. For how can the source of the inequality among men be known unless one begins by knowing men themselves? And how will man be successful in seeing himself as nature formed him, through all the changes that the succession of time and things must have produced in his original constitution, and in separating what he derives from his own wherewithal from what circumstances and his progress have added to or changed in his primitive state? Like the statue of Glaucus, which time, sea and storms had disfigured to such an extent that it looked less like a god than a wild beast, the human soul, altered in the midst of society by a thousand constantly recurring causes, by the acquisition of a multitude of bits of knowledge and of errors, by changes that took place in the constitution of bodies, by the constant impact of the passions, has, as it were, changed its appearance to the point of being nearly unrecognizable. And instead of a being active always by certain and invariable principles, instead of that heavenly and majestic simplicity whose mark its author had left on it, one no longer finds anything but the grotesque contrast of passion which thinks it reasons and an understanding in a state of delirium.

What is even more cruel is that, since all the progress of the human species continually moves away from its primitive state, the more we accumulate new knowledge, the more we deprive ourselves of the means of acquiring the most important knowledge of all. Thus, in a sense, it is by dint of studying man that we have rendered ourselves incapable of knowing him.

It is easy to see that it is in these successive changes of the human constitution that we must seek the first origin of the differences that distinguish men, who, by common consensus, are naturally as equal among themselves as were the animals of each species before various physical causes had introduced into certain species the varieties we now observe among some of them. In effect, it is inconceivable that these first changes, by whatever means they took place, should have altered all at once and in the same manner all the individuals of the species. But while some improved or declined and acquired various good or bad qualities which were not inherent in their nature, the others remained longer in their original state. And such was the first source of inequality among men, which it is easier to demonstrate thus in general than to assign with precision its true causes.

Let my readers not imagine, then, that I dare flatter myself with having seen what appears to me so difficult to see. I have begun some lines of reasoning; I have hazarded some guesses, less in the hope of resolving the question than with the intention of clarifying it and of reducing it to its true state. Others will easily be able to go farther on this same route, though it will not be easy for anyone to reach the end of it. For it is no light undertaking to separate what is original from what is artificial in the present nature of man, and to have a proper understanding of a state which no longer exists, which perhaps never existed, which probably never will exist, and yet about which it is necessary to have accurate notions in order to judge properly our own present state. He who would attempt to determine precisely which precautions to take in order to make solid observations on this subject would need even more philosophy than is generally supposed; and a good solution of the following problem would not seem to me unworthy of the Aristotles and Plinys of our century: *What experiments would be necessary to achieve knowledge of natural man? And what are the means of carrying out these experiments in the midst of society?* Far from undertaking to resolve this problem, I believe I have meditated sufficiently on the subject to dare respond in advance that the greatest philosophers will not be too good to direct these experiments, nor the most powerful sovereigns to carry them out. It is hardly reasonable to expect such a combination, especially with the perseverance or rather the succession of understanding and good will needed on both sides in order to achieve success.

These investigations, so difficult to carry out and so little thought about until now, are nevertheless the only means we have left of removing a multitude of difficulties that conceal from us the knowledge of the real foundations of human society. It is this ignorance of the nature of man which throws so much uncertainty and obscurity on the true definition of natural right. For the idea of right, says M. Burlamaqui, and even more that of natural right, are manifestly ideas relative to the nature of man. Therefore, he continues, the principles of this science must be deduced from this very nature of man from man's constitution and state.

It is not without surprise and a sense of outrage that one observes the paucity of agreement that prevails among the various authors who have treated it. Among the most serious writers one can hardly find two who are of the same opinion on this point. The Roman jurists—not to mention the ancient philosophers who seem to have done their best to contradict each other on the most fundamental principles—subject man and all other animals indifferently to the same natural law, because they take this expression to refer to the law that nature imposes on itself rather than the law she prescribes, or rather because of the particular sense in which those jurists understood the word "law," which on this occasion they seem to have taken only for the expression of the general relations established by nature among all animate beings for their common preservation. The moderns, in acknowledging under the word "law" merely a rule prescribed to a moral being, that is to say, intelligent, free and considered in his relations with other beings, consequently limit the competence of the natural law to the only animal endowed with reason, that is, to man. But with each one defining this law in his own fashion, they all establish it on such metaphysical principles that even among us there are very few people in a position to grasp these principles, far from being able to find them by themselves. So that all the definitions of these wise men, otherwise in perpetual contradiction with one another, agree on this alone, that it is impossible to understand the law of nature and consequently to obey it without being a great reasoner and a profound metaphysician, which means precisely that for the establishment of society, men must have used enlightenment which develops only with great difficulty and by a very small number of people within the society itself.

Knowing nature so little and agreeing so poorly on the meaning of the word "law," it would be quite difficult to come to some common understanding regarding a good definition of natural law. Thus all those definitions that are found in books have, over and above a lack of uniformity, and added fault of being drawn from several branches of knowledge which men do not naturally have, and from advantages the idea of which they cannot conceive until after having left the state of nature. Writers begin by seeking the rules on which, for the common utility, it would be appropriate for men to agree among themselves; and then they give the name *natural law* to the collection of these rules, with no other proof than the good which presumably would result from their universal observance. Surely this is a very convenient way to compose definitions and to explain the nature of things by virtually arbitrary views of what is seemly.

But as long as we are ignorant of natural man, it is futile for us to attempt to determine the law he has received or which is best suited to his constitution. All that we can see very clearly regarding this law is that, for it to be law, not only must the will of him who is obliged by it be capable of knowing submission to it, but also, for it to be natural, it must speak directly by the voice of nature.

Leaving aside therefore all the scientific books which teach us only to see men as they have made themselves, and meditating on the first and most simple operations of the human soul, I believe I perceive in it two principles that are prior to reason, of which one makes us ardently interested in our well-being and our self-preservation, and the other inspires in us a natural repugnance to seeing any sentient being, especially our fellow man, perish or suffer. It is from the conjunction and combination that our mind is in a position to make regarding these two principles, without the need for introducing that of sociability, that all the rules of natural right appear to me to flow; rules which reason is later forced to reestablish on other foundations, when, by its successive developments, it has succeeded in smothering nature.

In this way one is not obliged to make a man a philosopher before making him a man. His duties toward others are not uniquely dictated to him by the belated lessons of wisdom; and as long as he does not resist the inner impulse of compassion, he will never harm another man or even another sentient being, except in the legitimate instance where, if his preservation were involved, he is obliged to give preference to himself. By this means, an end can also be made to the ancient disputes regarding the participation of animals in the natural law. For it is clear that, lacking intelligence and liberty, they cannot recognize this law; but since they share to some extent in our nature by virtue of the sentient quality with which they are endowed, one will judge that they should also participate in natural right, and that man is subject to some sort of duties toward them. It seems, in effect, that if I am obliged not to do any harm to my fellow man, it is less because he is a rational being than because he is a sentient being: a quality that, since it is common to both animals and men, should at least give the former the right not to be needlessly mistreated by the latter.

This same study of original man, of his true needs and the fundamental principles of his duties, is also the only good means that can be used to remove those multitudes of difficulties which present themselves regarding the origin of moral inequality, the true foundations of the body politic, the reciprocal rights of its members, and a thousand other similar questions that are as important as they are poorly explained.

In considering human society from a tranquil and disinterested point of view it seems at first to manifest merely the violence of powerful men and the oppression of the weak. The mind revolts against the harshness of the former; one is inclined to deplore the blindness of the latter. And since nothing is less stable among men than those external relationships which chance brings about more often than wisdom, and which are called weakness or power, wealth or poverty, human establishments appear at first glance to be based on piles of shifting sand. It is only in examining them closely, only after having cleared away the dust and sand that surround the edifice, that one perceives the unshakeable base on which it is raised and one learns to respect its foundations. Now without a serious study of man, of his natural faculties and their successive developments, one will never succeed in making these distinctions and in separating, in the present constitution of things, what the divine will has done from what human art has pretended to do. The political and moral investigations occasioned by the important question I am examining are therefore useful in every way; and the hypothetical history of governments is an instructive lesson for man in every respect. In considering what we would have become, left to ourselves, we ought to learn to bless him whose beneficent hand, in correcting our institutions and giving them an unshakeable foundation, has prevented the disorders that must otherwise result from them, and has brought about our happiness from the means that seemed likely to add to our misery.

Learn whom God has ordered you to be, and in what part of human affairs you have been placed.

To The Republic of Geneva, Magnificent, Most Honored and Sovereign Lords

■ ■ ■

So far I have considered only physical man. Let us now try to look at him from a metaphysical and moral point of view.

In any animal I see nothing but an ingenious machine to which nature has given senses in order for it to renew its strength and to protect itself, to a certain point, from all that tends to destroy or disturb it. I am aware of precisely the same things in the human machine, with the difference that nature alone does everything in the operations of an animal, whereas man contributes, as a free agent, to his own operations. The former chooses or rejects by instinct and the later by an act of freedom. Hence an animal cannot deviate from the rule that is prescribed to it, even when it would be advantageous to do so, while man deviates from it, often to his own detriment. Thus a pigeon would die of hunger near a bowl filled with choice meats, and so would a cat perched atop a pile of fruit or grain, even though both could nourish themselves quite well with the food they disdain, if they were of a mind to try some. And thus dissolute men abandon themselves to excesses which cause them fever and death, because the mind perverts the senses and because the will still speaks when nature is silent.

Every animal has ideas, since it has senses; up to a certain point it even combines its ideas, and in this regard man differs from an animal only in degree. Some philosophers have even suggested that there is a greater difference between two given men than between a given man and an animal. Therefore it is not so much understanding which causes the specific distinction of man from all other animals as it is his being a free agent. Nature commands every animal, and beasts obey. Man feels the same impetus, but he knows he is free to go along or to resist; and it is above all in the awareness of this freedom that the spirituality of his soul is made manifest. For physics explains in some way the mechanism of the senses and the formation of ideas; but in the power of willing, or rather of choosing, and in the feeling of this power, we find only purely spiritual acts, about which the laws of mechanics explain nothing.

But if the difficulties surrounding all these questions should leave some room for dispute on this difference between man and animal, there is another very specific quality which distinguishes them and about which there can be no argument: the faculty of self-perfection, a faculty which, with the aid of circumstances, successively develops all the others, and resides among us as much in the species as in the individual. On the other hand, an animal, at the end of a few months, is what it will be all its life; and its species, at the end of a thousand years, is what it was in the first of those thousand years. Why is man alone subject to becoming an imbecile? Is it not that he thereby returns to his primitive state, and that, while the animal which has acquired nothing and which also has nothing to lose, always retains its instinct, man, in losing through old age or other accidents all that his *perfectibility* has enabled him to acquire, thus falls even lower than the animal itself? It would be sad for us to be forced to agree that this distinctive and almost unlimited faculty is the source of all man's misfortunes; that this is what, by dint of time, draws him out of that original condition in which he would pass tranquil and innocent days; that this is what, through centuries of giving rise to his enlightenment and his errors, his vices and his virtues, eventually makes him a tyrant over himself and nature.[9] It would be dreadful to be obliged to praise as a beneficent being the one who first suggested to the inhabitant on the banks of the Orinoco the use of boards which he binds to his children's temples, and which assure them of at least part of their imbecility and their original happiness.

Savage man, left by nature to instinct alone, or rather compensated for the instinct he is perhaps lacking by faculties capable of first replacing them and then of raising him to the level of instinct, will therefore begin with purely animal functions.[10] Perceiving and feeling will be his first state, which he will have in common with all animals. Willing and not willing, desiring, and fearing will be the first and nearly the only operations of his soul until new circumstances bring about new developments in it.

Whatever the moralists may say about it, human understanding owes much to the passions, which, by common consensus, also owe a great deal to it. It is by their activity that our reason is perfected. We seek to know only because we desire to find enjoyment; and it is impossible to conceive why someone who had neither desires nor fears would go to the bother of reasoning. The passions in turn take their origin from our needs, and their progress from our knowledge. For one can desire or fear things only by virtue of the ideas one can have of them, or from the simple impulse of nature; and savage man, deprived of every sort of enlightenment, feels only the passion of this latter sort. His desires do not go beyond his physical needs.[11] The only goods he knows in the universe are nourishment, a woman and rest; the only evils he fears are pain and hunger. I say pain and not death because an animal will never know what it is to die; and knowledge of death and its terrors is one of the first acquisitions that man has made in withdrawing from the animal condition.

Were it necessary, it would be easy for me to support this view with facts and to demonstrate that, among all the nations of the world, the progress of the mind has been precisely proportionate to the needs received by peoples from nature or to those needs to which circumstances have subjected them, and consequently to the passions which inclined them to provide for those needs. I would show the arts coming into being in Egypt and spreading with the flooding of the Nile. I would follow their progress among the Greeks, where they were seen to germinate, grow and rise to the heavens among the sands and rocks of Attica, though never being able to take root on the fertile banks of the Eurotas. I would point out that in general the peoples of the north are more industrious than those of the south, because they cannot get along as well without being so, as if nature thereby wanted to equalize things by giving to their minds the fertility it refuses their soil.

But without having recourse to the uncertain testimony of history, does anyone fail to see that everything seems to remove savage man from the temptation and the means of ceasing to be savage? His imagination depicts nothing to him; his heart asks nothing of him. His modest needs are so easily found at hand, and he is so far from the degree of knowledge necessary to make him desire to acquire greater knowledge, that he can have neither foresight nor curiosity. The spectacle of nature becomes a matter of indifference to him by dint of its becoming familiar to him. It is always the same order, always the same succession of changes. He does not have a mind for marveling at the greatest wonders; and we must not seek in him the philosophy that a man needs in order to know how to observe once what he has seen everyday. His soul, agitated by nothing, is given over to the single feeling of his own present existence, without any idea of the future, however near to may be, and his projects, as limited as his views, hardly extend to the end of the day. Such is, even today, the extent of the Carib's foresight. In the morning he sells his bed of cotton and in the evening he returns in tears to buy it back, for want of having foreseen that he would need it that night.

The more one meditates on this subject, the more the distance from pure sensations to the simplest knowledge increases before our eyes; and it is impossible to conceive how a man could have crossed such a wide gap by his forces alone, without the aid of communication and without the provocation of necessity. How many centuries have perhaps gone by before men were in a position to see any fire other than that from the heavens? How many different risks did they have to run before they learned the most common uses of that element? How many times did they let it go out before they had acquired the art of reproducing it? And how many times perhaps did each of these secrets die with the one who had discovered it? What will we say about agriculture, an art that requires so much labor and foresight, that depends on so many other arts, that quite obviously is practicable only in a society which is at least in its beginning stages, and that serves us not so much to derive from the earth food it would readily provide without agriculture, as to force from it those preferences that are most to our taste? But let us suppose that men multiplied to the point where the natural productions were no longer sufficient to nourish them: a supposition which, it may be said in passing, would show a great advantage for the human species in that way of life. Let us suppose that, without forges or workshops, farm implements had fallen from the heavens into the hands of the savages; that these men had conquered the mortal hatred they all have for continuous work; that they had learned to foresee their needs far enough in advance; that they had guessed how the soil is to be cultivated, grains sown, and trees planted; that they had discovered the arts of grinding wheat and fermenting grapes: all things they would need to have been taught by the gods, for it is inconceivable how they could have picked these things up on their own. Yet, after all this, what man would be so foolish as to tire himself out cultivating a field that will be plundered by the first comer, be it man or beast, who takes a fancy to the crop? And how could each man resolve to spend his life in hard labor, when, the more necessary to him the fruits of his labor may be, the surer he is of not realizing them? In a word, how could this situation lead men to cultivate the soil as long as it is not divided among them, that is to say, as long as the state of nature is not wiped out?

Were we to want to suppose a savage man as skilled in the art of thinking as our philosophers make him out to be; were we, following their example, to make him a full-fledged philosopher, discovering by himself the most sublime truths, and, by chains of terribly abstract reasoning, forming for himself maxims of justice and reason drawn from the love of order in general or from the known will of his creator; in a word, were we to suppose there was as much intelligence and enlightenment in his mind as he needs, and is in fact found to have been possessed of dullness and stupidity, what use would the species have for all that metaphysics, which could not be communicated and which would perish with the individual who would have invented it? What progress could the human race make, scattered in the woods among the animals? And to what extent could men mutually perfect and enlighten one another when, with neither a fixed dwelling nor any need for one another, they would hardly encounter one another twice in their lives, without knowing or talking to one another.

■ ■ ■

Questions for Further Exploration:

- How does Rousseau conceptualize the human "soul" or "constitution"? By what faculties does he distinguish what is natural from what is artificial in the human constitution? How does he describe "savage man" in contrast with the prevailing philosophical views of human nature?

- Compare and contrast Rousseau and Descartes on the nature of animals and humans.

- Where would Rousseau locate the root of the contemporary ecological crisis?

- How does Rousseau's metaphysical position support or justify his call for political equality and duties towards both other humans and animals? How does he define the "natural law"? What role does it play in his politics?

- Free-write your reaction to Rousseau's claim that man differs from an animal only in degree, or answer his question, "Why is man alone subject to becoming an imbecile?"

On the Origin of Species

6th Edition

Charles Darwin

Chapter IV. Natural Selection; or the Survival of the Fittest

How will the struggle for existence, briefly discussed in the last chapter, act in regard to variation? Can the principle of selection, which we have seen is so potent in the hands of man, apply under nature? I think we shall see that it can act most efficiently. Let the endless number of slight variations and individual differences occurring in our domestic productions, and, in a lesser degree, in those under nature, be borne in mind; as well as the strength of the hereditary tendency. Under domestication, it may truly be said that the whole organisation becomes in some degree plastic. But the variability, which we almost universally meet with in our domestic productions is not directly produced, as Hooker and Asa Gray have well remarked, by man; he can neither originate varieties nor prevent their occurrence; he can only preserve and accumulate such as do occur. Unintentionally he exposes organic beings to new and changing conditions of life, and variability ensues; but similar changes of conditions might and do occur under nature. Let it also be borne in mind how infinitely complex and close-fitting are the mutual relations of all organic beings to each other and to their physical conditions of life; and consequently what infinitely varied diversities of structure might be of use to each being under changing conditions of life. Can it then be thought improbable, seeing that variations useful to man have undoubtedly occurred, that other variations useful in some way to each being in the great and complex battle of life, should occur in the course of many successive generations? If such do occur, can we doubt (remembering that many more individuals are born than can possibly survive) that individuals having any advantage, however slight, over others, would have the best chance of surviving and procreating their kind? On the other hand, we may feel sure that any variation in the least degree injurious would be rigidly destroyed. This preservation of favourable individual differences and variations, and the destruction of those which are injurious, I have called Natural Selection, or the Survival of the Fittest. Variations neither useful nor injurious would not be affected by natural selection, and would be left either a fluctuating element, as perhaps we see in certain polymorphic species, or would ultimately become fixed, owing to the nature of the organism and the nature of the conditions.

Several writers have misapprehended or objected to the term Natural Selection. Some have even imagined that natural selection induces variability, whereas it implies only the preservation of such variations as arise and are beneficial to the being under its conditions of life. No one objects to agriculturists speaking of the potent effects of man's selection; and in this case the individual differences given by nature, which man for some object selects, must of necessity first occur. Others have objected that the term selection implies conscious choice in the animals which become modified; and it has even been urged that, as plants have no volition, natural selection is not applicable to them! In the literal sense of the word, no doubt, natural selection is a false term; but who ever objected to chemists speaking of the elective affinities of the various elements?—and yet an acid cannot strictly be said to elect the base with which it in preference combines. It has been said that I speak of natural selection as an active power or Deity; but who objects to an author speaking of the attraction of gravity as ruling the movements of the planets? Every one knows what is meant and is implied by such metaphorical expressions; and they are almost necessary for brevity. So again it is difficult to avoid personifying the word Nature; but I mean by nature, only the aggregate action and product of many natural laws, and by laws the sequence of events as ascertained by us. With a little familiarity such superficial objections will be forgotten.

We shall best understand the probable course of natural selection by taking the case of a country undergoing some slight physical change, for instance, of climate. The proportional numbers of its inhabitants will almost immediately undergo a change, and some species will probably become extinct. We may conclude, from what we have seen of the intimate and complex manner in which the inhabitants of each country are bound together, that any change in the numerical proportions of the inhabitants, independently of the change of climate itself, would seriously affect the others. If the country were open on its borders, new forms would certainly immigrate, and this would likewise seriously disturb the relations of some of the former inhabitants. Let it be remembered how powerful the influence of a single introduced tree or mammal has been shown to be. But in the case of an island, or of a country partly surrounded by barriers, into which new and better adapted forms could not freely enter, we should then have places in the economy of nature which would assuredly be better filled up if some of the original inhabitants were in some manner modified; for, had the area been open to immigration, these same places would have been seized on by intruders. In such cases, slight modifications, which in any way favoured the individuals of any species, by better adapting them to their altered conditions, would tend to be preserved; and natural selection would have free scope for the work of improvement.

We have good reason to believe, as shown in the first chapter, that changes in the conditions of life give a tendency to increased variability; and in the foregoing cases the conditions the changed, and this would manifestly be favourable to natural selection, by affording a better chance of the occurrence of profitable variations. Unless such occur, natural selection can do nothing. Under the term of "variations," it must never be forgotten that mere individual differences are included. As man can produce a great result with his domestic animals and plants by adding up in any given direction individual differences, so could natural selection, but far more easily from having incomparably longer time for action. Nor do I believe that any great physical change, as of climate, or any unusual degree of isolation, to check immigration, is necessary in order that new and unoccupied places should be left for natural selection to fill up by improving some of the varying inhabitants. For as all the inhabitants of each country are struggling together with nicely balanced forces, extremely slight modifications in the structure or habits of one species would often give it an advantage over others; and still further modifications of the same kind would often still further increase the advantage, as long as the species continued under the same conditions of life and profited by similar means of subsistence and defence. No country can be named in which all the native inhabitants are now so perfectly adapted to each other and to the physical conditions under which they live, that none of them could be still better adapted or improved; for in all countries, the natives have been so far conquered by naturalised productions that they have allowed some foreigners to take firm possession of the land. And as foreigners have thus in every country beaten some of the natives, we may safely conclude that the natives might have been modified with advantage, so as to have better resisted the intruders.

As man can produce, and certainly has produced, a great result by his methodical and unconscious means of selection, what may not natural selection effect? Man can act only on external and visible characters: Nature, if I may be allowed to personify the natural preservation or survival of the fittest, cares nothing for appearances, except in so far as they are useful to any being. She can act on every internal organ, on every shade of constitutional difference, on the whole machinery of life. Man selects only for his own good: Nature only for that of the being which she tends. Every selected character is fully exercised by her, as is implied by the fact of their selection. Man keeps the natives of many climates in the same country. He seldom exercises each selected character in some peculiar and fitting manner; he feeds a long and a short-beaked pigeon on the same food; he does not exercise a long-backed or long-legged quadruped in any peculiar manner; he exposes sheep with long and short wool to the same climate; does not allow the most vigorous males to struggle for the females; he does not rigidly destroy all inferior animals, but protects during each varying season, as far as lies in his power, all his productions. He often begins his selection by some half-monstrous form, or at least by some modification prominent enough to catch the eye or to be plainly useful to him. Under nature, the slightest differences of structure or constitution may well turn the nicely-balanced scale in the struggle for life, and so be preserved. How fleeting are the wishes and efforts of man! How short his time, and consequently how poor will be his results, compared with those accumulated by Nature during whole geological periods! Can we wonder, then, that Nature's productions should be far "truer" in character than man's productions; that they should be infinitely better adapted to the most complex conditions of life, and should plainly bear the stamp of far higher workmanship?

■ ■ ■

If under changing conditions of life organic beings present individual differences in almost every part of their structure, and this cannot be disputed; if there be, owing to their geometrical rate of increase, a severe struggle for life at some age, season or year, and this certainly cannot be disputed; then, considering the infinite complexity of the relations of all organic beings to each other and to their conditions of life, causing an infinite diversity in structure, constitution, and habits, to be advantageous to them, it would be a most extraordinary fact if no variations had ever occurred useful to each being's own welfare, in the same manner as so many variations have occurred useful to man. But if variations useful to any organic being ever do occur, assuredly individuals thus characterised will have the best chance of being preserved in the struggle for life; and from the strong principle of inheritance, these will tend to produce offspring similarly characterised. This principle of preservation, or the survival of the fittest, I have called natural selection. It leads to the improvement of each creature in relation to its organic and inorganic conditions of life; and consequently, in most cases, to what must be regarded as an advance in organisation. Nevertheless, low and simple forms will long endure if well fitted for their simple conditions of life.

Natural selection, on the principle of qualities being inherited at corresponding ages, can modify the egg, seed, or young as easily as the adult. Among many animals sexual selection will have given its aid to ordinary selection by assuring to the most vigorous and best adapted males the greatest number of offspring. Sexual selection will also give characters useful to the males alone in their struggles or rivalry with other males; and these characters will be transmitted to one sex or to both sexes, according to the form of inheritance which prevails.

Whether natural selection has really thus acted in adapting the various forms of life to their several conditions and stations, must be judged by the general tenour and balance of evidence given in the following chapters. But we have already seen how it entails extinction; and how largely extinction has acted in the world's history, geology plainly declares. Natural selection, also, leads to divergence of character; for the more organic beings diverge in structure, habits and constitution, by so much the more can a large number be supported on the area, of which we see proof by looking to the inhabitants of any small spot, and to the productions naturalised in foreign lands. Therefore, during the modification of the descendants of any one species, and during the incessant struggle of all species to increase in numbers, the more diversified the descendants become, the better will be their chance of success in the battle for life. Thus the small differences distinguishing varieties of the same species, steadily tend to increase, till they equal the greater differences between species of the same genus, or even of distinct genera.

We have seen that it is the common, the widely diffused, and widely ranging species, belonging to the larger genera within each class, which vary most; and these tend to transmit to their modified offspring that superiority which now makes them dominant in their own countries. Natural selection, as has just been remarked, leads to divergence of character and to much extinction of the less improved and intermediate forms of life. On these principles, the nature of the affinities, and the generally well defined distinctions between the innumerable organic beings in each class throughout the world, may be explained. It is a truly wonderful fact—the wonder of which we are apt to overlook from familiarity—that all animals and all plants throughout all time and space should be related to each other in groups, subordinate to groups, in the manner which we everywhere behold—namely, varieties of the same species most closely related, species of the same genus less closely and unequally related, forming sections and sub-genera, species of distinct genera much less closely related, and genera related in different degrees, forming sub-families, families, orders, sub-classes, and classes. The several subordinate groups in any class cannot be ranked in a single file, but seem clustered round points, and these round other points, and so on in almost endless cycles. If species had been independently created, no explanation would have been possible of this kind of classification; but it is explained through inheritance and the complex action of natural selection, entailing extinction and divergence of character, as we have seen illustrated in the diagram.

The affinities of all the beings of the same class have sometimes been represented by a great tree. I believe this simile largely speaks the truth. The green and budding twigs may represent existing species; and those produced during former years may represent the long succession of extinct species. At each period of growth all the growing twigs have tried to branch out on all sides, and to overtop and kill the surrounding twigs and branches, in the same manner as species and groups of species have at all times overmastered other species in the great battle for life. The limbs divided into great branches, and these into lesser and lesser branches, were themselves once, when the tree was young, budding twigs; and this connexion of the former and present buds by ramifying branches may well represent the classification of all extinct and living species in groups subordinate to groups. Of the many twigs which flourished when the tree was a mere bush, only two or three, now grown into great branches, yet survive and bear the other branches; so with the species which lived during long-past geological periods, very few have left living and modified descendants. From the first growth of the tree, many a limb and branch has decayed and dropped off; and these fallen branches of various sizes may represent those whole orders, families, and genera which have now no living representatives, and which are known to us only in a fossil state. As we here and there see a thin, straggling branch springing from a fork low down in a tree, and which by some chance has been favoured and is still alive on its summit, so we occasionally see an animal like the Ornithorhynchus or Lepidosiren, which in some small degree connects by its affinities two large branches of life, and which has apparently been saved from fatal competition by having inhabited a protected station. As buds give rise by growth to fresh buds, and these, if vigorous, branch out and overtop on all sides many a feebler branch, so by generation I believe it has been with the great Tree of Life, which fills with its dead and broken branches the crust of the earth, and covers the surface with its ever-branching and beautiful ramifications.

Questions for Further Exploration:

- What is the nature of the reality Darwin calls "Natural Selection, or the Survival of the Fittest"? What is his view of "human" and of "nature"? What is the place of agency (free will) in Darwin's theory?

- Is atheism a consequence of Darwinism? Could Darwin be read as pan-psychic or pantheist?

- Compare and contrast the theories of change offered by Darwin and Aristotle.

- Compare and contrast Darwin and Descartes on the nature of animals and humans.

- Where would Darwin locate the root of the contemporary ecological crisis?

- Free-write: Does the Darwinian view of reality instill optimism or pessimism at the prospect of solving environmental problems? Are you a Darwinian?

Darwin's Dangerous Idea

An Idea is Born

Daniel C. Dennett

2. Natural Selection—An Awful Stretcher

It is an awful stretcher to believe that a peacock's tail was thus formed; but, believing it, I believe in the same principle somewhat modified applied to man.

—Charles Darwin, letter quoted in Desmond and Moore 1991, p. 553

Darwin's project in *Origin* can be divided in two: to prove *that* modern species were revised descendants of earlier species—species had evolved—and to show *how* this process of "descent with modification" had occurred. If Darwin hadn't had a vision of a mechanism, natural selection, by which this well-nigh-inconceivable historical transformation could have been accomplished, he would probably not have had the motivation to assemble all the circumstantial evidence that it had actually occurred. Today we can readily enough imagine proving Darwin's first case—the brute historic fact of descent with modification—quite independently of any consideration of natural selection or indeed any other mechanism for bringing these brute events about, but for Darwin the idea of the mechanism was both the hunting license he needed, and an unwavering guide to the right questions to ask.[1]

---

[1] This has often happened in science. For instance, for many years there was lots of evidence lying around in favor of the hypothesis that the continents have drifted—that Africa and South America were once adjacent and broke apart—but until the mechanisms of plate tectonics were conceived, it was hard to take the hypothesis seriously.

The idea of natural selection was not itself a miraculously novel creation of Darwin's but, rather, the offspring of earlier ideas that had been vigorously discussed for years and even generations (for an excellent account of this intellectual history, see R. Richards 1987). Chief among these parent ideas was an insight Darwin gained from reflection on the 1798 *Essay on the Principle of Population* by Thomas Malthus, which argued that population explosion and famine were inevitable, given the excess fertility of human beings, unless drastic measures were taken. The grim Malthusian vision of the social and political forces that could act to check human overpopulation may have strongly flavored Darwin's thinking (and undoubtedly has flavored the shallow political attacks of many an anti-Darwinian), but the idea Darwin needed from Malthus is purely logical. It has nothing at all to do with political ideology, and can be expressed in very abstract and general terms.

Suppose a world in which organisms have many offspring. Since the offspring themselves will have many offspring, the population will grow and grow ("geometrically") until inevitably, sooner or later—surprisingly soon, in fact—it must grow too large for the available resources (of food, of space, of whatever the organisms need to survive long enough to reproduce). At that point, whenever it happens, not all organisms will have offspring. Many will die childless. It was Malthus who pointed out the mathematical inevitability of such a crunch in *any* population of long-term reproducers—people, animals, plants (or, for that matter, Martian clone-machines, not that such fanciful possibilities were discussed by Malthus). Those populations that reproduce at less than the replacement rate are headed for extinction unless they reverse the trend. Populations that maintain a stable population over long periods of time will do so by settling on a rate of overproduction of offspring that is balanced by the vicissitudes encountered. This is obvious, perhaps, for houseflies and other prodigious breeders, but Darwin drove the point home with a calculation of his own: "The elephant is reckoned to be the slowest breeder of all known animals, and I have taken some pains to estimate its probable minimum rate of natural increase: . . . at the end of the fifth century there would be alive fifteen million elephants, descended from the first pair" (*Origin,* p. 64).[2] Since elephants have been around for millions of years, we can be sure that only a fraction of the elephants born in any period have progeny of their own.

So the normal state of affairs for any sort of reproducers is one in which more offspring are produced in any one generation than will in turn reproduce in the next. In other words, it is almost always crunch

---

[2]This sum as it appeared in the first edition is wrong, and when this was pointed out, Darwin revised his calculations for later editions, but the general principle is still unchallenged.

time.[3] At such a crunch, which prospective parents will "win"? Will it be a fair lottery, in which every organism has an equal chance of being among the few that reproduce? In a political context, this is where invidious themes enter, about power, privilege, injustice, treachery, class warfare, and the like, but we can elevate the observation from its political birthplace and consider in the abstract, as Darwin did, what would—must—happen in nature. Darwin added two further logical points to the insight he had found in Malthus: the first was that at crunch time, if there was significant variation among the contestants, then any advantages enjoyed by any of the contestants would inevitably bias the sample that reproduced. However tiny the advantage in question, if it was actually an advantage (and thus not absolutely invisible to nature), it would tip the scales in favor of those who held it. The second was that *if* there was a "strong principle of inheritance"—if offspring tended to be more like their parents than like their parents' contemporaries—the biases created by advantages, however small, would become amplified over time, creating trends that could grow indefinitely. "More individuals are born than can possibly survive. A grain in the balance will determine which individual shall live and which shall die,—which variety of species shall increase in number, and which shall decrease, or finally become extinct" (*Origin,* p. 467).

What Darwin saw was that if one merely supposed these few general conditions to apply at crunch time—conditions for which he could supply ample evidence—the resulting process would *necessarily* lead in the direction of individuals in future generations who tended to be better equipped to deal with the problems of resource limitation that had been faced by the individuals of their parents' generation. This fundamental idea—Darwin's dangerous idea, the idea that generates so much insight, turmoil, confusion, anxiety—is thus actually quite simple. Darwin summarizes it in two long sentences at the end of chapter 4 of *Origin:*

> If during the long course of ages and under varying conditions of
> life, organic beings vary at all in the several parts of their organi-
> zation, and I think this cannot be disputed; if there be, owing to
> the high geometric powers of increase of each species, at some

---

[3] A familiar example of Malthus' rule in action is the rapid expansion of yeast populations introduced into fresh bread dough or grape juice. Thanks to the feast of sugar and other nutrients, population explosions ensue that last for a few hours in the dough, or a few weeks in the juice, but soon the yeast populations hit the Malthusian ceiling, done in by their own voraciousness and the accumulation of their waste products—carbon dioxide (which forms the bubbles that make the brad rise, and the fizz in champagne) and alcohol being the two that we yeast-exploiters tend to value.

age, season, or year, a severe struggle for life, and this certainly cannot be disputed; then, considering the infinite complexity of the relations of all organic beings to each other and to their conditions of existence, causing an infinite diversity in structure, constitution, and habits, to be advantageous to them, I think it would be a most extraordinary fact if no variation ever had occurred useful to each being's own welfare, in the same way as so many variations have occurred useful to man. But if variations useful to any organic being do occur, assuredly individuals thus characterized will have the best chance of being preserved in the struggle for life; and from the strong principle of inheritance they will tend to produce offspring similarly characterized. This principle of preservation, I have called, for the sake of brevity, Natural Selection. [*Origin,* p. 127.]

This was Darwin's great idea, not the idea of evolution, but the idea of evolution *by natural selection,* an idea he himself could never formulate with sufficient rigor and detail to prove, though he presented a brilliant case for it.

■ ■ ■

3. Did Darwin Explain the Origin of the Species

■ ■ ■

The theoretical power of Darwin's abstract scheme was due to several features that Darwin quite firmly identified, and appreciated better than many of his supporters, but lacked the terminology to describe explicitly. Today we could capture these features under a single term. Darwin had discovered the power of an *algorithm.* An algorithm is a certain sort of formal process that can be counted on—logically—to yield a certain sort of result whenever it is "run" or instantiated. Algorithms are not new, and were not new in Darwin's day. Many familiar arithmetic procedures, such as long division or balancing your checkbook, are algorithms, and so are the decision procedures for playing perfect tic-tac-toe, and for putting a list of words into alphabetical order. What is relatively new—permitting us valuable hindsight on Darwin's discovery—is the theoretical reflection by mathematicians and logicians on the nature and power of algorithms in general, a twentieth-century development which led to the birth of the computer, which has led in turn, of course, to a much deeper and more lively understanding of the powers of algorithms in general.

The term *algorithm* descends, via Latin (*algorismus*) to early English (*algorisme* and, mistakenly therefrom, *algorithm*), from the name of a Persian mathematician, Mûusâ al-Khowârizm, whose book on arithmetical procedures, written about 835 A.D., was translated into Latin in the twelfth century by Adelard of Bath or Robert of Chester. The idea that an algorithm is a foolproof and somehow "mechanical" procedure has been present for centuries, but it was the pioneering work of Alan Turing, Kurt Gödel, and Alonzo Church in the 1930s that more or less fixed our current understanding of the term. Three key features of algorithms will be important to us, and each is somewhat difficult to define. Each, moreover, has given rise to confusions (and anxieties) that continue to beset our thinking about Darwin's revolutionary discovery, so we will have to revisit and reconsider these introductory characterizations several times before we are through:

1. *substrate neutrality:* The procedure for long division works equally well with pencil or pen, paper or parchment, neon lights or skywriting, using any symbol system you like. The power of the procedure is due to its *logical* structure, not the causal powers of the materials used in the instantiation, just so long as those causal powers permit the prescribed steps to be followed exactly.

2. *underlying mindlessness:* Although the overall design of the procedure may be brilliant, or yield brilliant results, each constituent step, as well as the transition between steps, is utterly simple. How simple? Simple enough for a dutiful idiot to perform—or for a straightforward mechanical device to perform. The standard textbook analogy notes that algorithms are *recipes* of sorts, designed to be followed by *novice* cooks. A recipe book written for great chefs might include the phrase "Poach the fish in a suitable wine until almost done," but an algorithm for the same process might begin, "Choose a white wine that says 'dry' on the label; take a corkscrew and open the bottle; pour an inch of wine in the bottom of a pan; turn the burner under the pan on high; . . ."—a tedious breakdown of the process into dead-simple steps, requiring no wise decisions or delicate judgments or intuitions on the part of the recipe-reader.

3. *guaranteed results:* Whatever it is that an algorithm does, it always does it, if it is executed without misstep. An algorithm is a foolproof recipe.

It is easy to see how these features made the computer possible. *Every computer program is an algorithm,* ultimately composed of simple steps that can be executed with stupendous reliability by one simple mechanism or another. Electronic circuits are the usual choice, but the power of computers owes nothing (save speed) to the causal peculiarities of electrons darting about on silicon chips. The very same algorithms can be performed (even faster) by devices shunting photons in glass fibers, or (much, much slower) by teams of people using paper and pencil. And as we shall see, the capacity of computers to run algorithms with tremendous speed and reliability is now permitting theoreticians to explore Darwin's dangerous idea in ways heretofore impossible, with fascinating results.

What Darwin discovered was not really *one* algorithm but, rather, a large class of related algorithms that he had no clear way to distinguish. We can now reformulate his fundamental idea as follows:

> Life on Earth has been generated over billions of years in a single branching tree—the Tree of Life—by one algorithmic process or another.

What this claim mans will become clear gradually, as we sort through the various ways people have tried to express it. In some versions it is utterly vacuous and uninformative; in others it is manifestly false. In between lie the versions that really do explain the origin of species and promise to explain much else besides. These versions are becoming clearer all the time, thanks as much to the determined criticisms of those who frankly hate the idea of evolution as an algorithm, as to the rebuttals of those who love it.

■ ■ ■

5. Processes as Algorithms

When theorists think of algorithms, they often have in mind kinds of algorithms with properties that are *not* shared by the algorithms that will concern us. When mathematicians think about algorithms, for instance, they usually have in mind algorithms that can be proven to compute particular mathematical functions of interest to them. (Long division is a homely example. A procedure for breaking down a huge number into its prime factors is one that attracts attention in the exotic world of cryptography.) But the algorithms that will concern us have nothing particular to do with the number system or other mathematical objects; they are algorithms for sorting, winnowing, and building things.[8]

---

[8]Computer scientists sometimes restrict the term *algorithm* to programs that can be proven to *terminate*—that have no infinite loops in them, for instance. But this special sense, valuable as it is for some mathematical purposes, is not of much use to us. Indeed, few of the computer programs in daily use around the world would qualify as algorithms in this restricted sense; most are designed to cycle indefinitely, patiently waiting for instructions (including the instruction to terminate, without which they keep on going). Their subroutines, however, are algorithms in this strict sense—except where undetected "bugs" lurk that can cause the program to "hang."

Because most mathematical discussion of algorithms focus on their guaranteed or mathematically provable powers, people sometimes make the elementary mistake of thinking that a process that makes use of chance or randomness is not an algorithm. But even long division makes good use of randomness!

$$\frac{7?}{47)\overline{326574}}$$

Does the divisor go into the dividend six or seven or eight times? Who knows? Who cares? You don't have to know; you don't have to have any wit or discernment to do long division. The algorithm directs you just to choose a digit—at random, if you like—and check out the result. If the chosen number turns out to be too small, increase it by one and start over; if too large, decrease it. The good thing about long division is that it always works eventually, even if you are maximally stupid in making your first choice, in which case it just takes a little longer. Achieving success on hard tasks in spite of utter stupidity is what makes computers seem magical—how could something as mindless as a machine do something as smart as that? Not surprisingly, then, the tactic of finessing ignorance by randomly generating a candidate and then testing it out mechanically is a ubiquitous feature of interesting algorithms. Not only does it not interfere with their provable powers as algorithms; it is often the key to their power. (See Dennett 1984, pp. 149–52, on the particularly interesting powers of Michael Rabin's random algorithms.)

We can begin zeroing in on the phylum of evolutionary algorithms by considering everyday algorithms that share important properties with them. Darwin draws our attention to repeated waves of competition and selection, so consider the standard algorithm for organizing an elimination tournament, such as a tennis tournament, which eventually culminates with quarter-finals, semi-finals, and then a final, determining the solitary winner.

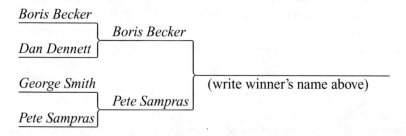

Notice that this procedure meets the three conditions. It is the same procedure whether drawn in chalk on a blackboard, or updated in a computer file, or—a weird possibility—not written down anywhere, but simply enforced by building a huge fan of fenced-off tennis courts each with two entrance gates and a single exit gate leading the winner to the court where the next match is to be played. (The losers are shot and buried where they fall.) It doesn't take a genius to march the contestants through the drill, filling in the blanks at the end of each match (or identifying and shooting the losers). And it always works.

But what, exactly, does this algorithm *do?* It takes as input a set of competitors and guarantees to terminate by identifying a single winner. But what is a winner? It all depends on the competition. Suppose the tournament in question is not tennis but coin-tossing. One player tosses and the other calls; the winner advances. The winner of this tournament will be that single player who has won n consecutive coin-tosses without a loss, depending on how many rounds it takes to complete the tournament.

There is something strange and trivial about this tournament, but what is it? The winner does have a rather remarkable property. How often have you ever met anyone who just won, say, ten consecutive coin-tosses without a loss? Probably never. The odds against there being such a person might seem enormous, and in the normal course of events, they surely are. If some gambler offered you ten-to-one odds that he could produce someone who before your very eyes would proceed to win ten consecutive coin-tosses using a fair coin, you might be inclined to think this a good bet. If so, you had better hope the gambler doesn't have 1,024 accomplices (they don't have to cheat—they play fair and square). For that is all it takes (2^{10} competitors) to form a ten-round tournament. The gambler wouldn't have a clue, as the tournament started, which person would end up being the exhibit A that would guarantee his winning the wager, but the tournament algorithm is sure to produce such a person in short order—it is a sucker bet with a surefire win for the gambler. (I am not responsible for any injuries you may sustain if you attempt to get rich by putting this tidbit of practical philosophy into use.)

Any elimination tournament produces a winner, who "automatically" has whatever property was required to advance through the rounds, but, as the coin-tossing tournament demonstrates, the property in question *may* be "merely historical"—a trivial fact about the competitor's past history that has no bearing at all on his or her future prospects. Suppose, for instance, the United Nations were to decide that all future international conflicts would be settled by a coin-toss to which each nation sends a representative (if more than one nation is involved, it will have to be some sort of tournament—it might be a "round robin," which is a different algorithm). Whom should we designate as our national representative? The best coin-toss caller in the land, obviously. Suppose we organized every man, woman, and child in the U.S.A. into a giant elimination tournament. Somebody would have to win, and that person would have just won twenty-eight consecutive coin-tosses without a loss! This would be an irrefutable historical fact about that person, but since calling a coin-toss is just a matter of luck, there is absolutely no reason to believe that the winner of such a tournament would do any better in international competition than somebody else who lost in an earlier round of the tournament. Chance has no memory. A person who holds the winning lottery ticket has certainly *been* lucky, and, thanks to the millions she has just won, she may never need to be lucky again—which is just as well, since there is no reason to think she is more likely than anyone else to win the lottery a second time, or to win the next coin-toss she calls. (Failing to appreciate the fact that chance has no memory is known as the Gambler's Fallacy; it is surprisingly popular—so popular that I should probably stress that it *is* a fallacy, beyond any doubt or controversy.)

In contrast to tournaments of pure luck, like the coin-toss tournament, there are tournaments of skill, like tennis tournaments. Here there *is* reason to believe that the players in the later rounds would do better *again* if they played the players who lost in the early rounds. There is reason to believe—but no guarantee—that the winner of such a tournament is the best player of them all, not just today but tomorrow. Yet, though any well-run tournament is guaranteed to produce a winner, there is no guarantee that a tournament of skill will identify the best player as the winner in any nontrivial sense. That's why we sometimes say, in the opening ceremonies, "May the best man win!"—because it is not guaranteed by the procedure. The best player—the one who is best by "engineering" standards (has the most reliable backhand, fastest serve, most stamina, etc.)—may have an off day, or sprain his ankle, or get hit by lightning. Then, trivially, he may be bested in competition by a player who is not really as good as he is. But nobody would bother organizing or entering tournaments of skill if it weren't the case that *in the long run,* tournaments of skill are won by the best players. *That* is guaranteed by the very definition of a fair tournament of skill; if there were no probability greater than half that the better players would win each round, it would be a tournament of luck, not of skill.

Skill and luck intermingle naturally and inevitably in any real competition, but their ratios may vary widely. A tennis tournament played on very bumpy courts would raise the luck ratio, as would an innovation in which the players were required to play Russian roulette with a loaded revolver before continuing after the first set. But even in such a luck-ridden contest, more of the better players would *tend,* statistically, to get to the late rounds. The power of a tournament to "discriminate" skill differences in the long run may be diminished by haphazard catastrophe, but it is not in general reduced to zero. This fact, which is as true of evolutionary algorithms in nature as of elimination tournaments in sports, is sometimes overlooked by commentators on evolution.

Skill, in contrast to luck, is *projectable;* in the same or similar circumstances, it can be counted on to give repeat performances. This relativity to circumstances shows us another way in which a tournament might be weird. What if the conditions of competition kept changing (like the croquet game in *Alice in Wonderland*)? If you play tennis the first round, chess in the second round, golf in the third round, and billiards in the fourth round, there is no reason to suppose the eventual winner will be particularly good, compared with the whole field, in *any* of these endeavors—all the good golfers may lose in the chess round and never get a chance to demonstrate their prowess, and even if luck plays no role in the fourth-round billiards final, the winner might turn out to be the second-*worst* billiards player in the whole field. Thus there has to be some measure of uniformity of the conditions of competition for there to be any *interesting* outcome to a tournament.

But does a tournament—or any algorithm—have to do something interesting? No. The algorithms we tend to talk about almost always do something interesting—that's why they attract out attention. But a procedure doesn't fail to be an algorithm just because it is of no conceivable use or value to anyone. Consider a variation on the elimination-tournament algorithm in which the *losers* of the semi-finals play in the finals. This is a stupid rule, destroying the *point* of the whole tournament, but the tournament would still be an algorithm. Algorithms don't have to have points or purposes. In addition to all the useful algorithms for alphabetizing lists of words, there are kazillions of algorithms for reliably *mis*alphabetizing words, and they work perfectly every time (as if anyone would care). Just as there is an algorithm (many, actually) for finding the square root of any number, so there are algorithms for finding the square root of any number except 18 or 703. Some algorithms do things so boringly irregular and pointless that there is no succinct way of saying what they are *for.* They just do what they do, and they do it every time.

We can now expose perhaps the most common misunderstanding of Darwinism: the idea that Darwin showed that evolution by natural selection is a procedure *for* producing Us. Ever since Darwin proposed his theory, people have often misguidedly tried to interpret it as showing that we are the destination, the goal, the point of all that winnowing and competition, and our arrival on the scene was guaranteed by the mere holding of the tournament. This confusion has been fostered by evolution's friends and foes alike, and it is parallel to the confusion of the coin-toss tournament winner who basks in the misconsidered glory of the idea that since the tournament had to have a winner, and since he is the winner, the tournament had to produce him as the winner. Evolution can be an algorithm, and evolution can have produced us by an algorithmic process, without its being true that evolution is an algorithm for producing us. The main conclusion of Stephen Jay Gould's *Wonderful Life: The Burgess Shale and the Nature of History* (1989a) is that if we were to "wind the tape of life back" and play it again and again, the likelihood is infinitesimal of *Us* being the product on any other run through the evolutionary mill. This is undoubtedly true (if by "Us" we mean the particular variety of *Homo sapiens* we are: hairless and upright, with five fingers on each of two hands, speaking English and French and playing tennis and chess). Evolution is not a process that was designed to produce us, but it does not follow from this that evolution is not an algorithmic process that has in fact produced us. (Chapter 10 will explore this issue in more detail.)

Evolutionary algorithms are manifestly interesting algorithms—interesting to us, at least—not because what they are guaranteed to do is interesting to us, but because what they are guaranteed to *tend* to do is interesting to us. They are like tournaments of skill in this regard. The power of an algorithm to yield something of interest or value is not at all limited to what the algorithm can be mathematically proven to yield in a foolproof way, and this is especially true of evolutionary algorithms. Most of the controversies about Darwinism, as we shall see, boil down to disagreements about just how powerful certain postulated evolutionary processes are—could they actually do all this or all that in the time available? These are typically investigations into what an evolutionary algorithm *might* produce, or *could* produce, or is *likely* to produce, and only indirectly into what such an algorithm would *inevitably* produce. Darwin himself sets the stage in the wording of his summary: his idea is a claim about what "assuredly" the process of natural selection will "tend" to yield.

All algorithms are guaranteed to do whatever they do, but it need not be anything interesting; some algorithms are further guaranteed to tend (with probability p) to do something—which may or may not be interesting. But if what an algorithm is guaranteed to do doesn't have to be "interesting" in any way, how are we going to distinguish algorithms from other processes? Won't *any* process be an algorithm? Is the surf pounding on the beach an algorithmic process? Is the sun baking the clay of a dried-up riverbed an algorithmic process? The answer is that there may be features of these processes that *are* best appreciated if we consider them as algorithms! Consider, for instance, the question of why the grains of sand on a beach are so uniform in size. This is due to a natural sorting process that occurs thanks to the repetitive launching of the grains by the surf—alphabetical order on a grand scale, you might say. The pattern of cracks that appear in the sun-baked clay may be best explained by looking at chains of events that are not unlike the successive rounds in a tournament.

Or consider the process of annealing a piece of metal to temper it. What could be a more physical, less "computational" process than that? The blacksmith repeatedly heats the metal and then lets it cool, and somehow in the process it becomes much stronger. How? What kinds of an explanation can we give for this magical transformation? Does the heat create special toughness atoms that coat the surface? Or does it suck subatomic glue out of the atmosphere that binds all the iron atoms together? No, nothing like that happens. The right level of explanation is the algorithmic level: As the metal cools from its molten state, the solidification starts in many different spots at the same time, creating crystals that grow together until the whole is solid. But the first time this happens, the arrangement of the individual crystal structures is suboptimal—weakly held together, and with lots of internal stresses and strains. Heating it up again—but not all the way to melting—partially breaks down these structures, so that, when they are permitted to cool the next time, the broken-up bits will adhere to the still-solid bits in a different arrangement. It can be proven mathematically that these rearrangements will tend to get better and better, approaching the optimum or strongest total structure, provided the regime of heating and cooling has the right parameters. So powerful is this optimization procedure that it has been used as the inspiration for an entirely general problem-solving technique in computer science—"simulated annealing," which has nothing to do with metals or heat, but is just a way of getting a computer program to build, disassemble, and rebuild a data structure (such as another program), over and over, blindly groping towards a better— indeed, an optimal—version (Kirkpatrick, Gelatt and Vecchi 1983). This was one of the major insights leading to the development of "Boltzmann machines" and "Hopfield nets" and the other constraint-satisfaction schemes that are the basis for the Connectionist or "neural-net" architectures in Artificial Intelligence. (For overviews, see Smolensky 1983, Rumelhart 1989, Churchland and Sejnowski 1992, and, on a philosophical level, Dennett 1987a, Paul Churchland 1989.)

If you want a deep understanding of how annealing works in metallurgy, you have to learn the physics of all the forces operating at the atomic level, of course, but notice that the basic idea of how annealing works (and particularly *why* it *works*) can be lifted clear of those details—after all, I just explained it in simple lay terms (and I don't know the physics!). The explanation of annealing can be put in *substrate-neutral* terminology: we should expect optimization of a certain sort to occur in any "material" that has components that get put together by a certain sort of building process and that can be disassembled in a sequenced way by changing a single global parameter, etc. That is what is common to the processes going on in the glowing steel bar and the humming supercomputer.

Darwin's ideas about the powers of natural selection can also be lifted out of their home base in biology. Indeed, as we have already noted, Darwin himself had few inklings (and what inklings he had turned out to be wrong) about how the microscopic processes of genetic inheritance were accomplished. Not knowing any of the details about the physical substrate, he could nevertheless discern that if certain conditions were somehow met, certain effects would be wrought. This substrate neutrality has been crucial in permitting the basic Darwinian insights to float like a cork on the waves of subsequent research and controversy, for what has happened since Darwin has a curious flip-flop in it. Darwin, as we noted in the preceding chapter, never hit upon the utterly necessary idea of a gene, but along came Mendel's concept to provide just the right structure for making mathematical sense out of heredity (and solving Darwin's nasty problem of blending inheritance). And then, when DNA was identified as the actual physical vehicle of the genes, it looked at first (and still looks to many participants) as if Mendel's genes could be simply *identified* as particular hunks of DNA. But then complexities began to emerge; the more scientists have learned about the actual molecular biology of DNA and is role in reproduction, the clearer it becomes that the Mendelian story is at best a vast oversimplification. Some would go so far as to say that we have recently learned that there really *aren't* any Mendelian genes! Having climbed Mendel's ladder, we must now throw it away. But of course no one wants to throw away such a valuable tool, still proving itself daily in hundreds of scientific and medical contexts. The solution is to bump Mendel up a level, and declare that he, like Darwin, captured an *abstract* truth about inheritance. We may, if we like, talk of *virtual genes,* considering them to have their reality distributed around in the concrete materials of the DNA. (There is much to be said in favor of this option, which I will discuss further in chapters 5 and 12.)

But then, to return to the question raised above, are there any limits at all on what may be considered an algorithmic process? I guess the answer is No; if you wanted to, you could treat any process at the abstract level as an algorithmic process. So what? Only some processes yield interesting results when you do treat them as algorithms, but we don't have to try to define "algorithm" in such a way as to include only the *interesting* ones (a tall philosophical order!). The problem will take care of itself, since nobody will waste time examining the algorithms that aren't interesting for one reason or another. It all depends on what needs explaining. If what strikes you as puzzling is the uniformity of the sand grains or the strength of the blade, an algorithmic explanation is what will satisfy your curiosity—and it will be the truth. Other interesting features of the same phenomena, or the processes that created them, might not yield to an algorithmic treatment.

Here, then, is Darwin's dangerous idea: the algorithmic level *is* the level that best accounts for the speed of the antelope, the wing of the eagle, the shape of the orchid, the diversity of species, and all the other occasions for wonder in the world of nature. It is hard to believe that something as mindless and mechanical as an algorithm could produce such wonderful things. No matter how impressive the products of an algorithm, the underlying process always consists of nothing but a set of individually mindless steps succeeding each other without the help of any intelligent supervision; they are "automatic" by definition: the workings of an automaton. They feed on each other, or on blind chance—coin-flips, if you like—and on nothing else. Most algorithms we are familiar with have rather modest products: they do long division or alphabetize lists or figure out the income of the Average Taxpayer. Fancier algorithms produce the dazzling computer-animated graphics we see every day on television, transforming faces, creating herds of imaginary ice-skating polar bears, simulating whole virtual worlds of entities never seen or imagined before. But the actual biosphere is much fancier still, by many orders of magnitude. Can it really be the outcome of nothing but a cascade of algorithmic processes feeding on chance? And if so, who designed that cascade? Nobody. It is itself the product of a blind, algorithmic process. As Darwin himself put it, in a letter to the geologist Charles Lyell shortly after publication of *Origin,* "I would give absolutely nothing for the theory of Natural Selection, if it requires miraculous additions at any one stage of descent. . . . If I were convinced that I required such additions to the theory of natural selection, I would reject it as rubbish . . ." (F. Darwin 1911, vol. 2, pp. 6–7).

According to Darwin, then, evolution is an algorithmic process. Putting it this way is still controversial. One of the tugs-of-war going on within evolutionary biology is between those who are relentlessly pushing, pushing, pushing towards an algorithmic treatment, and those who, for various submerged reasons, are resisting this trend. It is rather as if there were metallurgists around who were disappointed by the algorithmic explanation of annealing. "You mean that's all there is to it? No submicroscopic Superglue specially created by the heating and cooling process?" Darwin has convinced all the scientists that evolution, like annealing, *works.* His radical vision of *how* and *why* it works is still somewhat embattled, largely because those who resist can dimly see that their skirmish is part of a larger campaign. If the game is lost in evolutionary biology, where will it all end?

Questions for Further Exploration:

- According to Dennett, what is Darwin's dangerous idea?

- What is an "algorithm"? What key features help explain the power of an algorithm?

- According to Dennett, what role is played by algorithm in Darwin's theory of reality?

- What is dangerous about the idea of evolution by natural selection?

- What does Dennett mean by saying, "Chance has no memory"? What does this say about Dennett's view of "nature"?

- Explore the strength of Dennett's analogy between elimination tournaments and evolutionary processes. What are the relevant similarities and differences between them?

- What is Dennett's response to his opposition's claim that the purpose or goal of evolution was to produce human beings?

- Free-write: If we were to "wind the tape of life back" and play it again and again, as Stephen Jay Gould proposed, would evolution produce human beings every time? Or answer Dennett's question, "Can the biosphere really be the outcome of nothing but a cascade of algorithmic processes feeding on chance?" Explore the implications of affirmative and negative answers.

Beyond Good & Evil

IX. What is Noble?

Friedrich Nietzsche

257. EVERY elevation of the type "man," has hitherto been the work of an aristocratic society and so it will always be—a society believing in a long scale of gradations of rank and differences of worth among human beings, and requiring slavery in some form or other. Without the PATHOS OF DIS-TANCE, such as grows out of the incarnated difference of classes, out of the constant out-looking and down-looking of the ruling caste on subordinates and instruments, and out of their equally constant practice of obeying and commanding, of keeping down and keeping at a distance—that other more mysterious pathos could never have arisen, the longing for an ever new widening of distance within the soul itself, the formation of ever higher, rarer, further, more extended, more comprehensive states, in short, just the elevation of the type "man," the continued "self-surmounting of man," to use a moral formula in a supermoral sense. To be sure, one must not resign oneself to any humanitarian illusions about the history of the origin of an aristocratic society (that is to say, of the preliminary condition for the elevation of the type "man"): the truth is hard. Let us acknowledge unprejudicedly how every higher civilization hitherto has ORIGINATED! Men with a still natural nature, barbarians in every terrible sense of the word, men of prey, still in possession of unbroken strength of will and desire for power, threw themselves upon weaker, more moral, more peaceful races (perhaps trading or cattle-rearing communities), or upon old mellow civilizations in which the final vital force was flickering out in brilliant fireworks of wit and depravity. At the commencement, the noble caste was always the barbarian caste: their superiority did not consist first of all in their physical, but in their psychical power—they were more COMPLETE men (which at every point also implies the same as "more complete beasts").

258. Corruption—as the indication that anarchy threatens to break out among the instincts, and that the foundation of the emotions, called "life," is convulsed—is something radically different according to the organization in which it manifests itself. When, for instance, an aristocracy like that

of France at the beginning of the Revolution, flung away its privileges with sublime disgust and sacrificed itself to an excess of its moral sentiments, it was corruption:—it was really only the closing act of the corruption which had existed for centuries, by virtue of which that aristocracy had abdicated step by step its lordly prerogatives and lowered itself to a FUNCTION of royalty (in the end even to its decoration and parade-dress). The essential thing, however, in a good and healthy aristocracy is that it should not regard itself as a function either of the kingship or the commonwealth, but as the SIGNIFICANCE and highest justification thereof—that it should therefore accept with a good conscience the sacrifice of a legion of individuals, who, FOR ITS SAKE, must be suppressed and reduced to imperfect men, to slaves and instruments. Its fundamental belief must be precisely that society is NOT allowed to exist for its own sake, but only as a foundation and scaffolding, by means of which a select class of beings may be able to elevate themselves to their higher duties, and in general to a higher EXISTENCE: like those sun-seeking climbing plants in Java—they are called Sipo Matador,—which encircle an oak so long and so often with their arms, until at last, high above it, but supported by it, they can unfold their tops in the open light, and exhibit their happiness.

259. To refrain mutually from injury, from violence, from exploitation, and put one's will on a par with that of others: this may result in a certain rough sense in good conduct among individuals when the necessary conditions are given (namely, the actual similarity of the individuals in amount of force and degree of worth, and their co-relation within one organization). As soon, however, as one wished to take this principle more generally, and if possible even as the FUNDAMENTAL PRINCIPLE OF SOCIETY, it would immediately disclose what it really is—namely, a Will to the DENIAL of life, a principle of dissolution and decay. Here one must think profoundly to the very basis and resist all sentimental weakness: life itself is ESSENTIALLY appropriation, injury, conquest of the strange and weak, suppression, severity, obtrusion of peculiar forms, incorporation, and at the least, putting it mildest, exploitation;—but why should one for ever use precisely these words on which for ages a disparaging purpose has been stamped? Even the organization within which, as was previously supposed, the individuals treat each other as equal—it takes place in every healthy aristocracy—must itself, if it be a living and not a dying organization, do all that towards other bodies, which the individuals within it refrain from doing to each other it will have to be the incarnated Will to Power, it will endeavour to grow, to gain ground, attract to itself and acquire ascendancy—not owing to any morality or immorality, but because it LIVES, and because life IS precisely Will to Power. On no point, however, is the ordinary consciousness of Europeans more unwilling to be

corrected than on this matter, people now rave everywhere, even under the guise of science, about coming conditions of society in which "the exploiting character" is to be absent—that sounds to my ears as if they promised to invent a mode of life which should refrain from all organic functions. "Exploitation" does not belong to a depraved, or imperfect and primitive society it belongs to the nature of the living being as a primary organic function, it is a consequence of the intrinsic Will to Power, which is precisely the Will to Life—Granting that as a theory this is a novelty— as a reality it is the FUNDAMENTAL FACT of all history let us be so far honest towards ourselves!

■ ■ ■

Questions for Further Exploration:

■ What explanation for the origins of man and civilization does Nietzsche offer?

■ What view of reality underlies Nietzsche's view of the aristocracy in France at the beginning of the Revolution?

■ What does the analogy between the aristocracy and the Sipo Matador reveal about Nietzsche's view of humans and human relations?

■ What does Nietzsche mean by saying "life IS precisely Will to Power"?

■ Compare and contrast Nietzsche and Rousseau on nature and its corruption.

■ Free-write: What reasons are there for thinking that Nietzsche is or is not a Darwinian?

The Gay Science

Friedrich Nietzsche

108

New struggles.—After Buddha was dead, his shadow was still shown for centuries in a cave—a tremendous, gruesome shadow. God is dead;[1] but given the way of men, there may still be caves for thousands of years in which his shadow will be shown.—And we—we still have to vanquish his shadow, too.

109

Let us beware.—Let us beware of thinking that the world is a living being. Where should it expand? On what should it feed? How could it grow and multiply? We have some notion of the nature of the organic; and we should not reinterpret the exceedingly derivative, late, rare, accidental, that we perceive only on the crust of the earth and make of it something essential, universal, and eternal, which is what those people do who call the universe an organism. This nauseates me. Let us even beware of believing that the

---

[1]This is the first occurrence of this famous formulation in Nietzsche's books. We encounter it again in section 125 below, which has been anthologized again and again after it was quoted in the chapter on "The Death of God and the Revaluation" in the first edition of Kaufmann (1950), and then included in *The Portable Nietzsche.* It even brought into being a predictably stillborn movement in Christian theology that created a short-lived sensation in the United States. But most of those who have made so much of Nietzsche's pronouncement that "God is dead" have failed to take note of its other occurrences in his works which obviously furnish the best clues to his meaning. The most important passages include section 343 below and seven passages in *Zarathustra* (VPN, pp. 124f., 191, 202, 294, 371–79, 398f., and 426). This list includes only places in which death or dying are mentioned expressly. No less important are sections 109–56.

universe is a machine: it is certainly not constructed for one purpose, and calling it a "machine" does it far too much honor.

Let us beware of positing generally and everywhere anything as elegant as the cyclical movements of our neighboring stars; even a glance into the Milky Way raises doubts whether there are not far coarser and more contradictory movements there, as well as stars with eternally linear paths, etc. The astral order in which we live is an exception; this order and the relative duration that depends on it have again made possible an exception of exceptions: the formation of the organic. The total character of the world, however, is in all eternity chaos—in the sense not of a lack of necessity but of a lack of order, arrangement, form, beauty, wisdom, and whatever other names there are for our aesthetic anthropomorphisms. Judged from the point of view of our reason, unsuccessful attempts are by all odds the rule, the exceptions are not the secret aim, and the whole musical box repeats eternally its tune[2] which may never be called a melody—and ultimately even the phrase "unsuccessful attempt" is too anthropomorphic and reproachful. But how could we reproach or praise the universe? Let us beware of attributing to it heartlessness and unreason or their opposites: it is neither perfect nor beautiful, nor noble, nor does it wish to become any of these things; it does not by any means strive to imitate man. None of our aesthetic and moral judgments apply to it. Nor does it have any instinct for self-preservation or any other instinct; and it does not observe any laws either. Let us beware of saying that there are laws in nature. There are only necessities: there is nobody who commands, nobody who obeys, nobody who trespasses. Once you know that there are no purposes, you also know that there is no accident; for it is only beside a world of purposes that the word "accident" has meaning. Let us beware of saying that death is opposed to life. The living is merely a type of what is dead, and a very rare type.

Let us beware of thinking that the world eternally creates new things. There are no eternally enduring substances; matter is as much of an error as the God of the Eleatics.[3] But when shall we ever be done with our caution and care? When will all these shadows of God cease to darken our minds?[4] When will we complete our de-deification of nature? When may

---

[2]This is an allusion to the doctrine of the eternal recurrence (see sections 285 and 341 below).

[3]A group of early Greek philosophers who lived in Southern Italy. The most famous among them, Parmenides, was born about 510 B.C.

[4]Here, if not earlier, it becomes clear how continuous this section is with 108 and what has been *the central motif of section 109:* what Nietzsche goes on to call the "de-deification" of nature.

we begin to *"naturalize"* humanity in terms of a pure, newly discovered, newly redeemed nature?[5]

125

The madman.—Have you not heard of that madman who lit a lantern in the bright morning hours, ran to the market place, and cried incessantly: "I seek God! I seek God!"—As many of those who did not believe in God were standing around just then, he provoked much laughter. Has he got lost? asked one. Did he lose his way like a child? asked another. Or is he hiding? Is he afraid of us? Has he gone on a voyage? emigrated?—Thus they yelled and laughed.

The madman jumped into their midst and pierced them with his eyes. "Whither is God?" he cried; "I will tell you. *We have killed him*—you and I. All of us are his murderers. But how did we do this? How could we drink up the sea? Who gave us the sponge to wipe away the entire horizon? What were we doing when we unchained this earth from its sun? Whither is it moving now? Whither are we moving? Away from all suns? Are we not plunging continually? Backward, sideward, forward, in all directions? Is there still any up or down? Are we not straying as through an infinite nothing? Do we not feel the breath of empty space? Has it not become colder? Is not night continually closing in on us? Do we not need to light lanterns in the morning? Do we hear nothing as yet of the noise of the gravediggers who are burying God? Do we smell nothing as yet of the divine decomposition? Gods, too, decompose. God is dead. God remains dead. And we have killed him.

"How shall we comfort ourselves, the murderers of all murderers? What was holiest and mightiest of all that the world has yet owned has bled to death under our knives: who will wipe this blood off us? What water is there for us to clean ourselves? What festivals of atonement, what sacred games shall we have to invent? Is not the greatness of this deed too great for us? Must we ourselves not become gods simply to appear worthy of it? There has never been a greater deed; and whoever is born after us—for the sake of this deed he will belong to a higher history than all history hitherto."

Here the madman fell silent and looked again at his listeners; and they, too, were silent and stared at him in astonishment. At last he threw his

---

[5]"Naturalize" is here used in the sense of naturalism, as opposed to supernaturalism. Man is to be reintegrated into nature.

lantern on the ground, and it broke into pieces and went out. "I have come too early," he said then; "my time is not yet. This tremendous event is still on its way, still wandering; it has not yet reached the ears of men. Lightning and thunder require time; the light of the stars requires time; deeds, though done, still require time to be seen and heard. This deed is still more distant from them than the most distant stars—*and yet they have done it themselves."*

It has been related further that on the same day the madman forced his way into several churches and there struck up his *requiem aeternam deo.* Led out and called to account, he is said always to have replied nothing but: "What after all are these churches now if they are not the tombs and sepulchers of God?"[20]

129

The conditions for God.—"God himself cannot exist without wise people," said Luther with good reason. But "God can exist even less without unwise people"—that our good Luther did not say.

---

[20]This is one of the most famous sections in this book. See the first note on section 108 above, which calls attention to other passages in Nietzsche that use the same, or similar, imagery. Above all, however, it should be noted how this section fits into its immediate context, and how the de-deification in section 109 and all of the intermediate sections build up to the parable of the madman. It has often been asked what Nietzsche means by saying that "God is dead." One might fairly answer: what he means is what he says in sections 108 through 125—and in the sections after that. The problem is created in large measure by tearing a section out of its context, on the *false* assumption that what we are offered is merely a random collection of "aphorisms" that are intended for browsing.

Questions for Further Exploration:

■ What does Nietzsche mean by saying "God is dead" and "we still have to vanquish his shadow"?

■ What is Nietzsche's critique of the belief that the universe is a machine or a living being? What other theories of order in the universe are criticized by Nietzsche and on what grounds?

■ How does Nietzsche describe the character of the world?

■ What interpretive conclusions might be drawn from the allegory of the madman? What consequences of nihilism are alluded to in this allegory?

■ Free-write a response to Nietzsche's questions: "When will we complete our de-deification of nature? When may we begin to "naturalize" humanity in terms of a pure, newly discovered, newly redeemed nature?"

Nausea

Jean-Paul Sartre

6.00 *p.m.*

I can't say I feel relieved or satisfied; just the opposite, I am crushed. Only my goal is reached: I know what I wanted to know; I have understood all that has happened to me since January. The Nausea has not left me and I don't believe it will leave me so soon; but I no longer have to bear it, it is no longer an illness or a passing fit: it is I.

So I was in the park just now. The roots of the chestnut tree were sunk in the ground just under my bench. I couldn't remember it was a root any more. The words had vanished and with them the significance of things, their methods of use, and the feeble points of reference which men have traced on their surface. I was sitting, stooping forward, head bowed, alone in front of this black, knotty mass, entirely beastly, which frightened me. Then I had this vision.

It left me breathless. Never, until these last few days, had I understood the meaning of "existence." I was like the others, like the ones walking along the seashore, all dressed in their spring finery. I said, like them, "The ocean *is* green; that white speck up there *is* a seagull," but I didn't feel that it existed or that the seagull was an "existing seagull"; usually existence hides itself. It is there, around us, in us, it is *us,* you can't say two words without mentioning it, but you can never touch it. When I believed I was thinking about it, I must believe that I was thinking nothing, my head was empty, or there was just one word in my head, the word "to be." Or else I was thinking . . . how can I explain it? I was thinking of *belonging,* I was telling myself that the sea belonged to the class of green objects, or that the green was a part of the quality of the sea. Even when I looked at things, I was miles from dreaming that they existed: they looked like scenery to me. I picked them up in my hands, they served me as tools, I foresaw their resistance. But that all happened on the surface. If anyone

---

had asked me what existence was, I would have answered, in good faith, that it was nothing, simply an empty form which was added to external things without changing anything in their nature. And then all of a sudden, there it was, clear as day: existence had suddenly unveiled itself. It had lost the harmless look of an abstract category: it was the very paste of things, this root was kneaded into existence. Or rather the root, the park gates, the bench, the sparse grass, all that had vanished: the diversity of things, their individuality, were only an appearance, a veneer. This veneer had melted, leaving soft, monstrous masses, all in disorder—naked, in a frightful, obscene nakedness.

I kept myself from making the slightest movement, but I didn't need to move in order to see, behind the trees, the blue columns and the lamp posts of the bandstand and the Velleda, in the midst of a mountain of laurel. All these objects . . . how can I explain? They inconvenienced me; I would have liked them to exist less strongly, more dryly, in a more abstract way, with more reserve. The chestnut tree pressed itself against my eyes. Green rust covered it half-way up; the bark, black and swollen, looked like boiled leather. The sound of the water in the Masqueret Fountain sounded in my ears, made a nest there, filled them with signs; my nostrils overflowed with a green, putrid odour. All things, gently, tenderly, were letting themselves drift into existence like those relaxed women who burst out laughing and say: "It's good to laugh," in a wet voice; they were parading, one in front of the other, exchanging abject secrets about their existence. I realized that there was no half-way house between non-existence and this flaunting abundance. If you existed, you had to *exist all the way*, as far as mouldiness, bloatedness, obscenity were concerned. In another world, circles, bars of music keep their pure and rigid lines. But existence is a deflection. Trees, night-blue pillars, the happy bubbling of a fountain, vital smells, little heat-mists floating in the cold air, a red-haired man digesting on a bench: all this somnolence, all these meals digested together, had its comic side. . . . Comic . . . no: it didn't go as far as that, nothing that exists can be comic; it was like a floating analogy, almost entirely elusive, with certain aspects of vaudeville. We were a heap of living creatures, irritated, embarrassed at ourselves, we hadn't the slightest reason to be there, none of us, each one, confused, vaguely alarmed, felt in the way in relation to the others. *In the way:* it was the only relationship I could establish between these trees, these gates, these stones. In vain I tried to *count* the chestnut trees, to *locate* them by their relationship to the Velleda, to compare their height with the height of the plane trees: each of them escaped the relationship in which I tried to enclose it, isolated itself, and overflowed. Of these relations (which I insisted on maintaining in order to delay the crumbling of the human world, measures, quantities, and directions)—I felt myself to be the arbitrator; they no longer had their teeth into things. *In the way,* the chestnut tree there, opposite me, a little to the left. *In the way,* the Velleda. . . .

And I—soft, weak, obscene, digesting, juggling with dismal thoughts— I, too, was *In the way.* Fortunately, I didn't feel it, although I realized it, but I was uncomfortable because I was afraid of feeling it (even now I am afraid—afraid that it might catch me behind my head and lift me up like a wave). I dreamed vaguely of killing myself to wipe out at least one of these superfluous lives. But even my death would have been *In the way. In the way,* my corpse, my blood on these stones, between these plants, at the back of this smiling garden. And the decomposed flesh would have been *In the way* in the earth which would receive my bones, at last, cleaned, stripped, peeled, proper and clean as teeth, it would have been *In the way:* I was *In the way* for eternity.

The word absurdity is coming to life under my pen; a little while ago, in the garden, I couldn't find it, but neither was I looking for it, I didn't need it: I thought without words, *on* things, *with* things. Absurdity was not an idea in my head, or the sound of a voice, only this long serpent dead at my feet, this wooden serpent. Serpent or claw or root or vulture's talon, what difference does it make. And without formulating anything clearly, I understood that I had found the key to Existence, the key to my Nauseas, to my own life. In fact, all that I could grasp beyond that returns to this fundamental absurdity. Absurdity: another word; I struggle against words; down there I touched the thing. But I wanted to fix the absolute character of this absurdity here. A movement, an event in the tiny coloured world of men is only relatively absurd: by relation to the accompanying circumstances. A madman's ravings, for example, are absurd in relation to the situation in which he finds himself, but not in relation to his delirium. But a little while ago I made an experiment with the absolute or the absurd. This root—there was nothing in relation to which it was absurd. Oh, how can I put it in words? Absurd: in relation to the stones, the tufts of yellow grass, the dry mud, the three, the sky, the green benches. Absurd, irreducible; nothing— not even a profound, secret upheaval of nature—could explain it. Evidently I did not know everything, I had not seen the seeds sprout, or the tree grow. But faced with this great wrinkled paw, neither ignorance nor knowledge was important: the world of explanations and reasons is not the world of existence. A circle is not absurd, it is clearly explained by the rotation of a straight segment around one of its extremities. But neither does a circle exist. This root, on the other hand, existed in such a way that I could not explain it. Knotty, inert, nameless, it fascinated me, filled my eyes, brought me back unceasingly to its own existence. In vain to repeat: "This is a root"—it didn't work any more. I saw clearly that you could not pass from its function as a root, as a breathing pump, *to that,* to this hard and compact skin of a sea lion, to this oily, callous, headstrong look. The function explained nothing: it allowed you to understand generally that it was a root, but not *that one* at all. This root, with its colour, shape, its congealed movement, was . . . below all explanation. Each of its qualities escaped it a little, flowed out of it, half solidified, almost became a thing; each one was *In the way* in the root and the whole stump now gave me the impression of unwinding itself a little, denying its existence to lose itself in a frenzied excess. I scraped my heel against this black claw: I wanted to peel off some of the bark. For no reason at all, out of defiance, to make the bare pink appear absurd on the tanned leather: to *play* with the absurdity of the world. But, when I drew my heel back, I saw that the bark was still black.

Black? I felt the word deflating, emptied of meaning with extraordinary rapidity. Black? The root *was not* black, there was no black on this piece of wood—there was . . . something else: black, like the circle, did not exist. I looked at the root: was it *more than* black or *almost* black? But I soon stopped questioning myself because I had the feeling of knowing where I was. Yes, I had already scrutinized innumerable objects, with deep uneasiness. I had already tried—vainly—to think something *about* them: and I had already felt their, cold, inert qualities elude me, slip through my fingers. Adolphe's suspenders, the other evening in the "Railwaymen's Rendezvous." They *were not* purple. I saw the two inexplicable stains on the shirt. And the stone—the well-known stone, the origin of this whole business: it was not . . . I can't remember exactly just what it was that the stone refused to be. But I had not forgotten its passive resistance. And the hand of the Self-Taught Man; I held it and shook it one day in the library and then I had the feeling that it wasn't quite a hand. I had thought of a great white worm, but that wasn't it either. And the suspicious transparency of the glass of beer in the Café Mably. Suspicious: that's what they were, the sounds, the smells, the tastes. When they ran quickly under your nose like startled hares and you didn't pay too much attention, you might believe them to be simple and reassuring, you might believe that there was real blue in the world, real red, a real perfume of almonds or violets. But as soon as you held on to them for an instant, this feeling of comfort and security gave way to a deep uneasiness: colours, tastes, and smells were never real, never themselves and nothing but themselves. The simplest, most indefinable quality had too much content, in relation to itself, in its heart. That black against my foot, it didn't look like black, but rather the confused effort to imagine black by someone who had never seen black and who wouldn't know how to stop, who would have imagined an ambiguous being beyond colours. It *looked* like a colour, but also . . . like a bruise or a secretion, like an oozing—and something else, an odour, for example, it melted into the odour of wet earth, warm, moist wood, into a black odour that spread like varnish over this sensitive wood, in a flavour of chewed, sweet fibre. I did not simply *see* this black: sight is an abstract invention, a simplified idea, one of man's ideas. That black, amorphous, weakly presence, far surpassed sight, smell and taste. But this richness was lost in confusion and finally was no more because it was too much.

This moment was extraordinary. I was there, motionless and icy, plunged in a horrible ecstasy. But something fresh had just appeared in the very heart of this ecstasy; I understood the Nausea, I possessed it. To tell the truth, I did not formulate my discoveries to myself. But I think it would be easy for me to put them in words now. The essential thing is contingency. I mean that one cannot define existence as necessity. To exist is simply *to be there;* those who exist let themselves be encountered, but you can never deduce anything from them. I believe there are people who have understood this. Only they tried to overcome this contingency by inventing a necessary, causal being. But no necessary being can explain existence: contingency is not a delusion, a probability which can be dissipated; it is the absolute, consequently, the perfect free gift. All is free, this park, this city and myself. When you realize that, it turns your heart upside down and everything begins to float, as the other evening at the "Railwaymen's Rendezvous": here is Nausea; here there is what those bastards—the ones on the Coteau Vert and others—try to hid from themselves with their idea of their rights. But what a poor lie: no one has any rights; they are entirely free, like other men, they cannot succeed in not feeling superfluous. And in themselves, secretly, they are *superfluous,* that is to say, amorphous, vague, and sad.

How long will this fascination last? I *was* the root of the chestnut tree. Or rather I was entirely conscious of its existence. Still detached from it— since I was conscious of it—yet lost in it, nothing but it. An uneasy conscience which, notwithstanding, let itself fall with all its weight on this piece of dead wood. Time had stopped: a small black pool at my feet; it was impossible for something to come *after* that moment. I would have liked to tear myself from that atrocious joy, but I did not even imagine it would be possible; I was inside; the black stump did *not move,* it stayed there, in my eyes, as a lump of food sticks in the windpipe. I could neither accept nor refuse it. At what a cost did I raise my eyes? Did I raise them? Rather did I not obliterate myself for an instant in order to be reborn in the following instant with my head thrown back and my eyes raised upward? In fact, I was not even conscious of the transformation. But suddenly it became impossible for me to think of the existence of the root. It was wiped out, I could repeat in vain: it exists, it is still there, under the bench, against my right foot, it no longer meant anything. Existence is not something which lets itself be thought of from a distance: it must invade you suddenly, master you, weigh heavily on your heart like a great motionless beast—or else there is nothing more at all.

There was nothing more, my eyes were empty and I was spellbound by my deliverance. Then suddenly it began to move before my eyes in light, uncertain motions: the wind was shaking the top of the tree.

It did not displease me to see a movement, it was a change from these motionless beings who watched me like staring eyes, I told myself, as I followed the swinging of the branches: movements never quite exist, they are passages, intermediaries between two existences, moments of weakness, I expected to see them come out of nothingness, progressively ripen, blossom: I was finally going to surprise beings in the process of being born.

No more than three seconds, and all my hopes were swept away. I could not attribute the passage of time to these branches groping around like blind men. This idea of passage was still an invention of man. The idea was too transparent. All these paltry agitations, drew in on themselves, isolated. They overflowed the leaves and branches everywhere. They whirled about these empty hands, enveloped them with tiny whirlwinds. Of course a movement was something different from a tree. But it was still an absolute. A thing. My eyes only encountered completion. The tips of the branches rustled with existence which unceasingly renewed itself and which was never born. The existing wind rested on the tree like a great bluebottle, and the tree shuddered. But the shudder was not a nascent quality, a passing from power to action; it was a thing; a shudder-thing flowed into the tree, took possession of it, shook it and suddenly abandoned it, going further on to spin about itself. All was fullness and all was active, there was no weakness in time, all, even the least perceptible stirring, was made of existence. And all these existents which bustled about this tree came from nowhere and were going nowhere. Suddenly they existed, then suddenly they existed no longer: existence is without memory; of the vanished it retains nothing—not even a memory. Existence everywhere, infinitely, in excess, for ever and everywhere; existence—which is limited only by existence. I sank down on the bench, stupefied, stunned by this profusion of beings without origin: everywhere blossomings, hatchings out, my ears buzzed with existence, my very flesh throbbed and opened, abandoned itself to the universal burgeoning. It was repugnant. But why, I thought, why so many existences, since they all look alike? What good are so many duplicates of trees? So many existences missed, obstinately begun again and again missed—like the awkward efforts of an insect fallen on its back? (I was one of those efforts.) That abundance did not give the effect of generosity, just the opposite. It was dismal, ailing, embarrassed at itself. Those trees, those great clumsy bodies. . . . I began to laugh because I suddenly thought of the formidable springs described in books, full of crackings, burstings, gigantic explosions. There were those idiots who came to tell you about will-power and struggle for life. Hadn't they ever seen a beast or a tree? This plane-tree with its scaling bark, this half-rotten oak, they wanted me to take them for rugged youthful endeavour surging towards the sky. And that root? I would have undoubtedly had to represent it as a voracious claw tearing at the earth, devouring its food?

Impossible to see things that way. Weaknesses, frailties, yes. The trees floated. Gushing towards the sky? Or rather a collapse; at any instant I expected to see the tree-trunks shrivel like weary wands, crumple up, fall on the ground in a soft, folded, black heap. *They did not want to exist, only they could not help themselves*. So they quietly minded their own business; the sap rose up slowly through the structure, half reluctant, and the roots sank slowly into the earth. But at each instant they seemed on the verge of leaving everything there and obliterating themselves. Tired and old, they kept on existing, against the grain, simply because they were too weak to die, because death could only come to them from the outside: strains of music alone can proudly carry their own death within themselves like an internal necessity: only they don't exist. Every existing thing is born without reason, prolongs itself out of weakness and dies by chance. I leaned back and closed my eyes. But the images, forewarned, immediately leaped up and filled my closed eyes with existences: existence is a fullness which man can never abandon.

Strange images. They represented a multitude of things. Not real things, other things which looked like them. Wooden objects which looked like chairs, shoes, other objects which looked like plants. And then two faces: the couple who were eating opposite to me last Sunday in the Brasserie Vézelise. Fat, hot, sensual, absurd, with red ears. I could see the woman's neck and shoulders. Nude existence. Those two—it suddenly gave me a turn—those two were still existing somewhere in Bouville; somewhere—in the midst of smells?—this soft throat rubbing up luxuriously against smooth stuffs, nestling in lace; and the woman picturing her bosom under her blouse, thinking: "My titties, my lovely fruits," smiling mysteriously, attentive to the swelling of her breasts which tickled . . . then I shouted and found myself with my eyes wide open.

Had I dreamed of this enormous presence? It was there, in the garden, toppled down into the trees, all soft, sticky, soiling everything, all thick, a jelly. And I was inside, I with the garden. I was frightened, furious, I thought it was so stupid, so out of place, I hated this ignoble mess.

Mounting up, mounting up as high as the sky, spilling over, filling every-thing with its gelatinous slither, and I could see depths upon depths of it reaching far beyond the limits of the garden, the houses, and Bouville, as far as the eye could reach. I was no longer in Bouville, I was nowhere, I was floating. I was not surprised, I knew it was the World, the naked World suddenly revealing itself, and I choked with rage at this gross, ab-surd being. You couldn't even wonder where all that sprang from, or how it was that a world came into existence, rather than nothingness. It didn't make sense, the World was everywhere, in front, behind. There had been nothing *before* it. Nothing. There had never been a moment in which it could not have existed. That was what worried me: of course there was no *reason* for this flowing larva to exist. *But it was impossible* for it is not to exist. It was unthinkable: to imagine nothingness you had to be there al-ready, in the midst of the World, eyes wide open and alive; nothingness was only an idea in my head, an existing idea floating in this immensity: this nothingness had not come *before* existence, it was an existence like any other and appeared after many others. I shouted "filth! What rotten filth!" and shook myself to get rid of this sticky filth, but it held fast and there was so much, tons and tons of existence, endless: I stifled at the depths of this immense weariness. And then suddenly the park emptied as through a great hole, the World disappeared as it had come, or else I woke up—in any case, I saw no more of it; nothing was left but the yellow earth around me, out of which dead branches rose upward.

I got up and went out. Once at the gate, I turned back. Then the garden smiled at me. I leaned against the gate and watched for a long time. The smile of the trees, of the laurel, *meant* something; that was the real secret of existence. I remembered one Sunday, not more than three weeks ago, I had already detected everywhere a sort of conspiratorial air. Was it in my intention? I felt with boredom that I had no way of understanding. No way. Yet it was there, waiting, looking at one. It was there on the trunk of the chestnut tree . . . it was *the* chestnut tree. Things—you might have called them thoughts—which stopped halfway, which were forgotten, which for-got what they wanted to think and which stayed like that, hanging about with an odd little sense which was beyond them. That little sense annoyed me: I *could not* understand it, even if I could have stayed leaning against the gate for a century; I had learned all I could know about existence. I left, I went back to the hotel and I wrote.

■ ■ ■

Questions for Further Exploration:

- What commonalities in the views of Nietzsche and Sartre unite them as "existentialists"?

- What does Sartre's writing suggest about the nature of being human?

- Compare and contrast Roquentin's "meditation" and Descartes's First Meditation.

- Why is Roquentin nauseated? What does Roquentin's epiphany in the park reveal about Sartre's view of existence?

- Is it significant that the epiphany is sparked by a chestnut tree root? Could it have been by another human? Animal? Or non-organic thing?

- What is Sartre's view of nature?

- What light can Sartre's existentialism shed on the contemporary ecological crisis?

- If Sartre is right about the contingency and indeterminacy of existence, what are the consequences for projects devoted to sustainability and environmental problem-solving?

- Consider Sartre's philosophy in terms of Plato's allegory. In his view, what might each of the symbols (the cave, prisoners, shadows, escapee, outside, the sun, etc.) represent? What change(s) in the allegory would enable a better representation of Sartre's view?

- Free-write: What is revealed about reality from experiences in nature? Describe an epiphany you have had in nature and what it revealed to you about reality.

1 paragraph free write on each of the 2 films assigned.
No credit for summaries.
must show you thought about something raised in the film.

Metaphysical = "what is the nature of reality.

234

The Sane Society

The Human Situation

Erich Fromm

Erich Fromm (b. 1900), psychoanalyst and educator, was born in Germany and received his early education there. He has taught at various institutes and universities in Germany and the United States and at the National University of Mexico. His many books include *Psychoanalysis and Religion, Psychology and Culture, The Heart of Man,* and *The Crisis in Psychoanalysis.*

In the selection below, Fromm discusses man's physiological relation to the animal kingdom and the biological laws of nature. Yet, Fromm maintains, man is a unique creature who transcends his past and who can create and destroy. He is endowed with reason, imagination, and a sense of identity.

Man, in respect to his body and his physiological functions, belongs to the animal kingdom. The functioning of the animal is determined by instincts, by specific action patterns which are in turn determined by inherited neurological structures. The higher an animal is in the scale of development, the more flexibility of action pattern and the less completeness of structural adjustment do we find at birth. In the higher primates we even find considerable intelligence; that is, use of thought for the accomplishment of desired goals, thus enabling the animal to go far beyond the instinctively prescribed action pattern. But great as the development within the animal kingdom is, certain basic elements of existence remain the same.

The animal "is lived" through biological laws of nature; it is part of nature and never transcends it. It has no conscience of a moral nature, and no awareness of itself and of its existence; it has no reason, if by reason we mean the ability to penetrate the surface grasped by the senses and to understand the essence behind that surface; therefore the animal has no concept of the truth, even though it may have an idea of what is useful.

Animal existence is one of harmony between the animal and nature; not, of course, in the sense that the natural conditions do not often threaten the animal and force it to a bitter fight for survival, but in the sense that the animal is equipped by nature to cope with the very conditions it is to meet, just as the seed of a plant is equipped by nature to make use of the conditions of soil, climate, etcetera, to which it has become adapted in the evolutionary process.

At a certain point of animal evolution, there occurred a unique break, comparable to the first emergence of matter, to the first emergence of life, and to the first emergence of animal existence. This new event happens when in the evolutionary process, action ceases to be essentially determined by instinct; when the adaptation of nature loses its coercive character; when action is no longer fixed by hereditarily given mechanisms. When the animal transcends nature, when it transcends the purely passive role of the creature, when it becomes, biologically speaking, the most helpless animal, *man is born.* At this point, the animal has emancipated itself from nature by erect posture, the brain has grown far beyond what it was in the highest animal. This birth of man may have lasted for hundreds of thousands of years, but what matters is that a new species arose, transcending nature, that *life became aware of itself.*

Self-awareness, reason and imagination disrupt the "harmony" which characterizes animal existence. Their emergence has made man into an anomaly, into the freak of the universe. He is part of nature, subject to her physical laws and unable to change them, yet he transcends the rest of nature. He is set apart while being a part; he is homeless, yet chained to the home he shares with all creatures. Cast into this world at an accidental place and time, he is forced out of it, again accidentally. Being aware of himself, he realizes his powerlessness and the limitations of his existence. He visualizes his own end: death. Never is he free from the dichotomy of his existence: he cannot rid himself of his mind, even if he should want to; he cannot rid himself of his body as long as he is alive—and his body makes him want to be alive.

Reason, man's blessing, is also his curse; it forces him to cope everlastingly with the task of solving an insoluble dichotomy. Human existence is different in this respect from that of all other organisms; it is in a state of constant and unavoidable disequilibrium. Man's life cannot "be lived" by repeating the pattern of his species; *he* must live. Man is the only animal that can be *bored,* that can feel evicted from paradise. Man is the only animal who finds his own existence a problem which he has to solve and from which he cannot escape. He cannot go back to the prehuman state of harmony with nature; he must proceed to develop his reason until he becomes the master of nature, and of himself.

... He lacks the instinctive adaptation to nature, he lacks physical strength, he is the most helpless of all animals at birth, and in need of protection for a much longer period of time than any of them. While he has lost the unity with nature, he has not been given the means to lead a new existence outside of nature. His reason is most rudimentary, he has no knowledge of nature's processes, nor tools to replace the lost instincts; he lives divided into small groups, with no knowledge of himself or of others; indeed, the biblical Paradise myth expresses the situation with perfect clarity. Man, who lives in the Garden of Eden, in complete harmony with nature but without awareness of himself, begins his history by the first act of freedom, disobedience to a command. Concomitantly, he becomes aware of himself, of his separateness, of his helplessness; he is expelled from Paradise, and two angels with fiery swords prevent his return.

Man's evolution is based on the fact that he has lost his original home, nature—and that he can never return to it, can never become an animal again. There is only one way he can take: to emerge fully from his natural home, to find a new home—one which he creates, by making the world a human one and by becoming truly human himself.

When man is born, the human race as well as the individual, he is thrown out of a situation which was definite, as definite as the instincts, into a situation which is indefinite, uncertain and open. There is certainty only about the past, and about the future as far as it is death—which actually is return to the past, the inorganic state of matter.

The problem of man's existence, then, is unique in the whole of nature; he has fallen out of nature, as it were, and is still in it; he is partly divine, partly animal; partly infinite, partly finite. *The necessity to find ever-new solutions for the contradictions in his existence, to find ever-higher forms of unity with nature, his fellowmen and himself, is the source of all psychic forces which motivate man, of all his passions, affects and anxieties.*

The animal is content if its physiological needs—its hunger, its thirst and its sexual needs—are satisfied. Inasmuch as man is *also* animal, these needs are likewise imperative and must be satisfied. *But inasmuch as man is human, the satisfaction of these instinctual needs is not sufficient to make him happy; they are not even sufficient to make him sane. The archimedic point of the specifically human dynamism lies in this uniqueness of the human situation; the understanding of man's psyche must be based on the analysis of man's needs stemming from the conditions of his existence.*

The problem, then, which the human race as well as each individual has to solve is that of being born. Physical birth, if we think of the individual, is by no means as decisive and singular an act as it appears to be. It is, indeed, an important change from intrauterine into extrauterine life; but in many respects the infant after birth is not different from the infant before birth; it cannot perceive things outside, cannot feed itself; it is completely dependent on the mother, and would perish without her help. Actually, the process of birth continues. The child begins to recognize outside objects, to react affectively, to grasp things and to co-ordinate his movements, to walk. But birth continues. The child learns to speak, it learns to know the use and function of things, it learns to relate itself to others, to avoid punishment and gain praise and liking. Slowly, the growing person learns to love, to develop reason, to look at the world objectively. He begins to develop his powers; to acquire a sense of identity, to overcome the seduction of his senses for the sake of an integrated life. Birth then, in the conventional meaning of the word, is only the beginning of birth in the broader sense. The whole life of the individual is nothing but the process of giving birth to himself; indeed, we should be fully born, when we die—although it is the tragic fate of most individuals to die before they are born.

From all we know about the evolution of the human race, the birth of man is to be understood in the same sense as the birth of the individual. When man had transcended a certain threshold of minimum instinctive adaptation, he ceased to be an animal; but he was as helpless and unequipped for human existence as the individual infant is at birth. The birth of man began with the first members of the species homo sapiens, and human history is nothing but the whole process of this birth. It has taken man hundreds of thousands of years to take the first steps into human life; he went through a narcissistic phase of magic omnipotent orientation, through totemism, nature worship, until he arrived at the beginnings of the formation of conscience, objectivity, brotherly love. In the last four thousand years of his history, he has developed visions of the fully born and fully awakened man, visions expressed in not too different ways by the great teachers of man in Egypt, China, India, Palestine, Greece and Mexico. . . .

Another aspect of the human situation, closely connected with the need for relatedness, is man's situation as a *creature,* and his need to transcend this very state of the passive creature. Man is thrown into this world without his knowledge, consent or will, and he is removed from it again without his consent or will. In this respect he is not different from the animal, from the plants, or from inorganic matter. But being endowed with reason and imagination, he cannot be content with the passive role of the creature, with the role of dice cast out of a cup. He is driven by the urge to transcend the role of the creature, the accidentalness and passivity of his existence, by becoming a "creator."

Man can create life. This is the miraculous quality which he indeed shares with all living beings, but with the difference that he alone is aware of being created and of being a creator. Man can create life, or rather, woman can create life, by giving birth to a child, and by caring for the child until it is sufficiently grown to take care of his own needs. Man— man and woman—can create by planting seeds, by producing material objects, by creating art, by creating ideas, by loving one another. In the act of creation man transcends himself as a creature, raises himself beyond the passivity and accidentalness of his existence into the realm of purposefulness and freedom. In man's need for transcendence lies one of the roots for love, as well as for art, religion and material production.

To create presupposes activity and care. It presupposes love for that which one creates. How then does man solve the problem of transcending himself, if he is not capable of creating, if he cannot love? *There is another answer to this need for transcendence: if I cannot create life, I can destroy it. To destroy life makes me also transcend it.* Indeed, that man can destroy life is just as miraculous a feat as that he can create it, for life is *the* miracle, the inexplicable. In the act of destruction, man sets himself above life; he transcends himself as a creature. Thus, the ultimate choice for man, inasmuch as he is driven to transcend himself, is to create or to destroy, to love or to hate. The enormous power of the will for destruction which we see in the history of man, and which we have witnessed so frightfully in our own time, is rooted in the nature of man, just as the drive to create is rooted in it. To say that man is capable of developing his primary potentiality for love and reason does not imply the naive belief in man's goodness. Destructiveness is a secondary potentiality, rooted in the very existence of man, and having the same intensity and power as any passion can have. But—and this is the essential point of my argument—it is only the *alternative* to creativeness. Creation and destruction, love and hate, are not two instincts which exist independently. They are both answers to the same need for transcendence, and the will to destroy must rise when the will to create cannot be satisfied. However, the satisfaction of the need to create leads to happiness; destructiveness to suffering, most of all, for the destroyer himself. . . .

Man may be defined as the animal that can say "I," that can be aware of himself as a separate entity. The animal being within nature, and not transcending it, has no awareness of himself, has no need for a sense of identity. Man, being torn away from nature, being endowed with reason and imagination, needs to form a concept of himself, needs to say and to feel: "I am I." Because he is not *lived,* but *lives,* because he has lost the original unity with nature, has to make decisions, is aware of himself and of his neighbor as different persons, he must be able to sense himself as the subject of his actions. As with the need for relatedness, rootedness, and transcendence, this need for a sense of identity is so vital and imperative that man could not remain sane if he did not find some way of satisfying it. Man's sense of identity develops in the process of emerging from the "primary bonds" which tie him to mother and nature. The infant, still feeling one with mother, cannot yet say "I," nor has he any need for it. Only after he has conceived of the outer world as being separate and different from himself does he come to the awareness of himself as a distinct being, and one of the last words he learns to use is "I," in reference to himself.

In the development of *the human race* the degree to which man is aware of himself as a separate self depends on the extent to which he has emerged from the clan and the extent to which the process of individuation has developed. The member of a primitive clan might express his sense of identity in the formula "I am we"; he cannot yet conceive of himself as an "individual," existing apart from his group. In the medieval world, the individual was identified with his social role in the feudal hierarchy. The peasant was not a man who happened to be a peasant, the feudal lord not a man who happened to be a feudal lord. *He was* a peasant or a lord, and this sense of his unalterable station was an essential part of his sense of identity. When the feudal system broke down, this sense of identity was shaken and the acute question "who am I?" arose—or more precisely, "How do I know that I am I?" This is the question which was raised, in a philosophical form, by Descartes. He answered the quest for identity by saying, "I doubt—hence I think, I think—hence I am." This answer put all the emphasis on the experience of "I" as the subject of any *thinking* activity, and failed to see that the "I" is experienced also in the process of feeling and creative action.

The development of Western culture went in the direction of creating the basis for the full experience of individuality. By making the individual free politically and economically, by teaching him to think for himself and freeing him from an authoritarian pressure, one hoped to enable him to feel "I" in the sense that he was the center and active subject of his powers and experienced himself as such. But only a minority achieved the new experience of "I." For the majority, individualism was not much more than a façade behind which was hidden the failure to acquire an individual sense of identity.

Many substitutes for a truly individual sense of identity were sought for, and found. Nation, religion, class and occupation serve to furnish a sense of identity. "I am an American," "I am a Protestant," "I am a businessman," are the formulae which help a man experience a sense of identity after the original clan identity has disappeared and before a truly individual sense of identity has been acquired. These different identifications are, in contemporary society, usually employed together. They are in a broad sense status identifications, and they are more efficient if blended with older feudal remnants, as in European countries. In the United States, in which so little is left of feudal relics, and in which there is so much social mobility, these status identifications are naturally less efficient, and the sense of identity is shifted more and more to the experience of conformity.

Inasmuch as I am not different, inasmuch as I am like the others, and recognized by them as "a regular fellow," I can sense myself as "I." I am— "as you desire me"—as Pirandello put it in the title of one of his plays. Instead of the pre-individualistic clan identity, a new herd identity develops, in which the sense of identity rests on the sense of an unquestionable belonging to the crowd. That this uniformity and conformity are often not recognized as such, and are covered by the illusion of individuality, does not alter the facts.

The problem of the sense of identity is not, as it is usually understood, merely a philosophical problem, or a problem only concerning our mind and thought. The need to feel a sense of identity stems from the very condition of human existence, and it is the source of the most intense strivings. Since I cannot remain sane without the sense of "I," I am driven to do almost anything to acquire this sense. Behind the intense passion for status and conformity is this very good, and it is sometimes even stronger than the need for physical survival. What could be more obvious than the fact that people are willing to risk their lives, to give up their love, to surrender their freedom, to sacrifice their own thoughts, for the sake of being one of the herd, of conforming, and thus of acquiring a sense of identity, even though it is an illusory one.

Questions for Further Exploration:

- What criteria does Fromm use to distinguish humans from other animals?

- How does Fromm characterize human existence? What is the "dichotomy of human existence"? What does Fromm mean by the "human situation"?

- In contrast with Dennett's mechanistic view of evolution, how does Fromm conceptualize the evolution of homo sapiens?

- What are the ecological implications of Fromm's claim that human existence entails a "disequilibrium" with nature? Of his view of transcendence as creating or destroying life?

- How does Fromm characterize human freedom?

- Based on Fromm's view of human needs, what is the meaning and the hope of realizing the goal of sustainability defined as "meeting the needs of the present without jeopardizing the ability of those in the future to meet their needs"?

The Turning Point

The New Physics

Fritjof Capra

Reality is a process

At the beginning of modern physics stands the extraordinary intellectual feat of one man—Albert Einstein. In two articles, both published in 1905, Einstein initiated two revolutionary trends in scientific thought. One was his special theory of relativity; the other was a new way of looking at electromagnetic radiation which was to become characteristic of quantum theory, the theory of atomic phenomena. The complete quantum theory was worked out twenty years later by a whole team of physicists. Relativity theory, however, was constructed in its complete form almost entirely by Einstein himself. Einstein's scientific papers are intellectual monuments that mark the beginning of twentieth-century thought.

Einstein strongly believed in nature's inherent harmony, and throughout his scientific life his deepest concern was to find a unified foundation of physics. He began to move toward this goal by constructing a common framework for electrodynamics and mechanics, the two separate theories of classical physics. This framework is known as the special theory of relativity. It unified and completed the structure of classical physics, but at the same time it involved radical changes in the traditional concepts of space and time and thus undermined one of the foundations of the Newtonian world view. Ten years later Einstein proposed his general theory of relativity, in which the framework of the special theory is extended to include gravity. This is achieved by further drastic modifications of the concepts of space and time.

The other major development in twentieth-century physics was a consequence of the experimental investigation of atoms. At the turn of the century physicists discovered several phenomena connected with the structure of atoms, such as X-rays and radioactivity, which were inexplicable in terms of classical physics. Besides being objects of intense study, these phenomena were used, in most ingenious ways, as new tools to probe deeper into matter than had ever been possible before. For example, the so-called alpha particles emanating from radioactive substances were perceived to be high-speed projectiles of subatomic size that could be used to explore the interior of the atom. They could be fired at atoms, and from the way they were deflected one could draw conclusions about the atoms' structure.

This exploration of the atomic and subatomic world brought scientists in contact with a strange and unexpected reality that shattered the foundations of their world view and forced them to think in entirely new ways. Nothing like that had ever happened before in science. Revolutions like those of Copernicus and Darwin had introduced profound changes in the general conception of the universe, changes that were shocking to many people, but the new concepts themselves were not difficult to grasp. In the twentieth century, however, physicists faced, for the first time, a serious challenge to their ability to understand the universe. Every time they asked nature a question in an atomic experiment, nature answered with a paradox, and the more they tried to clarify the situation, the sharper the paradoxes became. In their struggle to grasp this new reality, scientists became painfully aware that their basic concepts, their language, and their whole way of thinking were inadequate to describe atomic phenomena. Their problem was not only intellectual but involved an intense emotional and existential experience, as vividly described by Werner Heisenberg: "I remember discussions with Bohr which went through many hours till very late at night and ended almost in despair; and when at the end of the discussion I went alone for a walk in the neighboring park I repeated to myself again and again the question: Can nature possibly be so absurd as it seemed to us in these atomic experiments?"[1]

It took these physicists a long time to accept the fact that the paradoxes they encountered are an essential aspect of atomic physics, and to realize that they arise whenever one tries to describe atomic phenomena in terms of classical concepts. Once this was perceived, the physicists began to learn to ask the right questions and to avoid contradictions. As Heisenberg says, "They somehow got into the spirit of the quantum theory,"[2] and finally they found the precise and consistent mathematical formulation of that theory. Quantum theory, or quantum mechanics as it is also called, was formulated during the first three decades of the century by an international group of physicists including Max Planck, Albert Einstein, Niels Bohr, Louis De Broglie, Erwin Schrödinger, Wolfgang Pauli, Werner Heisenberg, and Paul Dirac. These men joined forces across national borders to shape one of the most exciting periods of modern science, one that saw not only brilliant intellectual exchanges but also dramatic human conflicts, as well as deep personal friendships, among the scientists.

Even after the mathematical formulation of quantum theory was completed, its conceptual framework was by no means easy to accept. Its effect on the physicists' view of reality was truly shattering. The new physics necessitated profound changes in concepts of space, time, matter, object, and cause and effect; and because these concepts are so fundamental to our way of experiencing the world, their transformation came as a great shock. To quote Heisenberg again, "The violent reaction to the recent development of modern physics can only be understood when one realizes that here the foundations of physics have started moving; and that this motion has caused the feeling that the ground would be cut from science."[3]

Einstein experienced the same shock when he was confronted with the new concepts of physics, and he described his feelings in terms very similar to Heisenberg's: "All my attempts to adapt the theoretical foundation of physics to this [new type of] knowledge failed completely. It was as if the ground had been pulled out from under one, with no firm foundation to be seen anywhere, upon which one could have built."[4]

Out of the revolutionary changes in our concepts of reality that were brought about by modern physics, a consistent world view is now emerging. This view is not shared by the entire physics community, but is being discussed and elaborated by many leading physicists whose interest in their science goes beyond the technical aspects of their research. These scientists are deeply interested in the philosophical implications of modern physics and are trying in an open-minded way to improve their understanding of the nature of reality.

In contrast to the mechanistic Cartesian view of the world, the world view emerging from modern physics can be characterized by words like organic, holistic, and ecological. It might also be called a systems view, in the sense of general systems theory.[5] The universe is no longer seen as a machine, made up of a multitude of objects, but has to be pictured as one indivisible, dynamic whole whose parts are essentially interrelated and can be understood only as patterns of a cosmic process.

The basic concepts underlying this world view of modern physics are discussed in the following pages. I described this world view in detail in *The Tao of Physics,* showing how it is related to the views held in mystical traditions, especially those of Eastern mysticism. Many physicists, brought up, as I was, in a tradition that associates mysticism with things vague, mysterious, and highly unscientific, were shocked at having their ideas compared to those of mystics.[6] Fortunately, this attitude is now changing. As Eastern thought has begun to interest a significant number of people, and meditation is no longer viewed with ridicule or suspicion, mysticism is being taken seriously even within the scientific community. An increasing number of scientists are aware that mystical thought provides a consistent and relevant philosophical background to the theories of contemporary science, a conception of the world in which the scientific discoveries of men and women can be in perfect harmony with their spiritual aims and religious beliefs.

■ ■ ■

The experimental investigation of atoms at the beginning of the century yielded sensational and totally unexpected results. Far from being the hard, solid particles of time-honored theory, atoms turned out to consist of vast regions of space in which extremely small particles—the electrons—moved around the nucleus. A few years later quantum theory made it clear that even the subatomic particles—the electrons and the protons and neutrons in the nucleus—were nothing like the solid objects of classical physics. These subatomic units of matter are very abstract entities which have a dual aspect. Depending on how we look at them, they appear sometimes as particles, sometimes as waves; and this dual nature is also exhibited by light, which can take the form of electromagnetic waves or particles. The particles of light were first called "quanta" by Einstein—hence the origin of the term "quantum theory"—and are now know as photons.

This dual nature of matter and of light is very strange. It seems impossible to accept that something can be, at the same time, a particle, an entity confined to a very small volume, and a wave, which is spread out over a large region of space. And yet this is exactly what physicists had to accept. The situation seemed hopelessly paradoxical until it was realized that the terms "particle" and "wave" refer to classical concepts which are not fully adequate to describe atomic phenomena. An electron is neither a particle nor a wave, but it may show particle-like aspects in some situations and wave-like aspects in others. While it acts like a particle, it is capable of developing its wave nature at the expense of its particle nature, and vice versa, thus undergoing continual transformations from particle to wave and from wave to particle. This means that neither the electron nor any other atomic "object" has any intrinsic properties independent of its environment. The properties it shows—particle-like or wave-like—will depend on the experimental situation, that is, on the apparatus it is forced to interact with.[7]

It was Heisenberg's great achievement to express the limitations of classical concepts in a precise mathematical form, which is known as the uncertainty principle. It consists of a set of mathematical relations that determine the extent to which classical concepts can be applied to atomic phenomena; these relations stake out the limits of human imagination in the atomic world. Whenever we use classical terms—particle, wave, position, velocity—to describe atomic phenomena, we find that there are pairs of concepts, or aspects, which are interrelated and cannot be defined simultaneously in a precise way. The more we emphasize one aspect in our description the more the other aspect becomes uncertain, and the precise relation between the two is given by the uncertainty principle.

For a better understanding of this relation between pairs of classical concepts, Niels Bohr introduced the notion of complementarity. He considered the particle picture and the wave picture two complementary descriptions of the same reality, each of them only partly correct and having a limited range of application. Both pictures are needed to give a full account of the atomic reality, and both are to be applied within the limitations set by the uncertainty principle. The notion of complementarity has become an essential part of the way physicists think about nature, and Bohr has often suggested that it might also be a useful concept outside the field of physics. Indeed, this seems to be true, and we shall come back to it in discussions of biological and psychological phenomena. Complementarity has already been used extensively in our survey of the Chinese yin/yang terminology, since the yin and yang opposites are interrelated in a polar, or complementary, way. Clearly the modern concept of complementarity is reflected in ancient Chinese thought, a fact that made a deep impression on Niels Bohr.[8]

The resolution of the particle/wave paradox forced physicists to accept an aspect of reality that called into question the very foundation of the mechanistic world view—the concept of the reality of matter. At the subatomic level, matter does not exist with certainty at definite places, but rather shows "tendencies to exist," and atomic events do not occur with certainty at definite times and in definite ways, but rather show "tendencies to occur." In the formalism of quantum mechanics, these tendencies are expressed as probabilities and are associated with quantities that take the form of waves; they are similar to the mathematical forms used to describe, say, a vibrating guitar string, or sound wave. This is how particles can be waves at the same time. They are not "real" three-dimensional waves like water waves or sound waves. They are "probability waves"— abstract mathematical quantities with all the characteristic properties of waves—that are related to the probabilities of finding the particles at particular points in space and at particular times. All the laws of atomic physics are expressed in terms of these probabilities. We can never predict an atomic event with certainty; we can only predict the likelihood of its happening.

■ ■ ■

The discovery of the dual aspect of matter and of the fundamental role of probability has demolished the classical notion of solid objects. At the subatomic level, the solid material objects of classical physics dissolve into wave-like patterns of probabilities. These patterns, furthermore, do not represent probabilities of things, but rather probabilities of interconnections. A careful analysis of the process of observation in atomic physics shows that the subatomic particles have no meaning as isolated entities but can be understood only as interconnections, or correlations, between various processes of observation and measurement. As Niels Bohr wrote, "Isolated material particles are abstractions, their properties being definable and observable only through their interaction with other systems."[9]

Subatomic particles, then, are not "things" but are interconnections between "things," and these "things," in turn, are interconnections between other "things," and so on. In quantum theory you never end up with "things"; you always deal with interconnections.

This is how modern physics reveals the basic oneness of the universe. It shows that we cannot decompose the world into independently existing smallest units. As we penetrate into matter, nature does not show us any isolated basic building blocks, but rather appears as a complicated web of relations between the various parts of a unified whole. As Heisenberg expresses it, "The world thus appears as a complicated tissue of events, in which connections of different kinds alternate or overlap or combine and thereby determine the texture of the whole."[10]

The universe, then, is a unified whole that can to some extent be divided into separate parts, into objects made of molecules and atoms, themselves made of particles. But here, at the level of particles, the notion of separate parts breaks down. The subatomic particles—and therefore, ultimately, all parts of the universe—cannot be understood as isolated entities but must be defined through their interrelations. Henry Stapp, of the University of California, writes, "An elementary particle is not an independently existing unanalyzable entity. It is, in essence, a set of relationships that reach outward to other things."[11]

This shift from objects to relationships has far-reaching implications for science as a whole. Gregory Bateson even argued that relationships should be used as a basis for *all* definitions, and that this should be taught to our children in elementary school.[12] Any thing, he believed, should be defined not by what it is in itself, but by its relations to other things.

In quantum theory the fact that atomic phenomena are determined by their connections to the whole is closely related to the fundamental role of probability.[13] In classical physics, probability is used whenever the mechanical details involved in an event are unknown. For example, when we throw a die, we could—in principle—predict the outcome if we knew all the details of the objects involved: the exact composition of the die, of the surface on which it falls, and so on. These details are called local variables because they reside within the objects involved. Local variables are important in atomic and subatomic physics too. Here they are represented by connections between spatially separated events through signals—particles and networks of particles—that respect the usual laws of spatial separation. For example, no signal can be transmitted faster than the speed of light. But beyond these local connections are other, nonlocal connections that are instantaneous and cannot be predicted, at present, in a precise mathematical way. These nonlocal connections are the essence of quantum reality. Each event is influenced by the whole universe, and although we cannot describe this influence in detail, we recognize some order that can be expressed in terms of statistical laws.

Thus probability is used in classical and quantum physics for similar reasons. In both cases there are "hidden" variables, unknown to us, and this ignorance prevents us from making exact predictions. There is a crucial difference, however. Whereas the hidden variables in classical physics are local mechanisms, those in quantum physics are nonlocal; they are instantaneous connections to the universe as a whole. In the ordinary, macroscopic world nonlocal connections are relatively unimportant, and thus we can speak of separate objects and formulate the laws of physics in terms of certainties. But as we go to smaller dimensions, the influence of nonlocal connections becomes stronger; here the laws of physics can be formulated only in terms of probabilities, and it becomes more and more difficult to separate any part of the universe from the whole.

Einstein could never accept the existence of nonlocal connections and the resulting fundamental nature of probability. This was the subject of the historic debate in the 1920s with Bohr, in which Einstein expressed his opposition to Bohr's interpretation of quantum theory in the famous metaphor "God does not play dice."[14] At the end of the debate, Einstein had to admit that quantum theory, as interpreted by Bohr and Heisenberg, formed a consistent system of thought, but he remained convinced that a deterministic interpretation in terms of local hidden variables would be found some time in the future.

Einstein's unwillingness to accept the consequences of the theory that his earlier work had helped to establish is one of the most fascinating episodes in the history of science. The essence of his disagreement with Bohr was his firm belief in some external reality, consisting of independent spatially separated elements. This shows that Einstein's philosophy was essentially Cartesian. Although he initiated the revolution of twentieth-century science and went far beyond Newton in his theory of relativity, it seems that Einstein, somehow, could not bring himself to go beyond Descartes. This kinship between Einstein and Descartes is even more intriguing in view of Einstein's attempts, toward the end of his life, to construct a unified field theory by geometrizing physics along the lines of his general theory of relativity. Had these attempts been successful, Einstein could well have said, like Descartes, that his entire physics was nothing other than geometry.

▪ ▪ ▪

The conception of the universe as an interconnected web of relations is one of two major themes that recur throughout modern physics. The other theme is the realization that the cosmic web is intrinsically dynamic. The dynamic aspect of matter arises in quantum theory as a consequence of the wave nature of subatomic particles, and is even more central in relativity theory, which has shown us that the being of matter cannot be separated from its activity. The properties of its basic patterns, the subatomic particles, can be understood only in a dynamic context, in terms of movement, interaction, and transformation.

The fact that particles are not isolated entities but wave-like probability patterns implies that they behave in a very peculiar way. Whenever a subatomic particle is confined to a small region of space, it reacts to this confinement by moving around. The smaller the region of confinement, the faster the particle will "jiggle" around in it. This behavior is a typical "quantum effect," a feature of the subatomic world which has no analogy in macroscopic physics: the more a particle is confined, the faster it will move around.[22] This tendency of particles to react to confinement with motion implies a fundamental "restlessness" of matter which is characteristic of the subatomic world. In this world most of the material particles *are* confined; they are bound to the molecular, atomic, and nuclear structures, and therefore are not at rest but have an inherent tendency to move about. According to quantum theory, matter is always restless, never quiescent. To the extent that things can be pictured to be made of smaller constituents—molecules, atoms, and particles—these constituents are in a state of continual motion. Macroscopically, the material objects around us may seem passive and inert, but when we magnify such a "dead" piece of stone or metal, we see that it is full of activity. The closer we look at it, the more alive it appears. All the material objects in our environment are made of atoms that link up with each other in various ways to form an enormous variety of molecular structures which are not rigid and motionless but vibrate according to their temperature and in harmony with the thermal vibrations of their environment. Inside the vibrating atoms the electrons are bound to the atomic nuclei by electric forces that try to keep them as close as possible, and they respond to this confinement by whirling around extremely fast. In the nuclei, finally, protons and neutrons are pressed into a minute volume by the strong nuclear forces, and consequently race about at unimaginable velocities.

Modern physics thus pictures matter not at all as passive and inert but as being in a continuous dancing and vibrating motion whose rhythmic patterns are determined by the molecular, atomic, and nuclear configurations. We have come to realize that there are no static structures in nature. There is stability, but this stability is one of dynamic balance, and the further we penetrate into matter the more we need to understand its dynamic nature to understand its patterns.

■ ■ ■

The two basic theories of modern physics have thus transcended the principal aspects of the Cartesian world view and of Newtonian physics. Quantum theory has shown that subatomic particles are not isolated grains of matter but are probability patterns, interconnections in an inseparable cosmic web that includes the human observer and her* consciousness. Relativity theory has made the cosmic web come alive, so to speak, by revealing its intrinsically dynamic character; by showing that its activity is the very essence of its being. In modern physics, the image of the universe as a machine has been transcended by a view of it as one indivisible, dynamic whole whose parts are essentially interrelated and can be understood only as patterns of a cosmic process. At the subatomic level the interrelations and interactions between the parts of the whole are more fundamental than the parts themselves. There is motion but there are, ultimately, no moving objects; there is activity but there are no actors; there are no dancers, there is only the dance.

■ ■ ■

---

*The feminine pronoun is used here as a general reference to a person who may be a woman or a man. Similarly, I shall occasionally use the masculine pronoun as a general reference, including both men and women. I think this the best way to avoid being either sexist or awkward.

Questions for Further Exploration:

- What made the new physics (quantum mechanics) so absurd and shocking to the scientists who developed it?

- What has investigation of subatomic units revealed about the nature of matter? What is an electron? What principles/concepts are required to give a full account of atomic reality?

- In contrast to the Cartesian view of reality, what view of reality is emerging from modern physics? How do classical and quantum physics differ?

- What did Einstein mean by saying "God does not play dice"?

- What does it mean to say that "the cosmic web is intrinsically dynamic"?

- What are the implications of the shift from thinking of reality in terms of "objects" (things, substances) to thinking in terms of dynamic "processes" (probability patterns, relationships, interactions)?

- Free-write a response to Capra's claim, "There is motion but there are, ultimately, no moving objects; there is activity but there are no actors; there are no dancers, there is only the dance."

UNIT THREE:
Knowledge

Epistemology
The branch of philosophy concerned with the criteria, nature, and possibility of knowledge. Defining "knowledge" as "justified true belief" raises the question of what justification or explanatory account, if any, can establish the truth of a belief.

Introduction to Greening Epistemology

For a grasp of epistemology, let's return to Plato's *Allegory of the Cave*. If the prisoners inside the cave symbolize people with false beliefs or even just unchecked opinions, and the escapee outside the cave symbolizes someone with knowledge, then the pathway out of the cave symbolizes a method or manner of establishing the truth of a belief. For example, the pathway could symbolize logical analysis or generalization from empirical observation. Notice the narrative structure of the allegory assumes there *is* a way out (i.e., a way of establishing the truth about reality). Imagine if the story was about prisoners viewing shadows on the wall of a cave, or internal dwelling, with no way out. Changing the Allegory in this way could symbolize the view that knowledge of reality is impossible or that there is no fixed reality to have knowledge of.

In unit two we surveyed various philosophical views of reality. Although most of them were offered on the basis of argument, we did not focus our attention on the kind of *evidence* offered for the arguments. This is the work of epistemology.

Metaphysical debates lead naturally to epistemological questions. For example, the claim "God exists," is inevitably followed by "How do you *know?*" Inquiry into the basis or foundation of truth claims has led Western philosophers down several well-trodden paths, including rationalism, empiricism, skepticism, dialectical materialism, and phenomenology. Working through these epistemologies helps us to determine which truth claims about reality are based on the best explanatory account or justification. In particular, studying epistemology can help us determine the best approaches for understanding the natural world and analyzing environmental problems and solutions. Several philosophers in this unit are skeptical that "speculative metaphysics" can provide the necessary foundation for a shift to a sustainable order of values. Hence, this unit raises the question: "Can a justification be provided for a sustainable paradigm shift?"

As we survey the philosophical terrain of knowledge, including the distinctions between logic and empirical observation, objectivity and subjectivity, and the forces that impede our efforts to get at the truth, it makes sense to reflect on *how* and *why* we have sought to understand the natural world. Just as there are values embedded in metaphysical theories, there are values embedded in epistemological theories. In his pursuit of knowledge, Aristotle used the same method for getting at the truth about humans, animals, and artifacts. In 1641, Descartes broke with the Aristotelian tradition by establishing that "minds" and "bodies" require different sorts of inquiry, appropriate to their respective natures. In the process of seeking a foundation for modern science, the mode of inquiry appropriate for gaining knowledge of bodies, he initiated a long-standing epistemological debate. On one side stand the rationalists, who argue that innate ideas provide the only certain foundation for knowledge. On the other stand the empiricists, who argue that sensory experience provide the only possible, if less certain, foundation for knowledge. Efforts to resolve their differences generated new ways of looking at the work of knowledge-making. In the nineteenth century new skeptical questions arose in epistemology regarding the relationship between knowledge and power.

As you study the range of epistemic positions, seek to identify the values each approach embodies. Is rationality inherently anthropocentric? Are some forms of rationality more ecologically friendly than others, and if so, what makes them so? How does ideology function to obscure the interests motivating particular truth claims? Keep in mind as you sort through the annals of Western epistemology that urgent environmental problems await your answers.

Resources:

Anderson, Elizabeth, "Feminist Epistemology and Philosophy of Science," *The Stanford Encyclopedia of Philosophy,* edited by Edward N. Zalta, Fall 2010 Edition. http://plato.stanford.edu/archives/fall2010/entries/feminism-epistemology/

Aylesworth, Gary, "Postmodernism," *The Stanford Encyclopedia of Philosophy,* edited by Edward N. Zalta, Winter 2009 Edition. http://plato.stanford.edu/archives/win2009/entries/postmodernism/

Baraka: A World beyond Words, Dir. Ron Fricke, Magidson Films, 1993.

Bristow, William, "Enlightenment," *The Stanford Encyclopedia of Philosophy,* edited by Edward N. Zalta, Fall 2010 Edition. http://plato.stanford.edu/archives/fall2010/entries/enlightenment/

Gallagher, Shaun, and Zahavi, Dan, "Phenomenological Approaches to Self-Consciousness," *The Stanford Encyclopedia of Philosophy,* edited by Edward N. Zalta, Winter 2010 Edition. http://plato.stanford.edu/archives/win2010/entries/self-consciousness-phenomenological/

Klein, Peter, "Skepticism," *The Stanford Encyclopedia of Philosophy,* edited by Edward N. Zalta, Winter 2010 Edition, forthcoming. http://plato.stanford.edu/archives/win2010/entries/skepticism/

Markie, Peter, "Rationalism vs. Empiricism," *The Stanford Encyclopedia of Philosophy,* edited by Edward N. Zalta, Fall 2008 Edition. http://plato.stanford.edu/archives/fall2008/entries/rationalism-empiricism/

Phenomenon, Dir. Jon Turteltaub, Touchstone Pictures, 1996.

Steup, Matthias, "Epistemology," *The Stanford Encyclopedia of Philosophy* edited by Edward N. Zalta, Spring 2010 Edition. http://plato.stanford.edu/archives/spr2010/entries/epistemology/

Sypnowich, Christine, "Law and Ideology," *The Stanford Encyclopedia of Philosophy,* edited by Edward N. Zalta, Fall 2010 Edition. http://plato.stanford.edu/archives/fall2010/entries/law-ideology/

Wylie, Alison, Potter, Elizabeth, and Bauchspies, Wenda K., "Feminist Perspectives on Science," *The Stanford Encyclopedia of Philosophy,* edited by Edward N. Zalta, Spring 2010 Edition. http://plato.stanford.edu/archives/spr2010/entries/feminist-science/

Questions for Further Exploration:

■ What values are embedded in various ways of seeking the truth, including objectivity, subjectivity, and inter-subjectivity?

■ Can the causes of ecological destruction be found in particular Western assumptions about what knowledge is, and how it ought to be acquired?

■ What is the most ecologically sound manner of getting at the truth about humans and the natural world? Are some forms of rationality more ecologically friendly than others?

■ What do various epistemologies contribute to, and reveal about the cause(s) of ecological problems?

■ Is there an epistemological justification for the shift to a sustainable order of values?

■ Are there conceptual resources buried in Western epistemological theories that could open up fruitful directions for a more sustainable future?

Physics

Book II The Study of Nature

Aristotle
Translated by Robin Waterfield

3. The Four Types of Cause

With these distinctions in place, we should look into the question of how many causes there are, and what they are like. For the point of our investigation is to acquire knowledge, and a prerequisite for knowing anything is understanding *why* it is as it is—in other words, grasping its primary cause. Obviously, then, this is what we have to do in the case of coming to be and ceasing to be, and natural change in general. Then, once we know the principles of these things, we can try to analyse anything we are looking into in terms of these principles.

One way in which the word 'cause' is used is for that from which a thing is made and continues to be made—for example, the bronze of a statue, the silver of a bowl, and the genera of which bronze and silver are species.

Material 1. material

A second way in which the word is used is for the form or pattern (i.e. the formula for what a thing is, both specifically and generically, and the terms which play a part in the formula). For example, the ratio 2:1, and number in general, cause the octave.

2 formal

A third way in which the word is used is for the original source of change or rest. For example, a deviser of a plan is a cause, a father causes a child, and in general a producer causes a product and a changer causes a change.

3

A fourth way in which the word is used is for the end. This is what something is for, as health, for example, may be what walking is for. If asked, 'Why is he walking?', we reply, 'To get healthy', and in saying

4 means

Vocab: — Teleology

Aristotle: Physics translated by Robin Waterfield (OWC, 1996). Selection II.3 (pp. 38–39). Reprinted by permission of Oxford Univeristy Press.

this we mean to explain the cause of his walking. And then there is everything which happens during the process of change (initiated by something else) that leads up to the end: for example, the end of health may involve slimming or purging or drugs or surgical implements; they are all for the same end, but they are different in that some are actions and some are implements.

These are more or less all the ways in which we use the word 'cause'. The upshot is that there are a number of ways in which the word is used and also that a single thing has a number of causes, even without considering coincidence. For instance, both sculpturing and bronze are causally responsible for a statue, and are so for the statue in its own right, *qua* statue, although they are dissimilar *kinds* of causes, since one is a cause in the sense that matter is a cause, while the other is a cause in the sense that the source of change is a cause.

■ ■ ■

Questions for Further Exploration:

■ How does Aristotle describe the four types of causes of a thing one needs to understand to acquire knowledge of that thing?

■ Why does Aristotle believe that you know a thing when you know its four causes? Which among the four is the most suspect? (Hint: review his metaphysical assumptions.)

■ Using the four Aristotelian causes how would you explain each of the following: a tree, a spider, the Statue of Liberty, a television, and a human being? Which sort of thing does it work best to explain? What difficulties does each sort of thing raise in the explanatory process?

■ Challenge his view by thinking of a counter-example; i.e., something you "know" on some other basis than understanding the four causes.

■ Compare and contrast Aristotle's explanatory framework with that of modern science. What advantages does each offer in the pursuit of ecological knowledge?

Meditations on First Philosophy

René Descartes

Meditation Six: Concerning the Existence of Material Things, and the Real Distinction between Mind and Body

First, I know that all the things that I clearly and distinctly understand can be made by God such as I understand them. For this reason, my ability clearly and distinctly to understand one thing without another suffices to make me certain that the one thing is different from the other, since they can be separated from each other, at least by God. The question as to the sort of power that might effect such a separation is not relevant to their being thought to be different. For this reason, from the fact that I know that I exist, and that at the same time I judge that obviously nothing else belongs to my nature or essence except that I am a thinking thing, I rightly conclude that my essence consists entirely in my being a thinking thing. And although perhaps (or rather, as I shall soon say, assuredly) I have a body that is very closely joined to me, nevertheless, because on the one hand I have a clear and distinct idea of myself, insofar as I am merely a thinking thing and not an extended thing, and because on the other hand I have a distinct idea of a body, insofar as it is merely an extended thing and not a thinking thing, it is certain that I am really distinct from my body, and can exist without it.

Moreover, I find in myself faculties for certain special modes of thinking, namely the faculties of imagining and sensing. I can clearly and distinctly understand myself in my entirety without these faculties, but not vice versa: I cannot understand them clearly and distinctly without me, that is, without a substance endowed with understanding in which they inhere, for they include an act of understanding in their formal concept. Thus I perceive them to be distinguished from me as modes from a thing. I also acknowledge that there are certain other faculties, such as those of moving from one place to another, of taking on various shapes, and so on, that, like sensing or imagining, cannot be understood apart from some substance in which they inhere, and hence without which they cannot exist. But it is clear that these faculties, if in fact they exist, must be in a corporeal or extended substance, not in a substance endowed with understanding. For some extension is contained in a clear and distinct concept of them, though certainly not any understanding. Now there clearly is in me a passive faculty of sensing, that is, a faculty for receiving and knowing the ideas of sensible things; but I could not use it unless there also existed, either in me or in something else, a certain active faculty of producing or bringing about these ideas. But this faculty surely cannot be in me, since it clearly presupposes no act of understanding, and these ideas are produced without my cooperation and often even against my will. Therefore the only alternative is that it is in some substance different from me, containing either formally or eminently all the reality that exists objectively in the ideas produced by that faculty, as I have just noted above. Hence this substance is either a body, that is, a corporeal nature, which contains formally all that is contained objectively in the ideas, or else it is God, or some other creature more noble than a body, which contains eminently all that is contained objectively in the ideas. But since God is not a deceiver, it is patently obvious that he does not send me these ideas either immediately by himself, or even through the mediation of some creature that contains the objective reality of these ideas not formally but only eminently. For since God has given me no faculty whatsoever for making this determination, but instead has given me a great inclination to believe that these ideas issue from corporeal things, I fail to see how God could be understood not to be a deceiver, if these ideas were to issue from a source other than corporeal things. And consequently corporeal things exist. Nevertheless, perhaps not all bodies exist exactly as I grasp them by sense, since this sensory grasp is in many cases very obscure and confused. But at least they do contain everything I clearly and distinctly understand—that is, everything, considered in a general sense, that is encompassed in the object of pure mathematics.

As far as the remaining matters are concerned, which are either merely particular (for example, that the sun is of such and such a size or shape, and so on) or less clearly understood (for example, light, sound, pain, and the like), even though these matters are very doubtful and uncertain, nevertheless the fact that God is no deceiver (and thus no falsity can be found in my opinions, unless there is also in me a faculty given me by God for the purpose of rectifying this falsity) offers me a definite hope of reaching the truth even in these matters. And surely there is no doubt that all that I am taught by nature has some truth to it; for by "nature," taken generally, I understand nothing other than God himself or the ordered network of created things which was instituted by God. By my own particular nature I understand nothing other than the combination of all the things bestowed upon me by God.

There is nothing that this nature teaches me more explicitly than that I have a body that is ill-disposed when I feel pain, that needs food and drink when I suffer hunger or thirst, and the like. Therefore, I should not doubt that there is some truth in this.

By means of these sensations of pain, hunger, thirst and so on, nature also teaches not merely that I am present to my body in the way a sailor is present in a ship, but that I am most tightly joined and, so to speak, commingled with it, so much so that I and the body constitute one single thing. For if this were not the case, then I, who am only a thinking thing, would not sense pain when the body is injured; rather, I would perceive the wound by means of the pure intellect, just as a sailor perceives by sight whether anything in his ship is broken. And when the body is in need of food or drink, I should understand this explicitly, instead of having confused sensations of hunger and thirst. For clearly these sensations of thirst, hunger, pain, and so on are nothing but certain confused modes of thinking arising from the union and, as it were, the commingling of the mind with the body.

Moreover, I am also taught by nature that various other bodies exist around my body, some of which are to be pursued, while others are to be avoided. And to be sure, from the fact that I sense a wide variety of colors, sounds, odors, tastes, levels of heat, and grades of roughness, and the like, I rightly conclude that in the bodies from which these different perceptions of the senses proceed there are differences corresponding to the different perceptions—though perhaps the latter do not resemble the former. And from the fact that some of these perceptions are pleasant while others are unpleasant, it is plainly certain that my body, or rather my whole self, insofar as I am comprised of a body and a mind, can be affected by various beneficial and harmful bodies in the vicinity.

Granted, there are many other things that I seem to have been taught by nature; nevertheless it was not really nature that taught them to me but a certain habit of making reckless judgments. And thus it could easily happen that these judgments are false: for example, that any space where there is absolutely nothing happening to move my sense is empty; or that there is something in a hot body that bears an exact likeness to the idea of heat that is in me; or that in a white or green body there is the same whiteness or greenness that I sense; or that in a bitter or sweet body there is the same taste, and so on; or that stars and towers and any other distant bodies have the same size and shape that they present to my senses, and other things of this sort. But to ensure that my perceptions in this matter are sufficiently distinct, I ought to define more precisely what exactly I mean when I say that I am "taught something by nature." For I am taking "nature" here more narrowly than the combination of everything bestowed on me by God. For this combination embraces many things that belong exclusively to my mind, such as my perceiving that what has been done cannot be undone, and everything else that is known by the light of nature. That is not what I am talking about here. There are also many things that belong exclusively to the body, such as that it tends to move downward, and so on. I am not dealing with these either, but only with what God has bestowed on me insofar as I am comprised of mind and body. Accordingly, it is this nature that teaches me to avoid things that produce a sensation of pain and to pursue things that produce a sensation of pleasure, and the like. But it does not appear that nature teaches us to conclude anything, besides these things, from these sense perceptions unless the intellect has first conducted its own inquiry regarding things external to us. For it seems to belong exclusively to the mind, and not to the composite of mind and body, to know the truth in these matters. Thus, although a star affects my eye no more than does the flame from a small torch, still there is no real or positive tendency in my eye toward believing that the star is no larger than the flame. Yet, ever since my youth, I have made this judgment without any reason for doing so. And although I feel heat as I draw closer to the fire, and I also feel pain upon drawing too close to it, there is not a single argument that persuades me that there is something in the fire similar to that heat, any more than to that pain. On the contrary, I am convinced only that there is something in the first that, regardless of what it finally turns out to be, causes in us those sensations of heat or pain. And although there may be nothing in a given space that moves the senses, it does not therefore follow that there is no body in it. But I see that in these and many other instances I have been in the habit of subverting the order of nature. For admittedly I use the perceptions of the senses (which are properly given by nature only for signifying to the mind what things are useful or harmful to the composite of which it is a part, and to that extent they are clear and distinct enough) as reliable rules for immediately discerning what is the essence of bodies located outside us. Yet they signify nothing about that except quite obscurely and confusedly.

I have already examined in sufficient detail how it could happen that my judgments are false, despite the goodness of God. But a new difficulty now arises regarding those very things that nature shows me are either to be sought out or avoided, as well as the internal sensations where I seem to have detected errors, as for example, when someone is deluded by a food's pleasant taste to eat the poison hidden inside it. In this case, however, he is driven by nature only toward desiring the thing in which the pleasurable taste is found, but not toward the poison, of which he obviously is un-aware. I can only conclude that this nature is not omniscient. This is not re-markable, since man is a limited thing, and thus only what is of limited perfection befits him.

But we not infrequently err even in those things to which nature im-pels us. Take, for example, the case of those who are ill and who desire food or drink that will soon afterwards be injurious to them. Perhaps it could be said here that they erred because their nature was corrupt. How-ever, this does not remove our difficulty, for a sick man is no less a crea-ture of God than a healthy one, and thus it seems no less inconsistent that the sick man got a deception-prone nature from God. And a clock made of wheels and counter-weights follows all the laws of nature no less closely when it has been badly constructed and does not tell time accurately than it does when it completely satisfies the wish of its maker. Likewise, I might regard a man's body as a kind of mechanism that is outfitted with and composed of bones, nerves, muscles, veins, blood and skin in such a way that, even if no mind existed in it, the man's body would still exhibit all the same motions that are in it now except for those motions that pro-ceed either from a command of the will or, consequently, from the mind. I easily recognize that it would be natural for this body, were it, say, suffer-ing from dropsy and experiencing dryness in the throat (which typically produces a thirst sensation in the mind), and also so disposed by its nerves and other parts to take something to drink, the result of which would be to exacerbate the illness. This is as natural as for a body without any such ill-ness to be moved by the same dryness in the throat to take something to drink that is useful to it. And given the intended purpose of the clock, I could say that it deviates from its nature when it fails to tell the right time. And similarly, considering the mechanism of the human body in terms of its being equipped for the motions that typically occur in it, I may think that it too is deviating from its nature, if its throat were dry when having something to drink is not beneficial to its conservation. Nevertheless, I am well aware that this last use of "nature" differs greatly from the other. For this latter "nature" is merely a designation dependent on my thought, since it compares a man in poor health and a poorly constructed clock with the ideas of a healthy man and of a well-made clock, a designation extrinsic to the things to which it is applied. But by "nature" taken in the former sense, I understand something that is really in things, and thus is not without some truth.

When we say, then, in the case of the body suffering from dropsy, that its "nature" is corrupt, given the fact that it has a parched throat and yet does not need something to drink, "nature" obviously is merely an extrinsic designation. Nevertheless, in the case of the composite, that is, of a mind joined to such a body, it is not a pure designation, but a true error of nature that this body should be thirsty when having something to drink would be harmful to it. It therefore remains to inquire here how the goodness of God does not prevent "nature," thus considered, from being deceptive.

Now my first observation here is that there is a great difference between a mind and a body in that a body, by its very nature, is always divisible. On the other hand, the mind is utterly indivisible. For when I consider the mind, that is, myself insofar as I am only a thinking thing, I cannot distinguish any parts within me; rather, I understand myself to be manifestly one complete thing. Although the entire mind seems to be united to the entire body, nevertheless, were a foot or an arm or any other bodily part to be amputated, I know that nothing has been taken away from the mind on that account. Nor can the faculties of willing, sensing, understanding, and so on be called "parts" of the mind, since it is one and the same mind that wills, senses, and understands. On the other hand, there is no corporeal or extended thing I can think of that I may not in my thought easily divide into parts; and in this way I understand that it is divisible. This consideration alone would suffice to teach me that the mind is wholly diverse from the body, and I not yet known it well enough in any other way.

■ ■ ■

Questions for Further Exploration:

- What role does Descartes' "method of doubt" (used in the first *Meditation*) play in his theory of knowledge? Is he a skeptic?

- What does Descartes mean by "clear and distinct" apprehension? How is it achieved in contrast with "obscure and confused" modes of thinking? How can he distinguish between true and false judgments he is inclined to make?

- What human faculties insure that Truth is possible? Why call his view "rationalism"?

- What guarantee does he discover that ideas he grasps clearly and distinctly in his mind correspond to real things in the world; i.e., that he has *knowledge* of corporeal things?

- What does he mean when he refers to things he has been "taught by nature"? In contrast, what does he mean when he refers to "things known by the light of nature"?

- What are the implications of Cartesian mind/body dualism for his theory of knowledge and his knowledge of nature?

Discourse on the Method of Rightly Conducting the Reason, and Seeking Truth in the Sciences

René Descartes

But like one walking alone and in the dark, I resolved to proceed so slowly and with such circumspection, that if I did not advance far, I would at least guard against falling. I did not even choose to dismiss summarily any of the opinions that had crept into my belief without having been introduced by reason, but first of all took sufficient time carefully to satisfy myself of the general nature of the task I was setting myself, and ascertain the true method by which to arrive at the knowledge of whatever lay within the compass of my powers.

Among the branches of philosophy, I had, at an earlier period, given some attention to logic, and among those of the mathematics to geometrical analysis and algebra,—three arts or sciences which ought, as I conceived, to contribute something to my design. But, on examination, I found that, as for logic, its syllogisms and the majority of its other precepts are of avail—rather in the communication of what we already know, or even as the art of Lully, in speaking without judgment of things of which we are ignorant, than in the investigation of the unknown; and although this science contains indeed a number of correct and very excellent precepts, there are, nevertheless, so many others, and these either injurious or superfluous, mingled with the former, that it is almost quite as difficult to effect a severance of the true from the false as it is to extract a Diana or a Minerva from a rough block of marble. Then as to the analysis of the ancients and the algebra of the moderns, besides that they embrace only matters highly abstract, and, to appearance, of no use, the former is so exclusively restricted to the consideration of figures, that it can exercise the understanding only on condition of greatly fatiguing the imagination; and, in the latter, there is so complete a subjection to certain rules and formulas, that there results an art full of confusion and obscurity calculated to embarrass, instead of a science fitted to cultivate the mind. By these considerations I was induced to seek some other method which would comprise the advantages of the three and be exempt from their defects. And as a multitude of laws often only hampers justice, so that a state is best governed when, with few laws, these are rigidly administered; in like manner, instead of the great number of precepts of which logic is composed, I believed that the four following would prove perfectly sufficient for me, provided I took the firm and unwavering resolution never in a single instance to fail in observing them.

The first was never to accept anything for true which I did not clearly know to be such; that is to say, carefully to avoid precipitancy and prejudice, and to comprise nothing more in my judgement than what was presented to my mind so clearly and distinctly as to exclude all ground of doubt.

The second, to divide each of the difficulties under examination into as many parts as possible, and as might be necessary for its adequate solution.

The third, to conduct my thoughts in such order that, by commencing with objects the simplest and easiest to know, I might ascend by little and little, and, as it were, step by step, to the knowledge of the more complex; assigning in thought a certain order even to those objects which in their own nature do not stand in a relation of antecedence and sequence.

And the last, in every case to make enumerations so complete, and reviews so general, that I might be assured that nothing was omitted.

The long chains of simple and easy reasonings by means of which geometers are accustomed to reach the conclusions of their most difficult demonstrations, had led me to imagine that all things, to the knowledge of which man is competent, are mutually connected in the same way, and that there is nothing so far removed from us as to be beyond our reach, or so hidden that we cannot discover it, provided only we abstain from accepting the false for the true, and always preserve in our thoughts the order necessary for the deduction of one truth from another. And I had little difficulty in determining the objects with which it was necessary to commence, for I was already persuaded that it must be with the simplest and easiest to know, and, considering that of all those who have hitherto sought truth in the sciences, the mathematicians alone have been able to find any demonstrations, that is, any certain and evident reasons, I did not doubt but that such must have been the rule of their investigations. I resolved to commence, therefore, with the examination of the simplest objects, not anticipating, however, from this any other advantage than that to be found in accustoming my mind to the love and nourishment of truth, and to a distaste for all such reasonings as were unsound. But I had no intention on that account of attempting to master all the particular sciences commonly denominated mathematics: but observing that, however different their objects, they all agree in considering only the various relations or proportions subsisting among those objects, I thought it best for my purpose to consider these proportions in the most general form possible, without referring them to any objects in particular, except such as would most facilitate the knowledge of them, and without by any means restricting them to these, that afterwards I might thus be the better able to apply them to every other class of objects to which they are legitimately applicable. Perceiving further, that in order to understand these relations I should sometimes have to consider them one by one and sometimes only to bear them in mind, or embrace them in the aggregate, I thought that, in order the better to consider them individually, I should view them as subsisting between straight lines, than which I could find no objects more simple, or capable of being more distinctly represented to my imagination and senses; and on the other hand, that in order to retain them in the memory or embrace an aggregate of many, I should express them by certain characters the briefest possible. In this way I believed that I could borrow all that was best both in geometrical analysis and in algebra, and correct all the defects of the one by help of the other.

■ ■ ■

- What academic sources does Descartes consider in the design of his method? What strengths and weaknesses does the use of each entail for his project?

- What four precepts or laws comprise Descartes' method?

- How would you characterize Descartes' method of using reason rightly in pursuit of scientific truth? What other discipline does it most resemble? How does it compare to scientific method as we understand it today?

- Using Descartes' method how would you analyze each of the following: a tree, a spider, the Statue of Liberty, a television, and a human being? Which sort of thing does it work best to explain? What, if any, difficulties do you encounter in the process of analyzing each thing?

- Challenge his view with a counter-example; i.e., something you know on some other basis than his method.

- Some contemporary critics of Descartes charge that values embedded in his conception of rationality are wrecking havoc on the biosphere. Free-write: What values might be the source of the critics' criticisms?

An Essay Concerning Humane Understanding

John Locke

Introduction

■ ■ ■

Useful to know the Extent of our Comprehension.

If by this inquiry into the nature of the understanding, I can discover the powers thereof; how far they reach; to what things they are in any degree proportionate; and where they fail us, I suppose it may be of use to prevail with the busy mind of man to be more cautious in meddling with things exceeding its comprehension; to stop when it is at the utmost extent of its tether; and to sit down in a quiet ignorance of those things which, upon examination, are found to be beyond the reach of our capacities. We should not then perhaps be so forward, out of an affectation of an universal knowledge, to raise questions, and perplex ourselves and others with disputes about things to which our understandings are not suited; and of which we cannot frame in our minds any clear or distinct perceptions, or whereof (as it has perhaps too often happened) we have not any notions at all. If we can find out how far the understanding can extend its view; how far it has faculties to attain certainty; and in what cases it can only judge and guess, we may learn to content ourselves with what is attainable by us in this state.

■ ■ ■

Book I—Neither Principles nor Ideas are Innate
Chapter I. No Innate Speculative Principles.

■ ■ ■

2. General Assent the great Argument.

There is nothing more commonly taken for granted than that there are certain PRINCIPLES, both SPECULATIVE and PRACTICAL, (for they speak of both), universally agreed upon by all mankind: which therefore, they argue, must needs be the constant impressions which the souls of men receive in their first beings, and which they bring into the world with them, as necessarily and really as they do any of their inherent faculties.

3. Universal Consent proves nothing innate.

This argument, drawn from universal consent, has this misfortune in it, that if it were true in matter of fact, that there were certain truths wherein all mankind agreed, it would not prove them innate, if there can be any other way shown how men may come to that universal agreement, in the things they do consent in, which I presume may be done.

4. "What is is," and "It is possible for the same Thing to be and not to be," not universally assented to.

But, which is worse, this argument of universal consent, which is made use of to prove innate principles, seems to me a demonstration that there are none such: because there are none to which all mankind give an universal assent. I shall begin with the speculative, and instance in those magnified principles of demonstration, "Whatsoever is, is," and "It is impossible for the same thing to be and not to be"; which, of all others, I think have the most allowed title to innate. These have so settled a reputation of maxims universally received, that it will no doubt be thought strange if any one should seem to question it. But yet I take liberty to say, that these propositions are so far from having an universal assent, that there are a great part of mankind to whom they are not so much as known.

5. Not on Mind naturally imprinted, because not known to Children, Idiots, &c.

For, first, it is evident, that all children and idiots have not the least apprehension or thought of them. And the want of that is enough to destroy that universal assent which must needs be the necessary concomitant of all innate truths: it seeming to me near a contradiction to say, that there are truths imprinted on the soul, which it perceives or understands not: imprinting, if it signify anything, being nothing else but the making certain truths to be perceived. For to imprint anything on the mind without the mind's perceiving it, seems to me hardly intelligible. If therefore children and idiots have souls, have minds, with those impressions upon them, THEY must unavoidably perceive them, and necessarily know and assent to these truths; which since they do not, it is evident that there are no such impressions. For if they are not notions naturally imprinted, how can they be innate? and if they are notions imprinted, how can they be unknown? To say a notion is imprinted on the mind, and yet at the same time to say, that the mind is ignorant of it, and never yet took notice of it, is to make this impression nothing. No proposition can be said to be in the mind which it never yet knew, which it was never yet conscious of. For if any one may, then, by the same reason, all propositions that are true, and the mind is capable ever of assenting to, may be said to be in the mind, and to be imprinted: since, if any one can be said to be in the mind, which it never yet knew, it must be only because it is capable of knowing it; and so the mind is of all truths it ever shall know. Nay, thus truths may be imprinted on the mind which it never did, nor ever shall know; for a man may live long, and die at last in ignorance of many truths which his mind was capable of knowing, and that with certainty. So that if the capacity of knowing be the natural impression contended for, all the truths a man ever comes to know will, by this account, be every one of them innate; and this great point will amount to no more, but only to a very improper way of speaking; which, whilst it pretends to assert the contrary, says nothing different from those who deny innate principles. For nobody, I think, ever denied that the mind was capable of knowing several truths. The capacity, they say, is innate; the knowledge acquired. But then to what end such contest for certain innate maxims? If truths can be imprinted on the understanding without being perceived, I can see no difference there can be between any truths the mind is CAPABLE of knowing in respect of their original: they must all be innate or all adventitious: in vain shall a man go about to distinguish them. He therefore that talks of innate notions in the understanding, cannot (if he intend thereby any distinct sort of truths) mean such truths to be in the understanding as it never perceived, and is yet wholly ignorant of. For if these words "to be in the understanding" have any propriety, they signify to be understood. So that to be in the understanding, and not to be understood; to be in the mind and never to be perceived, is all one as to say anything is and is not in the mind or understanding. If therefore these two propositions, "Whatsoever is, is," and "It is impossible for the same thing to be and not to be," are by nature imprinted, children cannot be ignorant of them: infants, and all that have souls, must necessarily have them in their understandings, know the truth of them, and assent to it.

■ ■ ■

Book II–Of Ideas
Chapter I. Of Ideas in General, and Their Original.

■ ■ ■

2. All Ideas come from Sensation or Reflection.

Let us then suppose the mind to be, as we say, white paper, void of all characters, without any ideas:—How comes it to be furnished? Whence comes it by that vast store which the busy and boundless fancy of man has painted on it with an almost endless variety? Whence has it all the MATE-RIALS of reason and knowledge? To this I answer, in one word, from EX-PERIENCE. In that all our knowledge is founded; and from that it ulti-mately derives itself. Our observation employed either, about external sensible objects, or about the internal operations of our minds perceived and reflected on by ourselves, is that which supplies our understandings with all the MATERIALS of thinking. These two are the fountains of knowledge, from whence all the ideas we have, or can naturally have, do spring.

3. The Objects of Sensation one Source of Ideas

First, our Senses, conversant about particular sensible objects, do con-vey into the mind several distinct perceptions of things, according to those various ways wherein those objects do affect them. And thus we come by those IDEAS we have of yellow, white, heat, cold, soft, hard, bitter, sweet, and all those which we call sensible qualities; which when I say the senses convey into the mind, I mean, they from external objects convey into the mind what produces there those perceptions. This great source of most of the ideas we have, depending wholly upon our senses, and derived by them to the understanding, I call SENSATION.

4. The Operations of our Minds, the other Source of them.

Secondly, the other fountain from which experience furnisheth the un-derstanding with ideas is,—the perception of the operations of our own mind within us, as it is employed about the ideas it has got;—which oper-ations, when the soul comes to reflect on and consider, do furnish the un-derstanding with another set of ideas, which could not be had from things without. And such are perception, thinking, doubting, believing, reason-ing, knowing, willing, and all the different actings of our own minds;—which we being conscious of, and observing in ourselves, do from these receive into our understandings as distinct ideas as we do from bodies af-fecting our senses. This source of ideas every man has wholly in himself; and though it be not sense, as having nothing to do with external objects, yet it is very like it, and might properly enough be called INTERNAL SENSE. But as I call the other Sensation, so I call this REFLECTION, the ideas it affords being such only as the mind gets by reflecting on its own operations within itself. By reflection then, in the following part of this discourse, I would be understood to mean, that notice which the mind takes of its own operations, and the manner of them, by reason whereof there come to be ideas of these operations in the understanding. These two, I say, viz. external material things, as the objects of SENSATION, and the operations of our own minds within, as the objects of REFLEC-TION, are to me the only originals from whence all our ideas take their beginnings. The term OPERATIONS here I use in a large sense, as comprehending not barely the actions of the mind about its ideas, but some sort of passions arising sometimes from them, such as is the satisfaction or uneasiness arising from any thought.

5. All our Ideas are of the one or of the other of these.

The understanding seems to me not to have the least glimmering of any ideas which it doth not receive from one of these two. EXTERNAL OBJECTS furnish the mind with the ideas of sensible qualities, which are all those different perceptions they produce in us; and THE MIND furnishes the understanding with ideas of its own operations.

These, when we have taken a full survey of them, and their several modes, and the compositions made out of them we shall find to contain all our whole stock of ideas; and that we have nothing in our minds which did not come in one of these two ways. Let any one examine his own thoughts, and thoroughly search into his understanding; and then let him tell me, whether all the original ideas he has there, are any other than of the objects of his senses, or of the operations of his mind, considered as objects of his reflection. And how great a mass of knowledge soever he imagines to be lodged there, he will, upon taking a strict view, see that he has not any idea in his mind but what one of these two have imprinted;—though perhaps, with infinite variety compounded and enlarged by the understanding, as we shall see hereafter.

6. Observable in Children.

He that attentively considers the state of a child, at his first coming into the world, will have little reason to think him stored with plenty of ideas, that are to be the matter of his future knowledge. It is BY DEGREES he comes to be furnished with them. And though the ideas of obvious and familiar qualities imprint themselves before the memory begins to keep a register of time or order, yet it is often so late before some unusual qualities come in the way, that there are few men that cannot recollect the beginning of their acquaintance with them. And if it were worth while, no doubt a child might be so ordered as to have but a very few, even of the ordinary ideas, till he were grown up to a man. But all that are born into the world, being surrounded with bodies that perpetually and diversely affect them, variety of ideas, whether care be taken of it or not, are imprinted on the minds of children. Light and colours are busy at hand everywhere, when the eye is but open; sounds and some tangible qualities fail not to solicit their proper senses, and force an entrance to the mind;—but yet, I think, it will be granted easily, that if a child were kept in a place where he never saw any other but black and white till he were a man, he would have no more ideas of scarlet or green, than he that from his childhood never tasted an oyster, or a pine-apple, has of those particular relishes.

7. Men are differently furnished with these, according to the different Objects they converse with.

Men then come to be furnished with fewer or more simple ideas from without, according as the objects they converse with afford greater or less variety; and from the operations of their minds within, according as they more or less reflect on them. For, though he that contemplates the operations of his mind, cannot but have plain and clear ideas of them; yet, unless he turn his thoughts that way, and considers them ATTENTIVELY, he will no more have clear and distinct ideas of all the operations of his mind, and all that may be observed therein, than he will have all the particular ideas of any landscape, or of the parts and motions of a clock, who will not turn his eyes to it, and with attention heed all the parts of it. The picture, or clock may be so placed, that they may come in his way every day; but yet he will have but a confused idea of all the parts they are made up of, till he applies himself with attention, to consider them each in particular.

8. Ideas of Reflection later, because they need Attention.

And hence we see the reason why it is pretty late before most children get ideas of the operations of their own minds; and some have not any very clear or perfect ideas of the greatest part of them all their lives. Because, though they pass there continually, yet, like floating visions, they make not deep impressions enough to leave in their mind clear, distinct, lasting ideas, till the understanding turns inward upon itself, reflects on its own operations, and makes them the objects of its own contemplation. Children when they come first into it, are surrounded with a world of new things which, by a constant solicitation of their senses, draw the mind constantly to them; forward to take notice of new, and apt to be delighted with the variety of changing objects. Thus the first years are usually employed and diverted in looking abroad. Men's business in them is to acquaint themselves with what is to be found without; and so growing up in a constant attention to outward sensations, seldom make any considerable reflection on what passes within them, till they come to be of riper years; and some scarce ever at all.

■ ■ ■

Questions for Further Exploration:

- According to Locke, what limits the powers of understanding?

- What is the argument for innate ideas ("truths imprinted on the soul") that Locke intends to challenge? On what grounds does he challenge it?

- What speculative maxims does Locke use to make his case against universal consent? What counter-examples does he offer?

- What is Locke's view of the mind? How does he explain the acquisition of ideas? What reasons does he give in support of his explanation?

- Consider Locke's philosophy in terms of Plato's allegory. In his view, what might each of the symbols (the cave, prisoners, shadows, escapee, outside, the sun, etc.) represent?

- Free-write: In the debate on the foundation of knowledge between the rationalists represented by Descartes and the empiricists represented by Locke, where do you stand, and why?

An Enquiry Concerning Human Understanding

David Hume

Section IV. Sceptical Doubts Concerning the Operations of the Understanding.
Part I.

■ ■ ■

20. All the objects of human reason or enquiry may naturally be divided into two kinds, to wit, *Relations of Ideas,* and *Matters of Fact.* Of the first kind are the sciences of Geometry, Algebra, and Arithmetic; and in short, every affirmation which is either intuitively or demonstratively certain. *That the square of the hypothenuse is equal to the square of the two sides,* is a proposition which expresses a relation between these figures. *That three times five is equal to the half of thirty,* expresses a relation between these numbers. Propositions of this kind are discoverable by the mere operation of thought, without dependence on what is anywhere existent in the universe. Though there never were a circle or triangle in nature, the truths demonstrated by Euclid would for ever retain their certainty and evidence.

21. Matters of fact, which are the second objects of human reason, are not ascertained in the same manner; nor is our evidence of their truth, however great, of a like nature with the foregoing. The contrary of every matter of fact is still possible; because it can never imply a contradiction, and is conceived by the mind with the same facility and distinctness, as if ever so conformable to reality. *That the sun will not rise to-morrow* is no less intelligible a proposition, and implies no more contradiction than the affirmation, *that it will rise.* We should in vain, therefore, attempt to demonstrate its falsehood. Were it demonstratively false, it would imply a contradiction, and could never be distinctly conceived by the mind.

It may, therefore, be a subject worthy of curiosity, to enquire what is the nature of that evidence which assures us of any real existence and matter of fact, beyond the present testimony of our senses, or the records of our memory. This part of philosophy, it is observable, has been little cultivated, either by the ancients or moderns; and therefore our doubts and errors, in the prosecution of so important an enquiry, may be the more excusable; while we march through such difficult paths without any guide or direction. They may even prove useful, by exciting curiosity, and destroying that implicit faith and security, which is the bane of all reasoning and free enquiry. The discovery of defects in the common philosophy, if any such there be, will not, I presume, be a discouragement, but rather an incitement, as is usual, to attempt something more full and satisfactory than has yet been proposed to the public.

22. All reasonings concerning matter of fact seem to be founded on the relation of *Cause and Effect*. By means of that relation alone we can go beyond the evidence of our memory and senses. If you were to ask a man, why he believes any matter of fact, which is absent; for instance, that his friend is in the country, or in France; he would give you a reason; and this reason would be some other fact; as a letter received from him, or the knowledge of his former resolutions and promises. A man finding a watch or any other machine in a desert island, would conclude that there had once been men in that island. All our reasonings concerning fact are of the same nature. And here it is constantly supposed that there is a connexion between the present fact and that which is inferred from it. Were there nothing to bind them together, the inference would be entirely precarious. The hearing of an articulate voice and rational discourse in the dark assures us of the presence of some person: Why? because these are the effects of the human make and fabric, and closely connected with it. If we anatomize all the other reasonings of this nature, we shall find that they are founded on the relation of cause and effect, and that this relation is either near or remote, direct or collateral. Heat and light are collateral effects of fire, and the one effect may justly be inferred from the other.

23. If we would satisfy ourselves, therefore, concerning the nature of that evidence, which assures us of matters of fact, we must enquire how we arrive at the knowledge of cause and effect.

I shall venture to affirm, as a general proposition, which admits of no exception, that the knowledge of this relation is not, in any instance, attained by reasonings *a priori;* but arises entirely from experience, when we find that any particular objects are constantly conjoined with each other. Let an object be presented to a man of ever so strong natural reason and abilities; if that object be entirely new to him, he will not be able, by the most accurate examination of its sensible qualities, to discover any of its causes or effects. Adam, though his rational faculties be supposed, at the very first, entirely perfect, could not have inferred from the fluidity and transparency of water that it would suffocate him, or from the light and warmth of fire that it would consume him. No object ever discovers, by the qualities which appear to the senses, either the causes which produced it, or the effects which will arise from it; nor can our reason, unassisted by experience, ever draw any inference concerning real existence and matter of fact.

24. This proposition, *that causes and effects are discoverable, not by reason but by experience,* will readily be admitted with regard to such objects, as we remember to have once been altogether unknown to us; since we must be conscious of the utter inability, which we then lay under, of foretelling what would arise from them. Present two smooth pieces of marble to a man who has no tincture of natural philosophy; he will never discover that they will adhere together in such a manner as to require great force to separate them in a direct line, while they make so small a resistance to a lateral pressure. Such events, as bear little analogy to the common course of nature, are also readily confessed to be known only by experience; nor does any man imagine that the explosion of gunpowder, or the attraction of a loadstone, could ever be discovered by arguments *a priori.* In like manner, when an effect is supposed to depend upon an intricate machinery or secret structure of parts, we make no difficulty in attributing all our knowledge of it to experience. Who will assert that he can give the ultimate reason, why milk or bread is proper nourishment for a man, not for a lion or a tiger?

But the same truth may not appear, at first sight, to have the same evidence with regard to events, which have become familiar to us from our first appearance in the world, which bear a close analogy to the whole course of nature, and which are supposed to depend on the simple qualities of objects, without any secret structure of parts. We are apt to imagine that we could discover these effects by the mere operation of our reason, without experience. We fancy, that were we brought on a sudden into this world, we could at first have inferred that one Billiard-ball would communicate motion to another upon impulse; and that we needed not to have waited for the event, in order to pronounce with certainty concerning it. Such is the influence of custom, that, where it is strongest, it not only covers our natural ignorance, but even conceals itself, and seems not to take place, merely because it is found in the highest degree.

25. But to convince us that all the laws of nature, and all the operations of bodies without exception, are known only by experience, the following reflections may, perhaps, suffice. Were any object presented to us, and were we required to pronounce concerning the effect, which will result from it, without consulting past observation; after what manner, I beseech you, must the mind proceed in this operation? It must invent or imagine some event, which it ascribes to the object as its effect; and it is plain that this invention must be entirely arbitrary. The mind can never

possibly find the effect in the supposed cause, by the most accurate scrutiny and examination. For the effect is totally different from the cause, and consequently can never be discovered in it. Motion in the second Billiard-ball is a quite distinct event from motion in the first; nor is there anything in the one to suggest the smallest hint of the other. A stone or piece of metal raised into the air, and left without any support, immediately falls: but to consider the matter *a priori,* is there anything we discover in this situation which can beget the idea of a downward, rather than an upward, or any other motion, in the stone or metal? And as the first imagination or invention of a particular effect, in all natural operations, is arbitrary, where we consult not experience; so must we also esteem the supposed tie or connexion between the cause and effect, which binds them together, and renders it impossible that any other effect could result from the operation of that cause. When I see, for instance, a Billiard-ball moving in a straight line towards another; even suppose motion in the second ball should by accident be suggested to me, as the result of their contact or impulse; may I not conceive, that a hundred different events might as well follow from that cause? May not both these balls remain at absolute rest? May not the first ball return in a straight line, or leap off from the second in any line or direction? All these suppositions are consistent and conceivable. Why then should we give the preference to one, which is no more consistent or conceivable than the rest? All our reasonings *a priori* will never be able to show us any foundation for this preference.

In a word, then, every effect is a distinct event from its cause. It could not, therefore, be discovered in the cause, and the first invention or conception of it, *a priori,* must be entirely arbitrary. And even after it is suggested, the conjunction of it with the cause must appear equally arbitrary; since there are always many other effects, which, to reason, must seem fully as consistent and natural. In vain, therefore, should we pretend to determine any single event, or infer any cause or effect, without the assistance of observation and experience.

26. Hence we may discover the reason why no philosopher, who is rational and modest, has ever pretended to assign the ultimate cause of any natural operation, or to show distinctly the action of that power, which produces any single effect in the universe. It is confessed, that the utmost effort of human reason is to reduce the principles, productive of natural phenomena, to a greater simplicity, and to resolve the many particular effects into a few general causes, by means of reasonings from analogy, experience, and observation. But as to the causes of these general causes, we should in vain attempt their discovery; nor shall we ever be able to satisfy ourselves, by any particular explication of them. These ultimate springs and principles are totally shut up from human curiosity and enquiry. Elasticity, gravity, cohesion of parts, communication of motion by impulse;

these are probably the ultimate causes and principles which we shall ever discover in nature; and we may esteem ourselves sufficiently happy, if, by accurate enquiry and reasoning, we can trace up the particular phenomena to, or near to, these general principles. The most perfect philosophy of the natural kind only staves off our ignorance a little longer: as perhaps the most perfect philosophy of the moral or metaphysical kind serves only to discover larger portions of it. Thus the observation of human blindness and weakness is the result of all philosophy, and meets us at every turn, in spite of our endeavours to elude or avoid it.

27. Nor is geometry, when taken into the assistance of natural philosophy, ever able to remedy this defect, or lead us into the knowledge of ultimate causes, by all that accuracy of reasoning for which it is so justly celebrated. Every part of mixed mathematics proceeds upon the supposition that certain laws are established by nature in her operations; and abstract reasonings are employed, either to assist experience in the discovery of these laws, or to determine their influence in particular instances, where it depends upon any precise degree of distance and quantity. Thus, it is a law of motion, discovered by experience, that the moment or force of any body in motion is in the compound ratio or proportion of its solid contents and its velocity; and consequently, that a small force may remove the greatest obstacle or raise the greatest weight, if, by any contrivance or machinery, we can increase the velocity of that force, so as to make it an overmatch for its antagonist. Geometry assists us in the application of this law, by giving us the just dimensions of all the parts and figures which can enter into any species of machine; but still the discovery of the law itself is owing merely to experience, and all the abstract reasonings in the world could never lead us one step towards the knowledge of it. When we reason *a priori,* and consider merely any object or cause, as it appears to the mind, independent of all observation, it never could suggest to us the notion of any distinct object, such as its effect; much less, show us the inseparable and inviolable connexion between them. A man must be very sagacious who could discover by reasoning that crystal is the effect of heat, and ice of cold, without being previously acquainted with the operation of these qualities.

■ ■ ■

Section IX. Of the Reason of Animals.

82. All our reasonings concerning matter of fact are founded on a species of Analogy, which leads us to expect from any cause the same events, which we have observed to result from similar causes. Where the causes

are entirely similar, the analogy is perfect, and the inference, drawn from it, is regarded as certain and conclusive: nor does any man ever entertain a doubt, where he sees a piece of iron, that it will have weight and cohesion of parts; as in all other instances, which have ever fallen under his observation. But where the objects have not so exact a similarity, the analogy is less perfect, and the inference is less conclusive; though still it has some force, in proportion to the degree of similarity and resemblance. The anatomical observations, formed upon one animal, are, by this species of reasoning, extended to all animals; and it is certain, that when the circulation of the blood, for instance, is clearly proved to have place in one creature, as a frog, or fish, it forms a strong presumption, that the same principle has place in all. These analogical observations may be carried farther, even to this science, of which we are now treating; and any theory, by which we explain the operations of the understanding, or the origin and connexion of the passions in man, will acquire additional authority, if we find, that the same theory is requisite to explain the same phenomena in all other animals. We shall make trial of this, with regard to the hypothesis, by which we have, in the foregoing discourse, endeavoured to account for all experimental reasonings; and it is hoped, that this new point of view will serve to confirm all our former observations.

83. *First,* It seems evident, that animals as well as men learn many things from experience, and infer, that the same events will always follow from the same causes. By this principle they become acquainted with the more obvious properties of external objects, and gradually, from their birth, treasure up a knowledge of the nature of fire, water, earth, stones, heights, depths, &c., and of the effects which result from their operation. The ignorance and inexperience of the young are here plainly distinguishable from the cunning and sagacity of the old, who have learned, by long observation, to avoid what hurt them, and to pursue what gave ease or pleasure. A horse, that has been accustomed to the field, becomes acquainted with the proper height which he can leap, and will never attempt what exceeds his force and ability. An old greyhound will trust the more fatiguing part of the chace to the younger, and will place himself so as to meet the hare in her doubles; nor are the conjectures, which he forms on this occasion, founded in any thing but his observation and experience.

This is still more evident from the effects of discipline and education on animals, who, by the proper application of rewards and punishments, may be taught any course of action, and most contrary to their natural instincts and propensities. Is it not experience, which renders a dog apprehensive of pain, when you menace him, or lift up the whip to beat him? Is it not even experience, which makes him answer to his name, and infer, from such an arbitrary sound, that you mean him rather than any of his fellows, and intend to call him, when you pronounce it in a certain manner, and with a certain tone and accent?

In all these cases, we may observe, that the animal infers some fact beyond what immediately strikes his senses; and that this inference is altogether founded on past experience, while the creature expects from the present object the same consequences, which it has always found in its observation to result from similar objects.

84. *Secondly,* It is impossible, that this inference of the animal can be founded on any process of argument or reasoning, by which he concludes, that like events must follow like objects, and that the course of nature will always be regular in its operations. For if there be in reality any arguments of this nature, they surely lie too abstruse for the observation of such imperfect understandings; since it may well employ the utmost care and attention of a philosophic genius to discover and observe them. Animals, therefore, are not guided in these inferences by reasoning: Neither are children: Neither are the generality of mankind, in their ordinary actions and conclusions: Neither are philosophers themselves, who, in all the active parts of life, are, in the main, the same with the vulgar, and are governed by the same maxims. Nature must have provided some other principle, of more ready, and more general use and application; nor can an operation of such immense consequence in life, as that of inferring effects from causes, be trusted to the uncertain process of reasoning and argumentation. Were this doubtful with regard to men, it seems to admit of no question with regard to the brute creation; and the conclusion being once firmly established in the one, we have a strong presumption, from all the rules of analogy, that it ought to be universally admitted, without any exception or reserve. It is custom alone, which engages animals, from every object, that strikes their senses, to infer its usual attendant, and carries their imagination, from the appearance of the one, to conceive the other, in that particular manner, which we denominate *belief.* No other explication can be given of this operation, in all the higher, as well as lower classes of sensitive beings, which fall under our notice and observation.[19]

85. But though animals learn many parts of their knowledge from observation, there are also many parts of it, which they derive from the original hand of nature; which much exceed the share of capacity they possess on ordinary occasions; and in which they improve, little or nothing, by the longest practice and experience. These we denominate Instincts, and are so apt to admire as something very extraordinary, and inexplicable by all the disquisitions of human understanding. But our wonder will, perhaps, cease or diminish, when we consider, that the experimental reasoning itself, which we possess in common with beasts, and on which the whole conduct of life depends, is nothing but a species of instinct or mechanical

power, that acts in us unknown to ourselves; and in its chief operations, is not directed by any such relations or comparisons of ideas, as are the proper objects of our intellectual faculties. Though the instinct be different, yet still it is an instinct, which teaches a man to avoid the fire; as much as that, which teaches a bird, with such exactness, the art of incubation, and the whole economy and order of its nursery.

Questions for Further Exploration:

- According to Hume, what is the difference in the evidence for establishing truth in 'matters of fact,' and 'relations of ideas'? What is the nature of human understanding concerning matters of fact?

- How do humans arrive at the knowledge of cause and effect? What can be known with certainty to follow from a billiard-ball moving in a straight line towards another?

- How does Hume refute the idea that the laws of nature can be known *a priori?* What follows from his argument regarding knowledge of the natural world?

- What is Hume's view of "animals"? Does he agree or disagree with Descartes about the differences between humans and animals? What is the basis of the inference made by both animals and humans that similar causes will lead to similar effects?

- Free-write: What are the prospects of securing a foundation for sustainability in light of Hume's skepticism?

Skeptical Environmentalism

The Limits of Philosophy and Science

Robert Kirkman

The Nature of Nature

Environmentalism will succeed only if its advocates can bring about a change in the way people behave. How can environmentalists do this? Answers come from all sides: regulate, legislate, litigate, negotiate, innovate, and educate; restructure the marketplace to create new incentives; restructure the schools to create a new kinds of citizen; restructure civilization itself. In the midst of all these possibilities, environmental philosophy began with the belief that the best way to change the way people behave is to change the way they think. Not just any change would do. By and large, environmental philosophers have not been content to tinker with momentary opinions on matters of politics and economics. Instead, they have insisted that people rethink their answers to the most fundamental questions of human life in the world: What is the nature of nature, and what is my place within it? What is of value, and what are my obligations? For what may I hope?

So the search is on for a way of thinking about nature, about the cosmos, about reality itself that might fundamentally alter the ethical and political life of modern civilization. Many of those engaged in the search think of themselves as constituting a minority tradition, swimming against the intellectual current of modernity: in opposition to the fractured metaphysics of René Descartes, which they see as having set humans at odds with nature and with themselves, they propose an ecological worldview informed by a vision of relatedness. If nature is fundamentally relational, and if humans are caught up in those relations, then there may be some metaphysical leverage for ethical obligations toward nature. If humans have obligations toward nature, then there may be some ethical leverage for better public policies regarding environmental change. This, at least, is the hope of speculative environmentalists.

Descartes is important because he established the major problems of modern philosophy, contributed to the development of the modern sciences, and generally set the tone for the modern era. Critics charge that his doctrine of dualism introduced a schism into human thought, a wound that has not yet healed. Cartesian dualism holds that the world consists of two kinds of substance: mental substance, which thinks but takes up no space, and material substance, which takes up space and does not think. If Descartes is correct that material substance does nothing but take up space, it follows that material bodies can relate to each other only spatially. Suppose a number of billiard balls are resting on a pool table and that the cue ball is two feet away from the eight ball (proximity). I roll the cue ball toward the eight ball (relative motion), the cue ball strikes the eight ball (direct contact), and the two balls move off in different directions (relative motion again). Once these spatial relations—proximity, relative motion, and contact—have been measured and catalogued, there is nothing more to be learned about the situation on the pool table. In the Cartesian universe, the same applies to stars and planets, rocks and rivers, plants and animals, and even the human body.

For complex material objects such as animals, though, another feature of the dualistic conception of material substance comes into play. Matter is divisible, and so reduction becomes the proper method for studying complex systems. If I want to understand a clock, I need to disassemble it, study all of the parts, and account for their relationships to one another—in spatial terms, of course. The same holds if I want to understand a maple tree, a domestic cat, the workings of the human brain, or the cosmos as a whole. In effect, the Cartesian cosmos can be thought of as a great machine, designed and set in motion by a very powerful—and very clever—mechanic. Parts may come into contact with one another, and they may move relative to one another, but each can be understood in isolation from the others and each can be replaced if necessary.

A number of metaphysical and epistemological problems are associated with dualism, not least the problem of where to put the mind. If the mind takes up no space, how can it be located *in* space, in relation to a material body? This is an interesting puzzle, but many critics are more concerned with what they see as the pernicious ethical and political consequences of dualism—especially from an environmentalist point of view. When people see the natural world as a collection of material bodies, these critics charge, they come to treat the collection as nothing more than a stockpile of resources for human consumption. At the same time, reductionism and mechanism have allowed modern science to discover some of the inner workings of phenomena, adding to the variety of spatial and material relations to be catalogued and making possible more and more extensive and intrusive alterations of natural systems. Over all of this is spread an abiding modernist faith in the ability of humanity to solve its problems by rational, especially technological, means, which ensures the unending progress of human civilization as it conquers brute nature and secures its own future. Critics fear that this dominant paradigm (as some call it) of the modern era is a recipe for environmental disaster: civilization advances under Descartes' banner, blind to the destruction it leaves in its wake.

Those who call themselves deep ecologists are among the most strident critics of the dominant paradigm. Deep ecology is a political and philosophical movement first introduced into English-language philosophy by Norwegian philosopher Arne Naess in 1973. Naess distinguishes two different kinds of "ecology," two branches of the environmental movement: the shallow and the deep. Shallow ecology remains within the limits of the dominant paradigm; it simply adds some recognition that resources are not inexhaustible and that the continuing progress of civilization may require a good deal of prudence. The goal of shallow ecology, as Naess portrays it, is to fight pollution and resource depletion in order to ensure "the health and affluence of people in developed countries." It is "shallow" because it seeks to reform the system without challenging the dominant paradigm or the social and economic system to which it has given rise. Naess singles out the "man-in-environment image" as central to the worldview of the shallow ecologist: humans live out their lives against a neutral backdrop of material resources. He rejected this image in favor of a "relational, total-field image."[1] The foremost American interpreters of Naess's ideas, Bill Devall and George Sessions, argue that the task of deep ecology is to reverse what sociologist Max Weber called the "disenchantment of the world" which was brought about by the rise of "instrumental rationality."[2]

The way to reverse the destructive tendencies of modern civilization, according to many environmental philosophers, is to view nature instead as a kind of organism. Unlike machines, organic systems are so tightly integrated that to remove one part from its context is to render both the part and the system incomprehensible. The organism metaphor implies that the proper method for studying nature is not reduction but holistic synthesis: the goals of the investigator are to integrate and synthesize the scattered details of experience into a whole and to give some account of the unifying principles that connect everything together. The method tends to be speculative, on the assumption that the unifying principles in question can only be grasped by reason. The natural world as experienced through the senses and as studied by the natural sciences is a chaos of distracting details; the mind can only bring this chaos to order by the firm and consistent application of rational principles.

Advocates of the organicist worldview consider it to be more "ecological" than the alternative because it provides a more coherent—and more limiting—context for human activity. One feature that distinguishes life from non-life is that living things engage in goal-directed activity. Because organisms have goals and interests of their own, they can be harmed. If nature as a whole is really a kind of organic unity, then it has ends and interests of its own; nature can be harmed. Many environmental philosophers pick up on this implication, hoping that it might serve as a guide for human behavior. If human desires and projects can be brought into accord with nature's interests or nature's demands, they believe, then we may find a way out of the environmental crisis.

■ ■ ■

Hegel and the Limits of Philosophy

For Plato, the cosmos is intelligible to the human mind because both are patterned on the same rational principles. To gain knowledge, it is necessary only to bring the mind into harmony with the universe, to make distinctions in thought that copy distinctions in reality. If there is any difficulty in finding the truth of things, it is because there is another causal principle, necessity or materiality, which operates independently of the rational cause and distorts its appearance in the world. Here, then, is the basic challenge for speculative philosophy: to filter out all of the distortions and details of the world of appearance in order to grasp the underlying rational unity.

This challenge may well exceed the capabilities of the human mind. A skeptical reading of the history of speculative philosophy gives rise to the suspicion that whatever method we use, however carefully we proceed, the universe will ultimately evade our efforts to grasp it. These doubts extend also to the various proposals for an ecological worldview, at least insofar as they rest on a speculative foundation. If the finest, most rigorous philosophers in the Western tradition have all fallen short of the goal, has speculative philosophy progressed so far in its methods or principles that environmental thinkers might now succeed? This strikes me as unlikely.

I will take up the story in the early modern period, just after Descartes. Speculative philosophy in this period differed from what had come before, largely because Descartes introduced a representational model of consciousness. In the dualist universe, the mind is a substance that thinks, which is to say that it holds within itself a play of ideas. Ideas are like pictures held before the mind's eye, disembodied reflections of things both real and imagined. Knowledge, in this view, consists of a correspondence between ideas and the real things they are supposed to represent. The rationalists appealed to God to guarantee correspondence, while the empiricists appealed to the senses. Hume's skepticism is informed by the difficulties encountered by rationalists and empiricists alike and can be read as his recognition of the limits of the representational model of consciousness.

There has been quite a lot of speculative philosophy since Hume's time, of course, much of it based on modification or outright rejection of representationalism. One particularly fruitful tradition passes through Immanuel Kant and Romanticism to the nature philosophy of Hegel and concerns the possibility of unifying mechanistic and organic accounts of nature. This is particularly interesting for my purposes. Deep ecologists and others explicitly claim Romanticism as one of their sources of inspiration, and Hegel's attempt to construct a coherent, speculative nature philosophy stands as one of the most rigorous and systematic in the philosophical tradition. If he fails, others would be hard pressed to succeed.

Nature, Hegel writes, "confronts us as a riddle and a problem, whose solution both attracts us and repels us: attracts us, because spirit is presaged in Nature; repels us because Nature seems an alien existence, in which spirit does not find itself."[9] When I consider the world under the aspect of internality, each thing and event can be understood in terms of a larger whole. The tree outside the window and my own body share an irreducible, internal relationship to one another; each is part of the living order of nature. The human mind is drawn into the web of internal relationships because it recognizes itself there. Order responds to order. When I consider the world under the aspect of externality, however, things and events seem disconnected from me and from one another. My body and the tree outside my window have nothing essential in common. It just happens that both are material and both exist in space at the same time. The human mind can find no foothold in the shifting details of accidental material relationships. There is no order to which it can respond.

The unresolved contradiction of nature consists in the fact that the mind is caught between these two interpretations. Nature is at once familiar and strange, benevolent and hostile—or perhaps simply indifferent. Hegel insists that if there is to be any solution to the riddle of nature it can only be reached through a systematic internalization of the external world.

This means that the mind must seek out and articulate the basic rational unity of nature in such a way that no detail remains unconnected or unexplained.

Hegel can be read in various ways, and there is a good deal of debate over how seriously to take *The Philosophy of Nature*. It may be that Hegel introduces the riddle of nature because he intends to solve it once and for all. If so, then he promises nothing less than absolute and certain knowledge of the natural order. On the other hand, he may introduce the riddle because it has no solution. In that case, it is just an inescapably difficult moment in the development of human consciousness. But my interest in Hegel is hypothetical: if Hegel is seriously trying to solve the riddle of nature, then his success or failure will reflect on the efforts of speculative environmental philosophers to solve the riddle for themselves. For the sake of argument, then, I will assume that Hegel's nature philosophy is a careful systematic effort to attain absolute knowledge of nature.

First, though, I should provide some historical background to Hegel's work. The distinction between internality and externality I have just outlined is, in effect, a modern recasting of Plato's distinction between reason and necessity. In the wake of Cartesian dualism, all life, purpose, and value—all final causes—came to be attributed to the mental realm. Matter, as I have discussed, was thought to be inert, its only attributes being those of taking up space and of being infinitely divisible. For Descartes, everything in nature is external to every other thing and, because it is divisible, matter can always be made external to itself. If I break a stone in half, I am left with two stones which no longer bear any relation to each other aside from their proximity in space and the possibility that I could hit them together. If nature has any order or purpose, it is only the efficient purposiveness of a machine, the organizing principle of which resides in the rational mind of the machinist-god who created it and set it running. Even the human body is a machine, albeit a wondrous one; Gottfried Leibniz, a philosopher who followed and extended Descartes' rationalism, described the body as being so subtle that even its parts are themselves machines.[10]

This account of the origins of mechanism has the surprising consequence that mechanism and organicism actually have a lot in common. Insofar as they are speculative principles, both appeal to rationality as the model on which the natural world is patterned, and both emphasize the quintessentially rational capacity to set goals. The difference between organicism and mechanism comes down to the difference between internality and externality, which has consequences for where the organizing principle of nature is thought to reside. The development of an organism is interpreted as a process of striving to fulfill its own specific form, an organizing principle that resides within the organism itself and subordinates every part to the life of the whole. The orderliness of a machine, on the other hand, can be explained only in terms of the conscious intentions of the machinist, who shaped the parts and arranged them for some purpose or other. So to interpret the cosmos as an organism is to place the rational organizing principle within the cosmos itself, while to interpret the cosmos as a machine places the organizing principle in the mind of a supernatural creator.

The Romantic effort to internalize externality can be understood only in light of Kant's critical philosophy, which served as both predecessor to and foil for the Romantic imagination. Kant came to see early modern philosophy as a dead end: the rationalists' exclusive reliance on pure principles of reason without appeal to the senses rendered their systems empty and dogmatic, while the empiricists' exclusive reliance on sensory experience without appeal to pure rational principles rendered them blind. Kant sought a third way, but in doing so he had to change the terms of the debate. In essence, he turned his focus inward, away from the world and the hope for correspondence to the character and limits of human cognition.

From his investigation of the understanding, set out in the *Critique of Pure Reason,* Kant drew the conclusion that experience and knowledge of nature are possible only if some pure or rational element is brought to bear on the chaotic flux of sensation, organizing it into the world we experience and establishing the foundations of science. For example, Kant held that the idea of causality comes neither from the senses alone nor from pure reason alone. It is possible to know causal laws of nature, he insisted, because causality is a pure category of the understanding that is brought to bear on sensory perception. The human mind has the built-in capacity for making hypothetical assertions of the form "if x then y," which serves as the template for any causal law of nature. Sensation can provide only the material, the x and y that are plugged into the formula. All told, there are twelve pure categories of the understanding, and taken together they provide the foundation for the science of nature. The natural world as it is grasped by the understanding is very much as Isaac Newton envisioned it, consisting of material objects moving through space and governed in their (external) relations to one another by deterministic causal laws. As far as the understanding is concerned, every phenomenon can and must be explained in these terms.

This is not merely an endorsement of mechanistic metaphysics, however. By changing the terms of the debate over knowledge, Kant turned his back on any possibility of a direct link between mind and reality. Nature, as he understood it, is no longer the totality of things as they really are, but a construct of the understanding. Technically, he defined nature as the possibility of future experience, but he saw experience itself as generated by the understanding as it imposes the order of the categories on the chaos of sensation. I can have no knowledge of things in themselves, Kant insisted, only of things as they are for me. The product of the understanding is called knowledge, but not because it corresponds with what is really out there. Rather, human knowledge of nature is valid to the extent that it is consistent: the categories of the understanding are universally valid, so that any rational being would constitute its experience in precisely the same way. Nevertheless, because he construed the understanding as only one of the faculties of the human intellect, and because he denied that the understanding has any access to things as they really are, Kant left open the possibility that there are other, legitimate ways of thinking about the natural world and its relationship to human beings. This is important, because it made possible the reconciliation of opposites that had long been considered irreconcilable.

Consider Kant's treatment of final and efficient causality in *The Critique of Judgment*. In its reconstruction of experience, the understanding encounters entities that are beyond its grasp. The material causal connections within an organism, for example, interact reciprocally in such complex ways that the connections can only be judged to have been brought about for some purpose. The physiology of the human body, for example, only makes sense if it is the product of the conscious, free act of a rational being rather than the product of blind determinism. Unlike a watch, which has only a motive force based on the external relations among the parts, an organism is best thought of as possessing a "formative" or developmental force based on the internal relations among the parts. So, contrary to the understanding, we judge an organism to be "both cause and effect of itself." The eye is a condition for vision, but I can also judge that the eye exists for the sake of seeing, as though the idea of sight preceded the existence of the eye in the mind of some designer.

Kant calls such entities "natural purposes," which for a Cartesian would be a contradiction in terms. While he acknowledged that it would be impossible to give a scientific account of the coexistence of efficient and final causality in natural purposes, he insisted that it is not at all contradictory for the judgment to posit their coexistence. The two forms of causality do not contradict each other because they arise from different faculties of cognition: linear efficient causality grasped by the understanding is "real" while final causality posited by judgment is "ideal." Because I have no access to things in themselves, Kant believed, the best I can do is to follow the categories of the understanding as far as possible and to account for the rest as reason and judgment see fit.[11]

Following the pattern established with individual organisms, Kant argued for the possibility of judging nature as a whole to be a unified purposive system—one that has come into existence for the sake of supporting humanity as a community of free rational beings. Kant judged humanity to be the final purpose of creation because humans are the only earthly beings capable of setting purposes for themselves. "Only in man," he wrote, "and even in him only as a moral subject, do we find unconditioned legislation regarding purposes. It is this legislation, therefore, which alone enables man to be a final purpose to which all of nature is teleologically subordinated."[12] From this basis Kant formulated a "moral theology" in which God is the thinking and willing agent who has created the natural order in such a way that it harmonizes with and supports human culture. Hence, the unity of freedom and nature is established as a subjective principle of reflective judgment. This is part of his answer to the question "For what may I hope?" If I can judge nature to be a teleological system and its goal to support humans in their vocation as moral beings, then I can at least hope that good deeds will be rewarded, and bad deeds punished, by the system of nature itself.

Romanticism emerged in the early nineteenth century as a broad cultural and intellectual movement of reaction against modernism in philosophy and science, guided by the vision of a threefold unity: the unity of knowledge, the unity of nature, and the unity of human consciousness, or spirit, with nature. Among the literary, artistic, and religious expressions of the general Romantic movement, *Naturphilosophie* stands out as that form of Romanticism that seeks to arrive at this threefold unity by way of the study of the natural world.[13] Schelling, one of the leaders of the movement, declared that "Nature should be Mind made visible, Mind the invisible Nature. Here then, in the absolute identity of Mind *in us* and Nature *outside us,* the problem of the possibility of a Nature external to us must be resolved."[14] With this assertion, Schelling took up Kant's conclusions regarding the reconciliation of the natural and moral realms, but he and his compatriots cast aside Kant's caution by asserting the real truth of the reconciliation. For the Romantics, nature *really is* the self-externalization of mind, and the individual human mind is a product of nature that serves as the means by which nature awakens and becomes conscious of itself as spirit. This is also a departure from Kant in that knowledge of nature is to be formulated in terms of a dynamic process of development analogous to that of an organism rather than in terms of the static categories of traditional logic.

This brings my account back to Hegel, who gave this dynamic interpretation of nature its most powerful and sophisticated expression. This is not to say he was in full agreement with his contemporaries. In fact, Hegel made a point of distancing himself from Schelling and the other Romantics. In their "unskilled" hands, he asserted, nature philosophy had received "crude treatment" and so had been "brought low not so much by its opponents as by its friends." He identified the problem as simply laziness or, at best, sloppiness. The Romantics proceeded

> not by bringing consciousness out of its chaos back to an order based on thought, nor to the simplicity of the Notion, but rather by running together what thought has put asunder, by suppressing the differentiations of the Notion and restoring the *feeling* of essential being.

The result was not a coherent philosophical system but simply a kind of "rapturous haziness"; it lacked "the seriousness, the suffering, the patience and the labor of the negative."[15]

The "labor of the negative" is one way to describe dialectical logic, which Hegel developed as a logic for comprehending dynamic processes. The Concept (i.e., universality as such) begins as a simple unity; this is the first moment of the dialectic. When this unity is negated, it falls apart into a contradiction. In this, the second moment, consciousness vacillates between two interpretations of itself that are incompatible. The contradiction can only be overcome when consciousness recognizes that the two terms of the contradiction have something in common, which serves as the basis of a new unity. Hegel called this third moment "determinate negation": the contradiction is negated, but in such a way that the distinction it establishes is preserved as part of the new unity. As a result, the Concept becomes more comprehensive and less abstract; it becomes a unity-in-difference.[16] Ultimately, the new unity itself is negated, and the process begins again. To engage in the "labor of the negative" is to work through every step of the logic as carefully as possible, noting every distinction and every resolution, making sure that each step follows by logical necessity from the one before. The end result of this labor is "absolute knowing," in which the universal and the particular are unified. When the Concept has already comprehended every possible concrete distinction, reason can no longer extend itself because nothing remains that is other to it.

In Hegelian thought, the problem of nature arises as the second moment of an overarching triad. The Concept begins in unity and then falls apart into particularity and loses itself in the contingency and detail of externality. This is the unresolved contradiction, the riddle of nature. With fractal complexity, nature itself develops dialectically: each moment in each triad resolves into yet another triad. Mechanics gives way to physics, which gives way to organics; within organics, geological nature gives way to plant nature, which gives way to animal nature; animal nature resolves into a triad of its own, and so on. Overall, the process moves away from externality and the rule of efficient causality toward internality, subjectivity, and spontaneity, all of which paves the way for the development of human culture. At the end of the process, the fractured Concept comes back to itself and becomes aware of itself as spirit. What is to count as knowledge of nature is this "path of return . . . which overcomes the division between Nature and Spirit and assures to Spirit the knowledge of its essence in Nature."[17]

Organic nature is, for Hegel, the external expression of subjectivity. An organism has its existence in the external world, and yet it has the same kind of internality that characterizes human consciousness: it is both cause and effect of itself. As organic nature develops, this internality or subjectivity becomes stronger and more self-assertive. In the first moment, geological nature, the Earth as a whole is taken to be a kind of proto-organism, but one in which internality is still dominated by externality. In other words, the Earth-organism has the abstract shape of internality, but it does not have life of its own because it does not yet have the concept of itself. Plant nature is a significant improvement, possessing a "truer vitality," but it is still unable to express itself as a unity. An individual plant continually "falls apart" into modular parts that remain outside and relatively independent of one another; this is why it is possible to propagate a plant through cuttings or to graft part of one plant onto another. Animal life brings together the members of the organism into an ideal system of subjectivity; that is, into a self-sufficient organic unity. It is only with the emergence of the human animal, however, that the Concept is finally able to overcome the contingency of externality by attaining consciousness of its own essence as spirit. To paraphrase: human culture is a higher kind of order, one which is able to maintain its own integrity even in the face of the death of any individual human. More to the point, human culture can finally grasp that the purpose of nature, the goal of its entire development, is to produce human culture.

Many environmental thinkers would dismiss Hegel's nature philosophy out of hand because it is explicitly human centered. Even so, Hegel's conclusion is consistent with the historical pattern of speculative philosophy. To the extent that environmental philosophers engage in speculative nature philosophy, they must be aware of the pervasive tendency to anthropomorphize the natural order. For my purposes, however, the important question is this: Has Hegel succeeded in comprehending nature; has he really grasped the essence of things? If he has not, it will be helpful to see where he has fallen short and to consider the consequences for more recent efforts along these lines.

Scattered throughout the *Philosophy of Nature* are what can only be called "disclaimers" on behalf of speculative philosophy. Hegel repeatedly insists that it is not his responsibility to account for every detail of nature, citing either the difficulty of philosophy when confronted by externality or the "impotence" of the Concept in nature. In any case, it is clear that Hegel is primarily concerned with using nature as a stepping-stone to spirit. The *zusatz* of the final paragraph includes a particularly revealing statement:

> The difficulty of the Philosophy of Nature lies just in this: first, because the material element is so refractory towards the unity of the Notion, and, secondly, because spirit has to deal with an ever-increasing wealth of detail. None the less, Reason must have confidence in itself, confidence that in Nature the Notion speaks to the Notion and that the veritable form of the Notion which lies concealed beneath Nature's scattered and infinitely many shapes, will reveal itself to Reason.[18]

At first glance, it seems odd that Hegel should have to encourage reason to have "confidence" in itself "none the less"; that is, in spite of its own impotence in the face of externality. Consider the language he uses when he heralds the emergence of spirit from the death of nature: *"from this dead husk,* proceeds a more beautiful Nature, *spirit."*[19] What is this "dead husk" and what happens to it afterward? In one of the final passages of the *Philosophy of Nature,* Hegel recognizes that nature philosophy is difficult because the material element is "refractory" toward the unity of the Concept such that the Concept is "impotent" to hold itself together. This seems to imply that there is *something* "out there" that is *other* to the Concept; the Concept would not distort or conceal itself. The conclusion seems unavoidable that the materiality and diversity of the external world are *other* to reason and that Hegel can proceed only by actively ignoring them. It would seem that, since Plato's time, as the rational cause has been refined and more clearly grasped, necessity too has been refined so that it more completely evades reason's grasp. In Hegel, it would seem, necessity, or externality, has its ultimate revenge, receding to its place as the ultimate and intractable other of reason, the unintelligible core of nature.

Jacques Derrida offers a helpful metaphor that sheds some light on the problem: Hegel's system of speculative philosophy is a "restricted" economy, one that is

> limited to the meaning and to the established value of objects, and to their *circulation.* The *circularity* of absolute knowledge could dominate, could comprehend only this circulation, only the *circuit*

of reproductive consumption. The absolute production and destruction of value, the exceeding energy as such . . . all this escapes phenomenology as restricted economy.

With his determinate negation, Hegel hoped to negate and to conserve at the same time, while he ignored and externalized the possibility of an absolute negation, the "*indefinite* destruction of value."[20] Beyond the tidy circle of this economy, in which meaning is so carefully conserved, is "the exceeding energy," or simply "excess," the non-meaning out of which meaning is produced, into which it returns, and through which it is destroyed. Hegel must externalize excess because it is utterly other to reason and so cannot be brought into account. Even so, with his casual references to the dead husk and to the refractoriness of the material element, Hegel occasionally allowed externality to show up on the books, if only for a brief moment.

The endless details of nature open up the possibility that new discoveries about those details could render obsolete all of Hegel's carefully reasoned accounts of natural processes. After all, speculative nature philosophy has no self-correcting mechanism with which to keep pace with new and surprising phenomena as they emerge. Simply as a matter of historical observation, many of Hegel's accounts are simply wrong, often laughably so, in spite of his insistence that they are logically necessary. According to Hegel's speculative geology, for example, the geological Earth stands at the threshold of life: it embodies subjectivity, but only in an abstract form. Out of this diffuse sort of internality, "every stone breaks forth" into a profusion of "punctiform" proto-life; this is his account of the origin of lichens and mosses. The Earth also makes other "playful essays in organic formation," such as the shapes of trees that are sometimes found in coal seams. Hegel insists that these shapes could not be the remains of living things that have died but are rather "stillborn" organic formations that can be expected to occur on the cusp between two moments in the conceptual development of organic nature.[21] Hegel's denial of the possibility of fossils is grounded in his rejection of contingency in nature. The appeal to mere time, he insisted, does not account for the structure of the world, because all change in nature is to be understood as *logical* rather than merely mechanical and temporal.

Within a quarter-century of the completion of the *Philosophy of Nature,* Charles Darwin revolutionized natural history with the publication of his *Origin of Species.* Hegel, had he lived, could have responded in one of two ways. On the one hand, he could have ignored Darwin on the principle that scientists can only stumble around in the external world, chasing after details, while reason grasps at the essence of things. The consequence would be that the passage of time and the ongoing growth of the sciences would render Hegel's speculative nature philosophy obsolete and increasingly irrelevant to human affairs. The case of Darwin is especially troublesome for Hegelian thought: Darwin, more than any other, gave contingency and temporality a central role in explaining the apparent order of nature.

On the other hand, Hegel could have changed his own "logically necessary" accounts to integrate scientific theories of his contemporary. In response to Darwin, Hegel could have taken up and insisted on the necessity of evolution as a basic principle of nature, as many more recent speculative philosophers have done. At the very least, the idea of updating nature philosophy in order to keep up with the fruits of scientific "stumbling" is embarrassing for speculative reason. Worse, Hegel would probably have had to admit that the apparent strength of the sciences lies precisely in what he had identified as their weakness: the sciences have a self-correcting mechanism that allows scientists to adapt to new circumstances, while speculative reason is stuck with its own mistakes. The worst of it is that the appropriation of scientific theories for speculative purposes can only be carried out by misconstruing the scope and limits of scientific inquiry and the degree to which scientific concepts and theories may legitimately be transferred from one intellectual domain to another. This is a pervasive problem in speculative environmental philosophy.

If, according to the first principle of skepticism, my thinking is to be accompanied by doubt and caution, then Hegel's admonishment that reason should have faith in itself seems to be a bad bargain. As far as I know, the externality that evades reason continues to hide the springs and principles of nature, just as it hid from Hegel the basic insights of evolutionary biology. If, according to the second principle of skepticism, my inquiries should be confined to those that are suited to my limits, then it seems that I am compelled to abandon the hope that nature is ultimately intelligible to reason. Hegel's own difficulties suggest that belief in intelligibility can be sustained only by actively ignoring anything that is unintelligible; in effect, I must presuppose intelligibility in order to discover it.

■ ■ ■

Questions for Further Exploration:

- Kirkman begins his essay with the central premise of this textbook; i.e., that environmental change requires that "people rethink their answers to the most fundamental questions of human life in the world: What is the nature of nature and what is my place within it?" Having surveyed the field of metaphysics in Unit Two from the perspective of this premise, how convinced are you that philosophy is a good starting point for the greening project? Do you share Kirkman's skepticism about the existence of a way of thinking about nature and the cosmos that could steer civilization toward a sustainable future? If so, what follows? If not, where does he go wrong?

- What views does Kirkman include under the term "speculative environmentalism"? What hope does he attribute to its advocates? Which philosophical framework do the advocates define themselves in opposition to, and what are their criticisms of it? Where does Kirkman stand in relation to these two positions?

- What is the difference between the method of reduction and holistic synthesis? Why is one considered more "ecological" than the other?

- What is the "representational model of consciousness" and what is Hegel's alternative? What role does Hegel's (Romantic) philosophy of nature play in Kirkman's critique of speculative environmentalism?

- Why, according to Hegel, does nature confront humans as a riddle? What does it mean to consider the world "under the aspect of internality" in contrast with considering the world "under the aspect of externality"?

- What do "mechanism" and "organicism" have in common? How do they differ?

- How does Kant resolve the conflict between rationalism and empiricism? What is the new foundation for knowledge of nature? How is Kant's treatment of causality different than Hume's? What is "nature as a whole" for Kant? What hope does Kant's view offer those seeking a foundation for sustainability?

- How does Kirkman define Romanticism and Hegel's relation to it?

- How does Hegel conceptualize the logic necessary to grasp the dynamic process of nature? How does this logic help solve "the riddle of nature"? What is "nature as a whole" for Hegel?

- What is Kirkman's answer to the question, "Has Hegel succeeded in comprehending nature; has he really grasped the essence of things?"

- According to Kirkman, what challenges does Darwin raise for Hegel? What advantage does science have over speculative reason?

- What skeptical conclusion does Kirkman reach about the nature of nature?

- Free-write: In light of Kirkman's case, what are the implications for the project of discovering a foundation for an ecologically sound civilization?

The German Ideology

Karl Marx and Friedrich Engels

■ ■ ■

The Essence of the Materialist Conception of History
Social Being and Social Consciousness

The fact is, therefore, that definite individuals who are productively active in a definite way enter into these definite social and political relations. Empirical observation must in each separate instance bring out empirically, and without any mystification and speculation, the connection of the social and political structure with production. The social structure and the state are continually evolving out of the life-process of definite individuals, however, of these individuals, not as they may appear in their own or other people's imagination, but as they *actually* are, i.e., as they act, produce materially, and hence as they work under definite material limits, presuppositions and conditions independent of their will.

The production of ideas, of conceptions, of consciousness, is at first directly interwoven with the material activity and the material intercourse of men—the language of real life. Conceiving, thinking, the mental intercourse of men at this stage still appear as the direct efflux of their material behaviour. The same applies to mental production as expressed in the language of the politics, laws, morality, religion, metaphysics, etc., of a people. Men are the producers of their conceptions, ideas, etc., that is, real, active men, as they are conditioned by a definite development of their productive forces and of the intercourse corresponding to these, up to its furthest forms. Consciousness [*das Bewusstsein*] can never be anything else than conscious being [*das bewusste Sein*], and the being of men is their actual life-process. If in all ideology men and their relations appear upside-down as in a *camera obscura,* this phenomenon arises just as much from their historical life-process as the inversion of objects on the retina does from their physical life-process.

In direct contrast to German philosophy which descends from heaven to earth, here it is a matter of ascending from earth to heaven. That is to say, not of setting out from what men say, imagine, conceive, nor from men as narrated, thought of, imagined, conceived, in order to arrive at men in the flesh; but setting out from real, active men, and on the basis of their real life-process demonstrating the development of the ideological reflexes and echoes of this life-process. The phantoms formed in the brains of men are also, necessarily, sublimates of their material life-process, which is empirically verifiable and bound to material premises. Morality, religion, metaphysics, and all the rest of ideology as well as the forms of consciousness corresponding to these, thus no longer retain the semblance of independence. They have no history, no development; but men, developing their material production and their material intercourse, alter, along with this their actual world, also their thinking and the products of their thinking. It is not consciousness that determines life, but life that determines consciousness. For the first manner of approach the starting-point is consciousness taken as the living individual; for the second manner of approach, which conforms to real life, it is the real living individuals themselves, and consciousness is considered solely as *their* consciousness.

This manner of approach is not devoid of premises. It starts out from the real premises and does not abandon them for a moment. Its premises are men, not in any fantastic isolation and fixity, but in their actual, empirically perceptible process of development under definite conditions. As soon as this active life-process is described, history ceases to be a collection of dead facts, as it is with the empiricists (themselves still abstract), or an imagined activity of imagined subjects, as with the idealists.

Where speculation ends, where real life starts, there consequently begins real, positive science, the expounding of the practical activity, of the practical process of development of men. Empty phrases about consciousness end, and real knowledge has to take their place. When the reality is described, a self-sufficient philosophy [*die selbständige Philosophie*] loses its medium of existence. At the best its place can only be taken by a summing-up of the most general results, abstractions which are derived from the observation of the historical development of men. These abstractions in themselves, divorced from real history, have no value whatsoever. They can only serve to facilitate the arrangement of historical material, to indicate the sequence of its separate strata. But they by no means afford a recipe or schema, as does philosophy, for nearly trimming the epochs of history. On the contrary, the difficulties begin only when one sets about the examination and arrangement of the material—whether of a past epoch or of the present—and its actual presentation. The removal of these difficulties is governed by premises which certainly cannot be stated here, but which only the study of the actual life-process and the activity of the individuals of each epoch will make evident. We shall select here some of these abstractions, which we use in contradistinction to ideology, and shall illustrate them by historical examples. . . .

Primary Historical Relations, or the Basic Aspects of Social Activity: Production of the Means of Subsistence, Production of New Needs, Reproduction of Men (the Family), Social Intercourse, Consciousness

Since we are dealing with the Germans, who are devoid of premises, we must begin by stating the first premise of all human existence and, therefore, of all history, the premise, namely, that men must be in a position to live in order to be able to "make history". But life involves before everything else eating and drinking, housing, clothing and various other things. The first historical act is thus the production of the means to satisfy these needs, the production of material life itself. And indeed this is an historical act, a fundamental condition of all history, which today, as thousands of years ago, must daily and hourly be fulfilled merely in order to sustain human life. Even when the sensuous world is reduced to a minimum, to a stick as with Saint Bruno[5] it presupposes the action of producing this stick. Therefore in any conception of history one has first of all to observe this fundamental fact in all its significance and all its implications and to accord it its due importance. It is well known that the Germans have never done this, and they have never, therefore, had an *earthly* basis for history and consequently never a historian. The French and the English, even if they have conceived the relation of this fact with so-called history only in an extremely one-sided fashion, especially since they remained in the toils of political ideology, have nevertheless made the first attempts to give the writing of history a materialistic basis by being the first to write histories of civil society, of commerce and industry.

The second point is that the satisfaction of the first need, the action of satisfying and the instrument of satisfaction which has been acquired, leads to new needs; and this creation of new needs is the first historical act. Here we recognise immediately the spiritual ancestry of the great historical wisdom of the Germans who, when they run out of positive material and when they can serve up neither theological nor political nor literary rubbish, assert that this is not history at all, but the "prehistoric age". They do not, however, enlighten us as to how we proceed from this nonsensical

"prehistory" to history proper; although, on the other hand, in their historical speculation they seize upon this "prehistory" with especial eagerness
because they imagine themselves safe there from interference on the part
of "crude facts", and, at the same time, because there they can give full
rein to their speculative impulse and set up and knock down hypotheses by
the thousand.

The third circumstance which, from the very outset, enters into historical development, is that men, who daily re-create their own life, begin to
make other men, to propagate their kind: the relation between man and
woman, parents and children, the *family*. The family, which to begin with
is the only social relation, becomes later, when increased needs create new
social relations and the increased population new needs, a subordinate one
(except in Germany), and must then be treated and analysed according to
the existing empirical data, not according to "the concept of the family",
as is the custom in Germany.

These three aspects of social activity are not of course to be taken as
three different stages, but just as three aspects or, to make it clear to the
Germans, three "moments", which have existed simultaneously since the
dawn of history and the first men, and which still assert themselves in history today.

The production of life, both of one's own in labour and of fresh life in
procreation, now appears as a twofold relation: on the one hand as a natural, on the other as a social relation—social in the sense that it denotes the
co-operation of several individuals, no matter under what conditions, in
what manner and to what end. It follows from this that a certain mode of
production, or industrial stage, is always combined with a certain mode of
co-operation, or social stage, and this mode of co-operation is itself a "productive force". Further, that the aggregate of productive forces accessible
to men determines the condition of society, hence, the "history of humanity" must always be studied and treated in relation to the history of industry
and exchange. But it is also clear that in Germany it is impossible to write
this sort of history, because the Germans lack not only the necessary power
of comprehension and the material but also the "sensuous certainty", for
across the Rhine one cannot have any experience of these things since there
history has stopped happening. Thus it is quite obvious from the start that
there exists a materialist connection of men with one another, which is determined by their needs and their mode of production, and which is as old
as men themselves. This connection is ever taking on new forms, and thus
presents a "history" irrespective of the existence of any political or religious nonsense which would especially hold men together.

Only now, after having considered four moments, four aspects of primary historical relations, do we find that man also possesses "conscious-

ness". But even from the outset this is not "pure" consciousness. The "mind" is from the outset afflicted with the curse of being "burdened" with matter, which here makes its appearance in the form of agitated layers of air, sounds, in short, of language. Language is as old as consciousness, language *is* practical, real consciousness that exists for other men as well, and only therefore does it also exist for me; language, like consciousness, only arises from the need, the necessity, of intercourse with other men. Where there exists a relationship, it exists for me: the animal does not *"relate"* itself to anything, it does not *"relate"* itself at all. For the animal its relation to others does not exist as a relation. Consciousness is, therefore, from the very beginning a social product, and remains so as long as men exist at all. Consciousness is at first, of course, merely consciousness concerning the *immediate* sensuous environment and consciousness of the limited connection with other persons and things outside the individual who is growing self-conscious. At the same time it is consciousness of nature, which first confronts men as a completely alien, all-powerful and unassailable force, with which men's relations are purely animal and by which they are overawed like beasts; it is thus a purely animal consciousness of nature (natural religion) precisely because nature is as yet hardly altered by history—on the other hand, it is man's consciousness of the necessity of associating with the individuals around him, the beginning of the consciousness that he is living in society at all. This beginning is as animal as social life itself at this stage. It is mere herd-consciousness, and at this point man is distinguished from sheep only by the fact that with him consciousness takes the place of instinct or that his instinct is a conscious one. This sheep-like or tribal consciousness receives its further development and extension through increased productivity, the increase of needs, and, what is fundamental to both of these, he increase of population. With these there develops the division of labour, which was originally nothing but the division of labour in the sexual act, then the division of labour which develops spontaneously or "naturally" by virtue of natural predisposition (e.g., physical strength), needs, accidents, etc., etc. Division of labour only becomes truly such from the moment when a division of material and mental labour appears. From this moment onwards consciousness *can* really flatter itself that it is something other than consciousness of existing practice, that it *really* represents something without representing something real; from now on consciousness is in a position to emancipate itself from the world and to proceed to the formation of "pure" theory, theology, philosophy, morality, etc., come into contradiction with the existing relations, this can only occur because existing social relations have come into contradiction with existing productive forces; moreover, in a particular national sphere of relations this can also occur through the contradiction, arising not within the national orbit, but between this national consciousness and the practice of other nations, i.e., between the national and the general consciousness of a nation (as is happening now in Germany); but since this contradiction appears to exist only as a contradiction within the national consciousness, it seems to this nation that the struggle too is confined to this national muck, precisely because this nation represents this muck as such.

Incidentally, it is quite immaterial what consciousness starts to do on its own: out of all this trash we get only the one inference that these three moments, the productive forces, the state of society and consciousness, can and must come into contradiction with one another, because the *division of labour* implies the possibility, may the fact, that intellectual and material activity, that enjoyment and labour, production and consumption, devolve on different individuals, and that the only possibility of their not coming into contradiction lies in negating in its turn the division of labour. It is self-evident, moreover, that "spectres", "bonds", "the higher being", "concept", "scruple", are merely idealist, speculative, mental expressions, the concepts apparently of the isolated individual, the mere images of every empirical fetters and limitations, within which move the mode of production of life, and the form of intercourse coupled with it.

■ ■ ■

The Ruling Class and the Ruling Ideas. How the Hegelian Conception of the Domination of the Spirit in History Arose

The ideas of the ruling class are in every epoch the ruling ideas: i.e., the class which is the ruling *material* force of society is at the same time its ruling *intellectual* force. The class which has the means of material production at its disposal, consequently also controls the means of mental production, so that the ideas of those who lack the means of mental production are on the whole subject to it. The ruling ideas are nothing more than the ideal expression of the dominant material relations, the dominant material relations grasped as ideas; hence of the relations which make the one class the ruling one, therefore, the ideas of its dominance. The individuals composing the ruling class possess among other things consciousness, and therefore think. Insofar, therefore, as they rule as a class and determine the extent and compass of an historical epoch, it is self-evident that they do this in its whole range, hence among other things rule also as thinkers, as producers of ideas, and regulate the production and distribution of the ideas of their age: thus their ideas are the ruling ideas of the epoch. For instance, in an age and in a country where royal power, aristocracy and bourgeoisie are contending for domination and where, therefore, domination is shared, the doctrine of the separation of powers proves to be the dominant idea and is expressed as an "eternal law".

The division of labour, which we already saw above as one of the chief forces of history up till now, manifests itself also in the ruling class as the division of mental and material labour, so that inside this class one part appears as the thinkers of the class (its active, conceptive ideologists, who make the formation of the illusions of the class about itself their chief source of livelihood), while the others' attitude to these ideas and illusions is more passive and receptive, because they are in reality the active members of this class and have less time to make up illusions and ideas about themselves. Within this class this cleavage can even develop into a certain opposition and hostility between the two parts, but whenever a practical collision occurs in which the class itself is endangered they automatically vanish, in which case there also vanishes the appearance of the ruling ideas being not the ideas of the ruling class and having a power distinct from the power of this class. The existence of revolutionary ideas in a particular period presupposes the existence of a revolutionary class; about the premises of the latter sufficient has already been said above.

If now in considering the course of history we detach the ideas of the ruling class from the ruling class itself and attribute to them an independent existence, if we confine ourselves to saying that these or those ideas were dominant at a given time, without bothering ourselves about the conditions of production and the producers of these ideas, if we thus ignore the individuals and world conditions which are the source of the ideas, then we can say, for instance, that during the time the aristocracy was dominant, the concepts honour, loyalty, etc., were dominant, during the dominance of the bourgeoisie the concepts freedom, equality, etc. The ruling class itself on the whole imagines this to be so. This conception of history, which is common to all historians, particularly since the eighteenth century, will necessarily come up against the phenomenon that ever more abstract ideas hold sway, i.e., ideas which increasingly take on the form of universality. For each new class which puts itself in the place of one ruling before it is compelled, merely in order to carry though its aim, to present its interest as the common interest of all the members of society, that is, expressed in ideal form: it has to give its ideas the form of universality, and present them as the only rational, universally valid ones. The class making a revolution comes forward from the very start, if only because it is opposed to a *class,* not as a class but as the representative of the whole of society, as the whole mass of society confronting the one ruling class. It can do this because initially its interest really is as yet mostly connected with the common interest of all other non-ruling classes, because under the pressure of hitherto existing conditions its interest has not yet been able to develop as the particular interest of a particular class. Its victory, therefore, benefits also many individuals of other classes which are not winning a dominant position, but only insofar as it now enables these individuals to raise themselves into the ruling class. When the French bourgeoisie overthrew the rule of the aristocracy, it thereby made it possible for many proletarians to raise themselves above the proletariat, but only insofar as they became bourgeois. Every new class, therefore, achieves domination only on a broader basis than that of the class ruling previously; on the other hand the opposition of the non-ruling class to the new ruling class then develops all the more sharply and profoundly. Both these things determine the fact that the struggle to be waged against this new ruling class, in its turn, has as its aim a more decisive and more radical negation of the previous conditions of society than all previous classes which sought to rule could have.

This whole appearance, that the rule of a certain class is only the rule of certain ideas, comes to a natural end, of course, as soon as class rule in general ceases to be the form in which society is organised, that is to say, as soon as it is no longer necessary to represent a particular interest as general or the "general interest" as ruling.

Once the ruling ideas have been separated from the ruling individuals and, above all, from the relations which result from a given stage of the mode of production, and in this way the conclusion has been reached that history is always under the sway of ideas, it is very easy to abstract from these various ideas "the Idea", the thought, etc., as the dominant force in history, and thus to consider all these separate ideas and concepts as "forms of self-determination" of the Concept developing in history. It follows then naturally, too, that all the relations of men can be derived from the concept of man, man as conceived, the essence of man, Man. This has been done by speculative philosophy. Hegel himself confesses at the end of the *Philosophy of History* that he "has considered the progress of *the concept* only" and has represented in history the "true *theodicy.*"[8] Now one can go back again to the producers of "the concept", to the theorists, ideologists and philosophers, and one comes then to the conclusion that the philosophers, the thinkers as such have at all times been dominant in history: a conclusion, as we see already expressed by Hegel.

The whole trick of proving the hegemony of the spirit in history (hierarchy Stirner calls it) is thus confined to the following three attempts.

No. 1. One must separate the ideas of those ruling for empirical reasons, under empirical conditions and as corporeal individuals, from these rulers, and thus recognise the rule of ideas or illusions in history.

No. 2. One must bring an order into this rule of ideas, prove a mystical connection among the successive ruling ideas, which is managed by regarding them as "forms of self-determination of the concept" (this is possible because by virtue of their empirical basis these ideas are really connected with one another and because, conceived as *mere* ideas, they become self-distinctions, distinctions made by thought).

No. 3. To remove the mystical appearance of this "self-determining concept" it is changed into a person—"self-consciousness"—or, to appear thoroughly materialistic, into a series of persons, who represent the "concept" in history, into the "thinkers", the "philosophers", the ideologists, who again are understood as the manufacturers of history, as the "council of guardians", as the rulers. Thus the whole body of materialistic elements has been eliminated from history and now full rein can be given to the speculative steed.

This historical method which reigned in Germany, and especially the reason why, must be explained from its connection with the illusion of ideologists in general, e.g., the illusions of the jurists, politicians (including the practical statesmen), from the dogmatic dreamings and distortions of these fellows; this is explained perfectly easily from their practical position in life, their job, and the division of labour.

Whilst in ordinary life every shopkeeper is very well able to distinguish between what somebody professes to be and what he really is, our historiography has not yet won this trivial insight. It takes every epoch at its word and believes that everything it says and imagines about itself is true. . . .

■ ■ ■

Questions for Further Exploration:

- By what method do Marx and Engels seek to understand the nature of reality? How is their method different from Locke's empiricism? Does it overcome the skeptical challenges raised by Hume and Kirkman?

- According to Marx and Engels, what is the nature of the relationship between ideas/consciousness and the material realities of life? What is their critique of German philosophy's view of this relationship?

- What is "ideology"? What does it add to the traditional challenges of epistemology?

- What is the role of history in the conception of "mind" or consciousness set forth by Marx and Engels? How does their view of consciousness compare and contrast with the view shared by Darwin and Dennett?

- If Marx and Engels are right that "the ideas of the ruling class are in every epoch the ruling ideas," what class interests explain the dominance of the Cartesian legacy? In other words, in what sense is Cartesian mechanism ideological?

- Consider Marx & Engels philosophy in terms of Plato's allegory. In their view, what might each of the symbols (the cave, prisoners, shadows, escapee, outside, the sun, etc.) represent?

- How do you know your environmental awareness is not the product of "false consciousness"; i.e., "ideological brainwashing"?

The Will to Power

Book III—Principles
of A New Evaluation

Friedrich Nietzsche

■ ■ ■

Book III—Principles of A New Evaluation
2. The Epistemological Starting Point

480 (*March–June 1888*)

There exists neither "spirit," nor reason, nor thinking, nor consciousness, nor soul, nor will, nor truth: all are fictions that are of no use. There is no question of "subject and object," but of a particular species of animal that can prosper only through a certain relative rightness; above all, regularity of its perceptions (so that it can accumulate experience)—

Knowledge works as a tool of power. Hence it is plain that it increases with every increase of power—

The meaning of "knowledge": here, as in the case of "good" or "beautiful," the concept is to be regarded in a strict and narrow anthropocentric and biological sense. In order for a particular species to maintain itself and increase its power, its conception of reality must comprehend enough of the calculable and constant for it to base a scheme of behavior on it. The utility of preservation—not some abstract-theoretical need not to be deceived—stands as the motive behind the development of the organs of knowledge—they develop in such a way that their observations suffice for our preservation. In other words: the measure of the desire for knowledge depends upon the measure to which the will to power grows in a species: a species grasps a certain amount of reality in order to become master of it, in order to press it into service.

3. Belief in the "Ego." The Subject

481 (*1883–1888*)

Against positivism, which halts at phenomena—"There are only *facts*"—I would say: No, facts is precisely what there is not, only interpretations. We cannot establish any fact "in itself": perhaps it is folly to want to do such a thing.

"Everything is subjective," you say; but even this is interpretation. The "subject" is not something given, it is something added and invented and projected behind what there is.—Finally, is it necessary to posit an interpreter behind the interpretation? Even this is invention, hypothesis.

In so far as the word "knowledge" has any meaning, the world is knowable; but it is *interpretable* otherwise, it has no meaning behind it, but countless meanings.—"Perspectivism."

It is our needs that interpret the world; our drives and their For and Against. Every drive is a kind of lust to rule; each one has its perspective that it would like to compel all the other drives to accept as a norm.

482 (*1886–1887*)

instinct

We set up a word at the point at which our ignorance begins, at which we can see no further, e.g., the word "I," the word "do," the word "suffer":— these are perhaps the horizon of our knowledge, but not "truths."

483 (*1885*)

Through thought the ego is posited; but hitherto one believed as ordinary people do, that in "I think" there was something of immediate certainty, and that this "I" was the given *cause* of thought, from, which by analogy we understood all other causal relationships. However habitual and indispensable this fiction may have become by now—that in itself proves nothing against its imaginary origin: a belief can be a condition of life and nonetheless be false.[2]

---

[2]Cf. sections 487 and 493 and *Beyond,* section 4. This section, not in Nietzsche's handwriting, was evidently dictated.

484 (*Spring–Fall 1887*)

"There is thinking: therefore there is something that thinks": this is the up-shot of all Descartes' argumentation. But that means positing as "true *a priori*" our belief in the concept of substance—that when there is thought there has to be something "that thinks" is simply a formulation of our grammatical custom that adds a doer to every deed. In short, this is not merely the substantiation of a fact but a long-metaphysical postulate—Along the lines followed by Descartes one does not come upon something absolutely certain but only upon the fact of a very strong belief.

If one reduces the proposition to "There is thinking, therefore there are thoughts," one has produced a mere tautology: and precisely that which is in question, the "reality of thought," is not touched upon—that is, in this form the "apparent reality" of thought cannot be denied. But what Descartes desired was that thought should have, not an *apparent* reality, but a reality *in itself.*

485 (*Spring–Fall 1887*)

The concept of substance is a consequence of the concept of the subject: not the reverse! If we relinquish the soul, "the subject," the precondition for "substance" in general disappears. One acquires degrees of being, one loses that which *has* being.

Critique of "reality": where does the "more or less real," the gradation of being in which we believe, lead to?—

The degree to which we feel life and power (logic and coherence of experience) gives us our measure of "being," "reality," not-appearance.

The subject: this is the term for our belief in a unity underlying all the different impulses of the highest feeling of reality: we understand this belief as the *effect* of one cause—we believe so firmly in our belief that for its sake we imagine "truth," "reality," "substantiality" in general.—"The subject" is the fiction that many similar states in us are the effect of one substratum: but it is we who first created the "similarity" of these states; our adjusting them and making them similar is the fact, not their similarity (—which ought rather to be denied—).

486 (*1885–1886*)

One would have to know what *being* is, in order to decide whether this or that is real (e.g., "the facts of consciousness"); in the same way, what *certainty* is, what *knowledge* is, and the like.—But since we do not know this, a critique of the faculty of knowledge is senseless: how should a tool be able to criticize itself when it can use only itself for the critique? It cannot even define itself![3]

487 (*1883–1886*)

Must all philosophy not ultimately bring to light the preconditions upon which the process of reason depends?—our belief in the "ego" as a substance, as the sole reality from which we ascribe reality to things in general? The oldest "realism" at last comes to light: at the same time that the entire religious history of mankind is recognized as the history of the soul superstition. Here we come to a limit: our thinking itself involves this belief (with its distinction of substance, accident; deed, doer, etc.); to let it go means: being no longer able to think.

But that a belief, however necessary it may be for the preservation of a species, has nothing to do with truth, one knows from the fact that, e.g., we have to believe in time, space, and motion, without feeling compelled to grant them absolute reality.

488 (*Spring–Fall 1887*)

Psychological derivation of our belief in reason.—The concept "reality," "being," is taken from our feeling of the "subject."

"The subject": interpreted from within ourselves, so that the ego counts as a substance, as the cause of all deeds, as a doer.

The logical-metaphysical postulates, the belief in substance, accident, attribute, etc., derive their convincing force from our habit of regarding all our deeds as consequences of our will—so that the ego, as substance, does not vanish in the multiplicity of change.—But there is no such thing as will.—

We have no categories at all that permit us to distinguish a "world in itself" from a "world of appearance." All our categories of reason are of sensual origin: derived from the empirical world. "The soul," "the ego"—the history of these concepts shows that here, too, the oldest distinction ("breath," "life")—

If there is nothing material, there is also nothing immaterial. The concept no longer contains anything.

No subject "atoms." The sphere of a subject constantly growing or decreasing, the center of the system constantly shifting; in cases where it cannot organize the appropriate mass, it breaks into two parts. On the

---

[3]Cf. section 473.

other hand, it can transform a weaker subject into its functionary without destroying it, and to a certain degree form a new unity with it. No "substance," rather something that in itself strives after greater strength, and that wants to "preserve" itself only indirectly (it wants to *surpass* itself—).

489 (*1886–1887*)

Everything that enters consciousness as "unity" is already tremendously complex: we always have only a semblance of unity.

The phenomenon of the body is the richer, clearer, more tangible phenomenon: to be discussed first, methodologically, without coming to any decision about its ultimate significance.

490 (*1885*)

The assumption of one single subject is perhaps unnecessary; perhaps it is just as permissible to assume a multiplicity of subjects, whose interaction and struggle is the basis of our thought and our consciousness in general? A kind of aristocracy of "cells" in which dominion resides? To be sure, an aristocracy of equals, used to ruling jointly and understanding how to command?

My hypotheses: The subject as multiplicity.

Pain intellectual and dependent upon the judgment "harmful": projected.

The effect always "unconscious": the inferred and imagined cause is projected, *follows* in time.

Pleasure is a kind of pain.

The only force that exists is of the same kind as that of the will: a commanding of other subjects, which thereupon change.

The continual transitoriness and fleetingness of the subject. "Mortal soul."

Number as perspective form.

491 (*1885–1886*)

Belief in the body is more fundamental than belief in the soul: the latter arose from unscientific reflection on [the agonies of][4] the body (something that leaves it. Belief in the truth of dreams—).

---

[4]The words I have placed in brackets were interpolated by the German editors, on the basis of one of Nietzsche's other notes.

492 (*1885*)

The body and physiology the starting point: why?—We gain the correct idea of the nature of our subject-unity, namely as regents at the head of a communality (not as "souls" or "life forces"), also of the dependence of these regents upon the ruled and of an order of rank and division of labor as the conditions that make possible the whole and its parts. In the same way, how living unities continually arise and die and how the "subject" is not eternal; in the same way, that the struggle expresses itself in obeying and commanding, and that a fluctuating assessment of the limits of power is part of life. The relative ignorance in which the regent is kept concerning individual activities and even disturbances within the communality is among the conditions under which rule can be exercised. In short, we also gain a valuation of *not-knowing*, of seeing things on a broad scale, of simplification and falsification, of perspectivity. The most important thing, however, is: that we understand that the ruler and his subjects are of the same kind, all feeling, willing, thinking—and that, wherever we see or divine movement in a body, we learn to conclude that there is a subjective, invisible life appertaining to it. Movement is symbolism for the eye; it indicates that something has been felt, willed, thought.

The danger of the direct questioning of the subject *about* the subject and of all self-reflection of the spirit lies in this, that it could be useful and important for one's activity to interpret oneself *falsely.* That is why we question the body and reject the evidence of the sharpened senses: we try, if you like, to see whether the inferior parts themselves cannot enter into communication with us.

4. Biology of the Drive to Knowledge. Perspectivism

493 (*1885*)

Truth is the kind of error without which a certain species of life could not live. The value for *life* is ultimately decisive.[5]

494 (*1885*)

It is improbable that our "knowledge" should extend further than is strictly necessary for the preservation of life. Morphology shows us how the

---

[5]Cf. sections 483 and 487; but also 172.

senses and the nerves, as well as the brain, develop in proportion to the difficulty of finding nourishment.

495

If the morality of "thou shalt not lie" is rejected, the "sense for truth" will have to legitimize itself before another tribunal:—as a means of the preservation of man, as *will to power.*

Likewise our love of the beautiful: it also is our shaping will. The two senses stand side-by-side; the sense for the real is the means of acquiring the power to shape things according to our wish. The joy in shaping and reshaping—a primeval joy! We can comprehend only a world that we ourselves have made.

■ ■ ■

Questions for Further Exploration:

- What does Nietzsche mean by saying, "Knowledge works as a tool of power"? Compare and contrast his view with that of Marx and Engels.

- What evidence is there in the text for thinking Nietzsche is, or is not a Darwinian?

- What does Nietzsche's "perspectivism" entail?

- What is Nietzsche's critique of Descartes' philosophy?

- If "Truth is a kind of error," what basis for judgment does Nietzsche advocate?

- Are Nietzsche's claims reached by a discernible method? If so, how would you characterize it? If not, what follows?

On the Genealogy of Morals

Friedrich Nietzsche

Essay Three. Section 12

Given that such a living desire for contradiction and hostility to nature is used to practice philosophy, on what will it discharge its most inner arbitrary power? It will do that on something it perceives, with the greatest certainty, as something real. It will seek out error precisely where the essential instinct for life has established its most unconditional truth. For example, it will demote physical life to an illusion, as the ascetics of the Vedanta philosophy did. Similarly they will treat pain, the multiplicity of things, the whole ideational opposition between "subject" and " object" as error, nothing but error! To deny faith in their own ego, to deny their own "reality"—what a triumph—and not just over the senses, over appearances, but a much loftier triumph, an overpowering of and act of cruelty against reason: a process in which the highest peak of delight occurs when the ascetic self-contempt and the self-mockery of reason proclaims: "There is a kingdom of truth and being, but reason is expressly excluded from it." (By the way, even in the Kantian idea of the "intelligible character of things" there is still something of this old greedy ascetic dichotomy, which loves to turn reason against reason: for the "intelligible character" with Kant means a sort of composition of things about which the intellect understands just enough to know that it is wholly and completely unintelligible to the intellect).

But, as people who seek knowledge, the last thing we should do is be ungrateful for such determined reversals of customary perspectives and evaluations with which the spirit has for so long raged against itself, with such apparent wickedness and futility. To use this for once to see differently, the will to see things differently, is no small discipline and preparation of the intellect for its coming "objectivity," and not in the sense of "disinterested contemplation" (which is conceptual nonsense), but as the capability of having power over one's positive and negative arguments and to raise them and dispose of them so that one knows how to make the various perspectives and interpretations of emotions useful for knowledge.

324

From now on, my philosophical gentlemen, let us protect ourselves better from the dangerous old conceptual fantasy which posits a "pure, will-less, painless, timeless subject of cognition," let's guard ourselves against the tentacles of such contradictory ideas as "pure reason," "absolute spirituality," "knowledge in itself"—those things which demand that we imagine an eye which simply can't be imagined, an eye without any direction at all, in which the active and interpretative forces are supposed to stop or be absent—the very things through which seeing first becomes seeing something. Hence these things always demand from the eye something conceptually empty and absurd. The only seeing we have is seeing from a perspective; the only knowledge we have is knowledge from a perspective. The more emotional affects we allow to be expressed in words concerning something, the more eyes, different eyes, we know how to train on the same thing, the more complete our "idea" of this thing, our "objectivity," will be. But to eliminate the will in general, to suspend all our emotions without exception—even if we were capable of that—what would that be? Wouldn't we call that castrating the intellect?

Questions for Further Exploration:

■ How does Nietzsche characterize the conception of "objectivity" that is the target of his criticisms? What criticisms does he aim at this "customary perspective"?

■ In what sense is this conception of objectivity guilty of "castrating the intellect"?

■ What is the nature of the "objectivity" Nietzsche advocates? Why does he call it "objectivity" instead of "subjectivity," or "inter-subjectivity"?

■ Using Nietzsche's "objective" view, how would you explain each of the following: a tree, a spider, the Statue of Liberty, a television and a human being?

■ Compare and contrast Nietzsche's "objectivity" with a traditional scientific conception of "objectivity"? What are the advantages/ disadvantages of each as a basis for advocating ecologically sound policies and practices?

Spell of the Sensuous

David Abram

Philosophy on the Way to Ecology

■ ■ ■

Yet it was only after the publication of Descartes's *Meditations,* in 1641, that material reality came to be commonly spoken of as a strictly mechanical realm, as a determinate structure whose laws of operation could be discerned only via mathematical analysis. By apparently purging material reality of subjective experience, Galileo cleared the ground and Descartes laid the foundation for the construction of the objective or "disinterested" sciences, which by their feverish and forceful investigations have yielded so much of the knowledge and so many of the technologies that have today become commonplace in the West. The chemical table of the elements, automobiles, smallpox vaccines, "close-up" images of the outer planets—so much that we have come to assume and depend upon has emerged from the bold experimentalization of the world by the objective sciences.

Yet these sciences consistently overlook our ordinary, everyday experience of the world around us. Our direct experience is necessarily subjective, necessarily relative to our own position or place in the midst of things, to our particular desires, tastes, and concerns. The everyday world in which we hunger and make love is hardly the mathematically determined "object" toward which the sciences direct themselves. Despite all the mechanical artifacts that now surround us, the world in which we find ourselves before we set out to calculate and measure it is not an inert or mechanical object but a living field, an open and dynamic landscape subject to its own moods and metamorphoses.

My life and the world's life are deeply intertwined; when I wake up one morning to find that a week-long illness has subsided and that my strength has returned, the world, when I step outside, fairly sparkles with energy and activity: swallows are swooping by in vivid flight; waves of heat rise from the newly paved road smelling strongly of tar; the old red barn across the field juts into the sky at an intense angle. Likewise, when a haze descends upon the valley in which I dwell, it descends upon my awareness as well, muddling my thoughts, making my muscles yearn for sleep. The world and I reciprocate one another. The landscape as I directly experience it is hardly a determinate object; it is an ambiguous realm that responds to my emotions and calls forth feelings from me in turn. Even the most detached scientist must begin and end her study in this indeterminate field of experience, where shifts of climate or mood may alter his experiment or her interpretation of "the data": the scientist, too, must take time off from his measurements and analyses to eat, to defecate, to converse with friends, to interact straightforwardly with a familiar world that is never explicitly thematized and defined. Indeed, it is precisely from his experience in this preconceptual and hence ambiguous world that an individual is first drawn to become a scientist, to adopt the ways of speaking and seeing that are acknowledged as appropriate by the scientific community, to affect the proper disinterested or objective attitude with regard to a certain range of natural events. The scientist does not randomly choose a specific discipline or specialty, but is drawn to a particular field by a complex of subjective experiences and encounters, many of which unfold far from the laboratory and its rarefield atmosphere. Further, the scientist never completely succeeds in making himself into a pure spectator of the world, for he cannot cease to live in the world as a human among other humans, or as a creature among other creatures, and his scientific concepts and theories necessarily borrow aspects of their character and texture from his untheorized, spontaneously lived experience.

Indeed, the ostensibly "value-free" results of our culture's investigations into biology, physics, and chemistry ultimately come to display themselves in the open and uncertain field of everyday life, whether embedded in social policies with which we must come to terms or embodied in new technologies with which we all must grapple. Thus, the living world—this ambiguous realm that we experience in anger and joy, in grief and in love—is both the soil in which all our sciences are rooted and the rich humus into which their results ultimately return, whether as nutrients or as poisons. Our spontaneous experience of the world, charged with subjective, emotional, and intuitive content, remains the vital and dark ground of all our objectivity.

And yet this ground goes largely unnoticed or unacknowledged in scientific culture. In a society that accords priority to that which is predictable and places a premium on certainty, our spontaneous, preconceptual experience, when acknowledged at all, is referred to as "merely subjective." The fluid realm of direct experience has come to be seen as a secondary, derivative dimension, a mere consequence of events unfolding in the "realer" world of quantifiable and measurable scientific "facts." It is a curious inversion of the actual, demonstrable state of affairs. Subatomic quanta are now taken to be more primordial and "real" than the world we experience with our unaided senses. The living, feeling, and thinking organism is assumed to derive, somehow, from the mechanical body whose reflexes and "systems" have been measured and mapped, the living person now an epiphenomenon of the anatomized corpse. That it takes living, sensing subjects, complete with their enigmatic emotions and unpredictable passions, to conceive of those subatomic fields, or to dissect and anatomize the body, is readily overlooked, or brushed aside as inconsequential.

Nevertheless, the ambiguity of experience is already a part of any phenomenon that draws our attention. For whatever we perceive is necessarily entwined with our own subjectivity, already blended with the dynamism of life and sentience. The living pulse of subjective experience cannot finally be stripped from the tings that we study (in order to expose the pure unadulterated "objects") without the things themselves losing all existence for us. Such conundrums are commonly consigned to psychology, to that science that studies subjective awareness and perception. And so perhaps by turning to psychology we can expect to find a recognition and avowal of the preobjective dimension that permeates and sustains every reality that we know, and hence an understanding of the manner in which subjective experience both supports and sets limits to the positive sciences.

In psychology, however, we discover nothing of the sort. Instead, we find a discipline that is itself modeled on the positivism of the "hard" sciences, a science wherein the psyche has itself been reified into an "object," a thing to be studied like any other thing in the determinate, objective world. Much of cognitive science strives to model the computational processes that ostensibly underlie mental experience. While for Galileo and Descartes perceptual qualities like color and taste were illusory, unreal properties because of their ambiguous and indeterminate character, mathematical indices have at last been found for *these* qualities as well, or rather such qualities are now studied only to the extent that they can be rendered, by whatever process of translation, into *quantities*. Here as elsewhere, the everyday world—the world of our direct, spontaneous experience—is still assumed to derive from an impersonal, objective dimension of pure "facts" that we glimpse only through our instruments and equations.

It was his frustration with such assumptions, and with the early discipline of psychology—which, far from directing attention toward the fluid region of direct experience, was already at the start of the twentieth century solidifying the "mind" into another "object" in the mathematized and mechanical universe—that led Edmund Husserl to inaugurate the philosophical discipline of phenomenology. Phenomenology, as he articulated it in the early 1900s, would turn toward "the things themselves," toward the world as it is experienced in its felt immediacy. Unlike the mathematics-based sciences, phenomenology would seek not to explain the world, but to describe as closely as possible the way the world makes itself evident to awareness, the way things first arise in our direct, sensorial experience.[2] By thus returning to the taken-for-granted realm of subjective experience, not to explain it but simply to pay attention to its rhythms and textures, not to capture or control it but simply to become familiar with its diverse modes of appearance—and ultimately to give voice to its enigmatic and ever-shifting patterns—phenomenology would articulate the ground of the other sciences. It was Husserl's hope that phenomenology, as a rigorous "science of experience," would establish the other sciences at last upon a firm footing—not, perhaps, as solid as the fixed and finished "object" upon which those sciences *pretend* to stand, but the only basis possible for a knowledge that necessarily emerges from our lived experience of the things around us. In the words of the French phenomenologist Maurice Merleau-Ponty:

> All my knowledge of the world, even my scientific knowledge, is gained from my own particular point of view, or from some experience of the world without which the symbols of science would be meaningless. The whole universe of science is built upon the world as directly experienced, and if we want to subject science itself to rigorous scrutiny and arrive at a precise assessment of its meaning and scope, we must begin by reawakening the basic experience of the world, of which science is the second-order expression. . . . To return to things themselves is to return to that world which precedes knowledge, of which knowledge always *speaks,* and in relation to which every scientific schematization is an abstract and derivative sign-language, as is geography in relation to the countryside in which we have learnt beforehand what a forest, a prairie or a river is.[3]

Intersubjectivity

In the early stages of his project, Husserl spoke of the world of experience (the "phenomenal" world) as a thoroughly subjective realm. In order to explore this realm philosophically, he insisted that it be viewed as a wholly mental dimension, an immaterial field of appearances. That which experiences this dimension—the experiencing self, or subject—was similarly described by Husserl as a pure consciousness, a "transcendental" mind or ego.

Perhaps by designating subjective reality as a nonmaterial, transcendental realm, Husserl hoped to isolate this qualitative dimension from the apparently mechanical world of material "facts" that was then being constructed by the objective sciences (and thus to protect this realm from being colonized by those technological methods of inquiry). Yet his insistence upon the mental character of phenomenal reality led critics to attack Husserl's method as being inherently solipsistic—an approach that seals the philosopher inside his own solitary experience, rendering him ultimately unable to recognize anyone or anything outside of his own mind.

Husserl struggled long and hard to answer this important criticism. How does our subjective experience enable us to recognize the reality of other selves, other experiencing beings? The solution seemed to implicate the body—one's own as well as that of the other—as a singularly important structure within the phenomenal field. The body is that mysterious and multifaceted phenomenon that seems always to accompany one's awareness, and indeed to be the very location of one's awareness within the field of appearances. Yet the phenomenal field also contains many *other* bodies, other forms that move and gesture in a fashion similar to one's own. While one's own body is experienced, as it were, only from within, these other bodies are experienced from outside; one can vary one's distance from these bodies and can move around them, while this is impossible in relation to one's own body.

Despite this difference, Husserl discerned that there was an inescapable affinity, or affiliation, between these other bodies and one's own. The gestures and expressions of these other bodies, viewed from without, echo and resonate one's own bodily movements and gestures, experienced from within. By an associative "empathy," the embodied subject comes to recognize these other bodies as other centers of experience, other subjects.[4]

In this manner, carefully describing the ways in which the subjective field of experience, mediated by the body, opens onto other subjectivities—other selves besides one's own self—Husserl sought to counter the charge of solipsism that had been directed against his phenomenology. The field of appearances, while still a thoroughly subjective realm, was now seen to be inhabited by *multiple* subjectivities; the phenomenal field was no longer the isolate haunt of a solitary ego, but a collective landscape, constituted by other experiencing subjects as well as by oneself.

There remain, however, many phenomena in the experiential field that are not collective or commonly shared. When daydreaming, for example, my attention is carried by phenomena whose contours and movements I am able to alter at will, a whole phantasmagoria of images that nevertheless lack the solidity of bodies. Such forms offer very little resistance to my gaze. They are not, that is, held in place by gazes other than my own—these are entirely *my* images, *my* phantasies and fears, *my* dreamings. And so I am brought, like Husserl, to recognize at least two regions of the experiential or phenomenal field: one of phenomena that unfold entirely for me—images that arise, as it were, on this side of my body—and another region of phenomena that are, evidently, responded to an experienced by other embodied subjects as well as by myself. These latter phenomena are still subjective—they appear to me within a field of experience colored by my mood and my current concerns—and yet I cannot alter or dissipate them at will, for they seem to be buttressed by many involvements besides my own. That tree bending in the wind, this cliff wall, the cloud drifting overhead: these are not merely subjective; they are *intersubjective* phenomena— phenomena experienced by a multiplicity of sensing subjects.

Husserl's notion of *intersubjectivity* suggested a remarkable new interpretation of the so-called "objective world." For the conventional contrast between "subjective" and "objective" realities could now be reframed as a contrast within the subjective field of experience itself—as the felt contrast between subjective and intersubjective phenomena.

The sciences are commonly thought to aim at clear knowledge of an objective world utterly independent of awareness or subjectivity. Considered experientially, however, the scientific method enables the achievement of greater intersubjectivity, greater knowledge of that which is or can be experienced by many different selves or subjects. The striving for objectivity is thus understood, phenomenologically, as a striving to achieve greater consensus, greater agreement or consonance among a plurality of subjects, rather than as an attempt to avoid subjectivity altogether. The pure "objective reality" commonly assumed by modern science, far from being the concrete basis underlying all experience, was, according to Husserl, a theoretical construction, an unwarranted idealization of intersubjective experience.[5]

The "real world" in which we find ourselves, then—the very world our sciences strive to fathom—is not a sheet "object," not a fixed and finished "datum" from which all subjects and subjective qualities could be pared away, but is rather an intertwined matrix of sensations and perceptions, a collective field of experience lived through from many different angles.

The mutual inscription of others in my experience, and (as I must assume) of myself in their experiences, effects the interweaving of our individual phenomenal fields into a single, ever-shifting fabric, a single phenomenal world or "reality."

And yet, as we know from our everyday experience, the phenomenal world is remarkably stable and solid; we are able to count on it in so many ways, and we take for granted much of its structure and character. This experienced solidity is precisely sustained by the continual encounter with others, with other embodied subjects, other centers of experience. The encounter with other perceivers continually assures me that there is more to any thing, or to the world, than I myself can perceive at any moment. Besides that which I directly see of a particular oak tree or building, I know or intuit that there are also those facets of the oak or building that are visible to the other perceivers that I see. I sense that that tree is much more than what I directly see of it, since it is also what the others whom I see perceive of it; I sense that as a perceivable presence it already existed before I came to look at it, and indeed that it will not dissipate when I turn away from it, since it remains an experience for others—not just for other persons, but (as we shall see later in this chapter) for other sentient organisms, for the birds that nest in its branches and for the insects that move along its bark, and even, finally, for the sensitive cells and tissues of the oak itself, quietly drinking sunlight through its leaves. It is this informing of my perceptions by the evident perceptions and sensations of other bodily entities that establishes, for me, the relative solidity and stability of the world.

The Ecology of Magic
A Personal Introduction to the Inquiry

Late one evening I stepped out of my little hut in the rice paddies of eastern Bali and found myself falling through space. Over my head the black sky was rippling with stars, densely clustered in some regions, almost blocking out the darkness between them, and more loosely scattered in other areas, pulsing and beckoning to each other. Behind them all streamed the great river of light with its several tributaries. Yet the Milky Way churned beneath me as well, for my hut was set in the middle of a large patchwork of rice paddies, separated from each other by narrow two-foot-high dikes, and these paddies were all filled with water. The surface of these pools, by day, reflected perfectly the blue sky, a reflection broken only by the thin, bright green tips of new rice. But by night the stars themselves glimmered from the surface of the paddies, and the river of light whirled through the darkness underfoot as well as above; there seemed no ground in front of my feet, only the abyss of star-studded space falling away forever.

I was no longer simply beneath the night sky, but also *above* it—the immediate impression was of weightlessness. I might have been able, to reorient myself, to regain some sense of ground and gravity, were it not for a fact that confounded my senses entirely: between the constellations below and the constellations above drifted countless fireflies, their lights flickering like the stars, some drifting up to join the clusters of stars overhead, others, like graceful meteors, slipping down from above to join the constellations underfoot, and all these paths of light upward and downward were mirrored, as well, in the still surface of the paddies. I felt myself at times falling through space, at other moments floating and drifting. I simply could not dispel the profound vertigo and giddiness; the paths of the fireflies; and their reflections in the water's surface, held me in a sustained trance. Even after I crawled back to my hut and shut the door on this whirling world, I felt that now the little room in which I lay was itself floating free of the earth.

Fireflies! It was in Indonesia, you see, that I was first introduced to the world of insects, and there that I first learned of the great influence that insects—such diminutive entities—could have upon the human senses. I had traveled to Indonesia on a research grant to study magic—more precisely, to study the relation between magic and medicine, first among the traditional sorcerers, or *dukuns,* of the Indonesia archipelago, and later among the *dzankris,* the traditional shamans of Nepal. One aspect of the grant was somewhat unique: I was to journey into rural Asia not outwardly as an anthropologist or academic researcher, but as a magician in my own right, in hopes of gaining a more direct access to the local sorcerers. I had been a professional sleight-of-hand magician for five years back in the United States, helping to put myself through college by performing in clubs and restaurants throughout New England. I had, as well, taken a year off from my studies in the psychology of perception to travel as a street magician through Europe and, toward the end of that journey, had spent some months in London, England, exploring the use of sleight-of-hand magic in psychotherapy, as a means of engendering communication with distressed individuals largely unapproachable by clinical healers.[1] The success of this work suggested to me that sleight-of-hand might lend itself well to the curative arts, and I became, for the first time, interested in the relation, largely forgotten in the West, between folk medicine and magic.

It was this interest that led to the aforementioned grant, and to my sojourn as a magician in rural Asia. There, my sleight-of-hand skills proved invaluable as a means of stirring the curiosity of the local shamans. For magicians—whether modern entertainers or indigenous, tribal sorcerers—have in common the fact that they work with the malleable texture of perception. When the local sorcerers gleaned that I had at least some rudimentary skill in altering the common field of perception, I was invited into their homes, asked to share secrets with them, and eventually encouraged, even urged, to participate in various rituals and ceremonies.

But the focus of my research gradually shifted from questions regarding the application of magical techniques in medicine and ritual curing toward a deeper pondering of the relation between traditional magic and the animate natural world. This broader concern seemed to hold the keys to the earlier questions. For none of the several island sorcerers that I came to know in Indonesia, nor any of the *dzankris* with whom I lived in Nepal, considered their work as ritual healers to be their major role or function within their communities. Most of them, to be sure, *were* the primary healers or "doctors" for the villages in their vicinity, and they were often spoken of as such by the inhabitants of those villages. But the villagers also sometimes spoke of them, in low voices and in very private conversations, as witches (or "lejaks" in Bali), as dark magicians who at night might well be practicing their healing spells backward (or while turning to the left instead of to the right) in order to afflict people with the very diseases that they would later work to cure by day. Such suspicions seemed fairly common in Indonesia, and often were harbored with regard to the most effective and powerful healers, those who were most renowned for their skill in driving out illness. For it was assumed that a magician, in order to expel malevolent influences, must have a strong understanding of those influences and demons—even, in some areas, a close rapport with such powers. I myself never consciously saw any of those magicians or shamans with whom I became acquainted engage in magic for harmful purposes, nor any convincing evidence that they had ever done so. (Few of the magicians that I came to know even accepted money in return for their services, although they did accept gifts in the way of food, blankets, and the like.) Yet I was struck by the fact that none of them ever did or said anything to counter such disturbing rumors and speculations, which circulated quietly through the regions where they lived. Slowly, I came to recognize that it was through the agency of such rumors, and the ambiguous fears that such rumors engendered in the village people, that the sorcerers were able to maintain a basic level of privacy. If the villagers did not entertain certain fears about the local sorcerer, then they would likely come to obtain his or her magical help for every little malady and disturbance; and since a more potent practitioner must provide services for several large villages, the sorcerer would be swamped from morning to night with requests for ritual aid. By allowing the inevitable suspicions and fears to circulate unhindered in the region (and sometimes even encouraging and contributing to such rumors), the sorcerer ensured that *only* those who were in real and profound need of his skills would dare to approach him for help.

This privacy, in turn, left the magician free to attend to what he acknowledged to be his primary craft and function. A clue to this function may be found in the circumstance that such magicians rarely dwell at the heart of their village; rather, their dwellings are commonly at the spatial periphery of the community or, more often, out beyond the edges of the village—amid the rice fields, or in a forest, or a wild cluster of boulders. I could easily attribute this to the just-mentioned need for privacy, yet for the magician in a traditional culture it seems to serve another purpose as well, providing a spatial expression of his or her symbolic position with regard to the community. For the magician's intelligence is not encompassed *within* the society; its place is at the edge of the community, mediating *between* the human community and the larger community of begins upon which the village depends for its nourishment and sustenance. This larger community includes, along with the humans, the multiple nonhuman entities that constitute the local landscape, from the diverse plants and the myriad animals—birds, mammals, fish, reptiles, insects—that inhabit or migrate through the region, to the particular winds and weather patterns that inform the local geography, as well as the various landforms—forests, rivers, caves, mountains—that lend their specific character to the surrounding earth.

The traditional or tribal shaman, I came to discern, acts as an intermediary between the human community and the larger ecological field, ensuring that there is an appropriate flow of nourishment, not just from the landscape to the human inhabitants, but from the human community back to the local earth. By his constant rituals, trances, ecstasies, and "journeys," he ensures that the relation between human society and the larger society of beings is balanced and reciprocal, and that the village never takes more from the living land than it returns to it—not just materially but with prayers, propitiations, and praise. The scale of a harvest or the size of a hunt are always negotiated between the tribal community and the natural world that it inhabits. To some extent every adult in the community is engaged in this process of listening and attuning to the other presences that surround and influence daily life. But the shaman or sorcerer is the exemplary voyager in the intermediate realm between the human and the more-than-human worlds, the primary strategist and negotiator in any dealings with the Others.

And it is only as a result of her continual engagement with the animate powers that dwell beyond the human community that the traditional magician is able to alleviate many individual illnesses that arise *within* that community. The sorcerer derives her ability to cure ailments from her more continuous practice of "healing" or balancing the community's relation to the surrounding land. Disease, in such cultures, is often conceptualized as a kind of systemic imbalance within the sick person, or more vividly as the intrusion of a demonic or malevolent presence into his body. There are, at times, malevolent influences within the village or tribe itself that disrupt the health and emotional well-being of susceptible individuals within the community. Yet such destructive influences within the human community are commonly traceable to a disequilibrium between that community and the larger field of forces in which it is embedded. Only those persons who, by their everyday practice, are involved in monitoring and maintaining the relations *between* the human village and the animate landscape are able to appropriately diagnose, treat, and ultimately relieve personal ailments and illnesses arising *within* the village. Any healer who was not simultaneously attending to the intertwined relation between the human community and the larger, more-than-human field, would likely dispel an illness from one person only to have the same problem arise (perhaps in a new guise) somewhere else in the community. Hence, the traditional magician or medicine person functions primarily as an intermediary between human and nonhuman worlds, and only secondarily as a healer.[2] Without a continually adjusted awareness of the relative balance or imbalance between the human group and its nonhuman environ, along with the skills necessary to modulate that primary relation, any "healer" is worthless—indeed, not a healer at all. The medicine person's primary allegiance, then, is not to the human community, but to the earthly web of relations in which that community is embedded—it is from this that his or her power to alleviate human illness derives—and this sets the local magician apart from other persons.

The primacy for the magician of nonhuman nature—the centrality of his relation to other species and to the earth—is not always evident to Western researchers. Countless anthropologists have managed to overlook the ecological dimension of the shaman's craft, while writing at great length of the shaman's rapport with "supernatural" entities. We can attribute much of this oversight to the modern, civilized assumption that the natural world is largely determinate and mechanical, and that that which is regarded as mysterious, powerful, and beyond human ken must therefore be of some other, nonphysical realm *above* nature, "supernatural."

The oversight becomes still more comprehensible when we realize that many of the earliest European interpreters of indigenous lifeways were Christian missionaries. For the Church had long assumed that only human beings have intelligent souls, and that the other animals, to say nothing of trees and rivers, were "created" for no other reason than to serve humankind. We can easily understand why European missionaries, steeped in the dogma of institutionalized Christianity, assumed a belief in supernatural, otherworldly powers among those tribal persons whom they saw awestruck and entranced by nonhuman (but nevertheless natural) forces. What is remarkable is the extent to which contemporary anthropology still preserves the ethnocentric bias of these early interpreters. We no longer describe the shamans' enigmatic spirit-helpers as the "superstitious claptrap of heathen primitives"—we have cleansed ourselves of at least *that* much ethnocentrism; yet we still refer to such enigmatic forces, respectfully now, as "supernaturals"—for we are unable to shed the sense, so endemic to scientific civilization, of nature as a rather prosaic and predictable realm, unsuited to such mysteries. Nevertheless, that which is regarded with the greatest awe and wonder by indigenous, oral cultures is, I suggest, none other than what we view as nature itself. The deeply mysterious powers and entities with whom the shaman enters into a rapport are ultimately the same forces—the same plants, animals, forests, and winds—that to literate, "civilized" Europeans are just so much scenery, the pleasant backdrop of our more pressing human concerns.

The most sophisticated definition of "magic" that now circulates through the American counterculture is "the ability or power to alter one's consciousness at will." No mention is made of any *reason* for altering one's consciousness. Yet in tribal cultures that which we call "magic" takes its meaning from the fact that humans, in an indigenous and oral context, experience their own consciousness as simply one form of awareness among many others. The traditional magician cultivates an ability to shift out of his or her common state of consciousness precisely in order to make contact with the other organic forms of sensitivity and awareness with which human existence is entwined. Only by temporarily shedding the accepted perceptual logic of his culture can the sorcerer hope to enter into relation with other species on their own terms; only by altering the common organization of his senses will he be able to enter into a rapport with the multiple nonhuman sensibilities that animate the local landscape. It is this, we might say, that defines a shaman: the ability to readily slip out of the perceptual boundaries that demarcate his or her particular culture— boundaries reinforced by social customs, taboos, and most importantly, the common speech or language—in order to make contact with, and learn from, the other powers in the land. His magic is precisely this heightened receptivity to the meaningful solicitations—songs, cries, gestures—of the larger, more-than-human field.

Magic, then, in its perhaps most primordial sense, is the experience of existing in a world made up of multiple intelligences, the intuition that every form one perceives—from the swallow swooping overhead to the fly on a blade of grass, and indeed the blade of grass itself—is an *experiencing* form, an entity with its own predilections and sensations, albeit sensations that are very different from our own.

To be sure, the shaman's ecological function, his or her role as intermediary between human society and the land, is not always obvious at first blush, even to a sensitive observer. We see the sorcerer being called upon to cure an ailing tribesman of his sleeplessness, or perhaps simply to locate some missing goods; we witness him entering into trance and sending his awareness into other dimensions in search of insight and aid. Yet we should not be so ready to interpret these dimensions as "supernatural," nor to view them as realms entirely "internal" to the personal psyche of the practitioner. For it is likely that the "inner world" of our Western psychological experience, like the supernatural heaven of Christian belief, originates in the loss of our ancestral reciprocity with the animate earth. When the animate powers that surround us are suddenly construed as having less significance than ourselves, when the generative earth is abruptly defined as a determinate object devoid of its own sensations and feelings, then the sense of a wild and multiplicitous otherness (in relation to which human existence has always oriented itself) must migrate, either into a supersensory heaven beyond the natural world, or else into the human skull itself—the only allowable refuge, in this world, for what is ineffable and unfathomable.

But in genuinely oral, indigenous cultures, the sensuous world itself remains the dwelling place of the gods, of the numinous powers that can either sustain or extinguish human life. It is not by sending his awareness out beyond the natural world that the shaman makes contact with the purveyors of life and health, nor by journeying into his personal psyche; rather, it is by propelling his awareness laterally, outward into the depths of a landscape at once both sensuous and psychological, the living dream that we share with the soaring hawk, the spider, and the stone silently sprouting lichens on its coarse surface.

The magician's intimate relationship with nonhuman nature becomes most evident when we attend to the easily overlooked background of his or her practice—not just to the more visible tasks of curing and ritual aid to which she is called by individual clients, or to the larger ceremonies at which she presides and dances, but to the content of the prayers by which she prepares for such ceremonies, and to the countless ritual gestures that she enacts when alone, the daily propitiations and praise that flow from her toward the land and *its* many voices.

▪ ▪ ▪

Several months after my arrival in Bali, I left the village in which I was staying to visit one of the pre-Hindu sites on the island. I arrived on my bicycle early in the afternoon, after the bus carrying tourists from the coast had departed. A flight of steps took me down into a lush, emerald valley, lined by cliffs on either side, awash with the speech of the river and the sighing of the wind through high, unharvested grasses. On a small bridge crossing the river I met an old woman carrying a wide basket on her head and holding the hand of a little, shy child; the woman grinned at me with the red, toothless smile of a beetle nut chewer. On the far side of the river I stood in front of a great moss-covered complex of passageways, rooms, and courtyards carved by hand out of the black volcanic rock.

I noticed, at a end in the canyon downstream, a further series of caves carved into the cliffs. These appeared more isolated and remote, unattended by any footpath I could discern. I set out through the grasses to explore them. This proved much more difficult than I anticipated, but after getting lost in the tall grasses, and fording the river three times, I at last found myself beneath the caves. A short scramble up the rock wall brought me to the mouth of one of them, and I entered on my hands and knees. It was a wide but low opening, perhaps only four feet high, and the interior receded only about five or six feet into the cliff. The floor and walls were covered with mosses, painting the cave with green patterns and softening the harshness of the rock; the place, despite its small size—or perhaps because of it—had an air of great friendliness. I climbed to two other caves, each about the same size, but then felt drawn back to the first one, to sit cross-legged on the cushioning moss and gaze out across the emerald canyon. It was quiet inside, a kind of intimate sanctuary hewn into the stone. I began to explore the rich resonance of the enclosure, first just humming, then intoning a simple chant taught to me by a balian some days before. I was delighted by the overtones that the cave added to my voice, and sat there signing for a long while. I did not notice the change in the wind outside, or the cloud shadows darkening the valley, until the rains broke—suddenly and with great force. That first storm of the monsoon!

I had experienced only slight rains on the island before then, and was startled by the torrential downpour now sending stones tumbling along the cliffs, building puddles and then ponds in the green landscape below, swelling the river. There was no question of returning home—I would be unable to make my way back through the flood to the valley's entrance. And so, thankful for the shelter, I recrossed my legs to wait out the storm. Before long the rivulets falling along the cliff above gathered themselves into streams, and two small waterfalls cascaded across the cave's mouth. Soon I was looking into a solid curtain of water, thin in some places, where the canyon's image flickered unsteadily, and thickly rushing in others. My senses were all but overcome by the wild beauty of the cascade and by the roar of sound, my body trembling inwardly at the weird sense of being sealed into my hiding place.

And then, in the midst of all this tumult, I noticed a small, delicate activity. Just in front of me, and only an inch or two to my side of the torrent, a spider was climbing a thin thread stretched across the mouth of the cave. As I watched, it anchored another thread to the top of the opening, then slipped back along the first thread and joined the two at a point about midway between the roof and the floor. I lost sight of the spider then, and for a while it seemed that it had vanished, thread and all, until my focus rediscovered it. Two more threads now radiated from the center to the floor, and then another; soon the spider began to swing between these as on a circular trellis, trailing an ever-lengthening thread which it affixed to each radiating rung as it moved from one to the next, spiraling outward. The spider seemed wholly undaunted by the tumult of waters spilling past it, although every now and then it broke off its spiral dance and climbed to the roof or the floor to tug on the radii there, assuring the tautness of the threads, then crawled back to where it left off. Whenever I lost the correct focus, I waited to catch sight of the spinning arachnid, and then let its dancing form gradually draw the lineaments of the web back into visibility, tying my focus into each new knot of silk as it moved, weaving my gaze into the ever-deepening pattern.

And then, abruptly, my vision snagged on a strange incongruity: another thread slanted across the web, neither radiating nor spiraling from the central juncture, violating the symmetry. As I followed it with my eyes, pondering its purpose in the overall pattern, I began to realize that it was on a different plane from the rest of the web, for the web slipped out of focus whenever this new line became clearer. I soon saw that it led to its own center, about twelve inches to the right of the first, another nexus of forces from which several threads stretched to the floor and the ceiling. And then I saw that there was a *different* spider spinning this web, testing its tautness by dancing around it like the first, now setting the silken cross weaves around the nodal point and winding outward. The two spiders spun independently of each other, but to my eyes they wove a single interacting pattern. This widening of my gaze soon disclosed yet another spider spiraling in the cave's mouth, and suddenly I realized that there were *many* overlapping webs coming into being, radiating out at different rhythms from myriad centers poised—some higher, some lower, some minutely closer to my eyes and some farther—between the stone above and the stone below.

I sat stunned and mesmerized before this ever-complexifying expanse of living patterns upon patterns, my gaze drawn like a breath into one converging group of lines, then breathed out into open space, then drawn down into another convergence. The curtain of water had become utterly silent—I tried at one point to heart it, but could not. My senses were entranced.

I had the distinct impression that I was watching the universe being born, galaxy upon galaxy. . . .

Night filled the cave with darkness. The rain had not stopped. Yet, strangely, I felt neither cold nor hungry—only remarkably peaceful and at home. Stretching out upon the moist, mossy floor near the back of the cave, I slept.

When I awoke, the sun was staring into the canyon, the grasses below rippling with bright blues and greens. I could see no trace of the webs, nor their weavers. Thinking that they were invisible to my eyes without the curtain of water behind them, I felt carefully with my hands around and through the mouth of the cave. But the webs were gone. I climbed down to the river and washed, then hiked across and out of the canyon to where my cycle was drying in the sun, and headed back to my own valley.

I have never, since that time, been able to encounter a spider without feeling a great strangeness and awe. To be sure, insects and spiders are not the only powers, or even central presences, in the Indonesian universe. But they were *my* introduction to the spirits, to the magic afoot in the land. It was from them that I first learned of the intelligence that lurks in nonhuman nature, the ability that an alien form of sentience has to echo one's own, to instill a reverberation in oneself that temporarily shatters habitual ways of seeing and feeling, leaving one open to a world all alive, awake, and aware. It was from such small beings that my senses first learned of the countless worlds within worlds that spin in the depths of this world that we commonly inhabit, and from them that I learned that my body could, with practice, enter sensorially into these dimensions. The precise and minuscule craft of the spiders had so honed and focused my awareness that the very webwork of the universe, of which my own flesh was a part, seemed to be being spun by their arcane art. I have already spoken of the ants, and of the fireflies, whose sensory likeness to the lights in the night sky had taught me the fickleness of gravity. The long and cyclical trance that we call malaria was also brought to me by insects, in this case mosquitoes, and I lived for three weeks in a feverish state of shivers, sweat, and visions.

I had rarely before paid much attention to the natural world. But my exposure to traditional magicians and seers was shifting my senses; I became increasingly susceptible to the solicitations of nonhuman things. In the course of struggling to decipher the magicians' odd gestures or to fathom their constant spoken references to powers unseen and unheard, I began to *see* and to *hear* in a manner I never had before. When a magician spoke of a power or "presence" lingering in the corner of his house, I learned to notice the ray of sunlight that was then pouring through a chink in the roof, illuminating a column of drifting dust, and to realize that that column of light was indeed a power, influencing the air currents by its warmth, and indeed influencing the whole mood of the room; although I had not consciously seen it before, it had already been structuring my experience. My ears began to attend, in a new way, to the songs of birds—no longer just a melodic background to human speech, but meaningful speech in its own right, responding to and commenting on events in the surrounding earth. I became a student of subtle differences: the way a breeze may flutter a single leaf on a whole tree, leaving the other leaves silent and unmoved (had not that leaf, then, been brushed by a magic?); or the way the intensity of the sun's heat expresses itself in the precise rhythm of the crickets. Walking along the dirt paths, I learned to slow my pace in order to *feel* the difference between one nearby hill and the next, or to taste the presence of a particular field at a certain time of day when, as I had been told by a local *dukun,* the place had a special power and proffered unique gifts. It was a power communicated to my senses by the way the shadows of the trees fell at that hour, and by smells that only then lingered in the tops of the grasses without being wafted away from the wind, and other elements I could only isolate after many days of stopping and listening.

And gradually, then, other animals began to intercept me in my wanderings, as if some quality in my posture or the rhythm of my breathing had disarmed their wariness; I would find myself face-to-face with monkeys, and with large lizards that did not slither away when I spoke, but leaned forward in apparent curiosity. In rural Java, I often noticed monkeys accompanying me in the branches overhead, and ravens walked toward me on the road, croaking. While at Pangandaran, a nature preserve on a peninsula jutting out from the south coast of Java ("a place of many spirits," I was told by nearby fishermen), I stepped out from a clutch of trees and found myself looking into the face of one of the rare and beautiful bison that exist only on that island. Our eyes locked. When it snorted, I snorted back; when it shifted its shoulders, I shifted my stance; when I tossed my head, it tossed *its* head in reply. I found myself caught in a nonverbal conversation with this Other, a gestural duet with which my conscious awareness had very little to do. It was as if my body in its actions were suddenly being motivated by a wisdom older than my thinking mind, as though it was held and moved by a logos, deeper than words, spoken by the Other's body, the trees, and the stony ground on which we stood.

■ ■ ■

Questions for Further Exploration:

- What is Abram's critique of the objective sciences?

- How does Abram characterize the direct experience of humans in the everyday world?

- What is the work of "phenomenology" as conceived by Edmund Husserl? How did he counter the charge of solipsism leveled against his method?

- How does the notion of "intersubjectivity" resolve the dichotomy between subjectivity and objectivity? How does a phenomenologist characterize the "real world"?

- How is Abram's method evident in his writings about his experiences in Indonesia? What does he mean by the "the spell of the sensuous"? Have you ever experienced "the spell of the sensuous"?

344

- Compare and contrast the primary work of the modern scientist with that of the traditional shaman. With regard to their methods of understanding disease, what are the strengths and weaknesses of each? What explains Western researchers' misunderstanding of the shaman's work? To what extent is the shaman's method phenomenological?

- Consider Abram's philosophy in terms of Plato's allegory of the cave. In Abram's view, what might each of the symbols (the cave, prisoners, shadows, escapee, outside, the sun, etc.) represent? How does Abram's story of being caught in the monsoon challenge Plato's allegory?

- Free-write: What conceptual resources can phenomenology offer to those working for a shift to a more sustainable way of life?

Environmental Culture

Rationalism and the Ambiguity of Science

Val Plumwood

The Double Face of Science

Science is often identified as the ally and saviour of the environment, especially since scientists have spoken out on climate change and have added the authority of reason to environmental concern in many areas. This face is real enough: science has played an important and often crucial role in exposing environmental damage and aiding opposition to it. But modern technoscience also has an uglier but less remarked face: technoscience has contributed to producing the environmental crisis at least as much as to curing it, applying to highly complex situations and systems specialised and highly instrumentally-directed forms of knowledge whose aim is to maximise outputs, often with devastating results. Four out of five scientists now work for corporations which bring precisely such an orientation to bear: thus we can link overfishing to fisheries science and fishing technology, land salinisation and degradation to irrigation and agricultural technology, the disasters of intensive agriculture and genetic engineering to biological, agricultural and forestry science, exotic species introductions of agricultural science aimed at 'controlling pests' or maximising production to chains of indigenous extinctions, and transportation, combustion and refrigeration technology to global warming and the ozone hole. In fact to a large extent the environmental crisis *is* ratiogenic damage, the creation of technoscience aimed at increasing production without due regard for effects on larger self-regulating systems containing many unknowns.

Some would give the bad part of this technoscience complex the name 'technology' and call the good part 'science'. 'Science' then becomes a protean concept whose size and boundaries change in different contexts in a similar way to a basking reptile, expanding its form to take full credit for all the benefits of its applications when aiming to maximise its access to the sun of public funding, but retreating to a 'pure' form with minimised extension when confronted with the chilly task of taking responsibility for any damage or harm. One of the aims of such strategic boundary shifts in terminology is to maintain the ideology that 'science proper' can do no wrong by displacing attention and responsibility for any ill-effects onto externalised activities or onto parties identified as 'outside' science proper, for example, onto 'technology', or 'society' and its 'use' of science[1]. This strategy protects technoscience from critical appraisal but by the same token fails to encourage the development of self-critical thinking within technoscience. Evasive strategems of this kind cannot take the place of the responsible and ethical thinking technoscience needs and has yet to evolve.

To prioritise the kind face of technoscience over the ruthless one would be to ignore the fact that economic rationalism and productivism ensure that the research directions of technoscience are increasingly dominated by the narrowly instrumental and productivist goals of corporations, rather than by broader and more integrated knowledge agendas. If an ecosocially disembedded rational economy hand-in-hand with a sado-dispassionate productivist science were to become the twin forces shaping human history, the future would look very grim indeed. What relationship between these two can we discern here, and what forms of science might help us? Both capitalism and the state/military complex depend on technoscience to keep military and production forces ahead in competition. We might regard technoscience as involving a separable form of rationality that is influenced in various ways by the rationalist economy, or we might see closeness here as approaching identity, and view the rationalist engine of commodification that now dominates history as a hybrid form consisting of scientific reason developed and put in the service of the market under capitalism. The framework of the global order is not I think a singular, monolithic form of economic rationality which somehow selects or determines all the rest, but an oligarchy of collaborative rationalities that combine to produce outcomes that benefit associated elites, such as the ecological crisis. They work together (and sometimes against one another) as a system of interlinked rationalities in which each has some potential for independence and is not simply reducible to the economic form. But the present political context of neo-liberalism has encouraged the economic form to dominate over the others, which develop corresponding rationalist distortions.

For example scientific, political, ethical and administrative rationality failures have all played a role in producing the fishing overkill of the last two decades. This is borne out in the case of the Canadian Atlantic cod fishery, where scientific, administrative and political rationality all failed to stop over-fishing.[2] However we spell out the scenario of mutual selection, there can be no doubt that the love affair or at least excessive intimacy between technoscience and capitalism is strongly implicated in the fishery collapse scenario. Some of the effects of the capture of technoscience are illustrated in the way technology design and the research orientation of science in the fisheries case is dominated by the productivist goals of the rationalist market. Fisheries science in Canada during the period leading up to the collapse of the once-great Atlantic cod fishery in the 1990s exemplified what Rogers calls 'a production model view of nature', a reductionist conception which treats appropriate knowledge in the instrumental terms of development and production. The relationships so developed are monological because they are responsive to and pay attention to the needs of just one party to the relationship.

Such approaches are prudentially dangerous for a number of reasons. Monological approaches to nature are dangerous in the context where we press limits, especially limits we have not gauged. Another is that they are very narrow, focussing on just those aspects of the other that can be exploited rather than aiming at a more rounded form of knowledge. According to a Canadian analysis of the cod fishery collapse, 'In Canada, which exports $3 billion worth of seafood a year, research until recently focussed almost exclusively on ways to find, count, and catch more fish'.[3] Marine science here was an adjunct to maximising production goals and helped to legitimate excessive exploitation by claiming to establish safe levels that were not and could not in fact be established.[4] More basic research was neglected in favour of crudely instrumental and productivist goals— increasingly the kind of science corporations and economic rationalist bureaucrats are willing and able to find. 'In doing that' acknowledges marine researcher Richard Beamish 'we . . . sacrificed the opportunity to understand the mechanisms in the ecosystem batter'.[5] The neglect of nonproduction goals that aim to 'know the object in its fullness' feeds the mechanist illusions that nature is passive and open for the taking, and that that taking can be analysed down to some subset of self-contained technological problems that can always be solved. What is neglected in such instrumental, productivist science is hardly insignificant. Another ocean researcher states 'We think that photosynthesis and the carbon system have been affected [by overexploitation] in the eastern one-third of the Pacific, but we can't say for sure because we don't have the measurements'.[6] Narrowly instrumental, human-centred goals and methodologies aimed narrowly at prediction and control have been an established part of modern science since its inception, and can't just be written off as 'bad science'.[7]

The dominance of the economic sphere over other spheres means that scientific research and warning systems that have a potentially corrective role in the ecological crisis have themselves been largely compromised, both by this kind of crudely instrumental research direction and more directly by fear of offending privatised funding sources.[8] The outcome is that these different spheres of rationality tend to display complicity and convergence instead of correctiveness. It is a major compounding of the ecological irrationality of the rationalist economy that it is permitted to compromise potentially independent and corrective forms and sources.[9] The capture of an increasingly large part of science by the rationalist economy is part of a larger program of cooption of other systems of rationality, which I will discuss in subsequent chapters. In the case of science, mechanisms of capture range from the direct corporate sponsorship of science and employment of scientists to more indirect mechanisms of funding and political influence.

Disengagement as Sado-Dispassionate Practice

This kind of overt influence, although widespread and increasingly institutionalised, is the tip of the iceberg however;[10] the deeper conceptual structures that predispose science to such collaboration and capture are my concern here. They include basic conceptual frameworks like subject/object dualism and the demand for disengagement. In these, rationalism is again implicated, especially in the historical development of reductionist and nature-devaluing forms of scientific epistemology that make possible both the commodity form and the subservience of knowledge to it. Modern scientific knowledge prepares itself to be shaped as a servant of the corporation and the rationalist economy through endorsing sado-dispassionate rationalist models of personal objectivity as emotional neutrality and ethico-political disengagement. Such a science is aptly characterised in Brennan's terms as 'sado-dispassionate'; as we have seen, emotional neutrality or the absence of emotion in certain contexts (most obviously that of harmful experimentation) is not an admirable trait but an indication of a deep moral failing.[11] Disengagement and neutrality are as mythological in science as in the market, but the insistence on these ideals creates a commitment vacuum in science, reduces the ability to resist cooption by economic forces, and works systematically against a science committed to socially responsibility. In support of capitalist structures, modern science has invested strongly in subject/object dualism, the epistemic analogue of person/property dualism, which is basic to the commodification of nature. Methodologies of disengagement licence ratiogenic domination and damage to the other that is studied, an ethically-minimising stance with respect to that order, and neglect of the need for responsible and self-critical methodologies. Alternative forms of science are both possible and necessary for survival.

The concept of scientific disengagement is a powerful constituting and normative mythology for science, and perhaps, given the strong and continued gendering of reason/emotion dualism in dominant global culture, the one that most strongly marks science out as a masculinist activity. The rationalist construction of disengagement as objectivity demands the exclusion of considerations which have to be left out or put aside as corrupting in order to achieve a properly objective judgment. Objectivity is usually seen as excluding the emotional, the bodily, the particular, the personal, and of course especially the 'political'. Rationalist influences devaluing the body and emotionality and identifying them as feminine are clearly influential here. Although there is now a great deal of work which shows that the ideology accords poorly with actual scientific practice and scientific discovery,[12] the ideology of objectivity has its uses, one of them being the facilitation of control by privileged social groups, and this ideology shows no sign of weakening.

Interpretations of objectivity as oppositional to the body and the emotions (both thought of as forms of nature) have a long pedigree in rationalist thought. In Platonic rationalism, knowledge is gained in spite of the body, which is interpreted as a hindrance to knowledge. In later Cartesian rationalism, the ideal of knowledge as freedom from doubt and as objectivity is also interpreted as freedom from the body and its deceptions, weaknesses and hindrances, its personal and emotional ties.[13] Knowledge, interpreted oppositionally as pure thought, involves setting aside 'all distractions and passions which obscure thinking'.[14] Obstacles to knowledge according to such a rationalist interpretation include not only animality and the body itself, (both coded as female), but also material reality, practical activity, change, the emotions, sympathy, and subjectivity.

As Evelyn Fox Keller points out, the insistence on such a concept of impartiality or disengagement imposes a rigid barrier between subject and object which excludes relationships of care, sympathy and engagement with the fate of what is known, constructing connection as a source of error and the object known as alien to the knower. Such knowledges involve monological relationships: they imply the closure of the knower to the known, for the knower is construed as one who can change the other to make it conform to desire but who cannot be themselves changed by this other. The other can be known completely, and in the absence of consent— knowledge can be wrung from it, as a form of power over it. The withholding of recognition and respect (as forms of engagement), and the adoption of an ethically exclusionary or amoral knowledge stance towards the world, leaves the field for mechanism and for instrumentalism towards the object of study. The ruling out of care and respect as foundations for the knowledge relationship dictates an instrumentalising politics in which what is known becomes a means to the knower's ends, whether through direct manipulation or through simply figuring in the knower's schemes as a 'case', an experimental or observational means to intellectual or academic gratification or advancement. Apologists for rationalist science such as Hayward[15] picture the role of Enlightenment science in terms of the Hero of Reason overcoming human-centredness; however, such disengaged forms of science not only cannot challenge, but are actually major supports for human-nature dualism and human-centred worldviews.

In the absence of care and respect for what is studied and of responsibility to those who will be affected by it, it is inevitable that the knowledge relation is constructed as one in which the known is merely a means to the knower's ends or to the ends of power which they, in the absence of respect and care, will come to serve. The presence of a politics is particularly clear when the item known is itself threatened, and especially when it is threatened for ratiogenic reasons, as a direct result of what has been learnt about it. The politics of the emotionally-neutral anthropologist who does not care whether the indigenous people he or she studies are harmed or not through their knowledge-gathering illustrates this clearly, as does the politics of the natural scientist whose work opens the way for destructive exploitation of what is studied. Power is what rushes into the vacuum of disengagement; the fully 'impartial' knower can easily be one whose skills are for sale to the highest bidder, who will bend their administrative, research and pedagogical energies to wherever the power, prestige and funding is. Disengagement then carries a politics, although it is a paradoxical politics in which an appearance of neutrality conceals capitulation to power.

The objective knower must not only deny all relationship to and care for what they know, but also deny any elements which would 'locate' them or their perspective to present themselves and their knowledge as absolute and transcending location. The limits and social shaping of knowledge imposed by the knower's identity and their cultural or personal 'slant' or 'set' are disappeared in the presentation of such a knowledge as emerging from a universal perspective, or as transcending perspective, as 'the view from nowhere'.[16] One does not have to be an extreme epistemological relativist to reject these sorts of accounts of knowledge which disappear the knower. All viable and current epistemological theories have had to concede that the knower is active not only in seeking and selecting observational input but in constructing knowledge, that knowledge is a social activity, not the passive and 'neutral' reception of raw, 'pure' observational data by presocial individuals. The impossibility of fully unlocated and disengaged knowledge means that the demand for objectivity as disengagement in practice translates as the demand that there be no visible engagement.

This framework of disengagement is hegemonic, cloaking privileged perspectives as universal and impartial, and marking marginalised perspectives as 'emotional', 'biased' and 'political'. The 'value-free' stance will normally be taken to involve accepting the effects of power, since the powerful have the advantage of inertia, whereas the oppressed must act to disrupt the *status quo* from a passion for change. The demand for disengagement thus tends to favour the perspectives of the powerful, who have only to announce the realities created by power and to employ the well-practiced conceptual and emotional distancing mechanisms which legitimate the exploitation of the objectified and oppressed. The rationalist interpretation of objectivity as it stands is a mystifying notion that is useful in enabling dominant groups to pass their interests off as universal.[17] A less hegemonic form of scientific rationality and interpretation of objectivity could give us a more accountable and less dangerous science.[18]

My ethico-epistemological proposition is that knowledges that involve injustice to those who are known do not provide accurate or ethically acceptable forms of knowledge. Additionally, that the sado-dispassionate mode is prudentially irrational, especially as an ecological mode. We need, both for prudential and ethical reasons, for our own sakes and that of earth others, to develop communicative and caring rational and social forms and to cast off monological and sado-dispassionate forms—especially sado-dispassionate science, in favour of ones that affirm and nurture the earth. As Sandra Harding has pointed out, a 'purely rational' science that could somehow stand apart from all values could not be ethically or socially responsible or counter centric frameworks and values that reduce prospects for scientific accuracy. It could not distance itself from projects which are conceived in racist and sexist terms, such as those of Nazi science.[19] It is a very serious drawback of the presentation of knowledge as absolute and transcending location that it hinders self-critical forms of engagement which can acknowledge the limitations of particular knowledge locations and place the subject of knowledge on the same critical, causal plane as the objects of knowledge.[20] In the context of the ratiogenic complicity of science in over-exploitation, self-critical forms are surely what we need. As Harding argues, there are much more effective dialogical ways to counter partial and distorted beliefs that do not demand a generalised emotional detachment—for example in the form of dialogical contexts in which those most likely to be affected by and able to detect forms of bias (for example, women and other Others) are able to contest centric and undemocratic constructions of science. A more dialogical and less hyper-separated interpretation of the subject/object relationship together with a dialogical interpretation of objectivity would give us a better, more democratic and communicative form of scientific rationality, and one less open to capture by those economic forces that increasingly rule our world.

This kind of analysis points towards a complex, connected set of rationality failures linked to rationalism as the main factors in the fisheries collapse. In the background, high levels of human-centredness (as I will argue in Chapter 5, a prudential hazard) create blindspots, general lack of awareness in the dominant culture of ecological embeddedness, nature's agency and limits, and human dependency on the non-human sphere. Maximising economic rationalism is insensitive to or discounts ecological ill-effects, is inflexible and requires the constant 'throughput' of nature. There are other potentially corrective warning and control systems which might act as a check, (for example techno-bureaucratic and scientific rationality). But they either have their own reasons for seeking an economic maximisation,[21] or they are dominated and corrupted by economic forces and actors. All these players, including economic rationality, encourage and select for monological forms of scientific rationality which are strongly human-centred and consider non-human lives to be replaceable and sacrificeable. They reinforce narrow scientific goals of prediction and control, an orientation to instrumentalism and domination, an ethically-minimising stance for nature, and a minimally self-reflective science. We are dealing here with a set of systematic, self-reinforcing distortions to which the distortions of economic rationality are central, especially at present, but which are not simply reducible to a single factor or 'driver', and which combine and collaborate to produce the ecological crisis.

The Subject/Object Divide and the Ambiguity of Science

We have noticed that these economic forms go hand-in-hand with and select in favour of monological forms of science. Not only the history of science, but most of its theory and conceptual methodology, being based ultimately in rationalism, collude in endorsing monological forms. The radical separation of the subject of knowledge from its object is an epistemological foundation stone of monological science, of the commodification of nature, and of capitalism, one cemented in place by rationalist readings of surrounding concepts that devalue nature and treat it as replaceable. In this form of monological and dualistic thinking,[22] subjects set themselves radically apart from objects of knowledge in a way that refuses objects elements of commonality, mind or intentionality. The 'object' is an intentional nullity, never itself a reciprocal knower or active in disclosing knowledge, never itself the subject of a narrative we can hear. In the subject/object division the 'object' is treated as passive, the one acted upon, and the knower is the active party who forces knowledge from the reluctant or mute object. This passification of the objectified is a prelude to their instrumentalisation; since as a vacuum of agency, will and purpose, they are empty vessels to be filled with another's purpose and will. As a corollary to this passification, the subject/object division backgrounds or denies the agency of the one studied and any limits respect for this might impose on the knower. This kind of relationship fits very well with the treatment of knowledge as power over the one conceived as object; it is a monological account of the knowledge relationship because it is never envisaged as potentially reciprocal and because qualities of mind, activity and agency are assumed to fall onto one side, the side of the knower. In subject/object dualism we can recognise the distinctively 'modern' mechanistic view of nature as a purely material world empty of agency, mind and purpose, a 'clockwork' background to the master narrative of human consciousness and endeavour.

Evelyn Fox Keller has briefly outlined an account of the gendered development of this arrogant and monological approach to knowledge.[23] I will interpret and elaborate on this a little differently to bring out its rationalist origins and influences. The classical rationalist tradition, as we have seen, holds reason to be the supreme good in and the supreme force driving the universe, and sees human reason or intellect as the only proper basis of human knowledge and human culture. Reason, coded as male, maintains itself in a precarious and hostile relationship with the corrupted world of 'nature', thought of as the domain of emotionality, the senses, and the sphere of biological changes, of 'coming to be and passing away'. In this form nature, the body and the biological 'world of changes' were associated with women and other lower groups such as slaves and 'barbarians' or non-Greeks, in contrast to a strongly separate, higher realm of reason, ideas and 'spirit' associated with elite, Greek men. In this schema, the corrupted sensory and material world must be too unworthy to provide real knowledge, just as it cannot provide real love.

Knowledge is the product of reason, not of the senses or the body. Platonic rationalism held the proper locus of knowledge to be the semi-divine rational laws, the abstract and eternal mathematical and celestial bodies. These lent their rational prestige to knowledge and could be known by human reason as (male) like to (male) like. The rational, celestial realm is seen as active in disclosing knowledge, which is symbolically depicted as an erotic relationship of mutuality between male subjects of equal status.[24] True knowledge is knowledge of this higher realm, and the proper attitude of the knower to the known is respect, awe and wonder.[25] Plato thus delineates a highly respectful form of knowledge that can be interpreted as a subject–subject relationship but with a highly restricted cast of high prestige rational 'subjects' in what is now the 'object of knowledge' position. These are treated as other subjects rather than as objects, and are seen as active rather than as passive in the creation of knowledge. However despite this feature, it is essential not to universalise or romanticise the Platonic account: this true form of knowledge can be gained only when reason is maximally separated from the lower realm of the body and the senses, and is not available at all for the lower, material and sensory world of nature (coded female). And its male-to-male erotic imagery is 'respectful' in a highly exclusionary and non-extendable way, in contrast to the debased eroticism of sex with women, who, like the sensory world, are unworthy.

Rationalist interpretations of knowledge as a matter of the authority of rational tradition, of theory and principle rather than of observation and sense perception remain dominant until the great empiricist transition of the Enlightenment, uneasily so in their latter period. In the key movement which makes modernity and manipulative technoscience possible, Enlightenment empiricism shifts the locus of knowledge to the lowly material objects which the older Platonic rationalism held to be incapable of providing knowledge and to be unworthy of proper rational study. But although empiricism challenges this facet of the rationalist knowledge model, what it fails to challenge is the lowly status rationalism accorded the material and sensory realm, summed up in its symbolic status as female. It leaves this feature of its parent tradition unaltered, and instead recasts and regenders the knowledge relationship itself as a subject/object type of relationship between superior and inferior, between a rational active subject of knowledge, both typically and symbolically coded as male, and a mindless passive object of knowledge coded as female.

Empiricist philosophers and scientists re-present knowledge in terms of a new model which retains the nature-devaluing features of the old but which unlike the old now validates the pursuit of empirical knowledge. In this new model, knowledge of the inferior material and sensory sphere is not to be sought for its own sake, as in the rationalist model, but is strongly associated with power and manipulation. Male knowers are seen as wringing empirical knowledge from a nature pictured as a debased and passive female slave tortured to yield up her secrets. Because this model retains so many key features of rationalism there is a case for viewing it as a 'rationalist-empiricist' tradition rather than as an independently empiricist one.[26] In general terms, the Enlightenment transition that constitutes the empirical turn moves from a respectful model of knowledge directed towards a very restricted range of collaborating abstract subjects coded male to a disrespectful model directed towards an unrestricted range of passified objects in nature, coded female.

This puts a different light on the remarkable rash of metaphors presenting knowledge as sexual violence that emanated from early modern scientists in the newly enlightened empiricist mould, in which nature is depicted as a pliant female from whom knowledge is to be wrung by force. Through 'inquisition' and 'interrogation' Nature 'with all her children' is to be conquered and subdued, bound to service and made a slave.[27] In her classic 1980 book *The Death of Nature,* Carolyn Merchant contrasts the mechanistic account of nature arising with the Enlightenment with earlier respectful and organic models of nature as a living, maternal being. We can however see the articulation of these images of sexual violence as expressing *both* the shift from the organic model (present in both peasant and pre-urban European and indigenous non-European contexts) to the modern mechanistic model and *also* the shift from the rationalist to the rationalist-empiricist model of knowledge more influential among intellectual groups. What they indicate especially is the movement away from a respectful model to a power perspective.[28] This revolution opens the way for our modern view of nature as a purely material world empty of agency, mind and purpose, the 'object' or 'clockwork' background to the master element of human consciousness and endeavour. This arrogant model of knowledge as forced or tricked from a mindless and passive nature by a superior exclusively active and rational human mind replaces earlier rationalist models in which human reason meets its match in an actively disclosing, rational celestial world which evokes awe, wonder and a sense of human limitation from the knower. The new model in contrast evokes from the knower a sense of human superiority to nature and of freedom from its limits. The empirical object of knowledge remains unworthy, as in the older rationalist tradition, but its investigation can be justified in instrumental terms, as enabling the rationalisation of the world in ways beneficial to human knowers.

The modern rationalist-empiricist model is explicitly about power, instrumentalism, individualism, and human-centredness. The 'empire of man over things' (now 'mere things') becomes the explicit aim of the new subject/object science.[29] As we have seen, knowledge, instead of being a collaborative effort between knower and known, in part the creation of a nature conceived as rationally knowable, is reconceived as entirely the creation of a rational (male) knower who monopolises agency and reason. Since the knowledge forced from a passive nature by human effort is seen as generated exclusively by the work of the human knower, it can in effect be owned by that knower and be used for ends that are of benefit exclusively to that owner. Knowledge is simultaneously instrumentalised and privatised, open to be harnessed to private economic power.[30]

Most of all, the Enlightenment model, despite its orientation to external nature, makes the knowledge relationship monological and strongly anthropocentric, appropriating not only knowledge itself but its fruits and ends exclusively for the human. The ambition to 'establish and extend the power and dominion of the human race itself over the universe' is lauded as wholesome and noble, more so than any mere national or clan-based ambition.[31] In the monological modernist version of arrogant and anthropocentric knowledge, the hyper-separation between the subject and object positions in the knowledge relation, between human reasoner and non-human 'object', is now strongly marked. Not only are knowers as a group more strongly equated with the category of the human (since nothing now is willingly 'given' by nature), but both slave and machine models express the denial to nature of any uniqueness, agency and power. Both power and agency in the knowledge relation are exclusive to the scientific knower, the subject whose knowledge is construed as a means to power over another defined as object. As subject the knower is unique, agentic and has intrinsic value, but as an object of knowledge nature is passive, replaceable and has only instrumental value. A nature represented in mechanistic terms as inferior, passive and mindless, whose only value and meaning is derived from the imposition of human ends, is simply replaceable by anything else which can serve those ends equally well—it can be reduced and regimented, the more so as those ends are defined in monological and minimally interactive terms. As you wipe out one species of fish, it can be replaced with another, in theory without limit.

In the new Cartesian fantasy of mastery, the new human task becomes that of remoulding nature to conform to the dictates of this form of reason and achieving salvation on earth rather than in heaven, since man now becomes his own god. It is now through science rather than religion that man will achieve salvation, in the form of freedom from death and bodily limitation.[32] This doctrine is not just an abstract past concept but an active present ideology which touches all our lives. Arrogant monological knowledge is an effective tool for colonising programs which organise the world in favour of dominant elites; it can draw on older traditions in which knowledge is the most valuable thing in the universe, as well as on older rationalist assumptions concerning the primitive nature of women, indigenous and non-white peoples, to help shape the arrogant knowledge agendas of establishing gender and racial supremacy which were so influential in nineteenth century colonial science.[33] But it can also contribute to and draw on newer forms of domination. Its vision of mastery and salvation remains the underlying project of research into space colonisation and into genetic engineering, cloning and other life-extending technologies that seem set to further entrench a privileged 10 per cent at the eventual expense of immense ratiogenic harm to both human social groups and the earth's environment. Modernist science seems to lack any alternative imaginary that would allow it to forsake the rationalist-empiricist vision of the Enlightenment, even as its sinister aspects become more apparent.

Resolving the Ambiguity of Science: Integrating the 'Two Cultures'

What seems particularly useful in this understanding of the rationalist-empiricist transition of the Enlightenment is that, in addition to allowing us to put culturally dominant traditions of rationalism back into the explanatory picture, it clearly signposts an alternative road not taken, which appears as an uncompleted task for modernist science and its understanding of the subject-object division. The obvious question this kind of historical account throws up is: instead of accepting the original rationalist devaluation of non-human nature as too unworthy to provide knowledge, and recasting the empirical knowledge relationship towards nature in terms of superior/inferior and subject/object, as rationalist-empiricism does, why not take the other option, to challenge and recast the nature-devaluing aspect of rationalism and retain something like the mutualistic subject/subject relationship of the later Plato's vision—but now with a broader focus on the natural world rather than the ideal/abstract world? This alternative[34] then would aim for a form of subject/subject relationship more like that of Platonic rationalism—but without its restriction to rational objects of knowledge. It would be able to recast knowledge as a relationship of awe and wonder and nature as something to be known for its own sake, not just as a means to power over it or for the benefit of human beings.

Now this project is not a minor piece of conceptual technofix, rather it involves a major cultural project with ramifications through many areas beyond science and epistemology. To begin with, in making a respectful extension to include the world of nature it is essential to rework the Platonic male-to-male gender coding of the Platonic knowledge relationship. Since this coding makes knowledge an exclusionary relationship in which the respect due to the ideal male-coded realm gains its prestige and meaning in contrast to the disrespect extended to its contrast class in the female-coded material realm, we cannot simply extend the prestige of the hard form to the soft by adding in this latter class.[35] The implications for a larger cultural project of communicative and non-exclusionary ethical forms of relationship are explored in later chapters. For knowledge, the possibility of developing the alternative road not taken that would lead to a respectful orientation towards nature rather than the dominant manipulative one suggests a major epistemic and cultural program. In this project, a subject/subject knowledge orientation would legitimate and be expressed in different methodologies of reciprocity, generosity and communication, in place of the monological methodologies of reduction and human-centredness that abound in contemporary subject/object science. These reductionist projects include the minimisation of nature's mindfulness and agency (Ockemism)[36] and the maximisation of human empire and control at the expense of the rest of creation. They include also the assumption that the 'object' of knowledge lies outside the bounds of ethics, which is concerned exclusively with the human. This program too is pursued in later chapters of this book.

When we try to explore this alternative subject/subject road however, we soon discover that it is blocked off by a series of knowledge structures that owe their origins to the very same problem. These structures enforce a rationalist-influenced division, this time in the form of the 'two cultures' disciplinary divisions that frame the very foundations of western knowledges and which are based themselves on the very subject/object division we are trying to think our way around.[37] Development of the socially responsible and reflexive forms of knowledge that are so essential for democratic and ethical outcomes is impeded by the great split in the western episteme between the two cultures, corresponding to the split between nature (science) on the one hand and culture (philosophy and the humanities, cultural studies) on the other. It is not that the existence of multiple cultures of knowledge is itself problematic—multiple knowledge cultures can legitimately reflect different kinds of experiences and life orientations—but rather that the way the field is partitioned dualistically into the particular gender- and nature-coded forms I have identified hides from us certain hybrid possibilities and inhibits the development of certain mixed forms that are crucial for an ethically integrated science and an ecologically-integrated humanities knowledge field.

The idea that we humans are completely immersed in a self-enclosed sphere of our own we can call 'culture' while non-humans are part of a non-ethical sphere of 'nature' is the leading assumption that corresponds to and structures these disciplinary exclusions.[38] Indeed the problem can be taken to lie just as much in this concept of culture as in the concept of nature. The idea that human life takes place in a self-enclosed, completely humanised space that is somehow independent of an inessential sphere of nature which exists in a remote space 'somewhere else' is of course a major expression of culture/nature dualism. Its variant, human/nature dualism, has told us that there are totally separate narratives here with totally different casts of characters. The ecological crisis is forcing us to see that our apparent human immunity from the Heraclitean ecological narrative of nature is an illusion—that we too are positioned equally and along with the whole cast of non-humans in the drama of the ecological world of populations, species, and the flows of the food chain. The crumbling of human/nature dualism is also making us aware of our relationships with non-humans as subject to ethics as much as ecology. Both kinds of narratives must now be seen as applying to both groups; all our lives are situated in both culture and nature. We an no longer retain the comfortable human-centred illusion of separate casts of characters in separate dramas. Our disciplinary structures must reflect that knowledge.

Hyper-separation is also maintained by the same rationalist-empiricist collaboration we have analysed as lying behind the subject/object division, which has given us a corresponding hyper-separated division between the sciences and humanities. We find in the 'humanities' a form of knowledge that is subject/subject in orientation, which treats the other studied as a mindful, intentional or 'subjective' being who is the subject of a life narrative, and with whom we can experience solidarity and sympathy. This form of knowledge, however, conventionally sees its subject matter as confined to the human, and as extending to the non-human only in indirect and derivative ways. The non-human is supposed to be the sphere of the 'objective', of 'hard science' where subject/object constructions reign supreme. The ground of the 'eco-humanitis' and the subject-subject sciences we wish to reclaim has been artfully disappeared by these disciplinary divisions. Thus dualistic construction frames in hyper-separated terms the familiar distinction between subjective and objective realms, the first term identifying the 'soft' areas of 'cultural studies' and the humanities, the second the allegedly 'hard' areas of the natural sciences.[39] The first is conceived as a female-coded, self-reflective, positional form of knowledge oriented to the study of the human sphere, emphasising interpretation and relativity of construction, and leaning professionally towards a culture and philosophy of idealism as opposed to realism. Its focus on social construction and humanistic knowledge appears to exclude more than a passing and indirect concern with or for non-human nature, which tends to be identified as an extension of the human or social (it can be covered in terms 'nature writing' for example, a human study). The second identifies itself as a male-coded, superior 'hard' form, devoid of emotional or positional impurities and able to give detached consideration to external objects of knowledge. The non-human as subject misses out both ways, since it can appear only indirectly in the subjectively-oriented forms and only as object in the objectively-oriented ones.

In fact in this dominant conception, these dualised epistemic forms are not only hyper-separated (as we have seen, there is in fact far more continuity between these 'hard' and 'soft' realms of knowledge than dominant modes of conceiving them admit) but distorted in other reciprocal and complementary ways, in the same way as gender codes of the masculine and feminine self and hyper-separated and reciprocally distorted in multiple ways. If the 'soft' form, coded as feminine, is supposedly locked inside subjectivity and confined to internal forms of human self-knowledge that effectively exclude a concern with non-human nature, the canons of the second form that orient it exclusively to a hard external nature ensure that it is poorly able to reflect critically on itself and its positional aspects, since it has built its contrasting identity on 'objectivity', interpreted as the irrelevance of the subject's positionality and total exclusion of emotional and caring involvement.[40]

What we have is a science that is monological, instrumental, that has been encouraged not to question its ends, and these features make it a good servant of power. What we *need* for a viable future is an integrated democratic science that is dialogical, non-reductionist and self-reflective—a science that can bring itself and its ends under critical and democratic scrutiny. We need above all an *ethical* science; sado-dispassionate science has used the ideology of disengagement to wall itself off from ethics just as effectively as capitalism has done through the ideology of the private sphere. Both 'hard' and 'soft' forms are inadequate for the purpose of integrating ethics with the attempt to gain knowledge of non-human nature. The technoscientific form is prevented from attaining self-reflective and ethically integrated knowledges, to the extent that interrogation of the knower's own affiliations or limitations of perspective is inadmissible, along with ways to address 'soft' questions of ethics and responsibility. The softer 'feminine' literary paradigm which is often counter-asserted in postmodernism is only rarely able to break out of the limitations of enclosure within a human-centred epistemic idealism and use/mention confusion which makes everything thinkable into a human construction.[41] Since each form of knowledge operates by different canons and tends to define itself against the other, integration to create an ethically responsible form of technoscience and a form of the humanities not dedicated to human-self enclosure is especially difficult. The emphasis in hard, tough and cynical forms of science on ensuring that nature does not 'fool' us leads to a stress on manipulative experimental design and the control of nature, but relatively little effort goes into considering the equally important issue of whether and how we, the knowers, might be fooling ourselves, how our knowledge frameworks and perspectives may be limited or distorted by our sado-dispassionate ethical and epistemic positioning.

As an alternative to these dominant projects of domination, we can glimpse further, as yet only partially formally articulated, care models of knowledge that open up new possibilities for responsible forms of science and that empower rather than disempower ethical and socially engaged perspectives. Breaking the hold of the subject/object division is a big help; to begin with, we can turn to certain kinds of imaginative literature which write nature as agent, re-subjectivising and re-intentionalising the non-human as an ethical and intentional subject of narrative. This need not always be as radically intentionalising as Aldo Leopold's encounters with thinking mountains or Thoreau's with heraldry among the lichens, but it can still speak arrestingly of agency, learning, creativity and design among such 'spectacular beings' as winged dinosaurs, as in the scientific writing of Eric Rolls or the nature writing of Annie Dillard.[42] Although these blended genres do not as yet have the prestige of 'tough' science, they can help us retell the mechanistic narratives told by reductionist science in more memorable, more generous and more helpful ways. As well as imaginative science, we need corresponding narratives that can situate humans ecologically, as in the new discipline of environmental history and in the ecological humanities more generally.

We can also turn for help in envisaging a non-reductionist science and a compassionate and democratic rationality to disciplinary practices of care for the other that is studied. Anthropology is a discipline that sits astride the divide between subject/object and subject/subject orientation, and which has been challenged greatly in recent years to reconsider the subject/object model. Its highly articulate indigenous 'objects of study' have placed it under notice to move towards a subject/subject model in which knowledge is based on the consenting and cooperative disclosure of other active subjects, and which carries an ethic of care for, attention and accountability to those who are studied. In this case, those in the 'object' position speak of how and under what conditions they would wish to be studied as subjects, and in this they can be taken to speak also for others in the 'object' position and to define the conditions for an ethical and dialogical subject-subject knowledge relationship. The discipline of anthropology and its new-found ideals of respect, solidarity with and advocacy for an actively disclosing other to whom the student attends could provide a counter-framework to models of disengagement, disrespect, over-manipulation and reductionism that remain characteristic of the monological nature-oriented tradition of 'hard science' we have been tracing. The role of anthropologists employing rationalist subject-object models in the abuse of the Yanomami people of the Amazon detailed in Patrick Tierney's *Darkness in El Dorado* has been taken as a case of science illegitimately using methodologies for human subjects it should keep confined to non-human animals. Rather than being interpreted as a reason to further hyper-separate the treatment of humans from the treatment of non-humans, such cases provide an occasion to rethink the whole subject-object mode of knowledge, for both human and non-human subjects.

Realising the potential for an ethically-integrated science of care and responsibility means moving beyond the knowledge dualisms to an integrated form of knowledge which is able to escape the dualisms of subject/object, hard/soft and reason/nature. Caring rationalities are among the forms of ethical engagement made visible by a framework of scientific rationality that is socially engaged and accountable, but the term can also serve to identify an alternative model that resists the dominant sado-dispassionate rationalities. Caring rationality sees ethics and social responsibility as a crucial part of science and of the scientist's task, to be integrated at all levels, including especially that of the individual researcher. Some individual scientists may already operate wholly or partially within dialogical and care models rather than in the theoretically dominant frameworks demanding ethical and emotional disengagement and objectification, finding in the nature they study the basis for awe and environmental commitment rather than instrumentalism and an inflated sense of self.[43] Nevertheless the powerful monological models I have outlined above represent ideologies the dialogical model will have to displace in both practical and theoretical terms if it is to be re-born as a general institutional practice of science rather than remain as the unrecognised and largely disempowered personal ethical ideal of some individual knowers.

The subject/object doctrines of the disengagement of the knower and the passivity of the known not only help create the two cultures split that impedes the development of an ethical science, but are also leading assumptions behind the over-reliance on manipulative strategies for knowledge-gathering that helps to create the problem of ratiogenic damage in experimentation. Over-reliance on experimental manipulation is often supported by the contemporary institutional context in which knowledge is produced, which gives rise to unreflective adherence to legitimating formulae and professional intellectual schedules. This context for knowledge replaces the breadth of observation and experience of nature that could inspire the ideas of a Darwin and a Humboldt. In the knowledge factory situation, an emphasis on manipulative scientific study which rear-ranges nature according to rigid, set formulae sanctified as 'methodology' can make observation almost indistinguishable from the control of nature.

There is a strong convergence between contemporary manipulative models and the Baconian model in which nature is tricked or forced into disclosing information that is wrung from her with the destruction and travail of rearrangement. The manipulative model thus in effect assumes a passive nature and closes itself to the possibility that nature itself discloses and can be a partner in the production of knowledge.[44] In contrast, there are dialogical models of scientific discovery which treat nature as active in the production of knowledge, and articulate ethical and social engagement with respect for what is studied. When Darwin speaks of the Galapagos as 'the great laboratory of evolution', or when Humboldt speaks of rocks and pumice as speaking the history of the earth, we are encountering a practice of treating nature as active in the production of knowledge, as inviting the attentive observer to receive her disclosures.[45] The dialogical paradigm stresses instead communicative methodologies of sensitive listening and attentive observation, and of an open stance that has not already closed itself off by stereotyping the other that is studied in reductionist terms as mindless and voiceless.

■ ■ ■

Questions for Further Exploration:

- What is Plumwood's critique of techno-science? How does she refute those who defend the method of "pure" science by distancing it from its "use" by "outside" parties?

- Plumwood finds many forms of rationality at work in the world. What forms of rationality does she identify, and how does she distinguish them? How does each of these forms of rationality conceptualize "nature"?

- What are the conceptual structures that predispose science to corporate capture and how do they work? What is "the ideology of objectivity"? What values are embedded in the conception of scientific rationality that claims to be "value-free"?

- What values does Plumwood believe should be incorporated in a better form of scientific rationality? What examples does she give to help illustrate her alternative?

- How does the culture/nature dualism embedded in the disciplinary structures of higher education thwart the development of this alternative?

- Free-write your response to Plumwood's feminist critique of the dominant form of scientific objectivity.

Green Reason: Communicative Ethics for the Biosphere

John Dryzek

Introduction

The fields of environmental ethics and politics are currently home to a variety of lively and radical challenges to established institutions, practices, and moralities. Although deep ecologists, animal rights activists, ecofeminists, social ecologists, Heideggerians, pantheists, sociobiologists, and others find much to disagree about, they are united by rejection of the narrowly anthropocentric and utilitarian world views of industrial society and liberal morality. Unfortunately, however, the nefarious aspects of this rejected status quo can creep back in quietly through the back door in the form of what may be termed the subversion of ethics by epistemology. This subversion can be anticipated to the extent that an environmental ethic fails to attend fully to issues of knowledge and rationality. While connections between ethics and epistemology are readily identified (at least at the level of metaethics), in practice (i.e., at the level of applied ethics . . .) epistemology is often ignored. This neglect may be safe enough in many fields of human endeavor, but when it comes to the environment the oversight is dangerous. In this paper, I seek to correct this oversight and so close the back door.

One may expect the undermining of ethics by epistemology to the extent that an environmental ethic consorts—whether by design, accident, or oversight—with exclusively instrumental notions of reason.[1] The association with instrumental rationality applied most obviously if the ethic in question is seen as providing only the ends for instrumental actions; however, absolute prohibitions and compulsions (concerning, for example, respect for the rights of natural environments) are not immune, for such directives operate and make sense only in an environment of instrumental action—if only as constraints upon this action.

I begin my argument by outlining the threat to both the environment and environmental ethics posed by the lingering grip of instrumental reason. The search for a solution usually begins with the popular nostrum of ecological spirituality. I argue for a different cure, one that expands rationality to encompass communicative practices. Even though contemporary proponents of communicative rationality proceed in exclusively anthropocentric terms, a recognition of agency in the natural world, which a number of recent scientific developments point to, can overcome this limitation and render communicative rationality fit to regulate human dealings with the environment.

The Rational Roots of Environmental Decay

It can be argued that instrumental rationality underlies our current environmental predicament. Instrumental rationality, on this account, invokes a Cartesian dichotomy between subject and object. The human mind is subject; all else—including the natural world, and other people—consists of objects, to be manipulated, therefore dominated, in the interests of the mind's desires. Instrumental rationality is therefore abstract, estranged from nature (and society) and estranging to the extent that we subscribe to it. The expansion of this kind of rationality is often associated with the Enlightenment's disenchantment of the world, which paves the way for the destruction of that world for the sake of utility and industrialization at the hands of an arrogant humanism.[2] Ecofeminists equate such practices with patriarchal and masculine epistemology, which predates the Enlightenment by several thousand years.

The upshot is that in using the technological powers in our hands to turn the world to our use, we are destroying that world. No longer able to devise correctives for the proliferating secondary and tertiary effects of our instrumental interventions, we find that nature takes its revenge upon us in the form of environmental crisis.

This critique of instrumental rationality can also be extended to abstractly rational argument in favor of *general* moral principles. In this context, feminists argue that most contemporary political theory, whether liberal, Marxist, or Frankfurt School, works from a model of *man* which is universal, uniform, ahistorical, and transcendent, excluding a model of *woman* which is contextual, relational, and particularistic.[3] Ecofeminists add that the traditional model of man is alienated from natural contexts too.

One goal of environmental ethics is, of course, to generate solutions to the problems associated with our estrangement from the natural world. To what extent, then, are existing schemes crippled by their vestigial ties to exclusively instrumental rationality? Consider, first of all, deep ecology, which is claimed to be the most radically anti-anthropocentric (its critics would say misanthropic) ethic. When it comes to implementing this program, Devall and Sessions can suggest little more than that "policies must be changed."[4] In other words, instrumentally rational actions (such as population control) are commended to the very agencies (governments and other organizations) whose rationality is elsewhere condemned for contributing to environmental decay. In their inattention to the side effects of their proposed strategies Devall and Sessions are likely to discover that their ends are subverted by their means.

Further examples of a lingering stress on instrumental reason are readily identifiable. In his classic argument for the rights of natural objects, Stone asks that these rights be embodied in law—a system of instrumental-analytic rationality *par excellence*.[5] Lemons suggests that we take ideas promulgated by natural science, such as homeostasis and diversity, as the basis for an environmental ethic—and, implicitly, as the end for instrumental manipulations.[6]

A subtle extension of the dialectic of Enlightenment may come into play here. According to Horkheimer and Adorno, the dialectic of Enlightenment tells us that the more successful we become in securing the material conditions for human freedom (in part through control of the natural world), the more repressed we become as human subjects, unable to partake of freedom.[7] To overstate my proposed extension: the more assiduously we cultivate the ethical principles for benign but still instrumental action toward the environment, the less likely it becomes that we shall be able to reconcile ourselves to that environment in productive fashion. That is, nature will become still more firmly the "other" from which we are estranged, even if our instrumental manipulations of it are well motivated.

The challenge here then is to locate an epistemology less prone to the subversion of environmental ethics than the exclusively instrumental fixation associated with dominant (post-Enlightenment) conceptions of rationality. Another way of stating the same point is that we shold seek what Habermas disparages as the "resurrection of nature."[8] On this account, nature was not simply disenchanted by the Enlightenment—it was killed. As a result, no longer could meanings and purposes be discerned in the nonhuman world. How then may they be retrieved?

Two Ways to Resurrect Nature

Although the idea that nature merits resurrection is indeed current in the field of environmental ethics, most of those who subscribe to this idea seek resurrection through spirituality, religion, feeling, and intuition. That is, they accept the dichotomy established by Enlightenment rationalists and seek a return to pre-Enlightenment—or even prehistoric—sensibilities.

The idea that spirit is ultimately preferable to rationality is perhaps held most strongly by deep ecologists, although a host of other writers—including some critics of deep ecology—is equally enamoured of spirit and suspicious of any kind of reason. It is an easy step from condemnations of rationality to arguments for more holistic, intuitive, emotional, spiritual, or experiential "oneness" to mediate our relations with the natural world (and one another). Franciscan Christianity, Taoism, Buddhism, pagan religions, feminist spirituality, and American Indian beliefs all have their adherents and admirers.[9]

An advocacy of a particular spiritual position can be rooted in rejection of another spirituality, rather than in opposition to rationality. For example, Lynn White argues that because the source of environmental crisis is one kind of religion—specifically, the Judeo-Christian tradition that places man above nature—the solution must lie in adoption of a different kind of religion. Gary Snyder makes a similar point in bemoaning the establishment of "male deities located off the planet."[10]

Nevertheless, even if a particular spirituality is the problem, it does not follow that a different spirituality has to be the solution. Nor does it follow that if a particular rationality is the problem, then spirituality is the solution. Although the right kind of spirituality may be one answer, I argue that the right kind of rationality is a better one. I draw on the rationality debates now cutting across a variety of disciplines to argue that a broadened notion of rationality can meet the concerns of ecological antirationalists. I contend that provided our notions of rationality are expanded in the right direction, human dealings with the environment are indeed best governed by rational standards and that a regressive emphasis on spirit is therefore unnecessary. To be sure, because the rationality debates have for the most part missed the ecological dimension, some specifically green correctives must be brought to bear upon them. Thus, the kind of reason I argue for here is not only expanded beyond instrumental conceptions, but is also avowedly ecological.

The Hazards of Spiritual Alternatives

Before turning to an examination of this kind of rationality, let me identify some of the shortcomings inherent in excessive reliance upon is spiritual alternatives. Clearly an ecologically sensitive spirituality is not automatically to be commended. For an extreme negative model, we need look no further than the Third Reich and Hitler's invitation to good Aryans to think with their blood rather than their brains. Along with Teutonic mythology, Naziism embodied a peculiar kind of reverence for (German) nature and father*land*. Today's German Greens are well aware of this history, and so avoid any association with ecological spirituality.

Even if Naziism is dismissed as an irrelevant possibility involving only perversion and abuse of ecological spirituality, one can discern political dangers in the schemes of some contemporary ecological philosophers. For example, Devall and Sessions prescribe the true realization of the "self" in a larger communal "Self" of "organic wholeness" as an antidote to liberal individualism.[11] Even though the "Self" of Devall and Sessions is benign, extending beyond humanity to the natural world, willing immersion in a larger "Self" is also surely the essence of totalitarianism.

Some advocates of an ecological spirituality are impressed by the functions of myth and ritual in preliterate societies; nevertheless, as Luke points out, myth and ritual in primal societies can also form the substance of attempts to control and manipulate nature and other persons—the very sins of which instrumental rationality is accused.[12]

Although there are important differences between an earth ceremony at a gathering of contemporary environmentalists and a Nuremburg rally, spirituality as such cannot speak to these differences and help us choose one over the other. Thus, ecological spirituality by itself provides no defence against authoritarianism. As Bookchin points out, ecological religious sensibilities have often coexisted with despotic social order (as in ancient Egypt).[13]

Even if one dismisses these authoritarian possibilities to embrace a more tolerant and pluralistic spirituality, there are two reasons why any such orientation remains inadequate. First, natural systems are complex; it is a familiar adage that "everything is connected to everything else" in ecosystems.[14] It is also the case that interventions in complex systems often have counterintuitive results, as actions ramify extensively through these systems. As a result, intuitions, good intentions, and sympathetic sensibilities are insufficient guides to action. Think, for example, of the well-intentioned fire-control policies long followed in the forests of the American West which interrupted the life cycles of species and the well-being of ecosystems that depend on periodic scorching. To take another example, one might out of a reverence for all things living remove only deadwood from a forest for fuel, thereby undermining the key habitat dead trees provide.

Now it might be argued here that an appropriate spirituality could somehow be combined with a suitably tamed instrumental rationality to effectively cope with complexity. However, often ecological systems are *so* complex that they defy the efforts of instrumental rationalists to model them. In such cases, spirituality is not likely to be of much help either. I suggest below that a noninstrumental kind of reason can compensate for the deficiencies of instrumental rationality under complex conditions.

A second shortcoming of a spiritual approach is contingent on the conditions of our interactions with the natural world. One may assume that these conditions are in a state of some disequilibrium (otherwise, there would be little need to worry about environmental ethics, policies, and politics). Thus, even if a primarily spiritual orientation toward nature is adequate for maintaining an ecologically harmonious society, it contains no effective guidance about how to reach this happy state from our current plight (except perhaps through a massive exercise in spiritual empowerment). To put it crudely, there is no effective "theory of transition." Most of those who speak of ecological spirituality say little about this transition, let alone any practical political program.

Required here then is a noninstrumental capacity analogous to that of "resilience" in natural systems, which can be defined in terms of a capacity to return to stable operating range from a disequilibrium state. Natural systems can do this on their own without us. Moreover, if Lovelock is right about the ability of the planet's biota to sustain the physical conditions for all life—thereby constituting an entity he calls Gaia—these systems can also correct for many human excesses.[15] Nevertheless, larger stresses in systems with substantial human complicity require a human contribution to problem solving (as even Lovelock admits).

Communicative Reason

At this juncture we might seem in a bit of a quandary. On the one hand, instrumental rationality and abstract reasoning about values imply hierarchy and domination. On the other, spirituality is an inadequate alternative. Its inadequacy is implicitly confirmed by Spretnak, who qualifies her advocacy of green spirituality with a recognition that "holistic, or ecological, thinking is not a retreat from reason; it is an enlargement of it to more comprehensive and hence more efficient means of analysis."[16] Spretnak, of course, wishes to enlarge reason by incorporating spirituality, but, like other environmentalists who bemoan "dualistic thinking," she offers no hints as to how this might be done. In contrast, the alternative I propose is to expand reason in a different direction.

How then can an expanded, nonhierarchical conception of rationality point to what Whitebook calls a "non-regressive reconciliation with nature" that may allow us to escape from this impasse?[17] We may begin to chart this escape by noting that rationality is properly a property of community, and not just individuals, if for no other reason than that social isolates have no standards of judgment. As Dewey argues, "our intelligence is bound up . . . with the community of life of which we are a part."[18] We can describe a collective as *communicatively* rational to the extent that its interactions are egalitarian, uncoerced, competent, and free from delusion, deception, power, and strategy.[19] Communicative rationality is best thought of as a regulative ideal for human social practices, which can then be condemned to the extent of their violation of its precepts. No realizable blueprint is implied.

Most of those who recognize this kind of rationality believe it is embedded first and foremost in processes involving the creation of meaning—culture, socialization, friendship, and so forth. Nevertheless, communicative rationality may also be conducive to the resolution of complex problems, inasmuch as it promotes the free harmonization of actions by disparate individuals concerned with the different facets of such problems. Thus, communicative reason may rest more easily in a complex world than either spirituality or instrumental rationality.

One might argue that the ideal discursive community of communicative rationality is presupposed even in discussions about ecological spirituality, for if one accepts that some spiritualities have more benign ecological implications than others—and surely this is unarguable—then one needs some means of sorting them out. These mans cannot themselves be spiritual, since spirituality is internal to the schemes one is sifting. Within the Catholic schema, Catholics are right by revelation; within the pagan schema, pagans are right by revelation. Arguments across the boundaries of spiritual schemes, however, have to be reasoned arguments—of exactly the kind that proponents of such schemes deploy in the literature on environmental ethics. In deploying arguments, moreover, one is implicitly accepting the constitutive principles of a discursively rational community (however much one violates these principles in practice). My point here echoes Apel's analysis of scientific communities.[20] Apel points out that the practice of science presupposes a measure of communicative rationality within these communities. Just as scientists cannot deny their humanity, those who proclaim spirituality cannot, in this age of lost innocence, deny their rationality.

Communicative rationality as generally stated (e.g., by Habermas) is not, however, conducive to harmonious relationships with the natural world. A first defect arises from its transcendent, ahistorical leanings. In practice, all ecological contexts are different, and individuals are likely to interpret and experience them in diverse ways. This problem can be overcome by the explicit recognition of the ineliminable plurality in human discourse. In this way, communicative rationality becomes simply a *procedural* standard for human interaction, dictating no *substantive* resolution of disputes.

A second defect cuts deeper. If communication is seen merely as a property of human dealings with each other, then its rationality may co-exist easily with instrumental and dominating attitudes toward the non-human world. Indeed, Habermas proposes this coexistence as a *solution* to the problem posed by the dialectic of Enlightenment that will move critical theory beyond the impasse reached by the earlier work of Adorno and Horkheimer. Habermas tries to draw a clear line between the relationships we construct with the natural world and those we establish with one another. He avers that the only attitude toward the natural world which is fruitful in securing the material conditions for human existence is an instrumental one.[21] The domination of nature is a price that Habermas is willing to pay for fulfillment of the Enlightenment's promise of human emancipation: "the dignity of the subject . . . is attained at the price of denying all worth to nature."[22] To Habermas, there is ultimately no ontological distinction between inorganic and organic nature. A lump of iron and an ecosystem should be treated in the same terms, as objects for manipulation. Only in our relationships with other persons can instrumental rationality be overcome and communicative rationality flourish; Habermas's goal here is to "prevent social relations becoming like our relations with the natural world."[23]

Habermas believes that we can only truly know that which we have ourselves created—language—and that nature will always remain estranged and separate. We cannot truly *know* anything about nature; we can only observe the results of our interventions in it. Challenged on the potentially destructive environmental implications of this dichotomy, Habermas replies that one should not confuse ethics with epistemology.[24] Thus, he believes that an environmental ethic can be grafted onto our instrumental relations with the natural world—although, given that Habermas believes that the only entities that bear value are those which can participate in discourse, this ethic has to be anthropocentric. As a result, Habermas ends up just where the interesting problems in environmental ethics (and epistemology) begin. However, the best move here is not to reject communicative rationality, but to extend it.

From Communicative to Ecological Rationality

How may communicative rationality be extended to incorporate procedural standards which are not obviously intrinsic to human discourse, but which are essential to good order in human interactions with the natural world? One place to begin might be with the establishment of ecological principles—or ecosystem analogues—such as diversity, homeostasis, flexibility, and resilience as critical standards in human discourse. In so doing, we would not submit to nature's authority, in the manner advocates of biocentrism (the doctrine that value is created by and in natural system) sometimes seem to demand. Nor would we merely apply nature's standards to human communities. . . . Rather, individual ecological principles would always be applied, debated, redeemed, or rejected. In this sense, these principles would supplement the familiar standards intrinsic to the idea of communicative rationality (equality, noncoercion, truthfulness, etc.).

If we take away the dressing of communicative rationality, this first proposal is a bit facile, reducing as it does to advocacy of ecological principles in human debates. As such, it severs ethics from epistemology once again, though it grafts environmental ethics onto communicative, rather than instrumental, rationality. For their part, critical communications theorists would probably object that such a move is tantamount to the coercive imposition of an external, substantive, and transcendent judgment upon human discourse. One might equally well impose economic efficiency, political stability, or social harmony as a standard, for none of these principles is intrinsic to the idea of rational discourse, and so cannot be grounded in it.

How might one go about establishing the special claims of ecology upon human communication? One could start by arguing that intersubjective discourse presupposes some ecological—and not just linguistic—standards. Although it is easy to forget, our communications with one another can proceed only in and through the media made available by the natural world (in addition to our own medium of language). It is not just brute matter we are taking advantage of here, for, if Lovelock is right, the atmosphere in which we live, talk, hear, write, read, smell, and touch is composed and regulated by the planet's biota acting in concert.[25] This biota makes possible and maintains a physical environment fit for itself—and for us, and our communications. With this awareness in mind, we can no longer speak of communicative acts in a vacuum. Because any such act is made possible by this ecological system, it can be called to account in accordance with ecological standards. If indeed nature is a silent participant in every conversation, then perhaps it deserves a measure of the respect that we accord to human participants. If critical communications theorists argue that only entities capable of entering into communication can be assigned value, then there is a sense in which Gaia passes their test.

Assuming that the Gaia hypothesis holds, then we live *in* a highly differentiated, self-regulating global system whose "intelligence," which though not *conscious,* is of a complexity equal to that of any group of humans. Thus, "the Gaia hypothesis implies that the stable state of our planet includes man as a part of, or partner in, a very democratic entity."[26] Any special capabilities we do have—perhaps even, as Lovelock himself suggests, as Gaia's "nervous system and a brain"[27]—do not set us apart, but emphasize our embeddedness.

Lovelock himself equivocates between two extremes on the implications of his hypothesis for the standing of Gaia's "intelligence." On the one hand, he develops a reductionist model sufficient to explain climatic stability in the face of wide fluctuations in the flow of solar radiation. This model is demonstrated in a hypothetical "Daisyworld" populated only by light and dark daisies whose relative numbers, and hence the planet's albedo, change in response to the intensity of radiation.[28] Somewhat surprisingly, in the same volume Lovelock endorses a mystical view which interprets Gaia in religious terms.[29]

If one eschews these two extremes, then the Gaia hypothesis indicates that there is agency (but not divinity) in the natural world. But let me stress that this hypothesis and its supporting evidence are not the only indications of such agency, which can also be found at lower levels of biological organization. For example, in her discussion of the work of the celebrated geneticist Barbara McLintock, Keller argues that the key to McLintock's success is her "feeling for the organism," or, more precisely, for "the prodigous capacity of organisms to devise means for guaranteeing their own survival."[30] Thus, to McLintock, "the objects of her study have become subjects in their own right; they claim from her a kind of attention that most of us experience only in relation to other persons."[31]

To the biologist Charles Birch, this extension of subjectivity to nonhuman entities is the essence of "postmodern biology."[32] He treats "human experience as a high-level exemplification of entities in general, be they cells or atoms or electrons. All are subjects."[33] He argues that we should recognize the "self-determination exercised by natural entities in response to possibilities of their future."[34] Such an approach is also found in the work of Jane Goodall on chimpanzees and Donald Griffin on animal thinking.[35] Goodall and Griffin practice an essentially hermeneutic biology involving imaginative attempts to reconstruct the actions-in-context of other thinking beings.

Obviously there is a large gap between an "intelligent" Gaia and thinking organisms. In the early twentieth century this gap would have been handled by interpreting ecosystems as teleological entities seeking ever higher stages of ecological succession, culminating in climax. Today this superorganismic view of ecosystems is out of fashion in academic ecology, which has become thoroughly reductionistic and stochastic. Whether this epistemological commitment has more to do with academic ecology's desire for permission to worship in the temple of science than with the intrinsic superiority of the reductionist view remains an open question.

Regardless of its source, any recognition of agency in nature clearly undercuts the Cartesian subject–object dualism that legitimates the domination of nature—just as a recognition of *human* agency undermines the instrumental manipulation that legimates authoritarian politics. Nevertheless, agency in the natural world also makes the restriction of communicative rationality to purely human communities appear arbitrary. This world is not silent and passive, but *already* full of "values, purposes, and meanings," irrespective of what we ascribe to it.[36] As Abram argues, human perception can be reinterpreted in terms of reception of communication from the natural world.

In this discussion of communicative possibilities encompassing human and natural systems I have taken for granted the communicative competence of humans and sought analogues in nature; nevertheless, this issue may also be approached from the opposite direction by contemplating what is natural in humans. Human nature is not just human; it is also nature. We can communicate not only because we are human, but also because we are natural. This precondition for communicative competence applies to humans, other primates, cetaceans, and insects alike. True, human communication mechanisms, language in particular, are more elaborate than those of most other species; however, greater continuity across human and nonhuman species is evident in nonlinguistic forms of communication, such as body movements or pheromones.

If the idea of communicative interaction can indeed encompass the natural world, then so too can standards of communicative rationality. These standards, nevertheless, will not be the same as those enumerated above for speech among humans. So what standards are appropriate, and in what rational processes could such standards be embodied?

Toward a Communicative Ecological Ethic

The specification of a communicative ethic for interactions encompassing the natural world is no small task, and what follows is intended to be suggestive rather than definitive. The task becomes somewhat easier upon noting that the objective here is a set of procedural criteria to regulate actions, rather than a full resolution of the content of actions.

Any attempt at substantive resolution here would involve flirting with instrumental rationality (which, when all is said and done, is often unavoidable). Such resolution may, however, be appropriate with reference to one universal principle: respect for the perceptual media furnished by nature. This principle in turn implies special respect for any "vital organs" that sustain these media (most especially, the life-sustaining composition of the atmosphere). According to Lovelock, these organs may well be the tropical forests, wetlands, and continental shelves (we would do well to find out if they are!).[37]

For the most part, though, substantive norms will have to be contingent on time, place, and particular human and ecological circumstances. It is also worth bearing in mind that perfection is impossible. Procedural criteria should function as critical standards from which some practices depart more than others.

An approach to the specification of such criteria can begin by noting the sense in which there can be equality in interactions with the natural world. Although equality in communicative competence of the sort that one can hypothesize within human communities is out of the question here, one can still postulate equality in the minimal terms of the very ability to communicate. This recognition rules out two extremes. The first is the idea that ecological processes should be engineered by human minds that essentially transcend the natural world. This first extreme finds its culmination in the notion that a "noosphere" could supplant the ecosphere.[38] The second extreme is based on the idea that "nature knows best,"[39] carrying with it implicit rejection of the idea that human problem-solving intelligence has any meaningful role to play in environmental affairs. To avoid these extremes we need a symbiotic intelligence in which both human minds and the self-organizing, self-regulating properties of natural systems play a part.

"Intelligence" in natural systems does not arise through the existence of any communications center; Gaia may have vital organs, but she has no brain. Rather, the feedback processes which organize, regulate, and maintain natural systems are of a diffuse and internal type—signals do not pass through any central thermostat analog. Bearing in mind the principle of rough equality in communicative capability, we should be wary of highly centralized decision mechanisms—national environmental bureaucracies, multinational mining or logging corporations, international resource management agencies, and so forth—which could dominate, ignore, or suppress local ecological signals. The principle of rough equality suggests instead that diffuse feedback processes in the natural world should be matched by diffuse decision processes in human societies. This contention obviously provides further support to a presumption that "small is beautiful" in social organization—and, in practical political terms, to bioregionalism.

Obviously, though, not all of nature's feedback processes are localized. They can also be regional, even global. Think, for example, of ozone depletion or the greenhouse effect. The principle of rough equality does not limit the size and scope of political institutions in such cases. However, their designers should be careful to limit the purview of any such regional or global institutions to issues and problems which are themselves regional or global. Given the tendency of large organizations toward aggrandisement, the benefit of any doubt should probably go to the small-scale level.

Economic institutions, for their part, cannot escape size limitations so easily. Corporations whose reach is limited could not extend their operations to "pollution havens" in which they have no other interest. Similarly, the World Bank has no business making decisions for particular development projects based on universalistic, contextually inappropriate criteria. Such decisions have already led to numerous social and ecological disasters in the Third World, for example, in connection with the construction of large dams.[40]

What can we say about decision processes beyond questions of appropriate scale? Obviously there is much we do not know—and cannot know—about the workings of the natural world (and, for that matter, the human world). Thus, some kind of experimental practice in better living with the world seems to be appropriate. Yet experimentation in the image of science—manipulative, analytic, piecemeal, controlled, seeking generalizations across contexts—clearly violates the canons of communicative ethics. A more appropriate experimental practice would interpret any particular interaction of human and natural systems in terms of a complex, nonreducible, and unique entity. This kind of "holistic experimentation" (sketched in a nonecological context by Mitroff and Blankenship) makes no attempt to control conditions and keep them constant, generalize results beyond the case at hand, or distinguish between experimenters and subjects.[41] Nor does it impose any restrictions on the kinds of knowledge and perceptions admissible in experimental design, evaluation, and redesign. The trick is, of course, to extend participation in such experimentation to nonhuman entities.

This requirement returns us to the question of the perception of things natural and its relationship to communication. If in fact we can equate perception with communication, then the contemporary gross failings in human perception can be called to account by standards of communicative reason. Perceptual failure pervades industrial societies, as people simply fail to recognize the effects of their actions on the natural world (not to mention other people). Although these effects are sometimes visible, even to urban dwellers, who cannot escape the effects of pollution, in other ways nature is easy to ignore, especially by people who have no idea where and how their food is grown, or what resources go into making the goods they buy. Communicative ethics suggests improved perception.

Improvement could be sought at the level of social institutions. It is clear that small-scale, autonomous societies really do have to pay a great deal of attention to signals from their local environment. This necessity helps to explain the ecological sensibilities found in many preliterate societies: those without such orientations soon expire. These perceptual consideration obviously reinforce the argument for appropriate scale in social institutions—and in holistic experimentation.

Perceptual capabilities can also be addressed at the level of individuals. Again, it is possible to extend some critical theory notions here. In his most recent attempts to ground his theoretical project, Habermas appeals to the "reconstructive science" associated with figures such as Noam Chomsky, Lawrence Kohlberg, and Jean Piaget.[42] The stages of individual moral and cognitive development identified by Kohlberg and Piaget do, according to Habermas, serve as a fixed and true model for social evolution. Higher levels of individual development are characterized by increasing linguistic competence, by sensitivity to links with other individuals, by awareness of the interests of others—and, he adds, unfortunately, by recognition of the qualitively different status of human and nonhuman entities.[43] Again, though, Habermas has taken what are really just contingent empirical conjectures, generalized them into timeless and nonfalsifiable truths, and frozen their boundaries. Thus, he rules out the possibility that sensitivity to interconnections with the natural environment might also enter individual development. Habermas's perspective may be limited by what bourgeois society currently allows and encourages in the way of individual development, which he mistakes for timeless truth. One can imagine moral development that proceeds further.

Conclusion

By now I hope I have demonstrated the promise of a communicative episternology for environmental ethics which embraces the natural world in rational terms. There is no need here for mystical notions about spiritual communion with nature. Immersion in the world can be a thoroughly rational affair, provided we expand our notion of rationality in the appropriate directions. Reason too can be green. But clearly much remains to be done in the construction of a communicative ethics of rational interaction that embraces the natural world.

Notes

1. Instrumental rationality may be defined in terms of the capacity to devise, select, and effect good means to clarified ends.

2. D. Ehrenfeld, *The Arrogance of Humanism* (Oxford: Oxford University Press, 1978).

3. See S. T. Leonard, *Critical Theory in Political Practice* (Princeton, N.J.: Princeton University Press, 1990).

4. B. Devall and G. Sessions, *Deep Ecology: Living as if Nature Mattered* (Salt Lake City: Peregrine Smith, 1985), 70, 73.

5. C. D. Stone, "Should Trees Have Standing? Toward Legal Rights for Natural Objects," *Southern California Law Review* 45 (1972): 450–501.

6. J. Lemons, "Cooperation and Stability as a Basis for Environmental Ethics," *Environmental Ethics* 3 (1981): 219–30.

7. M. Horkheimer and T. Adorno, *Dialectic of Enlightenment* (New York: Herder & Herder, 1972).

8. J. Habermas, *Knowledge and Human Interests* (Boston: Beacon Press, 1971), 32–33. The reason Habermas disparages this resurrection is that he believes it could only occur in mystical form. Such romanticism may have been attractive to his Frankfurt School precursors, especially Adorno, Marcuse, and Horkheimer, but it has no place in Habermas's own rationalistic ambitions.

9. For suggestions, see L. White, Jr., "The Historical Roots of Our Ecologic Crisis," *Science* 155 (1967): 1203–17 [this volume, 5–14]; C. Spretnak, *The Spiritual Dimension of Green Politics* (Santa Fe: Bear, 1986); D. La Chapelle, *Earth Wisdom* (San Diego, Calif.: Guild of Tudors, 1978); Devall and Sessions, *Deep Ecology,* 8, 90–91, 100–101; W. Fox, "On Guiding Stars to Deep Ecology: A Reply to Naess," *Ecologist* 14 (1984): 203–4; and A. Naess, "A Defense of the Deep Ecology Movement," *Environmental Ethics* 6 (1984): 266. Clearly religions differ in their environmental implications and so constitute fit objects for comparative scrutiny in the light of ecological concerns. See, for example, E. C. Hargrove, ed., *Religion and Environmental Crisis* (Athens: University of Georgia Press, 1986).

10. Quoted in Spretnak, *Spiritual Dimension at Green Politics,* 33.

11. Devall and Sessions, *Deep Ecology,* 67.

12. T. Luke, "Deep Ecology and Distributive Justice" (Paper presented at the annual meeting of the Midwest Political Science Association, 1967), 17–18.

13. M. Bookchin, "Social Ecology Versus Deep Ecology: A Challenge for the Ecology Movement," *Green Perspectives* 4–5 (1987): 7–8.

14. B. Commoner, *The Closing Circle* (New York: Bantam, 1972).

15. J. E. Lovelock, *Gaia: A New Look at Life on Earth* (Oxford: Oxford University Press, 1979).

16. Spretnak, *Spiritual Dimension of Green Politics,* 29.

17. J. Whitebook, "The Problem of Nature in Habermas," *Telos* 40 (1979): 42.

18. J. Dewey, *Human Nature and Conduct* (New York: Modern Library, 1922), 314.

19. J. Habermas, *The Theory of Communicative Action,* vol. 1, *Reason and the Rationalization of Society* (Boston: Beacon Press, 1984).

20. Karl-Otto Apel, "The *A Priori* of Communication and the Foundation of the Humanities," *Man and World* 5 (1972): 3–37.

21. See, for example, J. Habermas, "A Reply to My Critics," in *Habermas: Critical Debates,* ed. J. B. Thompson and D. Held (Cambridge, Mass.: MIT Press, 1982), 243–45.

22. Whitebook, "Problem of Nature in Habermas," 53.

23. C. Alford, *Science and the Revenge of Nature* (Gainesville: University of Florida Press, 1985), 77.

24. Habermas, "Reply to My Critics," 241–42.

25. Lovelock, *Gaia.*

26. Ibid., 145.

27. Ibid., 147.

28. J. Lovelock, *The Ages of Gaia: A Biography of Our Living Earth* (New York: Norton, 1988), 45–61.

29. Ibid., 206.

30. E. F. Keller, *A Feeling for the Organism: The Life and Work of Barbara McLintock* (San Francisco: Freeman, 1983), 199.

31. Ibid., 200.

32. C. Birch, "The Postmodern Challenge to Biology," in *The Reenchantment of Science: Postmodern Perspectives,* ed. D. Griffin (Albany: State University of New York Press, 1988), 69–78. "Postmodern" used in this sense has no nihilistic or relativist connotations.

33. Ibid., 71.

34. Ibid., 75.

35. J. Goodall, *The Chimpanzees of Gombe: Patterns of Behavior* (Cambridge, Mass.: Harvard University Press, 1986); D. R. Griffin, *Animal Thinking* (Cambridge, Mass.: Harvard University Press, 1984).

36. D. Abram, "The Perceptual Implications of Gaia," *Ecologist* (1985): 88.

37. Lovelock, *Gaia,* 129–41.

38. V. I. Vernadsky, "The Biosphere and the Noosphere," *American Scientist* 33 (1945): 1–12.

39. Commoner, *Closing Circle.*

40. E. Goldsmith and N. Hildyard, *The Social and Environmental Effects of Large Dams* (Camelford: Wadebridge Ecological Centre, 1985).

41. I. Mitroff and L. V. Blankenship, "On the Methodology of the Holistic Experiment: An Approach to the Conceptualization of Large-Scale Social Experiments," *Technological Forecasting and Social Change* 4 (1973): 339–53.

42. Habermas, *Theory of Communicative Action.*

43. Ibid., 68–69.

Questions for Further Exploration:

■ What does Dryzek mean by "the subversion of ethics by epistemology"?

■ How does instrumental rationality pave the way for ecological destruction? How does the "dialectic of Enlightenment" play in our environmental predicament?

■ What are the two ways to "resurrect nature" and what is Dryzek's assessment of each? What is his point in bringing up Hitler and the Third Reich?

■ How does Dryzek characterize "communicative rationality"? What limitations surround Habermas' conceptualization of it? What obstacles must be overcome in order to incorporate ecological principles into an extended model of communicative rationality?

■ How does Dryzek propose to "green reason"? What role does David Abram's epistemology play in Dryzek's proposal? What does Dryzek include in his set of criteria for ecological rationality to extend and supplement the criteria Habermas finds implicit in human rationality (equality, non-coercion, truthfulness, etc.)?

■ Free-write: How might human perception be improved so that nature is not so easy to ignore? Return to suggestions made by Orr and Nietzsche regarding the best means and ends of education. Which among their suggestions would best support Dryzek's project of greening reason, and why?

UNIT FOUR:
Values

"The burdens of global citizenship continue to bind us together. Partnership among nations is not a choice; it is the one way, the only way, to protect our common security and advance our common humanity." —Senator Obama, "A World That Stands as One," Berlin, Germany, July, 2008

Introduction to Greening Global Citizenship

Is "a world that stands as one" the most viable path to the good life on Earth? Unit Four brings us full circle back to the "examined life" we considered in Unit One. In that unit we took up Plato's view that we ought to examine whether our choices are in accordance with justice before acting. In Unit Two, as we surveyed a range of philosophies of reality, we sought a metaphysical justification for the examined life—Is the value of justice, or any value, *given* in the nature of reality? We also took up the "green" version of this question, "Is there a metaphysical justification for the shift to a sustainable order of values?"

Trying to answer these questions led us naturally to epistemological questions, the subject of Unit Three. In that unit we encountered several theories regarding how truth about reality might be reached and what might prevent its being reached. In the face of skepticism regarding objective forms of rationality, we considered the possibility of reaching an intersubjective consensus through communicative rationality. Even if the values that will insure the good life, specifically the sustainable life, are not *given,* perhaps they can be *chosen.* Equipped with conclusions reached in the first three units, you are now in a position to think for yourself about exactly what values you believe ought to be examined before acting for the sake of a life worth living.

Ethics challenges us to think not just about the values we want to live by as individuals, but also the order of values we ought to examine to guide us collectively. For centuries we have construed community in terms of territories—cities, nation-states, regions. However, globalization, a constitutive feature of the modern world, is making one's location less important to one's sense of community. As our sense of social interconnectedness expands across geographical boundaries, new questions arise about where we ought to draw our moral and political boundaries.

Our problems are also crossing national borders, raising the question of whether justice, or any basic values, bounded by local constraints can lead to viable global solutions. Some contemporary value theorists have suggested that we can't realize the good life 'at home' without realizing an unbounded sense of home—'Earth as our home.' The debate is on. Cosmopolitans argue that humanity is at a crossroads that demands the embrace of universal values and a mission to live as a global community. Green Cosmopolitans argue "universal" must include not only humans, but also plants, animals, and ecosystems. Communitarians and Pluralists are skeptical, believing that attempts to globalize the moral order in the real world of power politics are naïve and dangerous. They ask, "What certainty is there that 'universal values' are not the ideological ploy of more powerful states to control and exploit less powerful states?" Is a shared order of values even possible at the global level given the growing disparities of power and wealth around the world?

The first call for a global order of values was articulated by the Enlightenment philosopher, Immanuel Kant. Kant's ethics, based on an absolute respect for humankind, led him to sketch an outline for "perpetual peace" in 1795. Kant was not calling for a global government, but for the establishment of a peaceful world community based on mutual respect for autonomy and universal hospitality. After World War I, Kant's call was answered by the formation of the first intergovernmental organization, the League of Nations. In 1945, after World War II, the United Nations (UN), which replaced the League of Nations, resisted fascism and created a venue for diplomatic negotiation to stop and prevent wars. In 1948, the UN developed and adopted the first internationally sanctioned order of values, called 'The Universal Declaration of Human Rights.' Widespread environmental degradation over the past half century has led to a growing awareness that the underlying principle of respect for humankind in the Declaration does not go far enough.

The Earth Charter (2000) represents a recent United Nations attempt to articulate a global order of values designed to promote the transition to sustainable societies, based on respect and care for the community of life. 'The Charter' was drafted, over six years, through a global consultation process overseen by Maurice Strong and Mikhail Gorbachev. It has been endorsed by organizations representing millions of people, including hundreds of universities and cities around the world. However, it has not yet been formally recognized and endorsed by the United Nations, which would give it the same standing as the Universal Declaration of Human Rights. The Charter is now being circulated, used as an educational tool, critically analyzed, and debated. Does the Charter offer an order of values well suited to solving global environmental problems? Does the examined life necessarily entail a moral relationship with the universe of life?

The pursuit of wealth by any means available without regard to the effects on others is often justified by claiming that's what survival requires in today's dog-eat-dog world. Self-interest, in this view, is the only enlightened basis for action, and the only reason people ever make moral choices is to avoid the consequences of ill repute. Part of the work of ethics is to make the case for choices based on the good of all.

While laws provide a guide for civil living, they don't serve two important functions ethics can serve. First, ethical values provide guidance for living the good life in areas the law does not touch. For example, there is no law against being a rude, anti-social miser, but it is hard to imagine a good life without courtesy, generosity and social bonding. Second, ethics provide critical leverage against unjust civil laws, as the lives of Socrates, Jesus, Gandhi and Martin Luther King exemplify.

The countdown to catastrophe has already begun. We stand at a critical crossroads: "every man for himself" or "all for one and one for all"? This question of what to make of our predicament challenges us to reconsider "the good life." What relationship between human civilization and the natural world will insure the good life? What values must govern relations among humans to insure our mutual flourishing? How can we meet the needs of the present without compromising the ability of future generations to meet their needs? What are we willing to do and sacrifice for a continued good life on planet earth? What ways of life are we willing to live and die for? These are genuinely open and urgent questions offered for your consideration and well-being.

Resources

Brennan, Andrew and Lo, Yeuk-Sze, "Environmental Ethics," *The Stanford Encyclopedia of Philosophy,* edited by Edward N. Zalta. Winter 2009 Edition. http://plato.stanford.edu/archives/win2009/entries/ethics-environmental/

Earthlings. Dir. Shaun Monson, Maggie Q and Nation Earth, 2005.

Flow: For the Love of Water. Dir. Irena Salina, Steven Starr, Gill Holland and Yvette Tomlinson, 2008.

Footprint Calculator. Global Footprint Network. http://www.footprintnetwork. org/en/index.php/GFN/page/calculators/

Kleingeld, Pauline and Brown, Eric, "Cosmopolitanism," *The Stanford Encyclopedia of Philosophy,* edited by Edward N. Zalta, Summer 2009 Edition. http://plato.stanford.edu/archives/sum2009/entries/cosmopolitanism/

Manufactured Landscapes. Dir. Jennifer Baichwal, Zeitgeist Films, 2006. Features by Edward Burtynsky's photography of landscapes transformed by human activity.

Sayre-McCord, Geoff, "Metaethics," *The Stanford Encyclopedia of Philosophy,* edited by Edward N. Zalta, Fall 2008 Edition. http://plato.stanford.edu/archives/fall2008/entries/metaethics/

Scheuerman, William, "Globalization," *The Stanford Encyclopedia of Philosophy,* edited by Edward N. Zalta, Summer 2010 Edition. http://plato.stanford.edu/archives/sum2010/entries/globalization/

The End of Poverty? Dir. Philippe Diaz, Cinema Libre Studio, 2009.

The Future of Food. Dir. Deborah Koons Garcia, Catherine Butler and Koons Garcia, 2005.

UN General Assembly, *Universal Declaration of Human Rights,* 10 December 1948. Accessed 7 November 2010 from http://www.unhcr.org/refworld/docid/3ae6b3712c.html

Questions for Further Exploration:

- How should we conceptualize "the good life" today?

  A life that is lived responsibly for all, not just I. We can all live a good life without taking from others, the good life is not just what we have but also what we have to give.

- Who is "we"? How should "moral community" be conceptualized? *give* On what basis should land, ecosystems, trees, animals, and humans be included or excluded from the moral community?

  "We" includes everyone on the planet

- What values ought to form the basis of an examined life for those who would be citizens of the Earth? What is "global citizenship"? What does it mean to "green" global citizenship?

- Should environmental problems be approached with a common purpose and a universal order of values? Or does the assertion of such a starting point close the door on the conflicts and debate needed for pragmatic progress?

- Should we develop our values in local, place-specific contexts, or seek common ground in global forums?

- Is a particular order of values at the root of our environmental problems? Is there a particular order of values that could help solve them? Does *The Earth Charter* offer an acceptable and/or praiseworthy articulation of values for a sustainable future?

Perpetual Peace

Immanuel Kant

First Section
Containing the Preliminary Articles
of Perpetual Peace Between States

I.   "No treaty of peace shall be regarded as valid, if made with the secret reservation of material for a future war."

For then it would be a mere truce, a mere suspension of hostilities, not peace. A peace signifies the end of all hostilities and to attach to it the epithet "eternal" is not only a verbal pleonasm, but matter of suspicion. The causes of a future war existing, although perhaps not yet known to the high contracting parties themselves, are entirely annihilated by the conclusion of peace, however acutely they may be ferreted out of documents in the public archives. There may be a mental reservation of old claims to be thought out at a future time, which are, none of them, mentioned at this stage, because both parties are too much exhausted to continue the war, while the evil intention remains of using the first favourable opportunity for further hostilities. Diplomacy of this kind only Jesuitical casuistry can justify: it is beneath the dignity of a ruler, just as acquiescence in such processes of reasoning is beneath the dignity of his minister, if one judges the facts as they really are.*

If, however, according to present enlightened ideas of political wisdom, the true glory of a state lies in the uninterrupted development of its power by every possible means, this judgment must certainly strike one as scholastic and pedantic.

---

*On the honourable interpretation of treaties, see Vattel (*op. cit.,* II. Ch. XVII., esp. §§ 263–296, 291). See also what he says of the validity of treaties and the necessity for holding them sacred (II. Ch. XII. §§ 157, 158: II. Ch. XV). [Tr.]

2. "No state having an independent existence—whether it be great or small—shall be acquired by another through inheritance, exchange, purchase or donation."*

For a state is not a property (*patrimonium*), as may be the ground on which its people are settled. It is a society of human beings over whom no one but itself has the right to rule and to dispose. Like the trunk of a tree, it has its own roots, and to graft it on to another state is to do away with its existence as a moral person, and to make of it a thing. Hence it is in contradiction to the idea of the original contract without which no right over a people is thinkable.† Everyone knows to what danger the bias in favour of these modes of acquisition has brought Europe (in other parts of the world it has never been known). The custom of marriage between states, as if they were individuals, has survived even up to the most recent times,‡ and is regarded partly as a new kind of industry by which ascendency may be acquired through family alliances, without any expenditure of strength; partly as a device for territorial expansion. Moreover, the hiring out of the troops of one state to another to fight against an enemy not at war with their native country is to be reckoned in this connection; for the subjects are in this way used and abused at will as personal property.

3. "Standing armies (*miles perpetuus*) shall be abolished in course of time."

For they are always threatening other states with war by appearing to be in constant readiness to fight. They incite the various states to outrival one another in the number of their soldiers, and to this number no limit can be set. Now, since owing to the sums devoted to this purpose, peace at last

---

*"Even the smoothest way," says Hume, (*Of the Original Contract*) "by which a nation may receive a foreign master, by marriage or a will, is not extremely honourable for the people; but supposes them to be disposed of, like a dowry or a legacy, according to the pleasure or interest of their rulers." [Tr.]

†An hereditary kingdom is not a state which can be inherited by another state, but one whose sovereign power can be inherited by another physical person. The state then acquires a ruler, not the ruler as such (that is, as one already possessing another realm) the state.

‡This has been one of the causes of the extraordinary admixture of races in the modern Austrian empire. Cf. the lines of Matthias Corvinus of Hungary (quoted in Sir W. Stirling Maxwell's *Cloister Life of Charles the Fifth*, Ch. I., *note*):—
    "Bella gerant alii, tu, felix Austria, nube!
    Nam quae Mars aliis, dat tibi regna Venus." [Tr.]

becomes even more oppressive than a short war, these standing armies are themselves the cause of wars of aggression, undertaken in order to get rid of this burden. To which we must add that the practice of hiring men to kill or to be killed seems to imply a use of them as mere machines and instruments in the hand of another (namely, the state) which cannot easily be reconciled with the right of humanity in our own person.* The matter stands quite differently in the case of voluntary periodical military exercise on the part of citizens of the state, who thereby seek to secure themselves and their country against attack from without.

The accumulation of treasure in a state would in the same way be regarded by other states as a menace of war, and might compel them to anticipate this by striking the first blow. For of the three forces, the power of arms, the power of alliance and the power of money, the last might well become the most reliable instrument of war, did not the difficulty of ascertaining the amount stand in the way.

4. "No national debts shall be contracted in connection with the external affairs of the state."

This source of help is above suspicion, where assistance is sought outside or within the state, on behalf of the economic administration of the country (for instance, the improvement of the roads, the settlement and support of new colonies, the establishment of granaries to provide against seasons of scarcity, and so on). But, as a common weapon used by the Powers against one another, a credit system under which debts go on indefinitely increasing and are yet always assured against immediate claim (because all the creditors do not put in their claim at once) is a dangerous money power. This ingenious invention of a commercial people in the present century is, in other words, a treasure for the carrying on of war which may exceed the treasures of all the other states taken together, and can only be exhausted by a threatening deficiency in the taxes—an event, however, which will long be kept off by the very briskness of commerce resulting from the reaction of this system on industry and trade. The ease, then, with which war may be waged, coupled with the inclination of rulers towards it—an inclination which seems to be implanted in human nature—is a great obstacle in the way of perpetual

---

*A Bulgarian Prince thus answered the Greek Emperor who magnanimously offered to settle a quarrel with him, not by shedding the blood of his subjects, but by a duel:—"A smith who has tongs will not take the red-hot iron from the fire with his hands."

(This note is a-wanting in the second Edition of 1796. It is repeated in Art. II., see p. 130.) [Tr.]

peace. The prohibition of this system must be laid down as a preliminary article of perpetual peace, all the more necessarily because the final inevitable bankruptcy of the state in question must involve in the loss many who are innocent; and this would be a public injury to these states. Therefore other nations are at least justified in uniting themselves against such an one and its pretensions.

5. "No state shall violently interfere with the constitution and administration of another."

For what can justify it in so doing? The scandal which is here presented to the subjects of another state? The erring state can much more serve as a warning by exemplifying the great evils which a nation draws down on itself through its own lawlessness. Moreover, the bad example which one free person gives another, (as *scandalum acceptum*) does no injury to the latter. In this connection, it is true, we cannot count the case of a state which has become split up through internal corruption into two parts, each of them representing by itself an individual state which lays claim to the whole. Here the yielding of assistance to one faction could not be reckoned as interference on the part of a foreign state with the constitution of another, for here anarchy prevails. So long, however, as the inner strife has not yet reached this stage the interference of other powers would be a violation of the rights of an independent nation which is only struggling with internal disease.* It would therefore itself cause a scandal, and make the autonomy of all states insecure.

6. "No state at war with another shall countenance such modes of hostility as would make mutual confidence impossible in a subsequent state of peace: such are the employment of assassins (*percussores*) or of poisoners (*venefici*), breaches of capitulation, the instigating and making use of treachery (*perduellio*) in the hostile state."

---

*See Vattel: *Law of Nations,* II. Ch. IV. § 55. No foreign power, he says, has a right to judge the conduct and administration of any sovereign or oblige him to alter it. "If he loads his subjects with taxes, or if he treats them with severity, the nation alone is concerned; and no other is called upon to offer redress for his behaviour, or oblige him to follow more wise and equitable maxims . . . . . . But (*loc. cit.* § 56) when the bands of the political society are broken, or at least suspended, between the sovereign and his people, the contending parties may then be considered as two distinct powers; and, since they arc both equally independent of all foreign authority, nobody has a right to judge them. Either may be in the right; and each of those who grant their assistance may imagine that he is giving his support to the better cause." [Tr.]

These are dishonourable stratagems. For some kind of confidence in the disposition of the enemy must exist even in the midst of war, as otherwise peace could not be concluded, and the hostilities would pass into a war of extermination (*bellum internecinum*). War, however, is only our wretched expedient of asserting a right by force, an expedient adopted in the state of nature, where no court of justice exists which could settle the matter in dispute, In circumstances like these, neither of the two parties can be called an unjust enemy, because this form of speech presupposes a legal decision: the issue of the conflict—just as in the case of the so-called judgments of God—decides on which side right is. Between states, however, no punitive war (*bellum punitivum*) is thinkable, because between them a relation of superior and inferior does not exist. Whence it follows that a war of extermination, where the process of annihilation would strike both parties at once and all right as well, would bring about perpetual peace only in the great graveyard of the human race. Such a war then, and therefore also the use of all means which lead to it, must be absolutely forbidden. That the methods just mentioned do inevitably lead to this result is obvious from the fact that these infernal arts, already vile in themselves, on coming into use, are not long confined to the sphere of war. Take, for example, the use of spies (*uti exploratoribus*). Here only the dishonesty of others is made use of; but vices such as these, when once encouraged, cannot in the nature of things be stamped out and would be carried over into the state of peace, where their presence would be utterly destructive to the purpose of that state.

Although the laws stated are, objectively regarded, (*i.e.* in so far as they affect the action of rulers) purely prohibitive laws (*leges prohibitivæ*), some of them (*leges strictæ*) are strictly valid without regard to circumstances and urgently require to be enforced. Such are Nos. I, 5, 6. Others, again, (like Nos. 2, 3, 4) although not indeed exceptions to the maxims of law, yet in respect of the practical application of these maxims allow subjectively of a certain latitude to suit particular circumstances. The enforcement of these *leges latæ* may be legitimately put off, so long as we do not lose sight of the ends at which they aim. This purpose of reform does not permit of the deferment of an act of restitution (as, for example, the restoration to certain states of freedom of which they have been deprived in the manner described in article 2) to an infinitely distant date—as Augustus used to say, to the "Greek Kalends", a day that will never come. This would be to sanction non-restitution. Delay is permitted only with the intention that restitution should not be made too precipitately and so defeat the purpose we have in view. For the prohibition refers here only to the *mode of acquisition* which is to be no longer valid, and not to the *fact of possession* which, although indeed it has not the necessary title of right, yet at the time of so-called acquisition was held legal by all states, in accordance with the public opinion of the time.*

Second Section
Containing the Definitive Articles
of a Perpetual Peace Between States

A state of peace among men who live side by side is not the natural state (*status naturalis*), which is rather to be described as a state of

---

*It has been hitherto doubted, not without reason, whether there can be laws of permission (*leges permissivæ*) of pure reason as well as commands (*leges præceptivæ*) and prohibitions (*leges prohibitivæ*). For law in general has a basis of objective practical necessity: permission, on the other hand, is based upon the contingency of certain actions in practice. It follows that a law of permission would enforce what cannot be enforced; and this would involve a contradiction, if the object of the law should be the same in both cases. Here, however, in the present case of a law of permission, the presupposed prohibition is aimed merely at the future manner of acquisition of a right—for example, acquisition through inheritance: the exemption from this prohibition (*i.e.* the permission) refers to the present state of possession. In the transition from a state of nature to the civil state, this holding of property can continue as a *bona fide,* if usurpatory, ownership, under the new social conditions, in accordance with a permission of the Law of Nature. Ownership of this kind, as soon as its true nature becomes known, is seen to be mere nominal possession (*possessio putativa*) sanctioned by opinion and customs in a natural state of society. After the transition stage is passed, such modes of acquisition are likewise forbidden in the subsequently evolved civil state: and this power to remain in possession would not be admitted if the supposed acquisition had taken place in the civilized community. It would be bound to come to an end as an injury to the right of others, the moment its illegality became patent.

I have wished here only by the way to draw the attention of teachers of the Law of Nature to the idea of a *lex permissiva* which presents itself spontaneously in any system of rational classification. I do so chiefly because use is often made of this concept in civil law with reference to statutes; with this difference, that the law of prohibition stands alone by itself, while permission is not, as it ought to be, introduced into that law as a limiting clause, but is thrown among the exceptions. Thus "this or that is forbidden",—say, Nos. 1, 2, 3, and so on in an infinite progression,—while permissions are only added to the law incidentally: they we not reached by the application of some principle, but only by groping about among cases which have actually occurred. Were this not so, qualifications would have had to be brought into the formula of laws of prohibition which would have immediately transformed them into laws of permission. Count von Windischgrätz, a man whose wisdom was equal to his discrimination, urged this very point in the form of a question propounded by him for a prize essay. One must therefore regret that this ingenious problem has been so soon neglected and left unsolved. For the possibility of a formula similar to those of mathematics is the sole real test of a legislation that would be consistent. Without this, the so-called *jus certum* will remain forever a mere pious wish: we can hare only general laws valid on the whole; no general laws possessing the universal validity which the concept law seems to demand.

war:* that is to say, although there is not perhaps always actual open hostility, yet there is a constant threatening that an outbreak may occur. Thus the state of peace must be *established*.† For the mere cessation of hostilities is no guarantee of continued peaceful relations, and unless this guarantee is given by every individual to his neighbour—which can only be done in a state of society regulated by law—one man is at liberty to challenge another and treat him as an enemy.‡

---

*"From this diffidence of one another, there is no way for any man to secure himself, so reasonable, as anticipation; that is, by force, or wiles, to master the persons of all men he can, so long, till he see no other power great enough to endanger him: and this is no more than his own conservation reuireth, and is generally allowed." (Hobbes: *Lev.* I. Ch. XIII.) [Tr.]

† Hobbes thus describes the establishment of the state. "A *commonwealth* is said to be *instituted*, when a *multitude* of men do agree, and *covenant, every one, with every one,* that to whatsoever *man,* or *assembly of men,* shall be given by the major part, the *right* to *present* the person of them all, that is to say, to be their *representative;* everyone, as well he that *voted for it,* as he that *voted against it,* shall *authorise* all the actions and judgments, of that man, or assembly of men, in the same manner, as if they were his own, to the end, to live peaceably amongst themselves, and be protected against other men." (*Lev.* II. Ch. XVIII.)

There is a covenant between them, "as if every man should say to every man, *I authorise and give up my right of governing myself, to this man, or to this assembly of men, on this condition, that thou give up thy right to him, and authorise all his actions in like manner.*" (*Lev.* II. Ch. XVII.) [Tr.]

‡It is usually accepted that a man may not take hostile step against any one, unless the latter has already injured him by act. This is quite accurate, if both are citizens of a law-governed state. For, in becoming a member of this community, each gives the other the security he demands against injury, by means of the supreme authority exercising control over them both. The individual, however, (or nation) who remains in a mere state of nature deprives me of this security and does me injury, by mere proximity. There is perhaps no active (*facto*) molestation, but there is a state of lawlessness (*status injustus*) which, by its very existence, offers a continual menace to me. I can therefore compel him, either to enter into relations with me under which we are both subject to law, or to withdraw from my neighbourhood. So that the postulate upon which the following articles are based is:—"All men who have the power to exert a mutual influence upon one another must be under a civil government of some kind."

A legal constitution is, according to the nature of the individuals who compose the state:—

(I) A constitution formed in accordance with the right of citizenship of the individuals who constitute a nation (*jus civitatis*).

(2) A constitution whose principle is international law which determines the relations of states (*jus gentium*).

(3) A constitution formed in accordance with cosmopolitan law, in as far as individuals and states, standing in an external relation of mutual reaction, may be regarded as citizens of one world-state (*jus cosmopoliticum*).

This classification is not an arbitrary one, but is necessary with reference to the idea of perpetual peace. For, if even one of these units of society were in a position physically to influence another, while yet remaining a member of a primitive order of society, then a state of war would be joined with these primitive conditions; and from this it is our present purpose to free ourselves.

First Definitive Article of Perpetual Peace

I. "The civil constitution of each state shall be republican."

The only constitution which has its origin in the idea of the original contract, upon which the lawful legislation of every nation must be based, is the republican.* It is a constitution, in the first place, founded in accor-

---

*Lawful, that is to say, external freedom cannot be defined, as it so often is, as the right [*Befugniss*] "to do whatever one likes, so long as this does not wrong anyone else."[1] For what is this right? It is the possibility of actions which do not lead to the injury of others. So the explanation of a "right" would be something like this:—"Freedom is the possibility of actions which do not injure anyone. A man does not wrong another—whatever his action—if he does not wrong another": which is empty tautology. My external (lawful) freedom is rather to be explained in this way: it is the right through which I require not to obey any external laws except those to which I could have given my consent. In exactly the same way, external (legal) equality in a state is that relation of the subjects in consequence of which no individual can legally bind or oblige another to anything, without at the same time submitting himself to the law which ensures that he can, in his turn, be bound and obliged in like manner by this other.

The principle of lawful independence requires no explanation, as it is involved in the general concept of a constitution. The validity of this hereditary and inalienable right, which belongs of necessity to mankind, is affirmed and ennobled by the principle of a lawful relation between man himself and higher beings, if indeed he believes in such beings. This is so, because he thinks of himself, in accordance with these very principles, as a citizen of a transcendental world as well as of the world of sense. For, as far as my freedom goes, I am bound by no obligation even with regard to Divine Laws—which are apprehended by me only through my reason—except in so far as I could have given my assent to them; for it is through the law of freedom of my own reason that I first form for myself a concept of a Divine Will. As for the principle of equality, in so far as it applies to the most sublime being in the universe next to God—a being I might perhaps figure to myself as a mighty emanation of the Divine spirit,—there is no reason why, if I perform my duty in the sphere in which I am placed, as that aeon docs in his, the duty of obedience alone should fall to my share, the right to command to him. That this principle of equality, (unlike the principle of freedom), does not apply to our relation to God is due to the fact that, to this Being done, the idea of duty docs not belong.

As for the right to quality which belongs to all citizens as subjects, the solution of the problem of the admissibility of on hereditary nobility hinges on the following question:— "Does social rank—acknowledged by the state to be higher in the case of one subject than another—stand above desert, or does merit take precedence of social standing?" Now it is obvious that, if high position is combined with good family, it is quite uncertain whether merit, that is to say, skill and fidelity in office, will follow as well. This amounts to granting the favoured individual a commanding position without any question of desert; and to that,

dance with the principle of the freedom of the members of society as human beings: secondly, in accordance with the principle of the dependence of all, as subjects, on a common legislation: and, thirdly, in accordance with the law of the equality of the members as citizens. It is then, looking at the question of right, the only constitution whose fundamental principles lie at the basis of every form of civil constitution. And the only question for us now is, whether it is also the one constitution which can lead to perpetual peace.

Now the republican constitution apart from the soundness of its origin, since it arose from the pure source of the concept of right, has also the prospect of attaining the desired result, namely, perpetual peace. And the reason is this. If, as must be so under this constitution, the consent of the subjects is required to determine whether there shall be war or not, nothing is more natural than that they should weigh the matter well, before undertaking such a bad business. For in decreeing war, they would of necessity be resolving to bring down the miseries of war upon their country. This implies: they must fight themselves; they must hand over the costs of the war out of their own property; they must do their poor best to make good the devastation which it leaves behind; and finally, as a crowning ill, they have to accept a burden of debt which will embitter even peace itself, and which they can never pay off on account of the new wars which are always impending. On the other hand, in a government where the subject is not a citizen holding a vote, (*i.e.* in a constitution which is not republican), the plunging into war is the least serious thing in the world. For the ruler is not a citizen, but the owner of the state, and does not lose a whit by the war, while he goes on enjoying the delights of his table or sport, or of his pleasure palaces and gala days. He can therefore decide on war for the most trifling

the universal will of the people—expressed in an original contract which is the fundamental principle of all right—would never consent. For it does not follow that a nobleman is a man of noble character. In the case of the official nobility, as one might term the rank of higher magistracy—which one must acquire by merit—the social position is not attached like property to the person but to his office, and quality is not thereby disturbed; for, if a man gives up office, he lays down with it his official rank and falls back into the rank of his fellows,

[1]Hobbes' definition of freedom is interesting. See *Lev.* II. Ch. XXI.:—"A Freeman, *is he, that in these things, which by his strength and wit he is able to do, is not hindered to do what he has a will to.*" [Tr.]

reasons, as if it were a kind of pleasure party.* Any justification of it that is necessary for the sake of decency he can leave without concern to the diplomatic corps who are always only too ready with their services.

■ ■ ■

The following remarks must be made in order that we may not fall into the common error of confusing the republican with the democratic constitution. The forms of the state (*civitas*)† may be classified according to either of two principles of division:—the difference of the persons who hold the supreme authority in the state, and the manner in which the people are governed by their ruler whoever he may be. The first is properly called the form of sovereignty (*forma imperii*), and there can be only three constitutions differing in this respect: where, namely, the supreme authority belongs to only one, to several individuals working together, or to the whole people constituting the civil society. Thus we have autocracy or the sovereignty of a monarch, aristocracy or the sovereignty of the nobility, and democracy or the sovereignty of the people. The second principle of division is the form of government (*forma regiminis*), and refers to the way in which the state makes use of its supreme power: for the manner of govern-

---

* Cf. Cowper: *The Winter Morning Walk:*—
  "But is it fit, or can it bear the shock
  Of rational discussion, that a man,
  Compounded and made up like other men
  Of elements tumultuous, ...
  . . . .
  Should when he pleases, and on whom he will,
  Wage war, with any or with no pretence
  Of provocation giv'n or wrong sustain'd,
  And force the beggarly last doit, by means
  That his own humour dictates, from the clutch
  Of poverty, that thus he may procure
  His thousands, weary of penurious life,
  A splendid opportunity to die?"
  . . . .
  . . . .
  "He deems a thousand or ten thousand lives
  Spent in the purchase of renown for him,
  An easy reckoning." [Tr.]

†Cf. Hobbes: *On Dominion,* Ch. VII. § I. "As for the difference of cities, it is taken from the difference of the persons to whom the supreme power is committed. This power is committed either to *one man,* or *council,* or some *one court* consisting of many men." [Tr.]

ment is based on the constitution, itself the act of that universal will which transforms a multitude into a nation. In this respect the form of government is either republican or despotic. Republicanism is the political principle of severing the executive power of the government from the legislature. Despotism is that principle in pursuance of which the state arbitrarily puts into effect laws which it has itself made: consequently it is the administration of the public will, but this is identical with the private will of the ruler. Of these three forms of a state, democracy, in the proper sense of the word, is of necessity despotism, because it establishes an executive power, since all decree regarding—and, if need be, against—any individual who dissents from them. Therefore the "whole people", so-called, who carry their measure are really not all, but only a majority: so that here the universal will is in contradiction with itself and with the principle of freedom.

Every form of government in fact which is not representative is really no true constitution at all, because a law-giver may no more be, in one and the same person, the administrator of his own will, than the universal major premise of a syllogism may be, at the same time, the subsumption under itself of the particulars contained in the minor premise. And, although the other two constitutions, autocracy and aristocracy, are always defective in so far as they leave the way open for such a form of government, yet there is at least always a possibility in these cases, that they may take the form of a government in accordance with the spirit of a representative system. Thus Frederick the Great used at least to say that he was "merely the highest servant of the state.* The democratic constitution, on the other hand, makes this impossible, because under such a government every one wishes to be master. We may therefore say that the smaller the staff of the executive—that is to say, the number of rulers—and the more real, on the other hand, their representation of the people, so much the more is the government of the state in accordance with a possible republicanism; and it may hope by gradual reforms to raise itself to that standard. For this reason, it is more difficult under an aristocracy than under a monarchy—while under a democracy it is impossible except by a violent revolution—to attain to this,

---

*The lofty appellations which are often given to a ruler—such as the Lord's Anointed, the Administrator of the Divine Will upon earth and Vicar of God—have been many times censured as flattery gross enough to make one giddy. But it seems to me without cause. Far from making prince arrogant, names like these must rather make him humble at heart, if he has any intelligence—which we take for granted he has—and reflects that he has undertaken an office which is too great for any human being. For, indeed, it is the holiest which God has on earth—namely, the right of ruling mankind: and he must ever live in fear of injuring this treasure of God in some respect or other.

the one perfectly lawful constitution. The kind of government,* however, is of infinitely more importance to the people than the kind of constitution, although the greater or less aptitude of a people for this ideal greatly depends upon such external form. The form of government, however, if it is to be in accordance with the idea of right, must embody the representative system in which alone a republican form of administration is possible and without which it is despotic and violent, be the constitution what it may. None of the ancient so-called republics were aware of this, and they necessarily slipped into absolute despotism which, of all despotisms, is most endurable under the sovereignty of one individual.

Second Definitive Article of Perpetual Peace

II. "The law of nations shall be founded on a federation of free states."

Nations, as states, may be judged like individuals who, living in the natural state of society—that is to say, uncontrolled by external law—injure one another through their very proximity.† Every state, for the sake of its own security, may—and ought to—demand that its neighbour should submit itself to conditions, similar to those of the civil society where the right

---

*Mallet du Pan boasts in his seemingly brilliant but shallow and superficial language that, after many years experience, he has come at last to be convinced of the truth of the well known saying of Pope [*Essay on Man,* III. 303]:—

"For Forms of Government let fools contest;
Whate'er is best administered is best."

If this means that the best administered government is best administered, then, in Swift's phrase, he has cracked a nut to find a worm in it. If it means, however, that the best conducted government is also the best kind of government—that is, the best form of political constitution,—then it is utterly false: for examples of wise administration are no proof of the kind of government. Who ever ruled better than Titus and Marcus Aurelius, and yet the one left Domitian, the other Commodus, as his successor? This could not have happened where the constitution was a good one, for their absolute unfitness for the position was early enough known, and the power of the emperor was sufficiently great to exclude them.

†"For as amongst masterless men, there is perpetual war, of every man against his neighbour; no inheritance, to transmit to the son, nor to expect from the father; no propriety of goods, or lands; no security; but a full and absolute liberty in every particular man: so in states, and commonwealths not dependent on one another, every commonwealth, not every man, has an absolute liberty, to do what it shall judge, that is to say, what that man, or assembly that representeth it, shall judge most conducing to their benefit. But withal, they live in the condition of a perpetual war, and upon the confines of battle, with their frontiers armed, and cannons planted against their neighbours round about." (Hobbes: *Leviathan,* II. Ch. XXI.) [Tr.]

of every individual is guaranteed. This would give rise to a federation of nations which, however, would not have to be a State of nations.* That would involve a contradiction. For the term "state" implies the relation of one who rules to those who obey—that is to say, of lawgiver to the subject people: and many nations in one state would constitute only one nation, which contradicts our hypothesis, since here we have to consider the right of one nation against another, in so far as they are so many separate states and are not to be fused into one.

The attachment of savages to their lawless liberty, the fact that they would rather be at hopeless variance with one another than submit themselves to a legal authority constituted by themselves, that they therefore prefer their senseless freedom to a reason-governed liberty, is regarded by us with profound contempt as barbarism and uncivilisation and the brutal degradation of humanity. So one would think that civilised races, each formed into a state by itself, must come out of such an abandoned condition as soon as they possibly can. On the contrary, however, every state thinks rather that its majesty (the "majesty" of a people is an absurd expression) lies just in the very fact that it is subject to no external legal authority: and the glory of the ruler consists in this, that, without his requiring to expose himself to danger, thousands stand at his command ready to let themselves be sacrificed for a matter of no concern to them.† The difference between the savages of Europe and those of America lies chiefly in this, that, while many tribes of the latter have been entirely devoured by their enemies, Euro-

---

*But see p. 136, where Kant seems to speak of a State of nations as the ideal. Kant expresses himself, on this point, more clearly in the *Rechtslehre*, Part. II. § 61:—"The natural state of nations," he says here, "like that of individual men, is a condition which must be abandoned, in order that they may enter a state regulated by law. Hence, before this can take place, every right possessed by these nations and every external "mine" and "thine" [*id est,* symbol of possession] which states acquire or preserve through war are merely *provisional,* and can become *peremptorily* valid and constitute a true state of peace only in a universal *union of states,* by a process analogous to that through which a people becomes a state. Since, however, the too great extension of such a State of nations over vast territories must, in the long run, make the government of that union—and therefore the protection of each of its members—impossible, a multitude of such corporations will lead again to a state of war. So that *perpetual peace,* the final goal of international law as a whole, is really an impracticable idea [*eine unausführbare Idee*]. The political principles, however, which are directed towards this end, (that is to say, towards the establishment of such unions of states as may serve as a continual approximation to that ideal), are not impracticable; on the contrary, as this approximation is required by duty and is therefore founded also upon the rights of men and of states, these principles are, without doubt, capable of practical realization." [Tr.]

†A Greek Emperor who magnanimously volunteered to settle by a duel his quarrel with a Bulgarian Prince, got the following answer:—"A smith who has tongs will not pluck the glowing iron from the fire with his hands."

peans know a better way of using the vanquished than by eating them; and they prefer to increase through them the number of their subjects, and so the number of instruments at their command for still more widely spread war.

The depravity of human nature* shows itself without disguise in the unrestrained relations of nations to each other, while in the law-governed civil state much of this is hidden by the check of government. This being so, it is astonishing that the word "right" has not yet been entirely banished from the politics of war as pedantic, and that no state has yet ventured to publicly advocate this point of view. For Hugo Grotius, Puffendorf, Vattel and others—Job's comforters, all of them—are always quoted in good faith to justify an attack, although their codes, whether couched in philosophical or diplomatic terms, have not—nor can have—the slightest legal force, because states, as such, are under no common external authority; and there is no instance of a state having ever been moved by argument to desist from its purpose, even when this was backed up by the testimony of such great men. This homage which every state renders—in words at least—to the idea of right, proves that, although it may be slumbering, there is, notwithstanding, to be found in man a still higher natural moral capacity by the aid of which he will in time gain the mastery over the evil principle in his nature, the existence of which he is unable to deny. And he hopes the same of others; for otherwise the word "right" would never be uttered by states who wish to wage war, unless to deride it like the Gallic Prince who declared:—"The privilege which nature gives the strong is that the weak must obey them."†

The method by which states prosecute their rights can never be by process of law—as it is where there is an external tribunal—but only by war. Through this means, however, and its favourable issue, victory, the question of right is never decided. A treaty of peace makes, it may be, an end to the war of the moment, but not to the conditions of war which at any time may afford a new pretext for opening hostilities; and this we cannot exactly condemn as unjust, because under these conditions everyone is his own judge.

---

*"Both sayings are very true: that *man to man is a kind of God;* and that *man to man is an arrant wolf.* The first is true, if we compare citizens amongst themselves; and the second, if we compare cities. In the one, there is some analogy of similitude with the Deity; to wit, justice and charity, the twin sisters of peace. But in the other, good men must defend themselves by taking to them for a sanctuary the two daughters of war, deceit and violence: that is, in plain terms, a mere brutal rapacity." (Hobbes: Epistle Dedicatory to the *Philosophical Rudiments concerning Government and Society.*) [Tr.]

†"The strongest are still never sufficiently strong to ensure them the continual mastership, unless they find means of transforming force into right, and obedience into duty.

From the right of the strongest, right takes an ironical appearance, and is rarely established as a principle." (*Contrat Social, I. Ch. III.*) [Tr.]

Notwithstanding, not quite the same rule applies to states according to the law of nations as holds good of individuals in a lawless condition according to the law of nature, namely, "that they ought to advance out of this condition." This is so, because, as states, they have already within themselves a legal constitution, and have therefore advanced beyond the stage at which others, in accordance with their ideas of right, can force them to come under a wider legal constitution. Meanwhile, however, reason, from her throne of the supreme law-giving moral power, absolutely condemns war* as a morally lawful proceeding, and makes a state of peace, on the other hand, an immediate duty. Without a compact between the nations, however, this state of peace cannot be established or assured. Hence there must be an alliance of a particular kind which we may call a covenant of peace (*foedus pacificum*), which would differ from a treaty of peace (*pactum pacis*) in this respect, that the latter merely puts an end to one war, while the former would seek to put an end to war for ever. This alliance does not aim at the gain of any power whatsoever of the state, but merely at the preservation and security of the freedom of the state for itself and of other allied states at the same time.† The latter do not, however, require, for this reason, to submit themselves like individuals in the state of nature to public laws and coercion. The practicability or objective reality of this idea of federation which is to extend gradually over all states and so lead to perpetual peace can be shewn. For, if Fortune ordains that a powerful and enlightened people should form a republic,—which by its very nature is inclined to perpetual peace—this would serve as a centre of federal union for other states wishing to join, and thus secure conditions of freedom among the states in accordance with the idea of the law of nations. Gradually, through different unions of this kind, the federation would extend further and further.

It is quite comprehensible that a people should say:—"There shall be no war among us, for we shall form ourselves into a state, that is to say,

---

*"The natural state," says Hobbes, (*On Dominion*, Ch. VII. § 18) "hath the same proportion to the civil, (I mean, liberty to subjection), which passion hath to reason, or a beast to a man."

Locke speaks thus of man, when he puts himself into the state of war with another:— "having quitted reason, which God hath given to be the rule betwixt man and man, and the common bond whereby human kind is united into one fellowship and society; and having renounced the way of peace which that teaches, and made use of the force of war, to compass his unjust ends upon another, where he has no right; and so revolting from his own kind to that of beasts, by making force, which is theirs, to be his rule of right, he renders himself liable to be destroyed by the injured person, and the rest of mankind that will join with him in the execution of justice, as any other wild beast, or noxious brute, with whom mankind can have neither society nor security." (*Civil Government*, Ch. XV. § 172.) [Tr.]

†Cf. Rousseau: *Gouvernement de Pologne*, Ch. V. Federate government is "the only one which unites in itself all the advantages of great and small states." [Tr.]

constitute for ourselves a supreme legislative, administrative and judicial power which will settle our disputes peaceably." But if this state says:— "There shall be no war between me and other states, although I recognise no supreme law-giving power which will secure me my rights and whose rights I will guarantee;" then it is not at all clear upon what grounds I could base my confidence in my right, unless it were the substitute for that compact on which civil society is based—namely, free federation which reason must necessarily connect with the idea of the law of nations, if indeed any meaning is to be left in that concept at all.

There is no intelligible meaning in the idea of the law of nations as giving a right to make war; for that must be a right to decide what is just, not in accordance with universal, external laws limiting the freedom of each individual, but by means of one-sided maxims applied by force. We must then understand by this that men of such ways of thinking are quite justly served, when they destroy one another, and thus find perpetual peace in the wide grave which covers all the abominations of acts of violence as well as the authors of such deeds. For states, in their relation to one another, there can be, according to reason, no other way of advancing from that lawless condition which unceasing war implies, than by giving up their savage lawless freedom, just as individual men have done, and yielding to the coercion of public laws. Thus they can form a State of nations (*civitas gentium*), one, too, which will be ever increasing and would finally embrace all the peoples of the earth. States, however, in accordance with their understanding of the law of nations, by no means desire this, and therefore reject *in hypothesi* what is correct *in thesi*. Hence, instead of the positive idea of a world-republic, if all is not to be lost, only the negative substitute for it, a federation averting war, maintaining its ground and ever extending over the world may stop the current of this tendency to war and shrinking from the control of law. But even then there will be a constant danger that this propensity may break out.*

---

*On the conclusion of peace at the end of a war, it might not be unseemly for a nation to appoint a day of humiliation, after the festival of thanksgiving, on which to invoke the mercy of Heaven for the terrible sin which the human race are guilty of, in their continued unwillingness to submit (in their relations with other states) to a law-governed constitution, preferring rather in the pride of their independence to use the barbarous method of war, which after all does not really settle what is wanted, namely, the right of each state in a quarrel. The feasts of thanksgiving during a war for a victorious battle, the hymns which are sung—to use the Jewish expression—"to the Lord of Hosts" are not in less strong contrast to the ethical ides of a father of mankind; for, apart from the indifference these customs show to the way in which nations seek to establish their rights—sad enough as it is— these rejoicings bring in an element of exultation that a great number of lives, or at least the happiness of many, has been destroyed.

"Furor impius intus—fremit horridus ore cruento." (Virgil.)*

Third Definitive Article of Perpetual Peace

III. "The rights of men, as citizens of the world, shall be limited to the conditions of universal hospitality."

We are speaking here, as in the previous articles, not of philanthropy, but of right; and in this sphere hospitality signifies the claim of a stranger entering foreign territory to be treated by its owner without hostility. The latter may send him away again, if this can be done without causing his death; but, so long as he conducts himself peaceably, he must not be treated as an enemy. It is not a right to be treated as a guest to which the stranger can lay claim—a special friendly compact on his behalf would be required to make him for a given time an actual inmate—but he has a right of visitation. This right† to present themselves to society belongs to all mankind in virtue of our common right of possession on the surface of the earth on which, as it is a globe, we cannot be infinitely scattered, and must in the end reconcile ourselves to existence side by side: at the same time, originally no one individual had more right than another to live in any one particular spot. Uninhabitable portions of the surface, ocean and desert, split up the human community, but in such a way that ships and camels —"the ship of the desert"—make it possible for men to come into touch with one another across these unappropriated regions and to take advantage of our common claim to the face of the earth with a view to a possible intercommunication. The inhospitality of the inhabitants of certain sea coasts—as, for example, the coast of Barbary—in plundering ships in neighbouring seas or making slaves of shipwrecked mariners; or the behaviour of the Arab Bedouins in the deserts, who think that proximity to nomadic tribes constitutes a right to rob, is thus contrary to the law of nature. This right to hospitality, however—that is to say, the privilege of strangers arriving on foreign soil—does not amount to more than

---

* Cf. *Aencidos,* I. 294 *seq.*
  "Furor impius intus,
   Saeva sedens super arma, et centum vinctus aënis
   Post tergum nodis, fremet horridus ore cruenio." [Tr.]

†Cf. Vattel (*op. cit.,* II. ch. IX. § 123):—"The right of passage is also a remnant of the primitive state of communion, in which the entire earth was common to all mankind, and the passage was everywhere free to each individual according to his necessities. Nobody can be entirely deprived of this right." See also above, p, 65, *note.* [Tr.]

what is implied in a permission to make an attempt at intercourse with the original inhabitants. In this way far distant territories may enter into peaceful relations with one another. These relations may at last come under the public control of law, and thus the human race may be brought nearer the realisation of a cosmopolitan constitution.

Let us look now, for the sake of comparison, at the inhospitable behaviour of the civilised nations, especially the commercial states of our continent. The injustice which they exhibit on visiting foreign lands and races—this being equivalent in their eyes to conquest—is such as to fill us with horror. America, the negro countries, the Spice Islands, the Cape etc. were, on being discovered, looked upon as countries which belonged to nobody; for the native inhabitants were reckoned as nothing. In Hindustan, under the pretext of intending to establish merely commercial depots, the Europeans introduced foreign troops; and, as a result, the different states of Hindustan were stirred up to far-spreading wars. Oppression of the natives followed, famine, insurrection, perfidy and all the rest of the litany of evils which can afflict mankind.

China* and Japan (Nipon) which had made an attempt at receiving guests of this kind, have now taken a prudent step. Only to a single European

---

*In order to call this great empire by the name which it gives itself—namely, China, not Sina or a word of similar sound—we have only to look at Georgii: *Alphab. Tibet.*, pp. 651–654, particularly *note* b., below. According to the observation of Professor Fischer of St. Petersburg, there is really no particular name which it always goes by: the most usual is the word *Kin*, *i.e.* gold, which the inhabitants of Tibet call *Ser*. Hence the emperor is called the king of gold, *i.e.* the king of the most splendid country in the world. This word *Kin* may probably be *Chin* in the empire itself, but be pronounced *Kin* by the Italian missionaries on account of the gutturals. Thus we see that the country of the Seres, so often mentioned by the Romans, was China: the silk, however, was despatched to Europe across Greater Tibet, probably through Smaller Tibet and Bucharia, through Persia and then on. This leads to many reflections as to the antiquity of this wonderful state, as compared with Hindustan, at the time of its union with Tibet and thence with Japan. On the other hand, the name Sina or Tschina which is said to be given to this land by neighbouring peoples leads to nothing.

Perhaps we can explain the ancient intercourse of Europe with Tibet—a fact at no time widely known—by looking at what Hesychius has preserved on the matter. I refer to the shout, Κονξ Ομπαξ *(Konx Ompax)*, the cry of the Hierophants in the Eleusinian mysteries (cf. *Travels of Anacharsis the Younger,* Part V., p. 447, *seq.*). For, according to Georgii *Alph. Tibet.*, the word *Concioa* which bears a striking resemblance to *Konx* means God. *Pah-cio* (*ib.* p. 520) which might easily be pronounced by the Greeks like *pax* means *promulgator legis,* the divine principle permeating nature (called also, on p. 177, *Cencresi*). *Om*, however, which La Croze translates by *benedictus, i.e.* blessed, can when applied to the Deity mean nothing but beatified (p. 507). Now P. Franz. Horatius, when he asked the Lhamas of Tibet, as he often did, what they understood by God (*Concioa*) always got the answer:— "it is the assembly of all the saints," *i.e.* the assembly of those blessed ones who have been people, the Dutch, has China given the right of access to her shores (but not of entrance into the country), while Japan has granted both these concessions; but at the same time they exclude the Dutch who enter, as if they were prisoners, from social intercourse with the inhabitants. The worst, or from the standpoint of ethical judgment the best, of all this is that no satisfaction is derived from all this violence, that all these trading companies stand on the verge of ruin, that the Sugar Islands, that seat of the most horrible and deliberate slavery, yield no real profit, but only have their use indirectly and for no very praiseworthy object—namely, that of furnishing men to be trained as sailors for the men-of-war and thereby contributing to the carrying on of war in Europe. And this has been done by nations who make a great ado about their piety, and who, while they are quite ready to commit injustice, would like, in their orthodoxy, to be considered among the elect.

The intercourse, more or less close, which has been everywhere steadily increasing between the nations of the earth, has now extended so enormously that a violation of right in one part of the world is felt all over it. Hence the idea of a cosmopolitan right is no fantastical, high-flown notion of right, but a complement of the unwritten code of law—constitutional as well as international law—necessary for the public rights of mankind in general and thus for the realisation of perpetual peace. For only by endeavouring to fulfil the conditions laid down by this cosmopolitan law can we flatter ourselves that we are gradually approaching that ideal.

born again according to the faith of the Lama and, after many wanderings in changing forms, have at last returned to God, to Burchane: that is to say, they are beings to be worshipped, souls which have undergone transmigration (p. 223). So the mysterious expression *Konx Ompax* ought probably to mean the holy (*Konx*), blessed, (*Om*) and wise (*Pax*) supreme Being pervading the universe, the personification of nature. Its use in the Greek mysteries probably signified monotheism for the Epoptes, in distinction from the polytheism of the people, although elsewhere P. Horatius scented atheism here. How that mysterious word came by way of Tibet to the Greeks may be explained as above; and, on the other hand, in this way is made probable an early intercourse of Europe with China across Tibet, earlier perhaps than the communication with Hindustan. (There is some difference of opinion as to the meaning of the words $ub\gamma\xi$ ′$b\mu\pi a\xi$—according to Liddell and Scott, a corruption of $ub\gamma\xi$, $\delta\mu o\iota\omega\varsigma$ $\pi\acute{a}\xi$.* Kant's inferences here seem to be more ban farfetched. Lobeck, in his *Aglaophamus* (p. 775), gives a quite different interpretation which has, he says, been approved by scholars. And Whately (*Historic Doubts relative to Napoleon Bonaparte*, 3rd. ed., Postcript) uses Konx Ompas as a pseudonym. [Tr.])

Questions for Further Exploration:

- What does Kant mean by "perpetual peace"? What articles does Kant propose as the basis for its realization?

- How does Kant conceptualize a "state" including its rights and responsibilities? What sort of state is required to insure perpetual peace? What distinction does he make between "Republican" and "Democratic" states?

- Among the articles of perpetual peace, which are consistent and inconsistent with U.S. policy today? What would follow from bringing U.S. policy into alignment with Kant's proposal?

- What arguments does Kant make for abolishing standing armies and national debts?

- How does Kant conceptualize international organization in the service of perpetual peace? What obstacles exist to the realization of this kind of organization and how does Kant think they can be overcome? What are the necessary conditions for a "law of nations"?

- What are the "rights of men as citizens of the world"? Do you agree that the law of world citizenship should be limited to conditions of universal hospitality or do you think global citizenship should entail a more substantive program?

- What are the strengths and weaknesses of Kant's proposal from the standpoint of the ecological principles set forth by Dryzek?

- Free-write: Where do you stand on the project of creating a "cosmopolitan constitution"?

The Earth Charter

Earth Charter Commission

Preamble

We stand at a critical moment in Earth's history, a time when humanity must choose its future. As the world becomes increasingly interdependent and fragile, the future at once holds great peril and great promise. To move forward we must recognize that in the midst of a magnificent diversity of cultures and life forms we are one human family and one Earth community with a common destiny. We must join together to bring forth a sustainable global society founded on respect for nature, universal human rights, economic justice, and a culture of peace. Towards this end, it is imperative that we, the peoples of Earth, declare our responsibility to one another, to the greater community of life, and to future generations.

Earth, Our Home

Humanity is part of a vast evolving universe. Earth, our home, is alive with a unique community of life. The forces of nature make existence a demanding and uncertain adventure, but Earth has provided the conditions essential to life's evolution. The resilience of the community of life and the well-being of humanity depend upon preserving a healthy biosphere with all its ecological systems, a rich variety of plants and animals, fertile soils,

---

Origin of the Earth Charter
The Earth Charter was created by the independent Earth Charter Commission, which was convened as a follow-up to the 1992 Earth Summit in order to produce a global consensus statement of values and principles for a sustainable future. The document was developed over nearly a decade through an extensive process of international consultation, to which over five thousand people contributed. The Charter has been formally endorsed by thousands of organizations, including UNESCO and the IUCN (World Conservation Union). For more information, please visit www.EarthCharter.org.

pure waters, and clean air. The global environment with its finite resources is a common concern of all peoples. The protection of Earth's vitality, diversity, and beauty is a sacred trust.

The Global Situation

The dominant patterns of production and consumption are causing environmental devastation, the depletion of resources, and a massive extinction of species. Communities are being undermined. The benefits of development are not shared equitably and the gap between rich and poor is widening. Injustice, poverty, ignorance, and violent conflict are widespread and the cause of great suffering. An unprecedented rise in human population has overburdened ecological and social systems. The foundations of global security are threatened. These trends are perilous—but not inevitable.

The Challenges Ahead

The choice is ours: form a global partnership to care for Earth and one another or risk the destruction of ourselves and the diversity of life. Fundamental changes are needed in our values, institutions, and ways of living. We must realize that when basic needs have been met, human development is primarily about being more, not having more. We have the knowledge and technology to provide for all and to reduce our impacts on the environment. The emergence of a global civil society is creating new opportunities to build a democratic and humane world. Our environmental, economic, political, social, and spiritual challenges are interconnected, and together we can forge inclusive solutions.

Universal Responsibility

To realize these aspirations, we must decide to live with a sense of universal responsibility, identifying ourselves with the whole Earth community as well as our local communities. We are at once citizens of different nations and of one world in which the local and global are linked. Everyone shares responsibility for the present and future well-being of the human family and the larger living world. The spirit of human solidarity and kinship with all life is strengthened when we live with reverence for the mystery of being, gratitude for the gift of life, and humility regarding the human place in nature.

We urgently need a shared vision of basic values to provide an ethical foundation for the emerging world community. Therefore, together in hope we affirm the following interdependent principles for a sustainable way of life as a common standard by which the conduct of all individuals, organizations, businesses, governments, and transnational institutions is to be guided and assessed.

Principles
I. Respect and Care for the Community of Life

1. **Respect Earth and life in all its diversity.**
    a. Recognize that all beings are interdependent and every form of life has value regardless of its worth to human beings.
    b. Affirm faith in the inherent dignity of all human beings and in the intellectual, artistic, ethical, and spiritual potential of humanity.

2. **Care for the community of life with understanding, compassion, and love.**
    a. Accept that with the right to own, manage, and use natural resources comes the duty to prevent environmental harm and to protect the rights of people.
    b. Affirm that with increased freedom, knowledge, and power comes increased responsibility to promote the common good.

3. **Build democratic societies that are just, participatory, sustainable, and peaceful.**
    a. Ensure that communities at all levels guarantee human rights and fundamental freedoms and provide everyone an opportunity to realize his or her full potential.
    b. Promote social and economic justice, enabling all to achieve a secure and meaningful livelihood that is ecologically responsible.

4. **Secure Earth's bounty and beauty for present and future generations.**
    a. Recognize that the freedom of action of each generation is qualified by the needs of future generations.
    b. Transmit to future generations values, traditions, and institutions that support the long-term flourishing of Earth's human and ecological communities. In order to fulfill these four broad commitments, it is necessary to:

II. Ecological Integrity

5. **Protect and restore the integrity of Earth's ecological systems, with special concern for biological diversity and the natural processes that sustain life.**
   a. Adopt at all levels sustainable development plans and regulations that make environmental conservation and rehabilitation integral to all development initiatives.
   b. Establish and safeguard viable nature and biosphere reserves, including wild lands and marine areas, to protect Earth's life support systems, maintain biodiversity, and preserve our natural heritage.
   c. Promote the recovery of endangered species and ecosystems.
   d. Control and eradicate non-native or genetically modified organisms harmful to native species and the environment, and prevent introduction of such harmful organisms.
   e. Manage the use of renewable resources such as water, soil, forest products, and marine life in ways that do not exceed rates of regeneration and that protect the health of ecosystems.
   f. Manage the extraction and use of non-renewable resources such as minerals and fossil fuels in ways that minimize depletion and cause no serious environmental damage.

6. **Prevent harm as the best method of environmental protection and, when knowledge is limited, apply a precautionary approach.**
   a. Take action to avoid the possibility of serious or irreversible environmental harm even when scientific knowledge is incomplete or inconclusive.
   b. Place the burden of proof on those who argue that a proposed activity will not cause significant harm, and make the responsible parties liable for environmental harm.
   c. Ensure that decision making addresses the cumulative, long-term, indirect, long distance, and global consequences of human activities.
   d. Prevent pollution of any part of the environment and allow no build-up of radioactive, toxic, or other hazardous substances.
   e. Avoid military activities damaging to the environment.

7. **Adopt patterns of production, consumption, and reproduction that safeguard Earth's regenerative capacities, human rights, and community well-being.**
   a. Reduce, reuse, and recycle the materials used in production and consumption systems, and ensure that residual waste can be assimilated by ecological systems.

b. Act with restraint and efficiency when using energy, and rely increasingly on renewable energy sources such as solar and wind.

c. Promote the development, adoption, and equitable transfer of environmentally sound technologies.

d. Internalize the full environmental and social costs of goods and services in the selling price, and enable consumers to identify products that meet the highest social and environmental standards.

e. Ensure universal access to health care that fosters reproductive health and responsible reproduction.

f. Adopt lifestyles that emphasize the quality of life and material sufficiency in a finite world.

8. **Advance the study of ecological sustainability and promote the open exchange and wide application of the knowledge acquired.**

a. Support international scientific and technical cooperation on sustainability, with special attention to the needs of developing nations.

b. Recognize and preserve the traditional knowledge and spiritual wisdom in all cultures that contribute to environmental protection and human well-being.

c. Ensure that information of vital importance to human health and environmental protection, including genetic information, remains available in the public domain.

III. Social and Economic Justice

9. **Eradicate poverty as an ethical, social, and environmental imperative.**

a. Guarantee the right to potable water, clean air, food security, uncontaminated soil, shelter, and safe sanitation, allocating the national and international resources required.

b. Empower every human being with the education and resources to secure a sustainable livelihood, and provide social security and safety nets for those who are unable to support themselves.

c. Recognize the ignored, protect the vulnerable, serve those who suffer, and enable them to develop their capacities and to pursue their aspirations.

10. **Ensure that economic activities and institutions at all levels promote human development in an equitable and sustainable manner.**

a. Promote the equitable distribution of wealth within nations and among nations.

    b. Enhance the intellectual, financial, technical, and social resources of developing nations, and relieve them of onerous international debt.

    c. Ensure that all trade supports sustainable resource use, environmental protection, and progressive labor standards.

    d. Require multinational corporations and international financial organizations to act transparently in the public good, and hold them accountable for the consequences of their activities.

11. **Affirm gender equality and equity as prerequisites to sustainable development and ensure universal access to education, health care, and economic opportunity.**

    a. Secure the human rights of women and girls and end all violence against them.

    b. Promote the active participation of women in all aspects of economic, political, civil, social, and cultural life as full and equal partners, decision makers, leaders, and beneficiaries.

    c. Strengthen families and ensure the safety and loving nurture of all family members.

12. **Uphold the right of all, without discrimination, to a natural and social environment supportive of human dignity, bodily health, and spiritual well-being, with special attention to the rights of indigenous peoples and minorities.**

    a. Eliminate discrimination in all its forms, such as that based on race, color, sex, sexual orientation, religion, language, and national, ethnic or social origin.

    b. Affirm the right of indigenous peoples to their spirituality, knowledge, lands and resources and to their related practice of sustainable livelihoods.

    c. Honor and support the young people of our communities, enabling them to fulfill their essential role in creating sustainable societies.

    d. Protect and restore outstanding places of cultural and spiritual significance.

IV. Democracy, Nonviolence, and Peace

13. **Strengthen democratic institutions at all levels, and provide transparency and accountability in governance, inclusive participation in decision making, and access to justice.**

    a. Uphold the right of everyone to receive clear and timely information on environmental matters and all development plans and activities which are likely to affect them or in which they have an interest.

    b. Support local, regional and global civil society, and promote the meaningful participation of all interested individuals and organizations in decision making.

    c. Protect the rights to freedom of opinion, expression, peaceful assembly, association, and dissent.

    d. Institute effective and efficient access to administrative and independent judicial procedures, including remedies and redress for environmental harm and the threat of such harm.

    e. Eliminate corruption in all public and private institutions.

    f. Strengthen local communities, enabling them to care for their environments, and assign environmental responsibilities to the levels of government where they can be carried out most effectively.

14. **Integrate into formal education and life-long learning the knowledge, values, and skills needed for a sustainable way of life.**

    a. Provide all, especially children and youth, with educational opportunities that empower them to contribute actively to sustainable development.

    b. Promote the contribution of the arts and humanities as well as the sciences in sustainability education.

    c. Enhance the role of the mass media in raising awareness of ecological and social challenges.

    d. Recognize the importance of moral and spiritual education for sustainable living.

15. **Treat all living beings with respect and consideration.**

    a. Prevent cruelty to animals kept in human societies and protect them from suffering.

    b. Protect wild animals from methods of hunting, trapping, and fishing that cause extreme, prolonged, or avoidable suffering.

    c. Avoid or eliminate to the full extent possible the taking or destruction of non-targeted species.

16. **Promote a culture of tolerance, nonviolence, and peace.**

    a. Encourage and support mutual understanding, solidarity, and cooperation among all peoples and within and among nations.

    b. Implement comprehensive strategies to prevent violent conflict and use collaborative problem solving to manage and resolve environmental conflicts and other disputes.

c. Demilitarize national security systems to the level of a non-provocative defense posture, and convert military resources to peaceful purposes, including ecological restoration.

d. Eliminate nuclear, biological, and toxic weapons and other weapons of mass destruction.

e. Ensure that the use of orbital and outer space supports environmental protection and peace.

f. Recognize that peace is the wholeness created by right relationships with oneself, other persons, other cultures, other life, Earth, and the larger whole of which all are a part.

The Way Forward

As never before in history, common destiny beckons us to seek a new beginning. Such renewal is the promise of these Earth Charter principles. To fulfill this promise, we must commit ourselves to adopt and promote the values and objectives of the Charter.

This requires a change of mind and heart. It requires a new sense of global interdependence and universal responsibility. We must imaginatively develop and apply the vision of a sustainable way of life locally, nationally, regionally, and globally. Our cultural diversity is a precious heritage and different cultures will find their own distinctive ways to realize the vision. We must deepen and expand the global dialogue that generated the Earth Charter, for we have much to learn from the ongoing collaborative search for truth and wisdom.

Life often involves tensions between important values. This can mean difficult choices. However, we must find ways to harmonize diversity with unity, the exercise of freedom with the common good, short-term objectives with long-term goals. Every individual, family, organization, and community has a vital role to play. The arts, sciences, religions, educational institutions, media, businesses, nongovernmental organizations, and governments are all called to offer creative leadership. The partnership of government, civil society, and business is essential for effective governance.

In order to build a sustainable global community, the nations of the world must renew their commitment to the United Nations, fulfill their obligations under existing international agreements, and support the implementation of Earth Charter principles with an international legally binding instrument on environment and development.

Let ours be a time remembered for the awakening of a new reverence for life, the firm resolve to achieve sustainability, the quickening of the struggle for justice and peace, and the joyful celebration of life.

Questions for Further Exploration:

- Which among the philosophies surveyed in this text support or challenge the values set forth in *The Earth Charter?* Does it have a metaphysical or epistemological bias?

- Could/would you live "the examined life" with the values set forth in the Charter as your guide? Which among the values set forth in the Charter are you most inclined to embrace or reject as part of your personal ethic?

- What do you believe are likely to be the most problematic or controversial principles in the Charter for citizens of the United States, and why?

- Select a principle; e.g., "Prevent cruelty to animals kept in human societies and protect them from suffering," and interpret it in terms of specific practices or concrete actions necessary to making it a reality.

- Free-write: Where do you stand on the Charter's claim that "We urgently need a shared vision of basic values to provide an ethical foundation for the emerging world community"?

The Ethic of Care

Leonardo Boff

Translated by Philip Berryman

Among so many other fine things, the Earth Charter proposes a new *way of seeing* that gives rise to a new *ethic*. The new way of seeing is understanding the inter- and retro-connections of all with all, for "Our environmental, economic, political, social, and spiritual challenges are interconnected, and together we can forge inclusive solutions."[1] Likewise, the new *ethic,* consistent with the new way of seeing, is based on the four creative energies of ecologically healthy human reality, called Parts in the Earth Charter, namely: (1) respect and care for the community of life; (2) ecological integrity; (3) social and economic justice; and (4) democracy, nonviolence, and peace.

The effect of these four interdependent principles, when reflected in society and culture, is "a sustainable way of life."[2] This sustainable way of life is equivalent to happiness in traditional versions of ethics deriving from the Greek, medieval, and modern traditions. The supreme value now, that which must save the system of life, of humankind, and of Earth, comes under the sign of care. It represents the new collective dream of humankind. The Earth Charter has given it a name: a sustainable way of life.

The New Dream: A Sustainable Way of Life

A sustainable way of life entails much more than "sustainable development," a key expression in official documents of governments and multilateral agencies, whose meaning is expanded by the Earth Charter.[3] A sustainable way of life is humankind's new ethical and cultural dream. It entails another way of conceiving the common future of Earth and humankind and, accordingly, it demands a true revolution in minds and hearts, values and habits, forms of production, and relationship with nature. It entails understanding that "Humanity is part of a vast evolving universe" and that

"Earth, our home, is alive"[4]; it also entails living "the spirit of human solidarity and kinship with all life," and assuming "responsibility for the present and the future well-being of the human family and the larger living world,"[5] taking care to use the scarce goods of nature rationally so as not to do harm to natural capital or to future generations who also have a right to a good quality of life and minimally just institutions, "being more, not having more"[6] and living "with reverence for the mystery of being, gratitude for the gift of life, and humility regarding the human place in nature."[7]

As is evident, this sustainable way of life demands a new human being, creating a new history different from that which humans have constructed thus far. Only through this sustainable way of life can we respond "together in hope"[8] to the challenges of life and death that we face.

The Preamble opens with an extremely important finding, one that prompted the creation of the Earth Charter: "We stand at a critical moment in Earth's history, a time when humanity must choose its future"[9] and "form a global partnership to *care* for Earth and one another or risk the destruction of ourselves and the diversity of life"[10] (emphasis added). the Preamble states: "The foundations of global security are threatened."[11]

These statements are not at all alarmist. They reveal the true crossroads that humankind has reached. It has created the principle of its own self-destruction with analytic reason and the project of technoscience used to dominate nature and persons. With biological, chemical, and nuclear weapons we can wreak profound havoc with the biosphere and block the planetary human project, conceivably even ending the human species, *homo sapiens* and *demens*.[12]

Thus far we foolishly allowed ourselves to cut down forests, pollute the atmosphere, contaminate waters, and wage wars with conventional weapons. We were operating under the assumption that natural resources were infinite and renewable, and that life and Earth would continue endlessly toward the future. That assumption is illusory. Resources are not infinite—and the earth can be completely wiped out.[13] Militarily powerful nations can carry out shameful wars against weaker countries. But they cannot do so with those that have weapons of mass destruction. It would be the end of civilization, perhaps of the human future itself. Hence either we care for the inheritance received from fifteen billion years of cosmic work, and 3.8 billion years of biotic activity, or we could share the fate of the dinosaurs who, in a short period of time, disappeared sixty-seven million years ago, after reigning supreme on the face of the Earth for over 130 million years.

In other words, humanity and Earth stand together facing the future. This future is not guaranteed by the forces leading the universe. We have to want it. Hence the Earth Charter goes on to say realistically "we must decide to live with a sense of universal responsibility."[14] Accordingly, the principle of self-destruction must be counteracted with the principle of care and of universal coresponsibility.

If the Earth Charter calls attention to these risks it also points to potential opportunities. In the spirit of the Earth Charter, the scenario is one of crisis, not tragedy. And every crisis is purifying and refining. It offers the chance of great changes and of the emergence of a higher and better order. "[G]reat peril, and great promise" . . . "These trends are perilous—but not inevitable" the Preamble rightly proclaims.[15]

This is the context in which the ethic of care proposed by the Earth Charter gains relevance as one of the axes around which the sustainable way of life revolves. It will either be oriented by care or it will not be sustainable.[16]

Care and its Echoes in the Earth Charter

The Earth Charter speaks of *care* four times, always in important contexts: "to *care* for Earth and one another"[17]; "Respect and *Care* for the Community of Life"[18]; "*Care* for the community of life with understanding compassion, and love"[19]; and "to *care* for their environments"[20] (emphasis added).

But echoes of care or similar terms permeate the entire text. Categories correlated with care, such as "sustainability" and "responsibility," are especially prominent. Sustainability is predicated not only on development, but on a "way of life,"[21] "life,"[22] "livelihood,"[23] "society"[24] and "global community."[25] Responsibility is "universal" and "to one another."[26] The term "concern" is likewise used for the global environment in the Preamble and Principle 5. Elsewhere the Earth Charter speaks of "preserving a healthy biosphere"[27] or it encourages us to "preserve our natural heritage."[28] The Earth Charter also seeks to protect, and calls to "protect . . . the integrity" of nature[29] or of natural reserves[30] or even safeguarding "Earth's regenerative capacities."[31] It also speaks of "applying a precautionary approach"[32] and urges preventing harm to the environment.[33]

We want to concentrate on the category of "care" because of its inner riches.[34] Care and sustainability are, we believe, the central categories of the new planetary paradigm. They are also the two principles that can make possible a globalized society and allow for a development that meets human needs and those of other beings in the biotic community. Such development can likewise preserve nature's integrity, beauty, and regenerative capacity with its resources for the sake of generations to come. That is what sustainability means.[35]

What is care? When does it arise? What is its function in the life process? How is an ethic based on care structured?

The Fable of Care and Its Implications

There is no better way to approach an understanding of care than the well-known fable number 220 of Hyginus (43 BCE–17 CE), a freedman who served Caesar Augustus as his librarian and philosopher. The fable goes like this:

> Once when "Care" was crossing a river she saw some clay; she thoughtfully took up a piece and began to shape it. While she was meditating on what she had made, Jupiter came by. "Care" asked him to give it spirit and this he gladly granted. But when she wanted her name to be bestowed upon it, he forbade this, and demanded that it be given his name instead. While "Care" and Jupiter were disputing, Earth arose and desired that her own name be conferred on the creature, since she had furnished it with part of her body. They asked Saturn to be their arbiter, and he made the following decision, which seemed a just one: "Since you, Jupiter, have given its spirit, you shall receive that spirit at its death; and since you, Earth, have given its body, you shall receive its body. But since 'Care' first shaped this creature, she shall possess it as long as it lives. And because there is now a dispute among you as to its name, let it be called 'homo' for it is made out of *humus* (earth)."[36]

This fable is filled with anthropological and ecological implications. Most importantly, care is prior to the spirit infused by Jupiter and prior to the body provided by Earth. The conception of body and spirit is accordingly not primordial. What is primordial is care, which "first shaped" the human being. Care did so with "care," zeal, and devotion, and thus with a loving attitude.

Care is the ontological *a priori,* that which must exist previously for the human being to emerge. Care is therefore at the core of the human being's makeup. Without it the human would not exist. Care thus constitutes the real and true essence of the human being. Hence, as the fable says, care "shall possess" the human being "as long as it lives." Whatever humans do with care will reveal us as we are.

The psychoanalyst Rollo May rightly says: "Our situation is that in our heyday of rationalistic and technicalistic episodes, we have lost sight of and concern for the human being; and we must now humbly go back to the simple fact of care. . . . It is the mythos of care—and that mythos alone—which enables us to stand against the cynicism and apathy which are the psychological illnesses of our day."[37]

Care in Cosmogenesis and Biogenesis

If we think about it, care is not just a category that defines who human beings, man and woman, are, but it also enables us to understand the universe. Care is as ancestral as the cosmos in evolution.

If, after the Big Bang, there had been no care on the part of the guiding forces by which the universe creates itself and regulates itself—that is, the gravitational and electromagnetic forces, and the weak and strong nuclear forces—everything would have expanded too much, preventing matter from condensing and forming the universe as we know it. Or everything would have been pulled in to the point where the universe would collapse upon itself in interminable explosions, preventing the formation of ordered matter. But it didn't. Everything proceeded with a care so subtle, in such a "careful" balance, of fractions of billionths of seconds, as calculated by cosmologists Steven Weinberg and Stephen Hawking, that it allowed us to be here and to talk about all these things.[38]

Care gained further momentum when life emerged 3.8 billion years ago. With utterly singular care, the first bacteria engaged in chemical dialogue with their environment to assure their survival and evolution.

Care acquired further complexity with the emergence of mammals, from which we have come, 125 million years ago, bringing with them the limbic brain, the organ of emotion, care, and tenderness.

Care gained centrality with the emergence of human beings, seven million years ago. Care is their underlying structure on which is built their essence, as in the lesson of the fable examined above.

We exist only because our mothers cared for us even in their wombs. And when we were born, they provided us with complete care, in an unconditional act of generosity and love. It was the extraordinary English pediatrician and psychoanalyst Donald W. Winnicott (1896–1962) who showed the fundamental importance of motherly care in the constitution of the basic psychological structures of the child, structures that will define its ethical direction, and its relationship to otherness.[39]

Care is that *a priori* condition that allows for the explosion of intelligence and loving; it goes before all behavior, guiding it to be free and responsible, and, in short, characteristically human. Care is loving gesture toward reality, gesture that protects and brings tranquility and peace. Care is always essential care.

No living thing survives without care. Care is the stronger force that stands up to the law of entropy, the natural wearing-out of all things, because everything for which we care lasts much longer.

Today we must rescue this attitude as a minimal and universal ethic if we want to preserve that inheritance that we receive from the universe and from culture and assure our common future.

Care and Cultural Crises

History has shown us that whenever crisis situations break out, care also emerges in consciousness. Let us simply put forth some illustrative instances that prove how right the Earth Charter is in choosing care as a core category for establishing a sustainable way of life.

Florence Nightingale (1820–1910) is the archetype of the modern nurse. In 1854 she set out with thirty-eight colleagues from London to a military hospital in Turkey, where the Crimean War was being fought. Imbued with the idea of care, she succeeded in reducing mortality from forty-two percent to two percent in two months.

World War I destroyed certainties and produced a deep metaphysical helplessness. That was when Martin Heidegger (1889–1976) wrote his brilliant *Being and Time* (1927), whose central sections (§§ 39–44) are devoted to care as ontology of the human being.[40] There he says, "care as a primary structural reality, lies 'before' ('*vor*') every factical 'attitude' and 'situation' of Dasein, and it does so existentially *a priori;* this means that it always lies in them" (§ 42). Care must be understood in the line of human essence. It responds to the question, "What is the human being?" By the very fact of being human, the human being is essentially a being of care. Formalizing the essential understanding Heidegger says "with the expression 'care' we have in mind a basic existential ontological phenomenon" (§ 42).

In 1972, the Club of Rome, a global think tank and center of innovation, sounded the ecological alarm on Earth's sickly condition. It identified the main cause, our pattern of predatory, wasteful, consumerist development. Sustainable development was proposed as the solution.

The United Nations Environment Programme, the World Wildlife Fund, and the World Conservation Union drew up a detailed strategy for the future of the Planet under the title "Caring for the Earth" (1991). It states: "The ethic of care applies at the international as well as the national and individual levels. All nations stand to gain from worldwide sustainability and are threatened if we fail to attain it."[41]

Drawing on this tradition, the drafting of the Earth Charter was completed in March 2000 and UNESCO accepted it on that same date. It is the text of the new ecological and ethical conscience of humankind in which the category of care occupies a central place.

Francis of Assisi, Mahatma Gandhi, Aldo Leopold, Mother Teresa of Calcutta, and Chico Mendes have all been marked by care, as have so many men and women, starting with our mothers, sisters, and grandparents. They are archetypes who inspire the path of care and of rescuing life and Earth.

We now want to comment on Principle 2 of Part I, Respect and Care for the Community of Life, which reads: "Care for the community of life with understanding, compassion, and love."[42] Let us examine each part.

Care for the community of life with understanding

Caring means being involved with the other or with the community of life showing zeal and indeed concern. But it is always an attitude of goodwill that wishes to be alongside, to accompany, and to protect. Understanding seeks to know the community of life emotionally. It wants to know with the heart and not simply the head. Hence, it is not at all about knowing in order to dominate (knowledge is power for moderns like Francis Bacon) but knowing in order to enter into communion with reality.[43] For that we need what Blaise Pascal calls *"espirit de finesse"* as opposed to the *"espirit de géometrie."* The spirit of kindness and courtesy grasps others as other, seeks to understand their inner logic and accept them as they are. This understanding entails love and goodwill and overcoming malice and suspicion. Saint Augustine rightly said, in Plato's wake, "we know insofar as we love."

Caring for the community of life with understanding thus means using science and technology always in consonance with this community, never against it, or sacrificing its integrity and beauty. Caring here is an invitation to ecologize everything we do with the community of life, that is, to refuse interactions that are harmful to ecosystems or that cause suffering to the representatives of the community of life as the Earth Charter urges in Principle 15: "Treat all living beings with respect and consideration"; it means maintaining the intermingling of beings, avoiding monocultures, and uniform thinking, so that the logic of inclusion and the holistic perspective prevails.[44]

Care for the community of life with compassion

In order to properly understand compassion, we must first devote some attention to our language, for in everyday understanding this word has pejorative connotations that rob it of its highly positive content. In everyday understanding, having compassion means "having pity" on the other, a feeling that lowers him or her to the condition of someone bereft of his or her own potentiality and inner energy to stand up. We suffer with such a person and share the pain of his or her situation.

We could also understand compassion in the sense of paleo-Christianity (primordial Christianity, before it took the form of churches) as synonym of mercy, a highly positive sense.[45] Having mercy (*misericór-dia*) means having a heart (*cor*) that can feel the poor (*míseros*) and emerge from self to aid them. That stance is suggested by the very philology of the word com-passion: sharing the passion of others and *with* other, suffering *with* them, rejoicing *with* them, walking the path *with* them. But this meaning has not prevailed in history. What has prevailed is the moralistic lesser sense of one who looks down from above and dispenses alms into the hand of the sufferer. Showing mercy comes to mean doing "charity" to the other, charity thus criticized by the Argentine singer and poet Atahualpa Yupanqui: "I have contempt for charity because of the shame wrapped in it. / I am like the mountain lion who lives and dies alone."[46]

The Buddhist conception of compassion is different, however. Compassion may be one of the greatest ethical contributions that the East offers humankind. Compassion has to do with the basic question that gave rise to Buddhism as an ethical and spiritual path. The question is: what is the best means to free us from suffering? The Buddha's answer is: "through compassion, through infinite compassion."

The Dalai Lama updates this time-honored reply as follows: "help others whenever you can, and if you cannot, never harm them."[47] This understanding is in line with the unconditional love and forgiveness proposed by Jesus.

The "great compassion" (*karuna* in Sanskrit) entails two attitudes: *detachment* from all beings in the community of life and *care* for all of them. By *detachment* we distance ourselves from them, relinquishing possession of them and learning to respect them in their otherness and difference. Through *care* we approach beings to enter into communion with them, accepting responsibility for their well-being and aiding them in their suffering.

We have here a behavior in solidarity that has nothing to do with pity and mere handout "charity." To Buddhists, the level of detachment reveals the degree of freedom and maturity that the person has reached. And the level of care shows how much goodwill and responsibility the person has developed toward the whole community of life and toward everything in the universe. Compassion encompasses two dimensions. Hence it demands freedom, altruism, and love.

The ethos that shows compassion knows no limits. The Buddhist ideal is the *bodhisattva,* that person who takes the ideal of compassion so far that he or she is willing to give up nirvana and even to agree to go through an infinite number of lives solely in order to help others in their suffering. This altruism is expressed in the *Prayer of the Bodhisattva:*

> As long as space abides
> and as long as sentient beings remain,
> May I too abide
> and dispel the sufferings of beings.[48]

Tibetan culture expresses this ideal through the figure of the Buddha with a thousand arms and two thousand eyes. With them, in compassion, it can serve an unlimited number of people.

From the Buddhist standpoint, the ethos that shows compassion teaches us how our relationship to the community of life ought to be: respect it in its otherness, live with it as a member, and care for it, and especially regenerate those beings that suffer or are threatened with extinction. Only then should we make use of their gifts, in a fair proportion, for what we need to live adequately and decently.

Care for the community of life with love

Love is the greatest force in the universe, in living beings, and in humans. For love is a force of attraction, union, and transfiguration. The ancient Greek myth formulated it as follows: Eros, the god of life, rose up to create the Earth. Before, everything was silence, naked and immobile. Now everything is life, joy, movement. Love is the highest expression of care because everything we love we also care for. And everything we care for is a sign that we also love.

Humberto Maturana, one of the greatest exponents of contemporary biology, has shown in his studies of *autopoiesis,* that is, on the self-organization of matter which issues in life, how love emerges from within the cosmic process.[49] In nature, says Maturana, are found two kinds of linkages, those of beings with the environment and those with each other. One is *necessary,* linked to the very subsistence of beings, and the other is *spontaneous,* connected to gratuitous relations, for sheer pleasure, in the flow of life itself. When this happens, even at very early stages of evolution, billions of years ago, love emerges as a cosmic and biological phenomenon. As the universe expands and becomes complex, this spontaneous loving linkage tends to increase. In human beings, it gains strength and becomes the primary motive of human actions. It was this relationship of loving and care that allowed our hominid and anthropoid ancestors to make the leap toward humanity. When they went out to gather food and hunt, they did not eat by themselves but brought their food to the group where they shared in a family spirit among everyone, likewise expressing their feelings. Language itself, which is characteristic of human beings, arose within dynamism of love and mutual care.

Love is always oriented to the Other. It always means an Abrahamitic adventure, that of leaving one's own reality and going out to meet what is different and establishing a relationship of covenant, friendship, and love with it. It is the birthplace of ethics.[50]

The irruption of the Other in my face is the beginning of ethics. For the Other forces me to take a practical stance, of welcome, of indifference, of rejection, of destruction. The Other signifies a proposal, which asks for a response with responsibility (*pro-posta, res-posta, res-ponsa-bilidade*).

The most onerous limit of the Western paradigm has to do with the Other, for whom it does not reserve any special place.[51] Indeed, it does not know what to do with the Other, whom it has either absorbed, brought under submission, or destroyed. This also applied to the community of life. The West has embodied a rigid anthropocentrism that has not allowed room for the otherness of nature. The relationship was not of communion and inclusion, but of exploitation and submission. By denying the Other, it has lost the chance for covenant and mutual learning. The paradigm of identity without difference has prevailed, following in the wake of the pre-Socratic Parmenides.

The Other causes the emergence of the ethos of loving. Paradigmatic of this ethos is the Christianity of origin, paleo-Christianity. It is distinguished from the Christianity of history and its churches, which in its ethics has been more influenced by the Greek masters than by the message and practice of Jesus. By contrast, paleo-Christianity gives absolute centrality to love of the Other, which for Jesus is the same as love for God. Love is so central that one who has love has all. It witnesses to this sacred conviction that God is love (1 John 4:8), love comes from God (1 John 4:7), and love will never die (1 Cor. 13:8). This love is unconditional and universal, for it encompasses even the enemy (Luke 6:35). The loving ethos is expressed in the golden rule, attested by all human traditions: "Love your neighbor as yourself"; "Do not do to the other what you do not want done to you."

Love is thus central because for Christianity the Other is central. Indeed God became other, through the incarnation. Without going by way of the Other, without the "more other" Other, i.e., the one who is hungry, poor, a pilgrim, or naked, God cannot be found, not can fullness of life (Matt. 25:31–46) be attained. This going out of self toward others to love them in themselves, to love them without return, unconditionally, lays the groundwork for the most inclusive possible ethos, the most humanizing ethos imaginable. This love is a single movement, it goes out to the other, to the community of life, and to God.

No one in the West has become an archetype of this loving and heartfelt ethos more than Saint Francis of Assisi. He united the two ecologies, internal ecology (by integrating his emotions and desires) and external ecology (by establishing kinship with all beings). Eloi Leclerc, one of the best contemporary Francisean thinkers, a survivor of the Nazi death camps at Buchenwald, observes:

> Rather than hardening himself and becoming enclosed in proud isolation, he allowed himself to be despoiled of everything, to become tiny, to take his place very humbly, in the midst of creatures, a neighbor to the most humble among them. He established kinship with Earth itself, with its original soil, with its obscure roots. And indeed, "our sister and Mother-Earth" opened before his marveling eyes a path of unlimited borderless brother- and sisterhood. A kinship that embraced all creation. Humble Francis became the brother of the Sun, the stars, the wind, the clouds, water, fire, and everything living.[52]

This is the result of an essential love that embraces the whole community of life with affection, tenderness, and love.

The loving ethos lays the groundwork for giving life new meaning. Loving the Other, whether the human being or each representative of the community of life, means giving it a reason for being. There is no reason for existing. Existence is sheer gratuity. Loving the Other means wanting the Other to exist because love makes the other important. Love is saying to another: you will not die, you must exist, you cannot die.

When someone or something becomes important to the Other, a value that mobilizes all vital energies appears. That is why when people love they are rejuvenated and have the sensation that they are beginning life anew. Love is the source of values.

Only this loving ethos can measure up to the challenges we face in the community of life, which finds itself devastated and threatened and futureless. This love respects otherness, opens up to it, and seeks a communion that enriches all. It brings close those who are afar, and makes brothers and sisters of those who are nearby.

Conclusion: Care and the Future of Life

If life can arise in a context of care, it is through ongoing care, through all the time in which it will exist on the face of the Earth, that life maintains itself, reproduces itself, and coevolves. Today we understand that the revolution of care has become imperative. As care belongs to the essence of the human being, it must serve as a minimum consensus on which a planetary ethic can be based, an ethic that everyone can understand and everyone can practice.[53]

In one of his songs the black Brazilian poet and singer Milton Nascimento sang: "há que se cuidar do broto para que a vida nos dê flor e fruto" (the seedling must be cared for so that life may give us flower and fruit). That applies to Earth and all ecosystems: we have to "care with understanding, compassion, and love" for Earth, understood as Gaia, Magna Mater, and the Pacha Mama of our indigenous peoples, so that she can secure her vitality, integrity, and beauty. We—Earth and Humankind—comprise a single entity, as the astronauts have been thrilled to see from their spacecraft out there in space. From that vantage point, there is no difference between Earth and Humankind. Both make up a single entity with a single origin and a single destiny. Only care will assure the sustainability of the Earth-system with all beings of the community of life, among which is situated the human being, one axis among others, of this vast current of life. Humankind's function is that of gardener, as portrayed in Genesis, chapter 2. The gardener's work is to care for the Garden of Eden, to make it fruitful and beautiful. The Earth Charter has awakened us, just in time, to this essential and urgent mission of ours.

Notes

1. Earth Charter, Preamble, paragraph four.
2. Earth Charter, Preamble, paragraph six.
3. Sustainable development is discussed in detail in L. Boff, *Ecology and Liberation: A New Paradigm* (Maryknoll, N.Y.: Orbis Books, 1995) and *Cry of the Earth, Cry of the Poor* (Maryknoll, N.Y.: Orbis Books, 1998).
4. Earth Charter, Preamble, paragraph two.
5. Earth Charter, Preamble, paragraph five.
6. Earth Charter, Preamble, paragraph four.
7. Earth Charter, Preamble, paragraph five.
8. Earth Charter, Preamble, paragraph six.
9. Earth Charter, Preamble, paragraph one.
10. Earth Charter, Preamble, paragraph four.
11. Earth Charter, Preamble, paragraph three.
12. See L. Boff, *Do iceberg à arca de Noé: o nascimento de uma ética planetária* (Rio de Janeiro: Garamond, 2002).
13. See, for example, D. Toolan, *At Home in the Cosmos* (Maryknoll, N.Y.: Orbis Books, 2001), part III, The State of the Earth, 75–125.
14. Earth Charter, Preamble, paragraph five.

15. Earth Charter, Preamble, paragraph three.
16. On the "ethic of care" see B. R. Hill, *Christian Faith and the Environment* (Maryknoll, N.Y.: Orbis Books, 1998); J. R. Des Jardins, *Environmental Ethics* (Belmont, Calif.: Wadsworth, 1977); A. Auer, *Umweltethik* (Düsseldorf: Patmos, 1985); and P. Schmitz, *Ist die Schöpfung noch zu retten?* (Würzburg: Echter, 1995).
17. Earth Charter, Preamble, paragraph four.
18. Earth Charter, Part 1.
19. Earth Charter, Principle 2.
20. Earth Charter, Subprinciple 13f.
21. Earth Charter, Preamble, paragraph six.
22. Earth Charter, Principle 5.
23. Earth Charter, Subprinciple 9b.
24. Earth Charter, Subprinciple 12c.
25. Earth Charter, The Way Forward, paragraph four.
26. Earth Charter, Preamble, paragraph one.
27. Earth Charter, Preamble, paragraph two.
28. Earth Charter, Subprinciple 5b.
29. Earth Charter, Principle 5.
30. Earth Charter, Subprinciples 5b, 12b, and 15b.
31. Earth Charter, Principle 7.
32. Earth Charter, Principle 6.
33. Earth Charter, Principle 6, Subprinciple 5d.
34. See the following primary bibliography: L. Boff, *Saber cuidar: ética do humano, compaixão pela Terra* (Petrópolis: Vozes, 1999); F. Torralba y Roselló, *Antropolgía del cuidar* (Barcelona: Fundación Mapfre Medicina, 1998); V. R. Waldow, *Cuidado humano—resgate necessário* (Porto Alegre: Sagra Luzzatto, 1998); S. T. Fry, A Global Agenda for Caring (New York: National League for Nursing Press, 1993), 175–79; S. T. Fry, "The Philosophical Foundations of Caring," in M. M. Leininger (ed.), *Ethical and Moral Dimensions of Care* (Detroit: Wayne State University Press, 1990); M. M. Leininger and J. Watson, *The Caring Imperative in Education* (New York: Nation League for Nursing, 1990); M. Mayeroff, *On Caring* (New York: Harper Perennial, 1971); J. M. Morse et al. "Concepts of Caring and Caring as a Concept," *Advances in Nursing Science,* vol. 13, n. 1, p. 1–14, 1990; N. Noddings, *Caring: A Feminine Approach to Ethics and Moral Education* (Berkeley: University of California Press, 1984); P. L., Chinn, *Anthology on Caring* (New York: Nation League of Nursing Press, 1991); M. J., dos S. Rossi, "O curar and o cuidar— a história de uma relação," *Revista Brasileira de Enfermagem* (Brasília), vol. 44, n. 1, 16–21, 1991.

35. On sustainability, see the classic, R. Goodland et al., *Medio ambiente y desarrollo sostenible. Más allá del informe Brundtland* (Madrid: Trotta, 1992).

36. Translated from Latin in Martin Heidegger, *Being and Time* (San Francisco: HarperSanFrancisco, 1962), 242.

37. Rollo May, *Love and Will* (New York: Dell, 1969), 202, 203.

38. On the careful balance, see Steven Weinberg, *The First Three Minutes Os Três primeiros minutos. Uma análise moderna da origem do universo* (Lisboa: Gradiva, 1987), and Stephen Hawking, *A Brief History of Time: From the Big Bang to Black Holes* (New York: Bantam, 1988).

39. Donald W. Winnicott, "Dependence in Infant Care, Child Care, Psychoanalytic Setting," *International Journal of Psychoanalysis,* vol. 44, 1963, 338–344; Winnicott, *Mother and Child: A Primer of First Relationship* (New York: Basic Books, 1957); Winnicott, *Human Nature* (New York: Schocken, 1988).

40. Heidegger, *Being and Time,* 238.

41. International Union for Conservation of Nature and Natural Resources, *Caring for the Earth: A Strategy for Sustainable Living* (Gland, Switzerland: IUCN [the World Conservation Union, UN Environment Programme, World Wide Fund for Nature], 1991).

42. Earth Charter, Principle 2.

43. Cf. J. Moltmann, "Die Entdeckung der Anderen. Zur Theorie des kommunikativen Erkennes," *Evangelische Theologie,* n. 5, 1990, 400–414.

44. J. B. McDaniel, *With Roots and Wings* (Maryknoll, N.Y.: Orbis Books, 1995).

45. Matthew Fox, *A Spirituality Named Compassion and the Healing of the Global Village, Humpty Dumpty, and Us* (San Francisco: Harper & Row, 1990); J. Sobrino, *The Principle of Mercy: Taking the Crucified People from the Cross* (Maryknoll, N.Y.: Orbis Books, 1994).

46. The lyric is from Atahualpa Yupanqui's "Milonga." The original is "Desprecio la caridad, / por la vergüenza que encierra. / Soy como el león de las sierras: / ¡vivo y muero en soledad!"

47. Dalai Lama, *The Good Heart: A Buddhist Perspective on the Teachings of Jesus* (Boston: Wisdom Publications, 1996), 170.

48. Ibid., 219; Dalai Lama, *Ethics for the New Millennium* (New York: Riverhead Books, 1999).

49. On love emerging from within the cosmic process, see *A ontologia da realidade* (Belo Horizonte: Editora da UFMG, 1997); *A árvore do conhecimento: As bases boilógicas do entendimento humano* (Campinas: Psy II, 1995); together with F. Varela, *De máquinas and*

seres vivos. *Autopoiese—a organização do ser vivo* (Porto Alegre: Artes Médicas, 1997).

50. L. Boff, *Etica e Moral. Fundamentos* (Petrópolis: Vozes, 2003).
51. See the classic D. de Rougemont, *L'amour et l'Occident* (Paris: Librairie Plon, 1972). Published in English as *Love in the Western World* (New York: Pantheon, 1956).
52. E. Leclerc, *Le soleil se lève sur Assise* (Paris: Desclée de Brouwer, 1999), 124.
53. L. Boff, *Ethos mundial. Um consenso mínimo entre os humanos* (Rio de Janeiro: Sextante, 2003).

Questions for Further Exploration:

- What does an ethic of care demand and what does it promise?

- How does Boff conceptualize "care"?

- What metaphysical and epistemology principles provide a foundation for Boff's ethic of care?

- What reasons does Boff give in support of his claim that care is the core value for establishing a sustainable way of life? In your view, how will his case for care fare against the core values of the existing paradigm?

- Do you agree/disagree with Boff that love "is the birthplace of ethics"?

- Free-write: What do you care about? How do you express care in your relations with others? How do you express care for yourself?

A Sand County Almanac

The Land Ethic

Aldo Leopold

When god-like Odysseus returned from the wars in Troy, he hanged all on one rope a dozen slave-girls of his household, whom he suspected of misbehavior during his absence.

This hanging involved no question of propriety. The girls were property. The disposal of property was then, as now, a matter of expediency, not of right and wrong.

Concepts of right and wrong were not lacking from Odysseus' Greece: witness the fidelity of his wife through the long years before at last his black-prowed galleys clove the wine-dark seas for home. The ethical structure of that day covered wives, but had not yet been extended to human chattels. During the three thousand years which have since elapsed, ethical criteria have been extended to many fields of conduct, with corresponding shrinkages in those judged by expediency only.

The Ethical Sequence

This extension of ethics, so far studied only by philosophers, is actually a process in ecological evolution. Its sequences may be described in ecological as well as in philosophic terns. An ethic, ecologically, is a limitation on freedom of action in the struggle for existence. An ethic, philosophically, is a differentiation of social from anti-social conduct. These are two definitions of one thing. The thing has its origin in the tendency of interdependent individuals or groups to evolve modes of co-operation. The ecologist calls these symbioses. Politics and economics are advanced symbioses in which the original free-for-all competition has been replaced, in part, by co-operative mechanisms with an ethical content.

A Sand County Almanac by Leopold (1996) Chp. "The Land Ethic" pp. 237-264 © 1949, 1977 by Oxford University Press, Inc. By permission of Oxford University Press, Inc.

The complexity of co-operative mechanisms has increased with population density, and with the efficiency of tools. It was simpler, for example, to define the anti-social uses sticks and stones in the days of the mastodons than of bullets and billboards in the age of motors.

The first ethics dealt with the relation between individuals; the Mosaic Decalogue is an example. Later accretions dealt with the relation between the individual and society. The Golden Rule tries to integrate the individual to society, democracy to integrate social organization to the individual.

There is as yet no ethic dealing with man's relation to land and to the animals and plants which grow upon it. Land, like Odysseus' slave-girls, is still property. The land-relation is still strictly economic, entailing privileges but no obligations.

The extension of ethics to this third element in human environment is, if I read the evidence correctly, an evolutionary possibility and an ecological necessity. It is the third step in a sequence. The first two have already been taken. Individual thinkers since the days of Ezekiel and Isaiah have asserted that the despoliation of land is not only inexpedient but wrong. Society, however, has not yet affirmed their belief. I regard the present conservation movement as the embryo of such an affirmation.

An ethic may be regarded as a mode of guidance for meeting ecological situations so new or intricate, or involving such deferred reactions, that the path of social expediency is not discernible to the average individual. Animal instincts are modes of guidance for the individual in meeting such situations. Ethics are possibly a kind of community instinct in-the-making.

The Community Concept

All ethics so far evolved rest upon a single premise: that the individual is a member of a community of interdependent parts. His instincts prompt him to compete for his place in that community, but his ethics prompt him also to co-operate (perhaps in order that there may be a place to compete for).

The land ethic simply enlarges the boundaries of the community to include soils, waters, plants, and animals, or collectively: the land.

This sounds simple: do we not already sing our love for and obligation to the land of the free and the home of the brave? Yes, but just what and whom do we love? Certainly not the soil, which we are sending helter-skelter downriver. Certainly not the waters, which we assume have no function except to turn turbines, float barges, and carry off sewage. Certainly not the plants, of which we exterminate whole communities without batting an eye. Certainly not the animals, of which we have already extirpated many of the largest and most beautiful species. A land ethic of course cannot prevent the alteration, management, and use of these 're-sources,' but it does affirm their right to continued existence, and, at least in spots, their continued existence in a natural state.

In short, a land ethic changes the role of *Homo sapiens* from conqueror of the land-community to plain member and citizen of it. It implies respect for his fellow-members, and also respect for the community as such.

In human history, we have learned (I hope) that the conqueror role is eventually self-defeating. Why? Because it is implicit in such a role that the conqueror knows, *ex cathedra,* just what makes the community clock tick, and just what and who is valuable, and what and who is worthless, in community life. It always turns out that he knows neither, and this is why his conquests eventually defeat themselves.

In the biotic community, a parallel situation exists. Abraham knew ex-actly what the land was for: it was to drip milk and honey into Abraham's mouth. At the present moment, the assurance with which we regard this assumption is inverse to the degree of our education.

The ordinary citizen today assumes that science knows what makes the community clock tick; the scientist is equally sure that he does not. He knows that the biotic mechanism is so complex that its workings may never be fully understood.

That man is, in fact, only a member of a biotic team is shown by an ecological interpretation of history. Many historical events, hitherto ex-plained solely in terms of human enterprise, were actually biotic interac-tions between people and land. The characteristics of the land determined the facts quite as potently as the characteristics of the men who lived on it.

Consider, for example, the settlement of the Mississippi valley. In the years following the Revolution, three groups were contending for its con-trol: the native Indian, the French and English traders, and the American settlers. Historians wonder what would have happened if the English at Detroit had thrown a little more weight into the Indian side of those tipsy scales which decided the outcome of the colonial migration into the cane-lands of Kentucky. It is time now to ponder the fact that the cane-lands, when subjected to the particular mixture of forces represented by the cow, plow, fire, and axe of the pioneer, became bluegrass. What if the plant suc-cession inherent in this dark and bloody ground had, under the impact of these forces, given us some worthless sedge, shrub, or weed? Would Boone and Kenton have held out? Would there have been any overflow into Ohio, Indiana, Illinois, and Missouri? Any Louisiana Purchase? Any transcontinental union of new states? Any Civil War?

Kentucky was one sentence in the drama of history. We are commonly told what the human actors in this drama tried to do, but we are seldom told that their success, or the lack of it, hung in large degree on the reaction of particular soils to the impact of the particular forces exerted by their occupancy. In the case of Kentucky, we do not even know where the bluegrass came from—whether it is a native species, or a stowaway from Europe.

Contrast the cane-lands with what hindsight tells us about the Southwest, where the pioneers were equally brave, resourceful, and persevering. The impact of occupancy here brought no bluegrass, or other plant fitted to withstand the bumps and buffetings of hard use. This region, when grazed by livestock, reverted through a series of more and more worthless grasses, shrubs, and weeds to a condition of unstable equilibrium. Each recession of plant types bred erosion; each increment to erosion bred a further recession of plants. The result today is a progressive and mutual deterioration, not only of plants and soils, but of the animal community subsisting thereon. The early settlers did not expect this: on the ciénegas of New Mexico some even cut ditches to hasten it. So subtle has been its progress that few residents of the region are aware of it. It is quite invisible to the tourist who finds this wrecked landscape colorful and charming (as indeed it is, but it bears scant resemblance to what it was in 1848).

This same landscape was 'developed' once before, but with quite different results. The Pueblo Indians settled the Southwest in pre-Columbian times, but they happened *not* to be equipped with range livestock. Their civilization expired, but not because their land expired.

In India, regions devoid of any sod-forming grass have been settled, apparently without wrecking the land, by the simple expedient of carrying the grass to the cow, rather than vice versa. (Was this the result of some deep wisdom, or was it just good luck? I do not know.)

In short, the plant succession steered the course of history; the pioneer simply demonstrated, for good or ill, which successions inhered in the land. Is history taught in this spirit? It will be, once the concept of land as a community really penetrates our intellectual life.

The Ecological Conscience

Conservation is a state of harmony between men and land. Despite nearly a century of propaganda, conservation still proceeds at a snail's pace; progress still consists largely letterhead pieties and convention oratory. On the back forty we still slip two steps backward for each forward stride.

The usual answer to this dilemma is 'more conservation education.' No one will debate this, but is it certain that only the *volume* of education needs stepping up? Is something lacking in the *content* as well?

It is difficult to give a fair summary of its content in brief form, but, as I understand it, the content is substantially this: obey the law, vote right, join some organizations, and practice what conservation is profitable on your own land; the government will do the rest.

Is not this formula too easy to accomplish anything worth-while? It defines no right or wrong, assigns no obligation, calls for no sacrifice, implies no change in the current philosophy of values. In respect of land-use, it urges only enlightened self-interest. Just how far will such education take us? An example will perhaps yield a partial answer.

By 1930 it had become clear to all except the ecologically blind that southwestern Wisconsin's topsoil was slipping seaward. In 1933 the farmers were told that if they would adopt certain remedial practices for five years, the public would donate CCC labor to install them, plus the necessary machinery and materials. The offer was widely accepted, but the practices were widely forgotten when the five-year contract period was up. The farmers continued only those practices that yielded an immediate and visible economic gain for themselves.

This led to the idea that maybe farmers would learn more quickly if they themselves wrote the rules. Accordingly the Wisconsin Legislature in 1937 passed the Soil Conservation District Law. This said to farmers, in effect: *We, the public, will furnish you free technical service and loan you specialized machinery, if you will write your own rules for land-use. Each county may write its own rules, and these will have the force of law.* Nearly all the counties promptly organized to accept the proffered help, but after a decade of operation, *no county has yet written a single rule.* There has been visible progress in such practices as strip-cropping, pasture renovation, and soil liming, but none in fencing woodlots against grazing, and none in excluding plow and cow from steep slopes. The farmers, in short, have selected those remedial practices which were profitable anyhow, and ignored those which were profitable to the community, but not clearly profitable to themselves.

When one asks why no rules have been written, one is told that the community is not yet ready to support them; education must precede rules. But the education actually in progress makes no mention of obligations to land over and above those dictated by self-interest. The net result is that we have more education but less soil, fewer healthy woods, and as many floods as in 1937.

The puzzling aspect of such situations is that the existence of obligations over and above self-interest is taken for granted in such rural community enterprises as the betterment of roads, schools, churches, and baseball teams. Their existence is not taken for granted, nor as yet seriously discussed, in bettering the behavior of the water that falls on the land, or in the preserving of the beauty or diversity of the farm landscape.

Land-use ethics are still governed wholly by economic self-interest, just as social ethics were century ago.

To sum up: we asked the farmer to do what he conveniently could to save his soil, and he has done just that, and only that. The farmer who clears the woods off a 75 percent slope, turns his cows into the clearing, and dumps its rainfall, rocks, and soil into the community creek, is still (if otherwise decent) a respected member of society. If he puts lime on his fields and plants his crops on contour, he is still entitled to all the privileges and emoluments of his Soil Conservation District. The District is a beautiful piece of social machinery, but it is coughing along on two cylinders because we have been too timid, and too anxious for quick success, to tell the farmer the true magnitude of his obligations. Obligations have no meaning without conscience, and the problem we face is the extension of the social conscience from people to land.

No important change in ethics was ever accomplished without an internal change in our intellectual emphasis, loyalties, affections, and convictions. The proof that conservation has not yet touched these foundations of conduct lies in the fact that philosophy and religion have not yet heard of it. In our attempt to make conservation easy, we have made it trivial.

Substitutes for a Land Ethic

When the logic of history hungers for bread and we hand out a stone, we are at pains to explain how much the stone resembles bread. I now describe some of the stones which serve in lieu of a land ethic.

One basic weakness in a conservation system based wholly on economic motives is that most members of the land community have no economic value. Wildflowers and songbirds are examples. Of the 22,000 higher plants and animals native to Wisconsin, it is doubtful whether more than 5 per cent can be sold, fed, eaten, or otherwise put to economic use. Yet these creatures are members of the biotic community, and if (as I believe) its stability depends on its integrity, they are entitled to continuance.

When one of these non-economic categories is threatened, and if we happen to love it, we invent subterfuges to give it economic importance. At the beginning of the century songbirds were supposed to be disappearing. Ornithologists jumped to the rescue with some distinctly shaky evidence to the effect that insects would eat us up if birds failed to control them. The evidence had to be economic in order to be valid.

It is painful to read these circumlocutions today. We have no land ethic yet, but we have at least drawn nearer the point of admitting that birds should continue as a matter of biotic right, regardless of the presence or absence of economic advantage to us.

A parallel situation exists in respect of predatory mammals, raptorial birds, and fish-eating birds. Time was when biologists somewhat over-worked the evidence that these creatures preserve the health of game by killing weaklings, or that they control rodents for the farmer, or that they prey only on 'worthless' species. Here again, the evidence had to be economic in order to be valid. It is only in recent years that we hear the more honest argument that predators are members of the community, and that no special interest has the right to exterminate them for the sake of a benefit, real or fancied, to itself. Unfortunately this enlightened view still in the talk stage. In the field the extermination of predators goes merrily on: witness the impending erasure of the timber wolf by fiat of Congress, the Conservation Bureaus, and many state legislatures.

Some species of trees have been 'read out of the party' by economics-minded foresters because they grow too slowly, or have too low a sale value to pay as timber crops: white cedar, tamarack, cypress, beech, and hemlock are examples. In Europe, where forestry is ecologically more ad-vanced, the non-commercial tree species are recognized as members of the native forest community, to be preserved as such, within reason. Moreover some (like beech) have seen found to have a valuable function in building up soil fertility. The interdependence of the forest and its constituent tree species, ground flora, and fauna is taken for granted.

Lack of economic value is sometimes a character not only of species or groups, but of entire biotic communities: marshes, bogs, dunes, and 'deserts' are examples. Our formula in such cases is to relegate their con-servation to government as refuges, monuments, or parks. The difficulty is that these communities are usually interspersed with more valuable private lands; the government cannot possibly own or control such scattered parcels. The net effect is that we have relegated some of them to ultimate extinction over large areas. If the private owner were ecologically minded, he would be proud to be the custodian of a reasonable proportion of such areas, which add diversity and beauty to his farm and to his community.

In some instances, the assumed lack of profit in these 'waste' areas has proved to be wrong, but only after most of them had been done away with. The present scramble to reflood muskrat marshes is a case in point.

Where is a clear tendency in American conservation to relegate to government all necessary jobs that private landowners fail to perform. Government ownership, operation, subsidy, or regulation is now widely prevalent in forestry, range management, soil and watershed management, park and wilderness conservation, fisheries management, and migratory bird management, with more to come. Most of this growth in governmental conservation is proper and logical, some of it is inevitable. That I imply no disapproval of it is implicit in the fact that I have spent most of my life working for it. Nevertheless the question arises: What is the ultimate magnitude of the enterprise? Will the tax base carry its eventual ramifications? At what point will governmental conservation, like the mastodon, become handicapped by its own dimensions? The answer, if there is any, seems to be in a land ethic, or some other force which assigns more obligation to the private landowner.

Industrial landowners and users, especially lumbermen and stockmen, are inclined to wail long and loudly about the extension of government ownership and regulation to land, but (with notable exceptions) they show little disposition to develop the only visible alternative: the voluntary practice of conservation on their own lands.

When the private landowner is asked to perform some unprofitable act for the good the community, he today assents only with outstretched palm. If the act costs him cash this is fair and proper, but when it costs only fore-thought, open-mindedness, or time, the issue is at least debatable. The overwhelming growth of land-use subsidies in recent years must be ascribed, in large part, to the government's own agencies for conservation education: the land bureaus, the agricultural colleges, and the extension services. As far as I can detect, no ethical obligation toward land is taught in these institutions.

To sum up: a system of conservation based solely on economic self-interest is hopelessly lopsided. It tends to ignore, and thus eventually to eliminate, many elements in the land community that lack commercial value, but that are (as far as we know) essential to its healthy functioning. It assumes, falsely, I think, that the economic parts of the biotic clock will function without the uneconomic parts. It tends to relegate to government many functions eventually too large, too complex, or too widely dispersed to be performed by government.

An ethical obligation on the part of the private owner is the only visible remedy for these situations.

The Land Pyramid

An ethic to supplement and guide the economic relation to land presupposes the existence of some mental image of land as a biotic mechanism. We can be ethical only in relation to something we can see, feel, understand, love, or otherwise have faith in.

The image commonly employed in conservation education is 'the balance of nature.' For reasons too lengthy to detail here, this figure of speech fails to describe accurately what little we know about the land mechanism. A much truer image is the one employed in ecology: the biotic pyramid. I shall first sketch the pyramid as a symbol of land, and later develop some of its implications in terms of land-use.

Plants absorb energy from the sun. This energy flows through a circuit called the biota, which may be represented by a pyramid consisting of layers. The bottom layer is the soil. A plant layer rests on the soil, an insect layer on the plants, a bird and rodent layer on the insects, and so on up through various animal groups to the apex layer, which consists of the larger carnivores.

The species of a layer are alike not in where they came from, or in what they look like, but rather in what they eat. Each successive layer depends on those below it for food and often for other services, and each in turn furnishes food and services to those above. Proceeding upward, each successive layer decreases in numerical abundance. Thus, for every carnivore there are hundreds of his prey, thousands of their prey, millions of insects, uncountable plants. The pyramidal form of the system reflects this numerical progression from apex to base. Man shares an intermediate layer with the bears, raccoons, and squirrels which eat both meat and vegetables.

The lines of dependency for food and other services are called food chains. Thus soil-oak-deer-Indian is a chain that has now been largely converted to soil-corn-cow-farmer. Each species, including ourselves, is a link in many chains. The deer eats a hundred plants other than oak, and the cow a hundred plants other than corn. Both, then, are links in a hundred chains. The pyramid is a tangle of chains so complex as to seem disorderly, yet the stability of the system proves it to be a highly organized structure. Its functioning depends on the co-operation and competition of its diverse parts.

In the beginning, the pyramid of life was low and squat; the food chains short and simple. Evolution has added layer after layer, link after link. Man is one of thousands of accretions to the height and complexity of the pyramid. Science has given us many doubts, but it has given us at least one certainty: the trend of evolution is to elaborate and diversify the biota.

Land, then, is not merely soil; it is a fountain of energy flowing through a circuit of soils, plants, and animals. Food chains are the living channels which conduct energy upward; death and decay return it to the soil. The circuit is not closed; some energy is dissipated in decay, some is added by absorption from the air, some is stored in soils, peats, and long-lived forests; but it is a sustained circuit, like a slowly augmented revolving fund of life. There is always a net loss by downhill wash, but this is normally small and offset by the decay of rocks. It is deposited in the ocean and, in the course of geological time, raised to form new lands and new pyramids.

The velocity and character of the upward flow of energy depend on the complex structure of the plant and animal community, much as the upward flow of sap in a tree depends on its complex cellular organization. Without this complexity, normal circulation would presumably not occur. Structure means the characteristic numbers, as well as the characteristic kinds and functions, of the component species. This interdependence between the complex structure of the land and its smooth functioning as an energy unit is one of its basic attributes.

When a change occurs in one part of the circuit, many other parts must adjust themselves to it. Change does not necessarily obstruct or divert the flow of energy; evolution is a long series of self-induced changes, the net result of which has been to elaborate the flow mechanism and to lengthen the circuit. Evolutionary changes, however, are usually slow and local. Man's invention of tools has enabled him to make changes of unprecedented violence, rapidity, and scope.

One change is in the composition of floras and faunas. The larger predators are lopped off the apex of the pyramid; food chains, for the first time in history, become shorter rather than longer. Domesticated species from other lands are substituted for wild ones, and wild ones are moved to new habitats. In this world-wide pooling of faunas an floras, some species get out of bounds as pests and disease, others are extinguished. Such effects are seldom intended foreseen; they represent unpredicted and often untraceable readjustments in the structure. Agricultural science is large a race between the emergence of new pests and the emergence of new techniques for their control.

Another change touches the flow of energy through plants and animals and its return to the soil. Fertility is the ability of soil to receive, store, and release energy. Agriculture, by overdrafts on the soil, or by too radical a substitution of domestic for native species in the superstructure, may derange the channels of flow or deplete storage. Soils depleted of their storage, or of the organic matter which anchors it, wash away faster than they form. This is erosion.

Waters, like soil, are part of the energy circuit. Industry, by polluting waters or obstructing them with dams, may exclude the plants and animals necessary to keep energy in circulation.

Transportation brings about another basic change: the plants or animals grown in one region are now consumed and returned to the soil in another. Transportation taps the energy stored in rocks, and in the air, and uses it elsewhere; thus we fertilize the garden with nitrogen gleaned by the guano birds from the fishes of seas on the other side of the Equator. Thus the formerly localized and self-contained circuits are pooled on a world-wide scale.

The process of altering the pyramid for human occupation releases stored energy, and this often gives rise, during the pioneering period, to a deceptive exuberance of plant and animal life, both wild and tame. These releases of biotic capital tend to becloud or postpone the penalties of violence.

■ ■ ■

This thumbnail sketch of land as an energy circuit conveys three basic ideas:

1. That land is not merely soil.
2. That the native plants and animals kept the energy circuit open; others may or may not.
3. That man-made changes are of a different order than evolutionary changes, and have effects more comprehensive than is intended or foreseen.

These ideas, collectively, raise two basic issues: Can the land adjust itself to the new order? Can the desired alterations be accomplished with less violence?

Biotas seem to differ in their capacity to sustain violent conversion. Western Europe, for example, carries a far different pyramid than Caesar found there. Some large animals are lost; swampy forests have become meadows or plowland; many new plants and animals are introduced, some of which escaped as pests; the remaining natives are greatly changed in distribution and abundance. Yet the soil is still there and, with the help of imported nutrients, still fertile; the waters flow normally; the new structure seems to function and to persist. There is no visible stoppage or derangement of the circuit.

Western Europe, then, has a resistant biota. Its inner processes are tough, elastic, resistant to strain. No matter how violent the alterations, the pyramid, so far, has developed some new *modus vivendi* which preserves its habitability for man, and for most of the other natives.

Japan seems to present another instance of radical conversion without disorganization.

Most other civilized regions, and some as yet barely touched by civilization, display various stages of disorganization, varying from initial symptoms to advanced wastage. In Asia Minor and North Africa diagnosis is confused by climatic changes, which may have been either the cause or the effect of advanced wastage. In the United States the degree of disorganization varies locally; it is worst in the Southwest, the Ozarks, and parts of the South, and least in New England and the Northwest. Better land-uses may still arrest it in the less advanced regions. In parts of Mexico, South America, South Africa, and Australia a violent and accelerating wastage is in progress, but I cannot assess the prospects.

This almost world-wide display of disorganization in the land seems to be similar to disease in an animal, except that it never culminates in complete disorganization or death. The land recovers, but at some reduced level of complexity and with a reduced carrying capacity for people, plants, and animals. Many biotas currently regarded as 'lands of opportunity' are in fact already subsisting on exploitative agriculture, i.e. they have already exceeded their sustained carrying capacity. Most of South America is overpopulated in this sense.

In arid regions we attempt to offset the process of wastage by reclamation, but it is only too evident that the prospective longevity of reclamation projects is often short. In our own West, the best of them may not last a century.

The combined evidence of history and ecology seems to support one general deduction: the less violent the man-made changes, the greater the probability of successful readjustment in the pyramid. Violence, in turn, varies with human population density; a dense population requires more violent conversion. In this respect, North America has a better chance for permanence than Europe, if she can contrive to limit her density.

This deduction runs counter to our current philosophy, which assumes that because a small increase in density enriched human life, that an indefinite increase will enrich it indefinitely. Ecology knows of no density relationship that holds for indefinitely wide limits. All gains from density are subject to a law of diminishing returns.

Whatever may be the equation for men and land, it is improbable that we as yet know all its terms. Recent discoveries in mineral and vitamin nutrition reveal unsuspected dependencies in the up-circuit: incredibly minute quantities of certain substances determine the value of soils to plants, of plants to animals. What of the down-circuit? What of the vanishing species, the preservation of which we now regard as an esthetic luxury? They helped build the soil; in which unsuspected ways may they be essential to its maintenance? Professor Weaver proposes that we use prairie flowers to reflocculate the wasting soils of the dust bowl; who knows what purpose cranes and condors, otters and grizzlies may some day be used?

Land Health and the A-B Cleavage

A land, ethic, then, reflects the existence of an ecological conscience, and this in turn reflects a conviction of individual responsibility for the health of the land. Health is the capacity of the land for self-renewal. Conservation is our effort to understand and preserve this capacity.

Conservationists are notorious for their dissensions. Superficially these seem to add up to mere confusion, but a more careful scrutiny reveals a single plane of cleavage common to many specialized fields. In each field one group (A) regards the land as soil, and its function as commodity-production; another group (B) regards the land as a biota, and its function as something broader. How much broader is admittedly in a state of doubt and confusion.

In my own field, forestry, group A is quite content to grow trees like cabbages, with cellulose as the basic forest commodity. It feels no inhibition against violence; its ideology is agronomic. Group B, on the other hand, sees forestry as fundamentally different from agronomy because it employs natural species, and manages a natural environment rather than creating an artificial one. Group B prefers natural reproduction on principle. It worries on biotic as well as economic grounds about the loss of species like chestnut, and the threatened loss of the white pines. It worries about whole series of secondary forest functions: wildlife, recreation, watersheds, wilderness areas. To my mind, Group B feels the stirrings of an ecological conscience.

In the wildlife field, a parallel cleavage exists. For Group A the basic commodities are sport and meat; the yardstick of production are ciphers of take in pheasants and trout. Artificial propagation is acceptable as a permanent as well as a temporary recourse—if its unit costs permit. Group B, on the other hand, worries about a whole series of biotic side-issues. What is the cost in predators of producing a game crop? Should we have further recourse to exotics? How can management restore the shrinking species, like prairie grouse, already hopeless as shootable game? How can management restore the threatened ratites, like trumpeter swan and whooping crane? Can management principles be extended to wildflowers? Here again it is clear to me that we have the same A-B cleavage as in forestry.

In the larger field of agriculture I am less competent to speak, but there seem to be somewhat parallel cleavages. Scientific agriculture was actively developing before ecology was born, hence a slower penetration of ecological concepts might be expected. Moreover the farmer, by the very nature of his techniques, must modify the biota more radically than the forester or the wildlife manager. Nevertheless, there are many discontents in agriculture which seem to add up to a new vision of 'biotic farming.'

Perhaps the most important of these is the new evidence that poundage or tonnage is no measure of the food-value of farm crops; the products of fertile soil may be qualitatively as well as quantitatively superior. We can bolster poundage from depleted soils by pouring on imported fertility, but we are not necessarily bolstering food-value. The possible ultimate ramifications of this idea are so immense that I must leave their exposition to abler pens.

The discontent that labels itself 'organic farming,' while bearing some of the earmarks of a cult, is nevertheless biotic in its direction, particularly in its insistence on the importance of soil flora and fauna.

The ecological fundamentals of agriculture are just a poorly known to the public as in other fields of land-use. For example, few educated people realize that the marvelous advances in technique made during recent decades are improvements in the pump, rather than the well. Acre for acre, they have barely sufficed to offset the sinking level of fertility.

In all of these cleavages, we see repeated the same basic paradoxes: man the conqueror *versus* man the biotic citizen; science the sharpener of his sword *versus* science the searchlight on his universe; land the slave and servant *versus* land the collective organism. Robinson's injunction to Tristram may well be applied, at this juncture, to *Homo sapiens* as species in geological time:

Whether you will or not
You are a King, Tristram, for you are one
Of the time-tested few that leave the world,
When they are gone, not the same place it was.
Mark what you leave.

The Outlook

It is inconceivable to me that an ethical relation to land can exist without love, respect, and admiration for land, and a high regard for its value. By value, I of course mean something far broader than mere economic value; I mean value in the philosophical sense.

Perhaps the most serious obstacle impeding the evolution of a land ethic is the fact that our educational and economic system is headed away from, rather than toward, a intense consciousness of land. Your true modern is separated from the land by many middlemen, and by innumerable physical gadgets. He has no vital relation to it; to him it is the space between cities on which crops grow. Turn him loose for a day on the land, and if the spot does not happen to be a golf links or a 'scenic' area, he is bored stiff. If crops could be raised by hydroponics instead of farming, it would suit him very well. Synthetic substitutes for wood, leather, wool, and other natural land products suit him better than the originals. In short, land is something he has 'outgrown.'

Almost equally serious as an obstacle to a land ethic is the attitude of the farmer for whom the land is still an adversary, or a taskmaster that keeps him in slavery. Theoretically, the mechanization of farming ought to cut the farmer's chains, but whether it really does is debatable.

One of the requisites for an ecological comprehension of land is an understanding of ecology, and this is by no means co-extensive with 'education'; in fact, much higher education seems deliberately to avoid ecological concepts. An understanding of ecology does not necessarily originate in courses bearing ecological labels; it is quite as likely to be labeled geography, botany, agronomy, history, or economics. This is as it should be, but whatever the label, ecological training is scarce.

The case for a land ethic would appear hopeless but for the minority which is in obvious revolt against these 'modern' trends.

The 'key-log' which must be moved to release the evolutionary process for an ethic is simply this: quit thinking about decent land-use as solely an economic problem. Examine each question in terms of what is ethically and esthetically right, as well as what is economically expedient. A thing is right when it tends to preserve the integrity, stability, and beauty of the biotic community. It is wrong when it tends otherwise.

It of course goes without saying that economic feasibility limits the tether of what can or cannot be done for land. It always has and it always will. The fallacy the economic determinists have tied around our collective neck, and which we now need to cast off, is the belief that economics determines *all* land-use. This is simply not true. An innumerable host of actions and attitudes, comprising perhaps the bulk of all land relations, is determined by the land-users' tastes and predilections, rather than by his purse. The bulk of all land relations hinges on investments of time, forethought, skill, and faith rather than on investments of cash. As a land-user thinketh, so is he.

I have purposely presented the land ethic as a product of social evolution because nothing so important as an ethic is ever 'written.' Only the most superficial student of history supposes that Moses 'wrote' the Decalogue; it evolved in the minds of a thinking community, and Moses wrote a tentative summary of it for a 'seminar.' I say tentative because evolution never stops.

The evolution of a land ethic is an intellectual as well an emotional process. Conservation is paved with good intentions which prove to be futile, or even dangerous, because they are devoid of critical understanding either of the land, or of economic land-use. I think it is a truism that as the ethical frontier advances from the individual to the community, its intellectual content increases.

The mechanism of operation is the same for any ethic: social approbation for right actions: social disapproval for wrong actions.

By and large, our present problem is one of attitudes and implements. We are remodeling the Alhambra with a steam-shovel, and we are proud of our yardage. We shall hardly relinquish the shovel, which after all has many good points, but we are in need of gentler and more objective criteria for its successful use.

■ ■ ■

Questions for Further Exploration:

- According to Leopold, what is the role of an ethic—ecologically and philosophically?

- Why is there "as yet no ethic dealing with man's relation to land"? How would a land ethic change the human/land relation? What obstacles stand in the way of a land ethic?

- How does Leopold conceptualize the "land mechanism"?

- How does Leopold conceptualize a "land ethic that reflects an ecological conscience"? What reasons does he offer for including nonhuman members in the moral community?

- What prohibitions, policies or practices follow from Leopold's assertion that "A thing is right when it tends to preserve the integrity, stability, and beauty of the biotic community"? Consider concrete examples including golf courses, commercial development, Farmers' Markets, clear cutting, community urban gardens, dam building, and industrial agriculture.

- Would endorsing *The Earth Charter* entail acceptance of Leopold's land ethic?

- Free-write a response to Leopold's suggestion that a land ethic is the next step in the process of social evolution.

All Animals Are Equal

Peter Singer

In recent years a number of oppressed groups have campaigned vigor-ously for equality. The classic instance is the Black Liberation movement, which demands an end to the prejudice and discrimination that has made blacks second-class citizens. The immediate appeal of the black liberation movement and its initial, if limited, success made it a model for other op-pressed groups to follow. We became familiar with liberation movements for Spanish-Americans, gay people, and a variety of other minorities. When a majority group—women—began their campaign, some thought we had come to the end of the road. Discrimination on the basis of sex, it has been said, is the last universally accepted form of discrimination, prac-ticed without secrecy or pretense even in those liberal circles that have long prided themselves on their freedom from prejudice against racial minorities.

One should always be wary of talking of "the last remaining form of discrimination." If we have learnt anything from the liberation move-ments, we should have learnt how difficult it is to be aware of latent preju-dice in our attitudes to particular groups until this prejudice is forcefully pointed out.

A liberation movement demands an expansion of our moral horizons and an extension or reinterpretation of the basic moral principle of equal-ity. Practices that were previously regarded as natural and inevitable come to be seen as the result of an unjustifiable prejudice. Who can say with confidence that all his or her attitudes and practices are beyond criticism? If we wish to avoid being numbered amongst the oppressors, we must be prepared to re-think even our most fundamental attitudes. We need to con-sider them from the point of view of those most disadvantaged by our atti-tudes, and the practices that follow from these attitudes. If we can make this unaccustomed mental switch we may discover a pattern in our atti-

Reprinted by permission of the author from *Philosophic Exchange,* Vol. 1, No. 5 (Summer 1974). Parts of this article also appeared in Peter Singer "Animal Liberation," *The New York Review of Books,* April 5, 1973. Copyright © Peter Singer, 1973, 1974.

tudes and practices that consistently operates so as to benefit one group—usually the one to which we ourselves belong—at the expense of another. In this way we may come to see that there is a case for a new liberation movement. My aim is to advocate that we make this mental switch in respect of our attitudes and practices towards a very large group of beings: members of species other than our own—or, as we popularly though misleadingly call them, animals. In other words, I am urging that we extend to other species the basic principle of equality that most of us recognize should be extended to all members of our own species.

All this may sound a little far-fetched, more like a parody of other liberation movements than a serious objective. In fact, in the past the idea of "The Rights of Animals" really has been used to parody the case for women's rights. When Mary Wollstonecraft, a forerunner of later feminists, published her *Vindication of the Rights of Women* in 1792, her ideas were widely regarded as absurd, and they were satirized in an anonymous publication entitled *A Vindication of the Rights of Brutes*. The author of this satire (actually Thomas Taylor, a distinguished Cambridge philosopher) tried to refute Wollstonecraft's reasonings by showing that they could be carried one stage further. If sound when applied to women, why should the arguments not be applied to dogs, cats, and horses? They seemed to hold equally well for these "brutes"; yet to hold that brutes had rights was manifestly absurd; therefore the reasoning by which this conclusion had been reached must be unsound, and if unsound when applied to brutes, it must also be unsound when applied to women, since the very same arguments had been used in each case.

One way in which we might reply to this argument is by saying that the case for equality between men and women cannot validly be extended to nonhuman animals. Women have a right to vote, for instance, because they are just as capable of making rational decisions as men are; dogs, on the other hand, are incapable of understanding the significance of voting, so they cannot have the right to vote. There are many other obvious ways in which men and women resemble each other closely, while humans and other animals differ greatly. So, it might be said, men and women are similar beings and should have equal rights, while humans and nonhumans are different and should not have equal rights.

The thought behind this reply to Taylor's analogy is correct up to a point, but it does not go far enough. There are important differences between humans and other animals, and these differences must give rise to some differences in the rights that each have. Recognizing this obvious fact, however, is no barrier to the case for extending the basic principle of equality to nonhuman animals. The differences that exist between men and women are equally undeniable, and the supporters of Women's Liberation are aware that these differences may give rise to different rights. Many feminists hold that women have the right to an abortion on request. It does not follow that since these same people are campaigning for equality between men and women they must support the right of men to have abortions too. Since a man cannot have an abortion, it is meaningless to talk of his right to have one. Since a pig can't vote, it is meaningless to talk of its right to vote. There is no reason why either Women's Liberation or Animal Liberation should get involved in such nonsense. The extension of the basic principle of equality from one group to another does not imply that we must treat both groups in exactly the same way, or grant exactly the same rights to both groups. Whether we should do so will depend on the nature of the members of the two groups. The basic principle of equality, I shall argue, is equality of consideration; and equal consideration for different beings may lead to different treatment and different rights.

So there is a different way of replying to Taylor's attempt to parody Wollstonecraft's arguments, a way which does not deny the differences between humans and nonhumans, but goes more deeply into the question of equality and concludes by finding nothing absurd in the idea that the basic principle of equality applies to so-called "brutes." I believe that we reach this conclusion if we examine the basis on which our opposition to discrimination on grounds of race or sex ultimately rests. We will then see that we would be on shaky ground if we were to demand equality for blacks, women, and other groups of oppressed humans while denying equal consideration to nonhumans.

When we say that all human beings, whatever their race, creed, or sex, are equal, what is it that we are asserting? Those who wish to defend a hierarchical, inegalitarian society have often pointed out that by whatever test we choose, it simply is not true that all humans are equal. Like it or not, we must face the fact that humans come in different shapes and sizes; they come with differing moral capacities, differing intellectual abilities, differing amounts of benevolent feeling and sensitivity to the needs of others, differing abilities to communicate effectively, and differing capacities to experience pleasure and pain. In short, if the demand for equality were based on the actual equality of all human beings, we would have to stop demanding equality. It would be an unjustifiable demand.

Still, one might cling to the view that the demand for equality among human beings is based on the actual equality of the different races and sexes. Although humans differ as individuals in various ways, there are no differences between the races and sexes as such. From the mere fact that a person is black, or a woman, we cannot infer anything else about that person. This, it may be said, is what is wrong with racism and sexism. The white racist claims that whites are superior to blacks, but this is false—

although there are differences between individuals, some blacks are superior to some whites in all of the capacities and abilities that could conceivably be relevant. The opponent of sexism would say the same: a person's sex is no guide to his or her abilities, and this is why it is unjustifiable to discriminate on the basis of sex.

This is a possible line of objection to racial and sexual discrimination. It is not, however, the way that someone really concerned about equality would choose, because taking this line could, in some circumstances, force one to accept a most inegalitarian society. The fact that humans differ as individuals, rather than as races or sexes, is a valid reply to someone who defends a hierarchical society like, say, South Africa, in which all whites are superior in status to all blacks. The existence of individual variations that cut across the lines of race or sex, however, provides us with no defense at all against a more sophisticated opponent of equality, one who proposes that, say, the interests of those with I.Q. ratings above 100 be preferred to the interests of those with I.Q.s below 100. Would a hierarchical society of this sort really be so much better than one based on race or sex? I think not. But if we tie the moral principle of equality to the factual equality of the different races or sexes, taken as a whole, our opposition to racism and sexism does not provide us with any basis for objecting to this kind of inegalitarianism.

There is a second important reason why we ought not to base our opposition to racism and sexism on any kind of factual equality, even the limited kind which asserts that variations in capacities and abilities are spread evenly between the different races and sexes: we can have no absolute guarantee that these abilities and capacities really are distributed evenly, without regard to race or sex, among human beings. So far as actual abilities are concerned, there do seem to be certain measurable differences between both races and sexes. These differences do not, of course, appear in each case, but only when averages are taken. More important still, we do not yet know how much of these differences is really due to the different genetic endowments of the various races and sexes, and how much is due to environmental differences that are the result of past and continuing discrimination. Perhaps all of the important differences will eventually prove to be environmental rather than genetic. Anyone opposed to racism and sexism will certainly hope that this will be so, for it will make the task of ending discrimination a lot easier; nevertheless it would be dangerous to rest the case against racism and sexism on the belief that all significant differences are environmental in origin. The opponent of, say, racism who takes this line will be unable to avoid conceding that if differences in ability did after all prove to have some genetic connection with race, racism would in some way be defensible.

It would be folly for the opponent of racism to stake his whole case on a dogmatic commitment to one particular outcome of a difficult scientific issue which is still a long way from being settled. While attempts to prove that differences in certain selected abilities between races and sexes are primarily genetic in origin have certainly not been conclusive, the same must be said of attempts to prove that these differences are largely the result of environment. At this stage of the investigation we cannot be certain which view is correct, however much we may hope it is the later.

Fortunately, there is no need to pin the case for equality to one particular outcome of this scientific investigation. The appropriate response to those who claim to have found evidence of genetically-based differences in ability between the races or sexes is not to stick to the belief that the genetic explanation must be wrong, whatever evidence to the contrary may turn up: instead we should make it quite clear that the claim to equality does not depend on intelligence, moral capacity, physical strength, or similar matters of fact. Equality is a moral ideal, not a simple assertion of fact. There is no logically compelling reason for assuming that a factual difference in ability between two people justifies any difference in the amount of consideration we give to satisfying their needs and interests. The principle of the equality of human beings is not a description of an alleged actual equality among humans: it is a prescription of how we should treat humans.

Jeremy Bentham incorporated the essential basis of moral equality into his utilitarian system of ethics in the formula: "Each to count for one and none for more than one." In other words, the interests of every being affected by an action are to be taken into account and given the same weight as the like interests of any other being. A later utilitarian, Henry Sidgwick, put the point in this way: "The good of any one individual is of no more importance, from the point of view (if I may say so) of the Universe, than the good of any other."[1] More recently, the leading figures in contemporary moral philosophy have shown a great deal of agreement in specifying as a fundamental presupposition of their moral theories some similar requirement which operates so as to give everyone's interests equal consideration—although they cannot agree on how this requirement is best formulated.[2]

---

[1] *The Methods of Ethics* (7th Ed.), p. 382.

[2] For example, R. M. Hare, *Freedom and Reason* (Oxford, 1963) and J. Rawls, *A Theory of Justice* (Harvard, 1972); for a brief account of the essential agreement on this issue between these and other positions, see R. M. Hare, "Rules of War and Moral Reasoning," *Philosophy and Public Affairs,* vol. 1, no. 2 (1972).

It is an implication of this principle of equality that our concern for others ought not to depend on what they are like, or what abilities they possess—although precisely what this concern requires us to do may vary according to the characteristics of those affected by what we do. It is on this basis that the case against racism and the case against sexism must both ultimately rest; and it is in accordance with this principle that speciesism is also to be condemned. If possessing a higher degree of intelligence does not entitle one human to use another for his own ends, how can it entitle humans to exploit nonhumans?

Many philosophers have proposed the principle of equal consideration of interests, in some form or other, as a basic moral principle; but, as we shall see in more detail shortly, not many of them have recognized that this principle applies to members of other species as well as to our own. Bentham was one of the few who did realize this. In a forward-looking passage, written at a time when black slaves in the British dominions were still being treated much as we now treat nonhuman animals, Bentham wrote:

The day may come when the rest of the animal creation may acquire those rights which never could have been witholden from them but by the hand of tyranny. The French have already discovered that the blackness of the skin is no reason why a human being should be abandoned without redress to the caprice of a tormentor. It may one day come to be recognized that the number of the legs, the villosity of the skin, or the termination of the os sacrum, are reasons equally insufficient for abandoning a sensitive being to the same fate. What else is it that should trace the insuperable line? Is it the faculty of reason, or perhaps the faculty of discourse? But a full-grown horse or dog is beyond comparison a more rational, as well as a more conversable animal, than an infant of a day, or a week, or even a month, old. But suppose they were otherwise, what would it avail? The question is not, Can they *reason?* nor, Can they *talk?* but, Can they *suffer?*[3]

In this passage Bentham points to the capacity for suffering as the vital characteristic that gives a being the right to equal consideration. The capacity for suffering—or more strictly, for suffering and/or enjoyment or happiness—is not just another characteristic like the capacity for language, or for higher mathematics. Bentham is not saying that those who try to mark "the insuperable line" that determines whether the interests of a being should be considered happen to have selected the wrong characteristic. The capacity for suffering and enjoying things is a prerequisite for having interests at all, a condition that must be satisfied before we can speak of interests in any meaningful way. It would be nonsense to say that it was not in the interests of a stone to be kicked along the road by a

---

[3] *Introduction to the Principles of Morals and Legislation,* ch. XVII.

schoolboy. A stone does not have interests because it cannot suffer. Nothing that we can do to it could possibly make any difference to its welfare. A mouse, on the other hand, does have an interest in not being tormented, because it will suffer if it is.

If a being suffers, there can be no moral justification for refusing to take that suffering into consideration. No matter what the nature of the being, the principle of equality requires that its suffering be counted equally with the like suffering—in so far as rough comparisons can be made—of any other being. If a being is not capable of suffering, or of experiencing enjoyment or happiness, there is nothing to be taken into account. This is why the limit of sentience (using the term as a convenient, if not strictly accurate, shorthand for the capacity to suffer or experience enjoyment or happiness) is the only defensible boundary of concern for the interests of others. To mark this boundary by some characteristic like intelligence or rationality would be to mark it in an arbitrary way. Why not choose some other characteristic, like skin color?

The racist violates the principle of equality by giving greater weight to the interests of members of his own race, when there is a clash between their interests and the interests of those of another race. Similarly the speciesist allows the interests of his own species to override the greater interests of members of other species.[4] The pattern is the same in each case. Most human beings are speciesists. I shall now very briefly describe some of the practices that show this.

For the great majority of human beings, especially in urban, industrialized societies, the most direct form of contact with members of other species is at mealtimes: we eat them. In doing so we treat them purely as means to our ends. We regard their life and well-being as subordinate to our taste for a particular kind of dish. I say "taste" deliberately—this is purely a matter of pleasing our palate. There can be no defense of eating flesh in terms of satisfying nutritional needs, since it has been established beyond doubt that we could satisfy our need for protein and other essential nutrients far more efficiently with a diet that replaced animal flesh by soy beans, or products derived from soy beans, and other high-protein vegetable products.[5]

---

[4]I owe the term speciesism to Richard Ryder.

[5]In order to produce 1 lb. of protein in the form of beef or veal, we must feed 21 lbs. of protein to the animal. Other forms of livestock are slightly less inefficient, but the average ratio in the United States is still 1:8. It has been estimated that the amount of protein lost to humans in this way is equivalent to 90 percent of the annual world protein deficit. For a brief account, see Frances Moore Lappe, *Diet for a Small Planet* (Friends of The Earth/Ballantine, New York 1971), pp. 4–11.

It is not merely the act of killing that indicates what we are ready to do to other species in order to gratify our tastes. The suffering we inflict on the animals while they are alive is perhaps an even clearer indication of our speciesism than the fact that we are prepared to kill them.[6] In order to have meat on the table at a price that people can afford, our society tolerates methods of meat production that confine sentient animals in cramped, unsuitable conditions for the entire durations of their lives. Animals are treated like machines that convert fodder into flesh, and any innovation that results in a higher "conversion ratio" is liable to be adopted. As one authority on the subject has said, "cruelty is acknowledged only when profitability ceases."[7] . . .

Since, as I have said, none of these practices cater for anything more than our pleasures of taste, our practice of rearing and killing other animals in order to eat them is a clear instance of the sacrifice of the most important interests of other beings in order to satisfy trivial interests of our own. To avoid speciesism we must stop this practice, and each of us has a moral obligation to cease supporting the practice. Our custom is all the support that the meat-industry needs. The decision to cease giving it that support may be difficult, but it is no more difficult than it would have been for a white Southerner to go against the traditions of his society and free his slaves: if we do not change our dietary habits, how can we censure those slaveholders who would not change their own way of living?

The same form of discrimination may be observed in the widespread practice of experimenting on other species in order to see if certain substances are safe for human beings, or to test some psychological theory about the effect of severe punishment on learning, or to try out various new compounds just in case something turns up. . . .

In the past, argument about vivisection has often missed the point, because it has been put in absolutist terms: Would the abolitionist be prepared to let thousands die if they could be saved by experimenting on a

---

[6]Although one might think that killing a being is obviously the ultimate wrong one can do to it, I think that the infliction of suffering is a clearer indication of speciesism because it might be argued that at least part of what is wrong with killing a human is that most humans are conscious of their existence over time and have desires and purposes that extend into the future see, for instance, M. Tooley, "Abortion and Infanticide," *Philosophy and Public Affairs*, vol. 2, no. I (1972). Of course, if one took this view one would have to hold—as Tooley does—that killing a human infant or mental defective is not in itself wrong and is less serious than killing certain higher mammals that probably do have a sense of their own existence over time.

[7]Ruth Harrison, *Animal Machines* (Stuart, London, 1964). For an account of farming conditions, see my *Animal Liberation* (New York Review Company, 1975) from which "Down on the Factory Farm," is reprinted in this volume [*Animal Rights and Human Obligations*].

single animal? The way to reply to this purely hypothetical question is to pose another: Would the experimenter be prepared to perform his experiment on an orphaned human infant, if that were the only way to save many lives? (I say "orphan" to avoid the complication of parental feelings, although in doing so I am being overfair to the experimenter, since the nonhuman subjects of experiments are not orphans.) If the experimenter is not prepared to use an orphaned human infant, then his readiness to use nonhumans is simple discrimination, since adult apes, cats, mice, and other mammals are more aware of what is happening to them, more self-directing and, so far as we can tell, at least as sensitive to pain, as any human infant. There seems to be no relevant characteristic that human infants possess that adult mammals do not have to the same or a higher degree. (Someone might try to argue that what makes it wrong to experiment on a human infant is that the infant will, in time and if left alone, develop into more than the nonhuman, but one would then, to be consistent, have to oppose abortion, since the fetus has the same potential as the infant—indeed, even contraception and abstinence might be wrong on this ground, since the egg and sperm, considered jointly, also have the same potential. In any case, this argument still gives us no reason for selecting a nonhuman, rather than a human with severe and irreversible brain damage, as the subject for our experiments).

The experimenter, then, shows a bias in favor of his own species whenever he carries out an experiment on a nonhuman for a purpose that he would not think justified him in using a human being at an equal or lower level of sentience, awareness, ability to be self-directing, etc. No one familiar with the kind of results yielded by most experiments on animals can have the slightest doubt that if this bias were eliminated the number of experiments performed would be a minute fraction of the number performed today.

Experimenting on animals, and eating their flesh, are perhaps the two major forms of speciesism in our society. By comparison, the third and last form of speciesism is so minor as to be insignificant, but it is perhaps of some special interest to those for whom this article was written. I am referring to speciesism in contemporary philosophy.

Philosophy ought to question the basic assumptions of the age. Thinking through, critically and carefully, what most people take for granted is, I believe, the chief task of philosophy, and it is this task that makes philosophy a worthwhile activity. Regrettably, philosophy does not always live up to its historic role. Philosophers are human beings, and they are subject to all the preconceptions of the society to which they belong. Sometimes they succeed in breaking free of the prevailing ideology: more often they become its most sophisticated defenders. So, in this case, philosophy as practiced in the universities today does not challenge anyone's preconceptions about our relations with other species. By their writings, those philosophers who tackle problems that touch upon the issue reveal that they make the same unquestioned assumptions as most other humans, and what they say tends to confirm the reader in his or her comfortable speciesist habits.

I could illustrate this claim by referring to the writings of philosophers in various fields—for instance, the attempts that have been made by those interested in rights to draw the boundary of the sphere of rights so that it runs parallel to the biological boundaries of the species homo sapiens, including infants and even mental defectives, but excluding those other beings of equal or greater capacity who are so useful to us at mealtimes and in our laboratories. I think it would be a more appropriate conclusion to this article, however, if I concentrated on the problem with which we have been centrally concerned, the problem of equality.

It is significant that the problem of equality, in moral and political philosophy, is invariably formulated in terms of human equality. The effect of this is that the question of the equality of other animals does not confront the philosopher, or student, as an issue itself—and this is already an indication of the failure of philosophy to challenge accepted beliefs. Still, philosophers have found it difficult to discuss the issue of human equality without raising, in a paragraph or two, the question of the status of other animals. The reason for this, which should be apparent from what I have said already, is that if humans are to be regarded as equal to one another, we need some sense of "equal" that does not require any actual, descriptive equality of capacities, talents or other qualities. If equality is to be related to any actual characteristics of humans, these characteristics must be some lowest common denominator, pitched so low that no human lacks them—but then the philosopher comes up against the catch that any such set of characteristics which covers all humans will not be possessed only by humans. In other words, it turns out that in the only sense in which we can truly say, as an assertion of fact, that all humans are equal, at least some members of other species are also equal—equal, that is, to each other and to humans. If, on the other hand, we regard the statement "All humans are equal" in some non-factual way, perhaps as a prescription, then, as I have already argued, it is even more difficult to exclude nonhumans from the sphere of equality.

This result is not what the egalitarian philosopher originally intended to assert. Instead of accepting the radical outcome to which their own reasonings naturally point, however, most philosophers try to reconcile their beliefs in human equality and animal inequality by arguments that can only be described as devious.

As a first example, I take William Frankena's well-known article "The Concept of Social Justice." Frankena opposes the idea of basing justice on merit, because he sees that this could lead to highly inegalitarian results. Instead he proposes the principle that

> all men are to be treated as equals, not because they are equal, in any respect, but simply because they are human. They are human because they have emotions and desires, and are able to think, and hence are capable of enjoying a good life in a sense in which other animals are not.[8]

But what is this capacity to enjoy the good life which all humans have, but no other animals? Other animals have emotions and desires and appear to be capable of enjoying a good life. We may doubt that they can think— although the behavior of some apes, dolphins, and even dogs suggests that some of them can—but what is the relevance of thinking? Frankena goes on to admit that by "the good life" he means "not so much the morally good life as the happy or satisfactory life," so thought would appear to be unnecessary for enjoying the good life; in fact to emphasize the need for thought would make difficulties for the egalitarian since only some people are capable of leading intellectually satisfying lives, or morally good lives. This makes it difficult to see what Frankena's principle of equality has to do with simply being human. Surely every sentient being is capable of leading a life that is happier or less miserable than some alternative life, and hence has a claim to be taken into account. In this respect the distinction between humans and nonhumans is not a sharp division, but rather a continuum along which we move gradually, and with overlaps between the species, from simple capacities for enjoyment and satisfaction, or pain and suffering, to more complex ones.

Faced with a situation in which they see a need for some basis for the moral gulf that is commonly thought to separate humans and animals, but can find no concrete difference that will do the job without undermining the equality of humans, philosophers tend to waffle. They resort to highs sounding phrases like "the intrinsic dignity of the human individual";[9] they talk of the "intrinsic worth of all men" as if men (humans?) had some worth that other beings did not,[10] or they say that humans, and only humans, are

---

[8]In R. Brandt (ed.), *Social Justice* (Prentice Hall, Englewood Cliffs, 1962), p. 19.

[9]Frankena, op. cit. p. 23.

[10]H. A. Bedau, "Egalitarianism and the Idea of Equality," in *Nomos IX: Equality,* ed. J. R. Pennock and J. W. Chapman, New York, 1967.

"ends in themselves," while "everything other than a person can only have value for a person."[11]

This idea of a distinctive human dignity and worth has a long history; it can be traced back directly to the Renaissance humanists, for instance to Pico della Mirandola's *Oration on the Dignity of Man.* Pico and other humanists based their estimate of human dignity on the idea that man possessed the central, pivotal position in the "Great Chain of Being" that led from the lowliest forms of matter to God himself; this view of the universe, in turn, goes back to both classical and Judeo-Christian doctrines. Contemporary philosophers have cast off these metaphysical and religious shackles and freely invoke the dignity of mankind without needing to justify the idea at all. Why should we not attribute "intrinsic dignity" or "intrinsic worth" to ourselves? Fellow-humans are unlikely to reject the accolades we so generously bestow on them, and those to whom we deny the honor are unable to object. Indeed, when one thinks only of humans, it can be very liberal, very progressive, to talk of the dignity of all human beings. In so doing, we implicitly condemn slavery, racism, and other violations of human rights. We admit that we ourselves are in some fundamental sense on a par with the poorest, most ignorant members of our own species. It is only when we think of humans as no more than a small sub-group of all the beings that inhabit our planet that we may realize that in elevating our own species we are at the same time lowering the relative status of all other species.

The truth is that the appeal to the intrinsic dignity of human beings appears to solve the egalitarian's problems only as long as it goes unchallenged. Once we ask why it should be that all humans—including infants, mental defectives, psychopaths, Hitler, Stalin, and the rest—have some kind of dignity or worth that no elephant, pig, or chimpanzee can ever achieve, we see that this question is as difficult to answer as our original request for some relevant fact that justifies the inequality of humans and other animals. In fact, these two questions are really one: talk of intrinsic dignity or moral worth only takes the problem back one step, because any satisfactory defence of the claim that all and only humans have intrinsic dignity would need to refer to some relevant capacities or characteristics that all and only humans possess. Philosophers frequently introduce ideas of dignity, respect, and worth at the point at which other reasons appear to be lacking, but this is hardly good enough. Fine phrases are the last resource of those who have run out of arguments.

---

[11]C. Vlastos, "Justice and Equality," in Brandt, *Social Justice,* p. 48.

In case there are those who still think it may be possible to find some relevant characteristic that distinguishes all humans from all members of other species, I shall refer again, before I conclude, to the existence of some humans who quite clearly are below the level of awareness, self-consciousness, intelligence, and sentience, of many non-humans. I am thinking of humans with severe and irreparable brain damage, and also of infant humans. To avoid the complication of the relevance of a being's potential, however, I shall henceforth concentrate on permanently retarded humans.

Philosophers who set out to find a characteristic that will distinguish humans from other animals rarely take the course of abandoning these groups of humans by lumping them in with the other animals. It is easy to see why they do not. To take this line without re-thinking our attitudes to other animals would entail that we have the right to perform painful experiments on retarded humans for trivial reasons; similarly it would follow that we had the right to rear and kill these humans for food. To most philosophers these consequences are as unacceptable as the view that we should stop treating nonhumans in this way.

Of course, when discussing the problem of equality it is possible to ignore the problem of mental defectives, or brush it aside as if somehow insignificant.[12] This is the easiest way out. What else remains? My final example of speciesism in contemporary philosophy has been selected to show what happens when a writer is prepared to face the question of human equality and animal inequality without ignoring the existence of mental defectives, and without resorting to obscurantist mumbo jumbo. Stanley Benn's clear and honest article "Egalitarianism and Equal Consideration of Interests"[13] fits this description.

Benn, after noting the usual "evident human inequalities" argues, correctly I think, for equality of consideration as the only possible basis for egalitarianism. Yet Benn, like other writers, is thinking only of "equal consideration of human interests." Benn is quite open in his defence of this restriction of equal consideration:

> . . . not to possess human shape is a disqualifying condition. However faithful or intelligent a dog may be, it would be a monstrous sentimentality to attribute to him interests that could be weighed

---

[12] For example, Bernard Williams, "The Idea of Equality," in *Philosophy, Politics, and Society* (second series), ed. P. Laslett and W. Rundman (Blackwell, Oxford, 1962), p. 118; J. Rawls, *A Theory of Justice,* pp. 509–10.

[13] *Nomos IX: Equality;* the passages quoted are on p. 62ff.

in an equal balance with those of human beings ... if, for instance, one had to decide between feeding a hungry baby or a hungry dog, anyone who chose the dog would generally be reckoned morally defective, unable to recognize a fundamental inequality of claims.

This is what distinguishes our attitude to animals from our attitude to imbeciles. It would be odd to say that we ought to respect equally the dignity or personality of the imbecile and of the rational man ... but there is nothing odd about saying that we should respect their interests equally, that is, that we should give to the interests of each the same serious consideration as claims to considerations necessary for some standard of well-being that we can recognize and endorse.

Benn's statement of the basis of the consideration we should have for imbeciles seems to me correct, but why should there be any fundamental inequality of claims between a dog and a human imbecile? Benn sees that if equal consideration depended on rationality, no reason could be given against using imbeciles for research purposes, as we now use dogs and guinea pigs. This will not do: "But of course we do distinguish imbeciles from animals in this regard," he says. That the common distinction is justifiable is something Benn does not question; his problem is how it is to be justified. The answer he gives is this:

... we respect the interests of men and give them priority over dogs not *insofar* as they are rational, but because rationality is the human norm. We say it is *unfair* to exploit the deficiencies of the imbecile who falls short of the norm, just as it would be unfair, and not just ordinarily dishonest, to steal from a blind man. If we do not think in this way about dogs, it is because we do not see the irrationality of the dog as a deficiency or a handicap, but as normal for the species, The characteristics, therefore, that distinguish the normal man from the normal dog make it intelligible for us to talk of other men having interests and capacities, and therefore claims, of precisely the same kind as we make on our own behalf. But although these characteristics may provide the point of the distinction between men and other species, they are not in fact the qualifying conditions for membership, to the distinguishing criteria of the class of morally considerable persons; and this is precisely because a man does not become a member of a different species, with its own standards of normality, by reason of not possessing these characteristics.

The final sentence of this passage gives the argument away. An imbecile, Benn concedes, may have no characteristics superior to those of a dog; nevertheless this does not make the imbecile a member of "a different species" as the dog is. Therefore it would be "unfair" to use the imbecile for medical research as we use the dog. But why? That the imbecile is not rational is just the way things have worked out, and the same is true of the dog—neither is any more responsible for their mental level. If it is unfair to take advantage of an isolated defect, why is it fair to take advantage of a more general limitation? I find it hard to see anything in this argument except a defense of preferring the interests of members of our own species because they are members of our own species. To those who think there might be more to it, I suggest the following mental exercise. Assume that it has been proven that there is a difference in the average, or normal, intelligence quotient for two different races, say whites and blacks. Then substitute the term "white" for every occurrence of "men" and "black" for every occurrence of "dog" in the passage quoted; and substitute "high I.Q." for "rationality" and when Benn talks of "imbeciles" replace this term by "dumb whites"—that is, whites who fall well below the normal white I.Q. score. Finally, change "species" to "race." Now retread the passage. It has become a defense of a rigid, no-exceptions division between whites and blacks, based on I.Q. scores, not withstanding an admitted overlap between whites and blacks in this respect. The revised passage is, of course, outrageous, and this is not only because we have made fictitious assumptions in our substitutions. The point is that in the original passage Benn was defending a rigid division in the amount of consideration due to members of different species, despite admitted cases of overlap. If the original did not, at first reading strike us as being as outrageous as the revised version does, this is largely because although we are not racists ourselves, most of us are speciesists. Like the other articles, Benn's stands as a warning of the ease with which the best minds can fall victim to a prevailing ideology.

Questions for Further Exploration:

- Do you agree/disagree with Singer that we ought to interrogate the prevailing ideology from the perspective of those most disadvantaged by the attitudes and practices justified by that ideology?

- How does Singer respond to the objection that because humans and nonhumans are different, there is no basis for extending to other species the principle of equality we recognize should be extended to all members of the human species?

- What reasons does Singer give for claiming we ought not to base opposition to racism and sexism on factual equality? What is the basis of the principle of the equality of human beings, if it is not a matter of fact?

- What is the basis of Singer's accusation that philosophy is "speciesist"?

- Is Singer's egalitarian ethic consistent with Leopold's land ethic?

- Would endorsing *The Earth Charter* entail acceptance of Singer's egalitarian ethic?

- Free-write a response to Singer's view that the practices of eating animals and experimenting on them are speciesist and unethical.

Ecofeminism, Integrity, and the Earth Charter:

A Critical Analysis

Victoria Davion

The concept of ecological integrity has received quite a lot of attention in the field of environmental philosophy, but little attention within ecological feminism, a constellation of theoretical positions linking forms of human oppression with environmental exploitation. The concept of ecological integrity and several core ecofeminist ideas are present in the Earth Charter (2002), a document which will be presented to the United Nations as a formal charter in 2002. The purpose of this chapter is to present important ecological feminist insights, and to examine both the concept of ecological integrity and the Earth Charter document through an ecological feminist lens. I shall argue that a focus on ecological integrity is consistent with ecological feminist concerns, provided that questions of ecological integrity are always seen as political in addition to scientific. I shall also argue that portions of the Charter are consistent with core ideas of ecological feminism, while others are problematic. I begin with a discussion of ecological feminism.

Ecological Feminism: Some Key Ideas

Ecological feminism refers to a constellation of positions bringing feminist insights to environmental philosophy. Feminists began to formulate theories about connections between abuses of nature and human oppression, such as sexism and racism, in the early 1970s. Although there are a wide variety of ecofeminist positions, a core position held by all is that there are important conceptual, epistemological, political, ethical, and theoretical links between abuses of nature and a variety of human oppressions. Ecological feminists agree that any environmental ethic failing to examine such links is conceptually and practically lacking (Warren 1990).

Analysis of value dualisms has been central in ecological feminist discussions of Western patriarchal culture. A value dualism is a pair of disjuncts in which each is seen as radically different from the other, and one is ranked above the other in a hierarchy of value. Ecological feminists such as Val Plumwood (1993) argue that a reason/nature dualism serves as a fault line underlying the conceptual framework of Western patriarchal cultures. This forms the basis for a series of related dualisms where whatever is associated with nature is seen as radically different and inferior to whatever is associated with reason. Examples commonly discussed in ecological feminist literature include civilized/primitive, masculine/feminine, mental/manual, and human/nature. These pairs legitimate a number of oppressions, including oppressions based on class, race, and sex.

Karen Warren (1990) distills the point about both conceptual and historical connections justifying dominations of women and nature within dominant Western frameworks. She argues that both rely on a "logic of domination," which asserts that certain differences constitute moral superiority, and uses alleged moral superiority to justify domination of the inferior group by the superior one. Warren provides the following as a typical argument using the logic of domination to justify human moral superiority over "nature."

(A1) Humans do, plants do not, have the conscious capacity to consciously change the community in which they live.

(A2) Whatever has this capacity is morally superior to whatever doesn't have it.

(A3) Humans are morally superior to plants and rocks.

(A4) For any X and Y, if X is morally superior to Y, then X is morally justified in subordinating Y.

(A5) Humans are morally justified in subordinating plants and rocks. (129)

Warren argues that the same kind of logic allows for the sexist domination of women in Western patriarchy due to the historical association of women with nature. She suggests that arguments of the following form are typical in justifying sexism.

(B1) Women are identified with nature and the realm of the physical; men are identified with the "human" and the realm of the mental.

(B2) Whatever is identified with nature and the realm of the physical is inferior to ("below") whatever is identified with the "human" and the realm of the mental.

(B3) Thus, women are inferior to men.

(B4) For any X and Y, if X is superior to Y, then X is morally justified in subordinating Y.

(B5) Men are justified in subordinating women. (130)

According to Warren, arguments A and B are conceptually connected because both use the logic of domination to justify subordination of one group by another. They are historically connected because premise (B2) relies on the acceptance of some version of argument A justifying the devaluation of nature presupposed in B. Warren and many other ecological feminists maintain that the justification for many oppressive institutions, such as American slavery, has relied on associating certain groups of humans with "nature." Because of these connections, fighting against the oppression of humans and the exploitation of nature are part of the same battle. Those working for social justice and those working for environmental protection should therefore be allies.

Concern for animals has also been a major theme in ecological feminist thought. Carol Adams (1991) suggests that concern for animals is part of the ecological feminist project, because acknowledging their value is part of disengaging the logic of domination, and because the exploitation of the Earth in general is part of much animal agriculture. Adams connects the exploitation of animals with the exploitation of black women, who as "lung runners" in U.S. poultry processing plants must scrape the lungs out of 5,000 chicken chest cavities per hour. According to Adams, "Both women workers and the chickens themselves are the means to the end of consumption, but because consumption has been disembodied, their oppressions as worker and consumable body are invisible" (131). Some ecological feminists have argued for universal vegetarianism except in cases where meat is required for survival. Others have argued for a more contextual approach, avoiding practices that are cruel and disrespectful to animals when possible, such as factory farming. The strategy of locating sites of multiple oppressions, such as poultry processing plants, has been a central one within ecological feminism.

The strategy of locating multiple oppressions is also evident in ecological feminist discussions of environmental racism. Ecological feminist analysis helps raise questions of how ethical, economic, and aesthetic discourses serve to justify environmental racism, and how lack of power and alienation make it especially difficult for certain communities to fight back. Other issues include ways in which racist conceptions of people and urban areas as dirty and hopeless justify mistreatment, and how in male-dominated societies women may be disproportionately affected by toxins. As always, ecological feminism focuses on the fact that toxic dumping affects not only humans, but nonhumans as well (Cuomo 1998).

Another concern central to ecological feminism has been the politics of "development." In the ecological feminist classic *Staying Alive* (1989), Vandana Shiva claims that in India, Western-style development has been highly problematic, and while both sexes have been affected, it is often women who lose most. Shiva refers to Western-style development as Western patriarchy. She argues that the devaluation of nature and women within Western patriarchy is imported in Western-style development projects. Hence, she argues that such development is often worse for women than for men. As in the West, knowledge associated with women is seen as unscientific and becomes discredited. "Scientific knowledge," mainly under the control of men, is considered real. Using India as an example, Shiva documents how, as these new "scientific methods" are employed, women—the primary providers of food, water, and fuel—are displaced. Because new methods tend to ignore nature's cycles and the interconnections between natural processes, results fail over time. They are unsustainable. Chapters on water, food, and forests document in impressive detail how and why many modern scientific techniques have been unsuccessful, destroying more sustainable ways of living.

The present discussion can provide only a glimpse of the highly textured and complex discussions often referred to by the umbrella term "ecological feminism." The key ideas that I shall be working with in my analysis of both ecological integrity and of the Earth Charter are as follows: Investigations into concrete environmental issues such as pollution, waste disposal, radiation, and extinction of wild species are always about more than they appear to be because they are in part results of destructive and inaccurate conceptions of reality (Cuomo 2001). We must address how power operates in areas pinpointed as environmental issues/problems. As Warren, Cuomo, Shiva, Plumwood, and others have pointed out, we need to examine underlying value systems that justify exploitation, and these have something to say not only about the value of nature, but about the value of various human beings as well. While looking at environmental problems, we must identify historically embedded assumptions lying beneath the surface of these problems, and look for the relationships between them. Ecofeminist critique of dualistic thinking reminds us that "the personal is political, the ecological is social, and culture is never completely separate from nature" (Cuomo 2001). Environmental issues are deeply political—and never separate from other issues of social justice.

Ecological Integrity

Among concerned environmentalists, some philosophers, scientists, and others have focused on the concept of ecological integrity in formulating an environmental ethic. According to Allan Holland, "Reduced to its simplest, integrity is wildness" (in Westra 1994, xii). In *The Principle of Integrity* (1994), Laura Westra suggests that in order for an ecosystem to have integrity, it must (a) retain the ability to deal with outside interference and, if necessary, regenerate itself; (b) its optimum capacity for the greatest ongoing possible development options within its time and location must be undiminished; (c) it must retain its ability to continue its ongoing change and development, unconstrained by human interruptions past or present. On this approach, questions of whether ecosystems possess integrity are largely scientific.

Using a biocentric approach, Westra and others argue that because human and nonhuman well-being depend on the existence of at least some ecosystems possessing integrity, protecting intact ecosystems must be a foundational concern of any environmental ethic. Therefore, Westra advocates for a general moral injunction to respect the integrity of ecological and biological processes, except in self-defense.

From ecological feminist standpoints, the need to preserve at least some level of ecological integrity is clear, and approaches such as Westra's are basically consistent with most ecological feminist thought. For example, Vandana Shiva's critique of development discussed above focuses on how development projects disrupt ecological integrity, although she does not use those exact words.

Ecological feminists have raised crucial questions about what it means to be "wild." And the idea that, in order to be wild, an area must have been free from both past and present human "interference" or "modification" requires analysis. It is important from ecological feminist perspectives to avoid dualistic thinking. Humans are part of "nature," even if this has been basically denied within much of the Western tradition. And, if humans are part of "nature," mere presence is not necessarily a threat to integrity. Ecofeminists have pointed out how the idea of wilderness as a place "untouched by man" has often been presented in an androcentric and ethnocentric manner in standard wilderness protection literature. Ecological feminists have argued that traditional approaches to environmentalism in the United States have focused on wilderness from privileged, white, middle-class perspectives in which concerns of working-class or racial minorities have been seen as marginal or as competing with wilderness preservation (Gaard 1997). While certain forms of human interference are clearly threats to ecosystem integrity, questions of what forms of interaction count as "interruption," as well as who benefits from various ways of construing "interruption" would all be interesting ecological feminist projects.

Ecological feminist analysis would examine how distributions of power and privilege might make it impossible for most people to live with integrity, as well as why living with integrity might simply be unattractive for those with the resources to make such choices. For example, what specific social/institutional configurations make it such that in developing and developed countries, many do not have resources to attempt to "live in integrity"—just surviving takes up more than all the time available. Unfortunately, in many situations, the ability to even conceive of "living in integrity" reflects power and privilege. And, ecological feminist analysis would ask about specific power distributions forcing many people into lifestyles that are clearly unsustainable in the long run, for the sake of short-term survival. A focus on the structural aspects of the distribution of power and privilege that make individual *choices* to live in integrity either inconceivable, impossible, or both, within particular concrete situations, is crucial for ecological feminist analysis. In addition, ecological feminist analysis would question why political, economic, and social structures make choices to live with integrity concretely, in particular times and places, unattractive or difficult even for people with fair amounts of power and privilege (such as whether choosing to live with integrity would require significant losses of both).

The Earth Charter

The Earth Charter (2002) contains much that is consistent with ecological feminist thinking. The basic aim is respect and care for the community of life. This is said to involve the following four broad commitments:

1. Respect Earth and life in all its diversity.
2. Care for the community of life with understanding, compassion, and love.
3. Build democratic societies that are just, participatory, sustainable, and peaceful.
4. Secure Earth's bounty and beauty for present and future generations. (2)

According to the Charter, fulfilling these broad commitments will require paying attention to maintaining ecological integrity, issues of social and economic justice, and the promotion of democracy, nonviolence, and peace.

From an ecological feminist perspective, all of these are worthy goals. And, it is important that the Charter seems to realize that preserving ecological integrity and promoting economic and social justice are highly interconnected enterprises. From this standpoint, the Charter is consistent with ecological feminism's commitment to seek connections between various environmental issues and other issues less obviously connected to environmental protection. The Charter specifies the importance of promoting human equality and minimizing animal suffering, central ecofeminist projects. In addition, the Charter does not merely imply the importance of eradicating sexism by speaking of the need for equality of all peoples. It has a specific subprinciple in the section on social and economic justice that calls for the affirmation of gender equality and equity as prerequisites to sustainable development and the ensuring of universal access to education, health care, and economic opportunity for women. This is clearly a key part of any ecological feminist vision. Finally, the Charter recognizes that the needed changes will require changes in dominant value systems and in particular, the notion of what it means to be human, which is again central in ecological feminist thought.

Although the broad goals of the Charter are consistent with some key insights of ecological feminism, there are several problems with the Charter from ecofeminist perspectives. The Preamble is troubling. The use of the word "we" for "humanity" raises critical issues. The Preamble begins "We stand at a critical moment in Earth's history, a time when humanity must choose its future." And "To move forward we must recognize that in the midst of magnificent diversity of cultures and life forms we are one human family and one Earth community with a common destiny" (1). Although there is a recognition that "the gap between rich and poor is widening," the Preamble asserts that "the choice is ours: form a global partnership to care for Earth and one another or risk the destruction of ourselves and the diversity of life" (1). Finally there is a call for the acceptance of "universal responsibility."

> To realize these aspirations, we must decide to live with a sense of universal responsibility, identifying ourselves with the whole Earth community as well as local communities. . . . Everyone shares responsibility for the present and future well-being of the human family and the larger living world. The spirit of human solidarity and kinship with all life is strengthened when we live with reverence for the mystery of being, gratitude for the gift of life, and humility regarding the human place in nature (2).

The Preamble ends by stating that the Charter is meant to be a standard for the conduct of all individuals, organizations, businesses, governments, and transnational institutions.

Most obviously, the uncritical use the term "family" is troubling. Ecological feminists and other feminists have paid a great deal of attention to the ways in which women have been abused within patriarchal families. Hence, the uncritical adoption of the notion of "family" with no discussion of questions of power within a family is highly problematic. Questions of leadership and authority are always loaded within ecological feminist discourse. Simply adopting this term as if it is friendly and unproblematic is deeply disturbing from an ecological feminist perspective.

The document has the tone of a message from those with political authority to "the people." Although framers claim to have sought input from a variety of people, the document speaks consistently of "empowering people," rather than helping people empower themselves. So, I am left wondering just who is the intended audience for this document. It is hard to believe that the "we" being addressed includes people whose only next concern is short-term survival.

The notion of "universal responsibility" is also troubling. "We" (all humans) are not responsible for the current situation, nor can "we" (all humans) make choices in favor of change. As I stated above, ecological feminism is more interested in why institutional structures make certain so-called "choices" either impossible, inconceivable, or both. Stating that every human has "universal responsibility" is at best empty, and at worst insensitive to the situation of many (most?) people on the planet. While there are subprinciples stating "we" must (a) "accept that with the right to own, manage, and use natural resources comes the duty to prevent environmental harm and to protect the rights of people," and (b) affirm that with increased freedom, knowledge, and power comes increased responsibility to promote "the common good" (2), nothing is stated about whether private ownership of natural resources is appropriate, or whether the differences in freedom assumed are fair. Hence, the implication that certain changes in patterns of ownership and distribution of resources are "unthinkable" seems implicit, an implication that is highly troubling from an ecological feminist perspective. While there is a subprinciple that calls for the promotion of equitable distribution of wealth within and among nations (4), this appears later in the document, and nothing about the tensions between this goal and the assumptions in (a) and (b) above is specifically mentioned. In closing, the Charter mentions the "common destiny" (5) of human beings. However, ecological feminists are committed to noticing key differences in the destinies of various human beings and in examining the power structures that make many such destinies intolerable.

In conclusion, the Earth Charter is a mixed bag from an ecological feminist perspective. On the positive side, it recognizes the link between environmental and other social issues, including the need for areas manifesting ecological integrity. It sees environmental issues *as* social, which is crucial. It also specifically calls for the eradication of sexism and other forms of oppression and of just distribution of wealth and resources, although as noted above, these calls seem to be in tension with certain other portions of the document. However, it calls for "choice" and "universal responsibility" for all, when responsibility is *clearly* not universal, and where choice of the sort called for is often (usually) impossible for most individuals living in the world. Hence, the document contains some significant flaws. In addition, from an ecological feminist standpoint, it is necessary not only to call for change but to examine the concrete conditions which make much of what the Charter calls for impossible, rather than simply calling for such changes.

References

Adams, Carol J. 1991. "Ecofeminism and the Eating of Animals." *Hypatia: A Special Issue, Ecological Feminism* 6 (1): 125–145. An article discussing the connections between ecological feminism and vegetarianism.

Cuomo, Chris J. 1998. *Feminism and Ecological Communities: An Ethic of Flourishing.* London: Routledge. The concept of flourishing is used to ground an ecological feminist ethic.

————. 2001. Unpublished manuscript.

The Earth Charter Initiative. 2002. "The Earth Charter." San José, Costa Rica: Earth Council. <http://www.earthcharter.org/earthcharter/charter.htm> (January 12, 2002).

Gaard, Greta. 1997. "Ecofeminism and Wilderness." *Environmental Ethics* 19 (1): 5–24.

Holland, Alan. 1998. "Foreword," in Laura Westra, *Living in Integrity.* Lanham, Md.: Rowman & Littlefield, xi–xvi.

Plumwood, Val. 1993. *Feminism and the Mastery of Nature.* London: Routledge. An analysis of the logic of dualistic thinking within Western patriarchies and some suggested alternatives.

Shiva, Vandana. 1989. *Staying Alive: Women, Ecology and Development.* London: Zed Books. A discussion of the negative impact of patriarchal style Western development in India.

Warren, Karen J. 1990. "The Power and Promise of Ecological Feminism." *Environmental Ethics* 12 (2): 125–146. A discussion of the conceptual connections between environmentalism and feminism.

Westra, Laura. 1994. *An Environmental Proposal for Ethics: The Principle of Integrity.* Lanham, Md.: Roman & Littlefield.

————. 1998. *Living in Integrity.* Lanham, Md.: Rowman & Littlefield.

Questions for Further Exploration:

- According to ecological feminism, what role do value dualisms play in the construction of Western patriarchal culture?

- According to Davion, why must resistance to human oppression and to the exploitation of nature be understood as part of the same battle?

- How is "ecological integrity" understood scientifically? Why are eco-feminists reluctant to define "ecological integrity" in terms of "wildness"? How does an eco-feminist view "ecological integrity"?

- What aspects of *The Earth Charter* are consistent with ecological feminism? What are the problems with the Charter from an eco-feminist perspective?

- Free-write a response to Davion's claim: "Stating that every human has 'universal responsibility' is at best empty, and at worst insensitive to the situation of many (most?) people on the planet."

The Greening
of the Global Reach

Vandana Shiva

The green movement grew out of local awareness and local efforts to resist environmental damage. The crisis of deforestation in the Himalaya
was a concern first voiced by the local peasant women of Garhwa. The crisis of toxic hazards was first recognized by the affected residents of the
Love Canal.

The pattern that emerged over the 1970s and 1980s was the recognition that major environmental threats were posed by globally powerful institutions, such as multinational corporations, and multilateral development banks such as the World Bank, whose operations reach every city,
village, field and forest worldwide.

In recent years, the two decades of the green movement are being
erased. The 'local' has disappeared from environmental concern. Suddenly, it seems, only 'global' environmental problems exist, and it is taken
for granted that their solution can only be 'global'.

In this chapter I shall look more closely at what the concept of the
'global' conceals and projects, how it builds power relations around environmental issues, and how it transforms the environmental crisis from being a reason for change into a reason for strengthening the status quo.

The 'Global' as a Globalized Local

Unlike what the term suggests, the global as it emerged in the discussions
and debates around the UN Conference on Environment and Development
(UNCED)—eventually held in June 1992—was not about universal humanism or about a planetary consciousness. The life of all people, including the poor of the Third World, or the life of the planet, are not at the centre of concern in international negotiations on global environmental issues.

The 'global' in the dominant discourse is the political space in which
a particular dominant local seeks global control, and frees itself of local,

national and international restraints. The global does not represent the universal human interest, it represents a particular local and parochial interest which has been globalized through the scope of its reach. The seven most powerful countries, the G-7, dictate global affairs, but the interests that guide them remain narrow, local and parochial. The World Bank is not really a Bank that serves the interests of all the world's communities. It is a Bank where decisions are based on voting power weighted by the economic and political power of donors, and in this decision-making it is the communities who pay the real price and are the real donors (such as the tribals of Narmada Valley whose lives are being destroyed by a Bank-financed megadam) but have no say. The 'global' of today reflects a modern version of the global reach of the handful of British merchant adventurers who, as the East India Company, later, the British Empire raided and looted large areas of the world. Over the past 500 years of colonialism, whenever this global reach has been threatened by resistance, the language of opposition has been co-opted, redefined, and used to legitimize future control.

The independence movement against colonialism had revealed the poverty and deprivation caused by the economic drain from the colonies to the centres of economic power. The post-war world order which saw the emergence of independent political states in the South, also saw the emergence of the Bretton Woods institutions such as the World Bank and IMF which took over the language of underdevelopment and poverty, removed these independent political states' history, and made them the reason for a new bondage based on development financing and debt burdens.

The environment movement revealed the environmental and social costs generated by maldevelopment, conceived of and financed by such institutions as the World Bank. Now, however, the language of the environment is itself being taken over and made the reason for strengthening such 'global' institutions and increasing their global reach.

In addition to the legitimacy derived from co-opting the language of dissent is the legitimization that derives from a false notion that the globalized 'local' is some form of hierarchy that reflects geographical and democratic spread, and to which lower order hierarchies should somehow be subservient. Operationalizing undemocratic development projects was based on a similar false notion of 'national interest', and every local interest felt morally compelled to make sacrifices for what seemed the larger interest. It was this moral compulsion that led each community to make way for the construction of mega-dams in post-independence India. Only during the 1980s, when the different 'local' interests met nation-wide, did they realize that what was projected as the 'national interest' was, in fact, the electoral interests of a handful of politicians financed by a handful of contractors, such as J.P. and Associates who benefit from the construction of all dams, such as Tehri and the Narmada Valley projects. Against the narrow and selfish interest that had been elevated to the status of 'national' interest, the collective effort of communities engaged in resistance against large dams began to emerge as the real though subjugated national interest.

In a similar way the World Bank's Tropical Forest Action Plan (TFAP) was projected as responding to a global concern about the destruction of tropical forests. When forest movements formed a worldwide coalition under the World Rainforest Movement, however, it became clear that TFAP reflected the narrow commercial interests of the World Bank and multinational forestry interests such as Shell, Jaako Poyry and others, and that the global community best equipped to save tropical forests were forest-dwellers themselves and farming communities dependent on forests.

Global Environment or Green Imperialism?

Instead of extending environmental concern and action, the recent emergence of a focus on 'global' environmental problems has in fact narrowed the agenda.

The multiple environmental concerns that emerged from the grassroots, including the forest, and the water crises, toxic and nuclear hazards and so on have been marginalized. Thus the Global Environmental Facility (GEF) set up at the World Bank addresses only four environmental issues: (1) a reduction in greenhouse gas emissions; (2) protection of biodiversity; (3) a reduction in pollution of international waters; and (4) a reduction in ozone layer depletion.

The exclusion of other concerns from the global agenda is spurious, since, for example, the nuclear and chemical industries operate globally, and the problems they generate in every local situation are related to their global reach.

'Global environmental problems' have been so constructed as to conceal the fact that globalization of the local is responsible for destroying the environment which supports the subjugated local peoples. The construction becomes a political tool not only to free the dominant destructive forces operating worldwide from all responsibility but also to shift the blame and responsibility for all destruction on to the communities that have no global reach.

Consider the case of ozone depletion. CFCs, which are a primary cause of ozone depletion, are manufactured by a handful of transnationals, such as Dupont, with specific locally identifiable manufacturing plants.

The rational mechanism to control CFC production and use was to control these plants. That such substances as CFCs are produced by particular companies in particular plants is totally ignored when ozone depletion becomes transformed into a 'global' environmental problem. The producers of CFCs are apparently blameless and the blame laid instead on the potential use of refrigerators and air-conditioners by millions of people in India and China. Through a shift from present to future, the North gains a new political space in which to control the South. 'Global' concerns thus create the moral base for green imperialism.

It also creates the economic base, since through conventions and protocols, the problem is reduced to technology and aid transfer. Dupont then becomes essential to the problem it has created, because it has patented CFC substitutes, for which a market must be found. The financial resources that go into the Montreal Protocol Fund for transfer of technology are in effect subsidies for Dupont and others, not for the Third World.

The erosion of biodiversity is another area in which control has been shifted from the South to the North through its identification as a global problem. Biodiversity erosion has occurred because of habitat destruction in diversity-rich areas, by dams, mines and highways financed by the World Bank for the benefit of transnational corporations (TNCs), and by replacing diversity-based agricultural and forest systems with monocultures of 'green revolution' wheat and rice and eucalyptus plantations, which were also supported and planned by the World Bank, in order to create markets for seed and chemical industries.

The most important step in biodiversity conservation is to control the World Bank's planned destruction of biodiversity. Instead, by treating biodiversity as a global resource, the World Bank emerges as its protector through the GEF (Global Environmental Facility), and the North demands free access to the South's biodiversity through the proposed Biodiversity Convention. But biodiversity is a resource over which local communities and nations have sovereign rights. Globalization becomes a political means to erode these sovereign rights, and means to shift control over and access to biological resources from the gene-rich South to the gene-poor North. The 'global environment' thus emerges as the principal weapon to facilitate the North's worldwide access to natural resources and raw materials on the one hand, and on the other, to enforce a worldwide sharing of the environmental costs it has generated, while retaining a monopoly on benefits reaped from the destruction it has wreaked on biological resources. The North's slogan at UNCED and the other global negotiation for a seems to be: 'What's yours is mine. What's mine is mine'.

The notion of 'global' facilitates this skewed view of a common future. The construction of the global environment narrows the South's options, while increasing the North's. Through its global reach, the North exists in the South, but the South exists only within itself, since it has no global reach. Thus the South can *only* exist locally, while *only* the North exists globally.

Solutions to the global environmental problems can come only from the global, that is, the North. Since the North has abundant industrial technology and capital, if it has to provide a solution to environmental problems, they must be reduced to a currency that the North dominates. The problem of ecology is transformed into a problem of technology transfer and finance. What is absent from the analysis is that the assumption that the South needs technology and finances from the North is a major cause of the environmental crisis, and a major reason for the drain of resources from South to North. While the governments of the South demand 'new and additional sources of finance' for the protection of the environment, they ignore the reverse transfer of $50 billion per year of capital from the poor South to the affluent North. The old order does not change through the environmental discussions, rather it becomes more deeply entrenched.

The Problem of False Causality

With the masking-out of the role of the globalized local in local environmental destruction worldwide, the multiple facets of destruction are treated as local causes of problems with global impact. Among the many simultaneously occurring impacts of maldevelopment and colonialism are: the rise of poverty; the increase of environmental degradation; the growth of population; polarization; and conflict between men and women, and between ethnic communities.

Extraction of surplus and the exploitation and destruction of resources have left people without livelihoods. Lacking access to resources for survival, the poor have been forced to generate economic security by having large families. The collapse of social cohesion and economic stability has provided the ground for ethnic conflict.

Instead of identifying the cause of these multifaceted problems as global domination of certain narrow interests of the North, however, these problems are selectively transformed from consequence to cause. Poverty and population are identified as *causes* of environmental degradation. Diversity is seen as a defect and indentified as a *cause* of ethnic conflict.

False causality is applied to explain false connections. Thus some UNCED documents went to the extent of pointing to population growth as a *cause* of the explosive growth in toxic chemicals. A problem caused by an irresponsible chemical industry is converted into a problem caused by fertility rates in the poor countries of the South. The 1991 cyclone in Bangladesh was similarly linked causally to the number of babies in Bangladesh.

The 'Global' is Not Planetary

The visual image of planet earth used in the discourse on global ecology disguises the fact that at the ethical level and global as construct dos not symbolize planetary consciousness. The global reach by narrow and self-ish interests is not based on planetary or Gaian ethics. In fact, it abstracts the planet and peoples from the conscious mind, and puts global institutions in their place. The planet's security is invoked by the most rapacious and greedy institutions to destroy and kill the cultures which employ a planetary consciousness to guide their concrete daily actions. The ordinary Indian woman who worships the *tulsi* plant worships the cosmic as symbolized in the plant. The peasants who treat seeds as sacred, see in them the connection to the universe. Reflexive categories harmonize balance from planets to plants to people. In most sustainable traditional cultures, the great and the small have been linked so that limits, restraints, responsibilities are always transparent and cannot be externalized. The great exists in the small and hence every act has not only global but cosmic implications. To tread gently on the earth becomes the natural way to be. Demands in a planetary consciousness are made on the self, not on others.

The moral framework of the global reach, however, is quite the opposite. There are no reflexive relationships. The G-7 can demand a forest convention that imposes international obligations on the Third World to plant trees. But the Third World cannot demand that the industrialized countries reduce the use of fossil fuels and energy. All demands are externally dictated—one way—from North to South. The 'global' has been so structured, that the North (as the globalized local) has all rights and no responsibility, and the South has no rights, but all responsibility. 'Global ecology' at this level becomes a moralization of immorality. It is devoid of any ethics for planetary living; and based on concepts not of universal brotherhood but of universal bullying.

Democratizing 'Global' Institutions

The creation of new mechanisms for responding to the global ecological crisis was one of UNCED's agendas. Problematizing the 'global' through collective articulation of all local concerns and interests, in all their diversity, is the creative intervention in the global/local conflicts as they are emerging.

To democratize the 'global' is the next step. What at present exists as the global is not the democratic distillation of all local and national concerns worldwide, but the imposition of a narrow group of interests from a handful of nations on a world scale. But if genuine democracy is to exist at local and national levels it is essential for international interests to become democratized.

The roots of the ecological crisis at the institutional level lie in the alienation of the rights of local communities to actively participate in environmental decisions. The reversal of ecological decline involves strengthening local rights. *Every* local community equipped with rights and obligations, constitutes a new *global* order for environmental care.

The current trend in global discussions and negotiations, however, is to move rights further upwards towards more distant, non-local centralization in such agencies as the World Bank.

Multilateralism in a democratic set-up must mean a lateral expansion of decision-making based on the *protection* of local community rights where they exist, and the institutionalization of rights where they have been eroded. Two central planks of local environmental rights include: (1) the right to information; and (2) right to prior consent; that is, any activity with potential impact on the local environment should be subject to consent by the local people.

Basing an environmental order on globally institutionalized local rights also avoids the impracticable issue of representation and the terrible bungling resulting from international NGOs 'selecting' national NGOs to 'select' local NGOs to represent 'people' at global negotiations.

The 'global' must accede to the local, since the local exists with nature, while the 'global' exists only in offices of World Bank/IMF and headquarters of multinational corporations. The local is everywhere. The real ecological space of global ecology is to be found in the integration of all locals. The 'global' in global reach is a political, not an ecological space.

Institutionally, we should not be concerned about how to enable the last tribal to be present at World Bank decisions in Washington. What we need to ensure is that no World Bank decision affecting the tribals' resources is taken without their prior informed consent.

Whether the local as global and the global as local will exist in a way different from the imperialistic order of the last 500 years depends on this process of democratization. The imperialistic category of global is disempowering at the local level. Its coercive power comes from abolishing limits for the forces of domination and destruction and imposing restrictions on the forces of conservation.

The ecological category of global is an empowering one at the local level because it charges every act, every entity, with the largeness of the cosmic and the planetary and adds meaning to it. It is also empowering because precisely by embodying the planetary in the local, it creates conditions for local autonomy and local control.

An earth democracy cannot be realized as long as global domination is in the hands of undemocratic structures. Neither can it be realized on an anthropocentric basis—the rights of non-human nature cannot be ignored. And it cannot be realized if the need to ensure the survival of the planet is made the reason for denying the right to survival of those who today are poor and marginalized because they have borne the accumulated burden of centuries of subjugation.

Questions for Further Exploration:

■ What is Shiva's critique of globalizing environmental solutions?

■ How is "global" conceptualized in the dominant discourse? What is "the globalized 'local'"? What is "green imperialism"?

■ Where does Shiva locate the roots of the environmental crisis? What is "the problem of false causality"?

■ What is obscured by the use of the image of planet earth in the discourse on global ecology? What's wrong with the moral framework of "global ecology"?

■ What does it mean to "democratize the 'global'"? What local right must be insured to realize this goal?

■ What are the implications of Shiva's critique for *The Earth Charter* as a tool for change?

■ Free-write: Should Shiva's "earth democracy" be affirmed even if it threatens national economic interests? Is cosmopolitanism unpatriotic or is nationalism hypocritical? Where does your allegiance lay, and why?

Reading the Earth Charter

Cosmopolitan Environmental Citizenship or Light Green Politics as Usual?

Sherilyn MacGregor

Introduction

My introduction to the Earth Charter came when an enthusiastic American college student thrust a pen into my hand and asked me to add my signature to the list of endorsees. After a quick skim of the accompanying brochure, with its blue planet image and key words 'ecological integrity', 'social justice', and 'peace', I happily obliged, bending down to sign the well-worn parchment scroll laid out in front of me. That it is a 'declaration of fundamental principles' for creating a socially just and ecologically sustainable global society and that it was to be presented to the United Nations (UN) General Assembly at the Johannesburg Earth Summit in September 2002 made it seem unquestionably endorsable. It felt like a significant act, perhaps an expression of my own global citizenship, to add my name to a list of people around the world who share this view. Weeks later, however, I began to wonder why I had uncharacteristically signed something so quickly without first reading the fine print and carefully thinking it through. I typically read petitions and political statements and try to debate the issues with their authors before publicly giving them my support. Why hadn't I done so in this case? Upon a close reading of the

From *Ethics, Place and Environment,* Volume 7, Issue 1, January 3, 2004 by Sherilyn MacGregor. Copyright © 2004 Routledge. Reprinted by permission of Taylor & Francis Group, http://www.informaworld.com.

Earth Charter, I began to feel uncomfortable not only with the process by which endorsement seemed to be taking place but also with several substantive aspects of the document. These are aspects that highlight significant tensions and contradictions in contemporary environmental politics that are best explored through open and continuous dialogue, rather than glossed over with the flourish of a pen or click of a mouse.[1]

The purpose of this paper is, first, to undertake a careful reading and second to inspire informed debate on the substance and process of the Earth Charter. I offer two possible readings that are informed by current scholarship in the field of environmental politics, most notably by what I call 'green cosmopolitanism' and by the writings of eco-democrats and eco-feminists. The first reading finds much in the document to suggest congruence with emerging discourses of cosmopolitanism and global environmental citizenship. With its espousal of universal responsibility and the inclusion of all human beings as members of 'the human family' in the status of world citizen, the Earth Charter appears to share key elements of the cosmopolitan visions articulated recently by social and political theorists and environmental ethicists. The second, more sceptical reading identifies aspects of the Earth Charter that seem more resonant with depoliticizing UN-style light green globalism, criticized by eco-feminist Vandana Shiva (1993), among others, as an elite form of 'globalitarianism', than with an inclusive vision of democratic transnational ecopolitics. After setting out these two readings, I argue that, although it may undermine its endorsability, thinking critically about the problematic aspects of the Earth Charter is an exercise that might help to illuminate approaches to cosmopolitan environmentalism that are less banal and instrumental and more dialogically open, reflexive, and democratic.

Reading #1: The Earth Charter as Cosmopolitan Environmental Vision

There has been growing interest in cosmopolitanism since the early 1990s. In response to economic and cultural globalization and the ongoing existence of national, ethnic, and religious conflict, many academics and activists involved in social change movements are seeking ways to make thinking and acting globally an ethically compelling approach to politics. Cosmopolitanism, a universalist ethical perspective with roots in ancient

---

[1]Visit the Earth Charter website and note that all one need to do to endorse it is 'click here!'.

Stoic and Christian traditions, seems to provide precisely this kind of stance (cf. Attfield, 1999). The origin of the term cosmopolis is the link between cosmos, the order of the universe, and polis, the order of society (Featherstone, 2002, p. 2). It is more recently associated with 18th-century philosopher Immanuel Kant, who believed that all human beings are endowed with a unique capacity for moral behaviour and that because respect for humanity is part of universal natural law, 'morality should be supreme over politics' (Nassbaum, 1997, p. 18; see also Kant, 1991a [1784]). Worried about war and other negative effects of nationalism in world politics, Kant argued that our sense of common humanity unites us in a more fundamental way than loyalty to rulers or states. Therefore, it is the duty of every human being to work toward a cosmopolitan society which would lead to perpetual peace (Kant, 1991b [1795]). Those who are inspired by Kantian thinking today find in cosmopolitanism a framework for global ethics that speaks to individuals, as 'citizens of the world' with universal rights and responsibilities, and an overarching institutional–legal model for peaceful global politics (cf. Attfield, 1999). Contemporary proponents of cosmopolitanism often look to the environmental crisis, which includes transboundary problems like ozone depletion and nuclear waste, as added justification for developing a universal ethical perspective, international law, and practices of 'global environmental citizenship'.

Although a relatively new concept, global environmental citizenship is typically defined as including the right to a non-polluted environment and the responsibility both to refrain from harming the environment and to participate in its preservation and rehabilitation (cf. Jelin, 2000). It demands an understanding of environmental problems as global in scope and a realization that acting locally—although necessary—will not be sufficient for solving them. While local loyalties are not ruled out, global environmental citizens must also hold allegiance to 'our planet, the shared environment of humanity and fellow creatures' (Attfield, 1999, p. 1). In that it departs from exclusively community- or nation state-based notions of citizenship and supports universal ethical principles that may improve intra-human as well as human–nature relationships, this approach might be given the name 'green cosmopolitanism' or 'cosmopolitan environmentalism'. International environmental non-governmental organizations that promote international solidarity and cooperation on environmental policy issues are often held up as evidence that this approach is already being practiced even though it is only recently being theorized by academics (Heater, 2002). The Earth Charter may be seen as an example of a global citizen initiative that supports and promotes a cosmopolitan environmental vision. Although there is no explicit call for global environmental citizenship in the Earth Charter, one can find three foundational elements or principles of cosmopolitanism in it, both in the drafting process and in the declaration itself.

The Need for Global Ethics

Nigel Dower (2002) writes that approaches to cosmopolitan citizenship should be informed by a core set of commonly held ethical principles that together make up global ethics. These principles include granting equal moral consideration to all human beings, universal responsibility to act accordingly, and the practice of balancing allegiances to local, national, and global communities. Several environmental scholars have embraced these principles, emphasizing that what the world needs now is a global ethical framework for guiding our efforts to address the complex environmental problematique (cf. Low, 1999). For example, environmental philosopher Robin Attfield (1999) suggests that the development of environmental ethics across spatial and temporal boundaries is important for sustainability. He argues that this ethical approach should include an attitude of identification with fellow people and fellow creatures, a sense of humility before nature, and a sense of global justice. And such an ethic, according to Attfield, needs to be institutionalized globally at the UN and in international agreements, policies, and laws.

On my first reading, the Earth Charter appears to respond to this call for a global ethics that blends respect for diverse human cultures (as a cosmopolitan virtue) and respect for the non-human and natural world (as an ecological virtue). Created through a participatory 'global dialogue' amongst members of the global ethics movement, grassroots organizations, and the 'world's great religions', the Charter claims to represent an 'emerging worldwide consensus' on the ethical principles needed to bring about a more just and sustainable world (Earth Charter, 2000, p. 50). It makes an ethical appeal to the common good for humanity while appearing to avoid an anthropocentric focus: 'Recognize that peace is the wholeness created by right relationships with oneself, other persons, other cultures, other life, Earth, and the larger whole of which all are a part' (Earth Charter Commission, 2002, Principle IV:16f). In the Earth Charter there is also explicit support for the development of internationally binding environmental laws, even though it is described as a soft law instrument.[2] It is

---

[2]Parallel to the Earth Charter there is an International Covenant on Environment and Development drafted by the Commission on Environmental Law of the International Union for the Conservation of Nature—World Conservation Union. It complements the Earth Charter but is still a work in progress. People involved believe it will take years of negotiation to come up with language that all states can support.

clear that the document is meant to be used as a guide for ethical action at the individual and institutional levels.

Membership in the Human Family

Derek Heater (2002) writes that the notion of membership in the human family is central to cosmopolitanism and this is what distinguishes it from other versions of citizenship that are based on separation of citizens from strangers (or non-citizens). Understandings of citizenship tied to nation states and to particular place-based communities tend to be exclusionary, a means of distinguishing 'us from them'. As Kant (1991b [1795]) observed, and as countless events have shown, drawing boundaries around political communities often leads to conflict and injustice. Cosmopolitanism on the other hand includes all people in the global community of citizens. This means that 'all human beings have equal moral status' (Dower, 2002, p. 150) and that one is a citizen by virtue of being a human being. This is an important point to consider in recognition of the exclusions that occur in a mobile world where for growing numbers of people the idea of being rooted in place is not possible, while others belong to multiple places at once (cf. Urry, 2000). While national and local level allegiances continue to exist, and continue to play necessary roles, the notion of a global community provides a level of membership that is infinitely inclusive (Dower, 2002; Heater, 2002).

The Earth Charter demonstrates this very principle. It is founded on awareness that various political spaces are interlinked and that people can have loyalties to more than one level at once. For example: 'We are at once citizens of different nations and of one world in which the global and local are linked' (Earth Charter Commission, 2002, Preamble). And with this point comes a typically cosmopolitan respect for diversity and the need for openness to and acceptance of people from other cultures/nations as if they were part of our own kin group. '[W]e must recognize that in the midst of a magnificent diversity of cultures and life forms we are one human family and one Earth community with a common destiny' (Earth Charter Commission, 2002, Preamble). In the face of ecological crisis, the Charter seems to be saying, we are all in the same boat and so might as well work together to keep it afloat.

Universal Responsibility

Cosmopolitanism is a concept founded on citizenship, which is a status that by nature attaches to individuals (recent discourse of corporate citizenship notwithstanding). All citizens have rights and duties, but cosmopolitanism places special emphasis on the responsibilities that individuals have to the well-being of humanity. Cosmopolitans believe that these responsibilities are universal: 'ethical responsibilities apply everywhere and to all moral agents capable of shouldering them' (Attfield, 1999, p. 29) not just to members of particular communities or traditions. In terms of environmental ethics, we find that cosmopolitan environmentalism places emphasis on individual duty to care for nature: to engage in behaviour that allows life on the planet to flourish. Bart van Steenbergen (1994) notes that environmental citizenship is all about our obligations to the human community and to the natural world (see also Steward, 1991). It is the acceptance of this responsibility by individuals that matters, along with the implementation of the kinds of behaviour that this acceptance demands. Attfield (1999) calls this sense of responsibility 'trusteeship'—others use the terms 'stewardship' (drawing on Christian tradition) and 'care' (sometimes drawing on 'maternal thinking' (Ruddick, 1989))—to describe how we ought to think of our individual environmental responsibility. Such an orientation is evident in the Earth Charter in the following passages: 'Everyone shares responsibility for the present and future well-being of the human family and the larger living world' (Earth Charter Commission, 2002, Preamble); and 'Affirm that with increased freedom, knowledge, and power comes increased responsibility to promote the common good' (Earth Charter Commission, 2002, Principle I:2b).

Obviously, there are aspects of the Earth Charter that do not fit perfectly with the cosmopolitan vision found in a growing number of scholarly texts. Most notable is its avoidance of the discourse of citizenship. This is not surprising given that citizenship is a contested term that lacks the kind of relevance and resonance with 'regular folk' that it has with social and political theorists. While citizenship theorists can find rhetorical ways of maneuvering around the legal and spatial constraints of more traditional meanings of citizenship in order to speak globally, most people find it difficult to envision what global environmental citizenship might mean, and how it might translate into practice. It is also important to remember that the Earth Charter is a popular document that involved negotiation on the part of thousands of differently situated participants with a wide range of beliefs rather than the product of abstract theorizing by a lone philosopher. The process undertaken by the Earth Charter drafters is in many ways commendable. But just because it is a product of cross-cultural dialogue does not mean it should be exempt from a more sceptical reading. Such a reading helps to illuminate aspects of cosmopolitan theory that are problematic as well as the kinds of problems that arise when an attempt is made to put it into practice.

Reading #2: Light Green Politics as Usual?

It is not the aim of my discussion to cover the many criticism of and debates about cosmopolitanism here but I will note a few that can inform a sceptical reading. Realists in the field of international relations tend to regard as naïve the Kantian idea that common values could ever unite the world in a perpetual peace. They may even call it an ignorant position especially now, in light of recent world events. Cultural relativists wonder who decides what ethics are universal in a culturally diverse world and what to do in the event of ethical conflicts. Marxists dismiss cosmopolitanism for emphasizing ethics over politics and economic power relations, thus obscuring the realities of global neoliberal capitalism. Indeed, there is little political economic content in cosmopolitan visions. In spite of its international appeal and inclusive process, there has also been some resistance to the Earth Charter. Most notably, and predictably, it has come under fire by the right in the US for rejecting national sovereignty and for imposing a totalitarian left-wing agenda on what should be a 'free world' (cf. Singer, n.d., p. 96, line 4; Dougherty, 2000). While few have assessed the strengths and weakness of the Earth Charter specifically, there will no doubt be left academics who express discomfort with some of its theoretical and political implications. For all his enthusiasm about the current trend toward global politics, for example, Ulrich Beck (1998, p. 29) asks: 'what are the unseen and unwanted consequences of the new rhetoric of "global community", "global governance" and "cosmopolitan democracy"? *What are the risks if the cosmopolitan mission succeeds?*' (emphasis added).

These are the kinds of questions that I want to consider in this section. The criticisms that I shall highlight have to do specifically with questions concerning the way the cosmopolitan ideals that have been embraced by drafters and supporters of the Earth Charter initiative fit with the concerns of those environmentalists who are wary of the risks involved in the globalization of ethics (which occurs alongside the globalization of capitalism). For many of these commentators, the Earth Charter would not be regarded as a positive move for environmentalism but as a continuation of old-style green approaches under the disguise of global participation and wrapped up in lofty United Nations-esque discourse. To them it is 'light' green politics as usual. I argue that it is worth considering these arguments because they provide grist for continuing rather than shutting down the global environmental debate.

Ethical Globalitarianism

A common criticism of cosmopolitanism is that it imposes the particular values and interests of an elite few on differently situated and less powerful others in the process of envisioning an ostensibly global ethic. In other words, it is claimed that these particular values come from those in the privileged position to articulate what they believe to be right for all. Cosmopolitanism has been called a Western or Eurocentric project and projection (Featherstone, 2002). This argument stems from an analysis of the contexts in which cosmopolitan ideas have been developed and promoted historically. For example, David Harvey (2000, pp. 559–600) writes that:

> 'A critical history shows that "Western" cosmopolitanism these last two hundred years has . . . been . . . infected by bourgeois sensibilities, pieties, and "feel-good" justifications for their hegemonic project of global domination of the world market. It is either that or being held captive (as in American political life) to local interests proclaiming noble universal values . . . Modern versions of cosmopolitanism cannot evade such connections'.

It seems important to consider, when reading the Earth Charter, whether such a criticism might apply in its case. Considering what has been written about similar documents and initiatives, it is altogether possible that scepticism about the Earth Charter's global ethics will come from those opposed to the 'greening of global reach' (Shiva, 1993).

Many critics, especially those who identify with the struggles of people in the South, will argue that their concerns have been marginalized or paid mere lip service throughout the past 15 or more years of global cooperation on sustainable development. It is often argued that sustainable development has been used to justify the imposition of development policies that privilege the urgency of environmental protection over the self-determination of peoples in the South. Vandana Shiva (1993) calls this a form of 'green imperialism', a process of imposing environmental values of the West on those who are paying the price for overdevelopment. Such critics will wonder whether the Earth Charter, initiated as it was by ex-UNCED (United Nations Conference on Environment and Development) officials and so deploying similar language (including the term sustainable development), offers anything different.

Wolfgang Sachs (1993) argues that the globalization of environmental concern, most notably in UN summits and declarations, has transformed environmentalism from a discourse of opposition to one of domination, stripping its transformative potential and disempowering politics at the local level. A central critique of global ethics discourse is that it takes attention away from local specificities and the need for grassroots action. Many in the environmental movement, especially those identifying with environmental justice, would rather embrace 'think locally, act locally' as a meaningful political slogan than buying into the increasingly popular discourse of globalization (cf. Mies and Bennholdt-Thomsen, 2000). Echoing communitarian critiques of cosmopolitanism, Sachs (1993) believes that ethics should emerge from local experience. Whilst the Earth Charter does attempt to balance the local and the global, it arguably gives pride of place to the global or planetary scale: its *raison d'être* is to unite local communities around a common global vision. With Harvey's (2000) comment in mind, one could arrive at the interpretation that in so far as it calls for the institutionalization of global ethics to guide sustainable development, it provides a kinder, gentler—and greener—face for already existing agendas that are not beneficial for local communities, such as neocolonial international aid policies. Sachs (1993, p. 19) expresses this concern clearly when he writes:

> 'indeed it is easy for an ecocracy which acts in the name of "one earth" to become a threat to local communities and their lifestyles. After all, has there ever, in the history of colonialism, been a more powerful motive for streamlining the world than the call to save the planet?'

Both Shiva (1993) and Sachs (1993) (in a collection of essays that reflect critically on the 1992 Rio Earth Summit) argues that the new discourse of 'global ecology' represents a globalitarian takeover of the environmental agenda by elite managers and bureaucrats from affluent regions of the world. Relatedly, van Steenbergen (1994) describes a kind of global ecological citizenship that is about management within existing unjust socioeconomic systems, under which lies a sense of optimism that all we need is a better way of organizing ourselves. He too associates this approach with experts who seek a clear list of ethical principles (such as sustainable development) to adopt on the simplistic assumption that it will lead to people changing our lifestyles accordingly. The Earth Charter can be read as giving support to just this kind of managerial approach, particularly in this passage:

> 'together in hope we affirm the following interdependent principles for a sustainable way of life as a common standard by which the conduct of all individuals, organizations, businesses, governments, and transnational institutions is to be guided and assessed' (Earth Charter Commission, 2002, Preamble).

On my sceptical reading, this might be an attempt to advance a 'greenprint'—a top-down ethical 'greenprint' for building a sustainable world. Some eco-democratic theorists have argued that this is an instrumental approach that compromises the politics in green politics. As Douglas Torgerson (1999) argues, for example, such instrumentalism leads to ethical principles becoming mere means to an idealized end and so are adopted without critical reflection, much less debate.[3] The Earth Charter appeals to us to adopt global ethics for the sake of survival rather than for its own sake: 'form a global partnership to care for Earth and one another or risk the destruction of ourselves and the diversity of life' (Earth Charter Commission, 2002, Preamble). The problem with this is that survivalist arguments tend to shut down, rather than open up, spaces for democratic dialogue.

Banal Globalism

It is interesting to look at the particular rhetoric that green cosmopolitans use to appeal to common human needs. As discussed earlier, the idea that we are all part of one 'human family' (or 'family of man' as they used to say) is central to cosmopolitanism. The Earth Charter not only contains many references to the human family, but also to caring, loving, and 'home'. One of the very first principles listed in the Earth Charter reads 'Care for the community of life with understanding, compassion, and love' (Earth Charter Commission, 2002, Principle I:2). Such rhetoric gives it a warmly emotional touch, something rarely found in policy documents. Yet the use of this kind of language and the notion that we are one human family raises a number of questions. Is it an approach that is appropriate to a pluralistic, postmodern age? Does it help or hinder the cause of cosmopolitan thinking in a complex world? Does the impulse to 'go global' in the Earth Charter end up 'bringing it home' in a way that threatens to depoliticize it?

Some scholars have used the term 'banal globalism' to refer to means by which those values 'which could help to create a sensibility conducive to the cosmopolitan rights and duties of being a "global citizen"' are made commonplace (Szerszynski *et al.*, 2000, p. 99). Such means include refer-

---

[3] A critic of this contradictory tendency, Torgerson (1999) prefers to focus on democratic procedural concerns rather than to accept a finalized list of ethical principles. Following democratic theorists like Habermas and Arendt, he argues that open and ongoing processes of negotiation over ethics (and what we mean by them) ought to be created and maintained, for in discussion and debate is where democratic politics can thrive. With the Earth Charter, in contrast, once the draft was final, the deliberative process stopped and all that is required of us now—or so it seems—is that we dutifully endorse it. One could point to Earth Charter community summits and some of the ongoing activities that Earth Charter initiative has promoted as evidence of a commitment to ongoing discussion and debate. However, I would argue—drawing in part on personal experience—that the emphasis is placed more heavily on packaging and 'selling' the document, collecting signatures, and working up to winning the ultimate endorsement—that of the UN General Assembly.

ences to popular cultural images, symbols, and narratives that evoke a sense of belonging and common identity across disparate individuals and groups in society. The Earth Charter pamphlet's graphic of smiling multicultural faces floating in space over images of wildlife and waterfalls serves to reinforce this message of unity very nicely. Szerszynski and Urry (2002), looking at the cultivation of cosmopolitan culture in Europe, identify a variety of global images that constantly bombard television viewers. In the Earth Charter not only do we find familist content but also images of the earth seen from space on the front cover (a 'luxuriously freefloating view from above' characteristic of cosmopolitanism (Cheah and Robbins, 1998, p. 1)) and of a human hand holding the planet (a graphic representation of human capacity to nurture it).

While the cultivation of cosmopolitan citizenship may be the intention behind invoking such language and imagery, the Earth Charter can also be read as promoting a simplistic Disneyfied 'it's a small world after all' kind of banal globalism, or what Beck (2002) calls 'banal cosmopolitanism', that gets in the way of deeper understandings of the desirability and impossibility of global community (see also Harvey, 2000). Familist rhetoric tends to suggest a degree of commonality of interest that is overly simplistic and in fact quite misleading. In the global environmental arena, it must not be forgotten that political associations are formed or destroyed on the basis of at times convergent and/or divergent needs, interests, and aspirations. As with most global declarations, the process of drafting the Earth Charter was fraught with conflict and power plays, negotiation, and compromise. But the fact that there were fundamental disagreements over the word choice, and even in the end, no consensus over what particular phrases actually mean is covered up with the language of cosmopolitan unity.[4]

My sense is that there is more to be learned from the debate than there is from the declaration of ostensibly common values. Characterizing the whole of humanity as a family threatens to depoliticize environmental debates. If we are all one big happy family, and we need urgently to act together in order to save the planet from collapse, then should we forget our

---

[4]For example, in the final drafting session of the Earth Charter there was a protracted debate between a representative of 'Arctic hunting cultures' from Finland and the rest of the participants over whether the Charter should include the principles of 'reverence and compassion' for animals. After much discussion of the meaning and implications of these and other such words, the Finnish representative's position was accommodated by using the words 'respect and consideration' instead (cf. Roberts, 2001). Surely the basic disagreement over the rights of animals remains, but the final document suggests consensus and resolution.

differences and just find a way to get along? Don't politics just get in the way?

Injunctions to 'care for people and the earth' are common in green cosmopolitan approaches and evident in the Earth Charter. Yet family relationships and intimate feelings like love and care are, in the minds of many political theorists, not appropriate to the political sphere; they are pre-political (cf. Dietz, 1998). Surely acting as a citizen in the public domain is qualitatively different from acting as a carer or family member in private (Arendt, 1958; Dietz, 1998). There are also gender implications of care rhetoric that, from a feminist perspective, are important to consider. Invoking the language of care is perhaps less risky for men than for women who are socially and culturally conditioned to practice care in self-sacrificial ways. When it is invoked in light green environmental discourse, care appears as a feeling rather than a practice, and seldom is noted the gendered connotations of the word itself, much less who takes on responsibility for the work of caring. Eco-feminists on the other hand call for greater recognition of the gender disparities in the division of caring labour. For example the Women's Environment and Development Organization (1992), in the Women's Action Agenda 21, have called for policies that help to redistribute the caring activities that sustain life and have asserted that it is everyone's responsibility to participate equally. Like most feminists, they argue that when such things go unsaid, the taken-for-granted gender relations remain unchallenged, beyond the realm of politics.

Privatization of Environmental Duty

A third key question that comes out of my sceptical reading is this: by resting responsibility on the shoulders of individual citizens, does a cosmopolitan approach to environmentalism in effect privatize ecological duty thereby taking the focus away from larger political relationships and power struggles? If so, does this not limit its ability to challenge the root causes of the environmental crisis?

The Earth Charter appears to speak to individuals rather than to states or corporations. When addressing its reader it uses the collectivizing language of an unspecified 'we' in order to create the sense of common situation. It fails to distinguish between, and thus speaks simultaneously to, individuals, organizations, communities, and states as if there were no difference in the burden of responsibility for putting principles into practice. But is it fair, or even accurate, to speak of this 'we' with respect to a sharing of responsibility? Do individual citizens have as much moral duty and capability to put these values into practice as do nation states and multinational corporations? Surely they do not. It is a rhetorical weakness of the Earth Charter that it is not addressed specifically to those institutions that are in the position to effect concrete change in law, policy, and economic relations. So why call it an Earth Charter? Most 'charters' in history have been drafted to express the demands of citizens to the state (or workers to an employer), to claim entitlements from those in the position to grant them. As a contemporary example, it is instructive to compare the Earth Charter with 'Charter 99 for Global Democracy' coordinated by the UK-based One World Trust.[5] Charter 99 starts: 'To the Governments of the World, this Charter is addressed to you, your representatives at the UN and peoples of the world you represent. It is a demand for global democracy' (www.charter99.org). In contrast, although the Earth Charter is ostensibly meant to guide decision making at all levels, it is clearly up to individual citizens to see that their governments take its principles seriously: 'Encourage your local government to use and endorse the Earth Charter; urge your national government to endorse the Earth Charter at the World Summit on Sustainable Development' (Earth Charter Commission, 2002, 'How you can participate in the Earth Charter Initiative'). It thus directs its 'demands' to individuals rather than institutions. And by using this universal 'we' it suggests that 'we' (citizens, civil servants, UN bureaucrats, and chief executive officers alike) are all in this together. It is, in effect, 'us speaking to ourselves' (Szerszynski, personal communication) in a united voice. This makes the Earth Charter seem more like a private prayer, a group credo, or a pledge of allegiance than a manifesto or charter for political change.

Conclusion

There are many positive aspects to be noted about the Earth Charter. Although difficult to measure, it is possible that it will contribute to a sense of common purpose that can unit diverse social groups around the world. It may provide the kind of rhetoric needed to inspire practices of global environmental citizenship and it has undoubtedly brought the concerns of hitherto excluded and marginalized people to the international policy table. In a hyper-cynical 'postmodern' era when it seems safer to dismiss the idea of a universal ethical position as at best naïve

---

[5]Charter 99 was inspired by the Chartists and modeled after the Commission of Global Governance's 1995 report 'Our Global Neighborhood'.

and at worst globalitarian, the Earth Charter represents courageous efforts to take a stand. And with its millions of supporters, claims of grassroots participation, and comprehensive list of things to be for and problems that need fixing, one feels reluctant not to endorse it. As noted at the outset, it is this aspect—that it so unreflexively envelops its reader into the global 'we' and makes dissent unthinkable (even unnatural?)—that I find most in need of critical reflection.

In *What is Globalization?* Ulrich Beck (1999, pp. 110–111) writes:

> 'We stand at a threshold where not only catastrophes but also cosmopolitan society are possible. To overlook this 'also-possibility' by focusing only on the catastrophes is an unrealistic attitude. I would expressly add, however, that unwavering scepticism in response to overhasty optimism about the pacification of world society is the necessary precondition for this also-possibility to be seized'.

With this comment in mind, I find it troubling that the Earth Charter does not allow much room for scepticism. Whereas Charter 99 contains a statement that not all of its endorsees agree with all of its demands, the Earth Charter presents a view of the world and the existence of a global consensus as a *fait accompli*. But politics needs debate and dissenting voices. Responsible global environmental citizenship requires more than simply adopting a pre-packaged list of ethical principles. Being cosmopolitan requires the capacity for reflexivity and constant scrutiny of one's own and others' perspectives, and the willingness to learn about humanity in all its cultural diversity (Turner, 2002). While education is foregrounded in the Earth Charter, it is important to notice what it actually teaches: the responsibilities we all must embrace, the perils we all face, and that we are all in the same boat as members of a global family. Readers are encouraged to think and act together as responsible earth citizens rather than to think independently or to be inquisitive about cultural, ethical, and political differences. It seems to me vitally important to keep in mind the limits of what we can know about people and places on this planet and to resist the temptation to find comfort in false universalisms. More good will come from constant conversation than one-off declaration. Perhaps it is best to embrace as a condition for global environmental citizenship the uncertainty and ambiguity that are inescapable in a postmodern, globalizing world (Bauman, 1993). If we try to approach it in this way, then space can be left open for the kind of epistemic humility that is needed (especially in the West) to counter the risks of moral and cultural imperialism often lurking beneath the surface of our universalist political projects.

Acknowledgements

Working drafts of this paper were presented at the annual conference of the Environmental Studies Association of Canada in June 2002 at the University of Toronto, and at an Institute for Environment, Philosophy and Public Policy colloquium at Lancaster University (where she is a visiting research associate) in December 2003. The author wishes to thank the audience participants from both occasions for their thoughtful comments. Thanks in particular to Adrian Ivakhiv (University of Vermont), Jenn Barth (York University, Toronto), and Bronislaw Szerszynski (Lancaster University). The author's research is funded by a postdoctoral fellowship awarded by the Social Sciences and Humanities Research Council of Canada.

References

Arendt, Hannah (1958) *The Human Condition,* Chicago, IL: University of Chicago Press.

Attfield, Robin (1999) *The Ethics of the Global Environment,* Edinburgh: Edinburgh University Press.

Bauman, Zygmunt (1993) *Postmodern Ethics,* Oxford: Blackwell.

Beck, Ulrich (1998) The cosmopolitan manifesto, *New Statesman,* 20 March, 28–30.

Beck, Ulrich (1999) *What is Globalization?,* Cambridge: Polity Press.

Beck, Ulrich (2002) The cosmopolitan society and its enemies, *Theory, Culture and Society,* 19(1–2), 17–44.

Cheah, P. and Robbins, B. (1998) *Cosmopolitics: Thinking and Feeling Beyond the Nation,* Minneapolis, MN: University of Minnesota Press.

Dietz, Mary (1998) Context is all: feminism and theories of citizenship, in: Gatens, M. (ed.) *Feminist Ethics,* Dartmouth, NH: Ashgate, 301–322.

Dougherty, Jon (2000) 'Earth Charter' calls for global society, *WorldNetDaily,* 3 April (http://www.mvcf.com/news/cache/00083/).

Dower, Niegel (2002) Global ethics and global citizenship, in: Dower, N. and Williams, J. (eds) *Global Citizenship: a Critical Reader,* Edinburgh: Edinburgh University Press, 146–157.

Earth Charter (2000) Annual report, *The Earth Charter in Action 2000,* Costa Rica: Earth Charter Initiative International Secretariat.

Earth Charter Commission (2002) *Earth Charter: Values and Principles for a Sustainable Future* (http://www.earthcharter.org).

Featherstone, Mike (2002) Cosmopolis: an introduction, *Theory, Culture and Society,* 19(1–2), 1–16.

Harvey, David (2000) Cosmopolitanism and the banality of cosmopolitan evils, *Public Culture,* 12(2), 529–564.

Heater, Derek (2002) *World Citizenship: Cosmopolitan Thinking and its Opponents,* London: Continuum.

Jelin, Elizabeth (2000) Towards a global environmental citizenship?, *Citizenship Studies,* 4(1), 47–63.

Kant, Immanuel [1784] (1991a) The idea of a universal history with a cosmopolitan intent, in: Reiss, Hans (ed.) *Kant's Political Writings,* 2nd edn, trans. Nisbet, H. B., Cambridge: Cambridge University Press, 41–53.

Kant, Immanuel [1795] (1991b) Perpetual peace: a philosophical sketch, in: Reiss, Hans (ed.) *Kant's Political Writings,* 2nd edn, trans. Nisbet, H. B., Cambridge: Cambridge University Press, 93–130.

Low, Nicholas (1999) Introduction: towards global ethics, in: Low, N. (ed.) *Global Ethics and Environment,* London: Routledge, 1–15.

Mies, Maria and Bennholdt-Thomsen, Veronika (2000) *The Subsistence Perspective: Beyond the Globalized Economy,* London: Zed Books.

Nussbaum, Martha (1997) Kant and Stoic cosmopolitanism, *Journal of Political Philosophy,* 5(1), 1–25.

One World Trust (n.d.) Charter 99: a Charter for Global Democracy (http://www.charter99.org/).

Roberts, Jan (2001) Earth Charter, *YES! Magazine,* Winter (http://www.futurenet.org/16culture/roberts.htm).

Ruddick, Sara (1989) *Maternal Thinking: Toward a Politics of Peace,* New York: Beacon Press.

Sachs, Wolfgang (ed.) (1993) *Global Ecology: a New Arena of Political Conflict,* London: Zed Books.

Shiva, Vandana (1993) The greening of global reach, in: Sachs, W. (ed.) *Global Ecology: a New Arena of Political Conflict,* Zed Books, 149–156.

Singer, S. Fred (n.d.) One World United under a UN Communist Dictatorship: the UN Earth Charter (http://www.unisevil.com/fs_earth_charter.htm). Accessed 16/04/2002.

Steenbergen, Bart van (1994) Towards a global ecological citizen, in: Steenbergen, B. van (ed.) *The Condition of Citizenship,* London: Sage, 141–152.

Steward, Fred (1991) Citizens of planet earth, in: Andrews, G. (ed.) *Citizenship,* London: Lawrence and Wishart, 65–75.

Szerszynski, Bronislaw and Urry, John (2002) Cultures of cosmopolitanism, *Sociological Review,* 50(4), 461–481.

Szerszynski, Bronislaw, Urry, John and Myers, Greg (2000) Mediating global citizenship, in: Smith, J. (ed.) *The Daily Globe: Environmental Change, the Public and the Media.* London: Earthscan, 97–114.

Torgerson, Douglas (1999) *The Promise of Green Politics: Environmentalism and the Public Sphere,* Durham, NC: Duke University Press.

Turner, Brian (2002) Cosmopolitan virtue, globalization and patriotism, *Theory, Culture and Society,* 19(1–2), 45–63.

Urry, John (2000) Global flows and global citizenship, in: Isin, E. (ed.) *Democracy, Citizenship, and the Global City,* New York: Routledge, 62–78.

Women's Environment and Development Organization (1992) *Women's Action Agenda 21* (http://iisdl.ca/women/action21/htm).

Questions for Further Exploration:

- According to MacGregor, what aspects of the Charter highlight significant tensions and contradictions in contemporary environmental politics?

- What is the difference between the two readings MacGregor gives the Charter? Which of the two are you most inclined towards, and why?

- What three principles from the Charter, does MacGregor use to conceptualize "global environmental citizenship"?

- What criticisms does MacGregor raise for the project of greening cosmopolitanism? Which among these are the most serious from your perspective, and why?

- What is the educational approach exemplified by the Charter according to MacGregor? What does she propose as an alternative approach?

- Free-write: How would you respond to a request that you endorse *The Earth Charter?* What would endorsing it mean to you? How would it translate into practice?

Ecological Ethics

Moral Pluralism and Pragmatism

Patrick Curry

The Poverty of Monism

Moral pluralism is the view that our ethical life consists of a number of different principles and values which can conflict, and which cannot be boiled down to just one. They can be compared practically in the course of arriving at a decision, but in themselves, to a greater or lesser extent, they are 'incommensurable', and any such decision, in taking one as its guide, always runs the risk of (so to speak) offending one or more of the others.

Such a view has been taken by some great thinkers: from Machiavelli and Nietzsche to William James, Max Weber and Isaiah Berlin.[1] In the latter's words:

 The notion that there must exist final objective answers to normative questions, truths that can be demonstrated or directly intuited,
 that it is in principle possible to discover a harmonious pattern in
 which all values are reconciled, and that it is towards this unique
 goal that we must make; that we can uncover some single central
 principle that shapes this vision, a principle which, once found,
 will govern our lives—this ancient and almost universal belief . . .
 seems to me invalid, and at times to have led (and still to lead) to
 absurdities in theory and barbarous consequences in practice.
 (1969: lv–lvi)

Nonetheless, pluralism remains a distinctly minority view. The reason is simple, if deep: the dominant kind of ethics in the West—from Greek philosophical and Christian religious to modernist/humanist—is profoundly

[1]See James 1977; Weber's seminal essay 'On Science as a Vocation' in his 1991; Berlin 1969 and his superb essay 'The Originality of Machiavelli' in his 1998.

monist. Its fundamental premise is that there is *a single reference point,* whereby, to quote Weber, 'one can, in principle, master all things by calculation' (1991: 139).[2] In terms of the logic of this belief, whether this single principle or value is spiritual (God) or material (scientific truth) is secondary, although not unimportant: the former, as the ultimate mystery, ultimately cannot be mastered, whereas the latter does hold out the promise of ultimate mastery. Such monism is necessarily also universalist, since if there is only one such principle it must, by definition, apply everywhere without exception. Of course, to ensure that the one truth is correctly perceived and promulgated, a cast of approved interpreters is also needed. The result, as Barbara Herrnstein Smith notes, is 'intellectual/political totalitarianism (the effort to identify the presumptively universally compelling Truth and Way and to compel it universally)' (1998: 179).

This worldview, and its operation, is one of the primary causes of our current ecological crisis, because, as Weber famously put it, the belief (note: *belief*) that everything can, at least in principle, be mastered by calculation results in 'the disenchantment of the world'. Now, as I mentioned earlier, the disenchantment of nature began with Greek philosophical monism (especially Plato) and monotheism, and in particular their combination in Christianity and later Islam. But it was sharply intensified by modern science. And we have seen that such disenchantment is a prerequisite to the physical desecration of nature by unrestrained exploitation.

It is also significant that it is virtually impossible to subscribe to a monist universalism without rejecting limits (since universal truth is, by definition, without any limits); and that rejection is another key element of anti-ecological modernity. Such monism is also deeply anthropocentric: it is humans alone who are licensed by God, or Truth, to work their will on nature without, in principle, any natural limits. Finally, it overrules our experience—perhaps particularly of nature—as worlds (plural) of effectively endless sensuous particulars.[3] In short, as William James demanded, 'Why should we envelop our many with the "one" that brings so much poison in its train?' (1977: 141).

Yet as we have also seen, any ecological fundamentalism would merely replace the one true and universal God with Nature. (It matters little whether the 'Nature' here is mystical or scientific.) Such a move would not only leave the destructive logic untouched, but ecocentrism, albeit of a pathological kind, would thereby become the enemy of nature. That would truly be a disaster.

---

[2]See also Kontos 1994.

[3]Abram 1996; Weston 1994.

It follows that the only way to resist and ultimately replace the inherently anti-ecological logic of monism is through pluralism. And that mans a *moral* as well as epistemological pluralism.[4] To quote Weber again: 'We are placed into various life-spheres, each of which is governed by different laws.' And being different, 'the ultimately possible attitudes toward life are irreconcilable, and hence their struggle can never be brought to a final conclusion' (1991: 123, 152). Furthermore, as I have already argued, in this situation science cannot make ethical choices for us. It 'presupposes that what is yielded by scientific work is important in the sense that it is worth being known. . . . [But] this presupposition cannot be proved by scientific means. It can only be *interpreted* with reference to its ultimate meaning, which we must reject or accept according to our ultimate position towards life' (ibid. 143).

It follows that different considerations can *validly* apply in different cases, and that each case can *properly* be viewed in different ways.[5] Connections must then be made, and decisions taken, on grounds to be argued and established contingently in each case, which is to say (in the broad sense), politically. And those taking the decisions must therefore take responsibility for them, rather than hiding behind supposedly transcendental abstract truth.[6]

Abandoning what the philosopher Bernard Williams called 'a rationalistic conception of rationality' (1993: 18)—which asks reason (including scientific reason) to do what it cannot—does not make choice arbitrary, any more than does dispensing with the notion that truth must be singular. (There is a strong parallel here with what we saw earlier about how realists view the consequences of *what they think of* as relativism.) Neither confused nor dishonest, moral pluralism is, in Midgley's words, 'simply a recognition of the complexity of life'.[7]

Nor is it an ethical disaster. On the contrary, as Christopher Stone writes, 'It is by the choices we affirm in this zone of ultimate uncertainty that we have our highest opportunity to exercise our freedoms and define

---

[4]On epistemological pluralism, see Feyerabend 1987 and Smith 1997; on axiological (value) pluralism see Smith's exemplary 1988; on moral pluralism, see Berlin 1969; on pluralism in a political context, and in relation to ecocentrism, see Stone 1987, 1995; Brennan 1995, 1995b; Midgley 1997; Curry 2003.

[5]Brennan 1995.

[6]See Stone 1995; Brennan 1995b; also Laclau and Mouffe 1985.

[7]She adds: 'The idea that reductive simplicity here is particularly rational or "scientific" is mere confusion' (1997: 100).

our characters' (1995: 525).[8] In other words, it is essential to the process of developing an ethically virtuous character—including ecologically virtuous—both individually and socially.[9]

The Consequences of Pluralism

We began this book by noting the gravity of the current ecological crisis. The subject of moral pluralism provides an opportunity to ask: what follows from this crisis as such? The short and perhaps unwelcome answer is that nothing *necessarily* follows from it, no matter how serious it is or may become. The reason is that any perception, assertion, valuation and meaning of ecocrisis is unavoidably only one among others, none of which is self-evidently true, let alone their implications. All of them are unavoidably contingent (partial, local, unstable)—which is *not* to say merely subjective—and competing in a complex rhetorical economy of claims and counter-claims, values and counter-values, all of them with actual or potential winners and losers (relatively speaking, of course). As Smith puts it, 'There is no way to give a final reckoning that is simultaneously total and final. There is no Judgement Day. There is no *bottom* line anywhere, for anyone or for "man"' (1988: 149). Indeed, when the end of the world for humans beings comes, the last two will probably be arguing about what it means (assuming, of course, that they notice in time). And if they aren't, the reason won't be because its meaning is obvious; it will be because they decided, and managed, to agree on something.

This is bound to be deeply frustrating for econcentric ethicists. You can almost hear them saying, 'Everything—human rights, health, the lot—depends on ecosystems! No Earth, no nothing!' But I'm afraid that even this truth, unavoidably, is a claim and a value competing in that economy; and as such it is not, even so baldly put as that, self-evident. Nothing that could happen, not even severe ecosystemic breakdown or ecological collapse, would *in itself* make ecocentrism universally accepted; people would, and will, be able to come up with other explanations. ('God's will' is always popular.) So illusions of 'self-evident objective truths' only make the ecocentric work that needs to be done still harder. (We will look at that work in the following chapter.) In short, the upshot of a pluralist world for ecocentrism is an apparent paradox: ecocentrics realize that since everything on this Earth depends on it and its vital constituent parts—the true

---

[8]This is also something that Machiavelli and Weber recognized.

[9]See Swanton 2004.

common good—*where human good, values or interests clearly conflict with the well-being of the Earth, the former must give way;* nonetheless, this realization cannot ever be taken for granted—as much as possible and wherever and whenever possible, *it must be argued, publicized, fought for and lived.*

There is a silver lining to this paradox, for pluralism helps relieve ecocentric ethicists of at least three burdens they are better off without:

1. A tendency to moral self-righteousness which is counterproductive in terms of its effect on members of the public whom they are trying to influence. However paradoxical it may seem, the intrinsic value of nature is something that must be established. And to proceed as if it was obvious (i.e., to everyone who isn't a fool or a knave) is not the most promising way to do so.

2. A tendency to despair when they dramatically fail to change the public and/or official mindset, *partly* because of the first problem, combined with underestimating just how hard it is to do so. Any positive change will be incremental, partial, uneven and contested, and a grasp of pluralism would make this clearer from the outset.

3. The potential, at least, to entertain a green version of 'intellectual/ political totalitarianism', which in this case takes the form of dogmatic misanthropy. It is usually nothing more than a side effect of the personal despair just mentioned, which is a more serious occupational hazard for ecocentrics. Full-blooded and dangerous green misanthropy is actually strikingly rare, especially compared with how common lethal anthropocentrism is.

The case for moral/ethical pluralism overlaps closely with that for **pragmatism.** That word commonly refers to a mindset primarily concerned with what works in practice as distinct from theory, and the philosophical version is not radically different; it simply fleshes out such concern theoretically and philosophically. Oversimplifying, practice, or *praxis,* in the relevant context, is both the starting point and terminus of theory, or what is considered to be true.[10]

The consequences for ecocentric ethics are practically identical with those of pluralism, with perhaps a slightly different emphasis. What follows is that ecocentrics must be able to work together with those who are committed to mid-green or intermediate, light green or shallow, and even outright anthropocentric, ethics when there is real potential common

---

[10]I am thinking of the work of William James and John Dewey (more than Pierce).

ground on a particular issue. An ecocentric point of view is one among many, not a revealed Truth, and allies are not exactly thick on the ground, so when the opportunity arises to do so without sacrificing ecocentric principles, alliances must be forged.

As Bryan Norton (1991) has pointed out, agreement on principles can *follow* agreement on practice, i.e., what to do in or about a concrete situation or problem. This is another aspect of the kind of labour-intensive, hands-on democracy-in-action just mentioned which ecocentric ethics requires in order to make a difference. Such agreement, however, is not a necessary 'principle'. There are absolutely no guarantees that policies in the interest of humanity and those in the interest of non-human nature will converge; all we can say is that they may.[11]

[11]See Plumwood 2002: 124–6.

Questions for Further Exploration:

- What does Curry mean by "moral pluralism"? Why it a minority view?

- How does Curry conceptualize "moral monism"?

- What reasons does Curry give in support of his claim that moral monism is "one of the primary causes of our current ecological crisis"?

- What are the consequences of pluralism? How should conflicts between human interests and the well-being of the Earth be decided?

- In what ways does pluralism 'unburden' ecocentric fundamentalism?

- What are the implications of moral pluralism for *The Earth Charter?*

- Free-write: Are you more inclined towards moral monism or moral pluralism, and why?